ETHNICITY
AND THE BIBLE

ETHNICITY AND THE BIBLE

EDITED BY

MARK G. BRETT

BRILL ACADEMIC PUBLISHERS, INC.
BOSTON • LEIDEN
2002

Library of Congress Cataloging-in-Publication Data

Ethnicity and the Bible / edited by Mark G. Brett
   p. cm.
  Originally published: Leiden ; New York : E.J. Brill, 1996, in series: Biblical
interpretation series.
   Includes bibliographical references and index.
   ISBN 0–391–04126–6
   1. Ethnology in the Bible. 2. Ethnicity—Biblical teaching. I. Brett, Mark G.

BS661 .E82 2002
220.8'3058—dc21

                                         2002066858

ISBN 0–391–04126–6

PRINTED IN THE UNITED STATES OF AMERICA

CONTENTS

ACKNOWLEDGMENTS

Patricia Marrfurra and Dominica Katyirr, both of the Merrepen Arts Aboriginal Corporation, Daly River (Northern Territory, Australia), kindly gave their consent for the reproduction in this volume of their paintings "Easter" and "Christ is Born."

Thanks are due also to the American Jewish Committee for permission to print a revision of Jon D. Levenson's essay "The Universal Horizon of Biblical Particularism," first published as a pamphlet in 1985.

I am very grateful to the members of the editorial board of the journal *Biblical Interpretation* who supported this project by contributing their own work in response to a research proposal which I first circulated at the end of 1993. Other members of the board offerred good advice along the way: Yairah Amit, Adela Yarbro Collins, Norman Gottwald, Jorge Pixley, John Rogerson, Christopher Rowland and Gerd Theissen. Susan Hawley gave helpful guidance on some of the relevant anthropological literature, and my introduction has benefitted from her perceptive critique. Thanks also to the translators who offerred their services: Alan Moss, David Orton, Sharon Ringe, and Rainer Shack. My own thinking on the subject of ethnicity has been influenced by all the authors who have contributed to this volume, but also by a number of friends, none of whom can be held responsible for the particular set of views represented here but all of whom have in some sense convinced me that this theme should be an important one in biblical studies: Danny Carroll (Guatemala), Terry Falla (Melbourne), Edea Kidu (Port Moresby), Philip Mosely (Melbourne), Thevathasan Premarajah (Colombo), Anna May Say Pa (Rangoon), and Gerald West (Pietermaritzberg).

Ron Ham, Ken Manley and the Executive Committee of Whitley College kindly granted me study leave in order to work on this and a related project on nationalism. Over the past few months, I have enjoyed the hospitality of the Department of Studies in Religion, University of Queensland (thanks, especially, to Ed Conrad), the Department of Biblical Studies, University of Sheffield, and Lincoln Theological College. The faculty and staff at all these places have provided stimulating environments in which to work. A somewhat "peripatetic" sabbatical has also left my family with a number of personal debts: Susan, Anusha, Mattheus and I would like to thank Lori Andrews and Matt Wiebe, Pippa and Alan Winton, Annette and David Orton, Chris and Noel Bailey, Christopher Rowland, Cheryl Exum, Gill and Rob Waszak, Melinda and Stephen Fowl.

In more general terms, I need to acknowledge my colleagues in Melbourne who, along with my former colleagues Stephen Fowl and Alan Winton, have helped me to reflect on the meaning of an academic vocation, especially, Jim Barr, Merryl Blair, Edwin Broadhead, Rosemary Dillon, Keith Dyer, Terry Falla, John Hirt, Trevor Hogan, David Hunter, Kate Hunter, Geoff Jenkins, Jeanette Mathews, Gwenith Measham, Frank Rees and Howard Wallace. There is an important sense in which my own teaching and research would not be possible without such a network of friendship.

M.G. Brett
Brisbane, June 1995

LIST OF CONTRIBUTORS

John M.G. Barclay
Department of Biblical Studies
University of Glasgow
Glasgow G12 8QQ
SCOTLAND

Mark G. Brett
Whitley College
271 Royal Parade, Parkville
  3052
AUSTRALIA

Pieter F. Craffert
Department of New Testament
UNISA, P.O. Box 392
Pretoria 0001
SOUTH AFRICA

Frank Crüsemann
Kirchliche Hochschule Bethel
Remterweg 45
33617 Bielefeld
GERMANY

Jonathan E. Dyck
School of Hebrew, Biblical &
  Theological Studies
Trinity College
Dublin
IRELAND

Diana Edelman
James Madison University
Dept. of Religion and
  Philosophy

Virginia 22807
USA

Philip F. Esler
Dept. of Divinity
St Mary's College
University of St Andrews
St Andrews, Fife KJ16 9JU
SCOTLAND

Reinhard Feldmeier
Universität Bayreuth
D-95440
Bayreuth
GERMANY

Susan Hawley
Mansfield College
Oxford OX1 3TF
ENGLAND

Lynne Hume
Dept. of Studies in Religion
University of Queensland
St. Lucia, 4072
AUSTRALIA

David Jobling and
  Catherine Rose
St Andrew's College
1121 College Drive
Saskatoon
Saskatchewan S7N OW3
CANADA

Jon D. Levenson
The Divinity School,
    Harvard University
45 Francis Avenue, Cambridge,
    Massachusetts 02138
USA

Rolf Rendtorff
(Professor Emeritus)
Ruprecht-Karls-Universität
6900 Heidelberg
GERMANY

Pablo Richard
Departamento Ecumenico de
    Investigaciones
Apartado 389-2070 Sabanilla
San José
COSTA RICA

John Riches
Department of Biblical Studies
University of Glasgow
Glasgow G12 8QQ
SCOTLAND

Fernando F. Segovia
The Divinity School
Vanderbilt University
Nashville, Tennessee 37240
USA

David C. Sim
Dept. of Religion and
    Philosophy
Australian Catholic University
McAuley Campus,
    P.O. Box 247
Everton Park, Qld 4053
AUSTRALIA

Daniel L. Smith-Christopher
Dept. of Theology
Loyola Marymount University
Loyola Blvd at W80th Street
Los Angeles, CA 90045
USA

Wolfgang Stegemann
Augustana Hochschule
Postfach 20
91561 Neuendettelsau
GERMANY

R.S. Sugirtharajah
Central House
Selly Oak Colleges
Birmingham B29 6LQ
ENGLAND

Thanzauva and R.L. Hnuni
Eastern Theological College
P.O. Rajabari
Jorhat 785014, Assam
INDIA

INTRODUCTION

INTERPRETING ETHNICITY:
METHOD, HERMENEUTICS, ETHICS

Mark G. Brett

Contrary to the expectations of many social theorists writing in the 1950s and early 1960s, ethnic identity is still a pressing feature of contemporary politics the world over. It was often suggested that although the new, post-colonial states would need to grapple for some time with the politics of ethnicity, they would gradually absorb the civic ideas of Western modernity which had, apparently, succeeded in amalgamating diverse peoples within nation states.[1] Communism, in a different way, attempted to construct a politics of homogeneity, often in an ironic alliance with nationalism. But whether communist or "democratic," there are now many examples in Africa and Asia where the fragile political unities constructed by post-colonial nationalisms have broken down with bloody consequences. The Soviet Union and communist Europe have also been deconstructed, and in the process, ethnic identities have been violently re-asserted. Ethnic nationalisms have emerged as potent forces, whatever the governing ideologies of previous regimes. Also in the homelands of civic democracy—France, Britain, North America—the politics of immigration and indigeneity have generated ethnic revivals of various kinds. Even if ethnic nationalisms have not been asserted there with comparable violence, a major social question has arisen of whether civic nationalism can encompass the diversity of multiculturalism.[2]

In most Western democracies, public life has been dominated by a discourse which tends to treat individuals primarily as equal citizens and economic actors—religion, culture and ethnicity therefore being regarded as private matters. In some contexts, such a discourse has been used with liberating consequences, such as in the American civil rights movement. The recent democratic reforms in South Africa

---

[1] See E. Ben-Rafael and S. Sharot, *Ethnicity, Religion and Class in Israeli Society* (Cambridge: Cambridge University Press, 1991), p. 3.

[2] See D.T. Goldberg (ed.), *Multiculturalism: A Critical Reader* (Oxford: Blackwell, 1994); for a fuller discussion of nationalism, see Mark G. Brett, "Nationalism and the Hebrew Bible," in J. Rogerson, M. Davies, M. Daniel Carroll R. (eds.), *The Bible in Ethics* (Sheffield: JSOT Press, 1995), pp. 136–63.

would be another case where the rhetoric of equal rights has been transformative. But in other contexts, such equalizing discourse is ill-prepared to deal with groups for whom ethnic or religious identity may be over-riding concerns.[3] The homogenizing presumptions of Western liberalism have been challenged by a "politics of difference" which emphasizes the uniqueness of particular social identities, like ethnicity and aboriginality, and adopts "affirmative action" pro-grammes which, by definition, are not universalizable.[4] Several au-thors have suggested that movements which project universal ethics and a uniform humanity have, ironically, turned out to be anti-Jew-ish,[5] but ideas of social homogeneity have also been directed against many other groups who have refused to sacrifice their particularity for the sake of the national good.

An example is provided by Australian Aborigines whose legal claims on traditional lands have only now been recognized in the High Court. Native title legislation based on the so-called "Mabo decision" rejects the presumption of *terra nullius* which has legitimated two centuries of British settlement, and suggests that Aboriginal tribes who can dem-onstrate a continual connection with crown land since pre-settlement days may claim it as their own; the land can no longer be conceived as a blank space to be filled by the civilizing power of Europe. The conspiracy of legal and poetic imagination which constructed a land with "no past, no story"[6] has been unmasked. The opponents of native title regard it as a threat to economic security and development, arguing that Aborigines should be regarded as Australian citizens like any other, with no rights or privileges which could not be universal-ized to include every citizen.[7] This kind of "difference-blind" liberal-

---

[3] P. Worsley, *The Three Worlds: Culture and World Development* (London: Weidenfeld and Nicholson, 1984), p. 243. Cf. J. Uyangoda, commenting on the situation in Sri Lanka: "We have had the Westminster type of democracy, which allowed an ethnic community with a numerical majority to control political power and resources... That in turn has given rise to another form of nationalism which I call minoritarian nationalism." "Understanding Ethnicity and Nationalism" *Ecumenical Review* 47/2 (1995), p. 191.

[4] C. Taylor, "The Politics of Recognition," in A. Gutman (ed.), *Multiculturalism and "The Politics of Recognition"* (Princeton: Princeton University Press, 1992), pp. 25–73.

[5] See, e.g., Frank Crüsemann's citation of Kant's statement "Pure moral religion is the euthanasia of Judaism." In W. Weischedel (ed.), *Werke Bd. 6: Der Streit der Fakultäten* (Frankfurt: Insel, 1964), p. 321.

[6] This phrase is from Marcus Clarke's introduction to the *Poems of Adam Lindsay Gordon*. See Veronica Brady's essay "Mabo: A Question of Space," in her *Caught in the Draught: On Contemporary Australian Culture and Society* (Sydney: Angus & Robertson, 1994), pp. 13–29.

[7] Cf. the U.S. Supreme Court ruling, in the case of *City of Richmond v. Croson*

ism might be summarized with some vocabulary borrowed from the apostle Paul: for those who are Australian, there is neither Jew nor Greek, slave nor free, English nor Aboriginal. From the perspective of the "politics of difference," however, such a view simply reflects the interests of the dominant culture, neglecting the constitutive role which land plays in Aboriginal identity.

Even if the land-centred worldviews of Australian Aborigines are in some senses distinctive, the legal and cultural conflicts in Australia are in many ways analogous with other contexts. The more general point here is that there are many ethnic groups who refuse, for good reasons, to be subsumed under homogenizing visions of national (or international) culture.

Whatever their geographical or social location, I would argue biblical critics have an ethical responsibility to address this complex web of issues.[8] There can be no denying that the Bible has had, and continues to have, an influence on many cultures, and a specialist knowledge of this ancient library is something which carries moral and political implications—whether scholars possess particular faith commitments or not. As the discipline of biblical studies begins to absorb the significance of reader-oriented literary theory, and the "cultural studies" movement,[9] it is becoming yet more clear that scholarly discourses themselves have histories and socio-economic locations (see especially, R.S. Sugirtharajah, John Riches and Fernando Segovia).[10] Whether we like it or not, we are implicated in contemporary ethnic issues in a variety of ways.

(1989), that a city ordinance which set aside 30% of public works funds for minority-owned construction companies was unconstitutional. For a detailed discussion of the issues, see S.L. Myer, "Measuring and Detecting Discrimination in the Post-Civil Rights Era," in J.H. Stanfield and R.M. Dennis (eds.), *Race and Ethnicity in Research Methods* (Newbury Park: Sage, 1993), pp. 172–97.

[8] Cf. N. Gottwald, "The Interplay of Religion and Ethnicity in Ancient Israel," in M. Bradbury (ed.), *Religion, Ethnicity and Violence* (College Park, MD.: University of Maryland Press, forthcoming).

[9] See Fernando Segovia's observation that the cultural studies movement has unmasked the "enduring construct of a universal and informed reader" which actually required all readers to divest themselves of constitutive identity factors and "to interpret like Eurocentric critics." See Segovia, "'And They began to speak in Other Tongues': Competing Modes of Discourse in Contemporary Biblical Criticism," in F.F. Segovia and M.A. Tolbert (eds.), *Reading from this Place* Vol. 1 (Minneapolis: Fortress, 1995), pp. 29–30. Cf. J.D. Levenson, *The Hebrew Bible, the Old Testament and Historical Criticism* (Louisville: Westminster/John Knox, 1993), pp. 95, 98, 122.

[10] Bracketed references in the text refer to essays in this volume. I do not mean to suggest that the discipline of biblical studies has only recently discovered the idea that all exegesis has presuppositions; this idea has been given lip service for some

Quite apart from the ethical implications of interpreters' social locations, there are issues of "ethnocentrism" which belong to the business of exegesis, however narrowly this may be conceived. For example, in spite of the frequently expressed (and logically vague) exhortation for biblical scholars to analyze a text "in its own terms," the interpretation of ancient texts requires, at decisive points, that cross-cultural comparisons and contrasts are made with the interpreter's own culture.[11] And insofar as the interpreter's own culture is an ineluctable feature of cross-cultural understanding, one could say that a certain kind of ethnocentrism is unavoidable: either one "goes native," in which case no *cross*-cultural understanding has been achieved,[12] or one attempts to describe the "other" in terms which would be intelligible within the interpreter's own culture (see further, Pieter Craffert).

This does not mean that cross-cultural understanding needs to find simple corresponding concepts; as Charles Taylor has argued, interpretation will often need to work with "perspicuous contrasts." In the case of a magical worldview, for example, a contrast is rarely made between the *social* dimensions and the *cognitive* claims of magic. Anthropologists coming from a scientific culture have, however, tended to introduce such a distinction since they are likely to regard the cognitive claims as false and to explain magical practices primarily in social terms. As soon as the charges of falsehood have (explicitly or implicitly) been laid, however, the logic of interpretation has moved from "the native point of view" (emics), towards a claim of critical superiority (etics). The anthropologist has, I would suggest, a choice between two kinds of ethnocentrism: (1) to observe that the native makes no distinction between the cognitive and social functions of magic, as we do, or (2) to explain what is *really* going on in magical

time, but sustained and detailed analyses of scholarly discourse (which go beyond the disciplinary limits of "*Forschungsgeschichte*") are still comparatively rare.
[11] See C. Taylor, "Understanding and Ethnocentricity," in his *Philosophy and the Human Sciences* (Cambridge: Cambridge University Press, 1985), pp. 116–33; C. Geertz, *Works and Lives* (Cambridge: Polity, 1988), pp. 144–45; H. Eilberg-Schwartz, *The Savage in Judaism: An Anthropology of Israelite Religion and Ancient Judaism* (Bloomington: Indiana University Press, 1990), pp. 87–102; D. Hoy, "Is Hermeneutics ethnocentric?" in J.F. Bohman, D.R. Hiley, and R. Shusterman (eds.), *The Interpretive Turn: Philosophy, Science, Culture* (Ithaca: Cornell University Press, 1991), pp. 155–75.
[12] See C. Geertz, *The Interpretation of Cultures* (New York: Basic Books, 1973), p. 13: "We are not, or at least I am not, seeking either to become natives (a compromised word in any case) or to mimic them. Only romantics or spies would seem to find point in that. We are seeking ... to converse with them."

practices, regardless of native accounts. No doubt the emic-etic contrast must be conceived as a continuum, rather than as a sharp dichotomy; either way, interpreters necessarily betray the categories of their own culture. But in the second case the goal of emic description has given way to explanation which is much less actor-oriented.

The conclusion to E.P. Sander's influential *Paul and Palestinian Judaism* represents a comparable example from New Testament studies. Sanders recalls that Rudolf Bultmann attempted to read all of Paul's discourse regarding the Christian life as existential demands relating to the believer's self-understanding. This was, at least in part, an exegetical claim: since a person who is already incorporated "in Christ" must still make decisions, Bultmann argued that Paul's language of incorporation did not imply magical or metaphysical transformation into the body of Christ. Sanders agrees up to a point, but then suggests that Bultmann and his followers set up the oppositions too rigidly: being one body with Christ was conceived as *either* cosmic speculation *or* a revision of self-understanding; receiving the Spirit was *either* a magical transfer *or* "accepting the word of grace." The difficulty, Sanders suggests, is that "we" lack a category "which lies between naive cosmological speculation and belief in magical transference on the one hand and a revised self-understanding on the other," but Paul certainly had one.[13] This kind of claim is a descriptive (emic) one which rightly betrays the limitations of the interpreter's culture; modern Western culture is shaped by a different system of semiotic contrasts. Sanders then makes an entirely different claim: what Paul thought cannot be directly appropriated by Christians today, because the *falsehood* of Paul's claims regarding the end of the present world undermines the plausibility of the cosmic dimensions of his thought.[14] These two claims, the one acknowledging a conceptual contrast and the second making a substantive critique, represent two different kinds of ethnocentrism, and there are different ethical issues arising from each. The co-operation of professional ethicists is much needed, I would suggest, if we are to take this analytical discussion further.

The issue of cross-cultural interpretation has, however, been discussed in some recent publications not so much as an emic-etic problem as a matter of global politics. African scholars have pointed out, for example, that there are enough analogies between the biblical

[13] E.P. Sanders, *Paul and Palestinian Judaism* (London: SCM, 1977), p. 522.
[14] Sanders, *Paul*, p. 523.

world and traditional, tribal societies to suggest that some biblical concepts may be more readily intelligible in Africa than in modern Europe (see John Riches but also R.S. Sugirtharajah's reservations concerning the homogenization of non-Western experience). A major problem, however, is that educational resources, theological institutions, and the means of publishing are all disproportionately concentrated in Europe and North America. Indeed, "contextual" and "cultural" hermeneutics have, in some cases, been developed in the Third World as forms of resistance to hegemonic Western theology and exegesis, and under the heading of "inculturation" such hermeneutics have often been governed, rightly, by a kind of ethnocentric logic.[15] This development within the domains of theology and biblical studies illustrates one the complexities which is to be found in the wider literature on ethnicity: ethnic categories have been used to manipulate and to rule, but they have also been used as modes of resistance.[16] Accordingly, a volume which deals with the general theme of "ethnicity and the Bible" will need to reflect the diversities of culture both within the biblical texts and among the interpretative communities for whom the Bible is a focus of thought and action.[17]

---

[15] See, e.g., R.S. Sugirtharajah (ed.), *Voices from the Margin* (New York: Orbis, 1991); idem. (ed.), *Commitment, Context and Text: Examples of Asian Hermeneutics*, special issue of *Bib.Int.* 2/3 (1994); G. West, *Contextual Bible Study* (Pietermaritzburg: Cluster, 1993); idem., "Difference and Dialogue: Reading the Joseph Story with Poor and Marginalized Communities in South Africa," *Bib.Int.* 2/2 (1994), pp. 152–70; idem., *Biblical Hermeneutics of Liberation* (New York: Orbis, rev. edn, 1995); see also the North American discussion of "Afrocentricity" in Cheryl J. Saunders (ed.), *Living the Intersection: Womanism and Afrocentrism in Theology* (Minneapolis: Fortress, 1995).

[16] Worsley, *Three Worlds*, pp. 239, 241. A particularly ironic case of this is to be found among the indigenous people of New Caledonia whose self-description as "kanaks" deliberately reverses the pejorative connotations of the French "canaque." See P. Wete, *Agis ou meurs-L'Eglise Évangélique: de Calédonie vers Kanaky* (Suva: Lotu Pacifika, 1991) and the discussion of "double-voiced" revision in H.L. Gates, *The Signifying Monkey: A Theory of Afro-American Literary Criticism* (Oxford: Oxford University Press, 1988), pp. 111–13. Another irony of *Wirkungsgeschichte*: Marshall Sahlins has recently argued that the very idea of "culture," in the relevant anthropological sense, was invented as a counter-Enlightenment strategy in the late eighteenth century by J.G. Herder, yet this "Western product" has been adopted as a common principle of resistance by peoples as diverse as Ojibway Indians, Tibetans, Kashmiris, Zulus, Maoris and Aborigines. Cf. Sahlins, *How "Natives" Think: About Captain Cook, for example* (Chicago: Chicago University Press, 1995).

[17] There are, I should emphasize, severe practical limits on the extent to which the diversity of interpretative communities can be represented (limitations which belong also to the present volume). In addition to the inequitable distribution of resources for research, there are a range of political reasons why some groups do not wish to be represented; they resist the idea of an "ideal speech situation." See especially James Scott's reservation concerning Jürgen Habermas's tendency to treat politics as

Our discussion has relied thus far on a rather loose association of the terms "culture" and "ethnicity," and broadly speaking, an ethnic group may indeed be defined as a social group which shares a culture. But such concepts obviously require closer definition, and there are a range of interpretative questions which need more detailed analysis.[18] For example, do modern ideas of ethnicity have direct parallels in ancient cultures, and by what method should any cross-cultural comparison proceed? How do particular groups go about constructing "ethnic" identities, as opposed to other kinds of identity? Under what conditions do people give priority to their ethnic identity, and what kinds of choices do they have in doing so? What is the relationship between ethnicity and class, or to put this more broadly, between ethnicity and asymmetrical social relationships—economic and political? (See especially Jonathan Dyck, Susan Hawley, David Jobling & Catherine Rose.) How much weight should be placed on self-descriptions (emics) and how much on ethnic labels imposed by outsiders?[19] As the essays in this volume make clear, there are several productive ways of construing ethnic identity, it may be unhelpful to pre-empt the conversation by defining our concepts too tightly; some approaches

---

if it ought to reflect "the perfect graduate student seminar." Scott, *Domination and the Arts of Resistance: Hidden Transcripts* (New Haven: Yale University Press, 1990), p. 115 n. 12. See, e.g., Habermas, *Moral Consciousness and Communicative Action* (Oxford: Polity, 1990). To mention just one example which complicates Habermas's ideal of undistorted communication, it is precisely the gender-differentiated *secrecy* of Australian Aboriginal sacred traditions regarding their land which limits the incorporation of such traditions in the public realm. To sacrifice this secrecy would entail a massive revision of aboriginal culture. Cf. Scott, *Arts of Resistance*, passim.

[18] See, especially, J.M. Yinger, "Ethnicity" *Annual Review of Sociology* 11 (1985), pp. 151–80.

[19] Two examples will suffice to suggest that, in my view, this last question should be decided on a case by case basis. During the Holocaust, the Nazi definition of a Jew was imposed without negotiation. On the other hand, in the context of current Israeli politics, it has been argued that the *edot ha'Mizrach* (communities of the East: Moroccan, Yemenite, etc.) have asserted their ethnic identity over against their perception of the secularized nationalism common amongst the Ashkenazi establishment. See further, E. Ben-Rafael and S. Sharot, *Ethnicity, Religion, and Class in Israeli Society*, pp. 43–47, 222. Cf. above n. 16 for the case in New Caledonia where the label "kanak" was ironically negotiated between insiders and outsiders. This latter example does not, however, undermine Pierre van den Berghe's well-argued case that social scientists should preserve a methodological distinction between emic and etic labels. See van den Berghe, "The Use of Ethnic Terms in the Peruvian social Science Literature," *International Journal of Comparative Sociology* 15 (1974), pp. 132–42. This article also illustrates the instability of emic labels, depending on who is using the term and in what setting. *Mestizo*, for example, was primarily a racial term in colonial times, whereas it has now lost practically all such connotations. Cf. the shifting usage of the terms "Hebrew" and "Philistine" (David Jobling and Catherine Rose).

to the theme may thereby be excluded. Let me risk a few introductory observations, however, which foreshadow some of the key issues.

Discussions of ethnicity are part of the formidable network of debates concerned with the description and explanation of social groups larger than the family. As with all social groups, the formulation of boundaries is crucial feature of self-definition. Who should be considered one of "us" and who should be considered "other"? Whether explicitly or implicitly, such a binary opposition is a common feature of social discourse. But as has frequently been observed, the most problematic social transactions occur precisely at the boundary, between "us" and those who are "like us." Binary divisions simplify the complexities of "proximate otherness;" otherness is "a matter of relative rather than absolute difference."[20]

Jonathan Z. Smith has emphasized that social taxonomies often obscure the fact that the construction of otherness is relational and transactional: "Something is 'other' only with respect to something 'else'." And if otherness is always a product of where one is standing, then it should be regarded not so much as a state of being but as "a political and linguistic project, a matter of rhetoric and judgement."[21] (Thus, for example, Kashmiri Brahmins, who think of themselves as white in contrast to dark-skinned South Indians, find themselves, on coming to Britain, treated as "Black" or "Coloured."[22]) Although *ethnie* can be exceptionally durable once formed, they are also symbolic constructions which have to be maintained by reiterated practices and transactions.[23] It seems that the majority of recent studies on ethnicity have envisioned this process as a dialectic of "structure" and "agency."[24]

---

[20] J.Z. Smith, "What a Difference a Difference Makes," in J. Neusner and E.S. Frerichs (eds.), *"To See Ourselves as Others see us": Christians, Jews, "Others" in Late Antiquity* (Chico: Scholars, 1985), p. 15; cf. E.S. Bogardus, "A Social Distance Scale," *Sociology and Social Research* 17 (1933), pp. 265–71. A paradigmatic biblical example of proximate otherness is supplied by the laws of warfare in Deut. 20:10–18 which (retrospectively) reserve the most violent treatment for the cities which are "near" rather than those which are "far." For a plausible account of the composition of this chapter, see M. Fishbane, *Biblical Interpretation in Ancient Israel* (Oxford: Clarendon, 1985), pp. 199–209; cf. also G. Braulik, *Deuteronomium II 16, 18–34, 12* (Würzberg: Echter Verlag, 1992), p. 150.

[21] Smith, "Difference," p. 46.

[22] Worsley, *Three Worlds*, p. 342.

[23] This is argued even by A.D. Smith, *Ethnic Origins of Nations* (Oxford: Blackwell, 1986), p. 16. For a recent review of the relevant social-scientific literature, see C. Calhoun, "Nationalism and Ethnicity," *Annual Review of Sociology* 19 (1993), pp. 211–39.

[24] The choice of vocabulary here resonates in particular with the social theory of

Studies of the Bible illustrate the complexity of such a dialectic. While controversy and doubt will always surround the dating of particular biblical traditions, there can be no doubt that the Bible records a long and heated conversation about how the boundaries of Israelite community are to be constructed and maintained.[25] Two extreme positions in this debate are well known: first, the "racialized" marriage policies of Ezra/Nehemiah,[26] and second, Paul's vision in Gal. 3:28–29 that within the social space defined by Jesus Christ "there is neither Jew nor Greek, male nor female, slave nor free;" Christ has erased the categories of ethnic group, gender and class.[27]

However, the extremes represented by Ezra/Nehemiah and Paul are not simply identifiable with a divergence between the Testaments, nor with a divergence between Judaism and Christianity. As several scholars have made clear, Ezra and Nehemiah represent a particularist strand of post-exilic political theology which is opposed to a great number of other traditions within the Hebrew Bible itself (see Jon Levenson, Frank Crüsemann, Rolf Rendtorff, Jonathan Dyck and Daniel Smith-Christopher). Complexities also arise within the New Testament material. If Paul appears to be prescribing a "new humanity of no difference," the wider contours of his argument constitute precisely an ascription of "ethnic" identity to the Galatians which is opposed to the Jewish *ethnos* (so Philip Esler).[28] And if we accept a

---

Anthony Giddens, but the general point has been advocated in different ways by most of the major sociological schools who have risen in revolt against the structural functionalism of Talcott Parsons—conflict theory, social exchange theory, symbolic interactionism and ethnomethodology. For a brief review, see W.H. Handel, *Contemporary Sociological Theory* (Englewood Cliffs: Prentice Hall, 1993). With specific application to ethnicity, see the detailed studies in Stanfield and Dennis (eds.), *Race and Ethnicity in Research Methods.*

[25] See, e.g., H.G.M. Williamson, "The Concept of Israel in Transition," in R.E. Clements (ed.), *The World of Ancient Israel* (Cambridge: Cambridge University Press, 1989), pp. 141–61.

[26] "Racialized" is here is scare quotes, alluding to the lineage-based or biological idea inherent in the reference to the "holy seed" (Ezra 9). One should recognize, however, that ideas of race are probably even more complicated than ideas of ethnicity. Over the last four centuries, race has been analysed in terms of lineage, type, sub-species, status and class. Whether such diversity has parallels in the ancient world is a matter for detailed historical investigation. See further M. Banton, *Racial Theories* (Cambridge: Cambridge University Press, 1987).

[27] Daniel Boyarin has summarized Paul's vision as "the new humanity of no difference." See his, *A Radical Jew: Paul and the Politics of Identity* (Berkeley: University of California Press, 1994), p. 5.

[28] Such a reading of Paul might seem to be stretching the concept of ethnicity too far, and Esler concedes at one point that the new *ethnos* in Christ implies perhaps only a "quasi-ethnicity." Several scholars have suggested that New Testament

recent trend in Matthean scholarship, represented in this volume by David Sim, the polemic against Jews in that Gospel is primarily an intra-Jewish affair, a case of "proximate otherness" generating more heat than we find between "distant others." Sim argues that Matthew's community is a Torah-centred but messianic Jewish sect which, unlike the apostle Paul, regards the Jewish practice of circumcision as self-evidently necessary for membership in the community of Jesus Christ— necessary but not sufficient.

These considerations lead us into a forest of contested concepts. One biblical concept of ethnicity seems to focus simply on blood-ties and genealogy (Ezra/Nehemiah), while another concept of peoplehood distinguishes between physical and spiritual descent (Gal. 4:29). Matthew's community, apparently, falls between these extremes by re-defining its boundaries (much as did the Qumran community) *within* the Jewish ethnos. The Bible thus presents us with a series of identity-forming interactions the social description of which depends on where one is standing. Is Matthew's Gospel "inside" or "outside" of Judaism?

And what about the modern social historians who are attempting to give some account of this whole process? Should their pre-fabricated social definitions resolve the biblical diversity by deciding what is "objectively" ethnic identity and what is not? It is indeed remarkable to notice just how some of the basic conflicts in biblical theology find a parallel in the recent social scientific debates about the nature of ethnicity. For example, the "primordialist" position, associated in particular with Edward Shils and Clifford Geertz, suggests that ethnicity is not just a function of interaction but a deeply rooted and durable affiliation based on kinship, shared territory and tradition: "Congruities of blood, speech, custom, are seen to have an ineffable, and at times overpowering coerciveness in and of themselves."[29] A different emphasis finds expression in "constructivist,"

---

concepts of peoplehood—and the early Christian self-description as a *tertium genus*— are deliberately opposed to any exclusive ideas of ethnicity (see Barclay, Stegemann and Feldmeier). Esler's argument, however, is explicitly working with constructivist, rather than "primordial," notions of ethnicity. See further below.

[29] E. Shils, "Primordial, Personal, Sacred, and Civil Ties," *British Journal of Sociology* 8 (1957), pp. 130–45; C. Geertz, "The Integrative Revolution: Primordial Sentiments and Civil Politics in the New States," *The Interpretation of Cultures* (New York: Basic Books, 1973), pp. 255–310, 259. This is a revised version of the paper which first appeared in C. Geertz (ed.), *Old Societies and New States* (Glencoe: Free Press, 1963), pp. 105–57. A.D. Smith rightly emphasizes that Geertz's position should be seen as

"instrumentalist" or "circumstantialist" positions which suggest that ethnicity is more manipulable and variable; the agency of the subjects concerned has a much higher profile. This it evidenced, for example, in Fredrik Barth's classic introduction to *Ethnic Groups and Boundaries*.[30] Over against Ezra/Nehemiah's "primordial" nativism, one might be justified in seeing Barth's volume as a kind of Pauline constructivism.

Barth argues that some older theories of ethnicity occluded the problems of boundary construction by imagining that cultures tend to work in isolation of each other, developing "mainly in response to local ecologic factors, through a history of adaptation by invention and selective borrowing." On the contrary, Barth suggests, although ecology may explain certain kinds of regional variation and social symbiosis with other groups, there are documented cases of single ethnic groups "occupying several different ecologic niches and yet retaining basic cultural and ethnic unity over long periods."[31] Barth's notion of ethnic unity here is not, however, static: cultural features which signal the boundaries of a community may change; organizational forms may change; structured interactions with other ethnic groups may change; but the continuing distinctions between outsiders and insiders permit us to identify the continuities of affiliation. Indeed, stable ethnic boundaries can be crossed by a flow of personnel without erasing the boundaries themselves. To mention just one study, the Yao of southern China have shown a remarkable capacity to incorporate outsiders into their kinship and ritual structures—10% of their population in a generation.[32]

"weak primordialism"; the claims are actor-oriented (emic) and not part of a stronger version advocated by certain sociobiologists. See Geertz's comment: "Simple primordial determinism is no more defensible a position than economic determinism." His main thesis is that although ethnic politics in Indonesia, Malaysia, India, Burma, Morocco and Nigeria "rest on historically developed distinctions, some of which colonial rule helped to accentuate (and others of which it helped to moderate), they are part and parcel of the very process of the creation of a new polity and a new citizenship" (p. 270). The replacement of colonial regimes with domestic states have configured primordial attachments in a new way, requiring a new set of social negotiations. See A.D. Smith, "The Politics of Culture: Ethnicity and Nationalism," in T. Ingold (ed.), *Companion Encyclopedia of Anthropology* (London: Routledge, 1994), p. 707.

[30] F. Barth (ed.), *Ethnic Groups and Boundaries: The Social Organization of Culture Difference* (London: Allen & Unwin, 1969), pp. 9–38.

[31] See Barth, *Ethnic Groups*, p. 13 and the literature cited there.

[32] Barth, p. 22.

For these reasons, Barth makes the important claim that "cultural" contents can vary

> without any critical relation to the boundary maintenance of the ethnic group. So when one traces the history of an ethnic group through time, one is not simultaneously, in the same sense, tracing the history of "a culture:" the elements of the present culture of that ethnic group have not sprung from the particular set that constituted the group's culture at a previous time, whereas the group has a continual organizational existence with boundaries (criteria of membership) that despite modifications have marked off a continuing unit.[33]

This thesis can be well illustrated by the Bible. In this sacred library we find the literary deposits of a people who have been clearly influenced by a range of ancient cultures—to mention a few: Egyptian, Canaanite, Assyrian, Babylonian, Persian, and Hellenistic. Yet we also find attempts to construct a continuity of peoplehood, even through the discontinuities envisaged by prophetic judgments (see Jon Levenson). There are, of course, limits to this continuity and varied reflections on the parting of ways—not least in the New Testament— but Barth's main point still goes through: any continuity an ethnic identity achieves is not simply to be equated with the continuity of a "culture."[34] This is particularly the case with regard to *material* elements of a culture, which are often borrowed more readily than ideologies.[35] Thus, the recent wave of scepticism regarding the question of whether archaeologists can identify distinctively "Israelite" artefacts in the premonarchic archaeological record would come as no surprise to most anthropologists (see Diana Edelman).

Barth's argument is also relevant to the contemporary debates

---

[33] Barth, p. 38. For a bold and detailed study along these lines, see Tony Swain's attempt to trace the influences of Melanesian, Indonesian and European ideas on Aboriginal worldviews in Australia, *A Place for Strangers: Towards a History of Australian Aboriginal Being* (Cambridge: Cambridge University Press, 1993).

[34] This is not to say that there is no connection between culture and ethnic identity, only that the connection is more problematic than has often been realized. Jews, for example, have usually regarded themselves as part of a unified "people," but the creation of the modern state of Israel has given rise to more self-conscious "ethnic" differences between Ashkenazi and Sephardic groups. These differences are largely a matter of "culture." See further, C.A. Rubenberg, "Ethnicity, Elitism, and the State of Israel" in J.F. Stack (ed.), *The Primordial Challenge: Ethnicity in the Contemporary World* (New York: Greenwood, 1986), pp. 161–84; cf. the illuminating comparisons between contemporary Israel and the conflicts in Ezra/Nehemiah in T.C. Eskanazi and E.P. Judd, "Marriage to a Stranger in Ezra 9–10," in T.C. Eskanazi and K. Richard (eds.), *Second Temple Studies* Vol. 2 (Sheffield: JSOT Press, 1994), pp. 266–85.

[35] See A.P. Royce, *Ethnic Identity: Strategies of Diversity* (Bloomington: Indiana University Press, 1982), p. 8.

concerning imperialism and its effects on dominated cultures. If Barth is correct, as I think he is, then we would need to note that attempts to preserve a "culture" do not, *ipso facto*, preserve the identity or dignity of an ethnic group. Clearly, the dignity of social groups is usually entwined with wider issues of economics and politics.[36] But it is also important to recognize ethnic identity can still be preserved in spite of cultural changes and influences.[37] And as the studies in this volume on the use of the Bible amongst indigenous people illustrate, the introduction of new cultural contents—even cultural contents which were imposed under the most unambiguously imperialist circumstances—*may* still be turned to serve the interests of a dominated group. It is one of the great ironies of Christian mission that, in spite of its dark history, indigenous peoples have in some contexts turned the Christian faith to anti-imperialist purposes.[38] In short, a "culture" is not, in itself, a social unit. Or to put it another way, ethnic groups are culturally permeable.[39]

A related point has been made by Etienne Balibar in his illuminating essay "Is There a 'Neo-Racism'?" Balibar argues that many anthropologists who have been involved in the struggle to preserve minority or dominated cultures have taken the view that the mixing of cultures is a contravention of nature—every culture is seen to be equally valuable and has a natural right to separate existence. The unintended consequence of this view is the expectation that inter-ethnic exchanges will inevitably be characterized by defensiveness and aggression.[40] What was originally an anti-imperialist strategy has ironically

---

[36] See Gottwald, "The Interplay of Religion and Ethnicity in Ancient Israel," and his discussion of E. Staub, *The Roots of Evil: the Origins of Genocide and Other Group Violence* (Cambridge: Cambridge University Press, 1989).

[37] In his classic article, "Nativistic Movements," Ralph Linton pointed out that nativistic cultural revitalization was always selective: it is concerned with "particular elements of culture, never with cultures as wholes." *American Anthropologist* 45 (1943), p. 230.

[38] A similar point can be made concerning the Maori Hau-hau rebellion against the British in late nineteenth century New Zealand. The Hau-hau synthesized their older religious traditions with their understanding of Judaism, seeing the British as "Egyptian" oppressors of the new elect, the Maoris. They also absorbed some Christian elements, such as the cross, which symbolized the crucifiction of natives at the hands of the whites. See V. Lantenari, *The Religions of the Oppressed* (London: MacGibbon & Kee, 1963), pp. 248–59.

[39] Cf. John Barclay's distinction between "acculturation" (e.g., the Jewish adoption of Greek language and thought-forms) and social "assimilation." Barclay, *Jews in the Mediterranean Diaspora* (Edinburgh: T. & T. Clark, forthcoming).

[40] Balibar, "Is there a 'Neo-Racism'?" in E. Balibar and I. Wallerstein, *Race, Nation,*

been turned by recent right-wing movements in Europe into xenophobia: since every culture has a right to separate existence, so this
response goes, people of other cultures should keep their distance.
There is an obvious parallel here between the resurgence of right-
wing movements in Balibar's France and the old apartheid system in
South Africa.

Building on the work of Balibar, Daniel Boyarin has distinguished
between rightist racism and liberal racism: the political goals of rightist
racism entail the subjugation or the expulsion of other "races;" liberal
racism, on the other hand, tends to advocate the construction of
new states within which the ethnic-nationalist aspirations for sovereignty may be fulfilled. The latter option, for Boyarin, simply reinscribes
homogeneity—the idea of "the One"—and the basic intolerance
towards difference is replicated.[41] His alternative is to allow the mixing of cultures while preserving a "polyphonic" ethnic identity. Although Boyarin has no detailed discussion of Fredrik Barth, it is clear
that this approach would make no sense unless one presumed something like Barth's account of how culture and ethnicity overlap, yet
are distinct phenomena—ethnic identity *with* cultural permeability.

In his important concluding chapter, Boyarin takes up that long
tradition of defending Judaism against charges of a malign ethnocentrism,[42] suggesting that there is nothing wrong with ethnocentricity
(a) when it is "polyphonic," and above all (b) when it is a strategy of
survival amongst subordinate groups. He argues that although Judaism has revolved around a tension between ideas of genealogy and

---

Class: Ambiguous Identities (London: Verso, 1991), pp. 21–23, implicating Claude Lévi-
Strauss in this problematic. The recent literature in sociobiology represents another
variant of this view by suggesting that altruistic sentiments "naturally" spread out-
wards from family to kin to ethnic group. Note, however, that some sociobiologists
argue explicitly that political ethics should seek to overcome this ethnocentrism;
sociobiology is an "anti-ethic." P. van den Berghe, *The Ethnic Phenomenon* (New York:
Oxford, 1981), p. 12; cf. M. Barker, *The New Racism* (London: Junction Books, 1981).
[41] Boyarin, pp. 247–50; see especially Balibar, "Racism and Nationalism," in *Race,
Nation, Class*, p. 53: "Nationalism emerges out of racism, in the sense that it would
not constitute itself as the ideology of a 'new' nation if the official nationalism against
which it were reacting were not profoundly racist: thus Zionism comes out of anti-
Semitism and Third World nationalisms come out of colonial racism." Cf. N. Harris,
National Liberation (London: I.B. Taurus, 1990), p. 221: "In the long history that lies
behind the civil war in Sri Lanka, we can see multiple layers of oppression generating nationalist responses—the British on the Ceylonese, the Sinhalese ruling order
on the Tamil."
[42] Cf. L.H. Feldman, *Jew and Gentile in the Ancient World* (Princeton: Princeton
University Press, 1993), pp. 123–49. See also the comparable charges laid against
early Christians, discussed by Reinhard Feldmeier below.

ideas of territory, genealogy should be given priority over territory, and ethnicity should be separated from all forms of political hegemony.[43] In short, ethnocentrism is only malign when it is combined with homogenizing political power. Genealogy is, in fact, opposed to autochthony, and the Bible makes no claim to Israel's autochthony; the rabbis rightly renounced the land until the final redemption, he suggests, and on this one point at least, his postmodern Jewish stance is in agreement with the example of the *Natorei Karta* who refuse to visit the Western Wall in Jerusalem without Arab "visas" because the Wall was taken by violence. Boyarin's view entails

> renunciation of sovereignty, autochthony, indigeneity (as embodied politically in the notion of self-determination), on the one hand, combined with a fierce tenacity in holding onto cultural identity, on the other.[44]

While such an approach might be perceived as "racism" in the hands of a dominating group, it is "resistance in the hands of a subaltern collective."[45] On this view, ethics are not simply universalizable; what is ethical cannot be decided independently of the social and economic power of those concerned.

Boyarin makes a notable concession at one point, however, when he argues that

> somewhere in the dialectic between the Pauline universalized human essence and the rabbinic emphasis on Israel a synthesis must be found, one that will allow for stubborn hanging on to ethnic, cultural specificity but in a context of deeply felt and enacted human solidarity. For that synthesis, Diaspora provides the model, and only in conditions of Diaspora can such a resolution be attempted. Within the conditions of Diaspora, many Jews discovered that their well-being was absolutely dependent on the principles of respect for difference.[46]

This line of argument supplies the background for Boyarin's critique of Galatians. Paul's gospel, he suggests, is shaped too much by his Hellenistic background:

---

[43] Boyarin, pp. 252–58.

[44] Boyarin, p. 259. The phrase "cultural identity" is unfortunately ambiguous: given the wider context, I read Boyarin to be advocating cultural *mixing* and ethnic continuity. As suggested above, this apparently paradoxical approach is perfectly intelligible within account of ethnicity provided by Barth.

[45] Boyarin, p. 242.

[46] Boyarin, p. 257. Cf. Julia Kristeva's suggestion that there is also a deconstructive potential in the Torah's legal protection of aliens insofar as it is based on the defining story of Israelites as aliens liberated from Egypt. She describes this defining story as "a primal inscription of foreignness." Kristeva, *Nations without Nationalism* (New York:

Paul was motivated by a Hellenistic desire for the One, which among other things produced an ideal of a universal human essence beyond difference and hierarchy. This universal humanity, however, was predicated (and still is) on the dualism of the flesh and the spirit, such that while the body is particular, marked through practice as Jew or Greek, and through anatomy as male or female, the spirit is universal.[47]

Pauline Christianity renounced "embodiedness" in various forms; it entailed "a disdain for the body, and disdain for the body entailed an erasure of 'difference.'" On the other hand, in rabbinic Judaism, we find "a commitment to such differences as race, parentage, and native country [which] entailed a commitment to the body and to 'difference' in general." The spiritualizing of circumcision in baptism, according to Boyarin, was a social practice with a hermeneutical counterpart: the new community of the spirit was shaped by interpretative habits of the spirit which supplanted the fleshly genealogy of Abraham, the literal Torah, the literal land of promise. In short, Jews refused "to be allegorized into a spiritual disembodiment."[48]

But Boyarin himself provides us with some clues as to how this opposition between rabbinic Judaism and Pauline Christianity may be deconstructed. First, he seems to concede that his real target is gnosticism when he says that Paul's universalized humanity is predicated on a dualism of flesh and spirit. The orthodox interpretations of Paul, as is well known, reacted against any gnostic or docetic tendencies to dis-embody Jesus Christ; it is precisely this point which lies at the centre of Christian debates about "incarnation." While it is true that many of the classical manuals of spirituality encouraged the loosening of family and local ties,[49] the anti-docetic tradition is a part of orthodox, not peripheral Christianity. One could argue that liberation theology constitutes a radical re-claiming of incarnational doctrine (see Pablo Richard). Second, we have seen that Boyarin recommends the rabbinic renunciation of political self-determination: the possession of the promised land is eschatologized, and diaspora identity should be the model to replace national self-determination.[50] Within the New Testament documents, indeed up until the time of

---

Columbia University Press, 1993), p. 23. Cf. Kristeva, *Strangers to Ourselves* (New York: Columbia University Press, 1991).

[47] Boyarin, *A Radical Jew*, p. 7.

[48] Boyarin, *A Radical Jew*, pp. 230–31.

[49] M. Miles, *The Image and Practice of Holiness* (London: SCM, 1988). Cf. Matt. 10:34–37.

[50] Boyarin, p. 249.

Constantine, the situation is hardly different: the life of the Christian is likely to be as that envisaged in 1 Peter—the life of a stranger and sojourner (see Reinhard Feldmeier).

Indeed, it would not be too far from the truth to suggest that the process of the separation of Judaism and Christianity took place in historical contexts within which both religious groups were minorities. Neither wielded significant political power, and it is really only when Christianity took on the institutional forms of Christendom that anti-Jewish rhetoric could be combined with political monopoly to form systematic anti-Semitic violence. It is precisely Boyarin who provides an ethical escape hatch both for rabbinic Judaism *and* early Christianity when he claims that ethnocentrism "is ethically appropriate only when the cultural identity is that of a minority, embattled or, at any rate, non-hegemonic."[51] On this point, he cites E.P. Sanders:

> We shall all agree that exclusivism is bad when practiced by the dominant group. Things look different if one thinks of minority groups that are trying to maintain their own identity. I have never felt that the strict Amish are iniquitous, and I do not think that, in assessing Jewish separatism in the Diaspora, we are dealing with a moral issue. (The moral issue would be the treatment of Gentiles in Palestine during periods of Jewish ascendancy.)[52]

The central ethical issue here is taken up by Jon Levenson in his contribution to the present volume. On the one hand, Levenson implicitly follows Boyarin and Sanders in resisting the Kantian version of ethics which requires universalizability (i.e., if a norm cannot be advocated for everyone, on Kant's view, then it is not a properly ethical norm). Judaism provides a paradigm counter-example: it does not hold that all the commandments are binding on everyone. On the other hand, Levenson also resists

> a common habit of stressing Jewish survival as a goal in its own right... At its worst, the absolutization of Jewish survival leads to the denial of ethical constraints on Jewry in danger. And since Jewry is usually in danger, this grants the Jews a moral *carte blanche*—quite the reverse of the biblical intent.

---

[51] Boyarin, p. 256.
[52] Sanders "Jewish Association with Gentiles and Galatians 2.11–14," in R.T. Fortna and B.R. Gaventa (eds.), *The Conversation Continues* (Nashville: Abingdon, 1990), p. 181. Cf. W.D. Davies, *The Territorial Dimension of Judaism* (Minneapolis: Fortress, 1992), pp. 133–38. D. Smith-Christopher has also defended the ethnocentric tendencies of groups suffering oppression in Smith, *Religion of the Landless* (New York: Meyer-Stone Books, 1989).

Similarly, following the logic of Sanders, I would suggest that if Christianity had a minority status before Constantine, it also would be given a moral *carte blanche* against biblical intent. It is ethically important to take asymmetries of power into account. But even if we agree that ethnocentrism is only pernicious when imposed by force, and it is a different matter when it is adopted as a strategy for subaltern resistance, there are nevertheless some ethical issues remaining for subaltern collectives. Even if we decide that the New Testament is not guilty of xenophobia, for example, the ethnic slurs which it contains cannot be dismissed as morally irrelevant, especially when one considers their later influence in history (see Wolfgang Stegemann). Dominated communities are not entirely free of ethical constraints.

One further issue, arising from the political stance of Daniel Boyarin's *A Radical Jew*, deserves discussion. Boyarin suggests that territoriality should be expendable within a postmodern diaspora Judaism. This might also be the case for Christians if they also regarded themselves as resident aliens on the model suggested by the letter of 1 Peter (see Reinhard Feldmeier, who discusses the model in relation to cultural resistance). It is not so clear, however, that land is such a negotiable item in the construction of the social identity of indigenous peoples. Certainly in the case of Australian Aborigines, it is difficult to see how they could renounce any claim on traditional land and still remain Aboriginal.[53] When the Aborigines first came into contact with Europeans, they could not grasp the significance of European settlement since in their own worldview to leave one's communal land would be to commit a kind of spiritual suicide.[54] Christian Aborigines are therefore placed in a dilemma with regard to their attitude to traditional land (see Lynne Hume).

---

[53] It is interesting, however, to note Swain's argument that there is a tension between place-based systems and patrilineal genealogical systems in Aboriginal worldviews. See Swain, *A Place for Strangers*, pp. 41–49.

[54] See Eve Mungwa D. Fesl, "Religion and Ethnic Identity: A Koori View," in A.W. Ata (ed.), *Religion and Ethnicity: An Australian Study* Vol. 2 (Melbourne: Spectrum, 1989), p. 9. While Aborigines were not "pacifists," wars of territorial conquest were initially inconceivable. See Swain, *A Place for Strangers*, who suggests that the pre-contact Aboriginal ontology of "structured locative interdependence" means that "to consume other people/lands is to destroy the world-pattern on which one depends" (p. 54). Cf. T.G.H. Strehlow, "Geography and the Totemic Landscape in Central Australia: A Functional Study," in R.M. Bernt (ed.), *Australian Aboriginal Studies* (Nedlands: University of Western Australia Press, 1970), p. 130.

Can they read themselves as aliens and sojourners as the New Testament suggests?

Speaking from their own experience in Mizoram, North-east India, Thanzauva and R.L. Hnuni argue below that the Bible does have resources for indigenous peoples, depending on how readers construct their identification with social groups in the biblical stories.[55] They tend to read "with the grain" of the biblical texts, and in this sense, their method has some affinities with so-called "intratextual" theology.[56] David Jobling and Catherine Rose, on the other hand, read the book of Samuel against the grain, or "contra-textually." What difference does it make, they ask, to read the text from the point of view of the Philistines? It is no accident that they begin their wide-ranging discussion of Philistines, ancient and modern, by reiterating a point made by Palestinian and American Indian critics: the biblical narratives are directed *against* the indigenous peoples of Canaan. How is it possible for Palestinians and Indians, who have experienced the violent consequences of being read "intratextually" as Canaanites,[57] to turn round and read themselves in some kind of continuity with "Israelites"?

Clearly, this is an important hermeneutical dispute, and it will surely be a matter of priority to examine the whole range of biblical theologies of land[58] and whether, or how, they should figure in the research programmes of Aboriginal cultural studies. This is just one of the questions for those of us who are struggling with the implications of multicultural politics for the discipline of biblical studies. The present volume raises a great number of other issues, and it is my hope that these diverse articles will generate more debate on the theme of ethnicity.

---

[55] Cf. Swain's comments on Aboriginal discourse concerning the "Promised Land" (*A Place for Strangers*, p. 289) and Lantenari's discussion of Maori appropriations of "Jewish" identity, above n. 38.

[56] See my discussion in Brett, *Biblical Criticism in Crisis?* (Cambridge: Cambridge University Press, 1991), pp. 156–67.

[57] See N.S. Ateek, *Justice, Only Justice* (Maryknoll: Orbis, 1989); S. Niditch, *War in the Hebrew Bible* (Oxford: Oxford University Press, 1992), pp. 1–2; E. Said, "Michael Walzer's *Exodus and Revolution*: A Canaanite Reading," in E.W. Said and C. Hitchens (eds.), *Blaming the Victims: Spurious Scholarship and the Palestinian Question* (New York: Verso, 1988), pp. 161–78; R.A. Warrior, "Canaanites, Cowboys and Indians," *Christianity and Crisis* 29 (1989), pp. 261–65; cf. K.W. Whitelam, *The Invention of Ancient Israel: The Silencing of Palestinian History* (London: Routledge, forthcoming).

[58] See, for example, N. Habel, *The Land is Mine: Six Biblical Land Ideologies* (Minneapolis: Fortress, 1995).

Some readers will, no doubt, wonder why such a diversity of top-
ics needed to be collected into a single volume. One of the virtues of
this collection is that it raises fresh questions for subjects which are
usually treated in isolation from each other. Interpretative issues which
are, strictly speaking, logically separable may nevertheless be enriched
by inter-disciplinary conversation. The goal is not to conflate separate issues but to examine their inter-relationship. Even the essays in
Part I, which are focussed on the ancient world, often have an eye
on present political realities. While the degree of cultural hybridity
evidenced in post-colonial societies[59] and postmodern cities is extreme,
this volume suggests that the ubiquity of cultural permeability might
cast a different light on the political questions of multiculturalism
(although we should be careful not to reduce the politics of identity
simply to questions of culture). The idea that cultures are, or should
be, hermetically sealed systems—all equally valuable, all equally need-
ing protection, all equally immune to critique—is probably as dam-
aging to the cause of dialogue as any presumed ideals of religion or
politics which propose the elimination of all cultural influences.[60]

---

[59] See the section of hybridity in B. Ashcroft et al. (eds.), *The Post-colonial Studies
Reader* (London: Routledge, 1995), pp. 183–209.
[60] See Taylor, "Politics of Recognition," pp. 67, 70; idem, "Understanding and
Ethnocentricity," pp. 123–24; J. Milbank, "The End of Dialogue," in G. D'Costa
(ed.), *Christian Uniqueness Reconsidered: The Myth of Pluralistic Theology* (Maryknoll: Orbis,
1990), p. 184.

PART I

ETHNICITY IN THE BIBLE

ETHNICITY AND EARLY ISRAEL

Diana Edelman

Introduction

Given the present state of textual and artifactual evidence, nothing definitive can be said about the ethnicity of premonarchic Israel. This realization has been growing during the last decade or so, as ancient Syro-Palestinian archaeologists and historians of ancient Israel and Judah have become more aware of the limitations of the evidence and have paid attention to the complex nature of ethnicity and how it functions in societies.[1] The reasons for our inability to learn anything about early Israel's ethnic composition and forms of ethnic expression will be explored in the balance of this paper.

Recent sociological studies of the development of ethnicity and forms of its expression have emphasized the genesis of ethnicity as a result of specific historical processes that structure relations of inequality between discrete social entities. Ethnic consciousness involves both an assertion of a collective self and the negation of collective other/s, creating a world of asymmetrical "we-them" relations.[2] It is

---

[1] See, for example, N.P. Lemche, *Early Israel* (VTSup, 37; Leiden: Brill, 1985), p. 406; R. Coote, *Early Israel: A New Horizon* (Minneapolis: Fortress, 1990), p. 78; T.L. Thompson, *Early History of the Israelite People From the Written & Archaeological Sources* (SHANE, 4; Leiden: Brill, 1992), pp. 154, 161–62, 223, 243–44, 281–82, 303–306, 314, 316, 322–23, 327; M. Skjeggestad, "Ethnic Groups in Early Iron Age Palestine: Some Remarks on the Use of the Term 'Israelite' in Recent Research," *SJOT* 6 (1992), pp. 159–86, esp. 163–68, 177–86; G.W. Ahlström, *The History of Ancient Palestine from the Palaeolithic Period to Alexander's Conquest* (JSOTSup, 146; Sheffield: JSOT, 1993), pp. 337–43. See esp. the following articles in I. Finkelstein and N. Na'aman, (eds.), From *Nomadism to Monarchy: Archaeological and Historical Aspects of Early Israel* (Jerusalem: Israel Exploration Society, 1994): I. Finkelstein and N. Na'aman, "Introduction," p. 17; A. Mazar, "Jerusalem and its Vicinity in Iron Age I," p. 91; Z. Herzog, "The Beer-sheba Valley: From Nomadism to Monarchy," pp. 146–49; I. Finkelstein, "The Emergence of Israel: A Phase in the Cyclic History of Canaan in the Third and Second Millennia BCE," p. 169; and N. Na'aman, "The 'Conquest of Canaan' in the Book of Joshua and History," p. 242.

[2] So J. and J. Comaroff, *Ethnography and the Historical Imagination* (Boulder: Westview, 1992), p. 56. I am indebted to my colleague, Rick Thompson, in the Dept. of Sociology and Anthropology at James Madison University, for steering me to this discussion. This "interactional" approach that involves both self-ascription and ascription by others has been acknowledged in previous discussions of the issue by

not an ontological feature of human organization, a "first cause" in
and of itself. While the meaningful construction of the world by classification is a necessary condition of social existence, the substance of
the identities varies from group to group and is determined by specific historical circumstances. Once ethnicity emerges, however, as
the basis of social classification and status relations, it seems on the
experiential level to become an independent principle that determines
social status, class membership, and social relations. It may be per-
petuated by factors quite different from those that caused its emergence and may have a direct and independent impact on the context in which it arose.[3]

The foregoing summary emphasizes that the factors leading to the
emergence of ethnicity within a given group cannot be predicted,
nor can the specific forms ethnicity will take and changes that it will
undergo over time. This means that there are no *artifactual* remains
that can consistently be used to understand a group's ethnicity; these
will vary from group to group, depending on historical circumstances.
While some cultural remains may reflect information about a given
group's ethnicity, it will not always be clear from the artifacts alone
how to extract such information and which artifacts can provide such
information.[4]

Textual Evidence

In order to examine the emergence of ethnicity in early Israel, as
well as its persistence and transformation, we need texts that accurately
record and transmit information about Israel's emergence as a recog-

e.g., F. Barth ("Introduction," in *Ethnic Groups and Boundaries* [ed. F. Barth; Boston:
Little, Brown and Co., 1969], pp. 9–38), G. Berreman ("Bazaar Behavior: Social
Identity and Social Interaction in Urban India," in *Ethnic Identity* [ed. G. de Vos
and L. Romanucci; Palo Alto, CA: Mayfield, 1975], pp. 71–105) and K.A. Kamp
and N. Yoffee ("Ethnicity in Ancient Asia During the Early Second Millenium BC,"
BASOR 237 [1980], pp. 85–104, esp. 87–88).
   [3] For a presentation of an analytic position that accounts for the genesis, persistence and transformation of ethnicity and ethnic consciousness, see J. and J. Comaroff,
Ethnography, pp. 49–67. I find this discussion more helpful than that, for example, by
R. McGuire ("The Study of Ethnicity in Historical Archaeology," *Journal of Anthropological Archaeology* 1 [1982], pp. 159–78), which has been cited as a good source for
the issue.
   [4] K.A. Kamp and N. Yoffee (above n. 2) have suggested that ethnic identification
may be derived from material cultural remains by using high probability correla-

nizable entity, whether geographical, social or cultural. Unfortunately, such texts do not now exist, and may never have existed. Moreover, it is highly unlikely that any additional ones will turn up in the future. We do need to examine, however, the potentially relevant material in the Bible and the Merneptah Stele.

A. *The Bible*

As emphasis has grown on studying the final form of the biblical text as a literary composition, whose meaning is the only level of meaning that can realistically be approached by scholarship, confidence in our ability to reconstruct the "original" form of a tradition has waned. At the same time, the recognition has grown that the biblical texts reflect the world view of the time in which their primary authors composed them, even allowing for subsequent editorial changes and "updatings." The primary composition of the books of Joshua and Judges, which deal with Israel's occupation of the land and life prior to the emergence of the monarchy, are variously dated to ca. 700,[5]

---

tions of the way data clusters for the following three types of behavior: behavior symbolizing ethnic identity; behavior resulting from socialization as a member of a group; and behavior associated with political or economic strategy based on group membership. They emphasize that home manufacturing techniques and stylistic preferences are especially good indicators ("Ethnicity in Ancient Asia," p. 96). Nevertheless, early in their article they acknowledge that ethnographic data are suggestive but in no way conclusive; researchers rely on many models (p. 93). Thus, since high probability correlations will vary depending on which ethnographic model they are measured against, or with which model they are compared, ultimately, all results will be tentative rather than conclusive. In spite of their optimism about being able to derive ethnic identification through the application of their proposed method, their results are not really open to verification when applied to ancient civilizations that left few or no texts and so remain proposals, not facts.

[5] So, e.g., H. Weippert, "Das 'deuteronomistischen' Beurteilungen der Könige von Israel und Juda und das Problem der Redaktion der Königsbücher," *Bib* 53 (1972), pp. 310–19, who points out reasons to posit a pre-Josianic date but does not specifically propose a date; W.B. Barrick, "On the 'Removal of the high Places' in 1–2 Kings," *Bib* 55 (1974), p. 259; M. Weinfeld, "The Emergence of the Deuteronomic Movement: The Historical Antecedents," in N. Lohfink, (ed.), *Das Deuteronomium: Enstehung, Gestalt, und Botschaft* (BETL, 68; Leuven: Leuven University, 1985), pp. 76–98. A. Lemaire posits a Hezekian edition, but believes that the first assembling of the extended history took place even earlier, under Jehoshaphat ("Vers l'histoire de la rédaction des livres de Rois," *ZAW* 98 [1986], pp. 224, 230, 232) while A. Campbell posits a northern prophetic record as the main base, dating to the reign of Jehu in the late 9th cent. BCE (*Of Kings and Prophets: A Ninth Century Document (1 Samuel 1–2 Kings 10)* [CBQMS, 17; Washington DC: Catholic Biblical Association, 1986]).

ca. 600,[6] or pre-515 BCE,[7] depending on one's preference for dating
the Deuteronomistic History. All dates are removed from the events
they recreate by hundreds of years and reflect the world view of a
monarchic society, either at the level of state or empire.

It is probably no coincidence that the office of "judge" as imagined
by the author of the book of Judges differs from that of kingship
only in hereditary succession, or dynasty. Both assign to the leader
the dual roles of military leadership and judicial leadership, which
specifically means holding the people to the terms of the Sinai covenant. The first task is made clear in Judg. 2:16 and 1 Sam. 9:16,
while the second is expressed in Judg. 2:17 and 1 Sam. 9:17.[8] The
office of judgeship has been modelled on the only system of leadership
the author knew from his own time and experience, that of kingship.

The second trait in particular, judicial leadership, has been artificially imposed on the source material used by the Judahite or Judean
writer to create the book of Judges. Details in the various accounts
of the lives of judges suggest that he has adapted a series of stories

---

[6] So, e.g., W.F. Albright, *The Biblical Period* (Pittsburgh: Pittsburg University, 1950),
pp. 45–46; J. Gray, *I and II Kings* (OTL; Philadelphia: Westminster, 1963), pp. 35–
36; F.M. Cross, Jr., *Canaanite Myth and Hebrew Epic* (Cambridge: Harvard University,
1973), pp. 274–89; P.K. McCarter, Jr., *1 Samuel* (AB, 8; Garden City, NY: Doubleday,
1980), p. 15; R.E. Friedman, *The Exile and Biblical Narrative* (HSM, 22; Chico, CA:
Scholars, 1981), pp. 1–26; R.D. Nelson, *The Double Redaction of the Deuteronomistic
History* (JSOTSup, 18; Sheffield: JSOT, 1981), pp. 120–21; A.D.H. Mayes, *The Story
of Israel Between the Settlement and Exile: A Redactional Study of the Deuteronomistic History*
(London: SCM, 1983), p. 136; I. Provan, *Hezekiah and the Books of Kings* (BZAW,
172; New York: Walter de Gruyter, 1988), p. 172.

[7] So, e.g., M. Noth, *The Deuteronomistic History* (tr. J. Doull *et al.*; JSOTSup, 15;
Sheffield: JSOT, 1981); R. Smend, "Das Gesetz und die Völker. Ein Beitrag zur
deuteronomistischen Redaktionsgeschichte," in H.W. Wolff, (ed.), *Probleme biblischer
Theologie: Gerhard von Rad zum 70. Geburtstag* (Munich: C. Kaiser, 1971), pp. 494–509;
W. Dietrich, *Prophetie und Geschichte* (FRLANT, 108; Göttingen: Vandenhoeck &
Ruprecht, 1972); T. Veijola, *Die ewige Dynastie: David und die Enstehung seiner Dynastie
nach der deuteronomistischen Darstellung* (AASF B, 193; Helsinki: Soumalainen Tiedea-
katemia, 1975); idem, *Das Königtum in der Beurteilung der deuteronomistischen Historiographie:
eine redaktionsgeschichtliche Untersuchung* (AASF B, 198; Helsinki: Suomalainen Tiedea-
katemia, 1977); H.D. Hoffmann, *Reform und Reformen: Untersuchung zu einem Grundthema
der deuteronomistischen Geschichtsschreibung* (ATANT, 66; Zurich: Theologischer Verlag,
1980); and B. Peckham, *The Composition of the Deuteronomistic History* (HSM, 35; Atlanta:
Scholars, 1985). Smend, Dietrich and Veijola recognize at least two layers of writ-
ing/editing but all date the initial composition to the exilic period.

[8] The failure of the people to listen to the judge and their breaking of the covenant by worshipping other gods indicates that the judge's role in peacetime, after
the overthrow of foreign oppression, was to tell the people the terms of the Sinai
covenant. The verb *'asar* in 1 Sam 9:17 should be translated in its primary sense,
"to constrain." The king is to hold the people to the terms of the covenant. The

dealing with military victories by local heroes associated with various regions that came to be or were part of the state of Israel to portray his vision of life before the monarchy. Martin Noth's theory that the minor judges stem from a list of supratribal judicial functionaries in the premonarchic period has not prevailed in the face of literary or historical investigations.[9] The minor judges seem rather to play the specific literary function of marking the passage of time within the schematized era of the judges, appearing in the incremental pattern 1–2–3.[10] Their stories may either have been presumed to have been known by the ancient audience, precluding the need to retell them fully, or they may have been obscure figures, like many of the so-called major judges prior to their development at the hands of the author of Judges. The author may have run out of potential weaknesses to point out in judgeship as a form of leadership, or he may simply have not been inspired by the details associated with these other six individuals to expand them into full accounts. None of the so-called major or minor judges seem to have been remembered for their function in a judicial capacity;[11] this aspect of office appears to have been assigned to them because it was an integral aspect of the royal office and because it helped the author underscore his point that the people continually chose to break the covenant in spite of their full knowledge of the laws contained therein, made known to them by their leaders.

In light of the centuries-long gap between the composition of Joshua and Judges and the actual premonarchic time period, questions need to be asked about the nature of sources that would have been created in such a socio-political setting, their means of preservation and transmission through the centuries, and how they would have become available to the southern writer responsible for the two books,

---

opposite of this term, *para'*, and its effects are illlustrated in Exod. 32:25, where Moses accuses Aaron of having "let the people loose" by failing to hold them to the worship of Yahweh.

[9] For a convenient statement of the position in English, see M. Noth, *The History of Israel* (New York: Harper & Row, 3rd edn, 1960), pp. 101–102.

[10] So E.T. Mullen, "The 'Minor Judges': Some Literary and Historical Considerations," *CBQ* 44 (1982), pp. 185–201.

[11] The only one who might potentially have fulfilled a judicial role is Deborah, but upon consideration of the sources used to create her story, this does not seem likely. She was remembered as a prophetess/seer in the poem in Judges 5, which served as the main source for the composition of the narrative in Judges 4. Her connection with a tree landmark in the central hill country may also reflect her historical status as religious functionary, since singular trees often had a sacred function.

given the amount of northern material contained within them.

It is generally agreed that poetic fragments incorporated into various narrative frameworks in different biblical books derive from pre-existing sources, though the nature and date of those sources remains disputed in many instances. Of sources specifically quoted by authors, there is the Scroll of the Wars of Yahweh (Num. 21:14) and the Scroll of Yashar (Josh. 10:13; 2 Sam. 1:18). Both seem to contain songs associated with wars, whether victories or defeats. Not surprisingly, a number of the poems quoted in the so-called historical books deal with situations of war: Miriam's Song (Exod. 15:20 and the expanded form in 15:1–18); Deborah's Song in Judges 5; the victory song claiming the capture of Heshbon in Num. 21:27–30. Even if all the battles referenced in the poetic fragments cited derive from the monarchic period, which is quite possible, it is still likely that the creation of such victory songs and laments in response to wars was a premonarchic practice that continued in the monarchic period. Wars are waged in prestate societies and the results become the basis of hero stories and poetic remembrances.

Whether any such literature, in story form or poetic form, either written or oral, survived from premonarchic Israel into the monarchic period cannot be known for certain, but it can be presumed that such material would have been produced by early Israelite society. The handing on of war-related traditions would explain the decision by the author of the book of Joshua to opt for the form of origin story common in ancient historiography that centered on claim to land through its conquest by ancestors, as opposed to the other common form in which a deity led an ancestor peacefully to a new homeland, found in the Abraham narrative.[12] If the writer had before him sources that focused on war stories or collections of victory songs stemming from early battles, he would logically have been swayed to recreate Israel's origins in terms of the conquest model rather than the more peaceful model. Even so, there is no guarantee that his sources went back to the premonarchic era; they may well reflect battles conducted during the monarchic period which, lacking specific dates or names of kings, were retrojected by him to the premonarchic period.

---

[12] For these two types of origin traditions, see esp. J. Van Seters, *Prologue to History: The Yahwist as Historian in Genesis* (Louisville: Westminster/John Knox, 1992), esp. p. 239. See also, M. Weinfeld, *The Promise of the Land: The Inheritance of the Land of Canaan by the Israelites* (Los Angeles: University of California, 1993), pp. 1–51.

Judges 5 may well be such a monarchic-era battle that has been used by the biblical writer to illustrate events in the premonarchic period. The original form of the poem can no longer be determined, but it appears that there have been a couple of stages of expansion. The northern origin of the tradition is made clear from the chastisement of various groups that did not participate; Judah and Simeon are not among the tribes or groups listed, and Reuben's mention should probably be connected with the tradition that places the stone of Bohan at the eastern edge of the central hill country (Josh. 15:5). The tribes named are traditionally associated with territory that was controlled at one time or another by the state of Israel.

According to v. 19, the kings of Canaan fought against Taanach. The battle was engaged between the Israelite forces from Taanach, led by Baraq, and Sisera's forces outside of the city, in the plain lying south of the Qishon River. The Israelites may have driven the enemy forces back to the river, which served as a barrier to their further retreat. The core details in the poem suggest that Taanach was an Israelite city that was unsuccessfully assaulted by Sisera's forces.[13]

As a lowland city adjoining the central hill country, Taanach's capture and incorporation into Israel has usually been dated to the monarchic period, under David or Solomon. Judg. 1:27 lists it as one of the Canaanite cities that fell within the tribal allotment of Manasseh but whose native population was never dispossessed, and it appears in the list of administrative districts attributed to Solomon in the Jezreel-Beth Shean corridor, one of the areas that lay outside of traditional tribal land, which was to have been created from newly conquered "Canaanite" territory (1 Kgs 4:12).[14]

---

[13] A. Rainey has suggested that Taanach was the mustering ground for the Canaanite forces and should not be read as the place where the battle was joined, but with the ensuing statement about the anticipated division of spoils ("The Military Campground at Taanach by the Waters of Megiddo," *Eretz Israel* 15 [1981], pp. 61*–66*). From where, then, would Sisera's troops have captured the expected female war trophies and made off with the fine cloth? Certainly not from the Israelite forces they engaged in battle in the open, since women were not part of the armed forces of the day. The situation presumes an attack on a specific settlement containing women, known for its fine cloth, and containing silver items worth spoiling, although the latter could arguably have been plundered from the bodies of slain warriors. His suggested interpretation can stand only if one argues that the list of anticipated war booty is generic, being an expected feature of such a composition.

[14] Whatever the date of the list, which could derive from a later Israelite administration, Taanach lies at the edge of the central hill country, the core of the territorial

Does the failure of poetic fragments memorializing Israelite victories to appear in most of the battle accounts in Joshua mean that poetic collections were not the primary source used by the author of each book? Probably. Otherwise, we would have expected each narrative account to have been followed by its victory song, on which it was based. Were any other sources used? Again, without the ability to confirm the use of sources, nothing definitive can be said. However, it is clear that the book of Judges is based on some sort of collection of hero stories stemming from northern state of Israel and not from the author's native Judah. Othniel is commonly acknowledged to be a secondary addition to the collection. His story illustrates the pattern of judgeship to a tee with no extraneous details, and quite suspiciously, he is the only judge from the south, who coincidentally illustrates that judgeship can work as a form of leadership, given the right person. The northern origin of the underlying traditions for the remaining judges suggests the use of some sort of source for this book at least. There is no way to know, however, if the individuals portrayed therein lived in premonarchic Israel or monarchic Israel or if they lived at all.

The book of Joshua appears to have been based in part on source material. Its author seems to have employed different kinds of administrative lists to delineate the division of the land into tribal allotments.[15] Some explanation for how a Judahite or Judean author came into possession of such lists for districts within the state of Israel must be given. Although a date under David or Solomon might be pos-

---

state of Israel, in non-traditional Israelite land. It is noteworthy that Taanach is mentioned in Egyptian accounts of the Battle of Megiddo (ca. 1468 BCE) and among the towns/cities conquered by Sheshonq ca. 918 BCE. Otherwise, it only appears in an 18th dynasty hieratic text among eleven towns that sent *maryannu* representatives to Pharaoh's court. On the basis of archaeological excavations, it has been surmised that the site was destroyed ca. 1350 BCE and resettled sometime in the 12th century BCE. Evidence for occupation during the 10th and 9th centuries was also uncovered. On the basis of currently available archaeological evidence, the site was not occupied during the conquest period that typically is assigned to the end of the Late Bronze Age (end of the 13th century BCE) or the early period of the judges, in the first half of the 12th century. Such results need to be used with caution, however, since exposure of early levels was very limited and the first excavations were done before modern methods were fully developed. See conveniently, A.E. Glock, "Taanach," in D.N. Freedman (ed.), *Anchor Bible Dictionary: Vol. 6* (New York: Doubleday, 1992), pp. 287–90.

[15] N. Na'aman has suggested that many of the battles contained in the first twelve chapters of the book are based on later monarchic-era battles, dating from David to the Assyrians. This is an attractive idea, even if it cannot be proven definitively ("The 'Conquest of Canaan,'" pp. 218–81, esp. 251–81).

sible, which would have been the last time that Judah would have controlled all this territory according to the author of Samuel and Kings, it is not the only viable explanation.

Noting the presence of northern material in the Deuteronomistic History, many scholars have argued that these traditions were carried south by fleeing northerners in the wake of the capture of Samaria in 721 BCE and the conversion of the former state of Israel to the Assyrian province of Samerina.[16] The great expansion of population in Jerusalem in the 7th century, when a second city wall was built to accommodate the new settlement outside the old city's perimeter, has been connected with this hypothetical refugee movement.[17] I have always found the picture of scribes fleeing the burning city with scrolls tucked under each arm to be highly amusing, although arguably, they could have carried their traditions in their heads and written them down once resettled in the south. Why the intelligentsia of the Jerusalemite court would have felt these traditions to be so superior to their own that they would have adopted them instantly, theology and all, has always been a mystery to me. Did they really have such an inferiority complex?

While some northern traditions could have been mediated to Judah by northern refugees after 721 BCE, two alternative explanations for the bulk of them are more appealing. According to most of the boundary lists in various books, Bethel and Gilgal were Israelite towns. However, in Josh. 18:21, both towns lie within the boundaries of Judah, in the northernmost district of Benjamin. Similarly, in Neh. 7:32 and 36 Bethel and Jericho are part of the Persian province of Yehud. This list in Joshua is frequently dated to the reign of Josiah, especially in light of the claim in 2 Kgs 23:4, 15–18 that Josiah had direct access to Bethel and defiled the former Israelite royal sanctuary there.[18] Even though it is unlikely that Josiah was able to take control

[16] So, e.g., E.W. Nicholson, *Deuteronomy and Tradition* (Philadelphia: Fortress, 1967), pp. 58–82, 94 and esp. 58, n. 1–2 and 59 n. 1–2 for others who have shared similar views.

[17] So, e.g., M. Broshi, "The Expansion of Jerusalem in the reign of Hezekiah and Manasseh," *IEJ* 24 (1974), pp. 21–26; N. Avigad, *Discovering Jerusalem* (Nashville: Thomas Nelson, 1983), pp. 54–56; Ahlström, *History of Ancient Palestine*, pp. 681–82. J. Hayes suggests that part of the population growth may have been due to northern refugees, but that part might equally have been Judahites who were displaced after the Assyrian confiscation of most of the land of Judah after 701 BCE (J.M. Miller and J.H. Hayes, *A History of Ancient Israel and Judah* [Philadelphia: Westminster, 1986], p. 354).

[18] So, e.g., A. Alt, "Judas Gaue unter Josia," *PJB* 21 (1925), pp. 100–111;

over most of the territory of the former Israelite state as Assyria's
empire crumbled, he could well have expanded his northern border
slightly to the north, in a test to see what the weakened Assyrians
would do. By taking control of Bethel and Gilgal, he would have
gained access to whatever northern records would have been preserved at those sanctuaries.

Two scenarios can be reconstructed on the basis of the citations
from Joshua and Nehemiah. The first is that control of a segment of
southern Mt. Ephraim passed from Samaria to the state of Judah
toward the end of the monarchy, perhaps during the reign of Josiah,
and remained connected to the South into the Persian period. The
second is that control of this region first passed to the South during
the Persian period, with the establishment of the province of Yehud,
when the old Assyrian and Neo-Babylonian district boundaries were
readjusted for some reason. In the latter case, the stories about Josiah
defiling the sanctuary at Bethel would be a retrojection to give fictional
credit for the change to this king, and the Benjaminite boundary list
would reflect the situation in the Persian period, not the late monarchy, as is frequently maintained.

Southern control over Bethel, whether established in the late monarchy or in the Persian period, would explain well the prominence of
Bethel in the biblical stories, and Gilgal, to a much lesser degree.
The stories of Elijah and Elisha tend to center around activities associated with these two sanctuaries, and the prophetical traditions of
Hosea and Amos could easily have been derived from Bethel's archives. A copy of northern royal annals might also have been kept
at the royal sanctuary, as a list of deeds performed by the kingdom's
earthly vice-regents on behalf of the national god. In fact, even a
cursory reading of the Hebrew Bible leaves the impression that Bethel,
not Samaria, was the most prominent northern royal sanctuary; there
are almost no traditions relating to the capital city proper, but many
associated with Bethel and Gilgal.

Since taxes were typically paid in the framework of religious festivals, local district lists should also have been kept at both sanctuaries.
Perhaps lists of all the northern state's districts were kept at regional

N. Na'aman, *Borders and Districts in Biblical Historiography* (Jerusalem Biblical Studies,
4; Jerusalem: Simor, 1986), p. 229. Contrast Z. Kallai, who dates it to the reign of
Abijah on the basis of his purported conquests in the region, which are found only
in 2 Chronicles 13 (*Historical Geography of the Bible* [Jerusalem: Magnes and Leiden:
Brill, 1986], p. 398).

administrative centers like Bethel, and those at Bethel survived the changeover to Assyrian administration. Certainly local lists would have served as the basis for ongoing taxation and conscription, regardless of the new head of state and the changes in population groups resident in towns.

The collection of stories lying behind the book of Judges and some of the boundary information and town lists for the North in the book of Joshua could have been derived from archival materials preserved at Bethel and/or Gilgal. For those who doubt the historicity of David or Solomon, or those who accept their existence as early kings over the combined entities of Israel and Judah but who suspect that very few records would have been preserved in the southern court from this early monarchic era, the proposed access either during the late monarchic period or during the Persian period by southern scribes to archival records stored at Bethel and Gilgal offers an alternative, viable explanation. It allows records from the end of the Israelite monarchy to have served as a data base for Judahite authors involved in the composition of a number of biblical books.[19]

B. *The Merneptah Stele*

The most important text for information about premonarchic Israel, the Merneptah Stele, yields almost no firm data about this unit or entity. As pointed out initially by O. Eissfeldt, the foreign group mentioned in line seven of the coda section, which describes a campaign to Hurru-land or Canaan that took place prior to his campaign against the Libyans, the main topic of celebration in the stele, cannot even definitively be read as Israel; it could just as well be Jezreel.[20]

---

[19] Since it is Jericho rather than Gilgal that appears in the town list in Nehemiah, a late monarchic date for the Gilgal traditions is more plausible if one wants to argue that they stem from actual sanctuary records. However, it could be argued that all the traditions mentioning Gilgal were derived from records kept at Bethel, since references to the two sanctuaries tend to cluster together. In this case, a date of origin in the Persian period could not be ruled out.

[20] This idea was put forward by O. Eissfeldt in the first version of his chapter in the *Cambridge Ancient History* entitled "Palestine in the Time of the Nineteenth Dynasty" (Cambridge: Cambridge University, 1965), p. 14. It was subsequently deleted from later editions of the chapter. In an earlier discussion, G.R. Driver had pointed out the possibility of this reading of the term on the stele, even though he had not adopted it himself (*Semitic Writing: From Pictograph to Alphabet* [The Schweich Lectures of the British Academy, 1944; London: Oxford University, 1948], p. 135). Recently,

While ultimately a geographical term, Jezreel could have become
the designation for the people who settled in the region, just as Israel, which is a personal name in form and thus, probably originated
as the name of a clan or group, came to be the designation of a
territory that included the area where the original group settled.

Assuming the name in line seven is to be read Israel, all that can
be learned definitively about this entity is that it existed somewhere
in ancient Palestine by the time of Merneptah's campaign in the
closing decade of the Late Bronze Age. It might have been a foreign
people, as the determinative suggests, but since it is not known whether
the Egyptian scribe who composed the stele had been involved in
the earlier campaign and had first-hand knowledge of Israel, nothing
certain can be concluded. It is equally possible that the determinative was used loosely, mistakenly, or deliberately in a complementary
way to the three preceding city-states to express the pharaoh's conquest of both the territory and its people.[21]

The geographical location of this Israel cannot be determined from
the information on the stele. Three proposals have been made: the
Galilee, Transjordan, and the central Cisjordanian hill country. The
first two presume that the order in which the three city-states and
Israel appear accurately reflects the course of the campaign. The
city-states move from south to north, up the coast, Ashkelon, Gezer,
and then turn east to Yeno'am. According to the first proposal,
Yeno'am is to be identified with el-'Abeidiyeh in the Jordan Valley
just south of Lake Kinneret and Israel would lie to the northeast, in
the Galilee.[22] The second proposal presumes Yeno'am is a Transjordanian city located at Tell esh-Shihab west of Edrei on the Yarmuk
River, controlling the main road to Ashtaroth and Damascus. Ac-

---

O. Margalith has taken up this idea again and favors the rendering as Jezreel rather
than Israel ("On the Origin and Antiquity of the Name 'Israel'," *ZAW* 102 (1990),
pp. 225–37, esp. 228–29, 235.

[21] A catalogue of the loose or careless use of determinatives in association with
foreign lands or peoples in texts dating from Merneptah's reign was presented by
John Huddlestun in a paper entitled "Merneptah's Revenge: The 'Israel Stela' and
its Modern Interpreters" at the 1991 Annual SBL/ASOR Meeting in Kansas City,
Kansas. For further discussion of this problem and related issues, see M. Hasel,
"Israel in the Merneptah Stele," *BASOR* 296 (1994), pp. 45–61.

[22] So, e.g., S. Yeivin, *The Israelite Conquest of Canaan* (Istanbul Nederlands
Historisch-Archaeologisch Instituut in het Nabije Oosten, 27; Leiden: Brill, 1971),
pp. 29, 30, 85; B. Peckham, "Israel and Phoenicia," in F.M. Cross *et al.* (ed.), *Magnalia
Dei: The Mighty Acts of God, Essays on the Bible and Archeology in Memory of G. Ernest
Wright* (Garden City, NY: Doubleday, 1976), p. 227; and Y. Aharoni and
M. Avi-Yonah, *The Macmillan Bible Atlas* (New York: Macmillan, rev. edn, 1977),
map 46.

cording to this view, the Egyptian troops continued east down the Beth She'an Valley and then crossed over the Jordan and continued east up the Yarmuk.[23]

The third proposal has been argued on the basis of two different rationales. The first, proposed by G.W. Ahlström and D. Edelman, assumes that the stela need not provide an accurate reflection of the course of campaign; instead, it sees the four destroyed entities to be a summary of the campaign highlights in which the first three represent lowland battles and the fourth a highland victory. It presumes that the scribe deliberately arranged the account to use the lowlands and highlands as complementary subdivisions of the land of Hurru-Canaan.[24]

An alternate approach has been taken by F. Yurco.[25] He has suggested that the three city-states and Israel mentioned in the coda can be correlated with the four battle scenes depicted on the eastern section of the eastern wall of the Cour de la Cachette in the temple of Karnak at Luxor. The four scenes appear alongside six other scenes involving the binding of shasu prisoners, the pharaoh leading Canaanite captives to his chariot, the pharaoh driving shasu prisoners back to Egypt, shasu and Canaanite prisoners being presented to Amun, and a final triumphal scene. Three of the battles involve attacks against cities while the fourth is a confrontation in open country with a host of enemies dressed in Canaanite garb. Assuming that the four scenes reflect the geographical sequence of the actual campaign, he suggests that Israel is to be equated with the fourth scene and to be located south of the Jezreel Valley, in the northern and central Cisjordanian highlands, and eastward across the Jordan River, in the Transjordanian highlands. He prefers this to the Galilee because he thinks that the earliest and densest archaeological traces of Israelite settlement lie in the former areas, not the latter area. Even if he is correct in his equation, which is not certain,[26] the pictures do not provide further

---

[23] So N. Na'aman, "Yeno'am," *Tel Aviv* 4 (1977), pp. 168–77, esp. 169, 171.

[24] So G.W. Ahlström and D. Edelman, "Merneptah's Israel," *JNES* 44 (1985), pp. 59–61.

[25] F.J. Yurco, "Merneptah's Canaanite Campaign," *JARCE* 23 (1986), pp. 189–201. His idea has been taken up and expanded by L.E. Stager, who was familiar with Yurco's work before it was published ("Merneptah, Israel and Sea Peoples: New Light on an Old Relief," *Eretz-Israel* 18 [1985], pp. 56*–64*).

[26] For a rejection of Yurco's dating of the four scenes to Merneptah and a counter proposal that they depict battle scenes from Ramses II, see D.B. Redford, "The Ashkelon Relief at Karnak and the Israel Stela," *IEJ* 36 (1986), pp. 188–200. A. Rainey has accepted Yurco's equation of the ten reliefs on the western face of

localization for Israel; the open country could be in the lowlands or
highlands, perhaps in an intermontance valley. It does not even help
settle the question of Israel's status as a people vs. some form of
state organization, since no details are known about the circumstances
under which the confrontation took place and the depiction is a highly
stylized portrayal. All four proposals about Israel's geographical location are possible; none can be proven.

The Merneptah Stele probably indicates that some sort of entity
called Israel was present in ancient Palestine already at the end of
the Late Bronze period and had a well-established enough presence
to be considered a threat worth attacking by Merneptah. Even the
latter statement is presumptuous; a review of Sheshonq's subsequent
campaign list reveals that small villages are listed alongside larger
walled towns and cities. If the scribe who composed the coda section
had been working from such a detailed list, Israel need not have
been a significant entity. The scribe might have chosen it among a
number of options because he wanted a population group, a people,
to balance his city-states, or because he wanted a highland encounter to balance the lowland ones. Other reasons are equally possible.
It might have been a major confrontation or a minor skirmish; there
are too many unknowns for us to second-guess why Israel is named.
We remain in that scribe's debt for including it in his summary for
whatever reasons and can only lament his failure to provide more
specific information.

Summary

A study of the ethnicity of premonarchic Israel needs to be based on
specific texts that indicate the geographical location and boundaries
of such a unit and which, ideally, provide information about its
socio-political structure and some of its cultural mores. Our inability

---

the western wall of the Cour de la Cachette with Merneptah's campaign that is
summarized in the coda section of the Merneptah Stele. He proposes, however, that
Israel is to be equated with the shasu depicted in the prisoner scenes and not with
the Canaanites being fought in the fourth battle scene ("Which Picture is the Israelites? Anson F. Rainey's Challenge," *BAR* 17/6 [1991], pp. 54–60, 93). His main
argument lies in his belief that the Bible has accurately portrayed the early Israelites
as semi-nomads and therefore, that they could not have used chariots, as depicted
in the reliefs. In response, F. Yurko points out that the four battle scenes should be
correlated with the four battles summarized in the coda section and that the shasu
do not fall within these scenes ("Yurco's Response," *BAR* 17/6 [1991], p. 61).

to determine definitively which traditions now found in various biblical books accurately reflect life and events in premonarchic Israel precludes such a study. This is particularly true since whatever early traditions might have used would almost certainly have been recast to reflect the world view of their authors who lived in the monarchic period or later. It seems likely that stories about local heroes and war-related poetry would have been produced by a premonarchic Israelite society. The same type of literature would also have been produced in monarchic Israel, however, making it extremely difficult, if not impossible, to distinguish between the two, should any of the first have survived.

[handwritten margin note: war poetry is premonarchic]

As outlined previously in this paper, two new alternative explanations can be proposed to account for the inclusion of a number of northern traditions in books authored by Judahites or Judeans. In addition to the possible use of southern records dating from the reign of David or Solomon, or of northern records that made their way south with refugees after the fall of the state of Israel in 721 BCE, the Judahite court may have gained access to northern records preserved in the archives of Bethel and Gilgal when these two sanctuaries were added to Judah's territory during the reign of Josiah. Alternatively, Judean scribes in the Persian province of Yehud may have gained access to northern records preserved in archives at Bethel.

The Merneptah Stele probably provides the earliest datable reference to Israel's existence as some form of definable entity somewhere in ancient Palestine but is not explicit enough to allow further conclusions to be drawn. A study of Israel's premonarchic ethnicity cannot be built on such a slim reference. The mention of Israel on the stele is best used as a clue to the minimum length of time that Israel existed as a prestate entity, although even this use presumes the accuracy of the characterization of Israel as a people, which is open to challenge.

Artifactual Evidence

Even though ethnicity will be expressed in different ways by different groups and there is no way to predict what specific forms it will take in a given society, it is possible to draw up a list of ways in which it typically is manifested in some form or another. It must be remembered that the following list is not exhaustive and that ethnicity need not find some form of expression for each item on the list in every society. Typical forms of ethnic expression can include, but are not limited to: ceramic repertoire, style, and forms of decoration, architecture, diet, religious beliefs and practices, burial customs, language, music, dance, clothing, hairstyles, lifestyles, customs, art, kinship reckoning, phenotypes, modes of production, and social structure.[27]

Only some of the forms listed above have traces that can be recovered through archaeological excavation as artifactual remains. In the quest to understand the ethnicity of premonarchic Israel, aspects of the following items have been analyzed using artifactual information: pottery repertoire, styles and forms of decoration, architecture, diet, religious beliefs and practices, burial customs, language, clothing, hairstyles, kinship reckoning, modes of production and social structure.

In each case, a presumption has been made that a specific site can be labelled "Israelite" or, in the case of the Karnak relief, that the fourth battle scene depicts Merneptah's encounter with Israelites. F. Yurco has drawn conclusions about early Israelite dress, hairstyles and lifestyle based on his tentative identification of one battle scene at Karnak with the reference in the Merneptah stela to the pharaoh's defeat of Israel. He suggests that the Canaanite-style dress indicates that a segment of early Israel had coalesced out of Canaanite society and that they can be equated archaeologically with farmsteads in the hill country in the late 13th and early 12th centuries BCE. At the same time, he accepts the accuracy of "the pastoral, nomadic images of proto-Israelites of Abraham's or Jacob's time" and thinks that early Israel contained a partially pastoral element alongside the partially settled element, even though this segment is not depicted on the reliefs and so is not documented pictorially.[28] Since his equation of the text and drawing is not certain, his conclusions need to be recognized as hypotheses, not established, verifiable facts.

Most Syro-Palestinian archaeologists and historians have concluded that premonarchic Israel can be located geographically by extending the boundaries of the later monarchic state at its fullest extent back in time to the premonarchic period or by accepting the main out-

---

[27] For a good discussion of different ways in which ethnicity can be conceived by a group and cautions about understanding the fluidity of such markers and their multipurpose functions that are not restricted to ethnicity alone, see M. Moerman, "Being Lue: Uses and Abuses of Ethnic Identification," in J. Helm (ed.), *Essays on the Problem of the Tribe* (Proceedings of the 1967 Annual Meeting of the American Ethnological Society; Seattle: University of Washington, 1968), pp. 153–69.

[28] "Yurco's Response," p. 61.

lines of the location of Israel as portrayed by the authors of the books of Joshua and Judges as essentially accurate. The second position fails to recognize that the boundaries as sketched in both books reflect the world view of their authors who lived in the monarchic period or later, rather than premonarchic reality, while the first assumes that the boundaries existed at some point in history and are not ideals. Neither presumption can be proven through independent information, and both are faulty.

Societies are not static units that remain unchanged over time; the boundaries and make-up of a group at any point in time is not identical to its past or its future. It is methodologically unsound to presume that premonarchic Israel would have been coterminous with monarchic Israel in its boundaries or its population composition. At most, it can be presumed that the later state included within its population some portion of the entity that had comprised premonarchic Israel and that the latter constituents bore a certain amount of power or prestige in the emergent state because their name was adopted by or transferred to the new political structure.

If information in the book of Kings and Assyrian annals can be presumed to reflect the boundaries of the later states of Israel and Judah at specific points in time with some degree of accuracy, the changing constituents that were included in either state fluctuated greatly over time. Without texts to provide information about changing borders, it would be very difficult, if not impossible, to chart these changing borders and the groups in border zones that became Israelite or Judahite for shorter or longer periods of time using only material cultural remains.

Since the state of Israel emerged in the central Cisjordanian highlands, it would be safe to assume that premonarchic Israel was located at least in part in this region in the period just prior to state formation. As already pointed out, however, more specific boundaries cannot be identified on the basis of biblical texts or the Merneptah stele. It might be tempting to try to use the list of districts in 2 Sam. 2:9 that the biblical writer claims Eshbaal inherited from Saul to establish the extent of premonarchic Israel on the eve of the move to statehood. However, since it cannot be determined how many non-Israelite regions Saul combined with Israelite regions to create the territorial state of Israel sometime during the first half of the 10th century, this list, should it derive from a genuine Saulide-era administrative list, cannot resolve the issue at hand.

A number of attempts have been made to identify ethnic markers

for premonarchic Israel in the material cultural Iron I remains of
the central Cisjordanian hill country. Specifically, ceramic style, architecture, site layout, modes of production, diet, religious beliefs and
practices, and social structure/kinship reckoning deduced from material remains have been argued to constitute distinctively "Israelite"
traits. None has proven to be an early Israelite ethnic marker in the
face of new data or further critical reflection.

A. *Pottery as an Ethnic Marker*

The collared-rim storage jar, which is ubiquitous in the central hill
country of Palestine on both sides of the Jordan River during the
Iron I period, was once held to be a marker of premonarchic Israelite
culture.[29] Its recovery at a number of small Iron I sites in territory
presumed to be Israelite because it lay within the tribal allotments
described in Joshua led to this postulation. As further excavations
were conducted in various regions, however, it became clear that the
storage jars were not limited to traditionally Israelite territory and
were also not found throughout traditionally Israelite regions. Examples were found on the one hand at Aphek, Megiddo, Tel Keisan,
Ta'anak, Aphek, Tel Mevorakh, Tel Zeror, Tell Qasile, and 'Afula
in the lowlands of Cisjordan and Sahab in the lowlands of Transjordan. On the other hand, examples were lacking in the northern
Negev and in the Galilee, where a variant form of the jar with a
taller neck prevailed. The latter form was traced back to local Late
Bronze forms used, for example, at Hazor.[30]

Further consideration of the function of the collared-rim storage
jars has now led to the suggestion that their prevalence is due to
their primary, though not exclusive use as water storage containers.[31]
Water was a scarce and precious commodity required by all inhabitants in the highlands, explaining the ubiquity of the jars. I. Finkelstein
has suggested additional use of the jars for the storage of wine, noting that such large containers would have been more suitable for use
in self-sufficient societies, which would explain their elimination in

---

[29] This was first proposed by Y. Aharoni, "New Aspects of the Israelite Occupation
in the North," in J.A. Sanders (ed.), *Near Eastern Archaeology in the Twentieth Century,
Essays in Honor of Nelson Glueck* (Garden City, NY: Doubleday, 1970), pp. 264–65.
[30] So, e.g., A. Mazar, *Archaeology of the Land of the Bible, 10,000–586 B.C.E.* (Anchor Bible Reference Library; New York: Doubleday, 1990), p. 348.
[31] I believe this was first suggested by A. Zertal ("The Water Supply Factor in
the Israelite Settlement in Manasseh," in *Settlements, Population and Economy in Ancient*

favor of smaller, transportable jars during the monarchy.[32] A. Mazar thinks that the jars were used to hold grain as well as water.[33] Variations in the shape and height of the rim of collared-rim jars have been noted, and although efforts to use the variations as chronological indicators have failed,[34] they may eventually provide evidence of regional preferences or pottery workshops.

Extreme caution must be used in using pottery as an ethnic marker. Even in rare cases like the Sea-Peoples, who brought with them their Mycenean tradition of pottery forms and decoration when they settled in Cisjordan, it is not always possible to distinguish among the different subgroups such as Philistines, Shekelesh, Denyen, Weshesh, Sherden and Teresh on the basis of locally made pottery that continues the Mycenean traditions. Without the aid of texts, such a distinction would not be possible.

The population groups that settled primarily in newly built farmsteads and villages in the hill country in the Iron I may have procured their pots from local pottery workshops or itinerant potters, regardless of their ethnic background. Pottery making is an acquired skill requiring knowledge of tempers, kilns, clay beds, and, in the Iron I, wheel techniques. There is no reason to believe that every village would have been able to secure and support its own potter. It is likely that regional pottery workshops[35] or itinerant potters[36] were

---

Israel: The Annual Memorial Day for Y. Aharoni, Abstracts of Lectures [Tel Aviv: Tel Aviv University, 1985], pp. 5–6) (Hebrew).

[32] *The Archaeology of the Israelite Settlement* (Jerusalem: Israel Exploration Society, 1988), p. 285.

[33] A. Mazar. "Giloh: an Early Israelite Settlement Site Near Jerusalem," *IEJ* 31 (1981), p. 30.

[34] For details, see the discussion by Finkelstein, *Archaeology of the Israelite Settlement*, pp. 276–83.

[35] The existence of the Galilean collared-rim storage jar has already been noted. In addition, the "Manassite bowl," "punched ware" and possibly "Einun ware," all of which were first identified by A. Zertal, may be regional Iron I phenomena (for a convenient summary in English, see "'To the Land of the Perizzites and the Giants: On the Israelite Settlement in the Hill Country of Manasseh," in I. Finkelstein and N. Na'aman (eds.), *From Nomadism to Monarchy: Archaeological and Historical Aspects of Early Israel* [Jerusalem: Israel Exploration Society, 1994], pp. 51–54). These types were initially discussed in his Ph.D. dissertation, "The Israelite Settlement in the Hill Country of Manasseh," Tel Aviv University, 1986 (Hebrew with English summary). Zertal is uncertain whether the latter pottery, which is characterized by a distinctive clay, should be dated to the Middle Bronze II period or the Iron I period (*ibid.*, p. 54). I. Finkelstein argues that it is MB II in date ("Emergence of Israel," p. 167). For a discussion of the possible role of pottery workshops in the production of Palestinian pottery in the Late Bronze-Iron Ages, see B. Wood, *The Sociology of Pottery in Ancient Palestine* (JSOTSup, 103; Sheffield: JSOT, 1990), pp. 33–50.

[36] The size of the collared-rim pithoi would have made transport extremely difficult.

responsible for supplying the local groups with their ceramic vessels. Under such circumstances, peoples of diverse ethnic origins would have quickly come to share a common ceramic tradition. The presence at Kh. Raddana of a multihandled krater decorated with bull heads, whose closest known parallels are from the Old Hittite Kingdom, provides some support for the presence of more than a single culture or ethnic group in Iron I Cisjordan.[37] The general homogeneity of the Iron I ceramic repertoire, which is considered by ceramic experts to be a direct continuation of the Late Bronze "Canaanite" ceramic tradition, should not erroneously be presumed to reflect the presence of a similar, ethnically homogenous population, nor necessarily be an ethnic marker.

B. *Architecture as an Ethnic Marker*

The four-room pillared house is another suggested ethnic marker of premonarchic Israelite society that has not withstood further examination. This type of dwelling is typically characterized by a broad room across one end of the structure, rooms along both sides, and a central courtyard, although there are a host of variant forms that are lumped together under the same rubric. The presence of a courtyard area and pillars, rather than a particular layout, seem to be the determining factors for the inclusion of a structure within this classification. A common variation is the "three-room house," with a courtyard, an adjacent, parallel area whose roof was supported by pillars, and a rear chamber across the back.[38]

The pillared house was typical of the new small settlements that sprang up in the hill country on both sides of the Jordan River in the Iron I period, leading early excavators to propose it was a new, specifically "Israelite" form.[39] However, ongoing excavations have

---

A logical deduction from this circumstance would be that itinerant potters made them *in situ* in various villages. This theory needs to be tested against petrographic results.

[37] For the jar, see J.A. Callaway and R.E. Cooley, "A Salvage Operation at Raddana, in Bireh," *BASOR* 201 (1971), p. 17. While the item could have arrived by trade, its probable use within the cult, which tends to be a conservative area of culture, provides a strong reason to suspect that it represents the native cultural and ethnic heritage of the settlers.

[38] So Mazar, *Archaeology of the Bible*, pp. 341–42.

[39] So esp. Y. Shiloh, "The Four Room House: Its Situation and Function in the Israelite City," *IEJ* 20 (1970), pp. 180–90.

revealed the use of pillared houses in lowland Cisjordanian urban centers like Megiddo VIB, Tell Keisan, in Philistia[40] and at Tell esh-Sharia[41] and in Transjordanian urban sites like Sahab and Khirbet Medeiyneh.[42] It has now been acknowledged that the form grew out of the local, Late Bronze Palestinian urban architectural tradition and is not a cultural innovation introduced by the arrival of a new ethnic group in the area.[43] Rather, it appears to have been an adaptation of a local urban building style to suit the needs of settlers in the hills who had limited labor power and resources, and multi-use needs.

C. *Site Layout as an Ethnic Marker*

Israel Finkelstein has proposed that the *ḥaṣer*-style layout of certain sites, in which housing units are built contiguously or continuously to form an ovoid or circular enclosure belted by buildings with open land in the center, is a marker of Israelite settlement in the hills and proof of their builders' pastoral origins.[44] His proposal is based on analogy with modern bedouin tent encampments, in which the large central courtyard is used as a shelter to protect flocks and the outer ring of tents as a windbreak and line of defense against hostile forces and in light of geographical considerations. He suggests a development among examples of courtyard-style layouts from excavated Iron I sites, in which the earliest form contains a belt of single-roomed rectangular or elliptical structures forming a solid ring around an open courtyard. Examples include 'Izbet Sartah III, Horvat 'Avot, Khirbet et-Tina, a site published by Bar Adon in the Judean desert, and four

[40] See e.g., G.W. Ahlström, "The Early Iron Age Settlers at Tel Masos (Hirbet el-Mšaš)," *ZDPV* 100 (1984), pp. 35–52; L.E. Stager, "The Archaeology of the Family in Ancient Israel," *BASOR* 258 (1985), pp. 2–12.

[41] See E. Oren, "Esh-Sharia, Tel," in M. Avi-Yonah and E. Stern (eds.), *Encyclopedia of Archaeological Excavations in the Holy Land* (5 vols.; Oxford: Oxford University, 1978) 4, pp. 1059–69.

[42] For details, see M.M. Ibrahim, "The Third Season of Excavations at Sahab, 1975 (Preliminary Report)," *ADAJ* 20 (1975), pp. 74–75.

[43] See especially K. Schaar, "The Architectural Traditions of Building 23A/13 at Tell Beit Mirsim," *SJOT* 2 (1991), pp. 75–98. He has built on the earlier work of G.W. Ahlström ("Early Settlers at Tel Masos;" "Giloh: A Judahite or Canaanite Settlement?," *IEJ* 34 [1984], pp. 170–72). A. Mazar has suggested that the roots of the style can be traced to large patrician houses that employed pillars in their courtyards, found, for example, at Late Bronze Tel Batash. *Archaeology of the Bible*, p. 247.

[44] See esp. *Archaeology of the Settlement*, pp. 237–59.

sites in the Negev Highlands, Ein Qadeis, Atar Haroʻa, Rahba, and Ketef Shivta. He then suggests a second stage characterized by Beersheba VII and Tel Esdar III, in which a belt of three or four-room houses are set contiguously to form an enclosure. The next major step is reflected in the move to a continuous line of three or four-room houses, whose rear broadrooms form a solid wall. Examples include Ai, Beersheba VII (sic), Refed, Hatira, Shiloh, Tell en-Nasbeh, and Khirbet ed-Dawwara.

For Finkelstein, these sites are Israelite because they lie within areas that come to be Israelite in the monarchic period—an approach which has already been challenged. They also are deemed Israelite because they reflect a pastoral way of life, which in turn is assumed to be the primary mode of production among prestate Israelites because of local geography and ecology and, I suspect, their tribal organization as reported by the biblical writers. The ecology, geography, and tribal organization did not change after the emergence of statehood, however,[45] and many of the small villages maintained the same strategies for production: a mixed economy based on dry farming and animal husbandry. It is true that the state eventually encouraged specialization in certain regions, especially in olive production and viticulture. It is conceivable, however, that such specialization already was in place in the premonarchic period, made possible through the existence of interregional trade.

It is noteworthy that Finkelstein does not discuss the layout of small sites in the hills during the Iron II period (under the monarchy) for comparative purposes, but this is probably due in large part to the lack of data. It is unlikely that the king would have used state resources to build a separate wall around every settlement within the kingdom's boundaries. The *haṣer*-style layout is a logical approach for any group of any background to use in a situation where they want to have some measure of defense against hostile outside attack with the minimum amount of investment in materials and labor. Allowing house walls to serve double-duty as settlement walls and having an open space in the interior of the site for the protection of animals, one of the mainstays of the local economy, is a common-sense

---

[45] With the emergence of kingship, a new administrative level was merely superimposed over the existing tribal structure in small towns; governance by local elders remained intact and traditional ways of transacting business in most instances. The *bet 'ab* and *mišpaḥah* units still functioned.

approach to living in the hill country. It reveals nothing about the origins of the inhabitants of a settlement, since animals would have been part of the economic strategy of all settlements, to a greater or lesser degree, in regions where rainfall was the primary source of water for crops.[46]

As indicated, there is no basis on which any sites in the Iron I period can be determined to be Israelite, because the boundaries of this premonarchic unit, and how they changed over time, are unknown throughout the period. The *ḥaṣer*-style site layout is something that could have been used by different ethnic groups as well as groups adapting different modes of production to life in the hill country. Its use was determined by environmental and ecological factors and concerns, not by socioeconomic or ethnic factors.[47]

D. *Diet as an Ethnic Marker*

The biblical prohibition against the consumption of pork has been put forward as another ethnic marker for premonarchic Israel that can be verified through archaeological remains.[48] The collection of animal bones has become routine at excavations in modern Israel and Jordan only within the last few decades, so the data pool available is fairly small. Notwithstanding, preliminary results have led to the conclusion that the law against the consumption of pork was already in place among the Israelites when they settled during the Iron I period because so few pig bones have been found at sites in

---

[46] The determination of whether a *ḥaṣer*-style site was settled by sedentarizing pastoralists or groups of primarily agricultural or a mixed economic background would be more profitably approached on the basis of ecology. The sites in the Negev highlands and other areas of marginal rainfall are most plausibly associated with sedentarizing pastoralists, since these areas are most conducive to grazing and there do not seem to be many, if any, silos used to store grains. By contrast, such courtyard-style sites in the central highlands often include a number of silos in the common open courtyard area, and/or grinding stones for processing grains, indicating an emphasis on grain production alongside the postulated keeping of herds.

[47] I think that Finkelstein's observations are likely applicable to the courtyard settlements that have irregular, ovoid structures, which seem to reflect the least amount of building skill and are the most reminiscent of bedouin tent-camps, although the latter could be sheer coincidence. Ecological considerations, especially the location of a number of these settlements in the Negev highlands, would bolster such a deduction, regardless of the modern tent-camp layout.

[48] So, e.g., L. Stager, "When Canaanites and Philistines Ruled Ashkelon," *BAR* 17/2 (1991), p. 31; R. Hess, "Early Israel in Canaan: A Survey of Recent Evidence and Interpretation," *PEQ* 125 (1993), pp. 125–42, esp. 138–39.

the highland areas associated with premonarchic Israel, while they
appear in larger numbers at lowland sites.

This is a sweeping assertion, given the small data base and its
incomplete nature.[49] It must be borne in mind that only a tiny fraction of the hundreds of sites that have been dated to the Iron I
period have been excavated, and even among that small fraction of
excavated settlements, less than 10% of a given site is usually able to
be systematically dug. It is premature to draw any conclusions about
a dietary prohibition against the consumption of pork at highland
sites. As B. Hesse points out, it is not always possible to distinguish
between the bones of wild and domesticated pigs in existing samples.[50]
In addition, he emphasizes the consumption of pork could reflect
dietary distinctions within differing social classes at a given site.[51] Given
the limited and random sampling of bones from the few sites that
have been excavated to date, there is no guarantee that the numbers
reflect trends throughout the entire site. It also needs to be noted
that the natural and preferred habitat for pigs is wet woodland, which
is found in the lowland areas but not in the highlands, although it
has been argued that wild pigs managed to occupy dry and rough
terrain not usually associated with them in most regions of the Le-
vant.[52] Should the absence of pig bones continue to occur as more
sites are dug, the influence of ecological factors would have to be
weighed carefully in a final decision about the reason for the absence. So, too, would the effect of social stratification on food bans
or avoidances, as well as economically or politically-based reasons
for avoiding certain types of food.[53]

The biblical law cannot be dated from internal evidence and cannot be presumed to have been in effect throughout the Cisjordanian

---

[49] For a discussion of the issue and preliminary data, see B. Hesse, "Pig Lovers
and Pig Haters: Patterns of Palestinian Pork Production," *Journal of Ethnobiology* 10
(1990), pp. 195–225; idem, "Husbandry, Dietary Taboos and the Bones of the Ancient
Near East: Zooarchaeology in the Post-Processual World," in D.B. Small (ed.), *Methods
in the Mediterranean: Historical and Archaeological Views on Texts and Archaeology* (Leiden:
Brill, 1995), pp. 197–232, esp. 217–232.

[50] "Pig Lovers and Pig Haters," pp. 202–204.

[51] *Ibid.*, pp. 212–14.

[52] D.L. Harrison, *The Mammals of Arabia* vol. 2 (London: Ernest Benn, 1964–1972),
p. 375.

[53] For a good presentation of the various theories that could be applied to explain the avoidance of pigs and which ones would fit the preliminary study of pig
bone distribution in ancient Palestine from the Chalcolithic-Iron Ages, see Hesse,
"Pig Lovers and Pig Haters."

highland sites of the Iron I period: the location of premonarchic Israel at a specific time during this 200-year period cannot be pinpointed. Thus, the law should not be used as a primary source of evidence for explaining the absence of pig bones in the Iron I highland villages. At some point in time it becomes an ethnic marker for Israelites, Judahites, Judeans, or Jews, but when is unclear.

E. *Aniconism as an Ethnic Marker*

There is a widespread presumption that the law prohibiting the representation of Yahweh or other deities in any known life form in the Second Commandment was in force among premonarchic Israelites and set them apart from their neighbors. The date of this legislation is uncertain, since there is no internal means by which to date the biblical law codes or individuals laws. Two recent studies have presented challenges to the mainstream presumption. First, B. Schmidt has suggested that the wording of the prohibition is meant to exclude single-form representations of deities as humans, birds, or marine life in favor of hybrid forms. Such an understanding is consistent with the drawings of Yahweh and his Asherah from the site of Kuntillet 'Ajrud in the monarchic period.[54] A study of the use of images on coins in Yehud, from their introduction during the Persian period through the end of the Hasmonean dynasty, reveals the use of single-form imagery of Yahweh and Athena in the Persian era and a gradual move away from such imagery during the subsequent periods. Thus, if the Second Commandment existed prior to the Persian period, it was not observed until after 333 BCE, and the motivation for the eventual avoidance of deified imagery could have developed out of concerns other than the existence of the Second Commandment.[55]

Confirmation of the existence of the aniconic tradition already in the premonarchic period has been sought in the archaeological record. To date, only two probable cultic sites have been excavated in the Cisjordanian hills that date to the Iron I period: the Mt. Ebal site

---

[54] B. Schmidt "The Aniconic Tradition: On Reading Images and Seeing Texts," in D.V. Edelman (ed.), *The Triumph of Elohim: From Yahwisms to Judaisms* (Contributions to Biblical Exegesis and Theology, 13; Kampen: Kok Pharos, 1995), pp. 75–105.

[55] See D.V. Edelman "Tracking Observance of the Aniconic Tradition through Numismatics," in Edelman, *The Triumph of Elohim*, pp. 185–225.

and the Bull Site. The former appears to have been in existence already at the end of the Late Bronze period,[56] while a proposal to date the latter to the Middle Bronze II period has recently been put forward.[57] The discovery of a bull figurine at the second locale, Dhahrat et-Tawila, has led to interesting suggestions concerning the identity of the deity being represented.

The Bull Site has been presumed by many who date it to the Iron I to be "Israelite" because it lies in the eastern Samarian hills, within the traditional tribal territory of Manasseh.[58] At the same time, however, the bull figure has been seen to be a possible representation of three different deities: the "Canaanite" storm god Ba'al/Hadad, El, or Yahweh.[59] The logical conclusion to be drawn, based on the earlier deduction that the site was Israelite, is that the figure represents Yahweh. This is not automatically done, however, probably because it goes against the prohibition of representations of Yahweh in the Second Commandment. While noting a tradition for the representation of Yahweh as a bull in the North, A. Mazar still concludes that the figurine most likely was a "Canaanite" object obtained through trade rather than a locally produced Israelite object.[60] G.W. Ahlström,

---

[56] A. Zertal, "Has Joshua's Altar been Found at Mt. Ebal?," *BAR* 11/1 (1985), pp. 26–43. The cultic nature of the site has been challenged by A. Kempinski ("Joshua's Altar—An Iron Age I Watchtower," *BAR* 12 [1986], pp. 42, 44–49). The presence of exotic materials and huge amounts of animal bones, including deer, tend to favor a cultic use for the site.

[57] Finkelstein, "Emergence of Israel," p. 167. The cultic nature of the site has been challenged by M. Coogan, who points to the lack of exotic materials apart from the figurine ("Of Cults and Culture: Reflections on the Interpretation and Context of Archaeological Evidence," *PEQ* 119 [1987], pp. 1–8, esp. 1, 5). The little pottery and lithics that are present are otherwise consistent with a domestic assemblage. The absence of almost all artifacts may suggest a deliberate abandonment of the site, with the removal of valuable items, making its function hard to determine. Also, the bull was found outside the walls of the building complex; was it dropped by mistake, ritually buried, or perhaps an original foundation deposit?

[58] So identified in the initial publication of the site by A. Mazar ("The 'Bull Site'—An Iron Age I Open Cult Place," *BASOR* 247 [1982], pp. 36–38) and followed widely by most others who have written subsequently. An exception is G.W. Ahlström, who argues that the site was used by an intrusive, non-Canaanite group who settled from the North ("The Bull Figurine from Dhahrat et-Tawila," *BASOR* 280 [1990], pp. 77–82).

[59] Mazar ("The 'Bull Site,'" pp. 29–32, 40) for Ba'al/Hadad and Yahweh; R. Wenning and E. Zenger ("Ein bäuerliches Baal-Heiligtum im samarischen Gebirge aus der Zeit der Anfänge Israels," *ZDPV* 102 [1986], pp. 81–82) and Coogan ("Of Cults and Culture," p. 2) for El, Ba'al or Yahweh; Ahlström ("Bull Figurine," p. 80) for El or Ba'al, but specifically not Yahweh.

[60] Mazar, "The 'Bull Site,'" pp. 32, 40.

on the other hand, has suggested that the figurine is a stylized depiction of a humpbacked Zebu bull, an animal not native to ancient Palestine. He concludes that it provides evidence of an intrusive, northern, non-Canaanite group of people who took their native religious tradition with them when they settled in the Samarian hills.[61]

The ethnic identity or affiliation of those who used the sanctuary at Dhahrat et-Tawila during the Iron I period cannot be established. The site cannot be declared "Israelite" at this date on the basis of later tribal boundaries; the problems with this common approach have already been discussed above. While the approach by G.W. Ahlström is sound methodologically, it is based on the questionable identification of the figurine as a representation of a Zebu bull. It needs to be noted that the "hump" is formed by the wrapping of a coil of clay over the top of the torso to form both front legs. The same technique is used to create the hind legs, although in the latter case, the coil is flattened out more than in the former. The result creates a small "hump" in the front, which is perhaps accentuated by the angle at which the legs are attached. What is not certain under the circumstances is whether the "hump" effect was intentional, meant to render the hump of a Zebu bull, or whether it is simply the result of the technique used to create the figurine and is not an attempt to depict a Zebu bull. Had the rear legs not been formed in the same manner as the front ones, or had the "hump" been more pronounced to indicate that it was indeed intentional, the bull figurine could have provided valuable evidence for the settlement of people of northern origin in the Samarian hills in the Iron I period, even though their original ethnic identity could not be pinpointed. Given the uncertain nature of the figure as a representation of a Zebu bull, however, such a conclusion must remain an unverified hypothesis.

F. *Social Organization as an Ethnic Marker*

As a final example, L. Stager has tried to link architectural compounds excavated at various sites in the hill country of Cisjordan with biblical references to the social unit known as the *bet 'ab* as a means of illustrating a form of social organization that was characteristic of premonarchic Israel and continued in use throughout the

---

[61] "Bull Figurine," pp. 77–82.

monarchic period.[62] By defining the period of investigation as the Iron Age in general, or 1200–587 BCE, he includes both premonarchic and monarchic Israel within the same study without further distinction. In so doing, he makes no attempt to date the various textual references to social organization and establish that there is clear textual evidence to support the existence of the *bet 'ab* within Israel in the premonarchic period. Instead, he uses monarchic era texts as his base and then presumes that the same organization would have existed in the earlier, prestate entity of that name. This is the same approach that has been used to define the boundaries of premonarchic Israel and the same weaknesses inhere in it. It can be noted that Stager makes the common presumption that the boundaries of early Israel correspond to those of the later state or are accurately delineated in the monarchic-era biblical texts.

The architectural examples Stager cites to illustrate the *bet 'ab* all are problematic since they come from excavations whose area is so limited that it often is not clear what lays contiguous to the walls being put forward as living compounds. In some instances, large segments of the walls themselves are hypothetical. Without knowing what adjoins a wall or lies on its other side, it is difficult to be certain that a whole complex has been uncovered and not just a segment or a series of isolated buildings. At the same time, without knowing where streets ran in relation to a postulated compound or how access was gained to the compound from the public area, it is hard to decide that a cluster of buildings in fact forms a larger intentional complex. I have not found one of his examples clearcut and convincing.

It is also suspicious that his postulated layout of the *bet 'ab* tends to be found in larger settlements. It is conspicuously absent from the *haser*-style settlements, which are characterized by contiguous dwellings but no internally shared courtyards between dwellings. Instead, there is the common "courtyard" in the center of the settlement. Since a number of these settlements have been dated to Iron I contexts and considered "Israelite" because of their geographical location in territory belonging to the later states of Israel or Judah—a premise Stager accepts—it seems odd that not all villages exhibit the architectural layout designated by Stager as illustrative of the *bet 'ab* social unit. Is this something that only crystallized in larger settlements under social pressure? Stager certainly seems to suggest that

---

[62] "Archaeology of the Family," pp. 1–35.

the *bet 'ab* was the smallest basic social unit that was used throughout premonarchic Israelite society, not just in certain tribes or segments of the society. If so, should we expect to find it expressed in a single manner architecturally, or is it possible that it took on multiple forms of architectural expression? If multiple, can they be contrasted with other forms of expression that can be linked to another social unit of organization? If no contrast can be established, the proposed link is meaningless.

G. *Burial Practices as Ethnic Markers*

In the quest to delineate ethnic groups within Cisjordan during the Iron I period, burial practices may be the best remains to use to distinguish the presence of such groups, even though specific ethnic labels cannot be assigned to each group so demarcated. The current data on Iron I burials is scanty, given the very limited amount of exposure of Iron I levels at excavated sites and the small fraction of total sites that have been even partially excavated. Systematic study of them is still underway. Even so, preliminary findings tend to indicate a range of tomb types and ritual objects buried with the deceased.[63] Since burial customs tend to be a conservative element within culture or society, they should be a good indicator to use to distinguish between the presence of different groups. The problem, however, is how to relate the groups once they are distinguished; do the distinctions reflect differences of status within a single larger society or ethnic group, do they represent a series of separate social or ethnic groups living side by side, or do they represent a combination of the two? Without texts that can be clearly dated to the Iron I period that provide contemporaneous witness to the ethnic configuration of the region, no specific ethnic labels can be associated with the groups distinguished by their burial practices.

---

[63] For details, see R. Wenning, "Eizenzeitliche Gräber in Jerusalem und Juda. Dokumentation des lokalen Bestattungswesens. Eine archäologische Untersuchung der Topographie, Architektur und Typologie der Gräber, der Grabinventare, der Bestattungssitten und der Totenpflege" (Habilitationsschrift, Eichstätt, 1994). His research is about to appear in print under the same title in the OBO Series.

Summary

No material cultural remains can be used as ethnic traits of pre-monarchic Israel, because the location of this entity cannot be established on the basis of current textual information. Without knowing its territory, it is impossible to find distinguishing traits within its cultural remains. Even if the boundaries of a given group can be established, the practices or means the group used to express its ethnicity and define itself over against neighboring groups may or may not leave traces in the material culture it produced.[64] It is quite likely that premonarchic Israelites used collar-rimmed storage jars, built four-room houses, laid out some of their settlements by building a belt of buildings around a common, central open space, had a mixed economy based on sheep/goats and agriculture, and had the *bet 'ab* as the basic social unit. None of these traits was uniquely Israelite, however, nor was the combination of all or part of them. Information about cultic practice and diet is too scarce or ambiguous to be adduced in a discussion of ethnic traits, and the uncertainty of the correlation of the battle scene at the Temple of Karnak with the coda section of the Merneptah Stele precludes any firm conclusions about the dress and hairstyle of early Israelites. Burial practices and tomb types seem to hold promise for the distinguishing of different groups resident in Cisjordan during the Iron I period, but without contemporaneous textual records, we have no way to assign ethnic labels to the different groups so delineated. In addition, some of these differences might reflect levels of social status within the same ethnic group, so it is not clear that the different practices would always reflect ethnic distinctions.

Conclusion

Little positive can be said about the ethnicity of premonarchic Israel. The lack of texts that can be firmly dated to the premonarchic era

---

[64] M. Skjeggestad questions the ability to use the archaeological material record to recover ethnic identity, pointing out that the remains need not necessarily correspond to or reflect the actual ethnic behavior behind the artifact. "Unless ethnic culture *consists* of artifacts, as if the artifacts as such constitute an ethnically defined culture, the supposed equivalence of material culture and ethnic identity of the inhabitants is objectionable" ("Use of the Term 'Israelite,'" p. 182).

precludes attempts to use material cultural remains to identify distinguishing traits or markers of the group. Biblical texts written in the monarchic, exilic or postexilic periods about the early history of the people of Israel cannot be taken at face value to portray life as it was in the prestate era. Rather, they must be seen to reflect those later societies' norms, political structures and customs; they represent how the intellegentsia in those periods imagined life would have been before there was a king in Israel. The writers may or may not have had access to a few traditions that arose in premonarchic Israel. If they did, they still would have framed those sources as they made use of them, according to their contemporary worldviews. Our inability to isolate and verify the use of such sources means that we must accept the inaccessibility of reliable, detailed information about premonarchic Israel. The Merneptah Stele indicates that some unit called Israel existed somewhere in Cisjordan by the last decade of the Late Bronze period. Nothing further can be known about it based on the present set of available texts.

Without the ability to locate premonarchic Israel and know something of its shifting boundaries over time, all attempts to use elements of the material cultural remains of Cisjordan in the Late Bronze and Iron I periods to define distinguishing characteristics of this group are also doomed to failure. Modern ethnographic studies have indicated the complexity of the formation and maintenance of ethnic identification and the inability to predict markers on the basis of practices of various living groups or cultures. No single list of traits can be generated and applied to all or any social unit(s). Defining ethnic traits of observable cultures using texts, interviews with natives and objects of their material culture is difficult and never yields a definitive, final list, since ethnicity is not a static category. To hope to be able to generate a list of ethnic traits without texts or informants, using only material cultural remains from a region that could have been home to a variety of ethnic groups, is to wish upon a star. To attempt such an undertaking is to put the cart before the ox.

HUMAN SOLIDARITY AND ETHNIC IDENTITY: ISRAEL'S SELF-DEFINITION IN THE GENEALOGICAL SYSTEM OF GENESIS[1]

Frank Crüsemann

The bloody excesses of new nationalisms illustrate, world-wide, how little success there has been in bringing ethics and ethnicity, universal human rights and group-specific identity, humanity and "people" (*Volk*), into a stable balance. "Hence, we stand before a dilemma," it is said, in one of the many contributions to the questions which have arisen out of this enigma: "On the one hand, a universal orientation towards the well-being of all is morally required. On the other hand, a group-related consciousness of identity, which particularizes the universalistic attitude, seems to be indispensable for the maintenance of our own personal identity." And this contradiction belongs "presumably, to the basic *aporia* of the *condition humaine*."[2] Whether genuine insights arise out of the present alarm, and out of the new debate, will depend not least on the extent to which the victims of past excesses are considered, and there are many victims on all sides. A fact which could turn out to have an important heuristic value is that an anti-Jewish attitude seems to be potentially inherent to both particularist and universalist orientations. As with almost the whole history of modern nationalism,[3] so also the new nationalism has quickly

---

[1] An abridged version of this paper appeared in a private Festschrift for Kristian Hungar marking his 60th birthday. It was also presented at the theological faculty of the Ernst Moritz Arndt University in Greifswald and the Catholic Theological Faculty in Paderborn.

[2] R. Schmücker and R. Hering, "Der Begriff der Nation berührt nur zwei Identitäten: Über Patriotismus, Nationalpatriotismus und die Suche nach Identität als Ausweg aus Unübersichtlichkeiten," *Rechtsphilosophische Hefte* (June 1994), quoted from *Frankfurter Rundschau* 142 (22.6.1994), p. 10.

[3] Already in the controversy concerning antisemitism in Berlin, 1879–80, Theodor Mommsen spoke of antisemitism as a "deformity of national feeling" and the "suicidal drive of national feeling" (see W. Boehlich (ed.), *Der Berliner Antisemitismusstreit* [Frankfurt: Insel, 2nd edn, 1965], p. 213). Cf. T. Nipperdey and R. Rürup, "Antisemitismus," in O. Brunner, W. Conze and R. Koselleck (eds.), *Geschichtliche Grundbegriffe Bd. I* (Stuttgart: Klett, 1972), pp. 129–153: Antisemitism is "a symptom of the loosing of radical and homogenizing nationalism from the moderate nationalism of the liberals" (p. 146).

shown itself to be enormously anti-Semitic. Even where there are no more Jews, the memory of the murdered still disturbs. But also movements orientated towards a universal ethic and a uniform humanity, such as Christianity,[4] the Enlightenment,[5] and socialism,[6] have often turned against a people, who could not, and did not wish to, abandon themselves for the sake of universal values and goals.

Against this background, I would like to explore the self-definition of Israel in Genesis. Here, at the entrance to the Tora, Israel has written itself into the world of peoples and has defined its location within the framework of the entire humanity created by God. What today often appears as a contradiction and an *aporia*—humanness and peoplehood—is here connected and mediated.

I

The chart on pp. 74–75 of this paper is an attempt to grasp the entire genealogical system of Genesis. With around three hundred names, and a representation of the relations between them, the chart follows the traditional Hebrew text. It shows a rather closed system of thoroughly patrilineal genealogies, i.e., pure father-son sequences. The names of women, or the mentioning of anonymous women, occur at relatively few, but central, places;[7] they are written in italics. For reasons of space, the arrangement cannot consistently reflect the same points of view. Thus, with respect to the names listed on the chart beneath each other, one has to distinguish on the one hand between father-son sequences where only the firstborn is mentioned—linear genealogies like the successors of Seth (Genesis 5) or of Shem (Genesis 11)—and on the other hand, the many sons of a father, segmentary genealogies, where the names would be better placed next to

---

[4] See K.H. Rengstorf and S. v. Kortzfleisch (eds.), *Kirche und Synagoge: Handbuch zur Geschichte von Juden und Christen* 2 vols. (München: dtv. Wiss. Reihe 4478, 1988).

[5] Cf. L. Poliakov, *Geschichte des Antisemitismus Bd. 5: Die Aufklärung und ihre judenfeindliche Tendenz* (German trans.; Worms: Heintz, 1983). Examplary is Kant's statement "Pure moral religion is the euthanasia of Judaism." In W. Weischedel (ed.), *Werke Bd. 6: Der Streit der Fakultäten* (Frankfurt: Insel, 1964), p. 321. Cf. M. Horkheimer and T.W. Adorno, "Elemente des Antisemitismus: Grenzen der Aufklärung," *Dialektik der Aufklärung: Philosophische Fragmente* (Amsterdam: de Munter, 1968), pp. 199ff.

[6] Cf. E. Silber, *Sozialisten zur Judenfrage* (German trans.; Berlin: Colloquium, 1962).

[7] See R.A. Freund, "Naming Names: Some Observations on 'Nameless Women' Traditions in the MT, LXX and Hellenistic Literature," *SJOT* 6 (1992), pp. 213–232.

each other on the same level, for example, the peoples descended from Egypt, Canaan, or Joktan (Genesis 10), the sons of Nahor (22:20ff.), or Jacob's grandsons (46:8ff.). The peoples listed from Gen. 14:5f. and 15:19 have neither a genealogical connection to each other, nor to the larger system.

At the beginning stands the first-created human, *Adam*. At the end, in Genesis 46, stands an enumeration of the grandchildren and great-grandchildren of Jacob, i.e., the entire group which (according to the Pentateuch) went to Egypt and from which the people of Israel originated. Here we reach the greatest depth of genealogical layering: there are twenty-five generations from the first human to the great-grandchildren of Jacob: Hezron and Hamul, Heber and Malkiel. Only with the grandchildren of Esau is a comparable depth reached. This depth of layering, however, does not simply mark a difference in time, since all other names which stand at the end of a genealogical branch are also present figures, living simultaneously with the descendants of Jacob and *cum grano salis* also with the readers of this text. Thus, especially through the table of nations in Genesis 10, all known humanity is grasped. The table of nations is arranged according to the three sons of Noah: Shem, Ham and Japhet. For the sake of a better graphical representation, the main line of descent through Shem forms the centre of the chart. The numbers in brackets after the names show the succession of birth. The three sons of Terah (Abraham, Nahor and Haran) mark the next important branching. The Abrahamites are divided into three by Abraham's wives: Sarah, Hagar and Keturah. Finally, we find the two sons of Isaac, Esau and Jacob, and their sons and descendants, listed according to their different mothers.

Only a brief account of some of the literary, tradition-critical (*traditionsgeschichtliche*) and historical aspects of the system is possible in this context. We must refrain from discussing problems associated with the identification and location of traditions, except for a few marginal comments.[8]

The genealogies summarized here, which pervade all of Genesis,

---

[8] See the extensive material in C. Westermann, *Genesis* (BK I/1–3; Neukirchen: Neukirchener Verlag, 1966–1982), as well as the works mentioned in note 12; T. Willi, *Chronik* (BK XXIV 1; Neukirchen: Neukirchener Verlag, 1991), pp. 30ff.; also, J. Simons, *The Geographical and Typographical Texts of the Old Testament* (Leiden: Brill, 1959); R.S. Hess, *Studies in the Personal Names of Genesis 1–11* (AOAT, 234; Neukirchen: Neukirchener Verlag, 1993).

form something like the skeleton of this book, a stable framework
which holds together and carries all other parts. This is true not
least because other elements which usually constitute the unity of
narratives, such as the temporal and spacial framework, are not always clearly or explicitly formulated in Genesis taken as a narrative
whole. It is, however, striking that I cannot find in Old Testament
scholarship any description of this system,[9] despite an intensified interest in the genealogies since the work of Wilson in the 1970s.[10] It
is also noticeable that, despite some new approaches,[11] research is
still resolutely fixed on questions of the genesis of Genesis, i.e., the
diachronic stratification, so that the conception of the final, canonical text has been given little attention. This article is thus to be
understood as a contribution to the understanding of this final text.

Neglecting, for the moment, the problem of the unconnected names
in Genesis 14; 15 and 36, everything else can be brought together
into a thoroughly meaningful and overtly intended system. Undoubtedly, older materials have been assimilated; thus, one finds the typical contradictions and tensions. Given the traditional division into a
Priestly and a "Yahwist" layer, say in the table of nations in Genesis

---

[9] However, a rough sketch can be found in the work of the anthropologist K.R.
Andriolo, "A Structural Analysis of Genealogy and Worldview in the Old Testament," *American Anthropologist* 75 (1973), pp. 1657–1669; cf. already E. Leach, "The
Legitimacy of Solomon: Some structural Aspects of Old Testament History," *AES* 7
(1966), pp. 58–101.

[10] R.R. Wilson, "The Old Testament Genealogies in Recent Research," *JBL* 94
(1975), pp. 169–189; idem, *Genealogy and History in the Biblical World* (New Haven:
Yale University Press, 1977; idem, "Between 'Azel' and 'Azel': Interpreting the Biblical
Genealogies," *BA* 42 (1979), pp. 11–22. Apart from the commentaries, see also:
M.D. Johnson, *The Purpose of the Biblical Genealogies, With Special Reference to the Setting
of the Genealogies of Jesus* (MSSNTS, 8; Cambridge: Cambridge University Press, 2nd
edn, 1988); T.J. Prewitt, "Kinship Structures and the Genesis Genealogies," *JNES*
40 (1981), pp. 87–98; R.B. Robinson, "Literary Functions of the Genealogies of
Genesis," *CBQ* 48 (1986), pp. 595–608; N. Steinberg, "The Genealogical Framework of the Family Stories in Genesis," *Semeia* 46 (1989), pp. 41–50; B. Renaud,
"Les généalogies et la structure de l'histoire sacerdotale dans le livre de la Genèse,"
RB 97 (1990), pp 5–30; T.D. Alexander, "Geneaologies, Seed and the Composi-
tional Unity of Genesis," *Tyndale Bulletin* 44 (1993), pp. 255–70; as well as (more
general) E. Blum, *Die Komposition der Vätergeschichte* (WMANT, 57: Neukirchen-Vluyn:
Neukirchener Verlag, 1984), pp. 438ff.; cf. K.F. Plum, "Genealogy as Theology,"
SJOT 1 (1989), pp. 66–91; G.A. Rendsburg, "The Internal Consistency and Histori-
cal Reliability of the Biblical Genealogies," *VT* 40 (1990), pp. 185–206.

[11] Exemplary would be Blum (n. 10 above); G.A. Rendsburg, *The Redaction of
Genesis* (Winona Lake: Eisenbrauns, 1986); E. Fox, "Can Genesis be Read as a Book?"
Semeia 46 (1989), pp. 31–40; T.W. Mann, "'All the Families of the Earth.' The
Theological Unity of Genesis," *Interp* 45 (1991), pp. 341–353.

10,[12] different linguistic realisations of the genealogies play a role, like, for example, the reduction to pure lists of names or the connection with anecdotal additions; or, the twin occurrence of names like Havilah and Seba under the descendants of Ham, on the one hand (10:7), and under the sons of Joktan, descendants of Shem, on the other hand (10:28f.). The name Uz, the home country of Job (Job 1:1), occurs three times: as the oldest son of Aram (10:23), as the oldest son of Nahor (22:21) and as the grandchild of Seir through Dishan (36:28), thus, as Horite. Especially the data concerning the names and origin of the wives of Esau in 26:34; 28:9 and 36 can hardly be brought into agreement.

Thus, unambiguously diverse materials have been used, but the confidence of source criticism proves to be misplaced. One need only consider how contradictory and malleable are the genealogies which have been empirically researched by anthropologists. Does the same name always imply the same figure? In any case, the present configuration produces an intended—or a tolerable—meaning. It is especially important to note that there are, among the texts usually ascribed to P, clear and enormous tensions. This is the case in Genesis 36, where, in the listing of the "princes" ('aluf) of Edom in vv. 15ff., a different organization of the tribes is evidenced, over against vv. 4–14 (which our chart follows). Also worth mentioning is the different classification of Aram, both as a son of Shem (10:22) and as a grandchild of Nahor (22:21). But given such a widespread and manifold phenomenon as the Arameans, are we really to seek for an explanation simply in literary layers? All this means that, on the whole, the problem of the genealogies is not essentially different from the rest of Genesis. Despite all the tensions, there arose a meaningful unity the significance of which may be grasped. The connection of narratives and genealogies, and indeed of priestly and non-priestly material, is obviously thought through and consciously shaped.[13]

---

[12] E.g., Westermann, *Genesis* I (n. 8 above), and Johnson, *Purpose* (n. 10 above). On Genesis 10, cf. G. Hölscher, *Drei Erdkarten. Ein Beitrag zur Erkenntnis des hebräischen Altertums* (SHAW.PH 3 [1947/48] 1949); J. Simons, "The Table of Nations (Genesis X): Its General Structure and Meaning," *OTS* 10 (1954), pp. 155–184. Cf. n. 33 below.

[13] Cf. R.H. Moye, "In the Beginning: Myth and History in Genesis and Exodus," *JBL* 109 (1990), pp. 577–598, esp. 590ff.; Robinson (n. 10 above); and esp. Steinberg (n. 10 above). Following Todorov's narratology, Steinberg sees the great genealogies in Genesis 11; 25 and 36 as representing a situation from which the narrative complications proceed.

Research cannot remain fixed on the unconnected fragments which are produced, not infrequently, by literary analysis. The basic pattern of the genealogical system undoubtedly stems from P.[14] But whether, and at which points, P employed and presupposed older material—which might even stand in a contradictory relationship with the content of P[15]—has not so far been clearly determined, and these shall remain open questions here also.

The names and traditions which remain unconnected, outside of the unified system, should perhaps be considered in a different way. These are the "giants" (nefilim) in Gen. 6:4,[16] the peoples mentioned in 14:5f.—the Rephaites, Zuzites, Emites and Horites, pre-inhabitants of the eastern Jordanian areas (cf. Deut. 2:8ff.)—and, in 15:19f., the Kenizzites, Kadmonites and Perizzites. With regard to the Horites: in 36:20ff. one finds a detailed Horite genealogy within the framework of the Edomite lists. There are also kinship connections with Edom: Oholibamah is introduced in 36:25 as the daughter of the Horite Anah; in the MT of 36:2, however, Anah is Hivite, i.e., designated as Canaanite. So should the Horites be identified with the Hivites? Or should one really think of beings not stemming from Adam, and thus "non-human beings"? Quite clearly, such is not the case for the pre-inhabitants of the land promised to Israel; they belong to Canaan (10:16ff.). Also the three additional names for the pre-inhabitants, which only occur in Gen. 15:19f., cannot change this fact. Yet, even if one presupposes the special position of Genesis 14, and assumes a later literary addition to 15:19, questions remain here, with regard to the genealogically unconnected names, which have so far received answers that are hardly sufficient for an interpretation of the whole text of Genesis.

An understanding of the Old Testament genealogies has really only been reached through comparisons with the oral genealogies of tribal societies.[17] For all peoples who are not organized by a state system,

---

[14] On this point, see, e.g., Renaud (n. 10 above), as well as the attempts to interpret the toledot schema, e.g., S. Tengström, *Die Toledotformel und die literarischen Strukturen der priesterlichen Erweiterungsschicht im Pentateuch* (CBOT, 17; Uppsala: Gleerup, 1982); P. Weimar, "Die Toledotformel in der priesterlichen Geschichtsdarstellung," *BZ* 18 (1974), pp. 65–93.

[15] On this concept, see E. Blum, *Studien zur Komposition des Pentateuch* (BZAW, 189; Berlin: de Gruyter,1990).

[16] On this, see, e.g., L. Perlitt, "Riesen im Alten Testament. Ein literarisches Motiv im Wirkungsfeld des Deuteronomiums" *NAWG* 61 (1990), pp. 381f.

[17] See especially Wilson (n. 10 above), as well as the discussion concerning the

genealogies play a role which hardly can be overestimated.[18] The whole social order is described by means of them. The place of each individual in society—and beyond that, in part, the entire creation—is grasped by them, i.e., rank and status, claims and expectations of all kinds.[19] The kinship connections remain, wherever a state is young or weak, the basic framework of order. The world is experienced and described as family. Many of the basic features of such empirically researched genealogies can be found in the Old Testament. There is their amazing flexibility and fluidity over the course of time, which, with regard to basic questions, does not exclude a continuity and confidence in the tradition.[20] There is a genealogical depth, which rarely exceeds ten to fourteen generations, which is achieved by dropping connecting links.[21] Persons are "naturalized" into the kinship system who, in a strict sense, are not biologically related but are nevertheless socially integrated.[22] However, none of the parallels known from ethnology, or from the ancient Near East, has a structure such as the system of Genesis. Genesis encompasses single families and entire ethnic groups, including connections with an ancestor from primordial time. Indeed, a system with the propensity to encompass all of humanity, all neighbouring peoples as well as the whole internal structure of one's own people, that is something extraordinary.[23]

segmentary social organization of premonarchic Israel, firstly in A. Malamat, "Tribal Societies: Biblical Genealogies and African Lineage System," *AES* 14 (1973), pp. 126–136. For an overview, see M. Oeming, *Das wahre Israel: Die "genealogische Vorhalle" 1 Chronik 1–9* (BWANT, 128; Stuttgart: Kohlhammer, 1990), pp. 9ff.

[18] Important ethnological material is easily accessible in F. Kramer and C. Sigrist (eds.), *Gesellschaften ohne Staat, Bd. 2: Genealogie und Solidarität* (Frankfurt, 1978); C. Sigrist and R. Neu (eds.), *Ethnologische Texte zum Alten Testament, Bd. 1: Vor- und Frühgeschichte Israels* (Neukirchen–Vluyn: Neukirchener Verlag, 1989), esp. ch. 2.

[19] Wilson, *Genealogy* (n. 10 above), pp. 37ff.

[20] Wilson, *Genealogy*, pp. 27ff.; on the Old Testament material, cf., e.g., the diverse genealogies of particular tribes in S. Yeivin, *The Israelite Conquest of Canaan* (Istanbul: Nederlands Historisch-Archaeologisch Institut, 1971), pp. 126–233; on the other hand, Rendsburg (n. 10 above).

[21] Wilson, *Genealogy* (n. 10 above), pp. 21ff.

[22] Cf., e.g., W.E. Mühlmann, "Ethnogonie und Ethnogenese: Theoretisch-ethnologische und ideologiekritische Studien," *ARWAW* 72 (1985), pp. 9–27: "I found that the assimilation of allogenic and ethnically alien elements plays a quite considerable role among 'primitive' peoples; this is termed 'Umvolkung' in European folk history" (p. 10). "Above all, the surprising element of assimilation among 'primitive' peoples stands in contrast to their ideological exclusiveness, their so-called 'ethnocentrism'." (p. 11).

[23] Thus, the judgment of F. Delitzsch (*Neuer Kommentar über die Genesis* [Leipzig: Dörffling und Franke, 1887], p. 199) on the table of nations may still be valid: "Nowhere can a comparable overview be found." In my opinion, this is true despite

As a whole, this system belongs to the Persian period. Certainly, some elements of the genealogical tradition of the Old Testament stem from the time of a pre-state, purely tribal society. This might be true of the basic features of the twelve-tribe system, but also of the connections with the closely related neighbouring peoples. But the beginnings of a written tradition are not to be ascribed to such an early time. It can be demonstrated that genealogies of the exilic/post-exilic time play an extraordinarily important role; one thinks of the rich material in 1 Chronicles 1–9,[24] but also elsewhere in the books of Chronicles, Ezra and Nehemia, and similarly, the Priestly texts. Quite clearly, the family and family-orientated thinking played again an astonishingly important role after the breakdown of the state.[25] The cohesiveness of the people, as well as their relationships with other peoples, could be described and grasped by genealogical thinking, independently of institutions like the kingship.

The hypothesis of a Persian date for the system cannot be contradicted by reference to the absence of the Persians in the table of nations. Babylon is also missing, although one can presume that it probably lies behind the otherwise unknown name Arpakshad.[26] The lack of these names cannot be explained simply by the hypothesis of an earlier origin of the texts; why have they not been added later? *Not* to mention the political power, under which Israel lived together with the predominant number of the peoples mentioned here, was

---

the opinion of E. Meyer, that "the connection of the individual traditions and the collection of all the tribes and peoples into a well-ordered whole" (by the "Yahwist") are of the same kind "as those by which Hesiod, and the other genealogical poetries of the Greeks, have systematically organised the Hellenists and the remaining known peoples into genealogical trees" (*Die Israeliten und ihre Nachbarstämme* [1st edn 1906; Hildesheim: Olms, 1966], p. 231, referring to Meyer, *Forschungen zur alten Geschichte I* [1st edn 1892; Hildesheim: Olms, 1966), pp. 91f.144f.). On the one hand, "the relationships of the peoples around the Mediterranean Sea" are genealogically interpreted (W. Speyer, "Genealogie," *RAC*, 9 [1976], pp. 1154f.), e.g., the Greeks, Egyptians and Barbarians are traced back to the same ancestors. On the other hand, the different Greek tribes are traced back to Deukalion, the Greek Noah (e.g., Apollodor I, 7.2). Thus, there seem to be comparable starting points but nowhere a comprehensive system which tends to encompass all human beings. We lack, however, a recent and thorough comparative investigation. For conversations on this point, I thank my friend and colleague Prof. Dr. Jens-Uwe Schmidt.

[24] For recent studies, see M. Kartveit, *Motive und Schichten der Landtheologie in I. Chronik 1-9* (Stockholm: Almquist and Wiksell, 1989); Oeming (n. 17 above).

[25] On the background, see, e.g. R. Albertz, *Religionsgeschichte Israels in alttestamentlicher Zeit* (GAT, 8/2; Göttingen: Vandenhoeck & Ruprecht, 1992), pp. 413ff.

[26] Cf., e.g., M. Görg, "Arpachschad," *NBL* I, pp. 175f.; recently, T. Willi, *Chronik* (n. 8 above), p. 37.

presumably simpler than to integrate it into such a system, in contradiction to their own view of things. Still the most probable solution[27] is that the Medes of 10:2 encompass the Persians, as is elsewhere occasionally the case in the Old Testament and in Greece.[28]

In any case, there is no doubt about where the readers find themselves. According to Nehemiah 11 and 1 Chronicles 9, there are descendants of the sons of Judah, Perez and Zerah, and perhaps also Shela, in postexilic Judah.[29] Along with these, of course, are members of the lineages of the Levites and descendants of Benjamin. Yet, unlike the Judahites, none of the ten sons of Benjamin mentioned in Gen. 46:12 appear as ancestors of the postexilic Benjaminites.[30] Here at the end, twenty five generations from the first human beings, the post-exilic addressees of Genesis find their own ancestors, and thus they find themselves.

II

We will explore now the relationship between humanity and a "people" (*Volk*), the connections between Israel and the whole world of peoples, without considering at this point specifically religious issues. The system as a whole links humanity and the peoples into a unity; or to be more precise, all of humanity and the kinships of Israel are grasped in one single system; between them there exists an

---

[27] In Genesis Rabba 37:1, "Tiras" of Gen. 10:2 is, among others, identified with Persia. E. Lipinski ("Les Japhétites selon Gen. 10, 2–4 et 1 Chr 1, 5–7," *ZAH* 3 (1990), pp. 40–53, 49f.) wants to read "Diphat" with 1 Chron. 1:6, instead of Riphat, and draws on an Iranian title *dahyu-pati* for his interpretation, which means "chef de peuple," witnessed to in texts from Persepolis. Here he is thinking, however, of local Median princes.

[28] See Isa. 13:17; 21:2; Jer. 51:11, 18 (cf. also the commentaries) on the one hand; on the other hand, Aischylos, *Persians* 236.765.791 and the linguistic usage of Herodotus and Thucydides; Hölscher, *Drei Erdkarten* (n. 12 above), p. 54; cf. already F. Schmidtke, *Die Japhetiten der biblischen Völkertafel* (Breslau: Müller & Seiffert, 1926), p. 59, and others.

[29] On Perez, cf. Neh. 11:4, 6 and 1 Chron. 9:4; on Serach, Neh. 11:24 and 1 Chron. 9:6. Behind "Shilonites" in 1 Chron. 9:5 one often presumes with Num. 26:20 an original "Shelanites", e.g. H.G.M. Williamson, *1 and 2 Chronicles* (NCBC; Grand Rapids: Eerdmans, 1982), p. 89; in opposition, Oeming (n. 17 above), p. 201.

[30] The post-exilic generations of Benjamin, mentioned in 1 Chron. 9:7ff. and Neh. 11:7 show, as far as I can see, no connections to the genealogies of the Benjamites in 1 Chron. 7:6ff.; 8:1ff. (nor to the fragmentary genealogy of a Shaharaim, 1 Chron. 8:8ff.).

abundance of intermediate stages and a continuous, sliding scale of linkages. We can discern an increasing concentration on Israel as the main line of descent:[31] of the three sons of Noah, Shem has special significance; of the three sons of Terah the main concern is with Abraham; of his descendants, it is Isaac, and then his younger son Jacob, who are central. In each case, the necessary divisions are described, and the aim is undoubtedly the origin of Israel. But who this Israel is, can only be grasped within the framework of the whole; this ethnic group is part of the entire coherence of humanity.

Humanity as a whole, which I will treat first, is traced back to a primal couple and then unfolds itself after the deluge out of the three sons of Noah. Thus, humanity is represented as family. Nothing less is at stake than the essential unity of all human beings.[32] Everyone is related to each other; human being as such presents no fundamental differences. Descendants of the other sons of Noah appear without any disqualification in the genealogical tree of Israel; Asenath, the Egyptian daughter of a priest, appears as the wife of Joseph and mother of the important tribes of Ephraim and Manasseh (41:45, 50ff.); the daughter of the Canaanite Shua appears as the wife of Judah (38:2) and a Canaanite woman as partner of Simeon (46:10). The biblical prohibitions concerning marriage cannot be presupposed here without further discussion, but they are in no way racially grounded. This decisive point may be missed when "races of men," or similar terms, are occasionally used in relation to the table of nations.[33] Some such concept might at most fit the *nefilim* mentioned in Gen. 6:4. The Genesis traditions lack any hint of an allusion to skin colour, or to other racially utilizable points of difference. In the Mishnah, the matter under consideration is formulated as follows: "Why did God create only one human being? So that no-one can say to a fellow human being: my father was better than yours" (Sanh.

---

[31] E.g., Moye (n. 13 above), pp. 590ff. with reference to M. Fishbane, *Text and Texture: Close Readings of Selected Biblical Texts* (New York: Shocken, 1979), pp. 27ff., and Andriolo (n. 9 above): "the separation of God's chosen people from the rest of humanity is the informing principle." (p. 592).

[32] As one example among many, cf. Westermann, *Genesis* I (n. 8 above), pp. 706f. with many references to older literature; recently, e.g., Willi (n. 8 above), p. 47. This is denied without any close reasoning by J. Grau, *The Gentiles in Genesis: Israel and the Nations in the Primeval and Patriarchal Histories* (PhD. diss. Southern Methodist University, 1980), pp. 124ff. in relation to the Canaanite peoples.

[33] Incidentally, e.g., J. Scharbert, *Genesis 1–11* (NEB: Würzburg: Echter Verlag, 2nd edn, 1980), p. 102.

10.5). The allotment of the peoples to the three sons of Noah cannot be explained unequivocally. In any case, neither linguistic categories (Elam with the Semites; Canaan and Egypt in one group) nor political categories (especially with Japhet; Lud/Lyder at Shem etc.) come into the question. Similarly, socio-cultural types are kept in the background.[34]

One of the great strengths underlying genealogical thinking is its capacity for complex differentiation. An important example is supplied by the relationships between the sons of Jacob, i.e., between the Israelite tribes: their assignment to the two main wives, Leah and Rachel, or their implication in the differentiation of mistress and maidservant (Zilpah and Bilhah), their succession of births, and finally the personal bias of Jacob to Rachel, so that her sons, although younger, achieve great significance—these are different, cross-cutting possibilities for describing social status. Israelites, for example in post-exilic times, who find themselves or their ancestors here, know that the internal differentiation goes further, that many generations and separations are necessary in order to grasp the position of an individual. All those differences are occluded when a modern racial nationalism wants to ground itself in pseudo-biology (and, for example, makes citizenship dependent on "German" origin). Even besides the liberal and "naturalizing" integration of strangers into the kinship system, already mentioned,[35] modernity lacks equivalents for both intra-ethnic and extra-ethnic differentiation: the internal differences among the Israelite people, the descendants of Jacob, are as great as those among the whole of humanity. And this point can be taken literally:[36] in Gen. 46:47 the number of persons who, in Egypt, belonged to Jacob's house is given as seventy (cf. also Exod. 1:5; Deut. 10:22). There are also seventy peoples who, according to Jewish tradition, originated from the sons of Noah,[37] a number which quite exactly accords with the number in Genesis 10 (if one does not

---

[34] See B. Oded, "The Table of Nations (Genesis 10)—A Socio-cultural Approach," *ZAW* 98 (1986), pp. 14–31; on the Japhethites and especially the phrase "Insel der Völker," cf. W. Horowitz, "The Isles of Nations: Genesis X and Babylonian Geography," in J.A. Emerton (ed.), *Studies in the Pentateuch* (VTS, 41; Leiden: Brill, 1990), pp. 35–43. A map with the most important names is provided by W. Zimmerli, *I. Mose 1–11: Die Urgeschichte* (ZBK; Zürich: Zwingli, 2nd edn, 1957).

[35] See above n. 22.

[36] On the following, see B. Jacob, *Das erste Buch der Tora. Genesis* (Berlin: Schocken, 1934), pp. 295f.

[37] See especially Targum Jonathan on Genesis 11; Sota VII,5 and others.

count Joktan himself).[38] The song of Moses, in Deut. 32:8, already suggests a correspondence between humanity on the one hand and ethnic identity on the other, between the macrocosm of humankind and the microcosm of Israel's people: "When the Most High (Elyon) assigned to the nations their inheritance, he separated the human children, he determined the boundaries of the peoples firmly, according to the number of the Israelites." Thus reads the traditional Hebrew text, and the statement is especially important if an older phenomenon of religious history shimmers dimly through this text.

So far, I have spoken of a "people" (*Volk*), and certainly the text is concerned with a social dimension which can be named as such. Even so, we have to take special care with this terminology bearing in mind all the problems which the concept of *Volk* carries within itself.[39] The problem is first of all discernable in the Genesis system itself. There is no pure opposition of humankind and *Volk*; the system knows many gradations in between. And many further layers lie between the fathers of the tribes and the concrete individuals of the time of composition. A human being is not just an Israelite but at least a member of a household (*bet 'ab*), of an extended family or a clan (*mišpaḥa*), as they appear here in the grandchildren of Jacob, and of a tribe. All these are levels of collective identity. However, the matter goes further, as our system illustrates nicely. There is not just the level of the people, i.e., Jacob-Israel, but, for example, the levels of the two sons of Isaac and all the descendants of Abraham. The ideal marriage relations fall within the group of Terah; this seems to be the ideal of endogamy.[40] What, then, of the level of the Hebrew peoples, to whom (apart from the sons of Terah) the peoples stemming from Joktan also belong? The Hebrews are spoken of, as is well known, many times in the Old Testament, especially in the stories of Joseph,[41] Exodus,[42] and Saul,[43] and much evidence suggests that such a social group could have been a political presence at some

[38] For this counting, Jacob (n. 36 above), p. 296; S. Krauss, "Die Zahl der biblischen Völkerschaften," *ZAW* 19 (1899), pp. 1–14.
[39] On the history of the term, cf. F. Geschnitzer, R. Koselleck, B. Schönemann, K.F. Werner, "Volk, Nation, Nationalismus, Masse," in *Geschichtliche Grundbegriffe: Bd.* 7 (Stuttgart: Klett-Cotta, 1992), pp. 144–432.
[40] See especially, Prewitt (n. 10 above).
[41] Gen. 39:14, 17; 40:15; 41:12; 43:32, and, e.g., 14:13.
[42] Exod. 1:15f., 19; 2:7, 11; 3:18; 5:3; 7:16; 9:1, 13; 10:3.
[43] 1 Sam. 4:6, 9; 13:3, 7, 19; 14:11, 21; 29:13.

stage.[44] Naturally, the level of Shem descendants offers a correlation. All of these levels are of importance, and many of them are not only fictive elements, but socially operative. Thus, there are multi-layered collective identities which encompass many peoples, such as the Hebrews or Terachites, and also the descendants of Abraham—from the closest connection which designates Esau/Edom a twin, through the twelve tribe unity of the people, down to the level of the extended families and households, which are determinative for everyday life.

Within the logic of genealogical thinking, all these levels are of equal importance. What we call a "people" plays only one role among many. Especially in comparison with all forms of modern nationalism, the manifold layers of identity should be stressed. Of course, the level of the people has importance, since this encompasses "Israel," the name which Jacob receives. At the same time, however, internal differentiation is also in view—the proximity and distance in relation to many other identities. The over-riding significance within modern nationalisms of the national layer, displacing all other relationships, is unthinkable. (And also today, over against this dangerous heightening, we should set a many-layered collective identity of familial, local, regional and international parameters.) Given these observations, one should take special care to keep a distance from the modern concept of the nation. In order to understand what is meant by "people" (in Hebrew, usually *'am*), one has to start from ancient[45] and especially from ethnological perspectives. Linguistically, it would be better, especially in scholarly terminology, to speak of *ethnos* or *ethnie*. Observations concerning the origin of peoples—ethnogenesis[46]— show that cultural differences play an important role. These can be understood in terms of language, habits, customs of all kinds, as well as religion. One speaks of a "limited" structure, a boundary which

---

[44] See, e.g., K. Koch, "Die Hebräer vom Auszug aus Ägypten bis zum Großreich Davids," *VT* 19 (1969), pp. 37–81.

[45] See, e.g., Geschnitzer and others (n. 39 above), pp. 151ff.

[46] Especially Mühlmann (n. 22 above) and R. Schott, "Die Ethnogenese von Völkern in Afrika," *ARWAW* 78 (1988), pp. 7–42. The latter refers with emphasis to Max Weber's differentiation of "common faith (Gemeinsamkeitsglauben)" and "concerted action (Gemeinschaftshandeln)" (*Wirtschaft und Gesellschaft*, Bd. 1 [Köln: Kiepenheuer & Witsch, 1964], p. 307). The ethnological material is analysed by E.A. Knauf (*Die Umwelt des Alten Testaments* [Neuer Stuttgarter Kommentar, Altes Testament, 24; Stuttgart: Katholisches Bibelwerk, 1994], pp. 184ff.) arguing that an identity like a "people" (Volk) did not exist before the time of the Persians. That does not accord with the great significance of the different forms of *ethnos*.

enables distinctions between one's own and the other.[47]

The possibilities of differentiation, both inside and outside of Israel's own *ethnos* (consciously in accord with each other), prove themselves in the ability to determine the proximities of the many ethnic identities to each other and to Israel. In the immediate neighbourhood, Edom is described as the most closely related; Moab and Ammon are also close, as are the Arameans descended from Nahor. The great abundance of proto-Arabic *ethnie* and tribes[48] are perceived in a very differentiated way as descendants of Cush, Joktan, Keturah as well as Hagar-Ishmael, but they are mostly perceived as quite closely related. On the other hand, the Canaanites,[49] Philistines[50] as Hamites[51] receive a quite remote position within the human family, along with all the Canaanite peoples who play an important role in the Deuteronomic tradition of the taking of the land. We should also notice the differentiation by defamation, as it is depicted in the origin of Moab and Ammon in incest (19:30ff.), but also Israel's own position arising out of pure deception (ch. 27). Of special interest is the integration of the peoples with whom Israel was connected by long and violent animosities. Assyria, which is responsible for the end of Israel's northern kingdom and most of the tribes, belongs to the descendants of Shem (10:22). Esau-Edom, connected by a long history of violence and hatred, is the twin brother of the father of Israel, defrauded of his blessing as the first-born.[52] Midian, viewed so variously in the Old Testament (Moses discovered the God of Israel in Midian [Exod. 3], yet Midian presents a deadly threat [Judges 6]), is an Abrahamite

---

[47] Cf. Mühlmann (n. 22 above), pp. 18ff.

[48] See, e.g., F.V. Winnett, "The Arabian Genealogies in the Book of Genesis," in *Translating and Understanding the Old Testament: Essays in Honor of H.G. May* (Nashville: Abingdon, 1970), pp. 171–196, and especially E.A. Knauf, *Midian: Untersuchungen zur Geschichte Palästinas und Nordarabiens am Ende des 2. Jahrtausends v.Chr.* (Wiesbaden: Harrassowitz, 1988); idem, *Ismael: Untersuchungen zur Geschichte Palästinas und Nordarabiens im 1. Jahrtausend v.Chr.* (Wiesbaden: Harrassowitz, 1985).

[49] Cf., e.g., A. van Selms, "The Canaanites in the Book of Genesis," *OTS* 12 (1958), pp. 182–213.

[50] On the problem of their origin, see G.A. Rendsburg, "Gen. 10:13–14: An Authentic Hebrew Tradition Concerning the Origin of the Philistines," *JNSL* 13 (1987), pp. 89–96.

[51] See also E. Lipinski, "Les Chamites selon Gen. 10, 6–20 et 1 Chr 1, 8–16," *ZAH* 5 (1992), pp. 135–162.

[52] F. Crüsemann, "Herrschaft, Schuld und Versöhnung: Der Beitrag der Jakobgeschichte der Genesis zur politischen Ethik," *Junge Kirche* 54 (1993), pp. 614–620 = "Dominion, Guilt and Reconciliation: The Contribution of the Jacob Narrative in Genesis to Political Ethics," *Semeia* 66 (1995), pp. 67–77.

(Gen. 25:2).[53] And Israel is connected even with Amalek—the memory of whom God wishes to extinguish, and with whom God is at eternal war (Exod. 17:14ff.; Deut. 25:17ff.)—not only by the strongest antagonism, but also by a close blood relationship: he is the grandchild of Esau (Gen. 36:2). This means that the worst enemies are not the ones who are markedly strange or different, as every racism perceives it; they belong to the closest relations.

Although everything is directed towards the special role of the one people within humankind, Israel's self-definition is to be distinguished fundamentally from all the decisive features of modern nationalisms: There is the essential unity of humankind in all its diversity; there is an internal differentiation within the people which corresponds to the whole of humanity; there are many levels which are important for a collective identity of which the ethnic level is only one.

III

If one attempts to connect the genealogies of Genesis with the book's religious and theological themes, one has first to consider their relationship to the important theological narratives. In the process it becomes evident just how complex the "theology" of the canonical text is and how little research has been focussed on it. Its usual division into relatively discreet literary units gives rise to small digestible pieces, a simplicity which becomes the yardstick of diachronic, frequently circular, reasoning. I will focus on a few basic questions, especially on those where genealogical connections and theological claims can illuminate each other.

Clearly, the blessing of creation (especially Gen. 1:28) and the commission to fill the earth, both repeated after the deluge (9:1), take shape in the abundance of the peoples listed in Genesis 10 and in the continuity through many generations suggested by the long sequences of names in Genesis 5 and 11.[54] Still before the expansion of human beings is reported in the table of nations, one finds in the form of the Noachic commandments (9:2ff.) the starting point for a human ethic the core of which is the legal prohibition of the killing of human beings, as well as the limitation of human violence against animals.

---

[53] See Knauf, *Midian* (n. 48 above).
[54] Cf., e.g., Westermann, *Genesis* I (n. 8 above) concerning Genesis 5; 10; 11.

What is decisive is the *theological evaluation* of the variety of the peoples and cultures, including what one could call their religions. This is finally dependent on an understanding of Genesis 11, the story of the tower of Babel. Following on the table of nations, and before the unfolding of the genealogical line through Terah and Abraham, the story points to the collapse of a uniform humanity. According to the usual reading, the story of the tower of Babel is concerned with an infringement on God by the still-uniform humanity, which is punished with dispersion and linguistic diversity. On such a view, a plurality of cultures seems to be a "graceless Judgment of God."[55] C. Uehlinger's new interpretation of Genesis 11[56] proves to be illuminating, also from the perspective of the text's function. He shows that behind the speech which gives rise to the building of the city and the tower, down to its linguistic details, stands the attempt of the Assyrian empire to bring together deported peoples from all countries, to homogenize their language and to have them work on one task, the building of the capital and the palace. The story is about the suppression of diversity. The nightmare of a uniform world order is prevented by God. The punishment is, above all, an act of liberation, the enabling of diverse identities. Every attempt to found the unity of humanity through the abolition of its variety must threaten Israel and finally destroy it.

Genesis is about the one creator-God and his distinct people in the midst of a divinely intended diversity of cultures and nationalities, to which belong also the diverse relationships with this God, i.e., their religions. It is most intriguing how this complexity of relationships is depicted. The topic appears first in Gen. 4:26 with the remark that the name of God has been called upon since Seth, i.e., including all of primordial humanity. At issue is *the* name, which is revealed again not until the call of Moses (Exodus 3; 6). The conflicts among the sons of Noah, especially the outrage of Ham (the father of Canaan!) in 9:20ff. lead not only to the founding of human domination (9:25) but also to an assignment of the one God to Shem alone: "Blessed be Yhwh, the God of Shem" (9:26), i.e., to only one third of humanity, with space for Japhet in the tents of Shem.

---

[55] So G. v. Rad, *Das erste Buch Mose: Genesis* (ATD; Göttingen: Vandenhoeck & Ruprecht, [1949] 9th edn, 1972), p. 117.

[56] C. Uehlinger, *Weltreich und "eine Rede": Eine neue Deutung der sogenannten Turmbauerzählung (Gen. 11, 1–9)* (OBO, 101; Fribourg: Universitätsverlag, 1990).

Genesis does not represent the process that Deuteronomic language calls "election" as *one* great step from the table of nations to the one nation. Instead, the texts form a most complex path which obviously knows relationships with God of various "shades." In order to illustrate this point, I will read the three great promises to Abraham in Genesis 12, 15 and 17 in relation to the genealogies of Abraham. After Terah had left Ur, a kind of proto-exodus which concerns all Terahites (11:31), Abraham is addressed by God with the famous words in 12:1–3. A separation is commanded—from land, from kin, and from the father's house—and this concerns all Abraham's descendants. The divine promise, to become a great nation, to receive a great name, but also the promise of the blessing, that all the families of the earth would bless each other with his name,[57] all that is valid for Abraham and that means for *all* of his descendants. There is no differentiation here, nor is there one later. Thus, 12:1–3 proves to be a key for understanding the canonical text of Genesis. All Abrahamites receive a mediating role for God's blessing on the whole human race, consisting of many peoples.

Gen. 15:1–5 contains the promise of God to Abraham that children from his own body will be as numerous as the stars of the sky. Again, the context allows no limitation; the promise concerns all Abrahamites. Even the most solemn self-commitment of God in the covenant ceremony of 15:7ff. is valid without limitation for the entire seed of Abraham (and that independent of what ch. 15 suggests, read in isolation). In the following chapter, the pregnancy of Hagar is then reported and the first attempt of Sarah to get rid of her competitor and child. The attempt fails, and the episode ends with an explicit promise of untold progeny for Hagar (16:10).

Genesis 17, then, represents a narrowing of some promises of God for a part of the children of Abraham. The initial promise of a covenant of a great progeny, peoples and kingdoms (17:2, 5, 6), the promise of the land (v. 8) as well as the sign of circumcision (v. 10ff.) is valid for all; it thus includes Ishmael and the sons of Keturah. Then, however, a special word about Sarah follows in vv. 15ff. This

---

[57] For a discussion of the philological problem, see Blum, *Komposition* (n. 10 above), pp. 350f. On the relation of the verses to the preceding primeval history, also the Priestly texts within it, cf. F. Crüsemann, "Die Eigenständigkeit der Urgeschichte: Ein Beitrag zur Diskussion um den 'Jahwisten'," in J. Jeremias and L. Perlitt (eds.), *Die Botschaft und die Boten. FS H.W. Wolff* (Neukirchen-Vluyn: Neukirchener Verlag, 1981), pp. 11–30, 29.

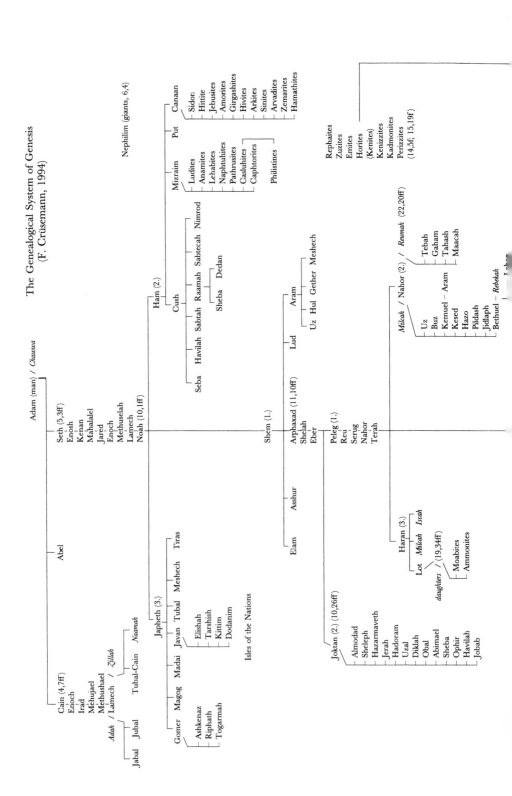

The Genealogical System of Genesis
(F. Crüsemann, 1994)

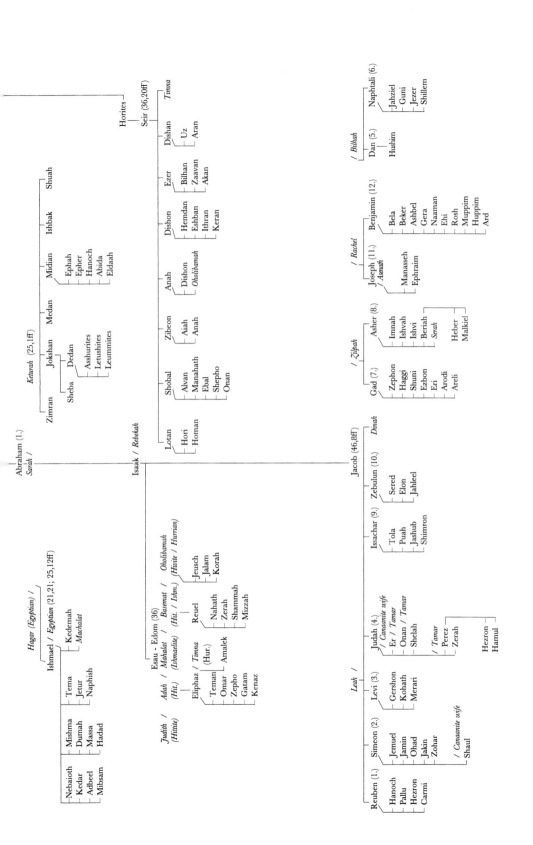

is by no means a superfluous act, as is occasionally claimed.[58] Abraham, who wants to relate everything to Ishmael (v. 18), is corrected by God, and Ishmael receives his own promise (v. 20). Recently, Irmtraud Fischer has correctly emphasized the significance of the words to Sarah: she sees behind them P's consideration of the older narrative in Genesis 18, with its central role for Sarah. A more basic issue here, however, is the constitution of the special role of the branch of Abrahamites which goes back through Sarah. The covenant is made with *Isaac* alone (vv. 19, 21); the promise to be God for him (v. 7) is directed towards his descendants.

Yet Esau is also a son of Isaac, indeed, the older one. Only through the tangled conflicts of the brothers, through deception, hatred to final reconciliation—not least through the highlight of all those conflicts in the night wrestling at the Jabbok (32:10ff.)—is the special blessing for Jacob and his descendants reached. They go to Egypt, and their oppression is then the motive for the communication of the divine name to Moses, which was honoured by all human beings in primordial times.

Again and again, one is reminded at key points in the Pentateuchal narrative that Israel's distinctive role is connected to the diversity of the world of peoples created by God. The theme of Gen. 12:1–3 reappears, e.g., at the beginning of the sojourn at Sinai, where Israel is described as a priestly people for the whole of humanity (Exod. 19:6), and then at the very end of the Pentateuch. Here, at the conclusion of the song of Moses, all peoples are called to praise the God of Israel (Deut. 32:43; cf. Rom. 15:10).

Translated by Rainer Schack and Mark G. Brett

---

[58] On the following, see I. Fischer, *Die Erzeltern Israels: Feministisch-theologische Studien zu Genesis 12–36* (BZAW, 222: Berlin: de Gruyter, 1994), p. 10; she engages critically with W. Zimmerli's devaluation of this passage (*1. Mose 1–11: Die Urgeschichte* [ZBK, 1; Zürich: Zwingli Verlag, 2nd edn, 1957], p. 72) as well as with the many attempts to emend the text, e.g., N. Lohfink, "Textkritisches zu Gn 17,5.13.16.17," *Bib* 48 (1967), pp. 439f.

THE *GĒR* IN THE PRIESTLY LAWS
OF THE PENTATEUCH

Rolf Rendtorff

"When the Lord told Moses that his people should love the stranger as themselves (Leviticus 19:34), who was the stranger?" This question, asked by an anthropologist,[1] is not easy to answer for a biblical exegete. First of all, for reasons of terminology: The Hebrew language uses a number of different expressions to refer to persons who do not belong to the majority, however the latter might be defined. Some of these expressions are generally used in a more negative sense, always emphasizing the otherness of those persons and their separateness from the majority, such as *nokrî* (e.g., Deut. 17:15) or *ben-nēkār* (e.g., Exod. 12:43), and *zār* (e.g., Isa. 1:7). In other cases the difference is not as evident and not always emphasized, as with *tôšāb* which is often used together with *gēr* (e.g., Gen. 23:4), the latter being the most frequent among these expressions. The question of terminology continues into translation: The "stranger" (e.g., JPS) is sometimes an "alien" (e.g., NRSV) or a "sojourner" (e.g., The Dictionary of Classical Hebrew, s.v. אֶזְרָח).

I.

The most interesting and most important among these expressions is the term *gēr*. This term shows a variety of aspects, and obviously its connotation is not always the same in different parts of the Hebrew Bible.[2] Let us begin with some observations about the way the *gēr* is

---

[1] Mary Douglas, "The Stranger in the Bible," *Archives européennes de sociologie* 35/2 (1994), pp. 283–298.

[2] There are two recent monographical studies on this topic: Christiana van Houten, *The Alien in Israelite Law* (JSOTSuppl, 107; Sheffield: JSOT Press 1991); Christoph Bultmann, *Der Fremde im antiken Juda. Eine Untersuchung zum sozialen Typenbegriff 'ger' und seinem Bedeutungswandel in der alttestamentlichen Gesetzgebung*, (*FRLANT, 153; Göttingen Vandenhoeck & Ruprecht, 1992*). See also Excursus 34: The "Ger" in Jacob Milgrom's

defined. First of all, it is important to note that the word *gēr* mainly appears in the singular. There are only a few exceptions: In some texts the term *gērîm* is used to describe Israel's situation in Egypt: "for you were *gērîm* in the land of Egypt" (Exod. 22:20; 23:9; Lev. 19:34; Deut. 10:19). This remembrance of Israel's fate serves as a reason not to oppress the actual *gēr* who in the immediate context is mentioned in the singular. In another small group of texts the term *gērîm* describes metaphorically Israel's position before God (Lev. 25:23; 1 Chr. 29:15; cf. Ps. 146:9). This use has no direct relation to the present *gēr* as a real person. The Books of Chronicles use the term *gērîm* in two contexts: First, to define the groups of non-Israelites whom David and Solomon forced to labor for the building of the temple (1 Chr. 22:2; 2 Chr. 2:16), which is an invention by the Chronicler in order to avoid the idea that Israelites had been forced to labor. Second, to specify "the *gērîm* who came out of the land of Israel" as one of the groups that participated in the great passover arranged by king Hezekiah (2 Chr. 30:25); this passover is also an invention of the Chronicler so that the text only shows his idea of Judah and Israel at the time of Hezekiah. Finally, in the Book of Ezechiel it is said that in the future division of the land "the *gērîm* who reside among you and have begotten children among you" shall be like a native (*'ezrāḥ*)[3] and therefore receive an allotment (Ezek. 47:22). In the following verse, for the detailed procedure of dividing the land the actual *gēr* who shall receive it is mentioned in the singular (v. 23).

This shows that the *gēr* is mainly dealt with as an individual. Another interesting aspect of defining the *gēr* is his being mentioned together with certain other groups of persons. One characteristic combination is that of *gēr* and *tôšāb*, the so-called "temporary resident."[4] Both words are based on verbal roots meaning "to reside" or the like: *gûr* and *yāšab*. In both cases the noun refers to a person that

---

commentary on *Numbers* (The *JPS Torah Commentary*; Philadelphia: *JPS, 1989*), pp. 298–402.

[3] See below note 8.

[4] Van Houten says that the juxtaposition of *gēr* and *tôšāb* in the "Priestly legislation" is "a new association, for neither in the Covenant Code nor in the Deuteronomic law was the alien classed with the temporary resident" (p. 125). But this is only half the truth, because the two mentioned legal codes do not use—and perhaps do not know!—the term *tôšāb* at all.

originally came from somewhere else and lives now in a surrounding that is not his or her own.[5] So Abraham calls himself a *gēr* and *tôšāb* among the inhabitants of the land (Gen. 23:4). This story shows that the *gēr* does not possess any part of the land, but that there could be friendly relations between him and the owners of the land and that he could even buy a certain piece of land. In other narrative texts that mention a *gēr* living in a foreign country, the emphasis sounds less peaceful (e.g., Gen. 15:13; Exod. 2:22; 18:3).

Interestingly, half of the number of occurrences of the word *tôšāb* (seven out of fourteen) appear in only one chapter, namely Leviticus 25. Here *gēr* and *tôšāb* sometimes are mentioned together, but it is evident that they are not identical. Of specific importance is the divine declaration in v. 23: "The land shall not be sold in perpetuity, for the land is mine; you are *gērîm* and *tôšābîm* with me." Here the Israelites themselves are called *gērîm* and *tôšābîm*, and the meaning is obvious: the land does not belong to them in a final sense. Therefore, in view of God the Israelites are in the same position as the *gēr* and *tôšāb* living among them.

In some cases the *tôšāb* is mentioned in juxtaposition with another social group, the *śākîr* (Lev. 25:6, 40; cf. 22:10; Exod. 12:45). This term describes a person working for wages, but being explicitly differentiated from the slave (Lev. 25:39f.) because of his or her personal freedom. The *gēr* is never mentioned together with the *śākîr*. Even more notable is the fact that out of the families of the *tôšābîm* children that are born in the country can be taken as slaves (v. 45) and even be left to the next generation (v. 46). Here the *tôšāb* is put into the same category with "the nations around you" (v. 44) which would never be the case with the *gēr*. This gives the impression of a certain social hierarchy: *gēr*—*tôšāb*—*śākîr*—slave, whereby the first three groups can be differently juxtaposed. But this hierarchy does not mean that the *gēr* will always be the most wealthy of these groups. In some texts he is mentioned together with the poor as to be given the right of gleaning (Lev. 19:10; 23:22).

Gēr and *tôšāb* together play a specific role in the framework of the law on slavery in Lev. 25:35–54. Here they are set in opposition to

---

[5] In Lev. 25:6, 45 both words are combined: the *tôšāb* is one of those who reside (*gûr*) with the Israelites.

"your brother" (v. 35 etc.), that is, to the brother of those to whom
the law is directed. The *gēr* and the *tôšāb* do not belong to those
"brothers." But this does not matter as long as land or house are to
be sold (vv. 25ff., 29ff.). If one "brother" has to sell it, there is no
specific mention about who might be the buyer. The reason is obvious: the land has to go back to the family of the original owner
anyhow, at the latest in the year of jubilee (v. 28). In case of personal poverty things are different. The first step is that the addressee
of the law, called "you" in the singular, has to support his brother
who is endangered to be reduced to poverty, so that he can live
alongside with him (v. 35). He shall do it as he would do with a *gēr*
and *tôšāb*.[6] This is an important remark. It shows that for these priestly
laws, even if they do not mention questions of charity too often, it
is quite self-evident to help one of the groups that do not belong to
the "brothers" (cf. in particular Lev. 19:33–34). The charity towards
those has to be the example for the behavior towards one's own
"brothers."

Later it is said that even if the "brother" has to sell himself he
should not be treated like a slave but like a *tôšāb* and *śākîr* (vv. 39–
42, see above). But then an interesting variant appears: It might
happen that the *gēr* and *tôšāb* become(s)[7] wealthy and the "brother"
has to sell himself to him (vv. 47–54). Then, of course, the "brother"
is not allowed to be taken as slave, but only as *śākîr* (v. 53). But in
addition, he need not serve until the year of jubilee, as usual (v. 40),
but there will be a special right of redemption, as generally in the
case of landed property (vv. 24, 29). The members of the family are
mentioned who could (and should) redeem him (vv. 48–49), and if
he prospers he might even redeem himself (v. 49b). Thus his situa-

---

[6] The text is a bit difficult because the two words גֵּר וְתוֹשָׁב are syntactically
unconnected with the context. LXX adds ὡς, and most modern translators and
commentators understand the text accordingly, e.g., "as though" in NRSV and JPS.
Others, as e.g., Rashi and Ibn Ezra, understand it saying that he should help the
person "even if he is a *gēr* or *tôšāb*"; but this is not convincing because in the next
verse the person is again called "your brother," and the remembrance of the exodus
in v. 38 refers also explicitly to the Israelites. Some commentators, like e.g., Elliger,
simply delete the two words because they do not understand the text.

[7] In the first half of v. 47 the MT says גֵּר וְתוֹשָׁב, in the second half only גֵּר
תוֹשָׁב. Is he taken to be only one person? At the end of the verse it only says "the
family of the *gēr*."

tion is qualitatively different from the one he would have been in had he sold himself to another "brother." His chance to get free is definitely higher, at least according to the wording of the law. This shows that the lawgiver would not exclude the possibility that a member of the community would have to sell himself to a *gēr* (and *tôšāb*), and there are no legal objections against that. But nevertheless, the family of this person, or even he himself, should have a special chance to free him from this uneasy situation.

These last observations show two things: First, the *gēr* is taken to be a permanent figure in the context of the society to which these laws are addressed. As such he is accepted and integrated in the rules of the daily life of the community. Second, he is still different. This is particularly clear if a member of the majority becomes financially and socially dependent on a *gēr*. Then there are special rules to make it easier to be extricated from this situation. But all this is formulated in the law without any bias.

II.

So far we have dealt with texts that emphasize the difference between the *gēr* (and the *tôšāb*) and the majority of the community that is addressed in the text of the law. I avoided calling the members of the majority by any ethnic or otherwise defining terms. Only where the text has a specific expression like "brother" I used it. On the other hand, we found some terms with whom the *gēr* could be juxtaposed, such as *tôšāb* and the poor. Both of these terms have a clear social connotation. But then we find another term with which the *gēr* is regularly juxtaposed: the term *'ezrāḥ*. This juxtaposition points in the opposite direction. The *'ezrāḥ* is exactly what the *gēr* is not: an original, native inhabitant of the land, a citizen. This word appears almost exclusively in priestly laws in the Pentateuch,[8] and in the majority of occurrences it is used in immediate relation to the *gēr*. The surprising fact is that in all those texts that mention the *gēr* and the *'ezrāḥ* together the point is not their difference or contrast

---

[8] In Josh. 8:33 *gēr* and *'ezrāḥ* are named together as integral part of the assembly. For Ezek. 47:22 see above note 3. In Ps. 37:35 the meaning is uncertain.

but what they have in common. Many of these texts look formulaic, albeit with several variations: "*gēr* like *'ezrāḥ*" (כגר כאזרח Lev. 24:16, 24:22); "all persons . . . *gēr* and *'ezrāḥ*" (כל־נפש . . . . באזרח ובגר 17:15); "the *'ezrāḥ* and the *gēr* who resides among you" (האזרח והגר הגר בתוככם 16:19; 18:26); in a very definite way "You shall have one ordinance (משפט) for the *gēr* and for the *'ezrāḥ*, for I am the Lord your God" (24:22, cf. Num. 15:16); "There shall be one law (תורה) for the *'ezrāḥ* and the *gēr* who resides among you" (Exod. 12:49, cf. Num. 15:16); "One single statute (חקה) shall be for you and for the *gēr*, a perpetual statute throughout your generations; you and the *gēr* shall be alike before the Lord" (Num. 15:15; cf. 9:14; 19:10). In addition, there are a number of texts that do not use the term *'ezrāḥ* but instead speak of Israelites. They are even more formulaic, often beginning with איש איש מבית ישראל or מבני ישראל "Anyone of the house (or: the people) of Israel" and then continuing "or from the *gēr* that resides among you" (Lev. 17:8, 10, 13; 20:2; 22:18).

All these texts explain certain aspects of the law that are valid for the *gēr* as well as for the *'ezrāḥ*. The latter is here identified belonging to the house or people of Israel. That makes it evident that the *gēr* does not belong to "Israel." But just from that point of view it is highly important to see in which fields the things in common are emphasized. The majority of these texts are dealing with cultic matters. Leviticus 17 contains a number of specifications of rules for sacrifices that are dealt with more generally in chs. 1–7. Here the *gēr* is fully included.[9] According to v. 8 he is entitled to offer *'ōlâ* and *zebaḥ* sacrifices. Like the Israelite, he has to bring every sacrifice "to the entrance of the tent of meeting," according to the basic laws in Lev. 1:3 and 3:2. Like the Israelite he is forbidden to eat any blood, be it from a sacrifice (v. 10, 12) or from a hunted animal (v. 13), and also to eat what has died or has been torn by beasts (v. 15). In certain cases, he is also subject to the "cut off" (*karet*) penalty like the Israelite (vv. 9, 10) or he becomes unclean (v. 15).

Numbers 15 brings also additional regulations for sacrifices such as additional grain and drink offerings. These rules are valid for the *'ezrāḥ* (v. 13) as well as for the *gēr* (v. 14). The latter is spoken

---

[9] Only in the first paragraph (vv. 3–7) the *gēr* is not mentioned. It is disputed whether he is therefore allowed to do things prohibited there, as e.g. to offer his sacrifices to the goat idols (v. 7).

of as one who "resides" (*gûr*), or who lives among the Israelites since generations.[10] A series of three formulae finalizes this paragraph, saying that there shall be one single *ḥuqqâ*, a perpetual one (v. 15), and one single *tôrâ* and *mišpāṭ* (v. 16) for the *'ezrāḥ* and the *gēr*. Another special aspect of sacrifices is emphasized in Lev. 22:17–25: Every animal presented for offering must not have and blemish "to be favorable for you" (v. 19, cf. Lev. 1:3[11]). This again is valid for the Israelite and for the "*gēr* in Israel" (v. 18). Together with the Israelite the *gēr* is responsible that the sacrifices are offered in a way expected and accepted by YHWH.

In some texts the *gēr* is explicitly made co-responsible, together with the *'ezrāḥ* or Israelite, for the purity of the land. In the summary of the sexual rules in Lev. 18:24–30 it is said that neither the *'ezrāḥ* nor the *gēr* should do all the abominations (v. 26) by which the earlier inhabitants had defiled the land. Not to defile themselves and not to defile God's land is of high importance for the life of both, Israelites and *gērîm*. Therefore, again both groups are responsible to prevent anyone in their midst giving of their offspring to Molech and thereby defiling God's sanctuary and his holy name (Lev. 20:1–5). There is also a perpetual *ḥuqqâ* for the Israelites and the *gēr* alike to purify themselves on the third and seventh day after touching a corpse. Otherwise they will remain unclean and by that defile the Lord's tabernacle (Num. 19:10b–13). For the same reason everyone who blasphemes the name of the Lord shall be put to death, the *gēr* like the *'ezrāḥ* (Lev. 24:16). And at the end of this chapter it is formulated anew: "You shall have one *mišpāṭ* for the *gēr* and for the *'ezrāḥ*, for I am the Lord your God" (v. 22).

The *gēr* is also included in the highest holy day of the year, the day of atonement. The final paragraph of the law of this day (Lev. 16:29–34) begins with the statement that it is a perpetual *ḥuqqâ* for the *'ezrāḥ* and the *gēr*, that they shall practice self-denial and do no

---

[10] J. Milgrom in his commentary (see above note 2) argues that *lᵉdōrōtêkem* in v. 14 "belongs here at the beginning of the verse." Then he wants to understand the "one who lives among you" as the *nokrî* "who does not actually reside among the Israelites . . . but who sojournes or visits" (120). But it seems to me quite impossible to exchange the two terms *gēr* and *nokrî*. This chapter speaks continuously of the *gēr*, and the *nokrî* does not appear in the priestly laws at all.

[11] Cf. Rolf Rendtorff, *Leviticus* (BK III, 1; Neukirchen-Vluyn: Neukirchener, 1985), pp. 30–32.

manner of work. There is disagreement among commentators whether the *gēr* is only included in the commitment of doing no work or also in that of self-denial. The New JPS Translation devides the verse by semicolon in favor of the first mentioned alternative: "you shall practice self-denial; and you shall do no manner of work, neither the citizen nor the alien who resides among you."[12] But then the question arises, who is included in the "you" in the following verse. "For on this day atonement shall be made for you to cleanse you; from all your sins you shall be clean before the Lord" (v. 31). Is the *gēr* included?[13] He is clearly included in several laws regarding the purity of the land (see above). Should he not be included in the cleansing? Whatever the answer might be, the *gēr* is mentioned anyhow in the perpetual *ḥuqqâ* for Israel's highest holy day alongside with the *'ezrāḥ*.

This group of texts shows the very close relations of the *gēr* with the majority of citizens, in particular in the cultic field. In several respects, the *gēr* is simply included in the cultic life of his surrounding. To what extent he remains unconcerned by certain laws is not quite clear. One theory is that "the *gēr* is bound by the prohibitive commandments but not by the performative ones."[14] But it is difficult to decide. Here we have to keep in mind that the laws we have before us in the biblical texts have not been worked out at one time and on one level. Therefore the mention of the *gēr* might have been added at certain places at different times and for different reasons without a consistent drive for systematics and completeness. Nevertheless, the general picture is quite clear.

III.

I include here some brief remarks on the role of the *gēr* in other law codes of the Hebrew Bible. In the "Book of the Covenant," as well as in Deuteronomy, the *gēr* is mentioned exclusively in a social con-

---

[12] Jacob Milgrom argues in detail in favor of this interpretation: see the Excursus "Ger" in the commentary on Numbers (s. above note 2); also his *Leviticus 1–16* (AB, 3; Garden City: Doubleday, 1991), pp. 1055–56.
[13] Van Houten (see note 2) does discuss this question while Milgrom (see note 12) does not.
[14] So Milgrom (see note 12).

nection: "You shall not wrong or oppress a stranger, for you were strangers in the land of Egypt" (Exod. 22:20; 23:9). The *gēr* is close to widows, orphans, and the poor (22:21, 24, cf. also Deut. 14:29; 16:11, 14; 24:14, 17, 19, 21; 26:13; 27:19), and also to the Levites (Deut. 14:29; 26:11, 13). But both these law codes never compare the *gēr* with the surrounding majority. They never use the term *'ezrāḥ*; possibly they do not know it at all. But they also never compare the *gēr* with the Israelite, as the priestly laws constantly do. There is just the opposition of "you" and "the *gēr*."

Now again: Who is the *gēr*? All the law codes agree that he is a person who lives more or less permanently among the Israelites but does not become one of them. But only the priestly laws reflect upon the relations between those to whom the laws are given and the *gēr*. We made the observation above that the term *'ezrāḥ* can interchange with "a person of the house of Israel" or "of the children of Israel." Then the other question arises: Who are the Israelites? In order to understand who is the *gēr* that is *not* an Israelite we should know who the Israelite is. But how can we know? In the Hebrew Bible the term "Israel" or "children of Israel" and the like has quite different meanings, beginning with the surname of the third of the patriarchs, Jacob (Gen. 32:28[29]; 35:10), through the name of the Northern Kingdom (1 Kgs. 12:19) up to the name for those who came back from the Babylonian Exile (Ezra 2:2; 7:13). Alongside those changing meanings there is always a general use of the term "Israel" embracing the whole people of the descendants of Abraham and Jacob notwithstanding the current political situation. Obviously this is also the case with the priestly laws for whom there is only *one* Israel.

But the moment there are persons who are not included in this "Israel" the question of borders arises. Who is in and who is out, who is an *'ezrāḥ* and who is a *gēr*? And why? We have seen how close the *gēr* is to the *'ezrāḥ* and how difficult it seems to be to define the difference. The prophet Ezekiel has felt this problem, and in his vision of the future he gave clear advice: The *gērîm* who live among the Israelites and who have begotten children among them shall receive an allotment, "and they shall be to you as an *'ezrāḥ* of the children of Israel" (Ezek. 47:22). According to this statement, the only thing that distinguishes a permanent *gēr* from an Israelite is the participation in the possession of the land. If this situation changes, there will no longer be any difference at all. The *gēr* will become an *'ezrāḥ*. Of course, this is an eschatological statement that could only be realized in a moment when the whole land is distributed anew. But we can learn from this what the difference between a *gēr* and an *'ezrāḥ* is really like.

Recently Mary Douglas wrote: "My idea is simply that the *gēr* was one of the other descendants of Jacob, not descended from Judah, nor from Levi or Benjamin, but those other remnants of the twelve tribes who had been defeated and scattered by invaders and who still lived in Canaan during and after the exile in Babylon. His special status at law would be precisely that he was neither a foreigner nor a Jew."[15] This seems to me to be exactly what Ezekiel had in mind, and it fits precisely the role of the *gēr* in the priestly laws. For the moment I want to stop here. It would be highly interesting and important to develop this idea further and to ask for the different connotations and implications of the terms "Israel," "house of Israel," children of Israel and the like. One could say: The *gēr* is an Israelite but not an "Israelite" according to the rule on which the priestly laws are based. Or: The *gēr* is an Israelite but not a Jew. In principal, this definition would be independent of the exact dating of the priestly laws, because some Israelites became landless at least from the Assyrian invasion in the eighth century BCE.

IV.

And what about Ezra? It is obvious that the whole problem of foreign marriages which Ezra treated in such a disturbing way is incompatible with the role of the *gēr* in the priestly laws. The term *gēr* never appears in the Book(s) of Ezra/Nehemiah; nor does the term *'ezrāḥ*. Instead the discussion is about marriages of members of the "people Israel," called "the holy seed," with women from the "peoples of the land," called by all kinds of anachronistic names in order to compare the present situation with that of the early times of the conquest of the land (Ezra 9:1–2). While in the priestly laws a spirit of closeness prevailed, and even the integration of the *gēr* is possible, in Ezra everything is dominated by the idea of separation

---

[15] Cf. note 1, "The Stranger in the Bible," p. 286.

and even hostility. One might understand this behavior in the context of the struggle for Israel's national and religious identity and survival. But one thing seems to be clear: This Ezra cannot be credited with the codification of the Priestly Torah as some scholars believe. If Mary Douglas is correct, this theory has it the wrong way around. It may be that the preservation of the laws of the *gēr* was directly opposed to the marriage policies represented in Ezra.

THE IDEOLOGY OF IDENTITY IN CHRONICLES

Jonathan E. Dyck

Introduction

The books of Chronicles do not immediately come to mind in thinking about ethnicity and the Bible. There are no texts to rival Ezra 9 and Nehemiah 13, no language to disquiet our minds like the language of "abominations," "the pure seed," and the "great evil" of "foreign women." The sociology of the Persian period is by and large a sociology of these and other texts in Ezra-Nehemiah which are the closest thing we have to a direct window onto post-exilic Judah. Chronicles scholars fall into two camps: those who paint Chronicles with the same brush as Ezra-Nehemiah, labelling the Chronicler's attitude to outsiders as equally exclusivist, and those who resist this tempting comparison and find the Chronicler to be rather more tolerant of others, an inclusivist and maybe even an ecumenist. Nineteenth century scholars, most of whom fall into the former camp, were not averse to judging openly "the good" and "the bad" and, more often than not, Chronicles was lumped in with "the bad" on account of his Judean-Jerusalemite-Priestly tendencies. In more recent scholarship there is a strong tendency to exonerate the Chronicler (and often at the expense of Ezra-Nehemiah) and to place him in the company of "the good." And times have changed even for Ezra-Nehemiah which is now getting an equally sympathetic reading. The community described therein is said to have had legitimate ethnic concerns which at times required strong measures such as those relating to intermarriage. The question of the Chronicler's concept of the identity his people, the people he calls "Israel," is thus a comparative one: What is the Chronicler's concept of Israel as compared to that found in Ezra-Nehemiah?[1] In light of what we find in Ezra-Nehemiah,

---

[1] The relationship between Chronicles and Ezra-Nehemiah also has a literary aspect in that scholars who argue that Chronicles is exclusivist have also tended to hold that Chronicles-Ezra-Nehemiah constitutes one larger "Chronistic" history. I am not at this point concerned with the literary question for the simple reason that one could defend either interpretations of Chronicles even if one judged it on its

is the Chronicler also though indirectly addressing the same contemporary problems? Would the Chronicler have supported Ezra and Nehemiah's attempts to rid the post-exilic community of foreign women or would he have sided with those who took wives from "the peoples of the lands" and other groups outside "the assembly of the exile"? Would the Chronicler have accepted these group divisions? My aim in this paper is to not only to answer these particular questions but to ask new questions which emerge from a closer examination of the concept of ethnic identity itself. The concept of identity is, as I hope to demonstrate in the following, a complex *sociological* notion which requires *sociological* terms and categories that do it justice.

Exclusivist or Inclusivist?

It may be helpful at this point to take a closer look at the two main positions taken with regard to the Chronicler's concept of identity and the textual evidence adduced in support of them. I begin with the *exclusivist interpretation* . . . an interpretation which goes all the way back to de Wette's[2] ground-breaking study of the biases of the Chronicler. De Wette argued that the Chronicler showed *a preference for Judah and hatred of Israel.*[3] The textual evidence he adduces in support of his interpretation forms the backbone of the exclusivist position. The most obvious, yet still implicit evidence, is the absence of a history of Israel after the division of the kingdom (2 Chron. 10ff.), which contrasts sharply with the book of Kings. More to the point perhaps is Abijah's speech to Jeroboam and the rebellious northern kingdom in 2 Chronicles 13 in which he claims that the Israelites cannot defeat "the kingdom of God in the hand of the sons of David" (v. 8) for to fight against the Davides is to "fight against the LORD" (v. 12). De Wette also cites 2 Chron. 19:3 which describes the northern kingdom of Ahab as "the wicked and those who hate the LORD."

---

own terms. Indeed, the first proponent of the exclusivist interpretation, W.M.L. de Wette, treated Chronicles as an independent work. Neither interpretation of Chronicles *requires* a particular view on the literary question. I will treat Chronicles as a separate book though I will continue to use Ezra-Nehemiah as a point of comparison.

[2] W.M.L. de Wette, *Beiträge zur Einleitung in das Alte Testament: Bd. 1, Kritischer Versuch über die Glaubwürdigkeit der Bücher der Chronik mit Hinsicht auf die Geschichte der Mosaischen Bücher und Gesetzgebung* (Darmstadt: Olms Verlag, reprint edn, 1971).

[3] De Wette, *Beiträge*, pp. 126–32.

It was Wellhausen who first suggested the link between this particular anti-Israel bias and the Samaritan problem, which was, supposedly, a major challenge facing the Chronicler's community. For
the Chronicler, argues Wellhausen, "Israel is the congregation of true
worship, and the last is connected with the temple at Jerusalem, in
which of course the Samaritans have no part."[4] Wellhausen's minor
insight was transformed by Torrey and Noth into the theory of an
anti-Samaritan purpose,[5] a theory which became an assured result of
biblical criticism. Noth reasons that if we observe what the Chronicler *included* in his history we must come to the conclusion that his
motive (stated in positive terms) was "to demonstrate the legitimacy
of the Davidic dynasty and of the Jerusalem temple as Yahweh's
valid cult centre."[6] If, on the other hand, we observe that the Chronicler excluded those traditions which the Jews and Samaritans had in
common (i.e., those contained in the Pentateuch, Joshua, and Judges)
and that he neglects the history of the northern kingdom we must
conclude that the opposition he had in view was "the Samaritan
community with a cult of their own on Mt. Gerizim."[7]

A somewhat more subtle approach is von Rad's analysis of the
use of the term "Israel" in Chronicles.[8] He observes that the Chronistic
history (i.e., Chronicles-Ezra-Nehemiah) contains *different and conflicting*
ideas of what Israel is. This conflict is a reflection of the clash between

---

[4] J. Wellhausen, *Prolegomena to the History of Ancient Israel*, trans. W. Robertson Smith
(Gloucestor, Mass: Peter Smith, reprint edn, 1973), pp. 187–8. "*Die Samarier*" is the
German word used which is better translated "Samarians."

[5] C.C. Torrey, "The Chronicler as Editor and Independent Narrator," in *Ezra
Studies* (New York: Ktav, reprint edn, 1970), p. 209. He follows Josephus in arguing
that the Samaritan priesthood was Jerusalemite in origin and that the Chronicler is
countering their claims to an ancient cultic legitimacy. A more recent study by
H. Kippenberg also suggests that Josephus' account of the origins of the Samaritan
priesthood has a basis in history: *Garizim und Synagoge: Traditionsgeschichtliche Untersuchungen
zur samaritanischen Religion der aramische Periode* (Berlin: De Gruyter, 1971), pp. 50–9.

[6] M. Noth, *The Chronicler's History* (trans. H.G.M. Williamson; JSOTS, 50; Sheffield:
JSOT Press, 1987), p. 100. Noth's stress on the "overall plan" was directed against
von Rad's view that the Chronicler's purpose in writing his history was to support
the claims of the Levites.

[7] Noth, *Chronicler's History*. The anti-Samaritan theory has fallen on hard times for
the simple reason that the sanctuary on Mt. Gerizim was probably established in
the Hellenistic period. Thus, the rivalry between the Jews and Samaritans as reported in Ezra-Nehemiah is not to be thought of as a rivalry between Jerusalem
and Mt. Gerizim. The schism between the two communities cannot with certainty
be traced back to the fifth century (see R.T. Anderson, "Samaritans," in *Anchor Bible
Dictionary*, vol. 5, pp. 940–7).

[8] G. von Rad, *Das Geschichtsbild des Chronistischen Werkes* (BWANT, 54; Stuttgart:
Kohlhammer, 1930).

theory and reality—the ideal of Israel as made up of the twelve tribes
of Jacob clashing with the historical reality of the post-exilic community of Judah, Benjamin and Levi.[9] To be sure, von Rad does not
assign all the material in the Chronistic History to the Chronicler.
He takes the Ezra and Nehemiah "memoirs" to be a largely authentic source material which gives us a direct insight into the Chronicler's
era.[10] Of particular note in this non-Chronistic material is the use of
the words "Jews"[11] and "Israel"[12] in these sources. The former is
used in political and organisational contexts whereas the latter is used
in religious contexts. Von Rad concludes from this that the post-
exilic community appropriated for itself, that is for Judah and Benjamin, the name "Israel" and the promises inherent in it.[13]

Such is the self-understanding of the Chronicler's contemporaries
and of the Chronicler himself. In the Chronistic material in Ezra-
Nehemiah the word "Jew" is not used. The emphasis is entirely on
the continuity between the community of returned exiles and Israel
of old. The same viewpoint is also found in the genealogies of
Chronicles (1 Chronicles 1–9) where we find an enumeration of all
the tribes of Israel.[14] But this ideal concept of Israel does, in von
Rad's view, eventually come into conflict with the narrower definition in the story of the divided kingdom, a definition rooted in the
self-understanding of the Chronicler's community. Von Rad argues
that when the Chronicler speaks of "all Israel in Judah and Benjamin" (2 Chron. 11:3) he means to say that the kingdom of Judah
(and the post-exilic "remnant" of that kingdom) is the *true Israel*.[15]
The northern kingdom is completely illegitimate and has, as it were,
excluded itself from salvation history.

Torrey and Noth represent the Chronicler as one who accepts
this narrowing of Israel. Their interpretations of Chronicles are tied
to a particular understanding of his motives. If you are going to
argue, with Noth, that the Chronicler is a polemicist you cannot

---

[9] Von Rad, *Geschichtsbild*, p. 18. Even in the genealogy which, on the surface
at least, attests to the twelve tribe ideal, the three "faithful" tribes stand out [pp.
25–6].
[10] Von Rad, *Geschichtsbild*, p. 19.
[11] Neh. 1:2; 2:16; 3:33, 34; 4:6; 5:1, 8, 17; 6:6; 13:23.
[12] Ezra 2:59; 6:17; 7:28; 8:25, 35; 9:1; 10:1ff., 5, 10; Neh. 8:1; 9:2; 13:18.
[13] Von Rad, *Geschichtsbild*, p. 24.
[14] Von Rad, *Geschichtsbild*, p. 29. Von Rad also notes the more lenient view of
intermarriage.
[15] Von Rad, *Geschichtsbild*, p. 31.

have a polemicist at odds with himself over such a fundamental issue. Von Rad's interpretation also centres on the question of motive, but he substitutes a *political* motive for a *theological* one. The Chronicler's history was not an ordinary secular history but the history of salvation, a history of the people of God. "Israel" is first and foremost a theological idea and this allows the Chronicler to equivocate in his use of it, argues von Rad. "All Israel" is readily transformed into "true Israel" and back again. This difference of approach can be seen in his interpretation of those texts in 2 Chronicles 10ff. which either suggest a more sympathetic attitude towards the people of the north (e.g., 2 Chron. 14:7ff.) or extend the sphere of influence of the Davidides into the north (e.g., 2 Chron. 31:1). Whereas Noth explains their presence by claiming that they reflect contemporary relations between inhabitants of Samaria-Galilee and Jerusalem or perhaps a contemporary claim to northern territory,[16] von Rad also sees in them a theological commitment to a particular idea.[17]

Those who argue that the Chronicler is an inclusivist have much in common with von Rad. Both Japhet[18] and Williamson,[19] for example, are particularly interested in the "all Israel" emphasis throughout Chronicles and in the "positive" notices about the North which at times contrasts sharply with the line taken in Ezra-Nehemiah.[20] Again, in line with von Rad, both scholars think the Chronicler takes this position because he is an "idealist;" neither of them thinks that the Chronicler is pursuing a political agenda. The difference between von Rad and the "inclusivists" is that the latter reach different conclusions as to the relative weight this textual evidence should have in the interpretation of the communicative intentions of the Chronicler. Their reassessment of the communicative intentions in turn necessitates, in their view, a reappraisal of the Chronicler's motive which is to be assessed independently from Ezra-Nehemiah.[21]

---

[16] Noth, *Chronicler's History*, p. 104.
[17] Von Rad, *Geschichtsbild*, p. 33.
[18] S. Japhet, *The Ideology of the Book of Chronicles and its Place in Biblical Thought* (BEATAJ, 9; Frankfurt aM: Lang, 1989).
[19] H.G.M. Williamson, *Israel in the Books of Chronicles* (Cambridge: Cambridge University Press, 1977).
[20] Von Rad also notes this contrast, especially in relation to intermarriage [Von Rad, *Geschichtsbild*, p. 29].
[21] According to Japhet and Williamson, the literary argument is crucial, but, as noted earlier, the exclusivist position is not absolutely dependent on the view that Chronicles-Ezra-Nehemiah are one work.

Japhet examines the use of "all Israel" in Chronicles,[22] and concludes that texts which apply this phrase to the Judah and Benjamin are referring to the southern *kingdom*, not just Judah and Benjamin. For example, a text such as 2 Chronicles 12:1, "When Rehoboam was established . . . he abandoned the LORD, he and *all Israel with him*," is to be understood in the context of 2 Chron. 11:13–17 which describes how priests and Levites from "*all the tribes* of Israel" (v. 16) were represented in the "southern kingdom."[23] According to Japhet, the Chronicler does not maintain the distinction between the ten northern tribes and the one southern tribe as does the Deuteronomistic historian (1 Kgs 11:35–6). Contrary to von Rad, Judah and Benjamin specify *geographical* regions in the phrase "all Israel in Judah and Benjamin" (2 Chron. 11:3).[24]

What about the Chronicler's attitude towards the northern kingdom? What about the texts which condemn the northern kingdom as illegitimate (e.g., 25:7)? Japhet's answer is simple: the condemnation applies only to the northern *kingdom* and not to the people of the North for "the northern kingdom, for all its sins, is an integral part of the people of Israel."[25] It is this attitude which, according to Japhet, contrasts sharply with the attitude to the inhabitants of the north in Ezra-Nehemiah. Whereas Ezra 4:1–2 (following 2 Kgs 17:24ff.) emphasises the foreign origins of the inhabitants in the North who are said to have been brought there by the Assyrians, the Chronicler continues to speak of Israelites in the North after the Assyrian invasion. Hezekiah's Passover celebration includes "the whole assembly that came out of Israel and the sojourners who came out of the land of Israel" (2 Chron. 30:25).

Williamson's *Israel in the Books of Chronicles* is a study of the use of the word "Israel" in Chronicles. Williamson contends, also contra von Rad, that when the term "Israel" is applied to the southern

---

[22] 1 Chron. 11:4; 13:6; 21:1–5; 2 Chron. 1:2–3 are Chronistic additions for the sake of special emphasis, where as 1 Chron. 14:8; 2 Chron. 7:4–6; 10:16; 11:3 are added for stylistic reasons only [Japhet, *Ideology*, pp. 272–4].

[23] Japhet, *Ideology*, p. 277.

[24] Japhet's also discerns a steady expansion of the kingdom of Judah into the North. The reign of Asa (see 2 Chron. 15:8–9), according to Japhet, marks the beginning of this *geographic* expansion which gains pace in the reigns of Hezekiah and Josiah reaching as far as Zebulun (2 Chron. 30:11) and Naphtali (2 Chron. 34:5–7) [Japhet, *Ideology*, pp. 295–8].

[25] P. 318. This is underscored by the use of the term "brother" (2 Chron. 12:40; 13:2 and 28:8).

kingdom it is not done in an exclusivist way.[26] For example, when the Chronicler applies the term "all Israel" to Judah in 2 Chron. 11:3, he is merely levelling the score between the North and the South, for the term "all Israel" had already been applied to the northern kingdom (2 Chron. 10:16). The Chronicler wanted to show that the term "all Israel" could be used for either kingdom.[27] In extending its usage to include Judah, the Chronicler did not wish "to exclude or contrast with the Northern Kingdom, but to make a positive point that there was to be found in Judah an unbroken continuation of the Israel of earlier days."[28] In terms of motive, Williamson contends that the Chronicler steers a middle course between assimilationists and separatists. "On the one hand, there can be no doubt about his unswerving loyalty to the Jerusalem cult . . . reconciliation with rebels could only be based on their return to complete allegiance to the authority of this cult."[29] On the other hand (and more importantly), the Chronicler is trying to reach out to all Israel on the basis of his belief in the unity of the twelve: "*a faithful nucleus* does not exclude others, but is a representative centre to which all the children of Israel may be welcomed if they will return."[30]

Evaluation. It should be clear from the above that ascertaining the Chronicler's concept of identity involves two distinct though related moves: determining the communicative intentions of the Chronicler and determining his motives. The contribution of Japhet and Williamson comes by way of offering a different interpretation of the Chronicler's communicative intentions, giving due weight to those texts which offer

---

[26] 2 Chron. 11:3 reads "Say to Rehoboam son of Solomon king of Judah, and to all Israel in Judah and Benjamin . . ." The parallel text in Kings reads "all the house of Judah and Benjamin and the rest of the people" (1 Kgs 12:23). Williamson disagrees with von Rad's claim that "Juda und Benjamin sind jetzt das wahre Israel" [Von Rad, *Geschichtsbild*, p. 31].

[27] Williamson, *Israel*, p. 109.

[28] Williamson, *Israel*, p. 107.

[29] Williamson, *Israel*, p. 139 (emphasis mine).

[30] Williamson, *Israel*. He expands on this interpretation in "The Temple in the Books of Chronicles," in W. Horbury (ed.), *Templum Amicitae: Essays on the Second Temple Presented to Ernst Bammel* (JSNTS, 48; Sheffield: JSOT Press, 1991), pp. 15–31. In it he argues that "the temple in Chronicles is not a litmus test of an orthodoxy that would exclude the non-conformist but rather a focus of unity for the people of Israel as a whole" (p. 21). Taking his cue from modern ecumenical theory, he suggests that the Chronicler (like any good ecumenist) links the Temple to the period before the divisions in Israel occurred. These "physical ties of unbroken continuity" make the Jerusalem temple "a focus of continuity with the nation's earliest history and one that should therefore override more recent differences" (pp. 24–5).

a "broader" view of Israel. In their opinion this precludes the idea
that the Chronicler was an exclusivist in terms of motives in line
with Ezra-Nehemiah. A different understanding of the Chronicler's
communicative intentions requires a different understanding of motive. But here both Williamson and Japhet run into trouble. Having
argued that we cannot paint the Chronicler with an Ezra-Nehemianic
brush, they reach for what appears to be the only alternative: the
Chronicler must have been an inclusivist. But this proposal presents
as many problems as it solves for what does one do with the texts
which present the narrow understanding of Israel? Japhet's geographical solution is not really a solution for although the text does clearly
recognise that there are representatives from all Israel in Judah, the
point surely is that *Judah's* territory is *the* representative centre of
Israel.

Williamson also asserts that Judah is conceived of as the representative centre of Israel, representing the "loyal" part of Israel. The
Chronicler, in effect, occupies the middle ground between "assimilationists" and "exclusivists." There are a number of difficulties with
this picture. It is, of course, possible that the Chronicler was a proto-
ecumenist, but is it not just as reasonable to lump the Chronicler in
with the assimilationists? I would contend that Williamson, as well as
the other interpreters surveyed, has unnecessarily restricted his options to a choice which turns on the presence or absence of boundary definitions. Yet his solution requires a middle ground seemingly
occupied by one person, the Chronicler. What is required, I would
argue, is a different approach to the question of ethnic identity that
begins with a sociological theory of identity of which the boundary
definitions are but a part.

Ethnicity and Identity

An ethnic group can be defined as a group which shares certain
characteristics or combination of characteristics including language,
religion, cultural traditions, and racial characteristics.[31] More often
than not one is born into an ethnic group and the tendency is to
think of ethnicity in terms of descent and race. This approach, how-

---

[31] A. Kuper and J. Kuper, *The Social Science Encyclopedia* (London: Routledge &
Kegan Paul, 1985), pp. 267–72.

ever, distracts attention from the constructive or dynamic nature of ethnic identity. Members of an ethnic group must *perceive* themselves to be distinct from other groups; *thinking* that one belongs is an essential aspect of belonging. One can therefore speak of ethnicity as a social construction of reality or as an aspect of the social consciousness of a group. This point is perhaps best underscored by the fact that ethnicity crystallises when different groups come into contact. Ethnic groups are not in this sense natural nor is ethnic identity a "given of all human association."[32]

Now there are, of course, important qualifiers to add to this dynamic definition of the ethnic group. Firstly, there is the question of the degree to which members of an ethnic group share in the sense of identity. The sense of solidarity is often most keenly felt by the ruling or elite classes. A similar case are those communities who have an ethnic label imposed on them by a different and politically dominant group.[33] Here "perceiving oneself to be distinct" is transformed into "perceiving that one is perceived to be distinct." Ethnic identity is thus vulnerable to ideological distortion in the context of the struggle for political power. As the title of this essay suggests, I want to raise our sensitivity to these dimensions of identity in Chronicles.

Another important consideration with regard to the above definition of ethnicity is to recognise that humans are "bounded by multiple identities."[34] The temptation is to use one rubric for exploring the social dynamics of a particular situation. It is quite common, for example, to divide Israelite history into the tribal (kinship group), monarchic (nation and or state), and post-monarchic (ethnic group) periods. It may be true that one or the other from of social organisation dominates one particular period, but not in the absence of another. Nor are these group types strictly delineated. The sense of solidarity felt by members of the nation may concern the very things which members of an ethnic group have in common: language, cultural traditions, and race. That which makes nationalism distinctive is "the people's" claim to sovereignty, a people which views itself as "only superficially divided by the lines of status, class, locality,

---

[32] A.D. Smith, "The Politics of Culture: Ethnicity and Nationalism," in T. Ingold (ed.), *Companion Encyclopedia of Anthropology* (London: Routledge, 1994), p. 707.

[33] N. Abercrombie and B.S. Turner (eds.), *Penguin Dictionary of Sociology* (London: Penguin, 2nd edn, 1988), p. 90.

[34] Smith, "Politics," p. 709.

and in some cases even ethnicity."[35] An ethnic group similarly contains
within itself kinship groups and may use kinship as a criterion of
membership.[36] The state, on the other hand, should not be thought
of an extension of the nation or ethnic group. It does not lie on the
same continuum because it is not defined in terms of the group
perception. The state is defined in terms of the existence of institutions of government which, like the nation, claim sovereignty over a
particular area. These institutions do not, however, exist in a vacuum,
but rather presuppose one or more of the other forms of group
identity.

The dynamic definition of ethnicity focuses attention on the factors that facilitate ethnic maintenance.[37] Smith puts forward the following four factors: territorialization, inter-state warfare, organised
religion and myths of common origin. Of these the last two are especially interesting. Myths of common origin and descent are rarely
if ever "secular" in nature. They are, for the most part, expressed in
religious categories which means that there is often considerable
overlap between religious and ethnic myths of origin. According to
Smith, myths of ethnic origin often contain "a myth of ethnic election, in which the ethnic community is promised redemption and
salvation on condition that religious or cultural obligations are properly fulfilled."[38] They legitimate the communities "'title-deeds' or land
charter" and the "reward for the fulfilment of religious duties is the
enjoyment of the sacred land as belonging to the community 'by
grace'."[39] Organised religion, then, can be a fundamental factor in
the maintenance of ethnic identity, and priests are often seen as the
primary guardians of ethnicity. Smith's "myth of common origin" is
part of what I call an "ideology of identity."

So far I have outlined a sociological understanding of ethnic identity
and have described factors which maintain identity over time. Prior
to using this theoretical perspective in a comparative analysis of ethnic

---

[35] L. Greenfeld, *Nationalism: Five Roads to Modernity* (Cambridge, Mass.: Harvard,
1992), p. 3; cited in M.G. Brett, "Nationalism and the Hebrew Bible," in J. Rogerson,
M.D. Carroll R., M. Davies (eds.), *The Bible in Ethics* (JSOTS, 207; Sheffield; JSOT
Press, 1995), p. 141.
[36] The post-exilic community is an example of this: see Ezra 2/Nehemiah 7.
[37] Smith, "Politics," pp. 711–13.
[38] Smith, "Politics," p. 710.
[39] Smith, "Politics," p. 712.

identity in Chronicles and Ezra-Nehemiah, it is necessary to introduce a typology of ethnic groups that takes into account the degree
to which ethnic culture penetrates different ethnic groups or *ethnie*.

> As a first step, it is useful to distinguish between two processes in eth-
> nic life: on the one hand, towards an extension of the *ethnie* in space
> at the cost of any social depth, and on the other hand, a social "deep-
> ening" of ethnic culture at the cost of its tight circumscription in space.
> The former process leads to what may be termed "lateral" *ethnie*, the
> latter to "vertical" *ethnie*.[40]

The survival of vertical *ethnie* has to do with the deep penetration of
culture which results in a relatively unified demotic culture. In lateral *ethnie*, identity is maintained on the strength of the group that
dominates the polyethnic state, but they also rely on a federalist
ideology which incorporates "lesser" vertical *ethnie* as "partners." Smith
cites the Hittites as an example of a lateral ethnic group comprising
a community of feudal nobles, priests and warriors who incorporated
lesser communities via an "unequal federalism" maintained in the
political sphere by treaties and in the religious sphere by a "spiritual
federalism." The argument to be presented here, that Ezra-Nehemiah
expresses a *vertical* ethnicity and Chronicles a *lateral* one, does not
mean that either is necessarily an ideal example of the type, but
rather that important characteristics of the ideology of identity of
both works can be elucidated with reference to these two ideal types.

Ezra-Nehemiah: A Vertical Ethnicity

Recent studies have suggested that Judah was a relatively small and
vulnerable community in the Persian empire. Carter's archaeological
survey suggests that Judah was a small province of approximately
620 square miles (excluding the Shephelah and the coastal plain)
with a population approximately 11,000 in Persian Period I (i.e.,
prior to Nehemiah's mission) rising to 17,000 in Persian Period II.[41]
These demographic figures are provisional at best but this does not
lessen the fact that they contradict the much larger estimates of the

---

[40] Smith, "Politics," p. 713.
[41] C.E. Carter, "The Province of Yehud in the Post-Exilic Period: Soundings in
Site Distribution and Demography," in T.C. Eskenazi and K.H. Richards (eds.),
Second Temple Studies: Vol. 2, Temple and Community in the Persian Period (JSOTS, 175;
Sheffield: JSOT Press, 1994), pp. 106–45.

population of Yehud, such as Weinberg's 200,000, by a huge margin.[42] The population in Jerusalem in Persian period II would have represented approximately ten percent of the total province's population, or 1250–1500, "well within the 5 to 10 per cent average of urban centres in the pre-industrial age."[43]

This sort of evidence points in the direction of a community that is tightly circumscribed in terms of space. The ideology of identity that we find in Ezra-Nehemiah "matches" this spatial dimension with its emphasis on ethnic depth. The focus of the identity of the post-exilic community is the experience of exile, and the story of the people begins with the story of the return from exile (Ezra 1). This is, of course, not a surprising claim for the writer of Ezra-Nehemiah to make for it is indeed quite probable that the Jewish community of the Persian period did in all likelihood originate in the return from exile. Nor should we be surprised that the experience in exile had a profound affect on their self-understanding.[44] Even the kinship structure of the community appears to be exilic in origin.[45] Ezra 2/Nehemiah 7 claims to be a list of "the sons of the province who came from the captivity of the exiles" (Ezra 2:1/Neh. 7:6) who are enumerated according to בתי אבות which together comprise "the whole assembly" (Ezra 2:64). These בתי אבות would, therefore, have helped to maintain the sense of a distinctly "exilic" identity long after the return.

This community of returnees has been described as a citizen-temple community similar to those found scattered throughout the Persian empire.[46] Membership in one of these communities, which were organised along kinship lines, determined access to the cult and established one's right to land.[47] In this way the "exilic" concept of ethnic identity, determined in the first instance by kinship, figured in every aspect of community life, helping to concentrate and focus social

---

[42] J.P. Weinberg, *The Citizen-Temple Community* (trans. D.L. Smith-Christopher; JSOTS, 151; Sheffield: JSOT Press, 1992), pp. 34–48.

[43] Carter "The Province of Yehud," p. 138.

[44] For a comparative study of "exile" groups, see D.L. Smith, *The Religion of the Landless: The Social Context of the Babylonian Exile* (Bloomington, IN: Meyer-Stone, 1989).

[45] This is indicated by the unusually large size of the groups and preponderance of post-exilic references. See Weinberg, *Citizen-Temple*, pp. 49–61.

[46] Ibid. See also M. Dandamaev, "Babylonia in the Persian Age," in *Cambridge History of Judaism. Vol. 1, Introduction: The Persian Period* (Cambridge: Cambridge University Press, 1984), pp. 330–1.

[47] Cf. Ezek. 11:15–17 and Lev. 25:23; M. Smith, *Palestinian Parties and Politics that Shaped the Old Testament* (London: SCM Press, 2nd edn, 1987), pp. 75, 81–2; and J. Blenkinsopp, *Ezra-Nehemiah* (London: SCM Press, 1988), p. 60.

interactions within the community and functioning as a redemption myth that legitimated the community's claim to the land. All this points in the direction of an ethnic group which emphasises vertical depth and territorial compactness.

Though the concept of ethnicity that we find in Ezra-Nehemiah was rooted in the experience of the exile, its full expression and further development was determined by the nature of the relationship between the post-exilic community and its neighbours. The conflicts mentioned in Ezra-Nehemiah centre on the building of the temple and walls of Jerusalem (Ezra 4; Nehemiah 4), but there was undoubtedly also conflict over the land which the new returnees claimed as their own. This is hinted at in Ezra 9 where the return is likened to the conquest with the "remainees" in the role of the Canaanites (Ezra 9:1–2).[48] Because control of the temple and of the land are thus linked, the concern for ethnic depth was part of the on-going struggle of the community to survive as a distinct entity in the face of outside pressures and competition. Or, to put it the other way around, the conflict with neighbouring *ethnie* helped to crystallise the ethnic identity of the returnees. The more rigorous the application of the "exile" criterion the more the community was committed to a vertical concept of ethnicity, and on this reading of the evidence, the choice of a vertical ethnic identity is no choice at all but a necessity.[49]

But this analysis is only one half of the equation, for a vertical ethnic identity paradoxically generates as many problems in terms of survival as it solves. I have just described the conflict between the returnees and their neighbours in roughly the same terms as it is described in Ezra-Nehemiah: that it was a question of their survival as an ethnically distinct community. But is this all that we need to know in order to understand the issues involved? Are we supposed to think (as the original readers were supposed to think) that a vertical ethnicity is the only right response? One can begin to answer these questions by observing the problem of intermarriage in the community in light of the inherent weakness of vertical ethnic groups. Its

---

[48] H. Williamson, "Concept of Israel in Transition," in R.E. Clements (ed.), *The World of Ancient Israel* (Cambridge: Cambridge University Press, 1989), p. 155; and S. Japhet "People and Land in the Restoration Period," in G. Strecker (ed.), *Das Land Israel in biblischer Zeit* (Göttingen: Vandenhoeck & Ruprecht, 1983), pp. 112–15.

[49] K. Hoglund argues that another reason for maintaining a vertical ethnic identity was because the Persian authorities required it ["The Achaemenid Context," in P.R. Davies (ed.), *Second Temple Studies: Vol. 1, Persian Period* (JSOTS, 117; Sheffield: JSOT Press, 1991), pp. 65–66].

emphasis on ethnic depth tends to restrict the community spatially and to reduce the scope for economic relationships with outsiders. Yet these same tendencies can also increase the dependence of the community on external relations, for the smaller the community the less likely it is to be self-sufficient. In Judah's case the emphasis on depth and separation threatened the economic relationships between the various local regions, Samaria, Ashdod, the Shephelah etc. which were important for all concerned. The requirements of a large temple would have only intensified the need for the movement of goods and people across ethnic boundaries. The approach recommended by the writers of Ezra-Nehemiah did not give the community the flexibility to address the need to broaden its territorial basis and to develop social and economic relations with its immediate neighbours.

With this in mind, what do we make of the intermarriage problem in Ezra 9 and 10?[50] In keeping with the small Judah hypothesis, Washington contends that intermarriage threatened the economic stability of the province by threatening its land base.[51] Smith-Christopher[52] similarly understands Ezra's call for endogamy in terms of group boundary maintenance. When a group's identity is under stress it tends to fall back "on the primary ties of the kinship network."[53] So why did the Jews practice exogamy in the first place? Again, starting with the small Judah hypothesis, Smith-Christopher wagers that lower status Jewish males were marrying up among higher

---

[50] The intermarriage problem in Nehemiah 13 involves a slightly different problem (intermarriage among the clergy) and will be left to the side for the purposes of this paper.

[51] H.C. Washington, "The Strange Woman of Proverbs 1–9 and Post-Exilic Judean Society," in *Second Temple Studies* 2, pp. 217–42. Washington interprets the warnings about the strange woman in Proverbs 1–9 in terms of the social context of Yehud in the Persian period. The best text for Washington's thesis is Prov. 2:21–2: "For the upright will abide in the land, and the innocent will remain in it; but the wicked will be cut off from the land and the treacherous will be rooted out of it." The strange/foreign (though not necessarily non-Israelite or even non-Judean) woman is an economic threat to the golah community because within the patrilineal land tenure system women were capable of inheriting and disposing of property. The citation of Num. 27:1–11 and 36:1–9 as evidence does not necessarily confirm the point since these are about *Israelite* women marrying outside the clan.

[52] D. Smith-Christopher, "The Mixed Marriage Crisis in Ezra 9–10 and Nehemiah 13: A Study of the Sociology of the Post-Exilic Judean Community," in *Second Temple Studies* 2, pp. 243–65.

[53] Smith-Christopher, "Mixed Marriage," p. 252 [citing E.L. Cerroni-Long, "Marrying Out: Socio-Cultural and Psychological Implications of Intermarriage," *Journal of Comparative Family Studies* 15 (1984), p. 28].

status females outside their community.[54] But these two observations do not cohere. Is it possible for exogamy to be a widespread practice and still be understood as a threat to the survival of the community? Was not the practice of exogamy a reasonable balance between the need for ethnic delineation and "lateral" interaction? Perhaps it was reasonable to some and not to others, or was the community not completely in touch with the consequences of the actions of its members? Looking at it from another angle, what are we to make of Ezra's objections to intermarriage? One possible explanation is that immigrant communities are initially willing to accept exogamy but that those who arrive later on, once the community is established, reject it.[55] In other words, economic necessity demands it early on but as time goes on it is no longer a compelling enough reason to override less pragmatic ethnic values. This mode of reasoning requires that we abandon the economic explanation for exogamy altogether.

What we are left with are the contradictions or tensions between different aspects of ethnic identity which constitute its internal dynamic. Ezra's concern for ethnic purity cannot be explained in terms of some unambiguous rationale. He may well have thought that he was acting in an unambiguous way, that he was protecting the unique identity of the post-exilic community, but that does not mean that his actions had these consequences. Nor can we assume that the "foreign" wives of Ezra 9 and 10 were really foreign. Eskenazi and Judd,[56] like Smith-Christopher,[57] interpret the conflict in terms of a

---

[54] Smith-Christopher, "Mixed Marriage," p. 249.

[55] Smith-Christopher, "Mixed Marriage," pp. 252–3.

[56] T.C. Eskenazi and E.P. Judd, "Marriage to a Stranger in Ezra 1–9," in *Second Temple Studies* 2, pp. 266–85. Eskenazi and Judd interpret it as a conflict between orthodox and non-orthodox Jews, especially as it pertains to the interpretation of the Torah. They compare this to the issue of marriage in modern Israel and the Haredim (a group that takes its name from the biblical text in question, namely Ezra 9:4 and 10:3). New rules of who constituted a Jew in 1970 excluded people who always considered themselves to be Jews. The Haredi call non-Haredi Jews "gentiles" and marrying such is considered a mixed marriage. The Chief Rabbinate and the Haredi rabbis will not recognize marriages because of their restricted definitions of who is a Jew. They also note that the foreigners are said to have commited abominations. The same claim is made in Trito-Isaiah about the opponents and one should not, therefore, take them literally as refering to non-Jewish practice but rather to less strict Jewish practice or different Jewish practice.

[57] For Smith-Christopher the issue is the definition of a "mixed" marriage. Ezra represents those who limit Jews to the returnees. The "outsiders" are Jewish remainees. He cites two types of evidence: more lenient texts (Isa. 60:1–6, Ruth, Jonah) and the use of perjorative anachronistic terms to describe the "outsiders."

104 JONATHAN E. DYCK

conflict between Jews over the definition of Jewishness and hence over what constitutes a "mixed" marriage.[58] The ideology of identity expressed in Ezra-Nehemiah is thus more problematic than it may appear at first glance. The ideology is clearly vertical in orientation, but we cannot assume that the authors of this ideology were representing the interests of the community at large nor that they were aware of the negative consequences such an ideology might have. The fact that we have other texts from roughly the same period[59] (including Chronicles) that present a different ideology of identity highlights again the need for a dynamic definition of ethnicity.

Chronicles: A Lateral Ethnicity

The ideology of identity in Chronicles represents, in my view, a different concept of identity—a lateral ethnicity versus a vertical one. The model the Chronicler uses for his community, the united monarchy of David and Solomon, represents the golden age of a greater Israel and contrasts sharply with the picture presented in Ezra-Nehemiah of a small community within a large and all-powerful empire. The contrast between the two ideologies of identity can be illustrated by the following simple two-dimensional diagram:

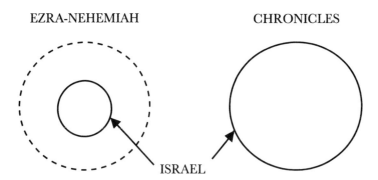

EZRA-NEHEMIAH   CHRONICLES

ISRAEL

---

[58] Sectarianism is another related explanation; cf. J. Blenkinsopp, "Interpretation and the Tendency to Sectarianism: An Aspect of Second Temple History," in E.P. Sanders (ed.), *Jewish and Christian Self-Definition: Vol. 2, Aspects of Judaism in the Graeco-Roman World* (Philadelphia: Fortress, 1981), pp. 1–26; and idem, "A Jewish Sect of the Persian Period," *CBQ* 52 (1990), pp. 5–20.

[59] Mary Douglas adds Numbers to the list of less exclusivist texts such as Isaiah 60, Jonah and Ruth [*In the Wilderness: The Doctrine of Defilement in the Book of Numbers* (JSOTS, 158; Sheffield: JSOT Press, 1993)].

The outer boundaries of "Israel" are similarly defined in both texts. Israel is clearly distinguished from her immediate neighbours such as the Arabs, the Ammonites, the Ashdodites and Edomites (Neh. 4:7 and 2 Chronicles 20). The Chronicler's sense of Israel among the nations is also presented in a systematic way in the genealogies. 1 Chronicles 1 begins with the generations from Adam to Noah (vv. 1–4), continues with a list of the "nations" of the world after the flood, those furthest away from Israel (the sons of Japheth; vv. 5–7) to those nearest to Israel (the sons of Ham; vv. 8–16), followed by the sons of Shem (vv. 17–23) and the generations from Shem to Abraham (vv. 24–27). The second half of the chapter deals with Israel's nearest rivals, Ishmael (vv. 28–33) and Esau (vv. 34–54). The frame of reference narrows in concentric circles from a view to the whole world down to the real focus of the Chronicler's interest, the descendants of Abraham, Isaac and Israel. Israel is a constituent member of a *world* order established by God at creation.[60]

But the internal boundaries are radically different. Whereas Ezra-Nehemiah makes a clear distinction between the "Israelite" community and the other people living in the land of Israel, the Chronicler maintains an "all Israel" perspective throughout the book. Again, one can illustrate this with reference to the genealogies. In Ezra-Nehemiah genealogies are used to establish the *exilic* origins of the community. The focus is on that which most clearly distinguishes the community of returnees from all the other inhabitants of the land of Israel. The Chronicler, on the other hand, uses the genealogies to present the Israel of the twelve tribes. The connection with pre-exilic Israel is important in both works (cf. Ezra 2:59/Neh. 7:61) but the Chronicler's genealogy links his community with *all* Israel. This is vividly illustrated in the closing chapter of the genealogy. 1 Chron. 9:1b states that "Judah was taken into exile in Babylon." The text continues with a note about the restoration using the same terms to describe the returnees that we find in Neh. 11:3 and elsewhere, namely, "Israelites, priests, Levites, and temple servants" (v. 2). But in the following verse we read that "some of the people of Judah, Benjamin, Ephraim and Manasseh lived in Jerusalem" (v. 3). This claim is all the more remarkable because of the close parallels between this text and Neh. 11:3–19 which *does not* include Ephraim and Manasseh. For the Chronicler, the exile and return does not

---

[60] Cf. 2 Chron. 20:5.

leave Judah as the sole remnant Israel on the basis of which it can
then claim to be the sole inheritor of the name Israel. *It does not
establish an inside/outside distinction.*[61]

To this text one could add all the texts cited by the inclusivist
interpreters such as those relating to Hezekiah's Passover. The reign
of Hezekiah saw the overthrow of the northern kingdom by the
Assyrians and the deportation of some of its people. The author of the
account in Kings represents this deportation as a more or less complete
de-population of Israel followed by the settlement of the land by
foreigners (2 Kgs 17:5–6, 24ff.). The Chronicler on the other hand
makes no mention of this exchange of peoples. Instead he tells how
"Hezekiah sent word to all Israel and Judah, and wrote letters also
to Ephraim and Manasseh, that they should come to the house of the
LORD at Jerusalem, to keep the Passover to the LORD the God of
Israel" (2 Chron. 30:1). Though the majority sent their regrets (vv.
10–11) the celebration was still a success and "the whole assembly of
Judah, the priests and the Levites, and the whole assembly that came
out of Israel, and the resident aliens who came out of the land of
Israel, and the resident aliens who lived in Judah, rejoiced" (v. 25).

Why the difference in approach? One could, of course, speculate
that the different approach stems from a different era when the
community felt more at ease with itself and could afford to be more
inclusive. One could also hypothesise that the Chronicler was addressing the contradictions inherent within a vertical *ethnie*, and was
seeking to take into account the need for interaction with communities outside of Judah. We do not, however, have access to information which could confirm or disprove these attempts to specify the
Chronicler's motives. Nevertheless, if one looks at the long-term trend,
the Jewish community centred in Judah and Jerusalem did eventually become the dominant ethnic group in Palestine. This did not
come about merely through the accident of history but, to my mind,
would also have required an "all Israel" ideology of the kind that we
find in Chronicles.

One can, however, make more general sociological observations
about how *the Chronicler transforms key elements of the vertical ideology of
identity into a lateral federalist ideology.* One can, for example, compare

---

[61] I have already mentioned above another important example of the same viewpoint, namely, Hezekiah's treatment of the survivors of Sennacherib's invasion as
Israelites (2 Chronicles 30).

this federalist vision to the federalist system of the Persians. The Persian empire of the Achaemenids was a federalist empire that grew out of the federalist kingdom of the Persians and Medes. The Persian kingdom is an example of large scale lateral *ethnie*.[62] The federalism at the kingdom level was, of course, an unequal federalism whereby the ruling families dominated the lesser communities and maintained a top-down ethnic and political identity. This same approach was used in the running of the empire; in other words, lesser communities such as kingdoms, city-states, tribes and ethnic groups of various kinds were integrated into the empire in the form of an unequal federalism. Of course the fundamental means of control in any empire is the threat of force, and the Persians were not averse to acting on this threat if need be.[63] More to the point, however, are the non-coercive means of administrative control and integration, such as ideology and propaganda.

The beginning of the inscription called DNa (the first inscription of Darius found at Naqs-i-Rustam) enunciates in a very straight-forward way the key elements of Achaemenid ideology.

> I am Darius the Great King, King of Kings, King of countries containing all kinds of men, King in this great earth far and wide, son of Hystaspes, an Achaemenian, a Persian, son of a Persian, an Aryan, having Aryan lineage (lines 8–15).[64]

Note that the Persian text the king is the "king of many" and the "king of countries containing all kinds of men." The Achaemenids saw themselves as ruling over a humanity that was ethnically and nationally differentiated.[65] Each nation also had its appropriate place.

> Ahuramazda, when he saw this earth in commotion, thereafter bestowed it upon me, made me king; I am king. By the favor of Ahuramazda I put it down in its place; what I said to them, that they did, as was my desire (lines 30–37).

Koch sees in this "ein föderalistisches Prinzip durch, welches begreiflich macht, warum die Grosskönige jene kultische Toleranz betreiben und

---

[62] Smith, "Politics," pp. 713–14.

[63] A. Kuhrt, "The Cyrus Cylinder and Achaemenid Imperial Policy," *JSOT* 25 (1983), pp. 83–97.

[64] R.G. Kent, *Old Persian: Grammar, Texts, Lexicon* (AOS, 33; New Haven: Yale University Press, 2nd edn, 1953), p. 138.

[65] K. Koch, "Weltordnung und Reichesidee im alten Iran," in H. Frei and K. Koch (eds.), *Reichsidee und Reichsorganization im Perserreich* (Göttingen: Vandenhoeck & Ruprecht, 1984), p. 59.

Gesetze sammeln lassen, welche den Landesbrauch aufgreifen . . ."[66]
One can, in other words, observe a parallelism between Persian ideology and Persian administrative policy. The administration of the
empire was a combination of central and local authorities that incorporated various local/national cultural and legal traditions within an
overarching administrative order.[67] As Frei remarks, "Der Untertan
war nicht Untertan, er war Reichsangehöriger."[68]

The effectiveness of Achaemenid ideology is illustrated by the remarkably positive attitude toward the Achaemenid rulers found in
the Old Testament, including Chronicles and Ezra-Nehemiah. The
author of Ezra-Nehemiah seems to accept the assembly's status as a
local administrative unit within the empire. Achaemenid imperial policy
allowed for local autonomy within a larger imperial order. From their
perspective, the empire was the centre and the local authorities were
the periphery, and so it would seem that the writers of Ezra-Nehemiah
were reconciled to the Achaemenid understanding.

The Chronicler seems to accept the basic premise that the Persian
empire was legitimate and indeed that it played a divine role in re-
establishing Israel after the exile (2 Chron. 36:22–23), but the Chronicler "recasts" Israel's place within the divine economy in terms of a
united federal nation in its own right, asserting cultic sovereignty over
the land of Israel. Instead of situating Israel within a large imperial
administration and ideology, he reapplies that same federalist model
to Israel, though on a smaller scale, setting Israel alongside the Persian empire rather than within it.

A Hierarchy Within

Up to this point I have used the concept federalism in conjunction
with lateral *ethnie* without its important qualifier "unequal." The reconstruction of the Chronicler's ideology of identity in these terms is

---

[66] Koch, "Weltordnung," p. 63.
[67] H. Frei, "Zentralgewalt und Lokalautonomie im Achämenidenreich," in *Reichsidee*,
pp. 1–48. Frei cites a number of examples in which the central administration recognizes and sanctions local law, including examples in the Old Testament. The
most important example is the 'Trilingual [stele] of Letoon' in which Satrap Pixodaros
endorses a local decree dealing with the establishment and maintenance of a local
Carian god.
[68] Frei, "Zentralgewalt," p. 27.

perhaps an exercise in re-stating what Williamson and Japhet have already said about the Chronicler portraying Judah as a *representative centre* for all Israel. But this is only half the picture, for they do not ask who is making this claim and why. Yes, one can find differences between Ezra-Nehemiah and Chronicles which point in the direction of a more tolerant attitude to the inhabitants in all the land of Israel, but why is it that Judah should be accepted as the centre? Why is it that the history of the northern kingdom is to be considered solely in relationship to Judah's? Yes, there are positive inclusivist notices but they occur within *Judah's* story. Thus the qualifier "unequal" is put on the agenda as much by a reading of Chronicles as it is from adopting a particular sociological model.

The question asked in this final section is this: who's ideology of identity do we find in Chronicles? Who had an interest in defining Israel, of telling her story in this particular way? The thesis to be put forward in this final section is that *the ideology of identity in Chronicles is at the same time an ideology which legitimates Jerusalem's role as the sole legitimate centre of Israel in the Chronicler's day.* I am not claiming that this ideology of legitimacy is what is *really* going on and that the concern for identity is an epiphenomenon. I would argue, for example, that the Chronicler's concern for the identity of Israel as a twelve tribe nation is a genuine concern, as is his concern for the legitimacy of the Jerusalem and its temple. But what the Chronicler feels to be two compatible ideas may not have been all that compatible to others. His interests may not have been the interests of "the whole assembly of Israel." Much of the evidence that supports this thesis has already been cited. The texts which have been used to illustrate the Chronicler's federalist vision of Israel can also be adduced as evidence in favour of my thesis. Identity and legitimacy go hand in hand.

Sacred Land / Sacred Centre. In the genealogies, the issue is not only the identity of all Israel but also the centrality and legitimacy of Judah, Benjamin and Levi. This latter aspect is reflected in the two structural principles by which chs. 2–8 are organised: status and geography.[69] The genealogy moves from *the centre* (Judah and Simeon), to the east (Reuben, Gad, E. Manasseh), to the north (Issacher, [Dan], Naphtali), and, making its way back through the heartland of northern Israel (Ephraim, W. Manasseh), to *the centre* again (Benjamin).

---

[69] Also indicated in listing of the settlements of the various tribes throughout the genealogy.

Judah is prominent because it is the first genealogy and the genealogy of David is the central feature of the Judahite genealogy (2:3–
4:23). Levi occupies the central spot in the list and is the longest
genealogy (81 verses) after Judah's. The genealogy of Benjamin
achieves prominence because it is included in three places (7:6–12;
8; 9:35–44).[70] These structural features of the genealogy suggest a
strong interest in underlining Judah's legitimacy as the leading tribe
in Israel, Levi's central role in relation to the cult, and Benjamin
completing the list of the tribes that are identified with the return.
This together with chapter nine, which directly links Israel of the
past with the Israel of the return, allows us to construe these claims
as the contemporary claims to legitimacy and centrality.

But the fact that these claims are made via a comprehensive genealogy is itself of interest. The genealogical picture of Israel is just
that, a *picture* of Israel, not a story. The time between Adam and
David is not historical time, if time is the right word. The genealogies describe Israel as it always was, its inner structure and hierarchy, and its geographical place.[71] It treats of space not time. There is
no contingency, no development, no promise to Abraham, no Moses,
no exodus, no Sinai, no conquest,[72] no point at which Israel came into
being. Israel emerged gradually and naturally from Adam, Abraham
and Israel. Israel emerged autochthonously in the land of Israel. This
is God's order. Israel among the nations. Israel as always in the land,
the sacred land with its sacred centre.

Redemption. The *story* of Israel really begins with the story of David
and Solomon, the account of Saul's death on Mt. Gilboa (ch. 10)
being a prelude to it. The story of David and Solomon is about two
things: the role of its first two monarchs in building the Temple and
organising the cult and the legitimacy of the Davidic dynasty. The
two issues, Temple and dynasty, are closely intertwined in the narrative
and in fact constitute one story. All the material from 1 Chronicles
11 to 2 Chronicles 9 is either directly or indirectly related to the
Temple project. The concern to establish the legitimacy of the temple

---

[70] The repetition of 8:29–38 in chapter 9 is understandable since it deals with
Saul (the subject of chapter ten).

[71] The genealogies abound with place names indicating the *where* of Israel: see
M. Kartveit, *Motive und Schichten der Landtheologie in I Chronik 1–9* (ConBOT, 28;
Stockholm: Almquist & Wiksell, 1989), pp. 166–7.

[72] S. Japhet, "Conquest and Settlement in Chronicles," *JBL* 98 (1979), pp.
205–18.

in Jerusalem is perhaps most obvious where the Chronicler parallels David and the temple with Moses and the tabernacle. For example, in the account of David's sacrifice on the threshing floor of Ornan, the future site of the Temple, the sacrifice is consumed by "fire from heaven" (1 Chron. 21:26). Aaron's sacrifice was consumed in like manner (Lev. 9:24) and the significance of this is not lost on David, who concludes "Here shall be the house of the LORD God and here the altar of burnt offering for Israel" (1 Chron. 22:1). The final transfer of the altar site under Solomon is marked in the same way: "When Solomon ended his prayer, fire came down from heaven and consumed the burnt offering and sacrifices; and the glory of the LORD filled the temple" (2 Chron. 7:1).[73]

The issue of the legitimacy of the temple does not, however, stand on its own. It is a fundamental part of the larger story of Israel's establishment as the *people* of God in the *land* of Israel. One notes for example that the "all Israel" perspective of the genealogies is continued in the narrative of David's reign as a way of emphasising not only that David had the support of all Israel from the beginning of his reign (1 Chron. 11:1, 4, 10; 12:38) but that they supported him in establishing the cult in Jerusalem (13:5). David and Solomon also establish Israel in the land, even though this idea conflicts with the genealogy's autochthonous tendency. The reason for this might have something to do with the Deuteronomic tradition making the conquest of the land a precondition for the setting up of the permanent sanctuary (Deut. 12:10–11). In the Chronicler's scheme of things, David is the conquerer and Solomon the temple builder. In his farewell discourse, David says to Solomon: "Has he not given you peace on every side? For he has delivered the inhabitants of the land into my hand; and the land is subdued before the LORD and his people" (1 Chron. 22:18). Solomon is, therefore, to "build the sanctuary of the LORD God so that the Ark of the covenant of the LORD and the holy vessels of God may be brought into a house built for the name of the LORD" (v. 19).

But there were conditions attached to Israel's "land ownership." In order for the people to maintain the state of redemption they had

---

[73] The Temple is also linked explicitly with the tabernacle in terms of its design. David gives Solomon the temple plans (תַּבְנִית: 1 Chron. 28:11–19) in the same way as God gave the tabernacle plan to Moses (Exod. 25:9, 40); see W. Riley, *King and Cultus in Chronicles: Worship and the Reinterpretation of History* (JSOTS, 160; Sheffield: JSOT Press, 1993), pp. 62–3.

to "observe and search out [*darash*] all the commandments of the LORD your God; that you may possess this good land, and leave it for an inheritance to your children after you forever" (1 Chron. 28:8). These "negative possibilities" are anticipated in the account of Saul's death at the hands of the Philistines. The closing verses of 1 Chronicles 10 are the Chronicler's own and are directed to the question of God's rejection of Saul and his house.

> So Saul died for his unfaithfulness; he was unfaithful to the LORD in that he did not keep the command of the LORD; moreover, he had consulted a medium, seeking guidance, and did not seek guidance from the LORD. Therefore the LORD put him to death and turned the kingdom over to David son of Jesse. (vv. 13–14)

The use of "unfaithfulness" (מעל) and "seek" (דרש)[74] to describe the end of Saul and his dynasty indicates the significance of this passage for understanding Chronicles as a whole. "Unfaithfulness" is a key word in Chronicles and in the Priestly tradition where it is used to refer to unfaithfulness to the cult.[75] "Seeking Yahweh" is a matter of showing proper concern for the legitimate cult.[76] Faithfulness to God results in rest in the land, unfaithfulness removal from the land.[77] The implication of all this for the narrative of Saul's death is that, in

---

[74] This text is an allusion to Saul's encounter with Samuel via the medium at Endor (1 Sam. 28). In this encounter Saul asks Samuel for advice before the battle with the Philistines. Samuel answers: "Why then do you ask me, since the LORD has turned from you and become your enemy? The LORD has done to you just as he spoke by me; for the LORD has torn the kingdom out of your hand, and given it to your neighbour, David" (1 Sam. 28:16–17).

[75] W. Johnstone, "Guilt and Atonement: The Theme of 1 and 2 Chronicles," in J.D. Martin and P.R. Davies (eds.), *A Word in Season: Essays in Honour of William McKane* (JSOTS, 42; Sheffield: JSOT Press, 1986), pp. 113–38.

[76] There are two words used for seeking Yahweh in Chronicles: דרש (17×; + 1× of Baal) and בקש (6×). The two words are synonymous as seen in the quote from Ps 105:4 found in 1 Chron. 16:11: "Seek [דרש] the LORD and his strength, seek [בקש] his presence continually." The former is more important to the Chronicler and is only used once in Samuel-Kings. Oddly enough the one time it is used is in the story of Saul and the medium of Endor (2 Sam. 28:7). The Deuteronomistic formulation of this idea maybe the basis for the Chronicler's use of it. "But you shall seek the place that the LORD your God will choose out of all your tribes to put his name there. You shall go there . . ." (Deut. 12:5).

[77] This link between unfaithfulness and the land is reminiscent of Lev. 26:40–43: "But if they confess their iniquity and the iniquity of their ancestors, in that they committed treachery [מעל] against me and, moreover, that they continued hostile to me—so that I, in turn, continued hostile to them and brought then into the land of their enemies; if then their uncircumcised heart is humbled and they make amends for their iniquity, then I will remember my covenant with Jacob; I will remember also my covenant with Isaac and also my covenant with Abraham, and I will remember the land. For the land shall be deserted by them, and enjoy its Sabbath

the Chronicler's view, Saul's failure was a failure with reference to the cult.[78] The people of Israel did not, of course, experience an exile in Saul's day, nor could Saul be faulted for not "seeking the LORD" in his temple, but the story makes the point just the same. The story does, however, have a paradigmatic, atemporal quality and serves as a fitting introduction to the story of Israel's defining moment under David and Solomon.[79] This *Urzeit*[80] has implications both backward and forward in time and sets in motion a cyclical pattern of punishment and forgiveness, exile and restoration.

Grace. This same pattern becomes the overarching thematic device in the narrative of the post-Solomonic period. The reigns of Ahaz and Hezekiah illustrate this pattern nicely. Ahaz did evil in the eyes of the LORD by worshipping Baal and engaging in other "abominable practices of the nations whom the LORD drove out before the people of Israel" (2 Chron. 28:4). He, therefore, suffers the consequence of a partial "exile" at the hand of Aram (and Israel; v. 8) who "take a great number of people captive" (v. 5). Hezekiah affects a "restoration" by restoring proper worship (2 Chronicles 29–31). This restoration under Hezekiah is, of course, the occasion of his generous and inclusive offer to the residents from the North. The letter of invitation, addressed to "the people of Israel" (30:6), advises them not to be like their ancestors who were "stiff-necked" but to "submit themselves before the LORD and come to his sanctuary" (v. 8). This is the Chronicler's concept of grace. To enjoy the grace of God requires one to recognise his sanctuary in Jerusalem. Yes, this grace is available to all those in the land of Israel, it is rooted in an inclusivist vision of all Israel under God, *but this concept of Israel is Judah's and Jerusalem's concept of Israel.* All the texts cited in support of the inclusivist interpretation are, like this text, about legitimacy. The "positive" references to the North in 2 Chron. 11:13–17, 15:9 and 28:8–15 refer to residents in the North who have a loyal and submissive attitude towards Judah and Jerusalem. These residents from

---

years by lying desolate without them, while they make amends for their iniquity, because they dared to spurn my ordinances, and they abhorred my statutes." The Chronicler also picks up of the idea of the land enjoying its Sabbaths; it is empty while the people are in exile (2 Chron. 36:21).

[78] 1 Chron. 13:3 makes this more explicit: "Then let us bring again the Ark of our God to us; for we did not turn to it in the days of Saul."

[79] R. Mosis, *Untersuchung zur Theologie des chronistischen Geschichtswerkes* (Freiburg: Herder, 1973), pp. 17–43.

[80] To use a term from Riley, *King and Cultus*, pp. 57–8.

the North are included in the "all Israel in Judah and Benjamin" *but on Judah's terms.*

Final Remarks

This brings us back to the model I used above to compare Chronicles and Ezra-Nehemiah. This two-dimensional model now needs to be modified into a three-dimensional model in order to represent the hierarchical nature of the ethnicity propounded in Chronicles.

EZRA-NEHEMIAH   CHRONICLES

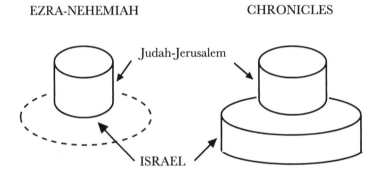

This diagram illustrates how the distinction between the post-exilic community and the "people of the land" is in fact retained in Chronicles though in the form of an internal hierarchy. The Chronicler's immediate community is still the community of returnees and thus he shares with the writer of Ezra-Nehemiah the "exile-(re)conquest" tradition of origin. The focus of Israel's identity on the centre is a transformation of the Ezra-Nehemiah ideology, not an abandonment of it. I would go on to argue that this had more than a nostalgic (von Rad, Japhet) or benignly ecumenical (Williamson) meaning in the Chronicler's day. *This was Jerusalem's claim to hegemony over all the land of Israel.*[81] Whereas the author of Ezra-Nehemiah merely asserts the continuity between his community and pre-exilic Israel, the Chronicler works this idea out in all its historical detail, amplifying the significance of this claim in the process.

---

[81] For an examination of the economic dimension of this claim see J.E. Dyck, *The Purpose of Chronicles and the Critique of Ideology* (PhD thesis; University of Sheffield, 1994).

But to whom was the Chronicler speaking? According to Tulpin, Persian ideology was "partly a matter of . . . manipulating high status local interest groups and taking advantage of low status groups' indifference to the identity of the ruling power,"[82] of harnessing "the energies and interests of native dominant classes to their own ends."[83] The objective of Achaemenid ideology would have been, in the first instance, the "self-indoctrination of [its own] ruling class"[84] and, secondly, the indoctrination of the dominant classes in the conquered territories. In the same way, I would contend, the Chronicler was addressing, in the first instance, the ruling class in Jerusalem. The Chronicler portrays Jerusalem as a centre in its own right, a centre which has a claim to the region associated with all Israel. In my opinion, *this is representative of the self-understanding of the elite (especially the clerical elite) within Jerusalem.* The Chronicler is asking his audience to imagine Jerusalem as the centre of a nation, not a small cultic community within an empire.[85] Whereas the author(s) of Ezra-Nehemiah exhibits a defensive posture, the Chronicler articulates the more confident understanding of Jerusalem's role as the *centre* of Israel. In comparison to Ezra-Nehemiah, the Chronicler recognised an opportunity for his community to expand its horizons, to claim its rightful place *over* Israel, and thereby restoring *all Israel* to a state of grace.

This is not to suggest, however, that the Chronicler was *only* addressing this immediate audience or that his ideology of identity is *merely* an expression of their limited interests. This is to misunderstand the nature of ideologies of identity and legitimacy. My conclusion regarding the ideology of identity in Chronicles, that it "contains" an ideology of legitimacy, does not mean that it could not have functioned in a truly integrative way for the inhabitants of "all Israel." If the Chronicler's motive was to create belief in his vision of a greater federalist Israel among the people in general, we cannot

---

[82] C. Tulpin "The Administration of the Achaemenid Empire," in I. Carradice (ed.), *Coinage and Administration in the Athenian and Persian Empires* (BAR International Series, 343; Oxford: BAR, 1987), p. 109.

[83] Tulpin, "Administration," p. 112.

[84] M. Liverani, "The Ideology of the Assyrian Empire," in M. Trolle Larsen (ed.), *Power and Propaganda: A Symposium on Ancient Empires* (Mesopotamia, 7; Copenhagen: Akademisk Vorlag 1979), p. 302. This concept is supported from the theoretical side by N. Abercrombie, S. Hill, and B.S. Turner, *The Dominant Ideology Thesis* (London: Allen & Unwin, 1980).

[85] As indicated in 1 Chron. 13:5, "So David assembled all Israel from the Shihor of Egypt [= an eastern tributary of the Nile] to Lebo-hamath [in northern Syria on the banks of the Euphrates] . . ."

assume that it did not in fact have this consequence. There is a danger, however, in taking ideologies of identity at face value without considering the social complexity of the concept of identity, without taking into consideration that ideologies of identity are the point at which the beliefs of the people are taken hold of for the purpose of power.[86] One is asked to believe, but can one disbelieve? In my view the Chronicler's ideology of identity, aimed at generating an integrating *belief* in a greater Israel, was simultaneously an ideology of legitimacy and power that functioned in the interests of Jerusalem, its institutions and its ruling classes.

---

[86] See C. Geertz, *The Interpretation of Culture* (New York: Basic Books, 1973), p. 100; and P. Ricoeur, *Lectures on Ideology and Utopia* (ed. G.H. Taylor; New York: Columbia University Press, 1986), pp. 259–61.

BETWEEN EZRA AND ISAIAH: EXCLUSION, TRANSFORMATION, AND INCLUSION OF THE "FOREIGNER" IN POST-EXILIC BIBLICAL THEOLOGY

Daniel L. Smith-Christopher

"It is not popular to speak of universalism in the Hebrew Bible . . ."[1]

I. *Introduction*

It seems hardly coincidental that a volume of biblical essays is dedicated to considering the theme of "Ethnicity and the Bible," and that such a collection also includes modern discussions as well as historical investigations. The two areas obviously relate closely—if only because the questions we bring to historical texts are often inspired by what otherwise worries us when we leave the library.

As the world marches toward the 21st century, those who are committed to the survival of the human enterprise have anguished over events that raise serious concerns about the possibility of co-existence. One of the most challenging aspects of modern conflict is the return of religious symbolism as fuel for opposing interests. This tendency, made complicated by histories of colonization and economic stress, is also creating new tensions between ethnic groups influenced by Christianity and Islam. Because of this, it is important to be reminded of the moments of hope within the annals of religious wars and violence. Even during the paradigm struggle between faiths, the Medieval Crusades, there were visions of alternative paths:

> Force having failed miserably in efforts to recover the Holy Land, thoughtful and pious men . . . began to insist that the crusades were misguided efforts. Men of this type, as capable of self-sacrifice and martyrdom as the early crusaders, felt that the recovery of the Holy Land could only come through the use of Christ's own methods: the preaching of the gospel. This pacifist missionary ideal, revived during the early 13th century, was deeply antagonistic to the militant crusading ideal of the 12th century . . .[2]

---

[1] David Peterson, *Haggai & Zechariah 1–8* (Philadelphia: Westminster, 1984).

[2] P. Throop, *Criticism of the Crusade: A Study of Public Opinion and Crusade Propaganda* (Amsterdam: N.v. Swets & Zeitlinger, 1940), p. 43.

Christians such as the Cistercian abbot, Isaac of Stella and the philosopher Walter Mapp, opposed the military campaigns completely, and advocated missionary-diplomats in their place.[3] Even more significantly, these brave souls point the way toward new religious interpretive strategies that could guide a renewed and authentic doctrinal expression of co-existence that is developed from within religious traditions, and their scriptural texts. In other words, as marginal as these historic voices may have been or however brief their moments, their importance for our future survival belies any attempt to discount their significance against a banal "majority." After all, what we seek is an alternative to the disappointing failures of the history and theology of the majority. How would such an alternative perspective within biblical studies alter analysis of such themes as ethnic tension in the biblical texts?[4]

Even the most casual familiarity with the Hebrew Bible enables one to see that there are many texts that could be used to justify racist and oppressive attitudes and policies toward anyone considered the "foreigner" or the "enemy." It is frequently noted in biblical scholarship that some of the more hopeful statements made with regard to the inclusion of foreigners in post-exilic Jewish worship were intended to counter the more xenophobic attitudes such as those of Ezra and his supporters who instigated the mixed-marriage crisis discussed in Ezra 9–10 and Nehemiah 13. Such exclusionary attitudes were, suggested Burrows, "the immediate object of the gentle but sharp satire of the book of Jonah," and Westermann argued that the open universalism of parts of later Isaiah (Third Isaiah particularly) were also directed against the attitudes reflected by Ezra and Nehemiah.[5]

---

[3] For those who bristle at the notion that this is a more "enlightened" strategy, believing it to be still a form of imperialist colonialism with or without arms, I suggest that readers merely consider what Saladin would have preferred, if given the only *historically valid* choice between soldiers and unarmed clerics.

The literature on opposition to the Crusades is a fascinating one. In addition to the early classic by Palmer Throop, *Criticism of the Crusades*, see Elizabeth Siberry, *Criticism of Crusading 1095–1274* (Oxford: Oxford University Press, 1985); Benjamin Kedar, *Crusade and Mission* (Princeton: Princeton University Press, 1984).

[4] I have often thought of the possibility of a critical "Friedensexegese," an analysis of scripture that *presumes* the task of highlighting the times and efforts, however brief or subsidiary to more widely held beliefs, when peace and co-existence was endorsed as the way of faith and righteousness. Such an approach would resemble some of the methodologies of feminist scholars who speak of "interested" perspectives in biblical analysis.

[5] This view is widely held, but note particularly C. Westermann, *Isaiah 1–12;*

In order to pursue this notion more fully, we will need to re-visit some traditionally vexing questions in the study of the post-exilic biblical community such as the nature of attitudes to gentiles and the meaning of "conversion" to Judaism. Along these lines, Cohen has recently suggested seven ways that foreigners were portrayed as showing "respect or affection" for Judaism, as noted in ancient sources:

(1) Admiring some aspect of Jewish religion
(2) Acknowledging the power of the God of the Jews, or including the Jewish God in a pantheon
(3) benefiting or otherwise being friendly toward the Jews
(4) practising some, or many, of the Jewish rituals
(5) venerating the Jewish God, and ignoring others
(6) joining the Jewish community
(7) converting and 'becoming a Jew'[6]

For the sake of argument, and also to facilitate the comparison of texts, I propose to collapse these shades of behavior into three contrasting attitudes toward gentiles that emerged as different strategies for the survival of the Jewish community (communities?) in post-exilic biblical theology. These are: Exclusion, Transformation, and Inclusion.

It would be misleading, however, to suggest that these different values were "sequential" or "chronological." It appears that in most periods of Israelite history, including the time of monarchical power, exclusionary attitudes co-existed with idealistic laws which sought, for example, to codify the traditions of "hospitality to the stranger" (Exod. 22:20; 23:9, 12). I would argue, however, that the exile experience "raised the stakes" on this discussion because of the particular circumstances of tension within the post-exilic communities seeking to rebuild their lives in Palestine during the Persian period. Therefore, the texts which I will discuss in this work will be limited largely to the post-exilic period.

The main point that I wish to argue is that in the midst of the theological voices of post-exilic biblical theology, there were those who began to conceive of Israel's relation to "foreigners" in a way

---

13–39; 40–66 (English translation of 1966 work in German; Philadelphia: Westminster Press, 1969) Vol. 3, pp. 312–313; M. Burrows, "The Literary Cateogry of the Book of Jonah", in H.T. Frank and W.L. Reed (eds.), *Translating and Understanding the Old Testament* [FS Herbert May], (Abingdon: Nashville, 1970), pp. 80–107, esp. 105; T. Fretheim, *The Message of Jonah* (Augsburg: Minneapolis, 1977).

[6] S. Cohen, "Crossing the Boundary and Becoming a Jew," *Harvard Theological Review* 82 (1989), pp. 13–33.

that ran counter to those who wished for the forced separation, if not subordination, *if not the death,* of all foreigners and especially former enemies.

It is important to clarify that the difference between these perspectives, held in circumstances of political occupation and subordination immediately following the Babylonian Exile and beyond, was *not* whether the present circumstances of political subordination needed to change. *The difference between these perspectives was a strategic discussion of how the change of circumstances should be brought about.* To focus the difference even more specifically—the difference of perspective was *what must happen to the foreigner in order for our present circumstances to change for the better.* With this in mind, let us turn to a brief examination of texts that illustrate the three different strategies of dealing with the foreigner.

1. *Excluding the Foreigner: The Nations vs. The 'Stranger Among Us'*

Attitudes toward the foreigner in the Bible exhibit a curious contradiction. As a group, or as "nations," foreigners are typically portrayed negatively, yet "resident aliens" are often defended in the legal tradition of Israelite society. These legal traditions appear to have sought to codify folk-traditions of "hospitality to the stranger." Another example—even though "Hittites" are often listed among the people to be "blotted out" (Exod. 23:23), yet Uriah the Hittite famously served under David (2 Samuel 11) as a mercenary soldier who is portrayed in a very favorable light by the Deuteronomistic Historian.

To suggest a simplistic dichotomy along the lines of: "foreigners as groups are bad, as individuals they are to be treated justly," is not possible. There is a clear aversion to foreign women as marriage partners in the later texts, which suggest that although individual foreign residents may be tolerable; "you wouldn't want your son to marry one."

Perhaps it is possible to trace a change over time? In her helpful study of the status of the alien in Israelite law, van Houten argues precisely this in relation to the laws regarding resident aliens. She follows the development of legal attitudes from an early call for just treatment in the older legal material (Covenant Code), to virtual inclusion in the community in the later legal material (notably in Deuteronomy):[7]

---

[7] C. van Houten, *The Alien in Israelite Law* (JSOTS, 107; Sheffield: JSOT Press, 1991), pp. 158–165.

> The laws dealing with the alien developed and became more inclusive. What began as an appeal for justice for the alien in the Covenant Code (Exod. 23:9), comes to be understood as a legal principle in the Priestly laws: 'There shall be one law for the alien and native-born'. This then opened the door for the inclusion of the alien into all the rights and privileges of Israelite society . . . the inclusive tendency is the working out, in the legal tradition, of God's purpose to include and save all.[8]

But is there indication that other discussions of foreigners, outside of laws pertaining to just treatment of resident aliens, developed along similar lines?

(a)   The Foreigner and the Foreign Woman

The observation that attitudes toward "the foreigner," especially in the monarchical period, are often quite negative in the Bible is one that hardly needs to be rehearsed in detail. Foreigners (often rendered in Hebrew as גֵּר "sojourner," or collectively as the נָכְרִים, although see also 1 Kgs 8:41, 43) are to be killed, conquered, or at the very least avoided. The theme of the destruction of the Canaanites at the time of the Conquest is a well-known theme in later biblical theology (The famous "enemy nations" were related to Canaanites in the Table of Nations: Gen. 10:16–17, and often repeated in circumstances where they are the people to be disinherited: Gen. 15:19–20; Exod. 3:8, 17; 23:23; 33:2; 34:11; Deut. 7:1; 20:17; Judg. 3:5; Josh. 3:10; 9:1; 11:3; 12:8, etc. But this continues in later periods: Neh. 9:8 and see the rehearsal of the enemy nations in Jdt 5:16. Finally, note the pejorative slur in Sus. 1:56, "You son of Canaanites!"—discussed below). In allusions to historic enemies like the Assyrians or Babylonians, there are typically also powerful motifs of the "reversal of fortune" when the enemies will be punished (Ps. 63:10–11, among the many examples in Psalms). These occupying foreigners are the ones who once conquered Palestine and stole the fruits of Jewish labor (Isa. 62:8–9); and the virulence directed at Babylon is legendary among the late additions to Jeremiah in chs. 51–52 and Psalm 137.

This attitude toward foreigners as enemies, however, was not only a product of warfare or conquest—the avoidance of foreigners was counseled in other matters of social intercourse, such as marriage. Note, for example, that a very similar list of the nationalities of foreign

---

[8] van Houten, *The Alien*, p. 175.

women that so revulsed Ezra in chs. 9 and 10 is also found in 1 Kgs 11:1–2, where Solomon's wives are mentioned, among whom were Ammonite, Moabite, Edomite, Sidonian and Hittite.[9] These stories of Solomon contain one of the few references to romantic love in the entire Bible (note also Isaac's love for Rebekah Gen. 24:67; Jacob's love for Laban and Rachel, Gen. 29:18, 30, and 32; Amnon's love for Tamar in 1 Sam. 13:1, 4) outside of Song of Solomon. The vast majority of cases deal with pious or religious "love" between God and the people. Furthermore, the only example of the phrase "I love you" between a man and woman is Judg. 16:4, 15, which is *also* dealing with a "mixed marriage" between Samson and Delilah.[10] The increasing interest in Proverbs 1–9 (but especially 5) shows how love/romance can lead to assignations with the "alien" woman, the results of which may be that, "your labors will go to the house of an alien." It appears to be the case, then, that romantic love is dealt with in the Bible with a certain circumspection, because it can lead to the unwise marital ties with "foreigners," and Blenkinsopp has suggested that the warnings about Solomon's wives now found in the Deuteronomic Historian may come from the post-exilic era.[11] The overall impression in later biblical material is that passions must be held in check, because unwise relationships may result.

(b) The Mixed Marriage Crisis in Ezra-Nehemiah

The paradigm case where aversion to foreigners is clearly observed in late biblical theology is the mixed marriage crisis of Ezra 9–10, also discussed in Nehemiah 13. In dealing with this episode in the Persian period, contemporary commentators are frequently unsettled from typical "scholarly reserve" when they approach these events— note Williamson's view that "The treatment described in these two chapters of how Ezra tackled the problem of mixed marriages is among

---

[9] There is a good discussion of this in Joseph Blenkinsopp, *Ezra-Nehemiah* (London: SCM Press, 1988), pp. 174–179.

[10] Although Delilah is never explicitly identified as Philistine, when one notes the parental concern over Samson's love for a Philistine woman in ch. 14, this appears to be a logical conclusion. See E. Lipinski, "Love in the Bible," columns 523–527, *Encyclopedia Judaica*, Vol. 11, Jerusalem. Mieke Bal's work, *Lethal Love—Feminist Literary Readings of Biblical Love Stories* (Bloomington: Indiana University Press, 1987) is an interesting analysis of the Samson/Delilah text, although she deals with themes not directly related to our concerns here.

[11] Blenkinsopp, *Ezra-Nehemiah*, p. 175.

the least attractive parts of Ezra-Nehemiah, if not the whole Old Testament,"[12] and David Clines' view that he is "appalled by the personal misery brought into so many families by the compulsory divorce of foreign wives [and] outraged at Ezra's insistence on racial purity, so uncongenial to modern liberal thoughts."[13]

I have previously suggested that approaching these events from a sociology of a threatened minority may shed considerably different light on these actions—by considering such actions as attempts to preserve identity and culture, etc.[14] Furthermore, in that same context, I also have argued that some of these "mixed" marriages—particularly in Ezra—were probably not "mixed" at all in any truly racial/ethnic sense of the term, and may well have represented marriages between Jews who were not a part of the exilic-formed "Sons of the Golah," with those who were. While this is not the place to review these arguments fully, it will be important to summarize the issue here.

Although there is some debate about whether Neh. 13:3 really deals with the mixed marriage issue, it is dealt with at great length in Ezra 9–10, and again in Neh. 13:23–31. This issue has usually been approached by commentators as two examples of the same problem within the post exilic community. But it seems clear that the Ezra texts deal with an *intra-Jewish debate* while it is only the Nehemiah texts that actually discuss "foreigners" in any modern sense of the term.

Note that sociologist Robert K. Merton describes mixed marriages as "marriage of persons deriving from those different in-groups and out-groups other than the family which are *culturally conceived as relevant* to the choice of a spouse."[15] This definition immediately raises further

---

[12] H.G.M. Williamson, *Ezra, Nehemiah* (Waco: Word, 1985), p. 159.

[13] D.J.A. Clines, *Ezra, Nehemiah and Esther* (NCB; Grand Rapids: Eerdmans 1984), p. 116.

[14] My own thinking about this event was considerably changed in my discussions with Native-Americans who express serious concern about native children being adopted by non-Native parents. The Native American elders saw the issue in terms of a threat to culture and identity. I have somewhat more sympathy for Ezra when seen in this light, even though I agree with the tone of Williamson and Clines' remarks as well. My more complete argument on the mixed-marriage crisis is D.L. Smith-Christopher, "The Mixed Marriage Crisis of Ezra 9–10 and Nehemiah 13: A study of the Sociology of Post-Exilic Judean Community," in T. Eskenazi and K. Richards (eds.), *Second Temple Studies, Vol. 2 Temple and Community in the Persian Period* (JSOTS, 175; Sheffield: JSOT Press, 1994), pp. 243–265.

[15] R.K. Merton, "Intermarriage and the Social Structure: Fact and Theory," *Psychiatry* 9 (1941), pp. 361–374.

questions about the biblical case by forcing modern readers to ask about the considerations considered "relevant" by Ezra. Ezra defined the terms of the marriage crisis both ethnically (by citing the national/ ethnic categories of Canaanite, Hivite, Perizzite, etc.) and religiously (by citing such terms as "the Holy Seed"). In this case, acceptable marriages would be those within a religious and ethnically defined group. *It is clear that Ezra conceived of "his" group as consisting only of former exiles* (Ezra 9:4). But even if this was a rigid definition for the writers of Ezra,[16] the possibility remains that these "mixed-marriages" were considered "mixed" *only* by Ezra and his supporters, and not in the first case by the married persons themselves. The issue is made more precise by Merton's considerations of "endogamy":

> Endogamy is a device which serves to maintain social prerogatives and immunities within a social group. It helps prevent the diffusion of power, authority and preferred status to persons who are not affiliated with a dominant group. It serves further to accentuate and symbolize the 're- ality' of the group by setting it off against other discriminable social units. Endogamy serves as an isolation and exclusion device, with the function of increasing group solidarity and supporting the social struc- ture by helping to fix social distances which obtain between groups. All this is not meant to imply that endogamy was deliberately insti- tuted for these purposes; this is a description in functional, not neces- sarily purposive, terms.[17]

Cerroni-Long furthermore observes that:

> When a human group finds itself uprooted and isolated and faced by a strong pressure to conform to alien standards it instinctively falls back on the primary ties of the kinship network both to reaffirm its indi- viduality in the face of threats of extinction and to maintain some form of normal existence amidst unforeseeable and stressful contingencies.[18]

Ezra's exilic, minority consciousness led to his extremism when con- fronted with a possible break-up of the recognized community of former exiles during the Persian period. But note that in Ezra (re- flecting both the specific priestly terminology and interest in purity) the sins of the Priests and Levites are prominent among the guilty

---

[16] Although I accept the notion that the books of Ezra and Nehemiah are now actually one work, I think that differences in the history of the Nehemiah materials which were later edited by the addition, among other things, of the Ezra material, allows us to still speak of "Ezra" as opposed to "Nehemiah."

[17] Merton, "Intermarriage," p. 368.

[18] Cerroni-Long, E.L., "Marrying Out: Socio-Cultural and Psychological Impli- cations of Intermarriage," *Journal of Comparative Family Studies* 15 (1984), pp. 25–46, p. 28.

(9:1, and note that the Priests and Levites are listed first among the guilty). The foreign peoples are blamed for "abominations" (תּוֹעֵבוֹת). Note the frequent cultic context of this term. Ezekiel uses it to describe the sins of the people, particularly their ritual/religious sins in Ezek. 5:9, 11; 7:3, 8; 16:22; describing idols in 16:36 and 14:6. In Proverbs, the term is used in reference to things that God "hates" (Prov. 3:32; 6:16; 15:8, 9) but this includes justice issues, such as a false balance or financial cheating (Prov. 11:1, 20 and 20:23). In ritual law, Lev. 18:24–30 associates foreign practices (of the "nations I am casting out before you" vs. 24) with "abominations." The use of this term is predominantly *late*, with some 33% of all instances found in Ezekiel alone. In short, Ezra's orientation reflects the priestly writer's obsessions with "separations" (note the use of the term *"bdl"* "to separate"[19]) between the pure and impure. Such concern with separation and identity maintenance in much of the priestly legislation is consistent with a group under stress.

But if Ezra is written from a "priestly" perspective, this raises troubling questions. Why are priests involved in this mixed marriage problem in the first place? We can establish quite clearly that it is the priestly writer of the exilic/post exilic period that is *most* passionately concerned with the maintenance of boundaries of separation. Ezekiel's concerns with purity are an excellent example of this, as are the concerns of Haggai and Zechariah. Are we to believe, then, that the mixed marriage "crisis" of Ezra, where the priests are so heavily implicated, represents a mass dereliction of duty on the part of exilic priests who abandon one of their central defining concepts? Or do the priests involved simply *disagree* with Ezra as to what constitutes a marriage that is actually "mixed"?

Van Houten's work on the priestly legislation regarding the resident alien tends to further support the notion that Ezra was engaged in a serious dispute *with other Priests* on the issue of "foreigner" and "insider." Van Houten argues that in a post-exilic redaction of priestly laws, the status of the alien "changed quite drastically."[20] In this later section, the laws tend to be cultic, and deal with the inclusion of foreigners as members of the Israelite society:

---

[19] D. Smith, *Religion of the Landless* (New York: Meyer-Stone Books, 1989), pp. 145–149.
[20] van Houten, *The Alien*, p. 162.

> ... the Israelite is instructed many times to treat the alien as a native-born in all things. This even includes an admonition to love the alien which is parallel to a previous admonition to love the fellow Israelite (Lev. 19:18, 34). According to the law, the alien is given the same status as the Israelite in all things. We do not find here the dualistic morality that was evident in the Deuteronomic laws or the first level of redaction of the Priestly laws.[21]

If there was a significant number of priestly legislators who were working on means of including aliens among the Israelite people on the basis of cultic observance, then we appear to have grounds for seeing Ezra 9–10 as a disagreement *between Jews, and specifically priests*, as to the acceptability of these people that Ezra is calling "foreigners."

But it is also quite possible that the *only* basis for Ezra's objection is that those he called "foreigners" were simply Jews who were not in exile. The strongest argument for this is the nature of the terms used, and especially the term "Canaanite": the women with whom these "mixed" marriages were sealed are identified partially with old terms that almost surely have become *stereotypically pejorative slurs* referring to those ethnic groups who have long since either disappeared or assimilated, but who were condemned *historically* as those unclean peoples "justifiably" destroyed by Joshua in the legendary patriotic tales of the founding of the Davidic House. Can one speak of Canaanites, Amorites, Jebusites, Perizzites, or even Hittites in the mid-5th Century BCE? If these are indeed terms of vilification, then such slurs suggest a debate within the community about the identity of the community itself in relation to others in the land. In short, I would argue that "boundary maintenance" ideas about "mixed marriage" (as emphasized by Merton and Cerroni-Long above) lead us to question whether the Ezra documents are really talking about "foreigners" at all.

Before developing this further, however, let us briefly note that the circumstances in Nehemiah 13 seem clearly different. Here, "the chief danger was perceived to come from outside Judah."[22] Political considerations seem predominant in Nehemiah, giving the impression of treacherous power-grabbing in both Temple and government through strategic marriages. Also in Nehemiah we are dealing with specific cases *which is the more typical biblical form for describing mixed marriage* (e.g., Solomon, Samson, etc.).

---

[21] van Houten, *The Alien*, p. 163.

[22] J. Blenkinsopp, "The Social Context of the 'Outsider Woman' in Proverbs 1–9," *Biblica* 74 (1991), pp. 457–473, p. 460.

Tobiah ("the Ammonite") and Sanballat ("the Horonite"), for example, were leaders of the opposition to Nehemiah's work of rebuilding Jerusalem. It appears that they have local authority, although the precise nature of their authority is not clear. Williamson suggests that "The context clearly presupposes that they were the leaders of those already in the land and not part of the group who returned with Ezra. Thus the suggestion that they were district governors . . . is attractive."[23]

The example that Nehemiah chooses to illustrate the problems of foreign marriage is an example of political leadership: Solomon. From Nehemiah, much more clearly than from Ezra, we gain the strong impression that the problem of foreign marriages is centrally a political problem, involving the Jewish aristocracy and local governmental leadership. In his recent commentary, Blenkinsopp also considered the political and economic advantages of such marriages: "As sparse as our information is, it reveals a network of relationships cemented by *mariages de convenance* between the Sanballats, Tobiads, and important elements of the lay and clerical aristocracy in Jerusalem."[24]

What we are clearly dealing with in Nehemiah is the attempt to intermarry the leadership of the Temple with the local political leadership, while in Ezra, we have no such suggestion. Indeed, the example of Solomon is only cited in Nehemiah, which suggests an even more explicitly political concern in the Nehemiah texts. The politics of associating with the descendants of Ammon and Moab is also much more explicitly a reference to local leadership than is the case with Ezra, where the ethnic categories in use seem more pejorative than informative.

Ezra's use of term like "Canaanite" (and in the context of the old lists of peoples to be driven from the land promised to Moses) is not our only example of anachronistic vilification. Consider the case of Susanna.

(c)   The Examination of Judges in Susanna

Among the Greek additions to the book of Daniel in the Septuagint, the story of Susanna stands in some of the Greek versions as the *first* of the Daniel stories, previous to the Hebrew ch. 1, but follows ch. 12 in others. The motivation to place the story before the Hebrew

---

[23] Williamson, *Ezra, Nehemiah*, p. 130.
[24] Blenkinsopp, *Ezra-Nehemiah*, p. 365.

ch. 1 was undoubtedly because Daniel is portrayed in this story as a
very young man who is wise beyond his years.

Although many theories have been suggested for the origin of the
story (a midrash on the evil prophets mentioned in Jeremiah 29? A
late polemic between Pharisees and Sadducees on court procedure?
A folktale that exhibits well-known themes in folklore such as "the
wisdom of the elders overturned by a child?")[25] no single view has
commanded wide agreement. While it is a tale that has clear similarities with the themes of Daniel 1–6, there is nothing within the
story that allows a clear date, or even socio-political context for the
Jewish community which treasured and maintained this story as part
of its religious folklore. It presumably reflects Hellenistic (post-333
BCE) developments of the Daniel legends.

Like Ezra (and unlike Daniel 1–6), Susanna is clearly set as an
intra-communal argument between Jews. The accusation brought
against Susanna in vv. 36–41a is adultery. But when one considers
the threat of their influence and power over Susanna, the behavior
of the corrupt elders is, in fact, a case of sexual harassment, which
itself can border on attempted rape. In order to cover for their own
lustful desire to rape Susanna,[26] the two corrupt elders claim that
they saw her with another young man. This young man, they continue,
escaped when the elders tried to confront the young couple in the
course of sexual intimacy (the Greek terms used here make the sexual
nature of their accusation clear, see Gen. 19:5; 39:10; and Jdt 12:16).
Although the entire community seems convinced by the corrupt elders'
accusations, Daniel is not. He calls out, in prophetic tones, that he
will not be a part of shedding innocent blood (compare Jer. 7:6 as
a classic example of this phrase in prophetic literature—it is used
extensively as an image of killing the innocent and especially God's
chosen messengers). Daniel is invited to come forward and finally reveal

---

[25] These and other suggestions are explained in more detail, with references to
the technical literature, in both J.J. Collins, *Daniel* (Hermeneia; Minneapolis: Fortress, 1993) and C. Moore, *Daniel, Esther, and Jeremiah: The Additions* (Garden City:
Doubleday, 1977).
[26] Glancy, J., "The Accused: Susanna and Her Readers," *JSOT* 58 (1993), pp.
103–116. Glancy makes it quite clear that rape is the issue here, not adultery. This
is supported by recent sociological and feminist studies of rape. See S. Brownmiller,
Against Our Will (New York: Simon and Schuster, 1975), p. 256; L. Baron and M.A.
Straus, *Four Theories of Rape in American Society* (New Haven: Yale University Press,
1989); P.B. Bart and E.G. Moran (eds.), *Violence Against Women* (London: Sage Publications, 1993); J.R. Schwendiger and H. Schwendiger, *Rape and Inequality* (London:
Sage Publications, 1983).

what has been hidden from virtually everyone by their own prejudices.

Daniel separates the two false judges, intending to examine each of them in turn. He requests that each judge be brought separately. When their stories differ in significant details, they are revealed in their treachery. But what is interesting is that Daniel greets each of them with abuse. The first is called "An old relic of evil days"[27] — presumably referring to the era before the exile as the "evil days," for which the exile itself was punishment (Isaiah 40, etc.). The beginning of the second interview in v. 56 mirrors the first in that, once again, Daniel meets the elder with abuse, and once again, the specific terms of abuse are noteworthy—Daniel calls him a "son of Canaan." Thus, such a use of the term "Canaanite" compares with Ezra 9:1 and Neh. 9:8, where "Canaanite" is also a term of abuse. It is possible that Ezek. 16:3 is intended to be a similar slur in the context of delivering a judgment.

Susanna reflects, therefore, an interesting association of ideas. The elders are condemned for their association with old sins by associating them with old enemies—those "foreigners," those "Canaanites." The point is this—the tradition of a conquest of the Canaanite peoples became symbolic of attitudes to foreigners—"outsiders"—long after the historical reference became obsolete. The use of the term "Canaanite" is a measure of social attitudes of exclusion much as the term "Babylon" (to denote foreign regimes) became a rallying point for Jewish spiritual and political resistance to empires that dominated their traditional homeland.

To summarize, it would appear that in addition to military propaganda about foreign nations, bigoted attitudes toward foreigners

---

[27] Moore translates "aged in evil days" or "You who have grown old in wickedness," but we argue that "old relic *of* evil days" makes more sense, especially in the light of Daniel's second appeal to history in the second examination of the other elder. Moore, *Additions*, p. 106.

As the "Day of Adversity" is noted in Isa. 50:9; 51:6; Amos 6:3, and Jer. 16:19, one wonders if what is referred to here is precisely the exile! If this entire story borrows from the Letter of Jeremiah in Jer. 29, then the "relic of evil days" may be a reference to the sins of the generation that caused the exile in the first place! After all, it was a central tenet of Deuteronomistic Theology (a theology where Jeremiah has a not insignificant contribution) that the exile was brought on by the sins of the people, *and the leaders particularly.* Daniel, therefore, delivers a searing condemnation of the generation of the exile in words similar to a Jeremiah or Isaiah. In v. 53, Daniel lists sins of leaders in a manner that is highly stylized in prophetic speech (Jer. 7:6; 19:4; 22:3, 17; Isa. 5:23, 29:21) but is also noteworthy in Wisdom literature (particularly Prov. 17:15; see also 24:24).

(especially the threat of foreign women), complete with pejorative terms, also co-existed within Israelite society with more open and welcoming attitudes. Even in late texts such as Ezra and the Greek additions to Daniel, we see a persistence of exclusionary attitudes at the same time that we will note more universalist attitudes.

2. *Transforming the Foreigner: The King in Exile Stories*

In some post-exilic texts, an alternative manner of dealing with foreigners was suggested in texts dealing with circumstances of conflict: the enemy will be defeated by its being transformed so that it is no longer a threat to the Jewish people. The book of Jonah is one of the boldest statements of this idea, but it was anticipated by other passages with similar notions about the potential for transformation. This idea can also be briefly illustrated in the attitudes towards the foreign Kings within the Daniel stories (chs. 1–6; not including the visions, which may reveal a more negative attitude).

(a)   Transforming the King in Daniel 1–6

It has frequently been argued in studies of the tales of Daniel 1–6 that the attitude toward the kings is favorable, or at least neutral. Collins, for example, has disputed the assignment of the Daniel stories to a Hellenistic/Maccabean era largely on the basis of these positive views of the foreign kings, which he considers incompatible with Jewish contempt for Antiochus Epiphanes IV in 2nd Century BCE (the undisputed date of Daniel 7–12). Concomitant to this view is the opinion that these tales reflect a Jewish appreciation for the rewards of a diaspora lifestyle, or at the very least the belief that it is possible to be successful in a foreign land.[28] Collins states that "we might assume that these stories reflect the aspirations and concerns of upper-class Jews in the eastern diaspora."[29] Collins furthermore states, in reference to Daniel 6, that:

> The benign attitude of Darius may, however, be a clue to the social setting of the tale. Problems for Jews in the Diaspora arose from envy and rivalry, but the benevolence of the king is assumed. The author

---

[28] The most important article along these lines, which began an extended tradition of comment, was W.L. Humphreys, "A Lifestyle for Diaspora: A Study of the Tales of Esther and Daniel," *JBL* 93 (1973), pp. 211–223.

[29] John Collins, *Daniel* (FOTL; Grand Rapids: Eerdmans, 1984), pp. 35–36.

does not wish to question Gentile rule as such. Given the benevolence of the king and the miraculous power of God, any problem can be overcome. We get the impression that the author of this tale was happy with his lot under the Gentile king, found the political status quo satisfactory, and was not eager to change it.[30]

Wills further comments:

> ... it is a popular genre, but it probably does not extend to the lower classes. It reflects the orientation of the administrative and entrepreneurial class. The scribal ideals inherent in the stories might restrict this circle somewhat to the extended court circles, for example, to the local administrative courts that might correspond to the training offered by Ben Sira's school.[31]

Similarly, the upper-class roots of Wisdom Literature, and the association of Wisdom themes with these tales (from the work of von Rad especially) has resulted in an interesting attempt to play down the defiance that is present in these tales. Lacocque suggests that "Daniel's resistance lies in his constancy and faithfulness. There is no bravado or provocation on his part,"[32] and Plöger had earlier argued that in ch. 6, for example, there was no intention to act in a provocative manner against the laws of the king.[33]

Some recent commentators are not so sanguine about the attitudes to foreign rulers, however. An important alternative view is represented by Fewell's study of the Daniel legends from a literary perspective: "In every story in Daniel 1–6, the sage is called upon to hold to values that somehow oppose the existent political authority."[34] Along these lines, I would argue that although it is true that very little hostility is ultimately shown toward the kings in Daniel 1–6, this is surely because they change. Their *transformation* is what eliminates the threat of deadly power and megalomaniac exercise of cruel and relentless oppression. The kings are originally portrayed as brutal monarchs who demand total allegiance, who fling obstinate subjects into fiery furnaces or lion pits—*it is the change from precisely these aspects of ancient Near Eastern oppressive realities that removes the threat to the Jews.* Let us examine two of these cases.

[30] Collins, *Daniel* (1984), p. 72.
[31] L. Wills, *The Jew in the Court of the Foreign King*, (Minneapolis: Fortress, 1990), p. 197.
[32] Andre Lacocque, *The Book of Daniel* (Atlanta: John Knox Press, 1979), p. 113.
[33] O. Plöger, *Daniel* (KAT; Leipzig: Gütersloh, 1965), p. 98.
[34] Dana Fewell, *Circle of Sovereignty: A Story of Stories in Daniel 1–6* (Sheffield: Almond Press, 1991), pp. 154–155.

When Daniel succeeds in interpreting the dream of the great statue for Nebuchadnezzar, in his relief at hearing the interpretation (even though it predicted the demise of his empire), Nebuchadnezzar is portrayed as saying: "Truly your God is God of gods, and Lord of lords and a revealer of mysteries, for you have been able to reveal this mystery!" (Dan. 2:47). The specific phrase "God of Gods/Lord of Lords" is also significant. In other contexts, the term is related to the greatness of God (Deut. 10:17) and particularly in the diaspora context where the power of God is contrasted to the power of worldly rulers (the exilic Psalm 136). While Collins suggests that this exclamation by Nebuchadnezzar may resemble Antiochus IV's supposed deathbed confession (2 Macc. 9:17),[35] Goldingay is more inclined to see the emphasis here on the elevation of Daniel, and therefore his God, rather than a theological statement on Nebuchadnezzar's part.[36] A statement of God's power and authority also follows Nebuchadnezzar's humbling "exile" among the beasts in Daniel 4: "I . . . praise and extol and honor the King of heaven, for all his works are truth, and his ways are justice; and he is able to bring low those who walk in pride" (Dan. 4:37). But these are not the strongest indications of change. Daniel 6 goes a significant step further:

> Then King Darius wrote to all peoples and nations of every language throughout the whole world: "May you have abundant prosperity! I make a decree, that in all my royal dominion people should tremble and fear before the God of Daniel:
> For He is the Living God
> enduring forever
> His Kingdom shall never be destroyed
> and his dominion has no end . . .
> (Dan. 6:25–26)

Collins wants to compare this to Persian declarations noted in Ezra 1 6, especially ch. 6, and thus see this as an expression of well-documented Persian sensibilities about respecting the religious traditions of its subjects.[37] Where the earlier statements by kings seem directed at simply preventing the Jews from being harassed and threatened, ch. 6 goes further in its statements about the "Living God" and this God's sovereignty.

The emphasis in late biblical texts on the "Living God" was im-

---

[35] Collins, *Daniel* (1993), p. 172.

[36] John Goldingay, *Daniel* (WBC 30, Dallas: Word, 1988), p. 52.

[37] Collins, *Daniel* (1993), p. 191.

portant in the context of idolatry. Note the views of Isaiah 40 and Psalm 115 about the impressive appearance of the idols of gold, silver, etc., but the fact that they do not *live*. Because they do not live, their rule is not permanent or everlasting, in contrast to the ultimate rule of the God of Israel. What is emphasized in the Daniel texts, as noted by Collins, Goldingay, and others, is similar to what is eventually the celebration of the book of Esther—the deliverance of the Jews as a result of the *transformation* of the foreign ruler.[38] In short, these transformations are more concerned with politics than religion. The transformation does not mean that these foreign rulers are part of the Jewish community—*only that the threat of the enemy is changed, and is no longer a threat*. As such, this represents an alternative strategy of dealing with foreign threat. If the first view we examined can be summarized as separation from or destruction of "the Canaanite"—this view is the transformation of the enemy.

(b) The Jonah Story as Hebrew Satyagraha[39]

Considering the theme of transforming the enemy helps to explain the relevance of the book of Jonah to this argument.[40] Scholars have tended to see Jonah as a very late text in Hebrew history (4th—3rd Cent. BCE),[41] but in any case, the salient text of this short book is the repentance by the residents of Nineveh:

---

[38] D. Clines is less certain that Esther is transformative: "this story, however sincerely it represents the position of the subject race self-evidently does not originate from the masses. However much they too may be affected by the imperial edict, this is a court-tale, told by haitues of the seat of power, reflecting the intrigue typical of the palace and the harem. For this reason, the narrative must be described as reactionary rather than progressive." (p. 45). In "Reading Esther from Left to Right: Contemporary Strategies for Reading a Biblical Text," D. Clines, S. Fowl, S. Porter (eds.), *The Bible in Three Dimensions* (Sheffield: JSOT Press, 1990).

[39] The reference to Gandhi's use of satyagraha (lit. "soul force" or "truth force") is intentional here. It was, after all, part of Gandhi's program that the enemy would be transformed by the campaigns in India and South Africa, and not only defeated.

[40] A. Lacocque, *The Jonah Complex* (Atlanta: John Knox, 1981); J. Magonet, *Form and meaning: Studies in Literary Techniques in the Book of Jonah* (Almond: Sheffield, 1983); T. Fretheim, *The Message of Jonah* (Minneapolis: Augsburg, 1977); H.W. Wolff, *Obadiah and Jonah* (Minneapolis: Augsburg, 1986); J. Sasson, *Jonah* (New York: Doubleday, 1990); John Day, "Problems in the Interpretation of the Book of Jonah," *Oudtestamentische Studiën* XXVI (Leiden: Brill, 1990), pp. 32–47.

[41] Wolff lists such arguments as Sirach's mention of "12" Prophets; terminology that is typical of post-exilic works such as "The God of Heaven" (Chronicles, Daniel); Nineveh sounding like a Persian principality in organization; familiarity with the Deuteronomic Theology of repentence; and the liturgical utterance of Yahweh's Mercy which was so typical of post-exilic psalms. See Wolff, pp. 75–83.

> Then he had a proclamation made in Nineveh: "By the decree of the
> king and his nobles: no human being or animal, no herd or flock, shall
> taste anything. They shall not feed, nor shall they drink water. Human
> beings and animals shall be covered with sackcloth, and they shall cry
> mightily to God. All shall turn from their evil ways and from the vio-
> lence that is in their hands. Who knows? God may relent and change
> his mind; he may turn from his fierce anger, so that we do not perish.
> (Jon. 3:6–9)

It is frequently noted in discussions of "conversion" in ancient Israel,
that the term most associated with such personal religious changes of
community is simply the Hebrew term for "turn" שׁוּב.[42] But focus
on this term is not fruitful for understanding the nuances of transformation in these texts. Certainly this is the term used in the Jonah
passage to indicate a "change" in God's intentions. But Wolff emphasizes the symbolism of the king's actions in this passage:

> By rising from his throne, he is stripping himself of his insignia as ruler
> and judge (cf. Jer. 36:22; 1 Kgs 1:46). He throws aside his royal robe,
> the token of his sovereignty; וַיַּעֲבֵר (hiphil) is a powerful word for "put
> away," and is used especially for things which are offensive to Yahweh
> cf. 1 Kgs 15:12; Zech. 3:4; 13:2 . . . finally the king sets down "in the
> dust" instead of on his throne . . .[43]

Further, Wolff's discussion of "violence" points out that the "violence of their hands" was bloodshed, also the "violence" that brought
on the flood (Gen. 6:5). What the people are repenting of, in short,
is the violence of empire—precisely that element which was most
threatening to the Jews. Fretheim agrees, suggesting that Jonah is
not a book about gentiles per se,[44] but about enemies: "It is always
their violence or wickedness which is in view."[45] Fretheim doubts
that this is to be read as a conversion passage, because the people
do not join the community—they are not viewed as streaming to
Jerusalem as in other passages such as Isaiah 2 or 60. The emphasis,
then, is not simply on "turning," but from *what* is one turning?

In summary, these famous passages of transformation do not have
as their aim a discussion of conversion—the expansion of the people
of Israel by the addition of gentiles as members in good standing.
The aim of these passages is to hold out the possibility that the steadfast, nonviolent resistance of faithful Jews may actually give witness
to God's existence and power, and thus invite a transformation of

---

[42] Beverly R. Gaventa, "Conversion," ABD Vol. 1, pp. 1131–33.

[43] Wolff, *Obadiah and Jonah*, p. 151.

[44] See also Burrows, "Literary Category," p. 100.

[45] Fretheim, *Message*, p. 22.

foreign enemies so that they are no longer a threat to the Jewish people. That this transformation typically involves a recognition of the power and/or wisdom of the God of the Jews should not lead to the hasty conclusion that a theological issue of conversion is at stake. The issue was political, not ecclesiastical, so to speak. Furthermore, let it not be presumed that I am arguing for some kind of ancient Hebrew "pacifist" ethic here—this transformation on the part of the enemy occasionally resulted in a blood bath for those who had earlier planned the destruction of the Jews (e.g., the end of Esther, Bel and the Dragon, Daniel ch. 6, etc.). However, to hold out such a possibility for change at least begins a process that will also leads to a questioning of the validity, or efficacy, of military tactics. Such a perspective is noted, for example, in the famous reference to the Maccabees in Daniel 11:34 as "little help."

There is clear evidence, however, that a third possibility did actually begin to be entertained in the minds of some late biblical theologians: the actual inclusion of gentiles as a part of the people of Israel. The similarity of religious language in this context leads one to suspect that this third option was *a logical development from the earlier possibility of transforming enemies from threatening emperors to defenders of Jewish rights.*

3. *Including the Foreigner among the People of God*

(a) Bel and the Dragon

We can see signs of this change already in the Greek additions to Daniel, one of our main sources for the "transformation" motif. The Greek addition known as Bel and the Dragon consists of two stories that are only loosely related. There is considerable scholarly debate as to whether these stories belong originally together—rather than artificially joined when they were made a part of the Daniel tradition.[46] Moore ingeniously suggests that just as the Susanna story represents Daniel as a precocious and wise youth, so the stories of Bel and the Dragon—taking place during Persian rule—represent the old and wise Daniel still true to his faith.[47] Certainly both parts of this chapter deal with idolatry, although in one case the idol is fashioned

---

[46] Moore, *Additions*, pp. 146–147.
[47] Moore, *Additions*, p. 9.

by human hands, and in the other case it is a living animal. Both obviously deal with the theme of idolatry in exile, already a major concern in Second Isaiah and in the canonical stories of Daniel 1–6. As we are only interested in a short aspect of the second story— specifically vv. 28–32, we cannot comment on these debates at great length here.[48]

Vs. 28 contains a startling concept. The Babylonians are angry with Daniel's influence on the King, and to express their frustration they use a surprising phrase:

Ἰουδαῖος γέγονεν ὁ βασιλεύς
"The King has become a Jew!"

The salient feature of the quote is the equative verb "to become"— the perfect suggesting "has become." Clearly, by the time of the Hellenistic period, we are in a context of Jewish thought that can conceive, even in a fiction, of a foreigner "becoming" a Jew—pre- sumably referring to a convert. Collins objects that even this does not necessarily refer to conversion in the modern sense,[49] but do we even know what "conversion" meant in this period? A clear transfor- mation of character and religious observance is suggested by the language of the passage. However, we must keep in mind that the story does not so much suggest that the King did, in fact, convert, *merely that the Babylonians accuse him of this!* In the context of a Jewish story of the late Persian, or Hellenistic period, this accusatory con- text lends credence to reading this phrase as an actual conversion precisely because it would be considered so shocking (in other words, the exaggeration fits the story). Furthermore, it is clear that in the context of the Daniel tradition—to which this story was editorially joined—this transformation is intended to be read in the context of the more startling "confessions" of faith that we have noted in the canonical stories of Nebuchadnezzar and Darius.

It can therefore be suggested that the confessions of the kings in Daniel, although perhaps not intending to suggest conversion in the first instance, eventually came to be understood as such by the time of the Greek additions to Daniel such as the story of the "Dragon" in "Bel and the Dragon." Do we have evidence that this possibility was held out for other gentiles besides kings?

---

[48] I go into detail on this matter in my commentary on Daniel for the *New Interpreter's Bible* (Vol. 7; Nashville: Abingdon Press, expected October, 1996).
[49] Collins, *Daniel* (1993), p. 415.

(b)   "Proselytes" in the Greek Texts

We have already noted in the study by van Houten that the priestly legislation moves decidedly toward a cultic inclusion of foreigners under certain ritual circumstances. She further notes in an appendix that by the time of the Hellenistic period and the translation of the Hebrew/Aramaic texts of the Bible into Greek, the term προσ-ήλυτος had come to be used for virtually *all* occasions of the Hebrew term גר, suggesting that by the time of the translations into Greek, the phenomenon of proselytes was so common among the Jewish people (and presumably especially in Egypt?) that it was assumed that this is what the texts were referring to, rather than resident aliens, etc.[50]

(c)   "Those who join with/to you."

In addition to this movement in legal discussions, however, there are a series of celebrated late biblical texts that speak of the inclusion of gentiles (although *never* using the terminology of the conquered peoples like "Canaanites") as equals among the people of God. In his study cited earlier, Cohen also illustrates that there is not a universal agree-ment in the sources as to the exact meaning of "conversion." However, Cohen himself suggests that actual conversion requires all of the following: (a) practise of Jewish law; (b) an exclusive devotion to the Jewish God; and (c) integration into the community (presum-ably the latter would take into consideration the wider communities' assessment of this "inclusion"). It is noteworthy that a paradigm case for Cohen's argument is clearly Ruth:

> Where you go, I will go;
> where you lodge, I will lodge;
> your people shall be my people,
> and your God my God. (Ruth 1:16b)

Note the various levels at which Ruth consciously mentions her trans-formation—including devotion to the God of the Jews *and* clear association with the people. Here we have a clear case of full-fledged conversion. But is Ruth an exception? Cases of full inclusion of the foreigner into the people of Israel can best be traced in an examina-tion of the use of the Hebrew term לְוָה, which means simply to

---

[50] van Houten, *The Alien*, pp. 179–183.

"attach to," or "join," but is used in a series of important passages to refer to gentiles who are "joined" to the people of God.

In Ps. 83:9, the term "joined" is coupled with עִם "with" to refer to an alliance of enemies against Israel, while in Num. 18:4 the context is the joining of the Tribe of Levi to the House of Aaron. Jer. 50:5, as in other places, refers to the reunification of Judah and Israel. In Gen. 29:34 it is used in the imperfect in reference to marriage (obviously not, however, a common use for the term). But what is noteworthy about this term is the number of occasion where it is specifically used to refer to the inclusion of foreigners among the people of Israel:

> And *the foreigners who join themselves to the Lord*,
> to minister to him, to love the name of the Lord,
> and to be his servants,
> all who keep the sabbath, and do not profane it,
> and hold fast my covenant
> these I will bring to my holy mountain,
> and make them joyful in my house of prayer;
> their burnt offerings and their sacrifices will be accepted on my altar
> for my house shall be called a house of prayer for all peoples.
> (Isa. 56:6–7)

In reference to this passage, Westermann writes:

> What is promised to the nation once it is delivered from Babylon are not new victories of the subjugation of foreign nations, but increase in numbers because of the distant and foreign people who come to Israel and want to belong to her because of the God of Israel.[51]

Compare this to other significant uses of the term לָוָה:

> But the Lord will have compassion on Jacob and will again choose Israel, and will set them in their own land; *and aliens will join them and attach themselves to the house of Jacob*.
> (Isa. 14:1)[52]

> Sing and rejoice, O daughter Zion! For lo, I will come and dwell in your midst, says the Lord. *Many nations shall join themselves to the Lord on that day*, and shall be my people, and I will dwell in your midst.
> (Zech. 2:10–11)

---

[51] C. Westermann, *Isaiah 40–66* (Philadelphia: Westminster Press, 1969), p. 285.

[52] Westermann already had doubts about 14:1, suggesting that it did not fit the context of the passage, and was probably added later (p. 25). Jensen, however, wonders if the enslavement of foreigners might not better be read as a spirit of service, and not in negative connotations at all. See J. Jensen, *Isaiah 1–39* (Wilmington, Glazier: 1984), p. 143. Kaiser had some doubts about the relation of these verses as well: "Aber der Gedanke an den Übertritt von Nichtjuden zum Gottesvolk kann auch

The Jews established and accepted as a custom for themselves and their descendants *and all who joined them*, that without fail they would continue to observe these two days every year, as it is written . . . (Esth. 9:27)[53]

These examples were enough for Westermann to suggest a "technical use" of the niphal participle of לוה, as in Esth. 9:27. The term is actually translated "proselyte" in important Greek texts.[54] A further consideration of the Greek terminology in these various passages is instructive. The first cited passage, Isa. 56:3, 6 refers to "foreigners" ὁ ἀλλογενής who have "joined to," the participle form is προσκείμενος which derives from προστίθεναι "to add, to be gathered" (see Gen. 25:8, 17, Bel 1, Acts 13:36—"gathered to fathers", a well-known Semiticism in reference to death; see also "added to" in Matt. 6:27, 33, Luke 3:20). Forms of the same term are noted in Isa. 14:1 and Esth. 9:27.

The Zechariah passage, however, differs in the Greek, even though the same Hebrew term is used. Here, the passage reads: καταφεύξονται ἔθνη πολλά.

The term καταφεύγειν seems clearly influenced by Isa. 55:5: ". . . nations that do not know you *shall run to you* . . ." (from Hebrew "run" רוץ) and Isa. 10:3 "to whom will you flee for help." Jer. 50:5, in the NRSV reads ". . . and they shall come and join themselves (Judah and Israel) to the Lord by an everlasting covenant." However, the Hebrew features לוה while once again the Greek reads καταφευγείν as in Zech. 2:11 (Gk v. 15). The same sense of "fleeing

deshalb vorgezogen worden sein, um v. 2 wirkungsvoller mit der Schilderung der bevorstehenden Umkehrung des Verhältnisses zwischen den Bedrückern und den Bedrückten schliessen zu lassen." *Der Prophet Jesaja, Kapitel 13–39* (Göttingen: Vandenhoeck and Ruprecht, 1973), p. 23.

[53] An interesting further case from Ezra is the following: "It was eaten by the people of Israel who had returned from exile, *and also by all who had joined them* and separated themselves from the pollutions of the nations of the land to worship the Lord, the God of Israel" (Ezra 6:21). This verse has a number of difficulties. The salient phrase, "all who joined them" is not specifically clear in either the Greek or Hebrew texts. The term we are examining, לוה certainly does not occur. Commentators are split with regard to who is being referred to here—Jews who separated themselves from the pollutions of the surrounding peoples, or *gentiles* who separated. If it were gentiles actually joining the community then this passage would alter considerably the general impression given by the books of Ezra-Nehemiah on attitudes to foreigners. For the view that gentiles are being referred to here, see J. Blenkinsopp, *Ezra-Nehemiah*, pp. 132–133. That these are other Jews, on the other hand, is argued by H. Schneider, *Die Bücher Esra und Nehemia* (Bonn: Peter Hanstein Verlag, 1959), p. 128; L. Batten *Ezra and Nehemiah* (Edinburgh: T&T Clark, 1913), p. 153; W. Rudolph, *Esra und Nehemia* (Tübingen: J.C.B. Mohr, Siebeck, 1949), p. 64.

[54] Westermann, *Isaiah 1–13*, p. 25

to/running to" in the Greek is captured in Ps. 143:9: "Save me from my enemies, O Lord, I have fled to you for refuge" (the Greek use of the form of κατέφυγον assumes, it appears, the Hebrew חסה "seek refuge" rather than כָּסָה "shelter, cover"). Does the use of the Greek term suggesting "seeking refuge/fleeing" in the Zechariah passage suggests that at least in some quarters, the "conversion" of gentiles was among those gentiles wanting to escape *to* the Israelites—perhaps to escape punishment or judgment? The translation may well have been influenced by the imagery of Zechariah 2, which is about the restoration of Jerusalem, and the call to the people in diaspora to "flee" the nations, who are about to experience such punishment that these nations will become subject to their own slaves.

In short, the "joining" of people to the Israelites appears to be an aspect of *restoration*. This is all the more significant given that in other texts, it was precisely restoration that involved the *punishment* of the foreign nations (Isa. 11:13–16; Ps. 137:7–9).

We appear to have a strong case for a conscious distinction between post-exilic writers in their attitudes toward foreigners in the time of restoration. Some writers look for a future bloody revenge, a punishment of the enemies, while others see deliverance by means of a dramatic transformation of the leaders of the enemy nations. Finally, a few writers begin to envision the possibility that some from among the foreign nations, even from the enemy nations, would seek to become a part of the worshipping people of God. The advocates of this last view even have moments of an incredible new era of multi-ethnic relations:

> On that day Israel will be the third with Egypt and Assyria, a blessing in the midst of the earth, whom the Lord of hosts has blessed, saying, "Blessed by Egypt my people, and Assyria the work of my hands, and Israel my heritage." (Isa. 19:24–25)

Summary

We have surveyed a considerable variety of opinion with regard to Israel's relationship to the foreigner in post-exilic biblical thought. The three options of exclusion, transformation, and inclusion clearly co-existed. But what is the meaning of this exercise? How does this relate to the thoughts with which we began this investigation—thoughts about the future of human co-existence?

I would argue that we can no longer can afford contemporary reflections on these passages that exhibit the tendency to cancel the universalist moments by attempting to "balance" them with texts dealing with conquest, destruction, enslavement, and reversal of fortune, as if to blunt the impact of the moments of insight. Note, for example, Stuhlmueller's comments on Zech. 2:11 which can be taken to be representative of a common tendency among contemporary scholars:

> The prophecy of Zechariah does not lay down the conditions for the admission of Gentiles, whether with dignity (Isaiah 56) or in chains (Isa. 45:14). *The other side of this movement* condemns the nations and separates Israel from them . . .[55] (emphasis mine)

Such an exegetical perspective about "sides" of "one movement" seems to involve a prior theological conviction that the Bible must speak with one united theological voice, however incoherent that voice may be after blending different strains of thought. The task of historical critical analysis is to present the diverse views. It is the task of theology, however, to attempt to deal with this diversity. But we need not insist, when reading the fine moments of profound hope that ancient Hebrew writers are capable of, that they be "balanced."

Hebrew visions of peaceful co-existence, and the possibility of including the foreigner among the people of God, advocated a more enlightened way to deal with enemies. These visionary passages are as much a part of post-exilic Hebrew theological development and religious life as are the motifs of exclusion. In short, the texts that call for destruction of enemies, avoiding foreigners as impure, and nationalistically reusing the terminology of the "impure peoples" who were driven from the land cannot be allowed to overshadow or rule out the tremendous hope engendered by a passage such as the last two verses of Isaiah 19.

The identification of alternative voices, then, is the beginning of an alternative history and exegesis that values the "brief moments" (or what Mieke Bal, in the context of feminist exegesis, identified as the supposedly "meaningless details" that nevertheless become *very* meaningful in the light of feminist analysis)[56] as lights on our path.

---

[55] C. Stuhlmueller, *Haggai and Zechariah: Rebuilding with Hope* (Edinburgh/Grand Rapids: Handsel/Eerdmans, 1988), p. 72.

[56] M. Bal, *Lethal Love: Feminist Literary Readings of Biblical Love Stories* (Bloomington: Indiana University Press, 1987), p. 2.

It is not a necessary step of critical analysis of the Bible that texts like Isa. 19:24–25, for example, must have their "epiphanous" character "balanced out" (and thus removed) by mundane human attitudes.

To return to our opening thoughts, then, it can be suggested that a critical, exegetical model that assumes differences of view within the biblical texts is a beginning of seeking alternative voices, and alternative symbols, from within religious traditions that are involved in conflict. To suggest that Isaac of Stella, or Walter Mapp, are far overshadowed by the thousands who marched to the "Holy Land" to liberate the cross is to miss the point. It is Isaac and Mapp who, like Isaiah 19:24–25, can light our path to a future co-existence by means of insights and hopeful ideals that are developed *from within* our textual and symbolic religious traditions.

THE UNIVERSAL HORIZON OF
BIBLICAL PARTICULARISM

Jon D. Levenson

I. *The Ambiguities of "Universalism"*

There is probably nothing in Judaism that has attracted so much attention and generated so much controversy as the biblical idea that the Jews are the chosen people. There were pagan authors in antiquity who resented what they saw as Jewish exclusiveness, and early Christianity often claimed to universalize the Hebrew Bible's supposedly parochial view of the divine covenant, making it available to all the nations of the earth. Anti-Semitism has historically focused on alleged Jewish clannishness and has charged that Jews' absorption with their own group leads to lack of concern for others. In response, many Jews have stressed the universalism that they perceive in prophetic ethics, downplaying evidence of Jewish particularism in the Bible. Other Jews, in the aftermath of the Holocaust, have reasserted and exaggerated the uniqueness of the Jewish people, even to the extent of denying the applicability to Jews of the outside world's moral standards.

Given this long history of polemics and apologetics, it is no easy task to sort out the biblical material on universalism and Jewish particularism in a scholarly way. But such an exercise is needed, not only to help non-Jews overcome confusion and bigotry about Judaism, but also to enable Jews to understand their own biblical heritage and its contemporary implications, for, as we shall see, the all-too-common contrast between "universal" and "particularistic" religion is, in every instance, simplistic, grossly misleading, and even dangerous.

The chief objective of the following pages is to reexamine the issue of universalism and particularism in the Hebrew Bible with an eye to the way in which the framing of the issue therein served a foundation for later Jewish reflection. As may already be apparent, I write not only as a student of biblical thought but also as a committed Jew interested in defining a defensible contemporary appropriation of the ancient legacy and in applying the resources of his tradition to the wide and increasingly vexatious problem of ethnicity in the modern world.

Predicated of a religious tradition, the term "universalism" can carry a number of divergent meanings. It may simply refer to the universality of the deity: No other god exists, and the whole world, without exception, is his. Such universalism, however, still allows for pockets of particularism. Although God may be lord of the world, he need not care about the world in its entirety, or he may care about different classes of creatures in different measures. He may, for example, favor persons over animals, although he is the creator of both, and even permit persons to kill animals without incurring guilt, but not the reverse. Or, he may single out one set of persons rather than another—such as the people of Israel, the Christian Church, or the Islamic *ummah*—for special favors and special responsibilities.

When this is held to have happened, hard questions have to be faced. What is the relationship of those who have not been so singled out to the universal deity and to his special group? The answers to this are several. The outsider may be condemned as an offense to the universal lord whom he does not acknowledge, or he may be respected as a person of dignity who is not to blame for his status. Or, again, he may be regarded as a person of diminished dignity whose true worth can be realized only by his electing to join the favored sub-group. Religious traditions that affirm both a universal God and a particular group as his elect face an especially difficult challenge on the question of moral standards and accountability. Has the God of all imparted knowledge of his ethical norms to those who have not experienced his revelation? If so, how? And what is the relationship of the universal ethical norms, if they exist, to the norms that govern the favored sub-group? If these two sets of norms are identical, then one can speak of a *moral* universalism that has been disclosed only to a special group: everyone should observe one group's ethic. In this case, the particular religious tradition will tend to identify itself with humanness itself, and to imply either the subhumanity of outsiders or their unwitting practice of the insider's religion, or both. There is another alternative: some norms oblige all persons, and others oblige only the sub-group. Here, universalism is affirmed on one tier, and particularism on another.

Although some religious traditions may on occasion conceive of themselves as representing or answering to a universal human condition, as a matter of historical fact all religious traditions are particular, since none includes everyone. There is no evidence that humankind has ever had only one religion. Religion is as much a creature of culture as it is of nature, and human culture is inevitably particular. To be sure, while no religion is universal, some aspire to be. In this sense, a "universal religion" may mean simply one that accepts proselytes, that is, one that is willing or eager to extend its particularity indefinitely. Or it may signify one that is found in a large number of different cultures. In this case, the term "universal" is misleading, since the religion has not transformed a highly diverse humanity into one universal body. Instead, it has formed symbiotic relationships with various enduring particularisms. In this case, the variety of human cultures has been eroded but not overcome, and there is no reason to assume that the erosion is irreversible, since few things are more characteristic of human experience than the fragmentation and disintegration of overarching structures of belief.

Yet another understanding of "universalism" may teach that in some future consummation, human variety will disappear altogether or submit permanently to an all-inclusive structure. In this case, particularism may be predicated of the present aeon, and universalism of the next. There is no contradiction between *historical* particularism and *eschatological* universalism, limited or total.

II. *The Universality of God and Human Dignity*

Before we attempt to determine where the Hebrew Bible fits into this rude typology of universalisms and particularisms, we must first acknowledge frankly that there is no one "biblical" position on this or on most other great theological issues. The Bible is an anthology of writings composed over a period of about a thousand years, in several lands, and by authors of various sorts. It presents a spectrum of positions, and although the spectrum is not endless, neither is it so limited as to facilitate generalization. Intellectual honesty requires us to avoid the popular tactic of citing a passage that appeals to us as if it were the entirety of the tradition.[1] Though the temptation to read our own values into the text is nearly overpowering, it must be

---

[1] On the hermeneutical issues involved, see Jon D. Levenson, *The Hebrew Bible, the Old Testament, and Historical Criticism* (Louisville: Westminster/John Knox, 1993), esp. chapters 1, 3, and 6.

resisted; complete objectivity is not humanly possible, but it remains a necessary ideal.

In spite of its anthological character, in Judaism the Hebrew Bible (especially the Torah, its first five books) is considered a coherent entity, not merely a concatenation of incompatibles. This postulate of coherence enables us to regard the separate elements as parts of a total picture that may not in reality have been affirmed by their original authors. Thus, some systematic statement is possible, so long as it is loose enough to allow for exceptions and self-aware enough to acknowledge its dependence on a canon that did not exist in the biblical period itself.

Universalism in the sense of the universality of the deity is most striking in those biblical traditions that speak of God as the creator of the world. The placement of the story of cosmic creation by God (*'elohim*) at the beginning of the entire Bible (Gen. 1:1–2:3) establishes a universal horizon for the particular story of Israel, which occupies most of the rest of that sacred book. Especially noteworthy is the lack of all spatial locality in that account of creation. Unlike the following creation story, that of the creation of Adam and then Eve by the Lord God (*YHWH 'elohim*, Gen. 2:4–24), this first account mentions no landmarks, no countries, no rivers, not even a Garden of Eden. Instead, men and women, created together, exist on undifferentiated dry land. No spot on earth can claim the prestigious status of primordiality: There is no "place" at which creation began and where its energies may yet be available. The familiar world is entirely and evenly the consequence of the creative act.

Here, it is instructive to contrast a Babylonian creation story, the *Enuma Elish*, in which Marduk's creation of the world culminates in the construction of Babylon, his city and therefore the capital of the cosmos, and of Esagila, its temple and his palace.[2] Like *'elohim*, Marduk is also a cosmic creator-god; his power is not limited to Babylon.[3] But, as is emphatically not the case in Gen. 1:1–2:3, his special relationship to a particular community is embedded in the very structure of cosmic order.

In the biblical story, the only *particular* vestige of the act of cre-

---

[2] See Alexander Heidel, *The Babylonian Genesis* (Chicago: University of Chicago Press, 2nd edn, 1951), p. 48.

[3] See H.W.F. Saggs, *The Encounter with the Divine in Mesopotamia and Israel* (London: University of London/Athlone, 1978), pp. 30–63.

ation is a cultic rite, the Sabbath, through which Israel replicates the rhythm of the protological events (2:1–3).[4] In this sense, the Sabbath is as universal as the deity whom Israel imitates, despite the fact that it is disclosed to Israel alone, and not until the generation of Moses (Exod. 20:8–11). In short, the "prestige of origins"[5] applies not to something so particular as a place, but to a way of organizing something universal—time. Like Esagila, the Sabbath recollects the divine repose after the work of creation, but in a nonspatial and therefore universalizable way. Unlike the *Enuma Elish*, Gen. 1:1–2:3 does not serve to buttress any particular political or cultic order.

It is also highly significant that in both creation accounts at the beginning of Genesis (1:1–2:3 and 2:4–24), it is humanity in general and not any people in particular that is created. Israel is not primordial. It emerges in history, twenty generations after the creation of the human species in the image of God (or the gods, 1:26–27). "Israel," in the words of a contemporary scholar, "has no particular supernatural status by birth and early history."[6] It is neither descended from the gods nor divine itself. All people are created equally in the divine image. The creation stories in Genesis serve as a powerful warrant for a Jewish doctrine of human solidarity and as a formidable obstacle to any attempt to mix Judaism and racism.

The relatedness of the members of the human family to each other and to God is underscored and formalized in the announcement of an eternal covenant with Noah in Gen. 9:1–17. Underlying this covenant is a theology that places all peoples in a relationship of grace and accountability with God. The subsequent establishment of covenants with all Abrahamites (Genesis 17) and with all Israelites (Exodus 24) is to be read against the background of this universal covenant. Israel's relationship to God is thus both unique and universal:

---

[4] See Moshe Weinfeld, "Sabbath, Temple, and the Enthronement of the Lord— The Problem of the Sitz im Leben in Genesis 1:1–2:3," in A. Caquot and M. Delcor (eds.), *Mélanges biblique et orientaux en l'honneur de M. Henri Cazelles* (Alter Orient und Altes Testament, 212; Kevalaer: Butzon and Bercker; Neukirchen-Vluyn: Neukirchener, 1981), pp. 501–512; and Jon D. Levenson, *Creation and the Persistence of Evil: The Jewish Drama of Divine Omnipotence* (San Francisco: Harper and Row, 1988; rept., Princeton: Princeton University Press, 1994), chap. 6.

[5] On this, see Mircea Eliade, *Myth and Reality* (New York and Evanston: Harper and Row, 1963), pp. 21–38.

[6] Carroll Stuhlmueller, "The Foundations for Mission in the Old Testament," in Donald Senior and Carroll Stuhlmueller (eds.), *Biblical Foundations for Mission* (Maryknoll, NY: Orbis, 1983), p. 11. Stuhlmueller notes especially Ezek. 16:3.

no other people has it, yet all humanity has something of the same order.

The Noahide Covenant, which is mentioned nowhere else in the Hebrew Bible, assumes greater importance in Rabbinic Judaism, where it serves as the functional equivalent of natural law, specifying the seven commandments incumbent upon all humanity, Jew and gentile alike.[7] The greater role of the Noahide Covenant in rabbinic than in biblical Judaism calls into question the too common notion that the rabbis abandoned the universal dimension of biblical theology and retreated into a cocoon of ethnocentricity. Indeed, one of the reasons for the absence of a missionary thrust in rabbinic theology is the doctrine of human dignity in general, whether Israelite or not. Those who think outsiders can have a proper relationship with God as they are will feel less of an impulse to make them into insiders.

It is significant that the primeval history (Genesis 1–11) presents humankind as primordially monotheistic and, in fact, YHWHistic (4:26). Idolatry, which, according to the rabbis, violates a Noahide commandment, is not intrinsic to human beings, and in the Hebrew Bible a gentile is not generally assumed to be idolatrous. It is possible to be a faithful and responsible worshiper of YHWH (the proper name of the God of Israel) without being an Israelite. In this, the YHWHistic source (J) in the primeval history goes beyond even the universalism of Gen. 9:1–17, derived from the priestly source (P). For the latter maintains that the name of YHWH was revealed only in the time of Moses (Exod. 6:2–3) and therefore uses only the more general terms 'elohim and 'el shadday before the revelation of the tetragrammaton to Moses.[8]

The YHWHist's lack of concern that the lips of a non-Israelite might contaminate the sacred name reflects a larger tendency in biblical tradition to acknowledge and honor gentiles who revere YHWH or otherwise play a special, positive role in his designs, such as Jethro (Exodus 18), Balaam (Numbers 22–24), Rahab (Joshua 2), Naaman (2 Kings 5), Job, and Cyrus (Isa. 44:24–45:10). This broadly inclu-

---

[7] See, e.g., *b.Sanh.* 56a. On the Noahide commandments, see David Novak, *The Image of the Non-Jew in Judaism* (Toronto Studies in Theology, 14; New York: Edwin Mellen, 1983).

[8] Conventionally, the proper name of the God of Israel, YHWH is translated "the Lord," whereas the word 'elohim is translated "God." For a convenient presentation of the hypothesis that underlies the source-critical distinctions, see E.A. Speiser, *Genesis* (AB, 1; Garden City, NY: Doubleday, 1964), pp. xxii–xliii.

sive theology demonstrates vividly the grave danger in using the term "pagan" to denote both a non-Israelite and a practitioner of a religion odious to the God of Israel: The two are not coterminous. Not every non-Israelite was thought to practice an abominated cult. Instead, biblical tradition seems to have thought that the knowledge of God, even in its most concentrated, YHWHistic form was not necessarily the result of some miraculous incursion into nature by the deity. Rather, "YHWH is near to all who call upon him/to all who call upon him in truth" (Ps. 145:18). Quite apart from the specific self-disclosure of God to Israel, then, the Bible assumes a natural knowledge of God available to all humanity.[9]

The technical term for this universally available religion is *yir'at 'elohim* or *yir'at YHWH*, "the fear of God" or "the fear of the Lord," and it is associated with moral rectitude. When the Philistine king Abimelech demands to know from Abraham why he passed his wife off as his sister, the latter responds, "because I thought there was surely no fear of God in this place and they would kill me for my wife" (Gen. 20:11). In the Hellenistic period, the term "God-fearers" (*phoboumenoi* or *sebomenoi ton theon*) came to denote a class intermediate between Jews, on the one hand, and "pagans" in the derogatory sense, on the other. The Noahide and the God-fearer, like the *ger toshav* of rabbinic literature (with whom they may be identical), testify to a theology that holds that the true religion is larger than the religion of the core of insiders, which it includes. The convenient dichotomy of insider-outsider is too crude to accommodate the Jewish conception of the divine-human relationship.[10]

This concept of the universal availability of God and his law remained alive and was never displaced in ancient Israel by more particularistic theologies. Wisdom teachers were especially inclined to speak in non-national terms. The books of Proverbs, Job, and Qohelet never refer to the people of Israel, the Exodus, the Covenant of Sinai, or the gift of the Land. Instead, they address what they perceive to be the general human condition and ground moral authority not in a historical revelation—there is no evidence the authors of these books knew of a Torah of Moses—but in direct

---

[9] On this, see especially James Barr, *Biblical Faith and Natural Theology* (Oxford: Clarendon, 1993), chap. 5.

[10] On the *ger toshav* and the God-fearer in rabbinic law, see Novak, *The Image*, pp. 14–28.

observation of the world.[11] Whereas the Pentateuchal and prophetic traditions celebrate the frightening irruption into the natural order of a passionate and unpredictable God, Wisdom literature relishes the reassuring constancy and reliability of nature and its creator. Injustice, like an imbalance in nature, cannot endure, for the world-order rights itself:

> He who digs a pit will fall into it.
> And he who rolls a stone—it will roll back on him. (Prov. 26:27)

With its high esteem for universal truths, Wisdom theology shows an inherent tendency toward cosmopolitanism. Israelite Wisdom writers took pride in their great culture-hero, King Solomon:

> Solomon's wisdom was greater than the wisdom of all the men of the East and than all the wisdom of Egypt. He was the wisest of men, wiser than Ethan the Ezrahite, Heman, Chalkol, and Darda, the sons of Mahol. His reputation spread among all the surrounding peoples. (1 Kgs 5:10–11)

It is telling that, although the biblical historian considers Solomon's wisdom a charismatic gift from YHWH (v. 9), he also stresses the international recognition of it. Solomon's sagacity, far from being something foreign and opaque to outsiders, is actually the quintessence of something they have esteemed and pursued, with no small success. The experience of Solomon's wisdom leaves the Queen of Sheba, for example, breathless with admiration (10:5). There is no hint that she is regarded as "pagan" in the pejorative usage, and her religion does not seem to interfere with her appreciation of Solomon's perspicacity. On the contrary, he passes *her* test (10:2–3).

In all likelihood, the Wisdom teachers considered the gods of the gentiles, or at least of the sagacious and ethical gentiles, as not different in kind from YHWH, the God of Israel. Perhaps they thought the different gods were really only different names for the one all-pervasive reality, which can be intuited in general human experience. It was a theology of this sort that enabled the Israelite sages to include in their proverb collections the dicta of foreign savants, such as those of the mysterious Agur ben Jakeh (Prov. 30:1) and Lemuel, king of Massa (Prov. 31:1–9), perhaps an Arabian emirate (cf. Gen. 25:14). The likelihood that these two men were indeed non-Israelite sages has

---

[11] See John J. Collins, "The Biblical Precedent for Natural Theology," *Journal of the American Academy of Religion* 45/1 Supplement (1977), pp. 35–67.

been advanced by the discovery that Prov. 22:17–24:22 is an Israel-ite adaptation of the thirty-chapter "Instruction of Amen-em-opet," an Egyptian Wisdom text that probably dates from the seventh cen-tury BCE.[12] The biblical Wisdom teachers provide a solid precedent for the Judaization of later philosophical movements, from Platonism to existentialism. A telling way in which Jewish practice continues this openness to non-Jewish wisdom to this day is the benediction to be pronounced upon seeing a gentile wise person: "Blessed are you, YHWH our God, master of the universe, who has imparted of his wisdom to flesh and blood."[13]

III. *Purpose and Mystery in the Election of Israel*

As the primeval history (Genesis 1–11) has it, the original unity of humankind could not endure increasing wickedness. From the expul-sion from the Garden of Eden through the first murder and the iniquity of the generation of the Flood, the dominant note is one of curse. With the incident of the Tower of Babel, the pristine unity of humanity is shattered: Persons now speak a variety of languages and dwell "over the face of the whole earth" (11:9). The familiar world of human fragmentation and diversity has been born. Its mother is rebellion, and its midwife, the curse of God.

At the beginning of the Patriarchal narratives, to our surprise, the note of curse is replaced by one of blessing: YHWH promises a Meso-potamian named Abram that he will inherit an unknown land, fa-ther a great nation, and become a byword of blessing, indeed a source of blessing to those who bless him (12:1–3). Apparently, God's high hopes for the world, continually frustrated throughout the dismal course of primeval history, are now focused on one man who will reverse the decline of a failing humanity. Unlike later rabbinic ex-egesis, the Torah itself offers no grounds for the selection of Abram for this awesome assignment. It makes no claim that he had earned

---

[12] See James B. Pritchard (ed.), *Ancient Near Eastern Texts Relating to the Old Testa-ment* (Princeton: Princeton University, 3rd ed, 1969), pp. 421–425. On Wisdom Lit-erature in general, see Joseph Blenkinsopp, *Wisdom and Law in the Old Testament: The Ordering of Life in Early Judaism* (Oxford Bible Series; New York: Oxford University, 1983).

[13] Cf. *b.Ber.* 58a, where the form is "to his creatures." On natural theology in Second Temple Judaism, see Barr, *Biblical Faith*, chap. 4.

it or that he was endowed with some innate predisposition that made his selection rational. Instead, the Torah presents the revelation to Abram as sudden and unanticipated, and his obedient response as an unalloyed act of faith. The backdrop is still universal; the relevance of his fate to the nations is announced at the outset (12:3). Yet he alone bears the promise.

The relationship of YHWH and Abraham is soon formalized as a "covenant" (Genesis 15 and 17), a treaty that the parties swear to uphold. When the parties are, as here, unequal, we speak of a "suzerainty treaty." The lord of the covenant, the suzerain, makes a pact with his subject, the vassal. In some biblical instances, as in the great covenant with all Israel concluded on Sinai, the treaty lists stipulations, in this case the *mitsvot* (commandments) of the Torah, which the suzerain enjoins upon his vassal.[14] In other cases, such as the covenant with Noah (9:1–17) and that with Abraham, the goal of the suzerain is not to secure the undivided allegiance of the vassal, but to reward his already demonstrated loyalty with a grant.[15] With Abraham, the grant includes a fiefdom, the land of Israel, as it will come to be called, and a dynasty, the people Israel, in whom kings will appear (17:6–8). In the second formulation of this covenant of grant (17:9–14), circumcision plays a central role. It is a visible "sign of the covenant" (v. 11), like the rainbow in the Noahide Covenant (9:12–17) and perhaps the Sabbath in the Sinaitic Covenant (Exod. 31:16–17).

It is significant that the Torah's promise to Abraham predates the existence of a people Israel, which indeed comes into being only as a result of YHWH's mysterious grace and the equally mysterious but edifying obedience of Abraham. By making the theology earlier than the people, the Torah underscores "the necessity of viewing the greatness of the nation in light of the greatness of her God."[16] Indeed,

---

[14] On covenant, see Delbert R. Hillers, *Covenant: The History of a Biblical Idea* (Seminars in the History of Ideas; Baltimore: Johns Hopkins, 1969); and Jon D. Levenson, *Sinai and Zion: An Entry into the Jewish Bible* (New Voices in Biblical Studies; Minneapolis: Winston Seabury, 1985; rpt., San Francisco: Harper and Row, 1987), pp. 23–86.

[15] See Moshe Weinfeld, "The Covenant of Grant in the Old Testament and in the Ancient Near East," *Journal of the American Oriental Society* 90 (1970), pp. 184–205; and Jon D. Levenson, "On the Promise to the Rechabites," *Catholic Biblical Quarterly* 38 (1976), pp. 508–514.

[16] Horst Seebass, "בחר bachar," in G.J. Botterweck and H. Ringgren (eds.), *Theological Dictionary of the Old Testament* (Grand Rapids: Eerdmans, 1975), Vol. 2, p. 84.

Israel exists only because of God's choice, and apart from God, it has no existence at all. Even those biblical traditions that date the selection of Israel from the generation of the Exodus and Sinai (e.g., Deut. 32:20; Hos. 11:1; Ezek. 20:5), rather than from Abraham, assume the inseparability of peoplehood from theology. Israel has no profane history, only a sacred history, a history of redemption, of backsliding and return, punishment and restoration.

Ancient Near Eastern covenants, whose signatories tend to be kings, illuminate for us the Bible's account of God's covenant with the Jewish people at Sinai. The covenanted Israelites, vassals though they be, are also described in royal terms:

> And if you truly obey me and observe my covenant, you will be my special possession from among all peoples—for the whole world is mine. But you are to be my priestly kingdom and sacred nation. . . . (Exod. 19:5–6)

It has even been argued that the word translated as "kingdom" actually means "king."[17] Whether or not this is so, the language describing Israel's chosenness in the Bible reflects the terms in which ancient Near Eastern kings described their relationships to their divine patrons. For example, an Egyptian text describes Hatshepsut, the female pharaoh, as "she whom he [the god] chose to protect Egypt." Mesopotamian kings were sometimes described as "the one chosen by the faithful heart of god," "the Chosen One of the gods," or "the one to whom the eyes of the gods have been directed."[18] Nebuchadrezzar I, king of Babylon in the twelfth century BCE, is described as "the prince beloved by Marduk—the king of the gods, Marduk commissioned him," and his younger contemporary Tiglath-Pileser I of Assyria is described as "the beloved prince, the desire of your [i.e., the gods'] hearts, the exalted shepherd, whom in your faithful hearts you have called. . . ."[19]

There are other biblical instances of God's referring to those he has selected in similarly exalted language. David, chosen as king, will say to YHWH, "You are my father," and YHWH "will make him [his]

---

[17] William L. Moran, "A Kingdom of Priests," in John L. McKenzie (ed.), *The Bible in Current Catholic Thought* (St. Mary's Theological Studies, 1; New York: Herder and Herder, 1962), pp. 7–20. But note that Moran considers the king in question to be the priesthood collectively.

[18] Jan Bergman and Helmer Ringgren, "בחר bachar" (see n. 16), pp. 73–74.

[19] J.M. Powis Smith, "The Chosen People," *American Journal of Semitic Languages and Literatures* 45 (1929), pp. 74–75.

firstborn son, highest of the kings of the earth" (Ps. 89:27–28; cf. 2 Sam. 7:8–16, Psalm 2). Israel, too, appears in the privileged role of YHWH's first-born son, whose desire to serve the divine father not even Pharaoh may thwart (Exod. 4:22–23). This concept of the people Israel collectively as God's son grounds the demand that Israel's ways are to be visibly different from the ways of the gentiles (Deut. 14:1–2), but it also insures that God's grace will not allow even the gravest sins of Israel to provoke him to disown them (Hosea 11; Jer. 31:18–20).[20] His paternal love elevates the covenantal relationship into something far more than a *quid pro quo* deal between two self-interested politicians.

To be sure, many Christian commentators have argued that God's choice of the Jews was conditional and instrumental rather than final. "In the thought of the Old Testament, it is always election to service," wrote an eminent Christian scholar of the last generation, "and it is held to be forfeited when it has no relation to that service."[21] This interpretation of election has support in both the Near Eastern analogues and in biblical texts themselves. Hammurabi, king of Babylon in the late eighteenth century BCE, tells us in the prologue of his famous law code that the gods singled him out "to promote the welfare of the people . . . to cause justice to appear in the land, to destroy the wicked and the evil, that the strong might not oppress the weak. . . ."[22] In similar language, the biblical God specifies his reasons for choosing Abraham, reasons that relate not to his past, but to his and his dynasty's future: "That he might charge his children and his household after him to keep the way of YHWH by doing what is right and just, so that YHWH may bring about for Abraham what he has promised him" (Gen. 18:19). While it remains mysterious why God needs a particular individual to realize these ends and why Abraham should have been that person, and while it might seem contradictory to promote the cause of justice through a plan that favors one family over the rest of humanity, the choice itself is neither mysterious nor autonomous. It is subordinate to a larger plan encompassing goals that extend beyond the covenant relationship itself—the essential goals of right action and justice.

---

[20] See Jon D. Levenson, *The Death and Resurrection of the Beloved Son* (New Haven: Yale University Press, 1993), esp. chap. 5.

[21] H.H. Rowley, *The Biblical Idea of Election* (London: Lutterworth, 1950), p. 94.

[22] *Ancient Near Eastern Texts* (see n. 12), p. 164. Cf. Ps. 72:1–4, 12–14.

Another rationale for the selection of Israel appears in the work of the anonymous prophet of hope who wrote toward the end of the Babylonian Exile (ca. 539 BCE):

> You are my witness—oracle of YHWH—
> And my servant whom I have chosen,
> In order that you may know and believe in me
> And understand that I am he:
> Before me no god was formed,
> And none will be after me. (Isa. 43:10)

In this case, the choice of Israel, or at least the Israelite community in Babylonia, is subordinate to a theological purpose: to establish a beachhead of monotheism, a sodality of witnesses to the uniqueness and eternity of YHWH. This concept of a witness implies a third party who receives the testimony, a judge or jury to be persuaded. Here, again, the horizon of particularism is universal. YHWH has commissioned Cyrus king of Persia

> For the sake of my servant Jacob
> And of Israel my chosen one. . . .
> So that they may know from east to west
> That there is none but me:
> I am YHWH and there is no other. (Isa. 45:4, 6)

Once more, chosenness serves a larger purpose. The chosen people does not withdraw from the human family, but exercises a special office within it, an office defined by the character and will of their universal God. They are the particular witnesses—and beneficiaries—of universalism.

These texts and others like them support the claim that biblical election was instrumental, telling of the ideas and values that God so esteemed that he chose one people to manifest them. But there is another side to the story. As we have seen, in much of the literature Israel's apostasy was not viewed as cancelling its original election; YHWH did not abandon it and try again with somebody else, though he did threaten to do so on occasion (Num. 14:12, cf. Exod. 33:14–15, Hos. 1:9 and 2:25). Thus, although the election was sometimes articulated in terms of larger purposes, Israel's failure to serve those purposes was not necessarily thought to have terminated the election. Conversely, simply serving those purposes—practising justice and worshiping YHWH alone—did not make one an Israelite, even if it did make one a responsible and worthwhile citizen of the universal theocracy.

The election of Israel was only partly grounded in universals. Even after these have been taken into account, the singling-out of Israel remains a mystery:

> Not because you were more numerous than all other peoples did YHWH take a passion to you (*hashaq*) and choose you—indeed, you are the least of the peoples; but it was because YHWH loved you and kept the oath that he swore to your Patriarchs that YHWH took you out with a strong hand and redeemed you from the house of bondage, from the power of Pharaoh, king of Egypt. (Deut. 7:7–8)

Here, the choice of Israel is grounded in passion. It is telling that the verb *hashaq* is also used of Shechem's tragic love for Dinah, whom he raped (Gen. 34:8), and of the feelings of an Israelite warrior upon sight of a captured woman whom he wishes to marry (Deut. 21:11). It suggests an affair of the heart, with all the irrationality and unpredictability of such things. Who can specify the reasons why he loves someone above all others of the same class, and even if he can, do those reasons ever account in full for that love? In this theology, God knows what he wants to do with Israel, but why he chose this people rather than another still remains a mystery of his love.

There is, then, a duality in the Bible's concept of election. On the one hand, election is at times articulated in terms of larger purposes that it is to serve, and, of necessity, those purposes extend beyond the confines of the chosen people. On the other hand, God bears with Israel even when it fails in its mission. The purposes do not override the chosenness, and chosenness cannot be reduced merely to the commitment to certain values. The specialness of Israel is neither altogether self-sufficient nor altogether instrumental. Should the Israelites imagine that their election is totally self-sufficient, they are reminded that their exodus is not unique (Amos 9:7) and that their relationship with YHWH brings with it greater accountability, not only greater privileges (Amos 3:2).[23] And should they imagine that their election is totally instrumental, depending only on their own very flawed obedience, they are reminded that the Covenant insures them an undeserved second chance (e.g., Lev. 26:39–45). Election implies service, but service renews election. God's grace implies his law, but

---

[23] On Amos' putative universalism, see Harry M. Orlinsky, "Nationalism-Universalism and Internationalism in Ancient Israel," in H.T. Frank and W.L. Reed (eds.), *Translating and Understanding the Old Testament: Essays in Honor of Herbert Gordon May* (Nashville: Abingdon, 1970), pp. 211–212.

his law implies his grace. Neither takes precedence over the other; they are inextricable.

For Jews in the post-Enlightenment West, where ideas of human equality and democratic government hold sway, there is a powerful temptation to stress the instrumental dimension of Jewish chosenness and to deny or ignore the self-sufficient dimension. We are sometimes told that the "chosen people" means the "choosing people," as if passive and active participles were not opposite in meaning. Judaism is often presented as a commitment to some rather amorphous "Jewish values," which, on inspection, turn out to be *universal* values, in which Jews and gentiles alike ought to believe. Covenant, if it is mentioned at all, appears only as the basis for a warm, meaningful community life. The fact that the Covenant distinguishes sharply between insiders and outsiders—although both are God's—is ignored.

In large measure, such attitudes are dictated by the exigencies of living as a minority in a mixed society with a high degree of openness. It is simply not prudent to affirm a distinctiveness of ultimate significance signaled by heredity, and what it is not prudent to express publicly often loses credibility, becoming peripheral or taboo even in private discourse. In addition, the contemporary theology in question represents a cognitive surrender to a Kantian theory of ethics in which morality entails universalizability: If the behavior cannot be advocated for everyone, it cannot be moral. On Kantian principles, Jewish ethics—a norm for one group only—is a contradiction in terms.[24] Hence the common substitution of ethics for Torah. "Ethics," as Michael Wyschogrod puts it, "is the Judaism of the assimilated."[25]

Despite the centrality of ethics to Judaism and despite the very real universalizing aspects of biblical thought, intellectual honesty obliges us to acknowledge that in the Hebrew Bible the ethic of the covenant-community was not thought to reduce to the universal moral

[24] On some implications of Kant for Judaism, see Emil L. Fackenheim, "The Revealed Morality of Judaism and Modern Thought: A Confrontation with Kant," in Arnold J. Wolf (ed.), *Rediscovering Judaism* (Chicago: Quadrangle, 1965), pp. 51–76, reprinted in Fackenheim, *Quest for Past and Future: Essays in Jewish Theology* (Boston: Beacon, 1968), pp. 204–228 and in Menachem Marc Kellner (ed.), *Contemporary Jewish Ethics* (New York: Sanhedrin, 1978), pp. 61–83. In the last book, see also Norbert Samuelson, "Revealed Morality and Modern Thought," pp. 84–99. On the parallel Christian problem, see James M. Gustafson, *Can Ethics Be Christian?* (Chicago: University of Chicago, 1975).
[25] Michael Wyschogrod, *The Body of Faith: Judaism as Corporeal Election* (New York: Seabury, 1983), p. 181.

law. The Israelite, for example, may eat no carrion, since he is a member of the "sacred people." The foreigner, however, may, and in Deuteronomic law (Deut. 14:21), he incurs no guilt by doing so.[26] In the Sabbatical Year one Israelite is not to dun another, but he may dun a foreigner (15:3), just as an Israelite may take no interest from another, but may take it from an outsider (23:20–21).

What is the basis for such discrimination? In some instances, these laws are based on Israel's sacrality, which must be guarded from pollution, and are of the same character as those that protect the priesthood. The Book of Ezekiel, for example (44:31), forbids priests (kohanim) any meat that is carrion or the result of tearing by beasts. This law, which may perhaps not know of the Pentateuchal extension of the prohibition to all Israel,[27] derives from the consecrated status of the priesthood, and it is reasonable that the people Israel, themselves a "priestly kingdom" (Exod. 19:6), should have fallen under some of the same protections. On the other hand, the prohibition on interest-taking from a fellow Israelite probably derives from the covenant theology and its concept of the special solidarity of the covenantal community. Israelites relate to each other as fellow vassals of the same liege lord; they relate to outsiders differently. "With my friend you shall be friend, and with my enemy you shall be enemy," a Hittite suzerain announced to his vassal.[28] In Israel, covenantal friendship seems to have involved the right to free loans. "You shall love your neighbor as yourself; I am YHWH," one of the most memorable verses in the Torah announces (Lev. 19:18). But the context makes it probable that the "neighbor" is one's "brother," a fellow worshiper of YHWH.[29]

Three points must be made about this nearly ubiquitous biblical phenomenon of the distinction—the discrimination—between Israel and the nations. The first is that the distinction does not coincide with the distinction between good and bad. The covenantal status of Israel does not necessarily imply any genetic superiority over other

---

[26] But cf. Lev. 17:15–16, where life in the Land seems to obligate the foreigner to observe purity prohibitions, whereas in Deuteronomy ethnic identity rather than place of residence seems to be the central factor.

[27] Exod. 22:30; Lev. 17:15–16, Deut. 14:21. But note Lev. 22:8, which, like Ezek. 44:31, imposes the prohibition only upon priests.

[28] *Ancient Near Eastern Texts* (see n. 12), p. 204.

[29] See Orlinsky, "Nationalism-Universalism," p. 210. But see also Ernst Simon, "The Neighbor (*Re'a*) Whom We Shall Love," in Marvin Fox (ed.), *Modern Jewish Ethics: Theory and Practice* (Columbus: Ohio State University, 1975), pp. 29–56.

nations, either before or after the fact. As we have seen, some biblical texts (e.g., Deut. 7:7–8) go out of their way to affirm that God's choice of Israel is not a response to any innate traits or special accomplishments, and others (e.g., Amos 3:2) see in the covenantal relationship a heightened vulnerability to punishment. The same texts that affirm Israel's specialness can also insist that the specialness has its source in the God who molds them for his purposes, often despite and not because of their character (e.g., Deut. 9:7). Whether, in the theology of the Hebrew Bible, non-Israelites can be excused for their ignorance of God and his will is doubtful. What is not doubtful is that the Hebrew Bible does not generally condemn them for their differentness from Israel. The difference between the chosen and the unchosen is not (as it often becomes in Christianity) the difference between the saved and the damned.

In light of this possibility of respect for the non-Israelite, my second point should come as no surprise: The same literature that insists, in intensely particularistic terms, upon the special, separate status of Israel can also insist, in intensely universalistic terms, upon special solicitude for the "stranger" or "resident alien," who is to be not only tolerated, but helped and even loved, in part because of Israel's own experience as strangers in Egypt (e.g., Exod. 23:9; Lev. 19:33–34; Deut. 23:8). In some instances, the "stranger" or "resident alien" is apparently a fellow Israelite who has lost his access to his ancestral land, but in others (e.g., Exod. 12:48) he seems to be a foreigner. It should not go unnoticed that this intense empathy for and sympathy with the outsider is not peculiar to the prophets, but, as the examples above show, is characteristic of the Priestly and Deuteronomic literatures, which insist at least as forcefully upon the importance of the distinction between Israel and the nations. The antique but resilient notion that involvement in covenant, ritual, and purity is inherently exclusivistic or even misanthropic must be laid to rest.

My last point about these discriminations involves the very definition of Israel. Here we must be very careful to understand the nettlesome problems involved in the conception of ethnicity in the Hebrew Bible. In the modern world, especially in the United States, there is an overwhelming tendency to define ethnicity according to physical characteristics (such as skin color) or language. In ancient Israel, the former seems to have played no role whatsoever, and not much more significance was attributed to the latter (we do not even know for sure what the Hebrews called their language, "Hebrew" never appearing in this meaning). Here the table of nations in Genesis 10 is highly revealing. The Canaanites, who among the primeval nations should be thought to resemble Israel most in race and language, are seen as descended not from Noah's son Shem, ancestor of Israel, but from his brother Ham (v. 6). This makes the Canaanites brothers with the Egyptians, whose language was much more distantly related to theirs than was Hebrew. The point is as simple as it is easily missed in the modern world: the ancients did not perceive ethnicity the way modern physical anthropologists and linguists do.[30] They did not think that their chosenness rested upon racial and cultural superiority or that the unchosen status of outsiders followed from some innate deficiency because they did not have a concept of *race* or *culture* at all in the sense in which the term is used by moderns, whether open-minded or bigoted, nationalistic or cosmopolitan. Indeed, one of the hardest points of biblical thought to understand is the concept of *peoplehood*, which is familial and natural without being racial and biologistic. Yet without a grasp of that concept, no understanding of the problem of universalism and particularism in the Hebrew Bible is possible.

There is a kind of pluralism inherent in those laws that distinguish Israel and the nations, a conceptuality that avoids applying the same norms to all families and nations, as if familial and national identities were insignificant. But the fact remains that just as classical Judaism is incompatible with racism, so is it incompatible with contemporary egalitarianism. The universalistic thrust of modern, democratic, capitalistic societies undermines all particularisms, especially those based on the claim of historical revelation.

Even when a particular biblical norm does not distinguish insiders from outsiders, something essential in the ancient vision is, for better or for worse, lost when the norm is described in the language of universal values rather than the language of commandments, as in the Torah itself. Commandments presuppose direct address: the king commands his subjects, the suzerain his vassal. The force of the commandment follows from the relationship in which it is embedded, in this case, the relationship of love and loyalty demonstrated to the satisfaction of all when YHWH took Israel out of Egypt to be his own. Values, however, which suggests meanings embedded in a uniform reality, presume no such relationship.

---

[30] See Robert R. Wilson, *Genealogy and History in the Biblical World* (New Haven: Yale University, 1977).

To be sure, this world of values is not altogether alien to the biblical traditions. Wisdom Literature, as we have seen, often speaks in such terms and, unlike the Torah, it does not ground ethics in the particularistic traditions of Exodus and Sinai. Even in the Torah itself, the larger meaning is sometimes noted (e.g., Exod. 23:25–26); not every commandment is a mysterious ukase incomprehensible to those upon whom it is enjoined. There is, in short, ample warrant in the biblical tradition for discourse in the language of values, and in contemporary Western culture, where claims of revelation are generally considered illicit in public disclosure,[31] this resort to the language of values is a necessity for the participation of religious Jews.

Nonetheless, we must not lose sight of the limitation that the structure of Judaism places upon such language. Unchecked, the tendency to recast commandments (*mitsvot*) as values renders the very existence of the Jews superfluous. Cut loose from their covenantal matrix, the commandments cease to bind those who observe them to the God of Abraham, Isaac, and Jacob. Thus, although the prerequisites of public discourse are not to be slighted, Jews interested in upholding their millennial tradition must guard against importing those extramural priorities into the discourse that takes place within the religious community, where a dialectical usage of the language of commandments and the language of values is appropriate. Neither vocabulary should be allowed to vanquish the other. Commandments and values are distinct but related.

IV. *Judaism for the Gentiles*

We have seen that one possible definition of a universalistic religion is a religion that accepts converts. On this issue, there seem to have been some ambiguity and significant evolution in biblical thought.

Some texts suggest that foreigners could indeed be integrated into Israel. One thinks, for example, of the "mixed multitude" (*'erev rav*) that went out of Egypt with the Israelites (Exod. 12:38). Rashi, the great medieval commentator, is perhaps correct in glossing this as a "mixture of converts from various nations" (although rabbinic definitions of Jewishness and conversion must not be anachronistically

---

[31] See Franklin I. Gamwell, "Religion and the Public Purpose," *Journal of Religion* 62 (1982), pp. 272–288.

retrojected into the biblical period). A more explicit case is that of Ruth, whose moving declaration to Naomi ("Your people will be my people/And your God will be my God," 1:16) may echo some sort of liturgy of naturalization. And then there is the enigmatic verse toward the end of Esther that reports that "many from the peoples of the country identified themselves with the Jews, for the fear of the Jews had fallen upon them" (Esth. 8:17), which may indicate some form of conversion.

Even if this is so, the degree of integration of a foreigner into ancient Israel remains shrouded in obscurity. Note that even after her naturalization, Ruth is still "Ruth the Moabite" (Ruth 4:5), and not the "Israelite." And while texts that exclude some groups altogether and admit others only after two generations imply the acceptability of those not so designated (Deut. 23:4, 8–9), Ezra and Nehemiah, in demanding the dissolution of all intermarriages, seem not to have known of any possibility of conversion for the foreign wives (Ezra 9–10, Neh. 13:23–31). Also, whereas biblical law insists that "the alien (*ger*) shall be to you like one of your citizens" (e.g., Lev. 19:34),[32] the very same equalizing law provides oblique evidence for the survival of his identity as an alien. In short, like the dichotomy of insider-outsider, the dichotomy between a religion that accepts converts and one that does not is too simplistic to accommodate the complex and shifting realities of biblical Israel.[33]

Whatever the precise status of the "foreigner" after his "conversion," it is clear that especially after the Babylonian Exile (sixth century BCE), we hear much about a class of people who wished to attach themselves (*nilwah*) to Israel, e.g.,:

Happy is the man who does this,
The person who holds fast to it:
Who observes the Sabbath and does not profane it,
Who guards his hand so that it does no evil.

Let not the foreigner say,
Who has attached himself to YHWH:

---

[32] This "theology of the stranger" has been astutely called an "anti-election theology" by Jeremy Cott, "The Biblical Problem of Election," *Journal of Ecumenical Studies* 21 (1984), pp. 205–207. On the large and complex question of the identity of the *ger*, see Christiana van Houten, *The Alien in Israelite Law* (JSOT Sup, 107; Sheffield: JSOT Press, 1991) and Christoph Bultmann, *Der Fremde in antiken Juda* (Göttingen: Vandenhoeck and Ruprecht, 1992).

[33] See Jacob Milgrom, "Religious Conversion and the Revolt Model for the Formation of Israel," *Journal of Biblical Literature* 101 (1982), pp. 169–176.

"ʏʜwʜ will keep me apart from his people."
. . .
As for the foreigners who attach themselves to ʏʜwʜ,
To minister for him and to love the name of ʏʜwʜ,
And to become his servants,
All who observe the Sabbath and do not profane it,
And hold tightly to my Covenant—

These I shall bring to my sacred mountain,
And to them I shall give joy in my House of Prayer.
Their whole-offerings and their sacrifices
Shall find acceptance on my altar,
For my Temple shall be called,
"A House of Prayer for All Peoples."

Oracle of the Lord ʏʜwʜ,
Who gathers the dispersed of Israel:
I will gather more to those already gathered.
(Isa. 56:2–3, 6–8)[34]

One should guard against the assumption that this text indicates the absorption of gentiles into Israel, as became possible in a later stage of Jewish history. The text does not imply naturalization—the foreigner may well remain just that—but it does endorse the acceptability of a gentile's participation in the cult of the God of Israel in Jerusalem, provided that the gentile, accepts the Covenant. Here the sign of the Covenant is the Sabbath, which functions as the *conditio sine qua non* for cultic participation, like circumcision in some Pentateuchal texts (e.g., Exod. 12:48–49).

Whether the oracle excerpted above anticipates the full absorption of the foreigner into Israel or not, it certainly envisions an international community of ʏʜwʜists centered upon the ʏʜwʜ-temple in Jerusalem. Another oracle from the same collection goes further, arguably envisioning foreigners serving as priests (*kohanim*) and Levites (*lewiyim*), previously hereditary offices (Isa. 66:18–21). Here, as in the previously quoted passage, the new Exodus, the return of Israel from its Babylonian dispersion, attracts the attention of the gentiles and converts them to the worship of ʏʜwʜ in his holy city and through his particular liturgy. Retrospectively, the image recalls the "mixed multitude" that went out of Egypt with Israel (Exod. 12:38). Prospectively, it anticipates the saying of the Talmudic authority Rabbi Elazar that "The Holy One (blessed be he) dispersed Israel into exile among the nations only so that converts may be added to them."[35]

---

[34] On this oracle, see further Jon D. Levenson, "The Temple and the World," *Journal of Religion* 64 (1984), pp. 291–293.
[35] *b.Pes.* 87b.

The fact that so much of late biblical eschatology envisions the reorientation of the nations toward yHwH is highly significant.[36] It suggests something like a restoration of the situation of the primeval history (Genesis 1-11), in which humanity was united, monotheistic, and yHwHistic. History has come full circle, except that Israel does not disappear into an undifferentiated humanity. Rather, it and the nations survive, only now centered upon the service of yHwH, the universal creator, king, and redeemer, in his cosmic capital, Jerusalem. Israelite particularism, in this vision of things, is not destined to disappear. It is destined to reach its universal horizon.

In post-biblical Judaism, it was certainly licit for a gentile to be absorbed completely into the people Israel without the retention of his foreign origin. A Greek who became a Jew was no longer, in *any* sense, a Greek; he was ethnically and religiously Jewish. It is this radical understanding of conversion that made possible the Talmudic discussion of whether a convert commits incest if he marries a close relative once the latter has also converted.[37] The question could arise only because of a presumption that conversion has created a new person who is now part of a new family, the biological family of Israel, and is no longer related to his blood relatives. So zealous were the rabbis to protect converts from discrimination that quite early they enunciated the ruling that a Jew may not say to a convert, "Remember your former ancestors," a remark that in their mind constituted the "oppression of the stranger" forbidden in Exodus 22:20.[38]

Some, following in the footsteps of the inspiring early twentieth-

---

[36] E.g., also Zech. 8:20-23; Isa. 19:16-25. It is important to note that this reorientation often occurs after the nations experience a catastrophic judgment of yHwH (e.g., Isa. 19:16). The pattern of calamity followed by restoration was an old one in Israel. On the dynamics of universalism and particularism in post-exilic literature, see Moshe Weinfeld, "Universalism and Particularism in the Period of Exile and Restoration," (in Hebrew) *Tarbiz* 33 (1964), pp. 228-242. On the dynamic in later Judaism, as illustrated through the *'aleynu* prayer, see Eugene B. Borowitz, "The Dialectic of Jewish Particularity," *Journal of Ecumenical Studies* 8 (1971), pp. 560-574.

[37] E.g., *b. Yeb.* 22a. See also *Mishneh Torah, Hilkhot 'Issurey Bi'ah* 14:10-16.

[38] *M.B. Metz.* 4:10 (*b.B.Metz.* 58b). See also *Shulkhan Arukh, Hoshen Hammishpat* 228:2. This is not, of course, to claim that the full acceptance of converts was (or is) a consistent social reality or that resistance to converts and suspicion of them is not to be found in rabbinic sources (note that a *kohen* may not marry a convert). It must not be missed, however, that powerful halakhic and aggadic currents oppose and mitigate this resistance and suspicion. Ironically, when the classic religious norms fall away, as they have for most Jews in modern times, the acceptance of the convert becomes more problematic and in some respects more difficult, since it becomes unclear what they have to do to become accepted and what it is exactly that they are to be accepted into. In some ways, religion—even a religion as all-encompassing as rabbinic Judaism—is more easily changed than ethnicity or culture.

century theologian Franz Rosenzweig, have described Christianity as the rays that shoot out into the dark night of "paganism" from the fiery star that is Judaism: Christianity is Judaism for the gentiles.[39] Be they right or wrong, they have surely obscured the essential fact that Judaism itself can also be Judaism for the gentiles.

V. *Election and Equality*

The early Christian Church claimed that it represented the universalistic eschatological fulfillment of biblical prophecy. According to this view, Judaism is to Christianity as exclusiveness is to inclusiveness, closedness to openness, particularism to universalism, or, not to put too fine an edge on the matter in this post-Enlightenment era, as bad is to good. The often cited prooftext for this assertion comes from an early letter of the apostle Paul:

> You are all sons of God through faith in Christ Jesus. As many of you as have been baptized into Christ have put on Christ as a garment. There is neither Jew nor Greek, neither slave nor freeman, neither male nor female. You are all one in Christ Jesus. If you are Christ's, then you are the seed of Abraham, and so heirs according to the promise. (Gal. 3:26–29)

In Paul's thinking, the way a person, Jew or gentile, falls heir to the Abrahamic promise is not, as it was for the rabbis, through birth or acceptance of the Torah, but through the pneumatic experience of baptism, which effects a spiritual transformation. Birth as a Jew and observance of the *mitsvot* are insufficient: It is faith that makes one an Israelite. Faithless Jews have lost the status of Abraham's offspring. They are like Ishmael, rejected in favor of Isaac, and like Esau, born of Isaac yet mysteriously rejected by God in favor of his brother Jacob.[40] Jews are branches mysteriously (and perhaps temporarily) lopped off the tree to make room for the gentiles graciously being grafted on through faith in Christ.[41]

---

[39] See Franz Rosenzweig, *The Star of Redemption* (New York: Holt, Rinehart, and Winston, 1970), pp. 336–379. This is a translation of the second German edition (1930). For a thorough discussion, see John T. Pawlikowski, *Christ in the Light of the Christian-Jewish Dialogue* (Studies in Judaism and Christianity; A Stimulus Book; New York: Paulist, 1982), pp. 8–35.

[40] Rom. 9:6–13. On this, see Levenson, *Death and Resurrection*, chap. 15.

[41] Rom. 11:13–18. But Paul's ambivalence does not allow us to make systematic sense of his letters. Note his implication of the continued election of the Jews in passages like Rom. 11:1–6, 19–24.

The community that Paul envisions in Galatians is indeed one
that has abolished fundamental Jewish distinctions. But Paul's thinking is hardly universalistic. He does not affirm the irrelevance of
Israelite identity, but only the uniqueness of faith and baptism as the
means of access to it. Whether one is heir to Abraham's promise still
means everything to Paul; although he specifies a different rite of
passage from that of the rabbis, like them, he still assumes that whether
one is in Israel or not is of supreme importance. He says that there
is neither Jew nor Greek among those *in Christ* and that whether one
is circumcised or not is of no account *in Christ*.[42] But he does not say,
his theology does not allow him or any other individual Christian to
say, that whether one is "in Christ" or not is inconsequential and
that whether one is baptized or not is of no account. Only if he said
these things could he be termed a universalist in a sense in which
the rabbis were not. Indeed, it is striking that Paul's theology seeks
to uphold gentile Christians as legitimate heirs not of Adam (whom
he makes into the negative antipode of the Christ in Rom. 5:12–21)
nor of Noah (whom he never mentions, despite the rabbinic traditions of Noah as the prototypical righteous gentile) but of Abraham,
the first Jew, as it were (see esp. Romans 4). To call early Christian
theology "inclusive," as is now often done, is to obscure the crucial
fact that it sought to include people only within a very particular
sub-category of universal humankind and did not affirm them within
their natural, Adamic state.

In point of fact, both Judaism and Christianity, to the extent that
they are true to their respective foundational literatures, must continue to affirm the essential dichotomy between insiders and outsiders, even as they mitigate and complicate the dichotomy in various
ways. The only difference is that the majoritarian character of Western Christianity tempts Christians to imagine that their religion is
universal, whereas minority groups are not similarly tempted. But
this seems to be changing. In a shrinking and often secularizing world,
Christians are becoming increasingly aware of their own particularity and culture-conditionedness. Undoubtedly, many of them will
continue to aspire to Christianize the globe; many will continue to
adhere to an exclusivism as extreme as any in all of Judaism and

---

[42] Gal. 3:26–29 and 5:6. For a hard-headed assessment of Paul's actual social
views, see G.E.M. de Ste. Croix, *The Class Struggle in the Ancient Greek World* (Ithaca,
N.Y.: Cornell University, 1981), pp. 103–111; 418–425.

more extreme than most, the exclusivism that affirms, in the words of the Jesus of Johannine tradition, "No one comes to the father except through me."[43] Nevertheless, the naive and unreflective contrast between a closed, ethnocentric Judaism and an open universal Christianity is likely to appear increasingly incredible.

Indeed, both Jewish and Christian identity are now threatened by an egalitarian theory of justice that is especially popular in contemporary America. This theory identifies justice not, as in the older liberalism, with equality before the law of the pluralistic state, but, increasingly, with equality of condition: inequities are seen as *ipso facto* proof of iniquities, and distinctive roles are seen as inherently oppressive, unless they are freely chosen (in which case they cease to be distinctive roles and become "lifestyles," or the like). Discrimination becomes the gravest of sins. (One sometimes suspects that in some people's ethics it is the *only* sin left.)

Neither Judaism nor Christianity can accede *in toto* to this egalitarian theory of justice without abandoning critical features of its foundational literature and undermining its own basis of existence, since, as we have seen, neither community advocates a natural and undifferentiated humanity, even one with the most commendable values. Rather, each community claims to be Israel and to give its members a unique and otherwise unavailable opportunity for participation in divine sonship. Neither Judaism nor Christianity can fully endorse an ethic of voluntarism in which obligations and roles are always freely chosen and can be resigned at will. Indeed, both communities call for a freely given assent to an identity not devised or chosen by persons, but conferred graciously by a mysterious deity, and both have classically refused to recognize conversion to another identity, religious or secular.[44] In the Bible, one sees an especially striking example of this curious simultaneous affirmation of choice and fate in Joshua's covenant ceremony at Shechem. In one breath Joshua offers Israel the choice of which god(s) to serve, and then in the next breath avers that if they choose any other than YHWH, YHWH will annihilate them (Josh. 24:15, 20). In classical biblical and rabbinic thought, whether Jews accept the *mitsvot* or not is their choice. But if they choose not to do so, they choose death (Deut. 30:15–20).

Judaism cannot survive the obliteration of the distinction between

---

[43] John 14:6.
[44] Similar statements could, *mutatis mutandis*, be made of Islam.

Jew and gentile (unless or until the nations convert to Judaism). Any theory of justice that engages in wholesale disparagement of accidents of birth and fated roles willy-nilly disparages Judaism. We have seen that the Bible offers impressive resources for a doctrine of human equality and that Talmud and midrash continue this stream of thought, endorsing a model of peoplehood that is non-racial and non-genetic, yet familial and earthly. But we have also seen that the sacred literature of Judaism legitimates and even mandates certain forms of inequality. Modern Jews, especially in the West, have been enthusiastic advocates of equality, in part because of their tradition, in part because a persecuted group stands to gain from equalization. But we must not lose sight of the essential distinction between the idea of *civic equality* and a thorough-going *egalitarianism* that undermines Jewish existence itself. The current tendency to identify equality with justice poses both a theoretical and a practical challenge to Judaism that we must not shrink from confronting.

VI. *Can Theology be Secularized?*

Our discussion of universalism and particularism in the Bible has sought to demonstrate the inadequacy of either term in dealing with the subtle, nuanced, and shifting biblical world view. On the one hand, the universality of God and of his realm are generally assumed. On the other, a single undifferentiated humanity is not assumed, except occasionally in primordial times and in some of the Wisdom Literature. The fractured unity of primeval humanity is to be restored in the reorientation of the nations toward YHWH enthroned in Jerusalem. Particularism is, on the one hand, very evident in the central concept of covenant: Israel is God's special possession, his firstborn son, who is assigned special obligations, special privileges, and a special destiny. Yet Israel exists only by the will and grace of God, and is constituted for divine service.

Can this world view, assembled synchronically out of the varying materials in Scripture, survive the demise of its theological matrix? I think not. We have already noted that when commandments are recast in the language of values, the effect is to undermine subtly and usually unintentionally the very basis of Jewish existence. Here, a convenient universalism is purchased at the price of an inconvenient and undemocratic particularism.

Ironically, secularization can also result in the opposite extreme, an exaggerated particularism purchased at the cost of the universal dimension of Judaism. I am thinking, for example, of the currently common habit of stressing Jewish survival as a goal in its own right. On occasion, we even hear Judaism itself commended on the grounds that it contributes to Jewish survival: "Keep kosher so that your children won't intermarry." Instead of Israel's existing for the service of God, God exists for the service of Israel. At its worst, the absolutization of Jewish survival leads to the denial of ethical constraints on a Jewry in danger. And since Jewry is usually in danger, this grants the Jews a moral *carte blanche*—quite the reverse of the biblical intent. If "ethics is the Judaism of the assimilated,"[45] then nationalism is the Judaism of the secularized.

Nothing is more delicate than the interplay of universalism and particularism in traditional Jewish theology. Take away the theology, and the interplay disappears or mutates. Observance is precious, but observance alone cannot ensure a Jew that it is the theology, rather than one of its modern derivatives, that is most active in his or her life. There is no substitute for theologically sophisticated scrutiny of the sacred sources.

---

[45] See n. 25.

CHRISTIANITY AND ETHNICITY IN THE GOSPEL OF MATTHEW

David C. Sim

The question of ethnicity was of paramount importance in the formative period of Christianity. That this was the case should occasion no surprise. The Christian church originated as a sect within Judaism which expressed certain convictions about a first century Jewish figure, Jesus of Nazareth. At that time, as in all periods of Jewish history, the various traditions which comprised Judaism took very seriously the notion of ethnicity, and the messianic movement associated with Jesus of Nazareth was no exception to this rule. So important was this issue that it threatened to tear apart the early church in the first few decades of its existence. In this paper I wish to revisit this ancient conflict between the various factions of the early church and focus in particular on the Gospel of Matthew. Is the question of ethnicity central for Matthew and, if it is, where do the evangelist and his community stand in relation to it? In order to answer these questions, it is necessary first to establish the relevant historical background. To this end, we shall discuss the issue of ethnicity in both first century Judaism and the primitive Christian movement prior to our analysis of the Gospel of Matthew and the community for whom it was written.

Ethnicity in First Century Judaism

As noted above, the question of ethnicity was of fundamental importance in all the traditions which comprised first century Judaism, and it was inextricably tied in with the distinctive Jewish notion of covenantal nomism.[1] The Hebrew scriptures detailed that God had chosen the Jews to be his elect people and that the two parties had entered into a holy covenant. The election of Israel gave this people special status vis-à-vis the other nations of the world; those born Jews were

---

[1] See E.P. Sanders, *Paul and Palestinian Judaism*, (London: SCM, 1977), pp. 75, 180, 236, 422–3, 426–8.

immediately members of the elect, while those born into the other nations were not. It was primarily this belief in the "racial" aspect of the covenant which made Judaism, in distinction to other religious traditions, a religion which emphasised ethnicity. But it should be noted that accompanying this privileged position of the Jews came great responsibility. The Jews, both individually and collectively, were expected to uphold the commandments of God which were collected in their sacred writings. This means that while Jews belonged to the covenant community by virtue of birth, they maintained their membership only by obedience to the torah which God had given specifically to them. These laws included, amongst others, the worship of one God, circumcision for men as a sign of the covenant, sabbath observance, and purity and dietary regulations.[2] Transgressions of these laws, which could place one outside the covenant and so liable for punishment, could be atoned for by true repentance and the performance of sacrifice as prescribed in the torah. Membership in ancient Judaism therefore involved two fundamental requirements; ethnicity (Jewishness) and the obligations which this entailed according to the covenant agreement.

When we turn to the sectarian groups which emerged in the second temple period, we find a slight variation on this basic pattern. As we might expect from minority groups which consciously differed from the mainstream, these sects had a more narrow definition of those Jews who were true to the covenant. Those who belonged to the sect were the faithful remnant, while the Jews who remained outside the sect were perceived to be apostates. For this reason, salvation was dependent upon membership in the sect rather than membership of the Jewish people. Outsiders could become members and so join the "true Israel," but they were required to submit to certain entrance requirements and then observe the distinctive regulations of the group, including its interpretation of the torah. This sectarian variation on the normal pattern is important and we shall return to it in due course. But before we leave this subject, it is important to bear in mind that despite their differences with the larger Jewish society, none of the major Jewish sects of this time eschewed the fundamental notion of the privileged position of the people of

---

[2] For a recent discussion of those laws affecting the majority of Jews, see E.P. Sanders, *Judaism: Practice and Belief 63 BCE–66 CE* (London: SCM, 1992), pp. 190–240.

Israel or the role of the torah. Membership in each sect was open only to Jews and obedience to the Mosaic laws (though interpreted differently by each sect) was always obligatory.

It is necessary at this point to examine more closely this concept of ethnicity within Judaism at the time of the formation of the Christian church. One point worthy of mention is that the Jewish emphasis on ethnicity did not lead the Jews to distance themselves from the Gentile world by remaining in the Jewish homeland. Most Jews of this period were content to live in the diaspora among larger populations of Gentiles, though they took steps to restrict their contact with Gentiles in order to preserve their social and ethnic identity. For example, there is good evidence that Jews were unwilling to share meals with their Gentile neighbours.[3] But an even more important point, particularly in view of the tendency of the Jewish people to erect boundaries between themselves and the Gentiles, is that their notion of ethnic privilege never led them to exclude those of the Gentile world from participation in their religion.[4] It is well known that in the ancient world many Gentiles were attracted to Judaism. They were especially impressed by its antiquity, its strict monotheism and its high moral character as expressed in the Hebrew scriptures and as exemplified by many of the Jews themselves.[5] Many of these Gentiles can be categorised as God-fearers or sympathetic supporters of Judaism who attended the synagogue and adopted certain Jewish ways but who had not converted completely to Judaism.[6] We find such people in the book of Acts (10:2, 22, 35; 13:16, 26, 43, 50;

---

[3] See the comprehensive discussion of this theme in P.F. Esler, *Community and Gospel in Luke-Acts: The Social and Political Motivations of Lucan Theology* (SNTSMS, 57; Cambridge: Cambridge University Press, 1987), pp. 73–86 and literature cited there.

[4] So correctly S. McKnight, *A Light Among the Gentiles: Jewish Missionary Activity in the Second Temple Period* (Minneapolis: Fortress Press, 1991), p. 30.

[5] On the attractiveness of Judaism to the Gentiles in the ancient world, see the detailed analysis by L.H. Feldman, *Jew and Gentile in the Ancient World* (Princeton: Princeton University Press, 1993), pp. 177–287.

[6] It has been argued that no such Gentile sympathisers existed in the ancient world. So A.T. Kraabel, "The Disappearance of the 'God-Fearers'," *Numen* 28 (1981), pp. 113–26. But Kraabel's views have been justly criticised and scholars continue to support the existence of these Gentiles, though it is still a matter of dispute as to whether they alone were known in the first century by the technical term "God-fearers." For discussion of these issues, see T.M. Finn, "The God-Fearers Reconsidered," *CBQ* 47 (1985), pp. 75–84; J.J. Collins. "A Symbol of Otherness: Circumcision and Salvation in the First Century," in J. Neusner and E.S. Frerichs (eds.), *"To See Ourselves As Others See Us": Christians, Jews, "Others" in late Antiquity* (Chico, California: Scholars Press, 1985), pp. 179–85; E. Schürer, *The History of the Jewish People in*

16:14; 17:4, 17; 18:7) and the picture there is confirmed by references in the writings of Josephus to Gentiles who revered and followed Jewish customs and laws (*Against Apion* 2.11, 40; *Jewish War*
2.20.2; 7.3.3; *Antiquities* 3.8.9; 20.8.11; cf. also 14.7.2).[7] Precisely which
aspects of Judaism were adopted by any given Gentile God-fearer
was presumably a matter of personal choice, but the evidence suggests that the laws concerning sabbath observance and dietary restrictions had widespread currency.[8] The status of these Gentile
sympathisers is evidenced by a passage in Josephus where he speaks
of a group of Gentiles in Antioch who were attracted to Jewish ceremonies and *in some measure* were incorporated with the Jews (*Jewish
War* 7.3.3). The fact that these Antiochene Gentiles were incorporated with the Jews only in some measure makes it clear that they
remained on the fringes of the Jewish community and were not fully
integrated into it.[9] We might conclude that from the standpoint of
the Jews themselves these Gentile sympathisers were clearly different
from and superior to those Gentiles who showed no interest in Judaism, but they were not counted as Jews and so they remained outside the covenant community.[10]

This brings us to a further important point in terms of Judaism
and its emphasis on ethnicity. Although the question of race was
crucial to their religion, the Jews never restricted membership of their
elect community only to those born Jews (though it would have been
understandable had they done so). In his apologetic response to Apion,
Josephus well makes the point that the Jewish practice of admitting
non-Jews into the people of Israel is more humane and magnani-
mous than the practice of the Spartans (and other Greeks) who rarely
granted citizenship to foreigners (*Against Apion* 2.37). Membership of
the people of Israel was therefore open to all, no matter whether
they were born Jewish or born to another race, and provision was

---

the *Age of Jesus Christ*, revised by G. Vermes, F. Millar, M. Black and M. Goodman,
(3 vols. in 4 parts; Edinburgh: T. & T. Clark, 1973, 1979, 1986, 1987), III.1, pp.
160–9; J.A. Overman, "The God-Fearers: Some Neglected Features," *JSNT* 32 (1988),
pp. 17–26; A.F. Segal, "The Costs of Proselytism and Conversion" in D.J. Lull
(ed.), *Society of Biblical Literature 1988 Seminar Papers* (Atlanta: Scholars Press, 1988),
pp. 350–3 and, more recently, McKnight, *A Light Among the Gentiles*, pp. 110–14 and
Feldman, *Jew and Gentile*, pp. 342–82.

[7] For non-Jewish and non-Christian references to such sympathisers, see Feldman,
Jew and Gentile, pp. 344–8.

[8] See Schürer *et al*, *History*, III.1, p. 169.

[9] Feldman, *Jew and Gentile*, p. 350.

[10] Schürer *et al*, *History*, III.1, p. 165.

made in Judaism for the full assimilation of converts into the covenant community. True converts or proselytes differed from the God-fearers or sympathisers insofar as they had chosen to embrace in full measure the Jewish way of life and all that the Jewish religion required. As a result of their conversion, proselytes were now counted as Jews and thus, unlike the God-fearers, they received the full benefits of membership in the elect community. Because the fully-committed proselyte was considered far superior to the less-committed God-fearer, it is probably accurate to say that the level of commitment attained by the God-fearer was never accepted by the Jews as an end in itself; it was merely a preparatory stage before the ultimate act of conversion.

For men such a conversion would normally have entailed circumcision of the foreskin.[11] This practice was a definitive sign of the covenant (Gen. 17:9–14) and there is good evidence that circumcision was the usual requirement for male proselytes in the second temple period. In the book of Judith (c. 160 BCE), Achior came to believe in the God of Israel, so he was circumcised and admitted to the people of Israel (14:10). Josephus reports that foreign male rulers who wished to marry into the Herodian household were expected to become Jews and be circumcised (*Antiquities* 20.7.1, 3; cf. 16.7.5). The Jewish historian also refers to two other instances of conversion. One of these concerns the conversion of the Roman general, Metilius, at the outbreak of the Jewish war (*Jewish War* 2.17.10). Having witnessed the massacre of his soldiers by the Jews, Metilius begged for mercy and promised to become a Jew by being circumcised. The other instance is the conversion of king Izates (*Antiquities* 20.2–4). Izates wished to convert to Judaism and supposed that to do so entirely he would need to be circumcised. His mother Queen Helena, though herself a Jewish convert, attempted to dissuade him on account of her belief that his subjects would not accept his conversion. Izates then consulted Ananias, a Jewish merchant who had taught the king and the royal household about Judaism. Like the king's mother,

---

[11] The entry requirements for women proselytes in this period are not known. It is possible, as some scholars have suggested, that they were baptised but there is no concrete evidence to support this. See McKnight, *A Light Among the Gentiles*, p. 148 n. 41 for scholars holding this view. The one text which details a female conversion to Judaism, the book of *Joseph and Asenath*, does not mention baptism as an essential ritual for the proselyte; on the contrary, the conversion of Asenath is accomplished by the rejection of idolatry (10:12–13; 11:4–5, 7–9), a long period of sincere repentance (10:1–8, 14–17) and the confession of her sins (11:3–13:15).

Ananias saw the political complications of such a conversion as well as the dangerous situation in which he himself would be placed, so he advised the king that he might worship God without being circumcised. God would forgive him this oversight on the grounds that circumstances dictated it. Izates was then visited by a Galilean named Eleazar who upbraided the king for not following what was clearly set down in the law, and Izates finally submitted to circumcision. This text is instructive insofar as it reveals that under certain conditions, in this case a set of extraordinary political circumstances and a sense of self-preservation, individual Jews were prepared to forgo the requirement of circumcision for converts. But the importance of this narrative lies in the fact that circumcision as the normal rite of entrance into Judaism is taken for granted. That Ananias says that God will forgive the king for not undergoing the operation is a clear indication that even in his understanding God expected his followers to be circumcised in accordance with his law. The point of view expressed by Izates himself and later by Eleazar, that (male) Gentiles must be circumcised for full incorporation into the Jewish people, must therefore be taken as the normative one.

The case of Ananias alerts us to the fact that there were some Jews who, for whatever reason, did not require proselytes to undergo circumcision. Philo provides another instance of this viewpoint when he speaks of certain Alexandrian Jews who dismissed physical circumcision in preference to an allegorical understanding of the ritual. In responding to these people, Philo himself accepts the allegorical interpretation of circumcision but maintains that the physical aspect is still essential and must be observed (*De Migratione Abrahami* 92). As interesting as these exceptions are, they should not be overemphasised. The evidence is clear that while a tiny number of Jews might have waived the requirement of physical circumcision, for reasons of ideology or expediency, the greater majority did not. For most Jews of this period, circumcision was an essential ritual which marked (for men) the crossing of the boundary between the Gentile and Jewish worlds.[12] It was no doubt the danger and pain associated with this

---

[12] Most scholars would largely agree with this judgement, though they might differ on how widespread were the exceptions to the rule. Those who play down the exceptions and claim that circumcision was always (with very few exceptions) a requirement for male converts, the correct view in my opinion, include Schürer *et al, History*, III.1 pp. 169, 173; Feldman, *Jew and Gentile*, pp. 157–8, 297–8, 299, 346, 347–8, 350–1 and J. Nolland, "Uncircumcised Proselytes?," *JSJ* 12 (1981), pp. 173–

operation that prevented many Gentile men from leaving the world of the God-fearer and entering the Jewish world in a complete manner.

The entry into the people of Israel by circumcision for Gentile men (and perhaps baptism for Gentile women) brought with it both privilege and obligation. As full members of the covenant community and no longer sympathisers on the fringe, proselytes were now counted among the elect and were, despite their origins, heirs to the ancient promises concerning the people of Israel. But alongside this privilege came the obligation to obey fully the law of God as given in the Hebrew scriptures (and as interpreted by the particular Jewish group into which they converted). This is evidenced by Paul when he tells the Galatians that any (Gentile) man who receives circumcision is bound to follow the law in its entirety (Gal. 5:3). Like any racial Jew, Gentile proselytes were expected to satisfy all the requirements for maintaining membership in the covenant community. By making these demands of its converts, Judaism was able to accept outsiders into its privileged community without sacrificing its ethnic identity.

Ethnicity in the Early Christian Church

It is appropriate at this point to turn to the early Christian church. What role did ethnicity play in the identity and character of this movement? The first thing which can be said is that in the first few years of the church all of its members were Jews. At this time the church counted among its numbers the disciples and the family of Jesus, all Jews by birth, and perhaps another hundred people (so Acts 1:15) who must also be reckoned as Jews since Luke refers to the whole group as 'Hebrews' (cf. 6:1). The author of Acts gives no hint that in this initial phase the Gentiles were ever approached by or accepted into the Christian community in Jerusalem. In his early speeches in Acts, Peter, the leader of the church, limits his proclamation solely to the Jews (Acts 2:5, 14, 22; 3:12), and only Jews are said to have been won over by his message (cf. 2:41), including priests

---

94. On the other hand, the alternative view which emphasises the exceptions and upholds that there was more diversity within Judaism on this issue is represented by McKnight, *A Light Among the Gentiles*, pp. 79–82; Collins, "A Symbol of Otherness," pp. 170–9; Segal, "Proselytism and Conversion," pp. 353–60 and N.J. McEleney, "Conversion, Circumcision and the Law," *NTS* 20 (1974), pp. 328–33.

(7:7) and Pharisees (15:5). Also converted at this early time were a number of Greek-speaking Jews from the diaspora who now resided in Jerusalem. Acts introduces these "Hellenists" in chapter 6 and they are said to count one proselyte, Nicolaus, among their number (6:5). It seems that the Hellenists conducted their own mission in the Greek-speaking synagogues of Jerusalem and attracted the anger of the Jews there (6:9) on account of their criticism of the basic institutions of Judaism, the law and the temple (6:13–14). The reason for this radical stance of the Hellenists is not immediately clear. Some scholars speculate that they were merely building upon Jesus' criticisms of the law and the temple cult,[13] but it is more probable that these diaspora Jews were influenced by the tendency, which Philo both noted and opposed, to allegorise the torah and abandon its literal interpretation.[14] In any event, the opposition the Hellenists encountered led to the martyrdom of Stephen (6:8–7:60) and the persecution of the rest which resulted in their hurried departure from Jerusalem (8:2). Though containing a large measure of legendary material, these initial chapters of Acts are probably correct in affirming that up to the time of the expulsion of the Hellenists the Jerusalem church was exclusively Jewish.[15] This is understandable, given that the church confined itself to Jerusalem which was the heart of the Jewish world and included few Gentiles among its permanent residents. Since no Gentiles had been actively approached and the church had no Gentile members (as distinct from proselytes who were counted as Jews), the grounds of admission for Gentiles into the primitive Christian movement had not yet become an issue on the agenda. But this situation was not to last.

It was the expulsion of the Hellenists from Jerusalem which proved to be the impetus for the Christian Gentile mission. And it was only when Gentiles were actively sought that the question of ethnicity in relation to the Christian movement became a practical problem.

---

[13] So M. Hengel, *Between Jesus and Paul: Studies in the Earliest History of Christianity* (London: SCM, 1983), pp. 22–4 and E. Haenchen, *The Acts of the Apostles* (Philadelphia: Westminster Press, 1971), pp. 267–8.

[14] See H. Räisenän, *Jesus, Paul and Torah: Collected Essays* (JSNTSS, 43; Sheffield: JSOT Press, 1992), pp. 190–1.

[15] Not all scholars agree with this conclusion. Some would argue that while in Jerusalem the Hellenists took their distinctive message not just to the Jews but to the Gentiles as well. So Räisenän, *Jesus, Paul and Torah*, pp. 186–8 and Esler, *Community and Gospel*, pp. 157–9. The problem with this thesis, however, is that there is no concrete evidence to support it.

Scholars are in general agreement that the initial approach to the Gentiles was begun by the law-critical Hellenists who travelled to Antioch (Acts 11:19–21).[16] Now situated in a firmly Gentile environment, the Hellenists took their law-critical attitude to its logical conclusion and announced to the Gentiles that they could become full followers of Jesus the messiah without requiring complete conversion to Judaism by circumcision (for men) and obedience to the requirements of the torah. In other words, they proclaimed a message about Jesus of Nazareth which effectively abandoned the Jewish notion of ethnicity and the privilege of the covenant community. It was this version of the Christian message which the converted Paul embraced when he settled in Antioch after his initial visit to Jerusalem (Gal. 1:18–20; Acts 11:25–6), and it was Paul who was destined to become its greatest defender. In taking up the banner of the Hellenists, Paul could later proclaim that since Christ is the end of the law (Rom. 10:4) there is no longer Jew or Greek (Rom. 10:12; 1 Cor. 12:13; Gal. 3:28; cf. Col. 3:11), circumcision or uncircumcision (Gal. 6:15); privilege now rests with all who have faith in Christ regardless of ethnicity and racial origins (Rom. 3:22). The fateful step of the Hellenists in initially granting full membership to the Gentiles without requiring them to convert in the normal Jewish manner is perhaps the single most important event in the entire history of the Christian church, and it raised for the first time the issue of ethnicity and the place of Gentiles within the fledgling Christian movement. Both Acts and the epistles of Paul testify that this development was strongly opposed by certain members of the Jerusalem church.

Luke describes these opponents as the circumcision party (οἱ ἐκ περιτομῆς; Acts 11:2), converted Pharisees who demanded that the Gentiles be circumcised (if male) and obey the requirements of the Mosaic law (Acts 15:1, 5). Paul refers to this group also as the circumcision party (Gal. 2:12) or false brethren (Gal. 2:4), who compel circumcision (Gal. 6:12) and mutilate the flesh (Phil. 3:2). Much of Paul's theological agenda, particularly in Galatians and Romans, was devoted to disproving their position and defending his own law-free

---

[16] So most scholars: see W.A. Meeks and R.L. Wilken, *Jews and Christians in Antioch in the First Four Centuries of the Common Era* (Missoula: Scholars Press, 1978), pp. 13–14; M. Hengel, *Acts and the History of Earliest Christianity* (London: SCM, 1979), pp. 99–100; J.P. Meier, "Antioch," in R.E. Brown and J.P. Meier, *Antioch and Rome* (New York: Paulist Press, 1983), p. 33 and G. Luedemann, *Early Christianity according to the Tradition in Acts: A Commentary* (London: SCM, 1989), p. 136.

stance. Despite the quite unflattering portrayal of these people in
Acts and the Pauline letters (and in much of the scholarly literature
for that matter!), these believers in Jesus as the prophesied messiah
should be treated with both sympathy and empathy. They were not
conservative legalists who failed to understand the implications of
the Christ event, but ordinary Jews who clearly took seriously the
ancient Jewish traditions in the Hebrew scriptures which emphasised
the eternal covenant between God and the nation of Israel, and the
role which the law played in the context of that covenant. Unlike
the Hellenists and Paul, the circumcision party[17] saw nothing in the
life, death and resurrection of Jesus the messiah which abrogated
this fundamental principle of Judaism. The new revelation of the
Christ complemented rather than rescinded the ancient covenant
between God and his people. Given the traditional views of these
people, their attitude towards Gentile converts to their messianic
movement within Judaism is both understandable and logical. Gentiles were welcome to join their Christian sect, but in accordance
with the covenant agreement they were expected to join the Jewish
people by circumcision (if male) and obey the demands of the torah.
It is essential to note, however, that this was only a preliminary step.
Despite the impression given by Paul and Acts, the circumcision party
had no intention of merely making Jews of Gentiles; on the contrary, they wished to make the Gentiles followers of Jesus the Christ.
On their terms this process involved Gentiles first becoming Jews in
the usual manner and then entering their messianic sect, probably
through the ritual of baptism. They would remain in the community
by obeying the law (as the circumcision party understood it) and by
adopting the distinctive sectarian beliefs and practices of this messianic group, whatever they might have been at that time. These
additional demands of initiation and adherence to specifically Christian beliefs and practices would also have been expected of Jewish
converts, a point which is often overlooked because our sources deal
only with the issue of Gentile converts. But it stands to reason that
the circumcision party, like the Qumran community and other sectarian groups, believed that mere Jewishness and obedience to the

---

[17] Despite the fact that the term "the circumcision party" was almost certainly
coined by their opponents and not used as a self-designation, I will retain it for
want of a better alternative. By contrast with Paul and the author of Acts, I do not
use the term in a pejorative sense; it is intended merely to be descriptive of the
viewpoint of these people.

law were no longer sufficient for salvation. While these two elements were still essential prerequisites for these followers of Jesus, they were now joined by other demands such as faith in Jesus as the prophesied messiah who was killed and then raised from the dead. When we look at the standpoint of these people from this perspective, it is simplistic to claim that they were interested only in "judaising" Gentiles. A fairer assessment would say that they were interested in converting all people, both Jew and Gentile, to the movement initiated by God's messiah, and for Gentiles this entailed a preliminary step of conversion to the Jewish community according to the ancient covenant between Israel and God.

The factional conflict between the Hellenists and the circumcision party posed such a serious threat to the primitive Christian movement that the so-called apostolic council was convened in the year 48 to settle the matter. The law-free gospel of the Hellenist Antiochene church was to be assessed by the leaders of the Jerusalem church—James, the brother of Jesus, and the disciples, Peter and John. Paul, Barnabas and at least one other person were chosen to represent the church in Antioch (Acts 15:2; Gal. 2:1–2). Precisely what happened at this important meeting is difficult to determine since our two accounts of these events, Acts 15 and Gal. 2:1–10, contradict one another at many points. One thing which can be said with some certainty is that the account in Acts of the outcome of this meeting is especially difficult to accept as it stands. James, the brother of Jesus proposes a compromise, the so-called apostolic decree, which is accepted by all the members of the church (15:13–29). According to this decree, the Gentile Christians do not need to be circumcised and obey the whole torah, but they must observe a number of laws akin to the levitical rules governing foreigners in the land of Israel (Lev. 17–18); they were to abstain from idolatry and unchastity, and refuse to eat blood and the meat from a strangled animal. This compromise of James in Acts means essentially that Gentiles could become followers of Jesus without converting to Judaism in the normal fashion. It granted full membership rights to uncircumcised Gentiles who obeyed some of the Jewish laws. In short, according to Luke's understanding, the decree gave God-fearers the same status as proselytes.[18] The narrative in Acts presents the solution of James as definitive. All parties agreed to it (15:22) and never

---

[18] So too T. Callan, "The Background of the Apostolic Decree (Acts 15:20, 29;

again does Acts refer to the status of the Gentiles in the Christian church. It is presumed that the edict from James became normative (cf. 21:25) and that the issue of ethnicity in the church had finally been decided.[19]

The Pauline version of the apostolic council and its aftermath gives an entirely different picture. Paul knows nothing of such a compromise of James, and he contradicts the Acts account by declaring that he would not compromise his position (Gal. 2:5) and that after hearing his defence of his gospel, the leaders of the Jerusalem church added nothing to him (Gal. 2:6). Apart from Paul's testimony, there is another reason to doubt the compromise of James as Acts reports. Such a solution would not have satisfied any of the disputants who were at extreme ends of the theological spectrum. The requirement that the Gentiles observe only some of the Mosaic laws would have been just as unacceptable to the Hellenists and Paul who demanded freedom from the law as to those of the circumcision party who demanded its full observance.[20] In addition to this and again by contrast with Acts, the Pauline epistles also make it clear that the conflict between the two factions continued after the meeting in Jerusalem. Although Paul affirms unequivocally that he successfully put his case to the Jerusalem church and was permitted to continue his law-free mission to the Gentiles, it seems likely that the situation was not as clear as Paul would have us believe. The old conflicts were not resolved in Jerusalem and they soon flared again. Immediately after his narration of the apostolic council, Paul describes an important incident which took place in Antioch (Gal. 2:11–14).

Not long after the meeting in Jerusalem, Peter came to Antioch and ate with the Gentile Christians until certain men came from James in Jerusalem. Upon their arrival and fearing the circumcision party, Peter withdrew from table-fellowship with the Gentiles. He was followed in this by Barnabas and the remainder of the Jewish Christians in Antioch. Paul then openly opposed Peter to his face and accused him of hypocrisy. How could Peter live like a Gentile and not like a Jew and yet compel the Gentiles to live like Jews?

21:25)," *CBQ* 55 (1993), pp. 295–7 and A.J.M Wedderburn. "The 'Apostolic Decree': Tradition and Redaction," *NovT* 35 (1993), pp. 376–7.

[19] P.J. Achtemeier, *The Quest for Unity in the New Testament Church* (Philadelphia: Fortress Press, 1987), p. 42.

[20] So correctly, Achtemeier, *Quest for Unity*, pp. 54–5. Even so, Achtemeier still accepts the historicity of James' compromise.

Although scholars vary widely over the precise meaning of these events, the simplest explanation is that the men from James represented the circumcision party and they came to Antioch with the blessing of James to impose their point of view. Gentile Christians could no longer be full members of the Christian movement unless they ful- filled the preliminary requirements of conversion to the Jewish faith by circumcision (for men) and observance of the torah.[21] That this was the case is suggested by Paul's statement that in abiding by the wishes of the visitors, Peter now compelled the Gentiles to live like Jews. As most scholars acknowledge, Paul lost the battle at Antioch.[22] He left the city and began new missions in Asia Minor and Greece where he converted many Gentiles to his law-free version of Chris- tianity. But as Paul's letters testify, his conflict with the circumcision party did not cease in Antioch. We know from the epistle to the Galatians that members of this group travelled to Galatia to impose their own form of Christianity on Paul's Gentile converts, and it is likely that they were expected to arrive in the Philippian church as well (Phil. 3:2–11). This evidence demonstrates that the issue of ethnicity within the Christian church and the related problem of the requirements for Gentile converts was not resolved either in Jerusa- lem or in Antioch; these important questions remained contentious throughout the lifetime of Paul and his opponents.

And these unresolved issues continued in the church for generations after the time of Paul. The successors of Paul upheld his conviction that Gentiles did not need to become Jews in order to become Christians and they disputed with any Christians who held the opposite point of view. This is well evidenced in the pastoral epistles (cf. 1 Tim. 1:4, 6–7, 14; 4:3–5, 7; 2 Tim. 4:4; Tit. 3:9) and the letters of Ignatius of Antioch (Mag. 8:1–10:3; Philad. 6:1–2; 8:2–9:2). On the other hand, the heirs of the circumcision party showed no incli- nation to relinquish their law-observant stance. We know of second century Jewish groups, such as the Nazarenes, the Ebionites and the Elkesaites, who not only required circumcision and torah-observance

---

[21] For defence of this interpretation, see Esler, *Community and Gospel*, pp. 87–8; F. Watson, *Paul, Judaism and the Gentiles: A Sociological Approach* (SNTSMS, 56; Cam- bridge: University Press, 1986), pp. 54–5; H.D. Betz, *Galatians* (Hermeneia; Phila- delphia: Fortress Press, 1979), pp. 111–12 and G. Howard, *Paul: Crisis in Galatia* (SNTSMS, 35; Cambridge: University Press, second edition, 1990), pp. 24–8.

[22] See, most recently, N. Taylor, *Paul, Antioch and Jerusalem: A Study in Relationships and Authority in Earliest Christianity* (JSNTSS, 66; Sheffield: JSOT Press, 1992), p. 137 and literature cited there.

as requirements for membership into the Christian community, but also were overtly critical of Paul.[23] Their theology is well preserved in a number of documents, including the pseudo-Clementine *Recognitions* and *Homilies*, and the *Kerygmata Petrou*. Bearing in mind that this intra-Christian conflict over the privileged position of Israel and the role of the law in the Christian church continued well after the time of Paul and his opponents, we may now turn our attention to the Gospel of Matthew and the community for whom he wrote. How did the evangelist and his church stand on this fundamental issue? Did they agree with Paul and the Hellenists, or were they in agreement with the circumcision party?

Ethnicity in the Gospel of Matthew

The answers to these questions are to be found in Matthew's statements about the conditions of entry to his particular Christian community. As many scholars have noted, the final pericope of the Gospel is of absolute importance in this respect. Here the risen Lord instructs his disciples to make disciples of all the nations (μαθητεύσατε πάντα τὰ ἔθνη) by baptising them in the name of the father, the son and the holy spirit and teaching them to observe all Jesus commanded them (28:16–20). For many commentators this final passage establishes two important things about the evangelist and his community.

First, it can be inferred from the command to evangelise all the nations that the Matthean church was directly involved in a mission to the Gentiles. The phrase πάντα τὰ ἔθνη in 28:19 obviously refers to the Gentile peoples, though there is some dispute as to whether it includes the Jews as well. While some commentators argue that the phrase alludes only to the Gentiles and so excludes the Jews from the Matthean mission,[24] others contend that it includes both the

---

[23] For discussion of these and other Jewish-Christian groups of the second and later centuries, see A.F.J. Klijn and G.J. Reinink, *Patristic Evidence for Jewish-Christian Sects* (Leiden: Brill, 1973). On the question of the antipathy toward Paul of Jewish-Christian groups and writings in the post-Pauline period, see G. Luedemann, *Opposition to Paul in Jewish Christianity* (Minneapolis: Fortress Press, 1989), pp. 119–99.

[24] See D.R.A. Hare and D.J. Harrington. "'Make Disciples of all the Gentiles' (Mt 28:19)," *CBQ* 37 (1975), pp. 359–69.

Gentiles and the Jews.[25] The second alternative is clearly the better of the two since it is fully consistent with the meaning of the phrase elsewhere in the Gospel, and it agrees with the evidence of the mission discourse in chapter 10 which implies that the Matthean community was to be actively involved in the Jewish mission until the parousia (cf. 10:23).[26] In any event, all scholars would agree that the risen Christ's command to evangelise definitely applies to the Gentile world, in which case it can be accepted that the Matthean community participated in the Gentile mission. The second inference usually drawn from this pericope is that the condition of entry to Matthew's community was baptism alone. Since there is no mention of circumcision in the charge of the risen Lord (or elsewhere in the Gospel), it must be concluded that the Matthean church did not expect its (male) Gentile converts to undergo this ritual operation. In other words, there was no expectation that Gentiles were to become Jews in order to become (Matthean) Christians. If this were the case, then by extension of the argument it can be concluded further that the Gentiles in the Matthean church were not bound by the obligation to uphold the torah.[27] On this understanding of this text, the evangelist and his community had abandoned the notion of Jewish privilege and the necessity of the law in the light of the Christ event. Consequently, they stood in the tradition of Paul and the Hellenists.

Both of these inferences can be questioned. Despite the widespread point of view that the Matthean community was directly involved in the Gentile mission, a careful reading of the Gospel supports the conclusion that the Matthean community had never conducted a Gentile mission prior to the time of the Gospel's composition and probably did not entertain initiating one in the foreseeable future.[28] The only text which seems to point to such a mission is indeed 28:19,

---

[25] See J.P. Meier, "Nations or Gentiles in Matthew 28:19?," *CBQ* 39 (1977), pp. 94–102.

[26] For detailed arguments, see S. Brown. "The Mission to Israel in Matthew's Central Section (9:35–11:1)," *ZNW* 69 (1978), pp. 74–5; J. Gnilka, *Das Matthäus-evangelium*, (HTKNT; 2 vols., Freiburg: Herder, 1986, 1988), I, p. 379 and W.D. Davies and D.C. Allison, *A Critical and Exegetical Commentary on the Gospel according to Saint Matthew*, (ICC; 2 vols.; Edinburgh: T. & T. Clark, 1988, 1991), II, p. 190.

[27] So Davies and Allison, *Matthew*, I, p. 193; Meier, "Antioch," p. 62; R.T. France, *Matthew: Evangelist and Teacher*, (Exeter: Paternoster Press, 1989), pp. 234–5 and D.A. Hagner, "The *Sitz im Leben* of the Gospel of Matthew," in K.H. Richards (ed.), *SBL 1985 Seminar Papers* (Atlanta: Scholars Press, 1985), p. 255.

[28] See D.C. Sim, "The Gospel of Matthew and the Gentiles," *JSNT* 57 (1995), pp. 39–44.

but we should be careful not to confuse acceptance of the validity of a mission with active involvement in it. This point can be illustrated by recalling Paul's account of the outcome of the apostolic council. According to Paul, the council agreed upon a strict demarcation of the Christian mission. He would continue his mission to the Gentiles and the Jerusalem authorities would conduct the mission to the Jews. If this version of events can be trusted, then it is clear that each party accepted the validity of the other's mission while taking no part in it. There is no reason why the same cannot apply to the Matthean community. It might have accepted the validity of the two missions, and yet only carried out such a mission to the Jews. One point in favour of this hypothesis is the well known fact that in Matthew's Gospel Peter assumes far greater importance than in any of the other three Gospels. On the basis of a number of texts (16:18–19; cf. 7:24–7), it seems likely that the Matthean community saw itself standing firmly in the Petrine tradition. Now if Peter was delegated the apostle to the Jews as Paul tells us in Gal. 2:7, then we should expect that Matthew's Petrine church would have followed suit. For our purposes, there is no need press this point. Even if it is conceded on the slim evidence of 28:19 that Matthew's church was involved in a mission to the Gentiles, does it follow that this was a law-free mission in the tradition of Paul and the Hellenists? I would argue that such a conclusion is not warranted by the evidence of the Gospel. Scholars have focused too much on the ritual of baptism in 28:19 and not sufficiently acknowledged the other requirements of the risen Lord in the following verse. The new disciples are certainly to be baptised, but they are also to be taught all that Jesus commanded and obey these teachings. When we examine the teaching of Jesus in Matthew's Gospel, we can hardly fail to notice that it places strong emphasis on obedience to the Mosaic torah.

This is nowhere more clearly stated than in 5:17–19. In this important section of the sermon on the mount, Jesus instructs his disciples on the continued validity of the law in the light of his mission. He begins with the strong affirmation that it should not be thought that he has come to abolish the law and the prophets. On the contrary, he has come to fulfil them. Jesus then states that not one iota will pass from the law until heaven and earth pass away (or all is accomplished), and he concludes by saying that whoever relaxes even the least of these laws and teaches others to do so will be called least (by those) in the kingdom of heaven. Despite the variety of scholarly interpretations of these verses,[29] their meaning for Matthew is crystal clear; the whole law remains valid and is not abolished in the light of the Christ event. In typical Jewish fashion, the Matthean Jesus summarises the law under the principles of love of God and neighbour (22:34–40; cf. 7:12), but in agreement with 5:19 he emphasises as well that the less weighty commandments, such as those which pertain to tithing mint, dill and cummin, must be obeyed to the full (23:23). It can be inferred from 5:18 that Matthew does set a temporal limit to the observance of the torah: the law remains in effect only until the time of the parousia (heaven and earth passing away).[30] Until that time, however, the demands of the torah remain valid and binding and must be obeyed by those who follow Jesus the messiah.

In response to the question of how the law is to be followed, the evangelist provides a christological answer. The torah is to be followed according to Jesus' definitive messianic exegesis; his authoritative exposition is what brings the law to its fulfilment. This is illustrated by the antitheses (Matt. 5:21–48) where the Matthean Jesus radicalises the law to include internal emotions along with external actions. The same can be said of the conflict stories in the Gospel where Jesus debates with his opponents on the subject of the law. In the Marcan tradition, Jesus disputes with the Pharisees over the validity of the law; Jesus either breaks the law or speaks against it and so comes into conflict with the law-observant Pharisees (cf. Mark 3:23–8; 3:1–6; 7:1–23; 10:2–12). But there is none of this in Matthew, as we would expect from an author who unquestionably affirms the necessity of keeping the whole torah (5:17–19). Rather, the conflict always centres on the proper exegesis of the law (cf. Matt. 12:1–14: 15:1–20; 19:3–9; 22:34–46). Jesus constantly opposes the Pharisaic oral interpretation of the torah, but he never speaks against the written law itself. These points cannot be defended here in detail. It is sufficient to draw attention to those recent studies of Matthew's treatment of the torah which reach these conclusions after close examination of the relevant texts.[31]

---

[29] See the major commentaries; for example, Davies and Allison, *Matthew*, I, pp. 482–98 and U. Luz, *Matthew 1–7* (Minneapolis: Augsburg Press, 1989), pp. 259–69.
[30] For discussion of this point, see D.C. Sim, "The Meaning of παλλιγγενεσία in Matthew 19:28," *JSNT* 50 (1993), p. 8 n. 12 and literature cited there.
[31] So, with varying nuances, R. Mohrlang, *Matthew and Paul: A Comparison of Ethical Perspectives* (SNTSMS, 48; Cambridge: University Press, 1984), pp. 7–26; J.A. Overman, *Matthew's Gospel and Formative Judaism: The Social World of the Matthean Community*

Matthew's emphatic insistence that the torah still remains operative in the light of the Christ event has certain corollaries. One of these is that Matthew and his community accepted the normative Jewish view regarding the covenant between Israel and God and the role which the Mosaic law plays in the context of that covenant. But although Matthew agrees that the people of Israel are in a privileged position vis-à-vis the other nations of the world, this point requires clarification. The latest studies of the social setting of the Matthean community have emphasised its sectarian nature vis-à-vis the remainder of the Jewish world. The church for whom the Gospel was written was a self-defined sect in opposition to the coalition of forces which comprised formative Judaism in the years following the first Jewish war.[32] In an attempt to legitimate his group's sectarian status, the evangelist denounces in the strongest terms the leaders of the opposition parent body, the scribes and Pharisees (cf. 23:4–39), and consigns these people as well as those who follow them to the eternal fires of Gehenna (3:7–12; 23:15, 33; cf. 8:11–12; 19:28; 25:31–46). Like other sectarian Jewish groups of the period, the Matthean community no longer saw membership in the people of Israel and obedience to the law as sufficient for salvation (cf. 3:8). For the evangelist, salvation now lay with following the Christ. Consequently, Jews who wished to be saved and not condemned at the judgement needed to take the extra step of conversion to Matthew's messianic sect and adopt its distinctive sectarian beliefs and practices with regard to Jesus the messiah, including obedience to his definitive exposition of the torah.

A second corollary of Matthew's viewpoint on the law concerns the question of his stance within the early Christian factional dispute. The complete contrast between Matthew's position on the torah and Paul's comment that Christ is the end of the law (Rom. 10:4) could not be more obvious,[33] and it reveals that the Matthean community stood in the tradition of, and chronologically between, the

(Minneapolis: Fortress Press, 1990), pp. 78–90 and A.J. Saldarini, *Matthew's Christian-Jewish Community* (Chicago: University of Chicago Press, 1994), pp. 124–64.

[32] See especially the comprehensive treatments by Overman, *Matthew's Gospel and Formative Judaism* and Saldarini, *Matthew's Christian-Jewish Community*. Cf. also B. Przybylski, "The Setting of Matthean Anti-Judaism," in P. Richardson and O. Granskou (eds.), *Anti-Judaism in Early Christianity, Vol. I* (Waterloo: Wilfred Laurier Press, 1988), pp. 181–200 and G.N. Stanton, *A Gospel for a New People: Studies in Matthew* (Edinburgh: T. & T. Clark, 1992), esp. pp. 85–107.

[33] See the comparison between Matthew and Paul on the issue of the law by Mohrlang, *Matthew and Paul*, pp. 42–7.

circumcision party which opposed Paul and the later Jewish Christian sects which so vilified him. In the light of this, the comparatively rare hypothesis that certain texts in the Gospel are directed specifically against Paul (e.g. 5:19) or his law-free gospel (7:15–23; 13:41–2) warrants far more attention than it currently commands.[34] The third corollary follows on from this. Matthew's acceptance of the continuing validity of the old covenant between God and Israel can only mean that any Gentile who wished to become a follower of the messiah must become a member of the Jewish people as the first decisive step prior to entering Matthew's sectarian (Christian) Jewish community. This means of course that any male Gentile converts were obliged to submit to circumcision. From Matthew's perspective, uncircumcised male Gentiles who claim to follow Jesus might be preferable to the scribes and Pharisees who oppose him, but without full conversion to the nation of Israel they remain outside the Matthean community just as much as any of Matthew's opponents.

It is sometimes suggested by scholars who acknowledge Matthew's insistence on obedience to the torah that the Matthean community differentiated between Jewish converts and Gentile converts on the issue of the law and the necessity of circumcision for Gentile men. W.D. Davies and D.C. Allison, for example, argue that Matthew wished Jewish Christians to keep the law (so 5:17–19), but exempted Gentile Christians from this requirement (so 28:16–20).[35] A similar view is proposed by U. Luz who suggests that Matthew distinguished between the many demands of the Mosaic law. The more weighty commandments concerned the moral law which all were expected to follow, while the cultic and ritual requirements (including circumcision) were of less importance and may have been dispensed with for Gentile converts.[36] Yet another argument is that recently proposed by A.J. Saldarini who builds his case on the diversity of Jewish opinion concerning the necessity of circumcision for entry to the Jewish

---

[34] Those who have argued for an anti-Pauline polemic in the Gospel of Matthew (or its sources) include T.W. Manson, *The Sayings of Jesus* (London: SCM, 1949), pp. 25, 154; S.G.F. Brandon, *The Fall of Jerusalem and the Christian Church* (London: SPCK, 1951), pp. 232–6; F.W. Beare, *The Gospel according to Matthew* (Oxford: Basil Blackwell, 1981), p. 141; H.D. Betz, *Essays on the Sermon on the Mount* (Philadelphia: Fortress Press, 1985), pp. 20–1 and A.F. Segal, "Matthew's Jewish Voice," in D.L. Balch (ed.), *Social History of the Matthean Community: Cross-Disciplinary Approaches* (Minneapolis: Fortress Press, 1991), pp. 21–2.

[35] Davies and Allison, *Matthew*, 1, pp. 492–3.

[36] Luz, *Matthew*, I, p. 86

community. Like some other Jews of this time, the Matthean community might have waived this ritual requirement for its (male) Gentile converts in favour of baptism.[37] The major problem with all these views is that the Matthean Jesus stipulates obedience to the whole law without qualification, no matter how the constituent parts of the law are ranked and no matter how many other Jews (no doubt a very small number outside the Christian sphere) had decided to abandon the need for circumcision. And he makes no distinction between those born Jews and those born Gentiles. The words of the Matthean Jesus in 5:17–19 have universal application which would have made it impossible for Matthew's community to have included Gentiles who did not obey all the regulations of the torah, including circumcision for male converts.

This point is supported by the often ignored material in 18:15–17 which relates to forgiveness within the confines of the Matthean community. It concludes on the solemn note that if a wrongdoer does not repent, then he or she is to be treated as a Gentile and a tax-collector (cf. also 5:46–7; 6:7–8, 32). While most scholars agree that what is enjoined is the expulsion of the offender from the community,[38] they fail to draw the correct inference from this observation. Since the unrepentant sinner is to be excluded in the same way as Gentiles and tax-collectors are excluded, it must be inferred that Gentiles *per se* were not a part of the Matthean church; the text would make little sense if they were. While this does not necessarily mean that there were no persons of Gentile origin in this church, it does mean that Matthew no longer considered them to be Gentiles. Consequently, he must have perceived such Gentile converts to his community as Jews who, like the ethnic Jews in his community, were to avoid contact with the Gentile world. And if these people were now counted as Jews and no longer as Gentiles, then it stands to reason that they had taken the preliminary step of conversion to Judaism before entering Matthew's sectarian Jewish community. This is as much as we would expect from a community for which not one jot or tittle of the law had been abrogated by the coming of the messiah.

---

[37] Saldarini, *Matthew's Christian-Jewish Community*, pp. 156–60.

[38] See G. Forkman, *The Limits of the Religious Community: Expulsion from the Religious Community within the Qumran Sect, within Rabbinic Judaism, and within Primitive Christianity* (CBNTS, 5; Lund: Gleerup, 1972), pp. 124–32. Cf. also Davies and Allison, *Matthew*, II, p. 785; Overman, *Matthew's Gospel and Formative Judaism*, pp. 103–4 and Meier, "Antioch," pp. 68–9.

Matthew's position on this question need not remain a theoretical proposition. He provides a concrete example of the manner in which Matthean Christians (as Jews) are to deal with those of the Gentile world, and the role model is none other than Jesus himself. P.F. Esler has drawn attention to the fact that in their respective narratives about Jesus, Matthew and Mark differ considerably on the issue of table-fellowship between Jews and Gentiles and much of the following discussion is indebted to Esler's work.[39] The relevant section in Mark is 7:1–30. In vv. 1–23 Jesus disputes with the Pharisees about defilement. The Pharisees accuse the disciples of eating with unwashed hands (vv. 2–5) to which Jesus responds, "There is nothing outside a man which by going into him can defile him, but the things which come out of him are what defile him" (v. 16). The things which come from within and lead to defilement are later identified as evil thoughts, fornication, envy, slander and a host of other wicked emotions (vv. 20–3). As for the things which enter a person but do not lead to defilement, Mark leaves his readers in no doubt that what Jesus meant here were the foods which the Pharisees (or the Jews) believed to be unclean. He makes this point by appending in v. 19b, "Thus he made all foods clean." This Marcan episode amounts essentially to an abolition of the Jewish dietary laws, and it is no coincidence that it is followed by a practical application of this new principle by the Marcan Jesus (vv. 24–30). Jesus travels to the Gentile region of Tyre and Sidon and enters a house there. While in this house he is asked by a Syro-Phoenician (Gentile) woman to heal her possessed daughter and, after some discussion, Jesus complies with her request. The significant aspect of this story for our purposes is not that Jesus heals a Gentile (from a distance!), but that he willingly enters the house of a Gentile and by implication eats with the Gentile householders (cf. the discussion about bread in vv. 27–8). Since Jews normally avoided such practices on account of the potential impurity of the food offered by Gentile hosts, the Marcan Jesus is putting into practice his earlier principle that all foods are clean so that now there is no barrier to separate table-fellowship between Jews and Gentiles. This very Pauline stance indicates very clearly Mark's position within the factional dispute in the early church, just as Matthew's redaction of this Marcan material informs us about his particular point of view.

---

[39] Esler, *Community and Gospel*, pp. 89–93.

Matthew's revision of Mark 7:1–30 appears in 15:1–28. In the conflict with the Pharisees over defilement (15:1–20), Matthew makes two significant redactional changes to his Marcan source. The first is that he omits Mark's interpretative statement that Jesus actually declared all foods to be clean. Secondly, he appends 15:20 which makes the point that, contrary to the Pharisaic teaching, eating with unwashed hands does not cause defilement. By editing his source in these ways, Matthew completely alters the meaning of the pericope. No longer does Jesus abolish the Jewish dietary laws concerning unclean food: rather, he speaks against the specific practice of the Pharisees with respect to handwashing prior to eating. In other words, he rejects the oral tradition of the Pharisees but he does not negate the demands of the torah. Matthew's acceptance of the Jewish food laws which restricted social intercourse between Jews and Gentiles is affirmed in his account of the Gentile woman who seeks Jesus' help (15:21–8). By contrast with the Marcan version, Matthew has the contact between the two occur out in the open and not in the house of a Gentile. This editorial change presents Jesus acting fully in accordance with the social conventions which Jews adopted in their dealings with Gentiles, and it forestalls any suggestion that he broke down the barriers between Jew and Gentile by sharing a table with a Gentile. The fact that Matthew follows Mark in having Jesus begrudgingly heal the woman's daughter does not alter this in any way. The messiah might have compassion on sick Gentiles, but he still observes the practices which preserved the social and ethnic identity of the Jews. The example of Jesus clearly serves as a role model for the Matthean community and it demonstrates in practical terms the outsider status of the Gentiles in relation to it (cf. 18:17). Like most Jews, including those of circumcision party which opposed Paul at Antioch, the evangelist and his church would not countenance mixing freely with Gentiles for risk of breaching the dietary and purity laws. This typically Jewish attitude would have made it impossible for there to have been uncircumcised (if male), law-free Gentiles in the Matthean church alongside circumcised (if male) law-observant Jews. Full incorporation of the Gentiles into this Jewish community required no less than full conversion to the people of Israel as a necessary preliminary step.

But if it is true that this Christian Jewish group demanded obedience to the torah of its Gentile converts, including circumcision for men, then why does Matthew in 28:19 mention baptism and not circumcision as the decisive ritual for entry into his Christian community? This is a valid question to which I would suggest one of two answers in response. The first of these takes as its starting point the thesis, which was stated above, that the Matthean community was engaged in a mission solely to the Jews and not to the Gentiles. If this were indeed the case, then a reference to circumcision as the mark of entry to the Matthean community would be superfluous, since any prospective male converts would already have been circumcised. Matthew understandably mentions baptism alone for this was the (Christian) ritual which inducted converting Jews to his messianic sect. But if it is accepted in accord with the scholarly consensus that the Matthean church conducted a mission to the Gentiles, then I would offer a second response which runs along similar lines.

The evangelist's acceptance of the privilege of Israel and the necessity of law-observance for remaining in the covenant means that only Jews could become followers of Jesus the messiah. It stands to reason then that Matthew focuses on the entry requirements for that ethnic group alone. There is no need to mention circumcision for (male) Gentile converts because Matthew was concerned not with the preliminary step of conversion to the Jewish nation, but with the specifically Christian ritual which admitted all Jews, whether by birth or proselytism, to his sectarian Jewish group. It is therefore presumed by author and reader alike that any Gentiles who wished to join their messianic sect must proselytise first in order to satisfy the basic requirements for admission; circumcision for male Gentiles is simply taken for granted.[40] We can illustrate this point by referring to the admission procedures of a contemporary Jewish sect, the Qumran community. This sectarian group counted proselytes among its members, even though they were ranked at the bottom of the hierarchy (CD 14:4–6). Yet the complex admission requirements of this community which took years to complete (cf. 1QS 6:13–23) say nothing about circumcision. The reason for this is that only Jews could join the Qumran community and its entry requirements simply presumed that potential Gentile members would become Jews as a necessary

---

[40] The view that Matthew assumes rather than states the necessity for circumcision is affirmed by Mohrlang, *Matthew and Paul*, pp. 44–5; A.-J. Levine, *The Social and Ethnic Dimensions of Matthean Salvation History: 'Go nowhere among the Gentiles...'* (*Matt. 10:5b*) (SBEC, 14; Lewiston: Edwin Mellen Press, 1988), pp. 178–85 and L.M. White, "Crisis Management and Boundary Maintenance: The Social Location of the Matthean Community," in Balch, *Social History*, pp. 241–2, n. 100.

first step. I would suggest that much the same applied to the Matthean community. As further evidence that Matthew presumes the necessity of circumcision, we might also mention that when the evangelist refers to Pharisaic proselytism, he does not mention circumcision for the obvious reason that again it would have been taken for granted by his readers. Matt. 28:19 should not be read any differently. Finally, had the Matthean community waived this most Jewish of practices for Gentile converts, we should expect that some account of it (and justification for it) would have been included in the pericopae which treat his community's conflict with formative Judaism.[41] That there is no mention of this subject must be taken to mean that circumcision was not an issue between the Matthean community and its opponents, and this could only be the case if both groups agreed on the necessity of this ritual.

Conclusions

The purpose of this study was to examine the question of Christianity and ethnicity in the Gospel of Matthew. The results, I would argue, take to the logical conclusion the latest studies on the social setting of the Matthean community which have emphasised its sectarian nature vis-à-vis the remainder of the Jewish world. It was argued that the sectarian Jewish Matthean community accepted the distinctive Jewish notion of the privileged position of the Jewish nation in the light of its ancient covenant with God. Consequently, it affirmed that the covenant agreement entailed following the torah as written in the Hebrew scriptures. The coming of Jesus the messiah in no way rescinded this notion, but served rather to confirm and clarify it. The Matthean community saw the revelation brought by the Christ, in both his earthly and risen states, as complementing the old revelation to Moses and providing it with its definitive interpretation. The corollary of this position is that only Jews could share in the salvation brought by the Christ. But Matthew is just as clear that not all Jews would find the salvation which was offered to them. True to his sectarian standpoint, the evangelist maintains that membership of the

[41] So correctly A.J. Saldarini, "The Gospel of Matthew and Jewish-Christian Conflict," in Balch, *Social History*, p. 49 n. 38. In view of Saldarini's latest study, he appears to have changed his mind on the significance of this point. See n. 37 above.

people of Israel cannot guarantee salvation; Jews must now become followers of the Christ and join the messianic movement (or Matthean community) which he initiated. This could be done by submitting to the Christian rite of baptism and adhering to its distinctive Christian beliefs and practices, including its exposition of the law.

Since Jews alone could be members of the Matthean community, it follows that it would have accepted Gentiles only after they had first joined the privileged but law-obligated people of Israel. For men this would have involved circumcision of the foreskin as the definitive mark of the covenant between God and his people, and for people of either gender obedience to God's commandments as laid down in the torah. After this necessary step such proselytes would then be inducted into Matthew's sectarian Jewish group in the same manner as those who were Jews by birth. Ethnicity was therefore part and parcel of Matthean Christianity and the Gospel which represented it. In terms of the factional dispute in the early church, the Matthean community stands firmly in the tradition of the earlier circumcision party which opposed Paul. By direct contrast with the proclamation of Paul, Matthew attests that Christ is *not* the end of the law (cf. Matt. 5:17–19) and that in view of the Christ event there *is* still Jew and Gentile, circumcision and uncircumcision (cf. Matt. 18:17).

'NEITHER JEW NOR GREEK': MULTICULTURALISM AND THE NEW PERSPECTIVE ON PAUL

John M.G. Barclay

What is at issue in Paul's critique of his contemporary Judaism? In Galatians, where it first comes to expression, Paul contrasts "faith" with "works of the law" (2:16), he plays off "spirit" against "flesh" (3:3) and he declares that, in Christ, "there is neither Jew nor Greek" (3:28). Such a multiplicity of motifs makes it possible to construe his critique in many different ways. Is there a principle by which "faith" is superior to "works (of the law)"? Is Judaism in some sense inherently "fleshly"? Is the issue the equalizing of Jew and Gentile in Christ? What is it about his "former life in Judaism" (1:13–14) that Paul now finds inadequate?

In their answers to such questions, interpreters of Paul reveal more than simply their attentiveness to the text. The framework within which they conduct their analysis of Paul indicates much about their own intellectual and social context. To assess how Paul's varied arguments hold together, and to do more than simply repeat the terms in which he expresses them, interpreters have to place Paul's theology within a conceptual framework which makes sense in their own day. The history of the interpretation of Paul shows the different modes in which Paul's theology has been construed, modes which naturally (and properly) reflect the social and cultural questions dominant in the interpreter's environment.

When F.C. Baur took Paul to articulate "the principle of Christian universalism as a thing essentially opposed to Jewish particularism," his reading of Paul was clearly influenced by nineteenth century notions of cultural and historical progress: according to these canons, Judaism was "a religion based on law" and had only "a subordinate and secondary place in the history of the religious development of mankind," while Christianity constituted "the absolute religion, the religion of the spirit and of freedom."[1] "Jewish particularism . . . is but a stage,

---

[1] F.C. Baur, *The Church History of the First Three Centuries* Vol. I (E.T. by A. Menzies from 3rd edition; London/Edinburgh: Williams & Norgate, 1878), pp. 47, 57; *Paul, The Apostle of Jesus Christ* Vol. I (E.T. by A. Menzies from 2nd edition; London/Edinburgh: Williams & Norgate, 1876), p. 255.

a stepping-stone to the universalism of Christianity, in which all nations should be embraced."[2] History determined that "it was necessary that the particularism of Judaism which opposed to the heathen world so repellent a demeanour and such offensive claims, should be uprooted, and that the baselessness of its prejudices and pretensions, of the privilege and the superiority it asserted, [be] fully exposed to the world's eye. This was the service which the apostle did to mankind by his magnificent dialectic."[3] From such soil grew the confident plant of "Culture Protestantism" and in it the seed of anti-Semitism could find fateful nourishment.

The new readings of Paul which developed out of the "theology of crisis" in the middle decades of this century were no less indebted to their social and intellectual milieu. From Bultmann's synthesis of Lutheran theology and existentialist philosophy Paul emerged as exposing a fundamental human perversion, our desire to justify ourselves. In Paul, to live "according to the flesh" designates "to trust in one's own self as being able to procure life by the use of the earthly and through one's own strength and accomplishment"—an illusory goal to which we are lured by the law.[4] Thus where Paul attacks Judaism under the rubric of "flesh" and "works of the law," it is this false hope of self-righteousness, and the false pride which it generates, which is his real target: "A specifically human striving has merely taken on its culturally, and in point of time, individually distinct form in Judaism."[5] Such a reading of Paul clearly represents a powerful combination of Lutheranism and Western, specifically existentialist, individualism.

At the present time a new reading of Paul has gained currency—in some circles the status of consensus—which radically opposes the "Lutheran" Paul and claims a greater historical sensitivity to the dynamics of Paul's controversies. Of course this interpretation, like all its predecessors, is influenced by current social and ideological

---

[2] *Paul,* p. 309.

[3] *Church History,* p. 73.

[4] R. Bultmann, *Theology of the New Testament* Vol. I (E.T. by K. Grobel; London: SCM Press, 1952), p. 239.

[5] "Christ the End of the Law," in *Essays Philosophical and Theological* (E.T. by J.C.G. Greig; London: SCM Press, 1955), p. 43. Cf. E. Käsemann, "Paul and Israel," in *New Testament Questions of Today* (E.T. by W.J. Montague, London: SCM Press, 1969), pp. 183–87. For further analysis see F. Watson, *Paul, Judaism and the Gentiles* (Cambridge: Cambridge University Press, 1986), pp. 2–10 and J.K. Riches, *A Century of New Testament Study* (London: Lutterworth Press, 1993), pp. 50–88.

currents, although such influences have rarely been noted and few of its practitioners seem conscious of the fact. In this essay I wish to outline, first, the main elements of this "new perspective" on Paul (I) and then attempt to identify the social and cultural factors which influence it and account for its popularity (II). I shall then describe a new and important discussion of Paul by Daniel Boyarin, who has built on the new perspective to address, from a Jewish standpoint, modern questions of multiculturalism (III). Finally, in dialogue with Boyarin, I shall outline my own reading of Paul as a potential resource for our multicultural society (IV).

I. *The New Perspective on Paul*

The new era in interpretation of Paul is generally recognized to have its starting point in an essay by Krister Stendahl on "The Apostle Paul and the Introspective Conscience of the West."[6] Here, claiming to "renew our acquaintance with Paul after nineteen hundred years" (p. 78, note), Stendahl challenged not just the Lutheran-Bultmannian consensus but the whole Western tradition of Pauline interpretation which had read Paul from the standpoint of the individual's troubled conscience and taken his doctrine of justification by faith to constitute the solution to the sinner's quest for a gracious God. For Stendahl, Paul's theology was primarily concerned not with any such general human predicament (first invented, he argued, by Augustine) but with the immediate social issue of the integration of Gentiles into the Messianic community. The law was a matter of controversy for Paul not because of its temptation to "legalism" but because some attempted to impose it on Gentile converts, while he asserted that salvation was "open to both Jews and Gentiles in Christ" (p. 80). Thus in Stendahl's view the doctrine of justification by faith "was hammered out by Paul for the very specific and limited purpose of defending the rights of Gentile converts to be full and genuine heirs to the promises of God to Israel."[7]

It is important to note the words "specific" and "limited" in this statement. In asserting that Paul struggled to make salvation "open

---

[6] First published in English in 1963 and subsequently available in *Paul among Jews and Gentiles* (London: SCM Press, 1977), pp. 78–96.
[7] *Paul among Jews and Gentiles*, p. 2.

to both Jews and Gentiles," Stendahl's reading of Paul bears some comparison with Baur's emphasis on Pauline "universalism" and might appear to renew Baur's view of Judaism as "particularist" and "secondary." But Stendahl insists that Paul's doctrine is *only* apologetic: it does not at the same time constitute a *polemic* against Judaism. Paul was merely concerned to defend "the right of Gentiles to be full members of the people of God;" he is only against "*Gentiles* submitting to circumcision and food laws."[8] Thus, although Stendahl is conscious that his reading of Paul "opens up a new perspective for systematic theology and practical theology," he is especially concerned that it should not be employed for any form of Christian anti-Semitism.[9]

As is well-known, the figure who ensured the full impact of the new perspective was E.P. Sanders, whose *Paul and Palestinian Judaism* changed the course of Pauline studies in English-speaking scholarship.[10] The most immediately significant aspect of this book was its demonstration, from detailed analysis of a huge range of literature, that Palestinian Judaism of the first century did not correspond to the Christian caricature of a legalistic religion, but was based on confidence in covenant grace, *within which* law-observance took place (constituting what Sanders called "covenantal nomism"). Yet, unlike Stendahl, Sanders saw Paul's theology as in some sense fundamentally *opposed* to Judaism, and if this was not for the reasons advanced by the Bultmannian consensus, what explanation could be offered? Sanders' analysis of Pauline theology marginalized the theme of justification by faith (following Schweitzer) and found the centre of Paul's thought to lie in the notion of the believer's new location "in Christ," awaiting his imminent return ("participationist eschatology"). Thus, the deficiency of non-believing Jews lay not in some inherent fault in their religion, but simply in their not being in Christ: "this is what Paul finds wrong in Judaism: it is not Christianity" (p. 552).

Sanders himself was aware that this was not an entirely satisfac-

---

[8] *Paul among Jews and Gentiles*, p. 130.
[9] *Paul among Jews and Gentiles*, pp. 95, 126–33. Note that the phrase "new perspective" was coined by Stendahl, and in a hermeneutical context: "a new perspective *for* systematic and practical theology" (p. 95, my italics). While combatting what he understood to be anachronistic readings of Paul, Stendahl did not regard his work as being of merely historical interest.
[10] London: SCM Press, 1977. Although it has been translated into German, its reception in German scholarship has been much less enthusiastic.

tory analysis, and he augmented it somewhat in his subsequent book, *Paul, the Law, and the Jewish People.*[11] Here he grappled at greater length with Paul's polemic against the law, noting the many different ways in which its deficiencies are described. He concluded that Paul did not critique Jews for boasting in the achievement of good works, but still had two principal reasons for excluding "justification by works of the law." One was Paul's Christological exclusivism (if justification was made available through Christ, it cannot be by means of the law, Gal. 2:21). The other was his commitment to the Gentile mission, which necessarily questioned the authority of the law and implicitly bracketed out those aspects of the law which Paul did not wish to have imposed on his Gentile converts (circumcision, Sabbath observance and food laws).

Thus both Stendahl and Sanders highlighted the social dimensions of Paul's theology, specifically his commitment to integrate Jews and Gentiles in the church. Sanders encapsulated the novelty of this reading of Paul when he wrote:

> The subject of Galatians is not whether or not humans, abstractly conceived, can by good deeds earn enough merit to be declared righteous at the judgment; it is the condition on which Gentiles enter the people of God . . . The supposed conflict between "doing" as such and "faith" as such is simply not present in Galatians. What was at stake was not a way of life summarized by the word "trust" versus a mode of life summarized by "requirements," but whether or not the requirement for membership in to the Israel of God would result in there being "neither Jew nor Greek."[12]

This new perspective on Paul has been widely adopted over the last ten years both in Britain and in North America.[13] A particularly prominent exponent has been James D.G. Dunn, who in numerous essays and in major commentaries on Romans and Galatians has

---

[11] Philadelphia: Fortress Press, 1983.

[12] *Paul, the Law, and the Jewish People*, pp. 18, 159.

[13] Among British scholars one may note, besides J.D.G. Dunn (see below), F. Watson, *Paul, Judaism and the Gentiles*; J. Ziesler, *Paul's Letter to the Romans* (TPI New Testament Commentaries; London: SCM; Philadelphia: Trinity Press International, 1989); N.T. Wright, *The Climax of the Covenant* (Edinburgh: T & T Clark, 1991); W.S. Campbell, *Paul's Gospel in an Intercultural Context* (Frankfurt am Main: Peter Lang, 1992). I made my own contribution in *Obeying the Truth: A Study of Paul's Ethics in Galatians* (Edinburgh: T & T Clark, 1988; Minneapolis: Fortress Press, 1991). In North America, besides J.G. Gager and L. Gaston (see below, n. 23) see, e.g., N. Elliott, *The Rhetoric of Romans: Argumentative Restraint and Strategy and Paul's Dialogue with Judaism* (Sheffield: JSOT Press, 1990) and S.K. Stowers, *A Rereading of Romans* (New Haven: Yale University Press, 1994).

employed the new perspective in exegesis of the key Pauline texts.[14] Particularly noticeable in Dunn's reading of Paul is his exploration of the social aspects of Paul's critical engagement with Judaism. Highlighting the "social function" of the law in distinguishing Jews from Gentiles, Dunn identifies the "works of the law" against which Paul polemicizes as particularly those "boundary markers" which identified Jews in Graeco-Roman society: circumcision, food laws and Sabbath observance. Thus, like Stendahl and Sanders, Dunn considers that "the leading edge of Paul's theological thinking was the conviction that God's purpose embraced Gentile as well as Jew, not the question of how a guilty man might find a gracious God."[15] But he develops this further than his predecessors in specifying that Paul's polemic was directed against:

> those who, in his judgement, were putting too much weight on the distinctiveness of Jews from Gentiles, and on the special laws which formed the boundary markers between them, those who rested their confidence in Israel's "favoured nation" status, those who invested their identity too far in the presumption that Israel was set apart from "the nations."[16]

In such statements it is possible to hear echoes of Baur's representation of Judaism as a "particularist" religion with special "prejudices" and "pretensions." But it is important to note that Dunn's analysis is shorn of Baur's claim for Christianity as the "absolute religion." Dunn is also at pains to insist that Paul was not rejecting Judaism as such, only a particular interpretation and application of the Jewish tradition. In Dunn's analysis, the objects of Paul's critique were "nationalistic presumption" and "ethnic restrictiveness," neither of which were, in Paul's view, a proper interpretation of the Jewish Scriptures.[17] And although these features may have been typical of the Judaism of his day, Dunn is careful to keep his discourse strictly historical and not to suggest that such features typify Judaism *as such*.[18]

---

[14] The chief essays are collected in *Jesus, Paul and the Law* (London: SPCK; Louisville: Westminster/John Knox Press, 1990). Dunn's commentaries are *Romans 1–8* and *Romans 9–16* (Word Biblical Commentary 38a and 38b, Dallas: Word, 1988); *The Epistle to the Galatians* (Black's New Testament Commentaries; London: A & C Black; Peabody, Mass.: Hendrickson, 1993).

[15] *Jesus, Paul and the Law*, p. 232.

[16] *The Epistle to the Galatians*, p. 172.

[17] *Jesus, Paul and the Law*, p. 248.

[18] E.g., *Jesus, Paul and the Law*, p. 249: "Paul objects to covenantal nomism understood as it *then* was consistently throughout Judaism" (my italics).

II. *The Social and Ideological Milieu of the New Perspective*

It is, of course, much harder to assess factors influencing contemporary interpretation than it is to discern, with hindsight, the influences on our predecessors. Nonetheless, there seem to be at least three aspects of our present social and ideological environment which undergird the new perspective and encourage its reception.[19]

1. *Theological Respect for Judaism*

This is the most obvious influence on the current readings of Paul, and is evident from the beginning in Stendahl's challenge to the consensus. When he clarifies the framework in which he reads Paul, Stendahl highlights his awareness of how, in relation to the Jewish people, "the Christian use of Scripture, and not least of the Pauline epistles, had caused developments of satanic dimensions." Thus he explicitly reads Paul "in an attempt to get at the roots of Christian anti-Semitism,"[20] and refuses to interpret Paul in any way that leads to "making Judaism a code word for all wrong attitudes toward God."[21] This is surely why, as we have seen, Stendahl is reluctant to accept that Paul was engaged in any sort of *critique* of Judaism: he is only defending Gentile converts, not attacking Jews. Indeed Stendahl suggested that Paul never expected Jews in general to believe in Christ. He took Romans 9–11 as the climax of that letter and was impressed by the fact that the name of Jesus Christ does not appear once in all of 10:17–11:36. Thus he suggested that "Paul's reference to God's mysterious plan [for the salvation of all Israel] is an affirmation of a God-willed co-existence between Judaism and Christianity in which the missionary urge to convert Israel is held in check."[22] This reading of Paul, which denies the presence of any serious critique of Judaism and suggests the prospect of a *Sonderweg* for Israel, has been

---

[19] In identifying these influences on the new perspective, I am not, of course, attempting to disqualify the historical study which has been its hallmark. But historians should not need reminding that historiography is not a value-free enterprise: it inevitably and properly operates within the framework of the social and cultural questions of the day. As those questions change, new perspectives on history are opened up, but careful historical research is not thereby to be dismissed, in a facile way, as a purely subjective enterprise.

[20] *Paul among Jews and Gentiles*, p. 126.

[21] *Paul among Jews and Gentiles*, p. 132.

[22] *Paul among Jews and Gentiles*, p. 4.

adopted by some other scholars as well, all acutely conscious of how
Paul could be, and has been, read to nourish Christian anti-Semitism.[23]

Most exponents of the new perspective hold that Paul *does* mount
some critique of his contemporary Judaism, but all are sensitized to
the horrendous potential of anti-Semitism in Pauline interpretation.
Sanders' massive rebuttal of caricatures of Jewish "legalism" is evidently a product of the new spirit of understanding between Jews
and Christians which characterizes our post-Holocaust, pluralist world.
Present unwillingness to portray first-century Judaism as a religion of
"works-righteousness" undoubtedly reflects our embarrassment that
Christians have for so long espoused such derogatory attitudes towards Jews. Neither Baur's nor Bultmann's construction of the relationship between Paul and Judaism could flourish again in the present
climate, even if some aspects of Baur's interpretation have been revived by Dunn and even if certain aspects of the Lutheran reading
remain influential and fruitful.[24]

2. *Community as the Goal of Christian Faith*

The shift in the new perspective from an individualistic to a communal
reading of Pauline theology is surely related to significant changes in
the social context of theology in the last thirty years. Bultmann's existentialist reading of Paul is now both philosophically and theologically
passé and even at a popular level one is now less likely to hear sermons
warning believers against trying to earn their salvation by good works.
In an age of ecumenism, Protestants are less inclined to define their
identity by contrast with the supposed "works-righteousness" of Catholicism, and the churches are in general more exercised about their
social identity and social roles than about ensuring their members
are individually put right with God on the correct terms. The current concern with ecclesiology—with the church as constituting and
creating community—thus dovetails neatly with a reading of Paul's
doctrine of justification which emphasizes its social origins and effects.[25]

---

[23] See e.g., J.G. Gager, *The Origins of Anti-Semitism* (Oxford: OUP, 1983); L. Gaston,
Paul and the Torah (Vancouver: University of British Columbia Press, 1987); S.G.
Hall III, *Christian Anti-Semitism and Paul's Theology* (Minneapolis: Fortress Press, 1993);
Stowers, *A Rereading of Romans*.

[24] S. Westerholm, *Israel's Law and the Church's Faith* (Grand Rapids: Eerdmans,
1988) represents a modified Lutheran reading of Paul, opposing some exaggerated
features of the new perspective.

[25] A pioneer in this regard was N.A. Dahl, "The Doctrine of Justification: Its

In the same post-60s climate social studies of early Christianity have gained a new lease of life and the research of G. Theissen and W.A. Meeks has focused attention on the social realities of the early church.[26] The use of sociology and anthropology in analysing those realities has discouraged a purely "theological" assessment of Paul's controversies; instead it encourages attention to social groups (synagogues and churches) and how they constructed and maintained their identities. By reading Paul within this framework, the new perspective thus mirrors a general change in both ecclesial and academic environments.

3. Multicultural Concerns

If the new perspective emphasizes the creation of communities in which "there is neither Jew nor Greek," this may also be seen to match contemporary concerns in multicultural politics. As we have seen, Dunn repeatedly refers to Paul's target as "nationalistic presuppositions" or "ethnic restrictions"—language redolent of social and political issues in the contemporary world. One cannot miss echoes of the contemporary rejection of colonialism and the current concern with "the politics of difference," in a statement such as:

> It was the attempt to enforce a uniform *Jewish* understanding of the gospel in *Gentile* Galatia which roused Paul to furious indignation. Integral to the freedom of the gospel is freedom to express it differently, with different emphases in different contexts.[27]

Within the Christian community, the bad conscience of Western churches in assessing their mission history, the development of non-Western theologies and the sanctioning of "inculturation" have induced a new awareness of the value of "difference." In the secular realm, the cultural crisis in the West and the questioning of its

---

Social Function and Implications," in *Studies in Paul* (Minneapolis: Augsburg, 1977), pp. 95–120. Cf. my "Justification by Faith: The Root of Christian Tolerance," in R.P. Carroll and A.G. Hunter (eds.), *Words at Work* (Glasgow: Trinity St. Mungo Press, 1994), pp. 1–13.

[26] G. Theissen, *The Social Setting of Pauline Christianity* (E.T. by J.H. Schütz; Edinburgh: T & T Clark, 1982); W.A. Meeks, *The First Urban Christians* (New Haven: Yale University Press, 1983).

[27] J.D.G. Dunn, *The Theology of Paul's Letter to the Galatians* (New Testament Theology; Cambridge: Cambridge University Press, 1993), p. 28. I was conscious of using such a conceptual framework in referring to Paul as combating a Jewish "cultural imperialism," *Obeying the Truth*, pp. 250–51.

Enlightenment legacy have undermined the presumption of Western
cultural hegemony. Thus the possibilities and problems of an interdependent and multicultural world have begun to loom large on the
agenda of serious thinkers. In this context it is understandable that the
Pauline motif of "neither Jew nor Greek" should come to the fore.

Of these three features of the current milieu, the third has been
perhaps the least noticed by Pauline interpreters and the least exploited for the current theological and social task. Interpreting Paul
as a cultural critic and exploring his vision of community in which
there is "neither Jew nor Gentile" is an agenda still largely unad-
dressed by Pauline scholars. It has, however, been opened up in a
significant fashion by Daniel Boyarin, and we may best pursue this
Pauline potential in dialogue with him.

III. *The Contribution of Daniel Boyarin*

Daniel Boyarin's *A Radical Jew: Paul and the Politics of Identity*[28] is a
rich and deeply engaging reading of Paul by a "talmudist and
postmodern Jewish cultural critic" (p. 1). As a practising and non-
Christian Jew, Boyarin inevitably resists some aspects of Paul's theology, but he reads Paul sympathetically enough to discern that he
issues an important challenge to Judaism, especially in its present
multicultural environment. Boyarin's refusal either to "blunt the force
of [Paul's] critique of Judaism" or to "render him a slanderer of
Judaism" (p. 6) enables him to resist some common temptations, and
his interpretation of Paul draws heavily on the main insights of the
new perspective. Ultimately he rejects Paul's universalism as naïve
and even dangerous, but he recognizes that equal dangers lurk in
the rabbinic insistence on Jewish "difference," especially if it is linked,
as in present-day Israel, with the possession of power and territory.

Foundational to Boyarin's interpretation of Paul is his conviction
that Paul was "motivated by a Hellenistic desire for the One, which
among other things produced an ideal of a universal human essence,
beyond difference and hierarchy" (p. 7). It is this "Greek longing for
universals" (combined with "Hebrew monotheism," p. 228) which
induced Paul to interpret Christ as enabling not just equality but
sameness (pp. 9, 156). For Boyarin, Gal. 3:28 indicates that Paul took

---

[28]   Berkeley: University of California Press, 1994.

Christ to fulfil "the moral and religious necessity of humankind, namely to erase all distinction between ethnos and ethnos, sex and sex and become one in Christ's spiritual body" (p. 85).[29]

Such a universalizing strategy is displayed, for Boyarin, in two interrelated features of Paul's theology: his dualism and his allegorical hermeneutics. Paul's dualism is, Boyarin insists, at least partially parallel to that of Philo: the two share a common background in eclectic middle-Platonism which influenced many Hellenistic Jews and encouraged them to operate "in a dualistic system in which spirit precedes and is primary over body" (p. 14). Boyarin finds his strongest evidence in Paul's "spirit"/"flesh" dualism which he takes to represent not complete rejection of the body, but a hierarchical schema in which physical and bodily phenomena are always subordinated to their spiritual counterparts (pp. 57–85). And this schema undergirds Paul's allegorization of Judaism. Whether in relation to circumcision (Rom. 2:25–29), Abrahamic lineage (Gal. 4:21–31), "Israel according to the flesh" (1 Cor. 10:18) or the Jewish interpretation of Scripture (2 Corinthians 3), Paul continually spiritualizes Jewish particulars and thus transforms the rites and the very existence of "a particular tribe" into "an ahistorical, abstract, and universal human 'truth'" (p. 96).

Boyarin understands this strategy as Paul's response to the tensions inherent in Judaism in which the God of all the world seems to have a disproportionate concern for one ethnic group.[30] By allegorizing circumcision and "the Israel according to the flesh," Paul's Christian perspective makes it possible for Judaism to become a world religion (pp. 230–31), but at the cost of eradicating Jewish difference and disqualifying its vital genealogical identity. Paul's treatment of circumcision is particularly crucial, and revealing, for Boyarin: it is the very physical character of this Jewish mark of identity which is fundamental to Jewish ethnicity, since it embodies the significance of parentage, family and historical memory. By spiritualizing and universalizing circumcision, Paul in effect deprives genealogy and ethnicity

---

[29] "Erasure" language is frequent: cf. pp. 24, 216, 231 etc. Elsewhere he talks of Pauline universalism as "dissolving all others into a single essence" (p. 9; cf. pp. 95, 257), "suppressing cultural difference (p. 26) and "eradicating" cultural specificities (p. 8).

[30] Boyarin finds Paul's Christology symbolic here, and biographically foundational for his whole theology: understanding the Christ "according to the Spirit" to supersede Christ "according to the flesh," Paul finds the "hermeneutic key to the resolution of that enormous tension that he experienced between the universalism of the Torah's content and the particular ethnicity of its form" (p. 29).

of value. To be sure, Paul does not outlaw circumcision (for Jews); he regards it as an *adiaphoron* which counts for nothing compared with "faith working through love" (Gal. 5:6; 6:15; 1 Cor. 7:19). But, Boyarin insists, even this apparent "tolerance" of difference is ultimately *intolerant* of the Jewish conviction that circumcision cannot be a matter of indifference:

> What will appear from the Christian perspective as tolerance, namely Paul's willingness—indeed insistence—that within the Christian community all cultural practice is equally to be tolerated, from the rabbinic Jewish perspective is simply an eradication of the entire value system which insists that our cultural practice is our task and calling in the world and must not be abandoned or reduced to a matter of taste. (p. 32; cf. pp. 9–10, 290 n. 10)

Thus Boyarin ultimately rejects Paul's multicultural transformation of the Jewish tradition despite its attractive embrace of all humanity; indeed, he regards the eradication of difference as a dangerous version of "coercive sameness" (p. 236) which suppresses cultural differences by absorbing them into a dominant cultural system. Such a strategy leads too easily into European cultural imperialism where one specific culture masquerades as nonspecific. As a Jewish response to the dilemmas of multiculturalism, Boyarin propounds what he calls "diasporized identity," in which Jewish ethnic loyalties are combined with cultural participation in their local environments and shorn of territorial claims. This, he suggests, is the only viable synthesis which can correct "in the 'Christian' system its tendencies toward a coercive universalism and in the 'Jewish' system its tendencies toward contemptuous neglect for human solidarity" (p. 235; cf. p. 257).

The above summary cannot convey the full richness of Boyarin's intense and often captivating dialogue with Paul.[31] In some respects it represents a Jewish riposte to Baur's Christian reading of Paul, which now at the close of the twentieth century appears painfully triumphalist and loaded with danger. In the light of European history it is remarkable that Boyarin can read Paul with such sympathetic attention, and it is his concern to give Paul (and his many interpreters) a fair hearing which constitutes one of the strengths of this book. Nonetheless, I consider that Boyarin's often acute reading of Paul sometimes misconstrues the apostle, and ultimately underval-

---

[31] I have perforce omitted Boyarin's discussions of gender, which he regards as an aspect of "difference" parallel to that constituted by Judaism.

ues the contribution he could make to our contemporary tasks. I shall therefore conclude with an alternative reading of Paul which, in dialogue with Boyarin, offers a different employment of the new perspective for our multicultural age.

IV. Paul and Multiculturalism

Paul's theology was forged in dispute with his contemporary Judaism and needs to be understood in its social context. All Jews in the Graeco-Roman world were affected to some degree by the dominant Hellenistic culture, which they encountered not only in the Diaspora but also in Palestine. Hellenization, however, had many different facets, and it is worth distinguishing (in an approximate manner) between "acculturation" (the adoption of Hellenistic speech, literary forms, values and philosophies) and "assimilation" (social integration into Hellenistic society). Highly acculturated Jews, who spoke and wrote sophisticated Greek and were conversant with the Greek intellectual tradition, were not necessarily highly assimilated: many indeed employed their Hellenistic training precisely to demarcate their social life from that of non-Jews. The bond which held Jews together was primarily social: their common life in observance of "ancestral customs." Of these customs the most significant for social relations were aniconic monotheism (the refusal to participate in non-Jewish religion), the male mark of circumcision (which, among other things, limited marriage relations), the dietary laws (which restricted social intercourse) and the observance of the Sabbath (which affected employment relations). Such customs defined Jewish difference: they created social boundaries between Jew and Greek, even where the two might otherwise speak the same language and employ the same thought-forms. Greeks who wished to become Jews (as some did), needed to adopt precisely these social practices to achieve full integration into the Jewish community.[32]

Paul's highly controversial claim was that Gentiles could become "children of Abraham" and heirs of the covenant promises simply by faith in Christ and receipt of the Spirit, thanks to the grace of

---

[32] On the distinction between acculturation and assimilation, and the social definition of Jewish identity in the Diaspora, see further my *Jews in the Mediterranean Diaspora* (Edinburgh: T & T Clark, 1996).

God. That led him to establish and maintain communities of believers whose common life could not be bounded or defined in the
same way as were Jewish communities. One of the defining "ancestral customs" he did in fact transfer to his churches: he continued
the ban on participation in Gentile religion, since his converts had,
as he put it, "turned from idols to the true and living God" (1 Thess.
1:9). But he did not allow the other three "social markers" to characterize the common life of believers: Gentiles should not be required
to "judaize" in such matters as food (Gal. 2:11–14), circumcision (Gal.
6:11–16) or the observance of "days" (Rom. 14:5–6). In this sense
Paul preached to Gentiles a partially "dejudaized Judaism"[33] and
attempted to create church communities which were multiethnic and
multicultural: in Christ "there is neither Jew nor Greek" (Gal. 3:28).

It is misleading, I believe, to interpret Paul as here engaged in a
"spiritualizing" or "allegorical" hermeneutic (*pace* Boyarin). Paul was
not reaching behind Jewish particulars to some abstract "essence" or
disembodied "ideal": he was placing alongside the Jewish community
another which was equally physical and embodied in social reality.
To be sure, he can relativize circumcision by claiming that what
counts is "faith working through love" (Gal. 5:6), but that faith and
love are designed to take extremely practical shape in the life of a
community (Gal. 5:13–6:10). Similarly, he will not allow the Roman
churches to define themselves by distinctions in food or drink, but
the "righteousness, peace and joy in the Holy Spirit" which he puts
in their place (Rom. 14:17) are meant to have immediate impact on
their common life, not least in their common meals (Rom. 14:1–
15:6). Hence Paul's apparent allegorization of Jewish particulars is
performed not in a quest for "the universal human essence," but to
enable an alternative form of community which could bridge ethnic
and cultural divisions by creating new patterns of common life.[34]

---

[33] G. Theissen speaks of a "Judaism for non-Jews," *Social Reality and the Early
Christians* (Edinburgh: T & T Clark, 1992), p. 205.

[34] In this respect there is far greater *distance* between Paul and Philo than Boyarin
allows. At first glance some of Paul's discussions of circumcision seem comparable
to Philo's allegorizations, and his practice as dangerous to Judaism as the allegorists
who advocated abandoning the practice of circumcision (Philo, *De Migratione Abrahami*
89–93). But Paul was not involved, like them, in an intellectual quest for the "human meaning" of Jewish customs: he was relativizing certain Jewish particulars in
the interests of establishing multiethnic communities. Paul was more assimilated than
Philo, but far less acculturated; hence the conceptual parallels between Paul and
Philo are in fact remarkably few.

For the same reason, Paul does not, I believe, "erase" or "eradicate" cultural specificities, but *relativize* them. Paul never loses his respect for Judaism, even for circumcision, which he regards as a sign of the advantage of the Jews (Rom. 3:1–2, even after 2:25–29!). He can still list Israel's privileges in Rom. 9:4–5 (sonship, glory, the covenants etc.) with genuine awe. It is important for him that Christ was a Jew and thus a "servant of the circumcised, to fulfil the promises to the patriarchs" (Rom. 15:8). But it is also important that Christ is now the Lord of both Jews and Gentiles, who call on him in faith on the same terms, whatever their cultural identity. Thus Jews and Gentiles are simultaneously *affirmed* as Jews and Gentiles and *humbled* in their cultural pretensions. In much of what he presents as the direction of the Spirit, Paul is indebted to his Jewish tradition, both in his response to "idolatry" and in his sexual ethics. He can also draw some resources from the Hellenistic cultural tradition, urging openness to "whatever is true, whatever is just, whatever is holy . . ." (Phil. 4:8).[35] No one's culture is despised or demonized, but by the same token none is absolutized or allowed to gain hegemony.

But from what vantage point does Paul relativize cultural specificities? Clearly, as he would say, from the vantage point of "the truth of the gospel" (Gal. 2:14). But Paul does not present the gospel as if it carries a whole new cultural package, designed to eradicate and replace all others. It is rather a cluster of values, focused in love, which enables the creation of a new community in which variant cultural traditions can be practised. When he describes himself, famously, as being all things to all people (1 Cor. 9:19–23) he indicates his ability to adapt his behaviour—at one time living under the law, at another without the law—because his ultimate commitment is not to the law (or to lawlessness) but to Christ (he is *ennomos Christou*, 1 Cor. 9:21). That does not install Christ as the founder of a new culture, but indicates how commitment to Christ can simultaneously *encompass* various cultural particularities. Thus Paul, although he dethrones the law, never forbids its practice by Jews or Jewish Christians, and in Romans 14 goes to some lengths to defend their rights to observe food and Sabbath customs. But as that chapter and others display (cf. 1 Corinthians 8–10), all such cultural commitments are of only penultimate significance: the overriding commitment is to

---

[35] See now T. Engberg-Pedersen (ed.), *Paul in his Hellenistic Context* (Edinburgh: T & T Clark, 1994).

love and the building of responsible and supportive communities. The gospel is not, for Paul, a philosophical principle which reveals universal human truths. His investments lie not in the abstractions of "knowledge" but in the practical and often complex demands of love (1 Cor. 8:1–3).

Thus far I have suggested that Paul's stance towards cultural difference was neither as brutal nor as naïve as Boyarin has suggested. At two points, however, I believe Boyarin is right to call attention to major difficulties in the Pauline prescription. In the first place, he rightly suggests that the very "tolerance" of cultural difference turns out to be subtly intolerant of those for whom the maintenance of their cultural traditions cannot be a matter of taste, but is the very core of their identity (see the citation above, p. 208). This is, as he says, one of the essential dilemmas of multiculturalism, since in this respect tolerance itself appears flawed (pp. 9–10). As Romans 14–15 indicates, Paul's protection of the rights of law-observant Christians to keep Sabbath and food laws in fact subtly undermines their social and cultural integrity, since they are forced to acknowledge the equal validity of *non-observance* even while being allowed (with some condescension) to observe.[36] Thus even if Paul does not "eradicate" cultural differences, his relativization of their significance somehow threatens the very seriousness with which they are taken by their practitioners. I can only agree with Boyarin that a dialectic between common values and cultural difference must be maintained and that "somewhere in this dialectic a synthesis must be found, one that will allow for stubborn hanging on to ethnic, cultural specificity but in a context of deeply felt and enacted human solidarity" (p. 257). I can only add that I believe Paul's ethic and his creation of cross-cultural communities is already pointing towards such "deeply felt and enacted human solidarity."

But isn't it true—and here we encounter Boyarin's second objection—that Paul's multicultural vision presupposes common *commitment to Christ* and in this Christological exclusivism refuses to recognize the "right" of Jews and others "to remain unconvinced by the gospel" (p. 10)? Does Paul's subtly "particularist claim to universalism"

---

[36] I have explored this irony in "'Do we Undermine the Law?' A Study of Romans 14:1–15:6," in J.D.G. Dunn (ed.), *Paul and the Jewish Law* (Tübingen: Mohr (Siebeck), forthcoming), a paper written before I encountered Boyarin's book but strongly supportive of his position at this point.

(pp. 205, 208) ultimately delegitimize Jews and all other non-Christians who cannot accept that they are simply "on the way to destruction" (1 Cor. 1:18)? Does Paul have anything at all to offer a world that is not only multicultural but also multireligious?

I think myself that Paul partially deconstructs his own Christological exclusivism by his pervasive appeal to the grace of God.[37] The foundation of Paul's gospel, and the basis of his relativization of all cultures, is his radical appreciation of the grace of God which humbles human pride and subverts the theological and cultural edifices which "flesh" constructs. The justification of the ungodly and the gift of the Spirit are, for Paul, acts of grace which undermine absolute commitment to the law (Rom. 4:4–5; Gal. 3:1–5); he himself had experienced God's grace as calling into question all his previous cultural assurances (Gal. 1:13–16; 1 Cor. 15:8–10). Paul discerns the gracious initiative of God through Israel's history, and its paradoxical triumph precisely through her unbelief (Romans 9–11), since the God who has consigned all to disobedience will ultimately have mercy on all (Rom. 11:32). This radical notion of divine grace, which Paul uses to destabilize the church at least as much as those outside it (cf. 1 Corinthians *passim*), could serve both to affirm and to relativize the Christian tradition itself. The church exists not for its own sake but to bear witness to the grace of God. Paul himself is ultimately speechless before the mercy of God and cannot find even Christian language in which to express its significance (Rom. 11:33–36). To this extent, even Pauline theology could be mobilized to serve a multiculturalism whose religious basis is the affirming and relativizing grace of God.

Thus the new perspective suggests that Paul could serve as a valuable resource in our struggles to fashion a harmonious but multicultural society. It reads Paul as the fashioner of multiethnic and multicultural communities, which function not to erase but to moderate between differing cultural specificities. It could be claimed that any community which relativizes difference sets itself up as, in effect, a new hegemonic culture. But I have suggested that Paul never intended to found a "Christendom," and his prescription, at its most basic, could

---

[37] This is a motif underappreciated by Boyarin who, influenced by Watson, takes Paul's contrast of "grace" and "works" as the *sociological* markers of different communities (p. 206) and fails to allow for their theological significance. Cf. his dialogue with Westerholm (pp. 295–96, n. 30).

be taken as elevating only what accords with love and enhances
community. Any social framework in which differing cultures are
enabled to share a common life necessitates the establishment of some
"common ground," and I am not convinced that Boyarin's stimulating advocacy of Jewish "diasporized identity" can circumvent this
requirement.[38] On one side we are faced by the injustices of cultural
suppression, but on the other lie the equally enormous dangers of
cultural incompatibility. And it is better that we create possibilities
for community on some common ground than that we tear the fabric
of societies whose cultural threads are already too interwoven to be
simply unravelled. A cautious use of our Pauline heritage could equip
us to undertake that long and difficult search for a polity which both
respects ineradicable difference and enables meaningful community.

---

[38] Precisely in the Diaspora, without the power to impose territorial or cultural
claims, Jews need to establish on what basis they can accept the conditions of their
social environment and perhaps contribute to its cultural life. If a diasporized identity entails being both Jewish and American (p. 244), on what basis can an individual (or community) justify the adoption of this double identity? In rejecting the
abstract notion of "a universal human essence" (p. 257), Boyarin leaves unclear the
basis of his own commitment to "human solidarity" (ibid.) and "social justice"
(p. 259). Josephus, writing on behalf of Jews in the Diaspora, articulated the need
for some common ground in their relations with non-Jews: "It is most advantageous
for all men, Greeks and barbarians alike, to practise justice; our laws are specially
concerned with this matter and they make us (if we keep to them sincerely) kind
and friendly to all. Thus we properly expect the same attitude from them, for foreignness should not be defined as a matter of difference of customs but in relation
to one's proper attitude to civilized behaviour (καλοκαγαθία); for this is common to
all and it alone enables society to survive" (Antiquities 16.177–78). Josephus' καλοκαγαθία
is, of course, a cultural product, manufactured no doubt by a privileged élite. But
on what other basis could (or can) minority groups hope to receive respect for their
difference?

GROUP BOUNDARIES AND INTERGROUP CONFLICT IN GALATIANS: A NEW READING OF GALATIANS 5:13-6:10[1]

Philip F. Esler

Introduction: The Galatian Context and Gal. 5:13-6:10

The principal issue in Galatia to which Paul responds in his letter to the congregations, the ἐκκλησίαι, which he had founded there, was the pressure being exerted upon Gentile members to accept circumcision and the other requirements of the Jewish law. It is clear from Gal. 6:12-13 that it was Jewish members of the congregations who were actively running this campaign, although, as I have argued elsewhere (Esler 1994: 52-69), they themselves were conforming to wider Jewish opinion. That this campaign was making some headway in Galatia is clear from 4:10-11, even if circumcision had not yet been widely accepted by the Gentile membership.

One of the great conundra of Galatians research, however, is that in Gal. 5:13-6:10, Paul seems to shift away from the question of circumcision and the primacy of justification by faith—and the forces in the external environment impelling him to such a discussion—and to turn instead to a problem internal to the communities of Galatia, namely, the way their members should behave toward one another. Further below I will outline various solutions which commentators have proposed to explain the alleged difficulty in relating the material in Gal. 5:13-6:10, traditionally described as "ethical," to the issue of circumcision.

In this essay I wish to outline a new approach to the problem. For present purposes my interest is the historical one of investigating what meaning or meanings this text conveyed to its original audience (listeners rather than readers). My starting point, however, is that since the context in which Paul was seeking to make an impact was a social one, we should augment traditional tools of historical

---

[1] This is a revised form of a paper delivered at the SBL Conference in Chicago on 21 November 1994.

analysis with perspectives developed during the last century or so of research into the social dimensions of human existence undertaken by anthropologists, sociologists and social psychologists. Ultimately, the walls which many biblical scholars deliberately erect around their work to keep out any ideas not strictly "historical" are social constructs, purity boundaries of the type explained by Mary Douglas (so Robbins 1995), and constitute an entirely unnecessary impediment to the understanding of early Christianity.

For the moment, I will set out the bipolar thesis of this essay, which ultimately derives from readily accessible social-scientific research: first, that the significance of 5:13–6:10 can only be appreciated in connection with the "external" forces, since both issues concern boundaries between insiders and outsiders, and, secondly, that this passage deals with Christian identity forged in a context of intergroup conflict rather than "ethics." My approach to arguing this position will involve five steps: (1) a short description of the data in Gal. 5:13–6:10; (2) a brief account of existing approaches to the alleged problem of its relationship to the wider context of the letter; (3) a resumé of my own view as to the underlying causes for the demand for circumcision, which will lead to (4) the description of certain social-scientific perspectives drawn from anthropology and social psychology on the establishment of group identity in a situation of largely ethnic interaction across group boundaries, and (5) an application of these perspectives to the textual data.

1. The Problem of Gal. 5:13–6:10

As already noted, New Testament commentators have traditionally regarded Gal. 5:13 as marking an important transition in the letter, in that here Paul seems to move on to an apparently new issue, one internal to the communities of Galatia, namely, the way their members should behave towards one another. He continues with this topic as far as 6:10, when he returns to the impact of external forces.

Within Gal. 5:13–6:10 Paul deals with a number of related issues, such as the meaning of Christian freedom as serving one another in love (5:13–15), the type of behaviour which comes from living according to the flesh as contrasted with the Spirit (5:16–24), particular consequences of life in the Spirit for behaviour within the community (5:25–6:6) and the ultimate fate of those who choose either the flesh or the Spirit (6:7–10). It has become a traditional feature of research into Galatians to categorise this material as "ethical" (especially Barclay 1988) or "paraenetic" (Dibelius 1934 and 1976). The extent to which such a classification depends upon significant unstated presuppositions and prejudgments and requires critical analysis will be a prominent theme in what follows.

Although a few critics regard the transition at 5:13 as quite unsurprising,[2] a far more common response has been to find the presence of 5:13–6:10 in the letter difficult to explain. The heart of the difficulty is that whereas in the first four chapters Paul has been at pains to attack reliance on the Jewish law, because there were Gentiles in Galatia attracted to adopting it (4:21: "You who wish to be under law"), in 5:13–6:10 he seems to have in his sights people who are acting in a lawless fashion. Thus, although he has previously told the Galatians they are free of the law, in this passage he seems to re-impose law on them, beginning at 5:14 when he says: "For the whole law is fulfilled in one word, 'You shall love your neighbor as yourself'," citing Lev. 19:18, part of the legal prescriptions given to Moses by Yahweh. The same theme emerges at 6:2: "Bear one another's burdens, and so fulfil the law of Christ." Scholars tend to abbreviate the point by saying that Paul's problem is "nomism" in the bulk of the letter but "anti-nomianism" or "libertinism" in 5:13–6:10.

2. *Existing Answers to the Problem*

The range of existing answers to the question of how this passage is connected with earlier parts of the letter, especially 2:15–5:12, has been helpfully set out by John Barclay (1988: 9–26). Commentators who take up this issue fall into two camps: first, those who consider 5:13–6:10 is not well integrated into the work as a whole[3] and, secondly, those who think that it is.[4]

---

[2] So Dunn (1993: 284–6), who sees the movement from "the exposition and appeal" of 3:1–5:12 to the "exhortation" of 5:13–6:10 as similar to the "natural pattern" found elsewhere in Paul, for example in the progression from Romans 1–11 to 12–15.

[3] Such as O'Neill (1972), Dibelius (1934: 238–9 and 1976: 1–11), Burton (1921), Lütgert (1919) and Ropes (1929).

[4] Such as Schmithals (1972: 13–64) Betz (1979: 8–9, 273–4 and 295–6), Howard (1979: 11–14), Brinsmead (1982: 164–92) and Barclay himself.

The most dramatic representative of the first approach is O'Neill (1972), who argues that the whole section is a non-Pauline interpolation. He cannot think that Paul would have been interested in the question of anti-nomianism. Dibelius thought the passage was by Paul, but was quite unrelated to the argument of the letter as a whole. It did not represent the apostle's own ethics, but, along with similar passages,[5] expressed a tradition of early Christian moral exhortation, which Dibelius subsumed under the literary genre of paraenesis (1934: 238–9 and 1976: 1–11). For E. de W. Burton, on the other hand, the passage was best understood as "an apologetic appendix" aimed at assuring those who might misunderstand Paul to mean that freedom from the law had removed all restraints that keep human beings from immorality (1921: 290). Another form of this broad approach was developed by Lütgert (1919) and Ropes (1929), both of whom argued that Paul actually had two quite different types of problem to cope with in Galatia: legalists who wanted to adopt the law and spiritualistic radicals whose freedom from the law led to anti-nomianism. In sum, they proposed that in this passage Paul was opening up a "second front," by initiating action against an enemy distinct from the main one in his sights.

One example of the second approach, which treats the passage as integrated into the letter as a whole, is that of W. Schmithals, who argued that Paul's opponents were Jewish Gnostics who advocated circumcision but were libertines as far as morality was concerned. His arguments for the presence of Gnostics in Galatia, however, have run into strong opposition (Wilson 1968). A more plausible line is taken by Betz, who suggests that one reason why the Galatians were attracted to the Jewish law was as a way of controlling the immorality otherwise present among them and that once Paul has demonstrated the error of taking on the law he must provide some alternative means of assisting them deal with the immorality which initially made it attractive to them (1979: 8–9, 273–4 and 295–6). For Howard (1979: 11–14), on the other hand, 5:13–6:10 constitutes a continuation of Paul's onslaught on the law, since what he attacks in this section is precisely the condition of being under the flesh which is a result of taking on the law. Similarly, Brinsmead sees the passage as directed against the ethical traditions of Paul's opponents (1982: 164–92).

---

[5] Romans 12–13; Col. 3:1–4:6; 1 Thess. 4:1–12; 5:1ff.

John Barclay also considers that the passage is integrated into the letter:

> our analysis of circumcision and law-observance has highlighted the dual aspect of the Galatian crisis: it raised questions concerning both identity and behavioural patterns. These two, of course, cannot be separated (73).

He proposes that in opposition to Jewish-Christian claims that the introduction of Jewish rites and ceremonies would provide a means whereby the Galatians could constantly reinforce their identity as the people of God (72), Paul establishes a relationship between his law-free Gospel and the moral life without which his earlier arguments would lose much of their force. Those who are led by the Spirit actually fulfil the law. Barclay's is the least problematic approach to the passage hitherto. We will see, however, that although he is not adverse to illustrating his argument with insights from the social sciences, especially the sociology of knowledge, his failure thoroughly to interrogate the heart of this proposal in social-scientific fashion prevents his judicious reading of the text from realising its full potential.

This brief discussion reveals the diversity of the attempts which have been undertaken to make sense of the data in Gal. 5:13–6:10. The fact that none of the other critics just mentioned, except (to a limited extent) John Barclay, have sought to utilise the social sciences in their work on Gal. 5:13–6:10 seems to me a depressing indictment of the narrowness of vision, and the consequent misinterpretation of the evidence, which comes from mono-disciplinary biblical research.

3. *The Causes of the Demand for Circumcision*

The immediate explanation for the pressure upon Gentile members of the congregations to become Jews was the scandal to wider Jewish opinion caused by the practice of mixed table-fellowship, pre-eminently in the eucharistic meal. We need to distinguish between the fact of opposition to such a practice and the reasons for the Jewish prohibition on it. At a general level Jews regarded Gentiles as sinful by reason of the idolatry in which they engaged. Some social intercourse with them was permitted and some was not. The particular reason for the ban on Jewish-Gentile eucharistic table-fellowship was probably that passing round from Gentile to Jew the one loaf of

bread and, even worse, one cup of wine (cf. 1 Cor. 10:16–17), implicated the Jews involved or, just as bad, might seem to implicate
them, in a specific act of idolatry (Esler 1994: 62–8 and 1995b).

Yet we must be wary of imagining that this factor standing alone
could explain the motivation for the Jewish position. The Jews concerned were not acting purely from an abstract, that is to say, socially disembodied, belief in the virtues of obeying the Mosaic law.
For the line they were taking also—perhaps we should say "principally"—involved defending and maintaining the Jewish *ethnos* in the
midst of a threatening Gentile world (see Esler 1987: 73–86). Making sense of the Jewish context of Paul's letter to the Galatians demands that we attend to the issue of ethnicity as much as to what
we moderns or post-moderns mean by "theology." Ethnicity is a field
which has been amply investigated by social scientists and in a moment
I will discuss how some of their findings shed light on Galatians.

4. *Social-Scientific Approaches*

Anthropology and the Boundary Question

Since it is clear from the rest of Galatians that the Gentile members
of the communities to whom Paul writes have crossed one boundary
which separates them from still-idolatrous Gentiles by becoming
members and are under pressure to cross another by becoming part
of the Jewish *ethnos*, the anthropological literature dealing with boundaries, boundary-crossing and boundary-consciousness, especially in the
context of ethnic groups, has an important role to play.

From an anthropological point of view the long-standing controversy as to why Paul would discuss the relationship of the Galatian
communities with the Jewish *ethnos* (the boundary issue) and the internal functioning of those congregations in the one letter is misplaced. Such a phenomenon could only furrow the brows of those
unaware that similar connections are commonplace in many social
contexts. A body of anthropological evidence suggests that there is
often a very close relationship between the position of a group, such
as a religious community, with respect to the outside world and its
internal conditions. The movement from one or more groups to
another is often a difficult one and the tensions generated in those
who join a community by crossing the boundary between it and the

wider world of competing groups or allegiances, in this case both Jewish and pagan, are likely to produce internal strains of the type which underly Paul's concerns in Gal. 5:13–6:10. The phenomenon has been admirably described by Anthony Cohen, professor of social anthropology at Edinburgh University. Drawing upon Arnold Van Gennep's explanation of ritual as a three-stage movement consisting of separation from an original group or status, an in-between or "liminal" period and a re-aggregation into a new group or status (Van Gennep 1960), Cohen rejects the idea that the confusion of liminality, of being "betwixt and between," ends as soon as one has been re-aggregated. He writes:

> Transformations of status, like crossing geo-political borders, require a process of adjustment, of rethinking... They require a reformulation of self which is more fundamental than admission to items of lore, or being loaded with new rights and obligations. The difficulties inherent in such self-adjustment may vary according to the nature of the frontiers which are crossed; but our experience of politics and travel should also alert us to the deceptively innocuous character of crossing between supposedly proximate statuses or cultures... Having crossed a boundary, we have to think ourselves into our transformed identity which is far more subtle, far more individualised than its predication on status (1993: 10; also see Cohen 1994: 128).

In other words, not only cannot we draw any sharp distinction between the boundary question and internal conditions of the group, but also the effective incorporation of members depends more upon their developing a new and appropriate sense of identity than the acquisition of teachings or ethics. This latter point is fundamentally important, since it raises a suspicion (although little more at this stage) that the categorisation of the material in Gal. 5:13–6:10 as ethics or paraenesis, rather than (say) identity-description, may be due to the thoroughly theological agendas of most New Testament critics, rather than to the social realities of the congregations in Galatia, or elsewhere in Paul's areas of activity. As we will soon see, a similar stress on the importance of identity characterises the research of social psychologists into the dynamics of inter-group relations. Thus, rather than following John Barclay in seeing the "ethics" of the passage as distinct from, although closely related to, the question of identity, we are led to ask rather whether the passage itself should not be categorised as relating to identity. In view of the obvious allure of Judaism for Paul's Galatian converts, the further development of this idea requires a consideration of the relevance of the ethnic dimension.

Ethnicity in Recent Anthropological Research

(a) Ethnic Boundaries: Insider and Outsider Perceptions

The publication of Fredrik Barth's symposium *Ethnic Groups and Boundaries* in 1969 constituted a watershed in research into ethnicity. Prior to its appearance research strategies were largely of a structural kind and focused on relations between "races." In his celebrated introduction to this volume, however, Barth located ethnicity "firmly in the realms of the interactional, the transactional and the symbolic" (Cohen 1993: 1). It is worthwhile to outline Barth's position, with a view to offering not an ontological description of ethnicity, but rather a heuristic tool or model with which to investigate the data in Galatians, especially in the critical area of boundaries, in a more socially realistic fashion than is customary in this field.

Barth begins with the proposition that the constitution of ethnic groups and the nature of the boundaries between them has not been adequately discussed. His principal theoretical departure is the notion that ethnic groups are categories of ascription and identification employed by the actors concerned with a view to organising interaction between themselves and others. Thus, an ethnic ascription is one which classifies persons in terms of their basic, most general identity, presumptively determined by their origin and background (Barth 1969: 13).

The *prima facie* relevance of this perspective to Galatia is that the Jews there were ascribing to themselves the status of an ethnic group by reference to their descent from their glorious ancestors Abraham (and Sarah) and that Paul sought to counter the appeal of such a status by re-defining Abrahamic descent to include only those who believed in Jesus as the Christ. Thus we find him saying, "So if you belong to Christ, you are the 'issue' of Abraham and heirs by virtue of the promise" (Gal. 3:29; JB) and again, "You see, then, my friends, we are no slave's children; our mother is the free woman" (Gal. 4:31; JB). It is clear that Paul is ascribing an ethnic status and identity to the Galatian Christians, even though we—and most Galatian Jews—would regard them, "objectively speaking," as "Gentile." Even Paul seems to appreciate he is stretching things a little here, since at one point he distinguishes between physical and spiritual descent (4:29).

On Barth's view, boundary maintenance, meaning how the actors themselves envision and maintain the boundaries, assumes a central importance. Other aspects, such as a distinctive culture, should be seen as the product or result rather than as the basis of ethnic differentiation (Barth 1969: 9–11). Cultural features do not matter for "objective" reasons, but because they are the ones which the actors themselves regard as significant. Some cultural features are used as emblems of ethnic distinctiveness, while others are played down or ignored. The cultural contents of ethnic dichotomies assume two broad types: first, *overt signals or signs*, the features that people look for and exhibit to show identity (such as dress, language, architecture and life-style) and, secondly, *basic value orientations*, the standards of morality and excellence by which performance is judged. The second aspect is important for its connection to the issue of identity: "Since belonging to an ethnic category implies being a certain kind of person, having that basic identity, it also implies a claim to be judged, and to judge oneself, by those standards that are relevant to that identity" (Barth 1969: 14).

It will be helpful at this stage to develop the argument by introducing a useful distinction which Anthony Cohen draws between two senses in which a relevant social boundary is perceived by insiders. Cohen distinguishes between (a) the sense insiders have of a boundary as it would be perceived by people on the other side, that is, the public face and "typical" mode of the boundary, and (b) their sense of community as refracted through all the complexities of their life and experience, the private face and idiosyncratic mode. The former corresponds to Barth's "overt signals" and the latter to his "value orientations." Of utmost importance for what follows is Cohen's view that the private and idiosyncratic mode is more important than the public mode, for here we have people thinking about and symbolizing their community (Cohen 1989: 74–75).

This phenomenon can be illustrated from my own experience. Prior to the reforms of the Second Vatican Council, many Roman Catholic children performed the devotion of attending morning Mass on the first Friday of each month for nine consecutive months, rain, hail or shine, with the aim of obtaining a plenary indulgence by so doing. Although this was a practice which did much to solidify the identity of the children as Catholics, it was not something of which non-Catholics were aware or, accordingly, which figured in the public face of Catholicism as seen by outsiders, or as Catholics understood would be perceived by the outside world.

Unfortunately, some New Testament scholars, such as J.D.G. Dunn, have adopted a notion of "boundary-markers" (or "identification-markers") in exploring the inter-relationships between Jew and Gentile in Galatia without reference to the subtleties of the concept as just outlined. This is one of many areas where biblical critics employ models without the explicit, or sufficiently explicit, discussion of their usefulness which characterises social-scientific interpretation. Thus, Dunn argues that just as non-Jews regarded the very visible signs of Judaism such as circumcision and food laws as marking out people as Jews, so the "Jews regarded them in the same way" (1990: 192). He summons this socially unrealistic proposition as key support for his broad view that in this letter Paul means by "works of the law" these visible signs of Jewishness (1990: 192–200) and, in particular, that the reference to the law which is spoken of as fulfilled in Gal. 5:14 is not the "boundary-marking" torah, but the more inclusive law, including the Mosaic ethical commandments, which he thinks Paul wishes to retain (1990: 200). Through failure to engage with the disciplined social-scientific research on point, Dunn and other commentators who follow him (such as Matera 1992: 15) fall into the error of supposing that the Jews did not regard the observance of the less visible aspects of the law, the Ten Commandments for example, as a vital part of the boundary between themselves and non-Jews and, moreover, that Paul did not understand them to hold that view. At a basic exegetical level, moreover, Dunn's attempt to drive something of a wedge between the (boundary-marking) "works of the law" and the "law" in all its fullness runs into the difficulties that the two are treated as equivalent in Gal. 3:7–14 and that his proposal would involve the unlikely consequence that righteousness by works of law (2:15–21 and 3:2–5) was distinguishable from righteousness by law (Gal. 5:4). I will return to the implications of Dunn's approach for the interpretation of 5:13–6:10 further below. Another obstacle for Dunn's view comes from the Jewish context, in as much as the expression מעשים, sometimes used in connection with תורה or התורה or בתורה, an expression for which ἔργα νόμου is a Greek equivalent, is widespread in the Second Temple period and onwards "as a term specifically designating the laws or commandments of the Bible" (Qimron and Strugnell 1994: 139).

(b) Ethnic Boundaries: Permeability and Resistance

Against the view that geographical and social isolation largely explain cultural diversity, Barth offers two research findings of critical importance for what follows:

> First, it is clear that boundaries persist despite a flow of personnel across them. In other words, categorical ethnic distinctions do not depend on absence of mobility, contact and information, but do entail social processes of exclusion and incorporation whereby discrete categories are maintained *despite* changing participation and membership in the course of individual life histories. Secondly, one finds that stable, persisting, and often vitally important social relations are maintained across such boundaries and are frequently based precisely on the dichotomized ethnic statuses (Barth 1969: 9–10).

Even if the cultural features which signal the boundary are changed, a boundary itself must be maintained to preserve the dichotomization between members and outsiders. Such boundaries persist even when different ethnic groups are in contact with each other, even though one might expect such a process to reduce the differences. This means that there must be some structuring of interaction which allows the persistence of cultural differences. The maintenance of inter-ethnic relations requires:

> a set of prescriptions governing situations of contact, and allowing for articulation in some sectors or domains of activity, and a set of proscriptions on social situations preventing inter-ethnic interaction in other sectors, and thus insulating parts of the cultures from confrontation and modification (Barth 1969: 16).

This is precisely the point I have previously made with respect to the Jewish prohibition on table-fellowship in the first century:

> But although Jews were happy to mix with Gentiles in synagogues or possibly even in market-places or streets, eating with them was a very different matter. Eating was an occasion fraught with the possibility of breaching the purity code, one of the most crucial aspects of the Mosaic law for the maintenance of the separate identity of the Jewish *ethnos* (Esler 1987: 84).[6]

The primary importance of this for Galatians is that mixed Jewish-Gentile table-fellowship was an area of interaction which the Jews and strict Jewish-Christians of Galatia could not tolerate. They perceived, quite correctly, that the Jewish identity of the Jews who took part would be seriously imperilled by this practice.

Yet while his primary concern was to insist on ethnic (or at least quasi-ethnic) boundaries for his congregations vis-à-vis Judaism, Paul

---

[6] Critics (such as J.D.G. Dunn [1990: 129–82]) who argue on the basis of more general forms of Jewish interaction that Jews were also relaxed about dining with Gentiles miss the point that while some contact was inevitable, there were, necessarily, also situations where it was forbidden.

himself was also concerned with keeping at bay the sinful world of pagan idolatry. This necessitated consideration of what types of interaction could be permitted and what proscribed, with the explicit practice of idolatry being among the most critical item in the latter category (5:20).

The Social Psychology of Intergroup Conflict and Social Identity

To explore further the way in which internal conditions of a group might be related to its relationships with external entities and forces, we turn to the area of social psychology. There has been a steady stream of research carried out into the social psychology of group dynamics since late in the nineteenth century (see Jones 1989). For this paper I have relied principally, although not solely, on the work of Henry Tajfel conducted in the 1960s, 1970s and 1980s because of its utility in prompting a fresh agenda of questions to pose to a number of New Testament texts, including Galatians. Tajfel was interested in exploring the manner in which group identity and the identity of the members of groups were largely an incident of intergroup relations. From his work, and research influenced by it (Brown 1988), I have developed a seven part model of this process which I will now set out and develop in detail below.

1. Identity and Group Membership

Our sense of who we are, of our identity, is intimately tied up with our group memberships. In joining a group we re-define who we are. If asked "Who am I?," part of my reply will be in terms of the groups to which I belong. Paul wanted the Galatians to see themselves as members of ἐκκλησίαι (1:2), as "brethren" (ἀδελφοί: 1:11; 3:15; 4:12, 28, 31; 5:11, 13; 6:1, 18), those justified in Christ (2:15–17 etc.), members of the one household (6:10), sons of God (3:26), those who are one in Christ (3:28–29) and as descendants of Abraham (and Sarah). As already noted, the last of these involves a claim to ethnic identity. But above all, as we will see below, Paul sought to present the identity of his Galatian readers as those who had become members of the congregations through their initial reception of the Holy Spirit (3:2–3) and who must continue to live in the Spirit thereafter (5:16–26).

Tajfel describes this recognition of belonging to a group as the "cognitive dimension." But this is only one of three dimensions of group belonging which he identifies:

(a) "Cognitive" – Recognition of belonging to a group,
(b) "Evaluative" – Positive or negative connotations of belonging,
(c) "Emotional" – Attitudes towards insiders and outsiders (Tajfel 1978: 28).

The evaluative dimension, and one which is positive in nature, is readily apparent in the approbation obviously attached to many of the modes of designating his addressees just mentioned, but also in other features, such as his distress that they could turn away from the Gospel which he preached (1:6). The emotional component emerges principally in the degree to which antipathy is directed toward members of various outgroups, to which we will return below. Tajfel defines "social identity" to mean that part of an individual's self-concept which derives from his or her knowledge of membership of a social group (or groups) together with the value and emotional significance attached to that membership (1978: 63).

2. The Dialectical Relationship between Social Setting and Group Belonging

Tajfel argues that there is a reciprocal or "dialectical" relationship between, first, social settings and situations and, secondly, the expression or reflection of them in subjective group memberships. There are two aspects to this:

(a) The number and variety of social situations seen as relevant to group membership will increase the stronger are a member's cognitive, evaluative and emotional connections with a group.
(b) Conversely, some social situations will force individuals to act in terms of group identification, however weak was their initial connection (1978: 39).

The main area of interest raised by this aspect of the model is the question of the extent to which the community perceives itself to be the subject of persecution by the outside world, Jewish especially, but to a lesser extent Gentile. There is no sign of Gentile persecution in Galatians, but persecution, or potential persecution, by the Jews is mentioned (Gal. 4:29; 5:11; 6:12), no doubt motivated by the danger which mixed table-fellowship posed to a critical ethnic boundary. This persecution is, in turn, inducing the Jewish-Christians to put pressure on the Gentiles to be circumcised and become Jews (5:2, 3, 11; 6:12). Paul's message for the Galatians is delivered in and has been shaped by a context of pronounced intergroup conflict.

3. Group Norms

Norms are values defining acceptable and unacceptable attitudes and behaviours for group members. They bring order and predicability to the environment, helping members to construe the world. They also point to appropriate behaviour in new and ambiguous situations. Norms enhance and maintain group identity (Brown 1988: 42–8).

Norms in this sense are related to "ethics" as employed by New Testament interpreters. But we should notice two areas of differentiation. We are not dealing here primarily with a topic which is distinct from identity, although related to it, as Barclay would have it, since norms are actually an *aspect of* identity. Nor are we primarily speaking of prescriptive assertions of what an *individual* should do to stay right with God and neighbour. From a social-psychological viewpoint, although its proponents would agree that ethical standards which individuals must embody exist in religious communities like those of the followers of Christ in Galatia, the emphasis falls on the much larger issue of the creation and maintenance of a group identity.

Thus, to employ a modern analogy, the ban on the consumption of meat on Fridays in force in the Roman Catholic Church prior to the Second Vatican Council did not merely function to specify a rule which it would be sinful for an individual to breach, it also served to stamp Catholics with a unique group identity. Gal. 5:10– 6:13 plainly falls to be understood in this light. It is to be interpreted as describing who the Galatian Christians are, or should be, with the notion of what they should do being subsidiary to that purpose. To see how and why, we need to set out further aspects of the model.

4. Group Conflict and Intergroup Behaviour

A critical aspect of the sense we have of belonging to one group is the existence of other groups to which we do not belong (Brown 1988: 192–200). For present purposes, however, the richly agonistic nature of so much of Galatians, where the *agon* is fought out in ethnic terms, induces us to focus our enquiry on a specific aspect of intergroup relationships, namely, the phenomenon of conflict between groups.

To understand the process of intergroup conflict, however, it is necessary to recognise that there is a continuum between behaviour which, at the one end, is entirely interindividual and, at the other, is entirely intergroup. Purely interindividual behaviour is determined solely by the personal characteristics of those involved and not by reference to any social categories; it is, however, difficult to imagine behaviour which is purely interindividual. Even a casual request for directions made on a street corner to someone passing by will probably mean evoking the roles of tourist and local inhabitant. Purely intergroup behaviour consists of behaviour solely determined by membership of social groups which disregards individual differences and personal relationships (Tajfel 1978: 44); an example can be seen in the action of bomber pilots releasing a load of bombs upon an enemy population (Tajfel 1978: 41).

Galatians reveals a strong intergroup emphasis, with barely any sign whatever of interindividual conduct. At one point Paul actually indicates that he does not know the identities of those who are disturbing the congregations (5:10), unless this is a way of saying personal status will have no effect on the punishment which will flow from such behaviour.

5. Stereotyping the Outgroup

The closer behaviour is to the intergroup extreme, the greater the tendency to treat outgroup members as undifferentiated items in a unified social category. This leads to:

(a) Clear awareness of ingroup-outgroup dichotomy,
(b) Attribution to all members of the outgroup of traits assumed to be common to their group as a whole (= "stereotyping"), and
(c) Usually negative value judgments of those traits (Brown 1988: 231–39).

Galatians has many signs of this. A good example is found at 6:12–13 and the characterisation of the opposing groups as "flesh" is another.

6. Social Immobility and Intergroup Inferiority

Extreme forms of animosity towards outgroup members usually require sharp boundaries between the two groups, so that movement from one to another is impossible (= "social immobility") (Tajfel 1978: 50–1). This aspect of the model, especially in view of the specifically

ethnic context of the issues, raises intriguing questions for Paul's letter
to the Galatians. In Galatia the position seems to be that the local
Jews, and the Jewish Christians doing their bidding, have begun to
insist that the Gentiles become Jews through adoption of circumcision and the rest of the law. At a theological level Paul is insisting
that to do so means forsaking the truth of the Gospel: "For if righteousness came through law, surely Christ died in vain" (2:21). At a
social level, Paul is opposing what will essentially mean the end of
the mixed communities he has founded in Galatia. He is defending
a boundary between their members and the Jews which is ethnic in
its intent to enlist Abraham as the true ancestor of the members
rather than of the Jews. This explains the sharp animosity expressed
at 1:9 (where he wishes that the proponents of the rival Gospel be
accursed) and at 5:12 (where he wishes they would castrate themselves).

Although it is possible to leave the group, this is presented as
extremely undesirable, as shown most clearly in the reminder that it
was through faith and not the law that the Galatians received the
Spirit (3:2–3), no doubt with the ecstatic consequences described
1 Corinthians 12–14 (see Esler 1994: 37–51), and in the problem of
being cut off from Christ (5:4). Thus, group members faced with
various disadvantages, such as a sense of deprivation vis-à-vis the
local Jews, yet wishing to remain within the community and to secure the benefits available within it, would have acted with the group
as a whole just as surely as if exit was impossible.

7. Group Differentiation Through Value Inversion

A group which does perceive itself to be subordinate to another in
terms of power and status will frequently respond through forms of
group differentiation which attack the basis for the perceived inferiority (Tajfel 1978: 67–76). Such responses involve sidestepping the
main dimensions of the comparison, either by changing those dimensions or inventing new ones. A possible strategy is the assertion
that the true positive values are the antithesis of those espoused by
the dominant group (Brown 1988: 250–251).

Based on the preliminary connection with this aspect of the model
that the Christian communities were probably no match for the local
synagogues in terms of power and influence, and that such dominance
was being exercised to persuade the Gentile Christians of Galatia to
become Jews, it is submitted that this strategy is pervasively present

in Gal. 5:13–6:10. As part of their advocacy of circumcision to end the scandal of mixed table-fellowship, the Jewish or Jewish-Christian opponents were advancing the claims of Judaism as a superior form of identity by arguing that sin was the inevitable concomitant of being a Gentile, even for those who had come to faith in Jesus Christ. This argument is reflected in Gal. 2:15–17 when Paul insists: "We are by nature Jews and not Gentile sinners (ἁμαρτωλοί) . . . If we seek to be justified in Christ and we are found to be sinners (ἁμαρτωλοί), does that mean that Christ is the agent of sin (ἁμαρτία)?"

Although the sin to which Gentiles most typically succumbed was idolatry, the sin referred to in 2:17 may transcend this. Possibly there was a measure of dissension within the ἐκκλησίαι (5:15) which gave credence to accusations of ἁμαρτία. The Jewish advocates of circumcision in Galatia were unfavourably comparing the sinful (because anomic) condition of the communities with the allegedly sinless (because nomic) one of the synagogue. Paul needs to sidestep the terms of this comparison by re-defining its terms. His primary means of achieving this is to stigmatise the world outside the congregations as the realm of "flesh" (σάρξ) in contrast to the Spirit-conditioned life within. In effect, he wants the Galatians to be able to define their identity with the assertion "We are the people of the Spirit" as against all others, Jew first but also Gentile, who are people of the flesh. Having made this observation we are now able to undertake a detailed application of the model to the textual data.

5. Detailed Application of the Social-Scientific Approaches to Gal. 5:13–6:10

Paul actually lays the foundation for his strategy of redefining the comparison being made by his opponents between the alleged sinfulness of the Christian congregations and allegedly nomic order among Jews somewhat earlier in the text—at Gal. 3:2–5. The word σάρξ occurs three times in the letter before this, on each occasion meaning little more than "human being" (1:16, 2:16 and 2:20).[7] At 3:3, however, Paul launches on a new tack by sharply contrasting the condition of being under the law, designated as "flesh" (σάρξ),

---

[7] For many of the subtleties of the meaning of σάρξ in Galatians, see Barclay 1988: 178–215.

compared with the experience of the "spirit" (πνεῦμα), which characterises the new dispensation (3:3): "Having begun with the Spirit,
are you now ending with the flesh?" (ἐναρξάμενοι πνεύματι νῦν σαρκὶ
ἐπιτελεῖσθε;). He reminds them of who they are by reference to the
circumstances of their turning to Christ. Since the context in which
they received the Spirit was presumably a meeting of the congregation, this reminder inevitably brings to their attention the manner in
which they joined the new Christian groups[8] or became committed
to them. No doubt σαρξ evokes here the spectre of circumcision and
the works of the Jewish law which Paul has just argued have no role
in justification (2:15–21), but the word is capable of carrying a fuller
meaning, to refer (by the process of stereotyping) to the whole social
order which beckons beyond the boundaries of the group. This sense
of σαρξ also emerges a little later in the allegory in 4:21–31, where
Paul links his congregations with Sarah, who was born according to
Spirit, as opposed to Hagar, who was born according to flesh (4:29),
and who represents the present-day Jerusalem which is still in a state
of slavery along with her children (4:25). As we will see below, Paul
provides the fullest explication of this meaning in 5:16–25, by
stigmatising unacceptable aspects of community life and individual
behaviour, which typify σάρξ, in contrast to acceptable ones, which
pertain to πνεῦμα (5:16–6:10). As already noted, none of this is surprising. For his Gentile readers, having crossed a boundary separating them from pagan idolatry to join the Christian communities and
being under pressure to cross another by taking on Jewish identity
(which utilised a detailed ethical code to contribute to its inner sense
of the boundary between itself and the wider world), desperately
needed to appropriate their own distinctive identity.

The theme begins at 5:13. Paul has previously made it clear that
the imposition of the law was a form of slavery (2:4; 4:8–9, 25; 5:1)
being forceably advocated (4:29; 6:12) by persons who were themselves enslaved (4:25). Now, paradoxically and yet in a way which
typifies the redefinition of the respective roles of the relevant groups
suggested by the model, he asserts that Christian freedom is not an
opportunity for the σάρξ, but a form of slavery-through-love (ἀγαπή).
As at 3:2–3 he recalls the occasion when they obtained their new
identity and contrasts it with the realm of flesh: "For you were called

---

[8] I am not suggesting that the word Christian was applied to them at this early stage.

to freedom, brethren, only not freedom as an opportunity for the flesh (σάρξ), but through love (ἀγάπη) be slaves to one another" (5:13). He is changing the dimensions of the comparison by suggesting that Christian freedom does not entail giving untrammelled licence to the flesh, but actually implies a type of slavery, one which is based on ἀγάπη. More significantly, he is about to go on to say that unsuitable modes of existence and activity within the congregations would leave one in a mess similar to that of being under the law, since σάρξ is an apt designation for both. The right identity and true positive values which are an aspect of it, which he will soon refer to as πνεῦμα (thus revisiting the blunt contrast of 3:3), are, in this stereotypical perspective, the precise antithesis of those of the Jews.

Gal. 5:14 is central to this project. We have already seen that an inadequate understanding of group boundaries led J.D.G. Dunn to suppose that Paul meant that the ethical elements of the Mosaic law were to be retained within the Christian congregations and Heikki Räisänen also sees in this verse "the reduction of the torah to the moral law" (1986: 23–7). But these views mistake Paul's intentions, which are, after all, expressed quite unequivocally at 5:18: "If you are led by Spirit, you are not under law." That Paul has the whole law in mind is clear from 5:3: "Everyone who is circumcised is obliged to carry out the whole law." When Paul taxes his opponents with not keeping the law themselves in 6:13 it is more likely to be the moral code thereof than the ceremonial elements to which he is referring. Paul's point is that if you have love (which, of course, you get as the first gift of the Spirit in the Christian community—5:22) you do not need the law. Christians have independent access to the best the law can provide: "If you are led by Spirit, you are not under law." Love, derived from the Spirit and not from the law, is being proposed as a substitute for the law. Paul has destroyed the law (2:18). This is a better explanation than the one proposed by John Barclay—that "the moral standards of the law are taken up into and fully realized in the life of the Spirit" (1988: 141). Paul opts for substitution, not realization. Paul ditches the Mosaic law in its entirety in order to create and maintain a boundary between his congregations and the Jews.

At 5:15 Paul provides a revealing glimpse of what it might be like if the Galatians do not serve one another in love, with people biting and tearing one another to pieces like wild animals. It is possible that Paul has actual conduct in mind, although this is not necessarily so and the language used is certainly hyperbolic (Betz 1979: 276–7). Either way, the verse constitutes a hard-headed acknowledgment by Paul that the process of acquiring a new identity could be a very difficult one, which is just what we would expect from the social-scientific material discussed above. The rival Jewish claimant to the loyalties of the Gentile members offered a mode of identity which its proponents were arguing provided a system of values which might restrain such behaviour. Paul's answer involves recognising that the Mosaic code does offer ethical guidance, encapsulated in the injunction to love neighbour as self in the previous verse, while setting out an entirely different mode of access to its benefits, coupled with a fundamental insistence that those advocating circumcision do not keep the law anyway (6:13).

In 5:16–22 Paul sets out as a sharp antithesis the experience of living in the σάρξ on the one hand and living in the πνεῦμα on the other. His language indicates that he is picking up a theme introduced earlier, at 3:2–5. Previously he had contrasted the beginning of the Galatians' life in Christ with their current inclinations: "Are you so stupid that having begun in Spirit (ἐναρξάμενοι πνεύματι) you are now being completed in flesh (σαρκὶ ἐπιτελεῖσθε)?" (3:3) and here, in very similar language, he expatiates in detail upon what it means to proceed in Spirit rather than in flesh: "Walk in Spirit (πνεύματι) and do not fulfil the desire of the flesh (ἐπιθυμίαν σαρκὸς οὐ μὴ τελέσητε) (5:16). In 5:16–21 the link back to the earlier connection between σάρξ and law is made even more pointed by the reference to "law" (νόμος) in v. 18 and "works of flesh" (ἔργα τῆς σαρκὸς) in v. 19, which seem to constitute an ironic parallel with the expression "works of the law" (ἔργα νόμου) used earlier (Gal. 2:16 (thrice); 3:2, 5 and 10). Paul is not suggesting that the works of the law are themselves works of the flesh, rather that those who rely on the law cannot escape the sway of the flesh (cf. Gal. 3:10).

For present purposes it is unnecessary to enter the discussion as to the extent to which Paul was directly indebted, if at all, to Jewish tradition as represented in 1QS 3:13–4:26[9] or to Stoic philosophy for the contents of the list in vv. 19–21 (Barclay 1988: 187–91). Never-

---

[9] Cf. 1 QS 4:9–11: "However, to the spirit of deceit belong greed, frailty of hands in the service of justice, irreverence, deceit, pride and haughtiness of heart, dishonesty, trickery, cruelty, much insincerity, impatience, much insanity, impudent enthusiasm, appalling acts performed in a lustful passion, filthy paths for indecent purposes, blasphemous tongue, blindness of eyes, hardness of hearing, stiffness of

theless, the fact that "vices"[10] similar to those in Gal. 5:19–21 have been found in a Jewish text such as 1 QS and attributed to other Jews who were purportedly living in accordance with the law of Moses strengthens the otherwise strong case that Paul primarily presents his list as (allegedly) constituting pathological dimensions of the Judaism proving so attractive to his Gentile converts in Galatia. Thus Paul suggests that the Jewish law, as advocated by the Galatian trouble-makers, will plunge those who adopt it into the realm of "flesh," which he castigated earlier (3:3). Although they are also seen as forms of behaviour which lead to loss of the Kingdom of God (5:21), their role in defining a reverse image of Christian identity is plain. At the same time, since the works of the flesh manifested by Jews who do not keep the law could also characterise idolatrous Gentiles, we should not exclude the latter from the persons whom Paul seeks to have his readers distance themselves from. To this extent he is seeking to keep them within the boundary they crossed in entering the congregations as much as discouraging their crossing the other boundary between themselves and Judaism. It may be that the inclusion of idolatry as the first topic in v. 20 is meant to underline the continuing menace of paganism. In the terms of the model from Tajfel's social psychology set out above, Paul is employing the particular works of the σάρξ listed in vv. 19–20 to stereotype the rival forms of ethnic and religious identity on offer in Galatia and to warn his congregations that they should be shunned.

Paul's interest in the group dimension of the works of the flesh is quite noticeable. Of the fifteen negative characteristics, nine of them relate to intra-community strife: sorcery (φαρμακεία), enmities (ἔχθραι), strife (ἔρις), jealousy (ζῆλος), outbursts of anger (θυμοί), selfish ambition (ἐριθεῖα), dissensions (διχοστασίαι), factions (αἱρέσεις) and envy (φθόνοι). In other words, the majority deal with aspects of inter-personal relations which have the potential to tear the community apart. They constitute elements of rival group identity which Paul wants to play no part in his congregations. The list tells the Galatian communities who and what they must not be, by warning them what not to do.

Paul also adopts the tactic of asserting that the true values are the

---

neck, hardness of heart in order to walk in all the paths of darkness and evil cunning"—Martínez 1994: 7.

[10] I hesitate to use this otherwise convenient word because it is somewhat too evocative of individual ethics which I am arguing should not be seen as the focus of the passage under discussion.

antithesis of those just described. He does this in 5:22–3. This possibility was raised by the seventh aspect of the social-psychological
model. The fruits of the Spirit which are listed here, beginning with
ἀγάπη, image the proper identity of the congregations in Christ. It is
apparent that ethical norms are only one aspect of this identity, both
from the general consideration of their role within the overall contrast between σάρξ and πνεῦμα as the diametric opposites characterising rival groups and because of the inclusion of joy and peace in
the list. Joy and peace are difficult to classify as norms but are easily
recognised as badges of identity.

Many of the social and personal delinquencies listed in 5:19–21
were widely recognised as such in the social world of the first century
Graeco-Roman world. Yet the admonition at 5:26—"Let us not
engage in empty boasting (κενόδοξοι), challenging (προκαλούμενοι) one
another, envying (φθονοῦντες) one another"—raises a somewhat different issue. What we have here is virtually a summary of Mediterranean
man,[11] always seeking to provoke others who were not kin to social
contests of challenge and response in order to win honour and to be
able to boast accordingly, as revealed to us by recent anthropological
research (Esler 1995b). In this verse Paul may have in his sights a general problem posed by the social environment more than the particular issue raised by Judaism. In counselling his audience to distance
themselves from such an outlook Paul has in mind for them a corporate identity which would be appropriate for members of one family,
who did not engage in the social pattern of challenge and response
with one another, since ἀδελφοί defend one another's honour.[12]

And it is the family to which Paul immediately proceeds in 6:1,
with an address to ἀδελφοί beginning a new section which is closed
with the reference to the members of the household of faith in 6:10.
Family imagery frames this section. In 6:1–6 Paul offers advice on
how ethically appropriate behaviour can be encouraged, but within
the context of how the maintenance of the right type of identity can
be guaranteed. First of all he advocates peer pressure (6:1), as one
would expect in Mediterranean society, given its strongly corporate
nature and the pressure customarily brought to bear on wayward

---

[11] The male gender is used deliberately. Challenge and response was a social
game played out between men in public.

[12] John Barclay, who never cites any works of Mediterranean anthropology in his
book on the passage, misses this aspect of the verse (1988: 156). I develop this point
in Esler 1997.

group members to conform. Secondly, he proposes the mutual sharing of burdens, suggesting, in one of the most difficult phrases in the letter, that by so doing they will "fulfil the law of Christ" (ἀναπληρώσετε τὸν νόμον τοῦ Χριστοῦ—6:2). The word νόμος is used thirty times in the letter and this is the only occasion on which there is any doubt that it refers to the Mosaic law. The expression "the law of Christ" is not likely to refer to a body of ethical teaching deriving from the historical Jesus. Nor, as John Barclay proposes (1988: 134) does it mean the Mosaic law redefined by Jesus, since this view is based on a failure to recognize that 5:13, in context, represents the stark substitution of the new dispensation for the old. Rather, Paul is employing "the law of Christ" as a bold metaphor for the manner in which love, originating in the Spirit, now becomes the guiding force in Christian life. This represents the high-point in the letter both of Paul's ascription to the congregations of an ethnic identity and the inversion of the values of the major group with which they are conflict: not only do the Galatian congregations have Abraham and Sarah as ancestors, they have their own law.

Lastly, we have Gal. 6:6–10. According to Betz (1979: 306), Paul expresses an "eschatological warning" in Gal. 6:7–9. The fact that the warning concerns the hard truth that as we sow, whether in Spirit or in flesh, so will we reap, suggests that it has a very general import, covering the basic dichotomy Paul inaugurated at Gal. 3:2 and began to develop at Gal. 5:13. Eschatological punishment or reward is attached to the choice his addressees make—either the way of the σάρξ (especially in the adoption of Jewish law and identity) or the way of the πνεῦμα, meaning continued membership of the congregations (without circumcision) and manifestation of ἀγάπη and the other gifts of the Spirit. Life in the *sarx* leads to destruction, life in the *pneuma* to eternal life. The connection between one's actions and one's ultimate moral responsibility for them is very direct and, moreover, not easy to reconcile with a Lutheran interpretation.[13] Even here, however, ethical norms form part, but only a part, of the preferable identity, which is created and maintained in the heat of intergroup conflict. The extent to which even eschatology can be deployed to legitimate the appropriate group identity is evident in the reversion to family imagery in the conclusion of this section: "Therefore

---

[13] Many of the difficulties of reconciling Paul with a Lutheran reading of his theology have been set out in Watson 1986.

238   PHILIP F. ESLER

since we have time let us do good to everyone, but mostly to our fellow-members in the household of faith" (6:10).

Conclusion

The analysis of Gal. 5:13–6:10 using social-scientific research into group boundaries, ethnicity and intergroup conflict supports both elements of the bi-polar thesis set out at the beginning of this essay: first, that understanding the passage requires an integrated account of the external and internal aspects of the context and, secondly, that the passage focuses on identity, of which ethical norms are one element, and that intergroup conflict has been fundamental in the creation of that identity. We are not dealing here, as John Barclay argues, with "ethical maxims" attached to the issue of identity, but with identity itself, in the establishment of which norms form only a part. By building on the unique experience of the Spirit, which brought the Galatian communities into being, as a means of sharply differentiating the life of the congregations from that of the Jewish and Gentile worlds, and by an idiosyncratic use of Jewish tradition and a more plausible application of family imagery, Paul seeks to forge an identity distinct from both Jew and Gentile. This is the social reality underlying his affirmation that "there is neither circumcision nor uncircumcision but a new creation" (Gal. 6:15).

List of References

Barclay, John M.G.
1988   *Obeying the Truth: A Study of Paul's Ethics in Galatians.* Edinburgh: T. & T. Clark.

Barth, Fredrik, ed.
1969   *Ethnic Groups and Boundaries: The Social Organization of Culture Difference.* Boston: Little, Brown and Company.

Betz, Hans Dieter
1979   *Galatians: A Commentary on Paul's Letter to the Churches in Galatia.* Hermeneia Commentary. Philadelphia: Fortress Press.

Brinsmead, B.H.
1982   *Galatians—A Dialogical Response to Opponents.* SBLDS, 65. Chico: Scholars Press.

Brown, Rupert
1988   *Group Processes: Dynamics Within and Between Groups.* Oxford: Basil Blackwell.

Burton, E. de W.
1921   *A Critical and Exegetical Commentary on the Epistle to the Gala-
              tians.* Edinburgh: T. & T. Clark.
Cohen, Anthony P.
1989   *The Symbolic Construction of Community.* London and New
              York: Routledge.
—— 1993   "Boundaries of Consciousness, Consciousness of Bound-
              aries." Plenary paper delivered the conference on *The
              Anthropology of Ethnicity: A Critical View,* The University of
              Amsterdam. 15th–18th December.
—— 1994   *Self Consciousness: An Alternative Anthropology of Identity.* Lon-
              don and New York: Routledge.
Dibelius, Martin
1934   *From Tradition to Gospel.* E.T. by Bertram Lee Woolf.
              London: Nicholson & Watson.
—— 1976   *A Commentary on the Epistle of James.* Revised by H. Gree-
              ven. Hermeneia Commentary. E.T. by Michael A. Wil-
              liams. Philadelphia: Fortress.
Dunn, James D.G.
1990   *Jesus, Paul and the Law.* London: SPCK.
—— 1993   *The Epistle to the Galatians.* Black's New Testament Com-
              mentaries. Peabody, MA.: Hendrickson.
Esler, Philip F.
1987   *Community and Gospel in Luke-Acts: The Social and Political
              Motivations of Lucan Theology.* Cambridge: Cambridge Uni-
              versity Press.
—— 1994   *The First Christians in their Social Worlds: Social-Scientific Ap-
              proaches to New Testament Interpretation.* London and New
              York: Routledge,
—— ed. 1995a *Modelling Early Christianity: Social-Scientific Studies of the New
              Testament in Its Context.* London and New York: Routledge.
—— 1995b   "Making and Breaking an Agreement Mediterranean
              Style: A New Reading of Galatians 2:1–14," *Biblical
              Interpretation* 3:285–314.
—— 1997   "Family Imagery and Christian Identity in Gal. 5:13–
              6:10," in Halvor Moxnes (ed.), *The Family as the Bearer
              of Religious Culture in Judaism and Early Christianity.* Lon-
              don and New York: Routledge, forthcoming.
Howard, George
1979   *Paul: Crisis in Galatia: A Study in Early Christian Theology.*
              Cambridge: Cambridge University Press.
Jones, Edward E.
1989   "Social Psychology," in Adam Kuper and Jessica Kuper
              (eds.), *The Social Science Encyclopedia.* London and New
              York: Routledge, 780–3.
Lütgert, W.
1919   *Gesetz und Geist. Eine Untersuchung zur Vorgeschichte des Galater-
              briefes.* Gütersloh: Bertelsmann.
Malina, Bruce J.
1993   *The New Testament World: Insights from Cultural Anthropology.*
              Revised edition. Louisville, KY: Westminster/John Knox
              Press.

Martínez, Florentino García
1994 *The Dead Sea Scrolls Translated: The Qumran Text in English.* Leiden: E.J. Brill.
O'Neill, J.C.
1972 *The Recovery of Paul's Letter to the Galatians.* London: SPCK.
Qimron, Elisha, and Strugnell, John
1994 *Qumran Cave 4. V. Miqsat Ma'ase Ha-Torah. Discoveries in the Judean Desert X.* Oxford: The Clarendon Press.
Räisänen, Heikki
1986 *Paul & the Law.* Philadelphia: Fortress.
Robbins, Vernon
1995 "Social-Scientific Criticism and Literary Studies: Prospects for Cooperation in Biblical Interpretation," in Esler 1995a.
Ropes, J.H.
1929 *The Singular Problem of the Epistle to the Galatians.* Cambridge: Harvard University Press.
Schmithals, W.
1972 *Paul and the Gnostics.* E.T. by J.E. Steely. Nashville: Abingdon Press.
Tajfel, Henri
1978 *Differentiation between Social Groups: Studies in the Social Psychology of Intergroup Relations.* London *et alibi*: Academic Press.
Van Gennep, Arnold
1960 *The Rites of Passage,* E.T. by Monika B. Vizedom and Gabrielle L. Caffee. Chicago: University of Chicago Press.
Watson, Francis
1986 *Paul, Judaism and the Gentiles: A Sociological Approach.* Cambridge: Cambridge University Press.
Wilson, R. McL.
1968 "Gnostics—In Galatia?," in F.L. Cross (ed.), *Studia Evangelica,* 4, (= Texte und Untersuchungen zur Geschichte der altchristlichen Literatur No. 102), 358–67.

THE 'NATION' OF STRANGERS: SOCIAL CONTEMPT AND ITS THEOLOGICAL INTERPRETATION IN ANCIENT JUDAISM AND EARLY CHRISTIANITY[1]

Reinhard Feldmeier

The terms "nation" and "stranger" are essentially sociological categories. As such they are opposed to each other: "nation" (German: *Volk*) is a common culture and tradition, fatherland and mother tongue; it is the part of the world I know and where I am known, the piece of mother earth in which life is rooted. If the term "nation" implies belonging, a homeland, also citizenship with its rights and responsibilities, the label "stranger" can have the opposite quality: it is used to separate off one group from those who do not, and are not supposed to, belong to it. The term stranger is thus used primarily to express something negative: not belonging, exclusion, mixed to some extent with the denigration of this other person (a "barbarian"). The state of being a stranger is experienced by those concerned as something that is *per se* thoroughly negative. This was especially the case in ancient times, when it was only the possession of citizenship that made someone legally and politically viable in the full sense.[2]

The title "the nation of strangers" thus appears at first sight to be a contradiction in terms: either one belongs to the nation, in which case one is a citizen and not a stranger, or one is a stranger, and one does not belong to the nation. However, both terms are in 1 Peter key terms for Christian self-understanding—with an interesting pre-history in the Jewish literature of the Hebrew Bible as well as a

---

[1] Translated by David E. Orton and Alan Moss. This article is a development of some ideas stemming from my Habilitationsschrift, *Die Christen als Fremde. Die Metapher der Fremde in der antiken Welt, im Urchristentum und im 1. Petrusbrief* (WUNT 64; Tübingen, 1992).

[2] In antiquity, which is oriented towards the ideal of the full citizen, the *peregrinus*, the stranger, is a second-class person, with limited rights and opportunities, and it was astonishing what an individual was prepared to put up with in order to leave this status behind him/her and become a citizen (e.g., 25 years of service in the reserve army!). And in ancient Israel too it is of course the member of a tribe who stands in the central position. The stranger is, it is true, placed under the special protection of divine law, alongside widows and orphans and other unfortunate characters, but this is precisely because of his/her miserable status (cf. Sir. 29:23–28).

notable history of influence in Christian tradition! We shall sketch both of these at this point. Our focus is, however, on 1 Peter, which is the first to make the exclusion of the "stranger" a constitutive element of the identity of the believer. It will become clear that in certain areas of the Jewish and Christian tradition the two apparently mutually exclusive terms complement and confirm one another in a remarkable way. To present the thesis of this article at the outset: *The affirmation and positive interpretation of their own strangerhood has contributed substantially to the fact that Jews scattered in the diaspora—and even more so Christians, who were in the minority, outsiders in society—were able to see themselves as the people of God, despite all attempts to make them into enemies, to exclude them, and despite all pressure on them to assimilate.* What follows will not only justify this thesis but at the same time make a contribution to the biblical understanding of "nationhood" or "peoplehood" (*Volkstum*).

1. *"Strangers" in the Old Testament People of God*

That Israel is God's people is one of the basic statements of the Hebrew Bible. The first thing that God does in the Bible after the exodus from Egypt is to make this group of fleeing nomads his people and thereby to give them their dignity and worth, at the same time placing his stamp upon them, a stamp which has made an extremely deep impression on the identity of Israel. However much Israel suffered, from time to time, under this characterisation, whatever attempts it made to divest itself of it, being God's people was (and is) central to Jewish self-understanding. It is so much the more surprising that the category of strangeness suddenly comes to the fore—even if only occasionally—in the Hebrew Bible and in Early Judaism.

1.1 *The Patriarchs: Identity by Identification*

The first people whose foreignness is extensively mentioned in the Bible are the patriarchs.[3] Ever since Abraham was called from his familiar surroundings and set on the road, he and his descendants have been strangers in the promised land. This foreignness is stressed time and again in the patriarchal narratives. Thus when buying the

---

[3] Cf. Gen. 12:10; 17:8; 19:9; 20:1; 21:23, 34; 23:4; 26:3; 28:4; 32:5; 35:27; 36:7; 37:1; 47:4; Exod. 6:4; Ps. 105:12 etc.

cave for his wife Abraham expressly describes himself to the indigenous population as "a stranger and a sojourner" (Gen. 23:4). There
is more than historical memory behind this. For on closer examination it is striking that among the Pentateuchal sources, the priestly
document in particular programmatically places "the time of the
patriarchs under the term 'sojourning'."[4] This is remarkable since
the priestly document was presumably written in the Babylonian
diaspora,[5] i.e. at a time and in a situation in which Israel had lost
everything that had previously characterised its life as a nation: It
had been driven out of the promised land of the fathers, no longer
had a king, its centre Jerusalem was destroyed, and above all there
was no longer a temple, the cultic centre of any religion. *Israel, it
must have appeared, was at an end as a nation.* In this situation the priestly
document now begins to retell the story of Israel and thereby also
the story of the patriarchs, all over again.[6] And one thing it underlines is that the patriarchs too were strangers, to whom no land
belonged. But though such strangers they had not been abandoned
by God. As "strangers and sojourners" they were people who went
on their way trusting in God's provision and were not disappointed!
The patriarchs thus become a sort of parable of living by faith, in
which God's word is valid even in foreign parts. *Being a stranger is life
according to the promise.* With these "strangers" the troubled Israelites
in the exile could identify themselves and thus gain in their desperate
situation the confidence they needed to enable them to survive.

1.2   *Being a Stranger and Relating to the Foreigner*

The reminder of foreignness does not only have a reassuring function, however. The exodus from the "house of slavery," Egypt, was
indeed the beginning of the existence of Israel, and this saving act of

---

[4] J. Schreiner, "Muß ich in der Fremde leben? Eine Frage des alten Israel," in
Dynamik im Wort: Lehre von der Bibel. Leben aus der Bibel (Stuttgart: Katholisches Bibelwerk,
1983), p. 140. According to Schreiner, P thereby clearly differentiates itself from the
earlier narratives: "A sign that the patriarchs felt themselves to be foreigners or that
their sojourn in Canaan seemed problematic to them, is not evident in this old
narrative layer (J)" (*ibid.*, p. 135). This formulation is not, however very sharply
defined since the patriarchs are described as נרים in the old pentateuchal sources
too (cf. Kellermann, "גר," p. 986).

[5] Cf. E. Zenger, *Gottes Bogen in den Wolken: Untersuchungen zu Komposition und Theologie
der priesterschriftlichen Urgeschichte* (SBS 112; Stuttgart, 1983), p. 48.

[6] Zenger (*Bogen*, p. 48) speaks of P as a critical utopia.

God became the foundational confession of the people of God, which time and again formed the justification for the commandments: "I am the Lord your God, who brought you out of the land of Egypt, out of slavery" (Exod. 20:2; Deut. 5:6). The reminder that Israel's roots themselves lie in foreign parts and that living in the land was made possible only by God's action, repeatedly formed the critical factor that stood in the way of an all-too self-glorifying separation from other strangers. Sometimes, meanwhile, a quite astonishing enhancement of the stranger is brought about by means of the divine commandment. In Lev. 19:33f., for example, we read: "When a stranger lives with you in your land, you shall not oppress him. He shall live among you like one of your own, and you shall love him as yourself, *for you were strangers in Egypt. I am the Lord your God.*"

This is a remarkable special feature of Israel: Its ancestors are not stylised as heroes of former times. One's origins lie not in demi-gods but, on the contrary, in a "wandering Aramaean, near to death," as the so-called concise historical creed puts it (Deut. 26:5)! To reassure oneself one does not here tell of *"the fame of the deeds of the dead," as is customary among other nations, but of God's action,* which created his people from miserable "outcasts." The result of this is not only the impetus to treat foreigners in one's midst in a different way, but also—as is shown by our next point—a "thorn in the flesh" against any kind of national hubris.

1.3   *Self-Description as Strangers before God*

Israel's unusual relationship with an intrinsically negative foreignness is also evident in the fact that the nation, or at least individual Israelites, can describe even themselves as strangers. This too seems to have *its basis in the post-exilic situation:* "After 538 there is a partial return to the old land, but this return is a return to a diaspora, it is a return to a new foreign country."[7] The security-giving unity found in a natural, common nation and faith can no longer be taken for granted;[8] the second temple, from which the ark of the covenant is

---

[7] R. Mosis, "Das Babylonische Exil Israels in der Sicht christlicher Exegese," in R. Mosis (ed.), *Exil—Diaspora—Rückkehr: Zum theologischen Gespräch zwischen Juden und Christen* (Düsseldorf, 1978), pp. 65f.

[8] Cf. Mosis, *Exil,* pp. 67ff. On the various ideas that followed from this separation, see J. Hausmann, *Israels Rest: Studien zum Selbstverständnis der nachexilischen Gemeinde* (BWANT 124; Stuttgart, 1987), pp. 237ff. Hausmann also shows, however, that in

missing, was not able completely to replace the first;[9] following the loss of sovereignty the land is much more a pawn of foreign powers and subject to their influence.[10] True, it is precisely the returning ones who claim to be the true inhabitants of Judaea, but such texts as Neh. 9:36f. testify to the feeling of no longer being at home, or of not yet being at home, in one's own land. "So the Babylonian exile leads to post-exilic Israel living as a minority, and often as an undervalued and disadvantaged minority, both in Judaea and elsewhere, and to its seeing itself as a diaspora people."[11] Typical in this regard are laments such as Psalm 73,[12] in which the individual righteous person is afflicted by his environment, which is no longer concerned with God. The surprising thing is that Israel does not fall apart as a result of these negative experiences but *is able to interpret this experience of alienation theologically and thus to integrate it in its self-understanding and its relationship to God.* This comes to expression for example in the self-designation as "strangers and sojourners," which is applied figuratively to the Israelites in the land.

---

the post-exilic concepts of "remnant" one cannot easily distinguish between nation and cultic community, since the two things always belong together. In the post-exilic situation there are, however, shifts in emphasis (*ibid.*, p. 246).

[9] This awareness remained alive in Judaism until later times (cf. *2 Bar.* 68:5f.).

[10] Mosis (*Exil*, pp. 64f.) suggests that "the recovered former homeland" is itself experienced "as a kind of diaspora . . . Judaea is without hope and not even a 'province' in the legal sense—perhaps not even an independent province but part of a province of the Persian world empire. This remains essentially true when the Persians are replaced by the Greeks, Alexander the Great and the Ptolemies and Seleucids, and remains so under the Romans, who from around 200 BCE onwards gain control of more and more of this area, until the destruction of the second temple and the defeat of the first and the second Jewish revolts remove all state independence from the Jews in Palestine." This general picture is certainly simplistic—the Maccabaean and Hasmonaean periods were not only periods of relative independence but also times of relatively great expansion and extension. The early Maccabaean period in particular was seen as a period of liberation, in which the Jewish nation was able successfully to resist being overwhelmed by foreign influences. Here too, however, history was taking place in the shadow of the great powers, and it was only a question of time before Israel again became fully dependent. To this extent I would agree with Mosis (with some qualifications).

[11] Mosis, *Exil*, p. 66; cf. C. Thoma, "Jüdische und christliche Exilserfahrungen und Exilstheologien: Deutung des nachbiblischen Judentums aus christlich-theologischer Sicht," in R. Mosis (ed.), *Exil—Diaspora—Rückkehr*, p. 81: "Already in early Jewish times it was taken for granted in Judaism that one could also be exiled and banished in one's homeland: if one was in trouble and isolation or if one was suffering persecution and war. To speak only of the allegorical use of the concept of exile, for example when this occurs in the context of the Seleucid persecution (ca. 170—ca. 160 BCE), is not to do justice to the Hebrew/Jewish mentality and forms of expression."

[12] On the date of this cf. Kraus, p. 667: "The Psalm is to be situated relatively late."

In Lev. 25:23 is found the ban on the selling of the land. This is justified by God with the words: "For the land is mine, and you are strangers and sojourners with me." The land is given, and is not disposable at anyone's whim. But at the same time this state of being a stranger is given a new reference point: God calls the Israelites "strangers before me." This expresses a dual idea: On the one hand it is remembered that Israel is not "autochthonic," i.e. that it is not what it is as a result of its own power and abilities, but that it receives this time and again as a gift from God's hand. This has consequences right through to the law of land ownership.[13] But this is not expressed negatively in the limitation of the enforcement of land rights, but is positively expressed in dependence on God alone. This is also liberating, especially where the land is administered by foreign powers.

This line is continued in David's great prayer of thanksgiving in 1 Chron. 29:10ff. The building of the temple seems, after the possession of the land and the securing of the land by the king, to complete the process of settlement by the people of God, in that God now gains a definitive position in Israel. But precisely in this prayer we find the interesting sentences: "What am I?" (the Chronicler's David is speaking, 29.14ff.), "What is my people, that we were able to give so much of our own free will? All things come from you; we give you what has come from your own hand. For we are strangers and guests before you like all our fathers. Our life on earth is like a shadow and gives no security." This prayer, authored around the end of the Persian period or in the early Hellenistic period,[14] (in any case in a time of great turmoil) does not only emphasise the grandeur of God. The text repeats: We are strangers before you! That fundamentally negative experience of the finiteness and uncertainty of human existence, the lack of control of one's own life and its fundamentals, is bound in with the relationship between finite humanity and the lord of the world. As a critical factor against national hubris, such a self-understanding should not be underestimated. At the same time, such estrangement is also an expression of the

---

[13] According to H.J. Boecker (*Recht und Gesetz im Alten Testament und im Alten Orient* [2nd edn., Neukirchen-Vluyn, 1984], p. 77), Lev. 25:23 can be called "the Magna Carta of the Old Testament land law."

[14] K. Galling (*Die Bücher der Chronik, Esra, Nehemia* [ATD 12; Göttingen, 1954], p. 17) dated the authorship of Chronicles to the "end of the 3rd century." Recently Chronicles has been dated a little earlier (cf. H.G.M. Williamson, *1 and 2 Chronicles* [New Century Bible Commentary; Grand Rapids/London, 1982], p. 16): "A dating within the Persian period is much more likely."

general dependence on God and thus it contains a positive feature. This recurs again in the prayers of Israel, the Psalms, in which this self-description is found variously in the context of petition and the expression of trust.[15]

1.4 The Stranger Metaphor in Early Jewish Literature

The relatively rare Old Testament self-description of the nation or of individual believers as "strangers" is not taken up in vast tracts of early Jewish literature. Indeed it is even suppressed. It is emphasised that the Jews are, and always were, full citizens in Israel. An illuminating early example is the speech of Achior in Jdt 5:5–21 (LXX). This outline of Jewish history, which dates from the Maccabaean period,[16] clearly reflects Jewish self-understanding.[17] It is striking how Israel's, or its forefathers' residence outside the promised land is invariably described as a life in the state of sojourning: in the land of the Chaldaeans (5:6), in Mesopotamia (5:7) and in Egypt (5:10). This παροκεῖν in a strange land is distinguished—in deliberate contrast—from living as κατοικεῖν in the land, which (all told, three times!) is emphatically represented as a successful occupation of the land: the ancestors already moved out of foreign parts and settled in the land of Canaan and became wealthy (Jdt 5:9), and the same thing is repeated after the exodus from Egypt (5:15) and after the return from exile.[18] Quite deliberately, then, *living in the land as a situation of fulfilled*

---

[15] In Ps. 39:13, by reference to his own estrangement, God effectively becomes duty-bound to help: "Hear my prayer, ΥΗΨΗ, and perceive my crying, be not silent at my tears, for I am a sojourner with you, a stranger like all my fathers." And in the famous Psalm 119 the twice emphasized alienation is just the backcloth against which the protective nearness of God is requested or praised: "I am a stranger in the land—do not hide your commandments from me" (v. 19); "Your commandments are my song in the house in which I am a stranger."

[16] Cf. E. Jenni, art. "Juditbuch," in *RGG* 3 III (1959), col. 1001.

[17] Here Achior gives a view of history which is reminiscent of the Deuteronomistic History; cf. Jdt 5:18f.: "But when they departed from the way which he (God) had determined for them, they were destroyed by many wars for a very long time . . . But now that they have returned to their God, they have reappeared from the dispersion in which they were dispersed. They have reoccupied Jerusalem where their sanctuary is . . ." It is not by chance that Achior, thrown out by the Assyrians after his speech, is received again by the Israelites with enthusiasm.

[18] Jdt 5:19: ἀνέβησαν ἐκ τῆς διασπορᾶς . . . καὶ κατέσχον τὴν Ιερουσαλημ . . . καὶ κατῳκίσθησαν ἐν τῇ ὀρεινῇ . . . Here it is noticeable how the notion of estrangement in relation to the Babylonian exile is no longer used but now the text speaks of the διασπορά—so there is an implied distinction between the period before and the period after the possession of the land.

promise is contrasted with the existence as strangers. The corollary of this is that in its own land Israel is not a sojourner at all, but a full citizen, designated as such by God. This connection is so close that even the foreignness of the patriarchs, so frequently emphasised in the book of Genesis, is suppressed and the text is emended accordingly. This attitude, expressed in an exemplary way here, which is clearly oriented towards the common ancient ideal of the full citizen, is typical of many parts of Judaism of the Hellenistic period.[19] Thus Josephus also plays down the foreignness of Abraham, and instead emphasises that he *lived in the land, left it to his descendants,*[20] *and possessed it.*[21] Accordingly Josephus is not at all inclined to take up the terms just mentioned and use them in a self-description.[22] This attitude is ap-

---

[19] In the "Praise of the Fathers" in Sirach, the motif of foreignness is entirely absent. Instead, the inheritance promised or given to the fathers is emphasized (Sir. 44:21, 23). As regards the fathers in Pseudo-Philo's *Liber Antiquitatum,* emphasis is also given only to the promise of the land and their dwelling in it. In 2 Maccabees Jerusalem or Israel is described as πατρίς (2 Macc. 8:21; 13:10, 14; 14:18; cf. 4:1; 5:8, 9, 15; 8:33; 13:3); accordingly, the Jews are citizens and fellow-citizens (2 Macc. 9:19; cf. 4:5, 50; 5:6, 8, 23; 14:8; 15:30). The same emphasis is found in Josephus, *Contra Apionem*—the law is even the "best version," and Judaism is a θεοκρατία as a political unit (*cAp* 2:164f.).

[20] *Ant.* 1:154: "... ἐν ᾗ (i.e. in the land of Canaan) κατῴκησε καὶ τοῖς ἀπογόνοις κατέλιπε.

[21] Cf. *Ant.* 1:157. In his efforts to show the full citizenship of the Jews, Josephus even stresses that Claudius confirmed the Alexandrian right of citizenship for the Jews (*Ant.* 19:280ff.), which is formulated misleadingly, to say the least. In the extant letter of Claudius (CPJ 153:88ff.) equal rights of citizenship are expressly ruled out. It is disputed whether this is a case of deliberate falsification by Josephus (so e.g. H. Conzelmann, *Heiden—Juden—Christen: Auseinandersetzungen in der Literatur der hellenistisch-römischen Zeit* [BHTh 62; Tübingen, 1989], p. 13, where other representatives of this view are listed). A much more cautious view is expressed by E.M. Smallwood, *The Jews under Roman Rule. From Pompey to Diocletian* (SJLA 20; Leiden, 1976), p. 229: "Josephus ... does not distinguish, possibly through ignorance, between the juridical and popular senses of the term 'Alexandrian', and in some places uses it of the Jews in such a way as to imply, deliberately or unconsciously, that they were Alexandrians in the juridical sense." A. Kasher (*The Jews in Hellenistic and Roman Egypt. The Struggle for Equal Rights* [Tübingen, 1985]) distinguishes between the citizens of Alexandria and the Jewish πολῖται (as members of the Jewish πολίτευμα). On this basis he views Josephus's statements much more positively, though he does admit that Josephus does not use his terms very precisely: "Admittedly, calling the Jews 'Alexandrian πολῖται' may be misleading, but probably unintentionally so. It does not seem likely that Josephus would have wanted to misinform his readers" (p. 275; on the meaning of ἰσοπολιτεία in Josephus, cf. pp. 281ff.). In whatever precise way this question is to be resolved, Josephus's interest in depicting the Jews from their positive side is in any case clear. Josephus's account is thus at best tendentious, if not misleading (cf. M. Hengel, *Juden, Griechen und Barbaren: Aspekte der Hellenisierung des Judentums in vorchristlicher Zeit* [SBS 76; Stuttgart, 1976], pp. 84f.)

[22] πάροικος is found only three times in the whole of his work, twice dependent

parently continued into rabbinic literature,[23] which thinks and argues from the premise of the land.[24] *The national map is paramount, so to speak.* However, there are two important exceptions:

The first exception is the community of the Essenes, who, in protest against the pollution of the land, had withdrawn to Qumran, in order to live in the hope of God's coming. The Essenes deliberately and provocatively describe themselves as those banished to the wilderness, as those who have converted from Israel and dwell in a strange land.[25] So for the Qumran community there is a clear connection

---

on the language of the LXX, and once in a quoted letter. In all case πάροικος is used only with its primary meaning, for the sojourner. Josephus of course knows of the estrangement of the Jews in ancient society, but when he comes to speak of it, he tries to justify it and to make it intelligible to the pagan mentality, for example by referring to the striving for good that is common to all (e.g., *Ant.* 16:174ff.; cf. J.N. Sevenster, *The Roots of Pagan Anti-Semitism in the Ancient World* [NTS 41; Leiden, 1975], p. 116).

[23] It is noticeable that Strack-Billerbeck (III, 762ff.) gives no parallels to 1 Pet. 1:1; 1:17 and 2:11.

[24] This is especially true of the Palestinian tradition; cf. G. Stemberger, "Die Bedeutung des 'Landes Israel' in der rabbinischen Tradition," *Kairos* NF 25 (1983), pp. 176ff.

[25] The most illuminating of all the texts are two passages in the so-called Damascus Document, which already by its—probably symbolic—use of the name Damascus (cf. CD 6:5) indicates the existence of the community in exile (J. Maier [ed.], *Die Texte vom Toten Meer* [2 vols.; München, 1960], II, pp. 49f.; T.W. Gaster, *The Dead Sea Scriptures* [Garden City, 3rd edn., 1976], p. 5). In that passage a derivative of גור is taken up, in order to describe the situation of the community. The context is interesting in each case: In CD 3f. Israel, which has gone astray, is contrasted with the community of those who keep God's commandments. God built them "a firm house in Israel, which has not seen its like either before or since" (CD 3:19f.), where as in other passages a description of the temple is applied figuratively to the community (cf. H. Lichtenberger, *Studien zum Menschenbild in Texten der Qumrangemeinde* [SUNT 15; Göttingen, 1980], p. 152). God has destined this community "to eternal life, and all the glory of Adam is theirs" (CD 3:20). This statement is reinforced by a quotation from Ezek. 44:15, in which "the priests and the Levites and the sons of Zadok" are honoured for their loyal sacrificial observance in contrast to the apostate people (CD 3:21–4:1). This word is interpreted in relation to the community: "The priests are the retournees of Israel (שבי ישראל) who had departed from the land of Judah; (and the Levites are those) who have joined them. And the sons of Zadok are the elect of Israel, those called by name, who will appear at the end of days." The following verse is not fully preserved; but it is clear that the election is connected with the contemporary situation, which is characterized by oppression (CD 4:5) and which is described as the years of their banishment. In contrast to this word to the community, in what follows judgment is announced to Israel, the reason given being their corruption, again in contrast with the new community (CD 6:2ff.). Remembering the covenant with the forefathers God raised up "insightful men from Aaron and wise men from Israel," who "dug the well," as the allusion to Num. 21:18 puts it. This intitially rather cryptic allusion is then explained further: "The well is the law, and those who dug it *are the returnees of Israel, who departed from*

between their election, the return to God's law and the withdrawal from the land, the consequence of which is the existence in a strange land. CD 19:33f. even speaks of the "new covenant in the land of Damascus."

The other exception is the great religious philosopher, Philo of Alexandria, who time and again represents the state of being a stranger in this world as the only admissible state for the wise (i.e., the Jew). The most detailed exposition of this theme is to be found in *Conf. Ling.* 75–82. In the context of his interpretation of the narrative of the construction of the Tower of Babel, Philo comes to Gen. 11:2: "they migrated from the rising (of the sun) and found a plain in the land of Shinar and settled there" (*Conf.* 60). The word κατοικῆσαι provides the occasion for an excursus beginning with the contrast between those who settle in evil-doing, and the οἱ κατὰ Μωυσῆν σοφοί. The latter become more closely defined as being here on earth only on a journey, and in a foreign land, but whose homeland is in the heavenly place.[26] Philo now refers back to Abraham, and interprets his saying, "I am a stranger and a sojourner among you" (Gen. 23:4) in the sense of a radical opposition between two kinds of existence: While some are "corpse-guardians and in-dwellers of the mortal," αὐτόχθονες, "who esteem dust and rubble above the soul," Abraham is one who "rose up from death-in-life and from the tomb."[27] This will subsequently be explained in the form of an exhortation, culminating in the challenge now to put this existence as a stranger into effect as a wise one, and as deliberate aversion from everything material,[28] not yielding to passion.[29] The wise one finds his true πατρίς—in the hellenised version of the popular conception—in the

---

the land of Judah and dwelt in the land of Damascus, in the strange land, whom God has called princes all" (CD 6:4–6). So the members of the Essene community are here deliberately described as those who returned from Israel (שבי ישראל, 4:2; 6:5). In 4:3f. further epithets of election are added to them. Both times, in connection with this return (and the rejection of Israel) there is a deliberate, express emphasis on their having departed from the land of Judah and having lived in a strange land.

[26] *Conf. Ling.* 78: πατρίδα μὲν τὸν οὐράνιον χῶρον ἐν ᾧ πολιτεύονται, ξένην δὲ τὸν περίγειον ἐν ᾧ παρῴκησαν νομίζουσαι. The opposition is once more underlined by a contrast between the colonist for whom the other city becomes home in place of the mother-city (μητρόπολις) and the traveller who wishes to return again to the city that sent him out.

[27] *Conf. Ling,* 79.

[28] *Conf. Ling.* 82: διαφερόντως οὐ μόνον ξένην τὴν ἐν σώματι μονὴν ὡς οἱ μέτοικοι νομίζων ἀλλὰ καὶ ἀλλοτριώσεως ἀξίαν οὐκ ἔμπαλιν οἰκειώσεως ὑπολαμβάνων.

[29] *Conf. Ling.* 81.

νοηταῖς ἀρεταῖς, immediately and directly equated by Philo with the Word of God (meaning the Law of Moses).[30] This is at least conditioned by the situation of the Egyptian Jews in the first century, for it was in Philo's time that Alexandrian nationalism began to turn vehemently against the Jews. The Roman prefect Flaccus too falls under the influence of nationalism, and belittles the Jews (some of whom had already been resident in Egypt for more than six hundred years) as "newcomers and foreigners."[31] There are eventually encroachments and pogroms, heralding the conflicts which escalate in the beginning of the second century and finally lead to the eradication of a flourishing Egyptian Judaism.

Whatever the differences between them, both Qumran and Philo have something in common: in virtue of their religious belief, they were outsiders in their surroundings. As such, they took up in a positive manner the Old Testament category of the stranger in order to provide a theological basis for their existence on the fringe of society. What is further striking in both of these is that now "being a stranger" includes an *elitist aspect*. God's faithful are strangers because they do not make themselves at home in a godless world. *Strangeness here expresses an alternative self-understanding resulting from a relationship to God.* Thereby those Jewish writers, with all that is special to them, preserve an essential feature of a biblical self-understanding.

2. The Category of Strangeness in 1 Peter as Suggesting a Christian Self-Understanding and Relationship to the World

Taken as a whole, the category of strangeness plays a rather subordinate role in the New Testament.[32] The significant exception, which moreover set in motion an enormous history of influence, is the First

---

[30] *Conf. Ling.* 81: ... κατοικεῖ δ' ὡς ἐν πατρίδι νοηταῖς ἀρεταῖς, ἃς λαλεῖ ὁ θεὸς ἀδιαφορούσας λόγων θείων.

[31] *Flaccus* 54: ξένοι καὶ ἐπήλυδες.

[32] Of course the NT is aware of what is designated by this, for example when the Son of Man says of himself that he has nowhere to lay his head, but nonetheless strangeness is not specifically spoken of. Paul can say positively that a Christian's homeland is in heaven (Phil. 3:20), but the negative consequence, that Christians are only strangers on earth, is not drawn. The deutero-pauline letter to the Ephesians can even describe conversion as overcoming foreignness. Hebrews is an exception. In chapter 11 it describes the life of faith of the Old Testament witnesses and there repeatedly emphasises their state as strangers. That this is aimed at the Christian community is apparent in that, at the end of the letter, it is once more made clear

Letter of Peter. Right at the beginning of the letter, thus in a decisive position, Christians are addressed as strangers, and then once more at the beginning of the main section, each time moreover with a compound expression: as "strangers of the dispersion" or "aliens and sojourners." In addition there are other places where the state of being a stranger is mentioned or alluded to. The metaphor of foreignness is here not only one attribute amongst others. In a bold recourse to a minor biblical and Jewish tradition, the negative experiences of non-identity are interpreted as the specific characteristic of Christian identity. And so, as already suggested at the outset, this letter has had a significant effect up to the present time. This merits further examination.

2.1   *Aliens and Strangers—the Situation of the Addressees*

No biblical writing speaks so often about suffering as 1 Peter. The discussion of it characterises the whole writing. A close inspection of the letter however reveals that "suffering" is not primarily what we usually understand as Christian persecutions. On the evidence of the letter, the Christians have first of all problems with their immediate society, which "is alienated" (4:4) from the new behaviour of its former fellow citizens and hence excludes and defames the Christian community, even makes them into enemies and denounces them (2:12,23; 3:14–17; 4:4, 14–16). The same picture is revealed in the other New Testament writings: Already in the earliest Christian writing, in 1 Thess. 2:14, in reference to both Jewish Christians and gentile Christians, there is mention of "suffering because of their fellow countrymen," and according to the presentation in the Acts of the Apostles, official proceedings against Paul always began with enraged citizens,[33] and the persecution logia speak of Christians being delivered up to judgment by their own neighbours, even by their own relatives.[34] The accounts in the Acts of the Apostles surely show how dangerous this could become: social discrimination meant a constant threat, and included pogrom-like excesses which the authorities then stopped mostly at the Christians' expense. To provide a reason for these

---

in summary form that Christians have here no lasting city, but seek one that is to come (Heb. 13:14). However even here the faithful are only indirectly designated as strangers.

[33] Acts 14:4f.; 16:19–22; 17:8,13; 19:23–40; 21:27–40.

[34] Cf. Mark 13:9–13; Matt. 10:17f.; Luke 21:12–17.

excesses, we must first refer to the striking fact that the Christians were inordinately hated. Nero's persecution is a typical example, as described by Tacitus. Apparently Nero had set fire to Rome. However the opposition of the population deprived of their homes was so great that Nero seized upon the most varied measures to quench the people's rage. When these all failed, he adopted a classic procedure: he sought a scapegoat. The ones best suited for this, it seemed to him, were "those whom the people hated for their abominations and whom they called Christians."[35] He singled out the most hated group to divert onto them the people's wrath. There are several remarkable aspects to this: first, Nero did not proceed against the Christians on his own initiative, but only used them. More importantly, this diversionary tactic succeeded where all other measures hitherto had failed to divert the people's anger. Tacitus' judgment shows the extent of this hatred, for in his account of Nero's action, Tacitus of course sees through the imperial tactic, and so in this case he does not believe in the Christians' guilt, but approves the emperor's deed as taking place in the interest of the public good:[36] the Christians are guilty (sontes), and their cruel execution as a public spectacle is justified.[37] "They were convicted less of arson than of hatred against the whole human race."[38] That Tacitus in his condemnation of the Christians was no exception is shown by Suetonius. In his biography of Nero he counts Nero's action against this "genus hominum superstitionis novae ac maleficae"[39] amongst the emperor's good deeds.[40] Now what reason is there for this plainly fanatical hatred of Christians which the most prominent Roman historians evidently shared with a large part of the population?

Amongst the various causes one is especially important. For the ancients, religion was a public affair, the spiritual basis of state and

---

[35] Tacitus, *Annals*, 15:44,2: "... quos per flagitia invisos vulgus Christianos appellabat." Even if it is taken into consideration that Tacitus writes this information about 50 years later and his opinion of Christians could be coloured by his own times and the standpoint of Trajan's circle, still there is no reason basically to distrust this assertion.

[36] Tacitus, *Annals* 15:44, 5 fin. For this translation and interpretation of "utilitate publica," cf. A. Wlosok, *Rom und die Christen: Zur Auseinandersetzung zwischen Christentum und römischem Staat* (Stuttgart, 1970), pp. 22, 26.

[37] Cf. *ibid.*, 44:5.

[38] 44:4: "... haud proinde in crimine incendii quam odio humani generis convicti sunt."

[39] *Nero* 16:2.

[40] Cf. Wlosok, *Rom*, p. 7.

society. Each person could believe what he wished, the essential thing
being that due regard was shown for the received religion and thereby
also to the *mos maiorum*. This is precisely what the Christians did not
do. They took up a position as an increasingly larger group outside
ancient society's life and social structure. They formed a group with
a rival reference system all their own.[41] The refusal of emperor worship
was only an outward sign of the fact that here was a group that
disputed the sacral foundations of state and society which were determinative for the whole of antiquity, and, at the expense of the
wider community, they committed themselves to their particular "superstition" with incomprehensible exclusiveness.

Clearly, this had social consequences. The Christians' religious separation severed social ties. The prohibition to consume sacrificed meat
excluded in practical terms any eating in common with pagans.[42]
This aroused indignation above all on the occasion of the feasts which
were so important for the community. Also the different burial customs[43] and burial grounds[44] created difficulty. Christianity had particularly destructive results in that this new belief and the new community formed by it invaded the hitherto prevailing social relationships
and threatened to destroy them. The New Testament refers to this
time and again. It is expressed in a plainly programmatic way in
Matt. 10:34–37 at the end of the mission discourse: "Do not think
that I have come to bring peace on earth, but the sword; for I have
come to set the son against his father, and the daughter against her
mother, and the daughter-in-law against her mother-in-law; and a
man's foes will be those of his own household. Whoever loves father
and mother more than me is not worthy of me; and whoever loves
son or daughter more than me is not worthy of me." Also 1 Peter
suggests that through conversion to Christianity intimate bonds (cf.
3:1ff.) and neighbourly ties (4:3f.) were jeopardised or destroyed.

---

[41] Cf. A. Wlosok, "Die Rechtsgrundlagen der Christenverfolgungen der ersten
zwei Jahrhunderte," in R. Klein (ed.), *Das frühe Christentum im römischen Staat* (Darmstadt,
1982), p. 280: "The christians appeared . . . to their pagan milieu as adherents of a
segregated organisation that rejected the pagans' way of life, in this respect determining its adherents' behaviour."

[42] A good example is the hatred of the mother of the emperor Galerius for
Christians. According to Lactantius, *De mortibus persecutorum* 11, this developed from
the Christians absenting themselves from the sacrificial meals she celebrated almost
daily in her native place.

[43] Cf. Minucius Felix, *Octavius* 38.

[44] Tertullian, *Ad Scapulam* 3.

Finally, not to be overlooked is that Christianity also encroached upon economic interests. This might often have been the concrete occasion for proceedings against the Christians.[45]

In every respect Christian belief and the way of life that came to expression through it were felt to be an extremely provocative assault on the most basic foundations of community life.[46] Time and again the charge of godlessness[47] recurs, of hatred of humankind,[48] of unbearable arrogance and insurrection,[49] and the charge of forming a race of their own that breaks away from common responsibility, and as a parasite destroys what it lives on. If, according to Plutarch, the characteristic of the superstitious person is that "he does not enjoy a world in common with the rest of the human race,"[50] this applies to Christians to particular degree. In short, the Christians had deliberately placed themselves outside life's religiously determined context, were "strangers" to it.[51] Accordingly ancient society saw them as a

[45] This is already shown in Acts 19:23ff. Also Pliny's action against the Christians seems at the least to have also been occasioned through economic problems (cf. A.N. Sherwin-White, *The Letters of Pliny: A Historical and Social Commentary* (Oxford, 1985), p. 709, Letter X, 96:10.

[46] The reason for the sentence pronounced on the Scilitanian martyrs is indicative of this (*Acta Scilitanorum* 14).

[47] The direct charge is found for example in Lucian, *Peregrinus* 13; Origen, Celsus 8:11; Minucius Felix, *Octavius* 8:1–9:2; in the *Martyrium* of Polycarp (Eusebius. *Hist. Eccl.* 4, 15,6). On this question see also Harnack's inquiry: *Der Vorwurf des Atheismus in den ersten drei Jahrhunderten* (TU 28,4 = NF. Bd. 13,4; Leipzig, 1905). Further, W. Schäfke, "Frühchristlicher Widerstand," in ANRW 2,23.1 (1979), pp. 460–723, esp. 627–630.

[48] The first was Tacitus, *Annals* 15:44,4. Cf. Tertullian, *Apologeticum* 37:8: "*hostes generis humani.*" Wlosok (*Rom*, p. 21) shows very nicely the link between this charge and the Christians' (religiously based) isolation: the Christians "were separated from the pagan milieu because of their exclusive religion and their community organisation. On religious grounds they had to renounce participation in public life, for there at every step they were confronted with pagan worship. That applied to apparently non-political events like performances, public games, and common meals, quite apart from public festivals, parades, and processions that related directly to the cult. Added to this, the Christians were organised as a community. To their surroundings they appeared as adherents of an exclusive association that as a group rejected on principle participation in public life. On the Roman side that necessarily led to being charged with an offence against state and society. Thus *odium humani generis* is 'an antisocial mind-set,' a charge on moral and political grounds."

[49] Celsus makes insurrection the origin and essence of christianity (Origen, *Contra Celsum*, 5:5ff.; cf. 3:14; 8:2, etc.), its effect consists in the production of chaos (8:68). Christianity is the "Theology of Revolt" (C. Andresen, *Logos und Nomos: Die Polemik des Kelsos wider das Christentum* (AKG 30; Berlin, 1955, p. 221), it disturbs the "world of divine ordinances" (*ibid.*, p. 222); cf. Tertullian, *Apologeticum* 35:1: "*publici hostes.*"

[50] Plutarch *Superst.* 166c.

[51] Tertullian vehemently and aggressively stresses the opposition to broad areas of civil life and in this context brings to pregnant expression the relation of Christians to public office: "nobis . . . nec ulla magis res aliena quam publica" *Apologeticum* 38:3.

foreign body, whose very existence jeopardised its foundations, whose spread disturbed peace and order, and hence in every respect *had destructive effects*.[52] The people in general may not have been in a position to understand it as clearly as did the historians and philosophers, but their experience was certainly similar: In the calumnies, the insinuations, and the ridicule, the separateness the pagan environment perceived in Christians is everywhere clear. It is but the consequence of this estrangement if in the end Christians were denied the right to exist:[53] "*Non licet esse vos*."[54] Jesus himself formulated it quite similarly in his last discourse: "You will be hated by all for my name's sake" (Mark 13:13 par).

2.2 What This Self-Description Achieves: From Social Non-Identity to Christian Identity

When the author of 1 Peter singles out Christians and in a decisive passage addresses them as "strangers" he formulates what they are in their society: outsiders, marked people, foreign bodies. What is special about 1 Peter, however, is that he makes this estrangement from the milieu, this social defect a decisive feature of Christian identity. This doubtless shows that he wants not only to react to this situation, but to take the offensive. *The Christians are strangers in this society—and this is precisely their vocation; that is what they are supposed to be.*

The language of sojourning in 1 Peter is noticeably different as compared with both the biblical and the extrabiblical tradition. Christians are addressed *absolutely* as "strangers and sojourners." Remarkably it is not stated in which place they are alien, such as in the (wicked) world, the evil cosmos and so on, though the concept of foreignness seems plainly to require such after it.[55] 1 Peter's dispensing with an

---

[52] Indicative in this context is how Suetonius (*Nero* 16:2) lists the emperor's action against the Christians between his measures for containing luxury and his action against the infringements of racing drivers, hence placing it in the context of other ordinances of the emperor which Suetonius considered beneficial.

[53] The right to exist is also denied Christians in Origen, *Contra Celsum* 8:55, and in Justin, *Apologies*, Appendix 4:1, the grim summons to extinction is handed over: "Kill yourselves, all of you, and make haste to travel to God, and give no more trouble."

[54] Tertullian, *Apologeticum* 4:4. Right at the beginning of his *Apologeticum* (1:4) Tertullian speaks of general hatred "erga nomen christianorum." This does not first occur in Tertullian's time, as witness the censure of the people's hatred already under Nero: Tacitus, *Annals* 15:44, 2.

[55] This indeed is shown when not a few translations saw themselves constrained to add a place indication to the Petrine statements about sojourning. Cf. the

antithetic object as a negative foil for comparison is revealing. It shows that 1 Peter does not derive the Christians' self-understanding as strangers in the first instance from their alienation from the society around them. This is also made clear by the fact that by adopting the thought-world of the LXX the author deliberately relates back to the experiences of the fathers, or the whole Old Testament people of God, who became strangers by God's call. This sometimes occurs in other New Testament places as well (cf. Hebrews), but what is new in 1 Peter is not only his establishing this trait indirectly through reference to the Hebrew Bible, but his directly addressing the Christians as strangers, and placing this stranger-existence in direct relation with election to, and participation in, the people of God.[56] To the chosen strangers in the dispersion—this is indeed how the letter begins. In short, strangerhood is not understood from opposition to society, but from response to God, and from belonging to his community, to his people.

At the same time in the context of the letter[57] the traditional language of sojourning receives a clearly eschatological focus. The Christians are "strangers" because they are reborn as such (1:3,23; 2:2). 1 Peter enlarges upon what this means: they are now redeemed from their fathers' futile way of life and placed in a new life context (cf. 1:18). They now have a future transcending this passing world.[58] Christian life, as constituted by "living hope"[59] is distinguished fundamentally from the self-understanding of the age we live in. Thus the specific foundation of estrangement is that the Christian community is moving towards God's future,[60] since living from hope places them

---

Einheitsübersetzung of 2:11: ". . . strangers and visitors . . . *in this world*"; Luther at 1:17: "as long as you sojourn *here* in foreign parts." In this connection, an indicative list particularly of the English translations is to be found in Elliott, *Home*, pp. 39ff.— probably a result of "pilgrim theology," strongly represented in the English-speaking world; cf. e.g. L.A. Barbieri, *First and Second Peter* (Chicago, 2nd edn., 1978), p. 34.

[56] 2:11, as externalisation of 2:9f.

[57] Likewise in Hebrews 11–13.

[58] Cf. the three *a*-privativa in 1:4 emphasising the other-worldly character of the Christian "inheritance in heaven."

[59] Cf. 1:3: "born anew to a living hope"; 1:13: τελείως ἐλπίσατε ἐπί . . .; finally in 1:21 it is stated that through the work of redemption, faith and "hope in God" are rendered possible to the christians. Women who hope in God are praised as examples (3:5), and in 3:15 Christians are supposed to account to others not for their faith but for the "hope that is in you." In 1 Peter hope is one of the essential elements, if not the essential element in Christian life.

[60] Cf. L. Goppelt, *Der erste Petrusbrief* (KEK, XII/1; Göttingen, 1978), p. 155: "To be strangers is the emblem of Christians in society, for this expresses sociologically the eschatological character of their way of life."

at a distance from this present age. Now if this be so, the problems arising from such remoteness must no more "surprise, as though something strange were happening to you" (4:12), but Christians can even rejoice in them since they are the reverse side of belonging to God.[61] The condition of social exclusion and persecution can be thus understood and embraced. Hence deliberately accepting estrangement and its consequences will integrate social non-identity into Christian identity, so that *the hitherto worrying and faith-threatening experiences* (cf. 1:6; 4:12) *now turn into a moment for assurance of faith.* The terms for foreignness, clearly negative from their origin, when revalued and preserved as a specific expression of Christian identity—according to the biblical and Jewish tradition we have described—gain positive, even elitist overtones.[62] 1 Peter, however, achieves even more. By distinguishing the "strangers" from their surroundings, as appropriate to the situation, he desires to free the Christians from pre-occupation with suffering (cf. 4:12ff.) and, from a stance of faith, to make possible a responsible public engagement with reality.

2.3 *Consequences for Self-Understanding and Relationship to the World*

(1) Hence, as we have seen, the Christians' negative experiences in a society that rejects them are explained, by recourse to the Hebrew Bible, as the reverse side of belonging to God's chosen people. Therefore *society's rejection of the faithful receives theological explanation.*[63] It must no longer hinder Christians and make them focus on opposition.[64]

---

[61] However it remains true that 1 Peter does not say that Christians must suffer. Unlike so many sects who seek opposition from others and suffering as confirmation of their identity, this letter speaks very carefully about tensions and time and again makes qualifications: if it be necessary, if it be God's will (employing the optative rarely used in the NT). The letter wants to say that Christian living from hope can time and again lead to tensions with a world that understands itself in terms of what has already come to pass, and that this is nothing unusual. Or again, suffering is not used as a means of self-approval. It is more a question of a reappraisal of experiences from the perspective of God's future already opened up by Christ.

[62] This is underlined also by the adjective ἐκλεκτός in 1 Pet 1:1 which emphasises the positive reverse-side of strangeness in the sense of 1 Pet (cf. J. Calloud and F. Genuyt, *La Première Épître de Pierre: Analyse Sémiotique* (LD 109; Paris, 1982), p. 33.

[63] Accordingly, in treatment met in concrete situations suffering is not judged from the perspective of persecution, but from that of discipleship and sharing in Christ's passion (cf. 2:20ff.).

[64] The challenge posed by this rejection is clearly expressed in 4:12. Significantly

The significance given the situation from a theological perspective enables it to be accepted and so releases energies tied up by resistance. Thus this distinction of Christians from the world around them has a liberating effect: for it is at least clear that estrangement, with the suffering that may ensue from it, belongs to the Christians' existence. Non-identity in this society is precisely a characteristic of Christian existence. On this basis, then, relationship to the social surroundings in regard to both activity and endurance can be considered afresh. The confirmation of their own identity also has *liberating consequences for their relationship to the world.*

(2) The otherness of Christians, so much emphasised in 1 Peter using the concept of "strangers," does not (as one might expect given an effective history of the term that is heavily marked by hellenistic philosophy and gnosis) justify the separation of the community from society. The opposite is in fact the case (and comparison with other NT writings strongly underlines this[65]): the differentiation of Christians as strangers rather justifies a freedom from their environment, which allows them not to succumb to the pressure of that environment, not to assimilate, to make their own identity clear, even in their way of life (ἀναστροφή) as the expression of a value system of its own.[66] But this is also expressed in a *Christian freedom towards the world and for the world.* In order to appreciate this fully one needs to compare the statements in 1 Peter with the way other oppressed and isolated minorities have reacted in similar situations. This is especially clear if one looks at the nightmarish desires for revenge that one finds for example in the Qumran scrolls[67] or in other early Jewish,

---

in this one verse the estrangement of Christians is rendered twice by ξενίζεσθαι and by ὡς ξένου accentuating its intensity.

[65] It is interesting in this context to compare 1 Pet. 1:13ff. with 2 Cor. 6:14ff. Despite a similarity in the basic structure in the fact that belonging to God contrasts with the surrounding world, the distinction is made much more sharply in 2 Cor. 6.

[66] Colloud/Genuyt, pp. 33f., emphasises the connection between talk of the stranger in 1 Peter and an alternative value system.

[67] Cf. 1 QS 2:4b–9: "And the levites shall curse all the men of the lot of Belial. They shall begin to speak and shall say: Accursed are you for all your wicked, blameworthy deeds. May he (God) hand you over to dread into the hands of all those carrying out acts of vengeance. Accursed, without mercy, for the darkness of your deeds, and sentenced to the gloom of everlasting fire. May God not be merciful when you entreat him, nor pardon you when you do penance for your faults. May he lift the countenance of his anger to avenge himself on you, and may there be no peace for you in the mouth of those who intercede." (F. Garcia Martinez, *The Dead Sea Scrolls Translated: The Qumran Texts in English* [Leiden: E.J. Brill, 1994]).

apocalyptically oriented writings,[68] but also in Christian apocalypses such as the *Apocalypse of Peter*[69] and not for the last time in the canonical Apocalypse of John[70] (and most of them have the emphasis of exclusion and strangeness in common with 1 Peter[71]). This is true also with reference to other NT writings which though they have no such apocalyptic scenarios, still emphasise the contrast to this world and its people much more strongly than 1 Peter does, and which criticise[72] the world around especially from the perspective of rejection of its fundamental corruption[73] and its punishment in the judgment.[74] The otherness of 1 Peter is noticeable here: the day of recompense will not in the first place be the day of revenge, but the day on which those who still do evil to Christians are won over by their manner of life, and praise God.[75] This clear reminder of a

---

[68] The whole of *6 Ezra*, for example, consists entirely of a threat and the associated woes.

[69] The whole of the central part of this text (5–12) represents an extensive description of the torments of the individual sinner—probably one of the sources for Dante's Inferno.

[70] Cf. esp. Rev. 8:6–9, 21; 14:14–16, 21.

[71] The Qumran community had already made its strangeness even over against the rest of the nation clear by its exodus into the wilderness. In CD 4:2–6 thus speaks in connection with the exodus, of those who have turned from Israel, out of the land of Judah (4:2f.) and of their election (4:3f.) and then expressly also of their sojourn in a foreign land, of the years of their banishment (שׁני התנוררם, 4:5f.). Particularly characteristic of the self-understanding of the community behind the Apocalypse is Rev. 12, the woman who has to flee into the wilderness in the face of the confrontation of the dragon. The motif of the heavenly home is clear (in contrast with the attempt to make oneself at home here), also at the end of the Apocalyse of Peter (16), where Peter, on his offer to build tabernacles (cf. Mark 9:5 par.), is first set straight in no uncertain terms, but then is taught: "Your eyes will be opened and your ears will open to understand that there is only one tabernacle: the one not made by human hands, but my heavenly Father . . ."

[72] Schärfke (*Widerstand*, 560ff.) has shown how the expectation of God's revenge on the persecutors has become a firm component of early Christian statements about suffering and martyrdom.

[73] We referred above to the frequent mentions of "this world" or "this age" especially in John and Paul; cf. also Eph. 4:18f.; 5:3f., 7f.; 2 Thess. 3:2; 2 Tim. 3:1ff.; Jas 4:4ff.; 1 Jn 2:15ff.; 4:3ff.; 2 Pet. 1:4.

[74] Cf. Eph. 5:5f.; 2 Thess. 1:5–9; 2:8–12; 2 Pet. 3:5ff.

[75] 2:12; similarly 3:1f.; cf. also 3:15ff. The meaning of the expression ἐν ἡμέρᾳ ἐπισκοπῆς is disputed. While some see in it the time of the gracious visitation or the conversion (cf. E. Schweizer, *Der erste Petrusbrief* [ZBK; Zürich, 3rd edn., 1972], pp. 56f.; B. Reicke, *The Epistles of James, Peter, and Jude: Introduction, Translation, and Notes* [AB 37; Garden City, 2nd edn., 1982], p. 94), others take it to refer to the final judgment (cf. N. Brox, *Der erste Petrusbrief* [EKK 21; Neukirchen-Vluyn, 2nd edn., 1986], pp. 114f.). But however this datum is to be understood, in any case the winning over of the opponents stands in the forefront, not the hope of revenge!

saying of Jesus[76] shows that in 1 Peter Christian existence is not
primarily determined by the expectation of revenge, but is oriented
towards reconciliation.[77] From all this it is clear that for 1 Peter it is
not the separation from "the world" and the judgment of it that
stands in the foreground. He certainly does not want to prepare
spiritually for a holy war against the sons of darkness. Rather, he
encourages those he addresses, as far as possible in following Jesus
Christ to overcome this contrast to other people!

(3) The last reason for all this, however, lies in the hope which
1 Peter emphasises so much, i.e. in the certainty of the coming turn
of the eras, which is already taking place in Jesus Christ. By their
foreignness, one could even say, the Christians are the representatives of this future of God's for a still fallen world. By a life that is
preparing for the heavenly inheritance (cf. 1:4) and the coming glory,
like newborns (1:3, 23; 2:2) the believers give account of the hope
that is in them (3:15). *In a world that is estranged from God, Christians*
have been ransomed by Christ's blood (1:18), freed from their sins
(2:24), have access to God through Christ (3:18) and are *finally strange*
precisely because they have come home.[78] For them the inheritance is prepared in the heavens (1:4), they have become one house and above
all one people, which God has mercifully accepted, has made his

---

[76] Transmitted in the Sermon on the Mount (Mt. 6:16). Probably 1 Peter has
received it through oral tradition, since his version is evidently more original than
that of Matthew (cf. especially the typically Matthean expression, "Father in Heaven").
[77] This is confirmed also by the conclusion of the central admonitions: 2:13–3:7:
Alongside the love commandment (3:8), which has reference to the community, the
reminder of the dominical prohibition of revenge and the challenge that belongs
with the commandment to love one's enemies, to react to inimical acts not by swearing
but by blessing. Here the concern in 3:8f. is certainly not only for "harmony in the
household" (D.L. Balch, *Let Wives Be Submissive: The Domestic Code in 1 Peter* [SBLMS
26; Chico, 1981], p. 88). In 2:11f. and 2:13–17 already, the opening bars of this
paraenetic section, the concern was for the relation of Christians to the world around
them, and this is clearly a central concern in 3:13ff. also. Further, as we shall see,
the concern in 2:18–3:7, too, is not simply for "domestic harmony" (p. 88). How
important this is for 1 Peter is shown also in the correspondingly portrayed example
of Christ: In 2:23 believers are shown Christ as the example they should follow,
who represents the one who "did not revile when he was reviled, who did not
threaten when he suffered, but gave (his case) in the hands of him who judges
rightly." This continues in the admonition to seek peace (3:11) as well as in the
challenge associated with this not to counter aggressively the unjust accusations and
reproaches towards being a Christian, but to meet them "with meekness and fear of
God" (3:16).
[78] Almost paradoxically 2:25 describes the conversion as a return from dispersion,
hence from the state of estrangedness: "For you had gone astray like sheep, but
now you are come home to the shepherd and bishop of your lives."

own possession (2:5; 2:9f.)—all terms which express the protective character of the new existence of the Christian churches.[79] *It is precisely as strangers that they belong to the divinely elected community.* The term λαός (people) is used as many as four times in this context—without going into the fact that this label is first and foremost a Jewish one.[80] The special position expressed by this term is not only one of privilege, however, but also carries with it the responsibility for those "strangers" to point the world around, caught up as it is in ignorance (1:14; 2:15), futility (cf. 1:18) and emphemerality (1:24) because of its separation from God, to the one who has already called them from darkness into his glorious light (2:9). As a visible foretaste of God's future, by means of their existence as strangers—such is the sense of the whole paraenesis of 2:11–3:9—they are to lead even their persecutors to the praise of God (2:12) and thus become a blessing to them (3:9).[81] *"Foreignness" and membership of the people of God are thus opposite sides of the same coin. The (Christian) people of God sees itself as the counterpart to a peoplehood that defines itself from* traditio *and the* mos maiorum. This also has consequences, finally, for the inner composition of this community—for its whole ethics, and for the way it deals with the social boundaries of the society and its evaluation of the "underdogs."[82]

---

[79] This is the *particula veri* of the study of J. Eillott, with the programmatic title: *A Home for the Homeless: A Sociological Exegesis of 1 Peter, its Situation and Strategy* (Philadelphia, 1981). For fundamental criticism of Elliott see Feldmeier, *Fremde*, pp. 203–210.

[80] From our present-day perspective, it is strange how matter-of-factly a central Jewish epithet is appropriated here by the Christians, without the merest reference to the Jewish people (at most, a salvation-historical break is alluded to in 2:10, there from an exclusively Christian perspective). This third-generation "forgetfulness" with regard to Israel (contrast e.g. Rom. 9–11) marks a not unproblematic departure from the Jewish root. Account should of course be taken of the fact that the pressure from the pagan environment, and the effort to stand firm against it, clearly peripheralised such questions and finally—regrettably—made it possible for them to be forgotten.

[81] It might be considered whether—at least indirectly—yet another aspect of foreignness plays a role here: otherness not only repels but also attracts. The foreign is not only something threatening, but also something promising, which opens up new horizons.

[82] On this cf. Feldmeier, *Fremde*, pp. 153ff.

3. Παροικία as Community Name
The Self-Understanding of Christians in the First Centuries

The Second Letter of Clement, composed between 130 and 150[83] describes the existence of Christians in this world as a sojourn in a foreign land (παροικία), which should be left behind (5:1), and he justifies this on the grounds that the followers of Jesus are like sheep among wolves in society (5:2). This statement shows in an exemplary way how the Christians of the first centuries understood themselves: "All Christians placed their citizenship in heaven. On earth they were but pilgrims and strangers."[84] So παροικία—the sojourn of the non-citizen in a foreign place, then foreign parts per se[85]—also became the self-description of the Christian community. It is significant that already in *1 Clement*, which is more or less contemporary with 1 Peter,[86] the self-designation ἐκκλησία ("congregation of the people") made more specific by means of a παροικοῦσα with a following *acc. loci*. Similar formulations are found in the *inscriptio* to the *Martyrdom of Polycarp*, the *inscriptiones* of the letters of Dionysius of Corinth[87] and the letter of Irenaeus to Victor of Rome,[88] and the letter of the gallic communities concerning their martyrs.[89] It is not by chance

---

[83] K. Wengst, *Didache (Apostellehre), Barnabasbrief, Zweiter Klemensbrief, Schrift an Diognet. Eingeleitet, herausgegeben, übertragen und erläutert* (SUC 2; Darmstadt, 1984), pp. 203–80 (227).

[84] R.H. Bainton, "The Early Church and War," *HTR* 39 (1946), p. 203, concerning the self-understanding of the early church in its relationship with the world; cf. already A. von Harnack, *Die Mission und Ausbreitung des Christentums in den ersten drei Jahrhunderten* (2 vols.; 4th edn., Leipzig, 1924), pp. 268f.: Christians saw themselves as "pilgrims and denizens; they walk in believing and not seeing, and their whole lifestyle is characterised by escape from the world, and is determined only by the kingdom of the world beyond, to which they are hastening." The meaning of this self-description is underlined also by C. Andresen, *Die Kirchen der alten Christenheit* (RM 29.1,2; Stuttgart, 1971), pp. 25ff. and K. Aland, "Das Verhältnis von Kirche und Staat in der Frühzeit," in W. Haase (ed.), *ANRW* II.23.1. Religion (Berlin, 1979), pp. 230ff., though Aland rightly underlines the political connotations of the terminology used here.

[85] W. Bauer, K. & B. Aland, *Griechisch-deutsches Wörterbuch zu den Schriften des Neuen Testaments und der frühchristlichen Literatur* (Berlin, 6th edn., 1988), col. 1270; H.G. Liddell & R. Scott (eds.), *A Greek-English Lexicon* (Oxford, 9th edn., 1968), col. 1342.

[86] J.A. Fischer (*Die Apostolischen Väter. Eingeleitet, herausgegeben, übertragen und erläutert* [SUC 1; 9th edn., Darmstadt, 1986], p. 19) comes to the conclusion that the letter must have been written before the end of the first century.

[87] Eus. *Hist. Eccl.* 4, 23, 5 cf. 4, 23, 7.

[88] Eus. *Hist. Eccl.* 5, 24,14f.

[89] Eus. *Hist. Eccl.* 5, 1, 3.

that in the third and fourth century the term παροικία then found its
way into the terminology of church administration[90] as "parish", "parochial" etc. The Latin equivalent, *peregrinatio*,[91] also terms the Christians' eschatologically oriented form of existence as "foreignness:"
"usque in huius saeculi finem inter persecutiones mundi et conso-
lationes Dei peregrinando procurrit ecclesia."[92] The meaning in Augustine is not, as in mediaeval Latin, "pilgrimage;"[93] rather, *perigrinari*
etc., as Schmidt[94] has shown in detail, means the "foreignness" of
Christians: "The metaphor derived from Augustine is a concept that
goes back to the primitive church: the Christian is a 'stranger and
denizen' with no citizenship on earth."[95]

With the concept of foreignness, expression is given not only to
the situation in which they found themselves, but also to a claim and
a task; the "state of affairs," one might say, in which the Christians

---

[90] P. De Labriolle, "Paroccia," *RSR* 18 (1928), pp. 60–72; see further Harnack,
Mission, pp. 421ff.

[91] On one occasion in the NT the Vulgate renders παροικεῖν by *peregrinari* (Lk.
24:18). On two occasions it translates παρεπίδημος by *peregrinus* (1 Pet. 2:11; Heb.
11:13). More frequently, in the OT it translates with *peregrinus* etc. where the LXX
has πάροικος κτλ (cf. Gen. 15:13; 23:4; Lev. 25:35, 47; Num. 35:15; Deut. 14:21; ψ
118:54 (Ps. 119:54).

[92] Aug. *Civ.D.* 18:51 (quoted again in *Lumen gentium* 8); cf. *idem*, *En. in Ps.* 136:1.
The vitality of this tradition in liturgy is attested to, for example, in the preface to
the communion in the dedication of a church: "This house, in which you gather
your pilgrim church, was erected in your honour. . . . Here you turn our eyes to the
heavenly Jerusalem and give us the hope to see your peace there" (*Schott-Meßbuch für
die Sonn- und Festtage des Lesejahres A. Originaltexte der authentischen deutschen Ausgabe des
Meßbuches und des Meßlektionars* [Freiburg, 1983], p. 437).

[93] Apart from the meaning it has in common with παροικία, "sojourn in foreign
parts" (*peregrinus* = foreign), in classical Latin *peregrinatio* also, in the majority of cases,
means foreign travel (so, the *Oxford Latin Dictionary*, ed. P.G.W. Glare [Oxford, 1968–
1982], col. 1335, with reference to Cicero, Seneca, Tacitus, Pliny et al.; cf. also
K.F. Georges, *Ausführliches latinisch-deutsches Handwörterbuch* [2 vols., Tübingen, 9th edn.,
1951], I, 1581). It is instructive to note that in ecclesiastical Latin *peregrinatio* was
understood as "pilgrimage," taking up the second meaning (just as, correspondingly, the theology of the *ecclesia peregrinans* is a *theologia viatorum*).

[94] On philological grounds alone, E.A. Schmidt (*Zeit und Geschichte bei Augustin*
[SHAW.PH 1985 Bericht 3; Heidelberg, 1985], pp. 84–88) rejects the translation of
peregrinatio in Augustine as "pilgrimage to a destination" as a "mistranslation" (p. 84).
"The concept of pilgrimage is impossible for the 'city of God', in the first place
because Augustine never uses the prepositional construction 'peregrinari ad . . .'. He
uses the verb absolutely, links it with locative prepositions or in constructions with
a (ab, abs)" (p. 87). Instead, Schmidt emphasises the continuity of Augustine's *peregrinatio*
statements with primitive Christian ideas.

[95] Schmidt, *Zeit*, p. 86. Further, the fact that "captivity" is a partial synonym of
"*peregrinatio*" shows that the "archetype of the Augustinian '*peregrinatio*'-concept is the
Babylonian captivity of the Jews with their sighing for Jerusalem, their home."

saw themselves situated, and on which their self-understanding rested, is being described. Clement of Alexandria demands—in the form of a regulation—this foreignness as a Christian duty: ὡς "ξένοι καὶ παρεπιδημοῦντες" πολιτεύεσθαι ὀφείλομεν.[96] The consequence of such an understanding of what constitutes the foreign is then the paraenetic exposition of this category, an exposition which—according to the character of the writing in question—can differ considerably. For the *Shepherd of Hermas*,[97] which stands in the apocalyptic tradition, the consequence of Christian foreignness[98] is the radical break with this world, the rejection of the acquisition of everything that goes beyond the essentials of life, because this world "stands under the power of another" (*Herm.* 1:3). The human being is thus situated between the competing law of two πόλεις[99] and must decide; there can be no compromise, and the consequence of a wrong decision is the irreversible banishment from the heavenly home (1:2–6). The description of Christian self-understanding and relationship to the world in the *Letter of Diognetus*, composed in the second or third century,[100] sounds similarly fundamental, but much less radical on the matter. Externally, Christians are in no respect different (according to Dg 5:1ff.) from other people; they do not live in different cities, and do not lead remarkable lives. They are, however, marked by a special inner attitude to all these things, which Dg 5:5 describes with the words: Πατρίδας οἰκοῦσιν ἰδίας, ἀλλ' ὡς πάροικοι. μετέχουσι πάντων ὡς πολῖται, καὶ πάνθ' ὑπομένουσιν ὡς ξένοι. πᾶσα ξένη πατρίς ἐστιν αὐτῶν, καὶ πᾶσα πατρὶς ξένη. Corresponding with this explanation of foreign parts is the fact that for the *Letter of Diognetus* the foreignness of Christians (basically a re-reading of 1 Cor. 7:29f. in a stoic light) is evident not in their complete antithesis to the world, as in the *Shepherd of Hermas*, but in an attitude which—in obedience to the

---

[96] Clem.Alex. *Strom.* III,14. Tertullian puts it similarly: "Non enim et nos milites sumus . . . non et nos peregrinantes—in isto saeculo—sumus. Cur autem ita dispositus es, o Christiane, ut sine uxore no possis?" (*De Exhotatione Castitatis* 12:1).

[97] According to B. Altaner & A. Stuiber (*Patrologie: Leben, Schriften und Lehre der Kirchenväter* [Freiburg, 8th edn., 1978], p. 55), the time of composition is likely to be the decade before 150.

[98] Cf. 1:1: ἐπὶ ξένης κατοικεῖτε.

[99] It is noticeable how the biblical image of the two masters (Mt. 6:24; Lk. 16:13) is replaced by the more political image of two cities.

[100] According to Wengst (SUC 2, pp. 305ff.), the only thing that can be said with certainty about the origin of the writing is that it was composed between the end of the second century and the beginning of the reign of Constantine; Altaner (*Patrologie*, p. 77), however, assumes an origin in the second half of the second century.

traditional laws—is manifested precisely in the supersession of these laws by their own lifestyle![101]

The self-designation "strangers" is thus also meant offensively, since it has an elitist connotation.[102] The category of strangeness can thus be directed critically against a church or a Christian society that settles too comfortably in this world.[103] Already in early Christian times, and then again and again in the history of the church, there had been outsiders in church and society who—often combined with direct criticism of a now worldly church and a worldly Christianity— saw themselves as "strangers" living from God's future, who do not intend to have their roots in this world. Frequently it was from these people that stimuli for a renewal of the church emerged. In the first place monasticism should be mentioned here, which consciously interpreted its form of existence as *peregrinatio*[104] and as a result not infrequently functioned as a critical factor within the church.[105] This monastic self-understanding—whatever its precise contours in individual cases—not only forms a link between the most varied movements of western monasticism such as the Iroscots,[106] Francis of Assisi[107]

---

[101] Dg 5:10: . . . τοῖς ἰδίοις βίοις νικῶσιν τοὺς νόμους.

[102] This is clear also in the Martyrdoms, when the Christians answer the question of their origin with Χριστιανός εἰμι (or "Christianus sum"), and thus provocatively link their not belonging to the earthly Polis with their belonging to God's πολίτευμα (as in the report about the martyrs of Lyon/Vienna, Eus. *Hist. Eccl.* 5,1,20; cf. Musurillo, *Acts* 22).

[103] In *De civitate Dei*, Augustine had emphasised the eschatological orientation of the church with *peregrinatio*, and used it to criticise a Christianity which had identified itself to a great extent as an imperial religion with the Imperium Romanum and had correspondingly met with a crisis situation after the sack of Rome by Alarich in 410. Augustine was certainly no isolated case.

[104] Cf. the data in C. du Cange, *Glossarium mediae et infimae latinitatis* (5 vols., repr. Graz, 1954), VI, p. 270. The roots of this idea stem from the ξενιτεία of early monasticism; cf. A. Guillaumont, "Le dépaysement comme forme d'ascèse dans le monachisme ancien," *Aux origines du monachisme chrétien* (Spiritualité Orientale 30; Bégrolles en Manges, 1979), pp. 89–116.

[105] It is no coincidence that the renewal and reform movements (up to the time of the Reformation) emerge from monasticism.

[106] The Iroscottish monks saw their life and their mission as "peregrinatio propter Christum."

[107] In the *regula bullata*, the definitive rule of the lesser brothers, these are called in the 6th chapter to strict poverty. They are not to acquire any property, including shelter, but rather to serve their Lord in this world "tamquam peregrini et advenae." In his Testament Francis expressly extends this lack of possessions to cover the possessions of a church; without any kind of possessions the brothers are to comply with their vow of poverty, "semper ibi hospitantes sicut advenae et peregrini" (*Testamentum* 7). In both cases Francis of Assisi quotes 1 Pet. 2:11 ("peregrini et advenae").

and Ignatius of Loyola,[108] but is also found in eastern monasticism.[109] These traditions are taken up also in the Protestant world, where from the "Pilgrim Fathers" of the 17th century to Zinzendorf's "Pilgrim Church" to the social-critical "Sojourners" movement of our own day, the concept of foreignness has found its way even into the self-designations of individual movements.

If one takes an overall view of these aspects of the history of the category of foreignness, the category's *clear situation-relatedness* is again striking here. It is characteristic that παροικία became the self-designation of the persecuted martyr-church of the 2nd century. Nor is it a coincidence that Augustine rediscovered the *peregrinatio* as a central category after the sack of Rome and the crisis in the Christian view of the empire that was caused by it. *Mutatis mutandis*, similar things will be true of later times: it is not accidental that J. Bunyan wrote his *Pilgrim's Progress* in a prison cell, after the failure of attempts to bring about the kingdom of God on earth. Dietrich Bonhoeffer discovers estrangement as an ecclesiological category, when in connection with the experiences of the church's struggle he seeks to determine the stand and the task of the followers of Jesus Christ in a

---

[108] In his memoirs, Ignatius never refers to himself by name, only by the term "pilgrim."

[109] Examples worth mentioning here would be Ephrem the Syrian, who in a penetrating homily describes the stranger-existence as in correspondence with God himself and thus as the only appropriate form of discipleship: "Whoever seeks Christ, should look for him in foreign parts (בܐܟܣܢܝܐ). And behold, he will indeed find him, God, in foreign parts (בܢܘ אܟܣܢܝܐ)." (v. 15), tr. A. Haffner, *Die Homilie des heiligen Ephräm von Syrien über das Pilgerleben. Nach den Handschriften von Rom und Paris herausgegeben und übersetzt* (SAWW.PH 135,9; Vienna, 1896), p. 13. Haffner's translation of the word בܐܟܣܢܝܐ (derived from Greek ξένος) as "pilgrimage" or "pilgrim existence" is not, however, accepted. According to J. Payne Smith (ed.), *A Compendious Syriac Dictionary, Founded upon the Thesaurus Syriacus of R. Payne Smith* (Oxford, repr. 1985), p. 16, בܐܟܣܢܝܐ has the meaning "strange or foreign country, living abroad, exile." On this etymology it can then mean also the lifestyle of the Anachorete, a meaning which certainly plays a role here: The anachorete realises Christian existence in the most perfect way. To render the word with "pilgrim existence" hides the danger of a considerable anachronism. In the forefront is the idea of an existence in abstinence and also in social exclusion, as is clear in paragraphs 6ff.: "And while everyone else makes himself comfortable in his house,/ a soul is tormented,/ and he is despised like a cripple,/ and contemned with importunity./ One calls him a thief,/ and the other a bad slave,/ one calls him a beggar,/ and the other a vagabond./ One calls him a seducer,/ and the other an enemy of his country,/ one calls him a spy,/ and the other a burglar./ One calls him possessed by the devil,/ and the other ignorant./ And again one calls him Thor,/ and the other irrational./ Such and like insults/ are prepared for the whole of life in foreign parts."

society which is no longer the "Christian West."[110] John XXIII, on the basis of his insight into the necessity of an *aggiornamento*, a fundamental reform of the fossilised church, takes up the *peregrinatio* into the self-understanding of the church, and in *Lumen gentium* now underlines, over against the hitherto usual one-sided emphasis of the institutionalised side of the church, its eschatological orientation as *ecclesia peregrinans*. Its "being" is defined as being en route: "Dum vero his in terris Ecclesia peregrinatur a Domino, ... tamquam exsulem se habet, ita ut quae sursum sunt quaerat et sapiat."[111]

The history of influence (*Wirkungsgeschichte*) thus confirms the surprising findings of the exegesis: to be found again and again are indeed the world-fleeing tendencies of a "pilgrims' theology," which interprets the estrangement as the self-egotising of Christians over against the evil earthly "vale of tears." But this should not be allowed to obscure the fact that taken as a whole the category of strangeness has developed a primarily positive, reality-embracing (and not reality-excluding) effect:

– not least as a corrective against the identification of the people of God and the earthly nation, it demanded again and again as a critical ideal the *distinction* (not separation) of Christians from the world around them;

– this brought them especially in difficult situations into public

---

[110] Cf. D. Bonhoeffer, *Nachfolge* (München, 9th edn., 1967), pp. 83f.: "The world celebrates and they stand aside; the world cries: Enjoy life, and they mourn. They see that the ship on which the festive rejoicing is taking place, has sprung a leak. The world fantasises about progress, power, future, the disciples know about the end, the judgment and the coming of the kingdom of heaven, for which the world is not at all suited. Therefore the disciples are strangers in the world, unwelcome guests, trouble-makers who are rejected ... They stand as strangers in the power of him who was so alien to the world that they crucified him." Bonhoeffer goes on to develop this idea of the "alien church"—to some extent as an ecclesiological counterpart to the crucified Christ—and returns to it several times (cf. 84, 89, 94, 146); further, the quotations of corresponding songs by Teerstegen (p. 149) or Richter (p. 245), while the latter concludes the section "The visible church" (220–45) which basically leads to the right understanding of foreignness as the Christian community's form of existence (cf. esp. 242–44). This idea also determines the following section about the church as "the saints," where the sanctification is described as the separation of the church from the world—determined by God's election: "Like a sealed train in a foreign land, so the church goes through the world" (253).

[111] *Zweites Vatikanisches Konzil: Dogmatische Konstitution über die Kirche. Authentischer lateinischer Text. Deutsche Übersetzung im Auftrage der deutschen Bischöfe. Mit einer Einleitung von J. Ratzinger* (Münster, 1965), art. 6. According to the example of the peregrinatio of Israel in the wilderness, the church too is on the way to an "abiding city" (art. 9), and is thus *Ecclesia peregrinans* (art. 14; 48, cf. 8; 21), or *Ecclesia viatorum* (art. 50). These designations are then also applied to believers (art. 7; 13; 62, cf. 58).

discussion and thus made possible a theological perspective on crises and the overcoming of crises—in the life of a church community, but also in the life of individuals (cf. the hymn book);

– it thereby opened up the possibility of a constructive reorientation on God's word, a renewed self-understanding and relationship to the world.

4. *Prospects: The Existence of Believers between Foreignness and 'Nationhood'*

Membership of the people of God could, in early Judaism, imply a clear distance from the endeavour to overcome state and political constructions in a religious manner. This was especially the case where other peoples and cultures had made their mark on the milieu. But Philo already shows clearly that this did not have to be understood in the sense of complete separation. Rather, precisely the self-understanding of believers as "strangers" implied both things: distinction and encounter, loyalty to one's own belief and coming to terms with the foreign. This tendency is continued in 1 Peter: his addressees had been alienated from their milieu by their conversion, and had become strangers. Despite the enormous difficulties of the early Christians, this letter affirms state and society, with their various tasks. It does not go the way of sectarian self-isolation which rubbishes everything else. The maintenance of such a legally and politically secured environment is, for him, also an act of practical worship! At the same time, however, this primitive Christian pastoral letter sharply distinguishes itself from any religious overexaltation of this "human creation," as 1 Pet. 2:13 deliberately calls the state. Any attempt to derive their identity from what they have become, from their inheritance, the traditions of their fathers, is rejected.[112] Alongside an acceptance of the nation and the bonds to it, being a Christian also implies a distance from nationalism where this has become absolute and takes on quasi-religious features. The polemic of 1 Peter against the "futility of the lifestyle inherited from the fathers" (as 1 Pet. 1:18

---

[112] It should be borne in mind that the opposition to pagan religiosity in 1 Peter leads to a sharpness of conflict which we must not replicate. On the other hand, the nation with its history, its traditions and its symbols can become an idol even in our own century. This is always the case where the notion of people or nation becomes the determinative measure of self-understanding and thus denigrates everything that is foreign.

puts it) is conditioned by the particularities of the situation, but its one-sidedness brings to expression something decisive: *The future home, towards which believers are walking, is not the unbroken extension of the earthly one.* The expectation of God's new world applies a critical yardstick to the old world, *a measure to which Christians, as members of the people of God, are also committed in their own nation.* As regards their nation and land, their task remains to work not just to reaffirm it, but also to be παροικία, practising strangers.

ANTI-SEMITIC AND RACIST PREJUDICES IN TITUS 1:10-16[1]

Wolfgang Stegemann

> Racism in all its forms is a fundamental evil in humanity and remains
> the cause of many conflicts in and between nations and states. The
> task of attaining the most objective possible knowledge of its historical
> preconditions is ever more urgent. The points of departure and refer-
> ence will always be the two most extreme forms of racism: Auschwitz
> for racial hatred and apartheid for race discrimination.

With the sentences just quoted, I. Geiss begins his *Geschichte des
Rassismus*, which was published in 1988.[2] Since then the world has
been able to see the end of institutionalized racism in South Africa,
as well as the end of the confrontation between East and West, in
my country the fall of the Wall and the unification of the two German
states. People are speaking of the end of the era of the Cold War or
the Post-War period. Many things seem to have come to an end—
but unfortunately not anti-semitism and racism. Acts of violence against
foreigners and asylum-seekers in Germany and elsewhere, race riots
in Los Angeles (1992), the Bosnian Serbs' war of conquest against
the Bosnian Moslems, to which the aweful phrase "ethnic cleansing"
has been applied, but also a new increase in anti-semitic attitudes
and actions (e.g., in Germany, Italy and Switzerland), all these things
make us painfully aware of this fact. The renewed kindling of nationalistic feeling, xenophobia, ethnocentrism and anti-semitism has
a social, economic and political background. But the way has been
prepared by spiritual authorities, and in the case of anti-semitism
these unfortunately include the Christian churches and Christian
theology. U. Tal, among many others, has analysed this relationship,
taking as an example the situation in Germany before the Nazi period,
and has come to the conclusion that racist anti-semitism and the
subsequent Nazi movement were not the result of mass hysteria or
the work of individual propagandists. The racist anti-semites, despite
their opposition to traditional Christianity, learned much from it and

---

[1] Translated from the German by David E. Orton.
[2] I. Geiss, *Geschichte des Rassismus* (Frankfurt, 1988).

successfully created a well-prepared, systematic ideology with a logic
of its own, which reached its climax in the Third Reich. The French
historian and writer, J. Isaac, was one of the first to make a careful
analysis of the significance of anti-Judaism in the Christian churches,
which he characterized as "instruction in contempt for the Jews"
and a "system of denigrating the Jews."[3] R.R. Ruether, similarly,
states:[4] "The Nazis, of course, were not Christians. They were indeed
anti-Christians . . . Nevertheless, the church must bear a substantial
responsibility for a tragic history of the Jew in Christendom which
was the foundation upon which political anti-Semitism and the Nazi
use of it was erected."[5] Ruether then comes to the thesis that Christian anti-semitism is to be found not just in later periods of Church
history but already in the earliest period of the origins of Christian
communities, including the New Testament period itself. Anti-semitism
is the "left hand" of Christology, the negative side of the Christian
claim that Jesus is the Christ.[6] The connection between religious and
secular anti-Judaism is confirmed also by modern empirical-socio-
logical findings.[7]

If exegetes are to take seriously the task demanded by Geiss, to
analyse the "historical preconditions" of racism and anti-semitism "as
objectively as possible," then a critical analysis of New Testament texts
is also unavoidable. On the question of anti-semitism in the New
Testament such an analysis has long since been undertaken, though
the assessments—sometimes regarding the very same New Testament
texts—vary. This is evident for instance in the most recent discussion
about the Lukan relationship to Judaism. According to bias, the range

---

[3] On this see, for example, J. Isaac, "Hat der Antisemitismus christliche Wurzeln?,"
EvTh 21 (1961), pp. 339–354.

[4] R.R. Ruether, *Faith and Fratricide: The Theological Roots of Anti-Semitism* (New York,
1974), p. 184 (German translation: *Nächstenliebe und Brudermord*, München, 1978).

[5] Ruether, *Faith and Fraticide*, p. 184.

[6] Ruether, *Faith and Fraticide*, pp. 64–65. Cf. also R.L. Wilken, *The Myth of Christian Beginnings: History's Impact on Belief* (New York, 1972), p. 197: "Christian antisemitism
did not arise by the importation of ideas foreign to Christianity through some historical accident. Christian antisemitism grew out of the Christian Bible, i.e., the
New Testament, as it was understood and interpreted by Christians over centuries . . . We must learn, I think, to live with the unpleasant fact that antisemitism is
part of what it has meant historically to be a Christian, and is still part of what it
means to be a Christian."

[7] On this cf., e.g., C. Glock & R. Stark, *Christian Beliefs and Anti-Semitism* (New
York, 1966); G. Lämmermann, "Christliche Motivierung des modernen Anti-semitis-
mus? Religionssoziologische und—pädagogische Überlegungen zu einem sozialen
Phänomen," *ZEE* 28 (1984), pp. 58–84.

of verdicts stretches from anti-semitic to pro-Jewish.[8] The debate also concerns the question of what constitutes "anti-semitism." And it appears that the anti-semitism of the history of Christian exegesis (professional exegesis expressly included) is rather more serious than the anti-Jewish tendencies of the New Testament itself. Less attention, however, has been paid to questions of ethnocentrism, xenophobia or even racist prejudice in the New Testament.[9] This has also no doubt to do with the New Testament itself and the earliest groups of Christian believers represented in it. For in the first place they are characterized by their crossing of ethnic-religious boundaries.

Overview and Thesis

In my first section I would like briefly to show that ethnicity or an ethnocentric self-understanding could play no role in the beginnings of Christian communities. For these newly forming groups defined themselves on the basis of their *religious* identity as a third entity alongside the nations and Judaism. While Paul resorted to religious symbols from Judaism in the self-definition of Christian believers and took account of the different heritage of believers from the nations or from Judaism, in the Pastoral Epistles, for example, there was a dominant perspective which evened out these differences. The claim to superiority associated with this is reflected in religio-ethical terms here too, but not ethnically. The letter to Titus does however contain xenophobic prejudices, which will be considered in more detail in my second section where I make provisional observations concerning Tit. 1:10–16. In my third section this text will be analysed from a sociology-of-deviance point of view. It can be demonstrated that the xenophobic prejudices against Jews and Cretans by the author of the letter to Titus can be placed in the framework of a so-called "negative labelling" of a heterodox Christian group. In my fourth section the two xenophobic prejudices will again be considered in more detail and evaluated as anti-semitic or racist. Finally, the fifth section suggests some considerations regarding the use of this text.

---

[8] On this see the collection of essays: J.B. Tyson (ed.), *Luke-Acts and the Jewish People: Eight Critical Perspectives* (Minneapolis, 1988).

[9] W.R. Herzog, "The New Testament and the Question of Racial Injustice," *American Baptist Quarterly* 5 (1988), pp. 12–32; J. Brown, "Racism in the Bible" (1/2), in R. Rollason (ed.), *Racism in Australia in the 1980's* (Sydney, 1981), pp. 36–42, 43–47.

1. *Christian Self-understanding beyond Ethnic-Religious Boundaries*

A fundamental given as far as the earliest Christian communities is concerned is this: ethnic or religious borders were crossed in the course of the establishment of permanent Christian communities in the cities of the Roman empire. Their (presumed) historical origin in Syrian Antioch is a relevant example in this respect. For it was here that Christ-believing Jews *and* non-Jews (ἔθνη) first formed a community in which an unrestricted social intercourse was practised (Gal. 2:11ff.). It is evidently not by chance that Luke connects this occurrence with the new label Χριστιανοί for the disciples, male and female (Acts 11:27). I cannot go into this matter more deeply at this point. The important thing for the moment is this: urban Christianity, in the process of development outside the land of Israel, could certainly not resort to ethnic identities in its self-definition. *Ethnicity*— that is bonding through common racial heritage, territory, history, concepts, feelings and actions, which at the same time differentiate them from others—was necessarily unable to play a role in the determination of "Christian" identity. It is true that the awareness of a differentiated ethnic-religious *origin* of Christ-believers was present for a long time, expressed from the perspective of Judaism in the asymmetrical opposing concepts of "Israel"—"the nations/heathen," or "Jews"—"Greeks." Earliest Christianity stands in a well-profiled tradition. For in the differentiation of one's collective identity from others, "asymmetrical opposing concepts,"[10] such as "Greeks" and "Barbarians," "Romans" (*Romani*) and "foreigners" (*peregrini*), were in use already in antiquity. Examples can also be found in the New Testament. I would refer simply to the Pauline letters in this respect.[11] There we encounter for example the differentiation between "Israel" and "the nations" (ἔθνη),[12] and the contrast between "Greeks" and "Jews,"[13] or between "circumcision" and "uncircumcision."[14] Pejorative

---

[10] On this, cf. R. Kosellek, "Zur historisch-politischen Semantik assymetrischer Gegenbegriffe," in R. Kosellek, *Vergangene Zukunft: Zur Semantik geschichtlicher Zeiten* (Frankfurt, 1979), pp. 211–59.

[11] On Paul as a whole see U. Heckel, "Das Bild der Heiden und die Identität der Christen bei Paulus," in R. Feldmeier & U. Heckel (eds.), *Die Heiden: Juden, Christen und das Problem des Fremden* (Tübingen, 1994), pp. 269–96.

[12] Cf., e.g., Rom. 9:30f.; 11:25; in contrast to the "Jews": Rom. 3:29; 9:24; 1 Cor. 1:23; Gal. 2:15.

[13] Rom. 1:16; 2:9f.; 3:9; 10:12; Gal. 3:28; 1 Cor. 1:22, 24; 10:32; 12:13.

[14] Rom. 2:25–27; 3:30; 4:9–12; 1 Cor. 7:18f.; Gal. 2:7; 5:6; 6:15.

associations certainly play a role here, for instance by reference to the immorality or the idolatry of the "heathen."[15] But the apostle can also use the differentiating concepts in a neutral way. Paul, indeed, wants to be a Jew to the Jews, to those without the law as one without the law (1 Cor. 9:20–22). And according to Gal. 3:28, in Christ the religious-national differences between Jews and Greeks are removed.[16]

Double Self-understanding

The special character of the self-understanding of the ἐκκλησία, for Paul, lies in the fact that he developed the notion for the Christian community that they were on the one hand something new, a third entity, in relation to Jews and Greeks (or the heathen/the nations), while on the other hand he kept the specific affinity with Judaism alive by calling them, for instance, "God's beloved" and "called to be saints" (Rom. 1:7), and even "the seed of Abraham" (Rom. 4:11–14:16). But it should be recognized that Paul *distinguishes* the ἐκκλησία from empirical Judaism, "Israel" or "Israel according to the flesh" (1 Cor. 10:18). So Paul speaks of the ἐκκλησία *from the nations* not as "Israel" or even as "the true or spiritual Israel."[17] He sees them not as part of Judaism, as a Jewish movement or sect, but as an eschatological community in its own right, called from the nations. He is thus able to express the particularity of the Christ-believing group also as the removal of ethnic-religious differences between pagans and Jews (Rom. 3:22; 10:12; Gal. 3:28; cf. Eph. 2:11ff.). This "double" self-understanding[18] found expression in the second century in the notion of the church as *tertium genus*. There are already hints in this direction within the New Testament. 1 Cor. 10:32, for example, makes it explicitly clear that the Apostle Paul sees in the ἐκκλησία a third empirical entity alongside Jews and Greeks (cf. also

---

[15] E.g., 1 Thess. 1:9; 4:5; Gal. 2:15; 1 Cor. 12:2; Rom. 1:18ff.

[16] I will not enter into the complex discussion of this verse at this point.

[17] The Pauline formulation, "Israel of God" (Gal. 6:16) could mean Israel itself or the community of God in Judaea, that is, the early church; cf. E. Stegemann, "Zwischen Juden und Heiden, aber "mehr" als Juden und Heiden? Neutestamentliche Anmerkungen zur Identitätsproblematik des frühen Christentums," *Kirche und Israel* 9 (1994), pp. 53–69 (62); cf. also 1 Pet. 2:9, where Israel's titles of honour are transferred to the churches; similarly, Heb. 3:1; 8:7ff.

[18] I am borrowing this concept from E. Stegemann "Zwischen Juden und Heiden."

2 Cor. 11:24–29). But remarkably enough he does not use "ethnic" vocabulary in this context, but speaks, among other things, of a "new creation" (καινὴ κτίσις), in which there is neither circumcision nor uncircumcision (Gal. 6:15), or of unity in Christ, of the body of Christ or the Temple of God.[19]

Because of the particular composition of the urban Christian communities it was thus not possible to determine the self-understanding of Christ-believers by reference back to an *ethnic* identity of their own. In defining themselves they began above all by resorting to Jewish identity terms.[20] But an increasingly polemical division is discernible between Judaism and the formation of a "gentile Christian" self-understanding or arrogance (evidently already in the church in Rome, as may be inferred from Romans 9–11), which then later—in Justin, for example—even found it difficult to accept so-called "Jewish Christianity." The only opponents of the Christ-believers were now, in the main, the nations/pagans.

The Perspective of the Pastoral Epistles: All People

This new situation is also reflected in the *Pastoral Epistles*, which also display a clear difference from the older (authentic) letters of Paul.[21] For even if Paul already had a universal perspective, humanity still consisted of Jews and Gentiles, and so also did the community of those who believed in Christ (the churches in Judaea, the churches among the nations).[22] He saw himself as the "Apostle to the nations" and the non-Jews as the addressees of his proclamation, while Peter was entrusted with taking the gospel to the Jews (Gal. 2:7f.). In the Pastoral Epistles, which claim his authority, only the heathen/nations are in view, which represent all humanity equally (Tit. 3:2). Their Christian addressees differ from them in their religious self-understanding and also in ethical respects (implied in Tit. 3:3–6), but

---

[19] Cf., e.g., 1 Cor. 3:16f.; 10:17; 12:27; 2 Cor. 6:16; Rom. 12:5.

[20] Among other things perhaps by the use of the term λαός, in principle used exclusively in reference to Israel, for the Christ-believers. At the beginning already in Paul (2 Cor. 6:16; Rom. 9:25), (at least once) also in Acts: 18:10. In 1 Pet. 2:9f. several titles of honour for Israel—including λαός—are applied to the Christ-believers.

[21] That the Pastoral Epistles see themselves in the Pauline tradition will not be contested here; cf. esp. M. Wolter, *Die Pastoralbriefe als Paulustradition* (Göttingen, 1988). But I do assume that the historical Paul is not their author.

[22] Rom. 16:4; Gal. 1:22; 1 Thess. 2:14.

by the same token this shows their proximity to, and their origin in, the nations.[23] So the perspective of the Pastoral Epistles is that of the whole of humanity—no longer, it is true, distinguishing between Israel and the nations. This perspective is reflected also in theological or christological formulae: God desires that "all people should be saved and come to the knowledge of the truth" (1 Tim. 2:4; cf. 4:11; Tit. 2:11f.); Christ came into the world to save sinners (1 Tim. 1:15); he is the βασιλεὺς τῶν αἰώνων (1 Tim. 1:17); he mediates between God and human beings and gave himself as a ransom for all (1 Tim. 2:5; Tit. 2:14). Israel and its prerogatives—i.e. an awareness of the special religious situation of the Jewish people—are no longer in the picture,[24] and quotations or allusions to the Jewish Bible have to be sought with an exegetical microscope. Furthermore, in the Pastoral Epistles Paul is also teacher of the nations/heathen (1 Tim. 2:7; 2 Tim. 4:17; cf. 1 Tim. 3:16), but an awareness of the difference as is found in the authentic letters of Paul is no longer associated with this. If we knew no better, we would not even be able to conclude from the Pastoral Epistles that Paul was himself a Jew. Nothing of a "double self-understanding" of Christianity (as in Paul), i.e., of a special proximity and connection to the Jewish tradition, remains discernible in the Pastoral Epistles. Judaism—if it plays any role at all!—plays a critical or negative role (1 Tim. 1:7–10; Tit. 1:10, 14f.; 3:9).

We may now summarize: Ethnicity and/or ethnocentrism are not discussed in the Pastoral Epistles either. This is connected with the specific self-understanding of the Christianity represented in these pseudo-Pauline letters. This Christianity does know about the origin of believers from the "nations" and understands itself as a community of the elect,[25] which differs from other people (cf. 1 Tim. 6:1f.). Indeed, it is prepared for the contempt of other people because of its convictions (1 Tim. 4:10). But its difference is not reflected in ethnic concepts but in the self-confident expectation of eschatological salvation and ethical superiority (2 Tim. 2:11–14; Tit. 3:2ff.). The claim to an ethical superiority of their own does indeed have its counterpart in a negative estimation of all other people. The lack of ethnic identification resulting from the religious self-definition of the

---

[23] The opposing party are non-believers or apostates (cf., e.g., 1 Tim. 5:8; 6:2, 21).

[24] This lies at the root of the comment, for example, that Christ is from the seed of David (2 Tim. 2:8).

[25] Cf., e.g., 1 Tim. 3:5f., 15; 2 Tim. 1:9; 2:10f.; Tit. 1:1.

Christianity of the time does not, however, mean that xenophobic prejudices are entirely lacking. On the contrary: in Titus we find crass prejudices towards Jews and Cretans. The text in question, Tit. 1:10–16, requires more detailed treatment.

2. *Preliminary Observations on Titus 1:10–16*

Tit. 1:10–16 is a single polemic against a group and its protagonists, whom the author of the letter understands as a sort of "party" (cf. Tit. 3:10) within the Christian communities of Crete. He does not use a group label, but on the other hand we find in the text a conglomeration of terms of abuse and slogans. The writer to Titus says of the group he is criticizing:

–   They are numerous (πολλοί),
–   they are insubordinate (ἀνυπότακτοι)
–   they are gossips (ματαιολόγια), i.e. they teach superfluities (διδάσ-κοντες ἃ μὴ δεῖ),
–   for the sake of shameful gain (αἰσχροῦ κέρδους χάριν),
–   they are spiritual deceivers (φρεναπάται) who destroy whole families with their teachings (ὅλους οἴκους ἀνατρέπουσιν),
–   they are described as unbelieving (ἄπιστοι)
–   and as impure (βδελυκτοί),
–   cannot be persuaded (ἀπειθεῖς);
–   and ethically they are totally unreliable (πρὸς πᾶν ἔργον ἀγαθὸν ἀδόκιμοι).

These relatively general labels are interwoven with two fundamental identifications. On one hand it is maintained that these negative characteristics are particularly, or primarily (μάλιστα) applicable to "those of the circumcision" (οἱ ἐκ τῆς περιτομῆς). Shortly afterwards a warning is given not to subscribe to Jewish fables ('Ιουδαικοὶ μύθοι). On the other hand the "opponents" are also identified with negative prejudices concerning the Cretans. For one of them, their own prophet, is supposed to have said of the Cretans: "They are always liars, evil beasts and lazy gluttons." Precisely this testimony is true, says the author, which evidently means: the predictions of the "prophet" have turned out to be true. Of the content of the false teaching we read almost nothing. Apart from the "Jewish fables" already mentioned, human commandments (ἐντολαὶ ἀνθρώπων) are mentioned, and these are linked with the purity regulations. By this means they turn people away from the truth. Tit. 3:9 further describes silly discussions or investigations (μωραὶ ζητήσεις), genealogies, squabbles or legal disputes with them as pointless. The apostates evidently include in their creed (ὁμολογοῦσιν) the conviction that they know God, but they deny him with their works (1:16). The addressee of the letter is strictly to set the false teachers straight so that they become healthy in the faith (cf. also 3:9f.). So the letter to Titus does not deal with the false teaching of the "opponents" in detail; indeed, Titus is told not to look into it (3:9).

There has been some controversy in exegetical research concerning the profile of the "opponents" and the "errant doctrine" they propound—with reference also to the other Pastoral Epistles. Are these "Jewish Christians" or "Gnostics" or a mixture of the two?[26] All attempts to illuminate the convictions of this group from the letter to Titus (or the two other Pastoral Epistles) run the danger of succumbing to the strategy of "stigmatization" or "negative labelling," which the letter itself uses.[27] We shall not be able to extract the beliefs and teachings, or praxis, of the Christians who are so sharply rejected here, from the Pastoral Epistles. They have disappeared in the sea of polemic. For our purposes this discussion does not have to be resolved. For now the important thing is this: we are dealing with intra-Christian "opponents" who should be persuaded and healed in

---

[26] On this cf., e.g., N. Brox, *Die Pastoralbriefe* (5th edn, Regensburg, 1989), pp. 31ff.; M. Dibelius (ed. H. Conzelmann), *Die Pastoralbriefe* (3rd edn, Tübingen, 1955), pp. 14f., 52–54; G. Haufe, "Gnostische Irrlehre und ihre Abwehr in den Pastoralbriefen," in K.-W. Tröger (ed.), *Gnosis und Neues Testament: Studien aus Religionswissenschaft und Theologie* (Gütersloh, 1973), pp. 325–39. Dibelius-Conzelmann (3rd edn, 1955): Gnosis "with clear Jewish components" (p. 53); Haufe (1973): "early form of Gnosis with strong Jewish influence" (pp. 332f.); Brox: "Jewish (or Jewish-Christian) and gnostic features" (p. 33). On the question of the relationship to Judaism see below.

[27] Quinn is one who uses historicizing imagination. He thinks it likely that "those of the circumcision" are Palestinian Jewish-Christians who fled to Crete before the destruction of the Temple (70 CE). The theological and pastoral "battle" for the Christian community there had long since been lost at the time the letter to Titus was written. For the Christians there "had deadened into Judaism." Titus, in this view, presents the Cretans as an example of what happens if one rejects Paul: J.D. Quinn, *The Letter to Titus: A New Translation with Notes and Commentary and an Introduction to Titus, I and II Timothy, the Pastoral Epistles* (New York, 1990), 105–107.

the faith (1:13) or admonished or rejected (3:10). Since there is no clear division between protagonists and their supporters, but it is clear that the group portrayed so negatively here is to be found within the Christian community, I use the term "deviant Christian group."

3. *Interpretation of Tit. 1:10–16 and the Sociology of Deviance*

Two polemical strategies of argumentation are intertwined: on the one hand the author labels the deviant group with various derogatory terms. On the other hand he is concerned to identify them with Judaism or the Cretans, whereby certain prejudices are clearly intended to be transferred to the deviant group. In sociological terms this strategy of exclusion can be termed *deviance accusations* and be described with the aid of deviance theory.[28] Deviance theories deal with the relationships and function of non-conformists, outsiders or other deviants from the point of view of society as a whole or for superior groups. A detailed presentation of the various sociological theories can be found, among other writers, in the work of J.T. Sanders.[29] Here we may sketch only a few aspects.

Social groups possess norms and structures of behaviour which are more or less met, or transgressed, with a wide range of variation. The borders of social groups define the normative and divergent behaviour. A fundamental insight of Becker's is that deviance is created by the social groups themselves: "Social groups create deviance by making the rules whose infraction constitutes deviance, and by applying those rules to particular people and labeling them as outsiders." This makes possible the fundamental statement that "Deviant behavior is

---

[28] Deviance theories have been made particularly fruitful in the understanding of New Testament conflicts by Saldarini, Malina-Neyrey and Sanders: A.J. Saldarini, "The Gospel of Matthew and the Jewish-Christian Conflict," in D.L. Balch (ed.), *Social History of the Matthean Community: Cross-disciplinary Approaches* (Minneapolis, 1991), pp. 38ff.; B.J. Malina & J.H. Neyrey, "Conflict in Luke-Acts. Labelling and Deviance Theory," in B.J. Malina & J.H. Neyrey (eds.), *The Social World of Luke-Acts: Models for Interpretation* (Peabody, 1991), pp. 97–122; J.T. Sanders, *Schismatics, Sectarians, Dissidents, Deviants: The First One Hundred Years of Jewish-Christian Relations* (London, 1993), pp. 129ff. They rely on such authors as H. Becker, *Outsiders: Studies in the Sociology of Deviance* (New York, 1966); N. Ben-Yehuda, *Deviance and Moral Boundaries: Witchcraft, the Occult, Deviant Sciences and Scientists* (Chicago, 1985). For further literature see e.g., Saldarini 1989, pp. 44f.

[29] Sanders 1993, pp. 130ff.

behavior that people so label."[30] The labelling of certain persons as outsiders or deviants cannot be explained by a static definition of the content and aspects of the divergent behaviour. Rather, deviant behaviour is defined by the majority society or group. The reasons for the fact that some persons or institutions are able to brand others officially as deviants is, in Becker's view, not so much a matter of recourse to particular values. Rather, deviance occurs in a process of interaction between people, in which some, in the service of their own interests, set up particular rules, which declare others to be deviants. Conversely, others (the deviants) transgress these rules in the pursuit of *their* interests. Such rules, which give shape to particular values, are fixed in "problem situations" in which particular areas are regarded as "critical" and require action.[31] In his theory, Erikson emphasizes the significance of crisis situations for deviance. In his view deviance is a constant element of groups which is not in every case regulated by specific measures. The interest in a control of deviance arises from factors which demand the change of a group or society (due either to internal or external factors). Especially favourable conditions for the establishment of the norms of the majority group or society against deviants are thus provided by crises. Deviance control is a form of boundary maintenance or boundary construction in crisis situations. By means of the exclusion of others, or the reinforcement of their boundaries, a society reconfirms its identity. Ben-Yehuda has developed this idea, showing that deviance is inseparably connected with the identity of a society or group. She shows that where a society/group draws its boundaries indicates fundamental structures and values in its social and symbolic system.[32] It should be borne in mind that deviant positions appear as such outside a society, but sociologically and historically they form part of a whole.[33]

An Application of Deviance Theory to Tit. 1:10–16

Let us now apply these insights to our text. It can be seen that the letter presupposes a "crisis situation" which concerns differing value-

---

[30] Becker 1963, pp. 8f.
[31] Becker 1963, p. 131.
[32] Ben-Yehuda 1985, pp. 19f.
[33] Saldarini 1989, p. 47.

conceptions among the *Christian* groups. The author reacts to the
value-conceptions of the deviant group on the one hand with a reinforcement of the structures of institutional order. On the other hand
he labels the deviance of the group with wholesale "deviance accusations" and applies heterophobic[34] prejudices (Jews/Cretans) to the
deviants.

On the crisis situation: The text does indeed give some indications of a
"crisis situation" of the Christian communities in Crete. It reckons
(Tit. 1:10) with a large number of group members who refuse to
submit (ἀνυπότακτοι) to the order structure favoured by the author.
Indeed, according to Tit. 1:11 the deviants have evidently already
brought about the collapse or ruin (ἀνατρέπουσιν) of whole families
or households (οἶκοι). This may mean that—in line with 2 Tim. 2:18—
they have departed from what the author considers to be "sound"
faith. But it is also possible that the deviants' activities have caused
social conflicts within Christian families. In any case, the author of
the letter to Titus takes the "crisis situation" very seriously. He regards himself as on the side of the conventional group. This is evident not least from the fact that with the aid of the authority of the
apostle Paul the author gives the addressee of the letter (Titus) instructions for the extension or establishment of institutional structures for the Christian communities in Crete (Tit. 1:5–9), as well as
instructions for relations between the Christian communities (Tit. 2:1ff.)
and regarding relationships with the institutions of pagan society (Tit.
3:1ff.). So it must be borne in mind that the instructions for the
extension or establishment of institutional structures refers precisely
to the task of setting the deviants straight. This is clear on the one
hand from the contextual connection between our text (1:10–16) with
the institutional instructions in 1:5–9,[35] but also from the fact that
the deviants in various respects embody the opposite of the ideal
picture of the church official, or of Christians per se.[36]

On the values: The text also reveals that particular values in the Christian group were subject to debate. It is possible that for the "virtues"
of the functionaries the author refers back to values that had already
become conventional in the Christian communities (cf. Tit. 1:6–9

[34] This term is defined below.
[35] Cf. the closing sentence of v. 9: καὶ τοὺς ἀντιλέγοντας ἐλέγχειν and the link to
v. 10 by the conjunction γάρ.
[36] Cf. Brox (5th edn, 1989), p. 286.

with 1 Tim. 3:1ff.). But they are in principle so non-specific and correspond to such an extent with general cultural values,[37] that extensive extrapolations are problematic. One may, however, take it that the deviant group to some extent drew tighter boundaries than the conventional group as far as its values were concerned. The expression in v. 15, "To the pure all things are pure," sounds apologetic. The fact that the deviants are immediately described as "blemished" (μεμιαμμένοι) supports this impression. The author does not, however, tie this judgment to the transgression of *particular* regulations, but accuses his opponents of impurity of attitude (νοῦς; συνείθησις). He further discredits the values of the deviant group as "human laws" and links them with Judaism (1:14). We have good reason to believe, then, that certain values of the deviant group were not shared by the author of the letter.[38] The deviant group did, however, possess concrete and tight regulations, to which the corresponding position of the author was quite indifferent. The author connects the corresponding values of the deviant group either intentionally or with justification, rightly or wrongly, with Jewish tradition (see below). Whatever the case, this connection with Judaism is reason enough for him to reproach the opposing group with falling away from the truth (1:4). There is an early indication here, then, that a heterophobic attitude on the part of the author towards Judaism has either given rise to, or reinforced, the ostracism of the deviant Christian group.

On the general labelling (deviance accusations): From the above survey of the negative labels which the author produces against the deviant group, the following accusations can be summarized: The deviant group will not submit to the conventional authority of the Christian communities. Its attitude is headstrong, since it refuses to be won over. By means of its teachings the deviant group leads other Christians astray, causing them to fall away from the the truth and bringing about the collapse of (or instigating discontent in) whole Christian households. The motive of its teachings is dishonourable, since the apostates are concerned with personal enrichment.[39] The teachings

---

[37] On 1 Tim. 3 cf. Dibelius & Conzelmann (3rd edn, 1955), pp. 42ff.; Brox (5th edn, 1989), pp. 283f.

[38] Conclusions can certainly not be drawn concerning the "actual immorality of the false teachers:" so, rightly, Haufe, "Gnostische Irrlehre," p. 336.

[39] Should the current prejudice concerning the "sophists" be reactivated here?

of the apostates are specious gossip and are closely connected with Judaism. Their more demanding values are discredited since they are impure in their thinking and their consciences.[40] In fact they are abhorrent (βδελυκτοί), i.e. abnormal, and thus fall out of the basic categories of order in human society.[41] To this belongs also the identification with the Cretans, to the extent that according to the letter-writer the group is one which fulfils the prophecies concerning the negative national characteristics of the Cretans. Their "theological" convictions (θεὸν εἰδίναι) too are unbelievable in view of the contradictory character of their ethical praxis (πρὸς πᾶν ἔργον ἀγαθὸν ἀδόκιμοι).

Results of the Sociology-of-Deviance Analysis

Tit. 1:10–16 represents a strategy of negative labelling which is intended to highlight the deviance of the opposing group. This polemic, characterized as "deviance accusations," makes use of stereotypes and generalizing suspicions. The strategy of identifying the deviants with Judaism is part of it. The author does not flinch even from evaluating the apostates as abnormal, or "animals" (κατὰ θηρία in the context of the "Cretan" quotation), and thus to place them outside the human species. The author's concern is doubtless by these accusations to undermine the position and role of the opposing group within the Christian community. The derogatory labelling of the deviants corresponds to severe treatment: their mouths must be stopped (ἐπιστομίζειν: 1:11),[42] they must be strictly admonished (ἀποτόμος; 1:13) or be rejected (παραιτοῦ; 3:10) after having twice been admonished (νουθεσία). Disputes with them on matters of substance should be avoided (3:9). The aggressive rejection of an intra-Christian deviance group is not only a feature of Tit. 1:10–16. It is typical of the Pastoral Epistles as a whole. However, it is particularly striking in our text that the rejected group is connected with *implicit* prejudices about Judaism and *explicit* prejudices about the Cretans. The heterophobic

---

[40] Cf. the opposite position in 1 Tim. 1:5; 3:9; 2 Tim. 1:3; 2:22; Dibelius & Conzelmann (3rd edn, 1955), pp. 16f.

[41] Basic for the significance of the distinction between "pure" and "impure:" B.J. Malina, *The New Testament World: Insights from Cultural Anthropology* (rev. edn, Westminster, 1993), pp. 149–183.

[42] The verb can also be used figuratively, in the sense of ending a rebellion (Jos. *Ant.* 17:252). This interpretation suggests itself here too.

attitude to the deviant Christian group is here reinforced, then, by specific identifications. These have, in my view, anti-semitic and racist contours.

4. *The Stigmatization of the Deviant Group with Heterophobic Prejudices*

Tit. 1:10–16 shows the whole syndrome of discrimination by prejudices. The author is experiencing disputes within his own Christian community. An intra-Christian group has departed from the dominant opinion, which the author immunizes as "sound doctrine." Instead of responding in detail to the arguments of the dissidents— something the author expressly rejects (cf. e.g., Tit. 3:9f.)—the opponents are discriminated against. The procedure of discrimination is typical: first they are subjected to general contempt. Not content with this, the writer moves them into the close proximity of a negatively conceived Judaism and brands them with heterophobic prejudices about the Cretans. Before proceeding further, I should like to explain the term "heterophobic."

A. Memmi introduced the term "heterophobia" in his book about racism.[43] By this he wants to render the concept of "those phobic and aggressive constellations which are directed against others and are justified with various—psychological, cultural, social or metaphysical—arguments.[44] This comprehensive term seems to me to be useful. It is more comprehensive than the imported term *xenophobia* (fear of, or animosity towards, strangers), which grounds the otherness of others and the resulting fear in the fact that such people belong to a foreign people. A phobic and aggressive rejection of the other can, however, also concern those who belong to one's own ethnic group, as for example in the case of those with other sexual orientations (homosexuality)—or, as in our text, in connection with other religious convictions and ethical practices. Xenophobia would then be a subcategory within heterophobia. Memmi then distinguishes racism from the basic constellation of heterophobia. According to his definition this is also a form of heterophobia, but in this case one in which

---

[43] A. Memmi, *Rassismus* (Frankfurt, 1987), esp. pp. 97–124; these pages are reprinted in D. Claussen *Was heißt Rassismus?* (Darmstadt, 1994), pp. 203–222. I quote from the more easily accessible edition of Claussen.
[44] Memmi (in Claussen), pp. 220–221.

biological features of the other prompt fear and aggressive rejection. Essentially I agree with this conceptual distinction, but would add to "biological features" (e.g., skin colour) the feature of ethnic "origin," to the extent that this is understood as a kind of "biological" characteristic. Racism would then be the discrimination of other people, in word or deed, on account of their biological features or their ethnic origins, to the extent that these origins are at the same time seen in terms of biological features. This extension of the definition seems more appropriate precisely for historical research into racism, since in the Mediterranean culture of antiquity, for example, the estimation of the personality of a person was not oriented towards the modern ideal of individuality. Rather, membership of a group played a decisive role, in principle also membership of a particular people (Roman, Greek, Egyptian, Jew etc.). Knowledge of biological features could also be linked with this, as with regard to the dark skin of Ethiopians, which did not necessarily, however, lead to negative prejudices.[45]

Stigmatization of the Deviant Group with Prejudices about Judaism

At the beginning of his polemic against the deviant group the author places them in the close proximity to Judaism. "Those of the circumcision" (οἱ ἐκ τῆς περιτομῆς), especially, are "gossips" and "seducers." In the context of the other three names they are called in verse 10, it seems that the syntagm οἱ ἐκ τῆς περιτομῆς is also used pejoratively. It is true that it is theoretically possible that the author is alluding to the fact that the deviant group also includes Christ-believers of Jewish origin (so-called "Jewish-Christians").[46] But this is not at all certain.

If a dispute between Christians of Jewish and pagan origin is reflected in Tit. 1:10–16,[47] it would be untypical. First of all, it is strik-

---

[45] A. Dihle, *Die Griechen und die Fremden* (München, 1994), pp. 7–10; F.M. Snowden, *Blacks in Antiquity: Ethiopians in the Greco-Roman Experience* (Cambridge, Mass., 1970).

[46] In the New Testament Christ-believers of Jewish origin can be called by this syntagm (Gal. 2:12; Col. 4:11; Acts 10:45; presumably also Acts 11:2; cf. Rom. 4:12).

[47] See e.g., P.W. van der Horst, "The Jews of Ancient Crete," *JJS* 39 (1988), pp. 183–200 (188).

ing that of all the Pastoral Epistles, only Titus uses two expressions which explicitly make a connection between the deviant group and Judaism: "those of the circumcision" and "Jewish fables" (1:10, 14). In 1 Tim. 1:4, 4:7 and 2 Tim. 4:4, there is a less precise mention of "fables," which are linked in 1 Tim. 1:4 with "genealogies" (cf. Tit. 3:9). The connection between fables and genealogies is traditional, and could therefore be polemic in a familiar form.[48] It can be directed against gnostic reception of Old Testament texts.[49] This does not necessarily have anything to do with Judaism itself or with "Jewish-Christian" backgrounds.[50] The syntagm ἐντολαὶ ἀνθρώπων, too, is fundamentally non-specific.[51] The outworking of this is clearly found in the following v. 15, which itself, however, reveals nothing more precise. The key term καθαρός in the near context (1:15f.) indicates differences in ethical behaviour. At least a special Jewish background can be assumed. This is so even if in 1 Tim. 4:3–5 we have more precise indications of what is meant by "purity" (ban on marriage, abstinence from food). The ban on marriage is itself hardly traceable to Jewish tradition. And as far as the abstinence from food is concerned, one need not necessarily think of Jewish food regulations (*kashrut*) but in connection with the marriage ban (or is it a general ban on sexual relations?), ascetic tendencies may be meant which could allude also to the key term μάχαι νομικαί (Tit. 3:9).[52] In general terms, then, Jewish backgrounds may be assumed for the behaviour of the deviant group. But this certainly does not have to indicate that they were Jews[53] or so-called "Jewish-Christians." Nor does the writer of the letter to Titus become a Jew or "Jewish-Christian" when in Tit. 2:14

---

[48] Cf. Plato, Tim. 22a; Polybius IX 2:1; V. Hasler, art. γενεαλογία, in H. Balz & G. Schneider (eds.), *Exegetisches Wörterbuch zum Neuen Testament* (EWNT), I (2nd edn, Stuttgart, 1992), pp. 581f.

[49] Irenaeus and Tertullian already apply 1 Tim. 1:4 to the gnostics. Brox supposes gnostic exegesis of the "primeval and patriarchal narratives" of the Old Testament (Brox, 5th edn, 1989, 102f.). Similarly Dibelius & Conzelmann (3rd edn, 1955), pp. 14f.

[50] Sanders (1993), p. 222: "Such people need be Jews or even influenced by Jews no more than Christian clergy today who admonish or advise their congregations on the basis of the Old Testament."

[51] Even for Col. 2:22 there is no necessary connection with Judaism.

[52] Cf. Dibelius & Conzelmann (3rd edn, 1955), pp. 113: "here too a dispute about ascetic (not particularly Jewish) laws could be implied."

[53] F. Büchsel (art. γενεά κτλ., *TWNT* I, 660–663) posits Jews behind the νομοδιδάσκαλοι of 1 Tim. 1:7.

he applies one of Israel's titles of honour (λαὸς περιούσιος)⁵⁴ to the Christ-believers.

So I regard it as probable that the author *deliberately* moves the protagonists of the deviant group into the proximity of Judaism, which he clearly sees in a negative light. Whether the deviants themselves fell back on Jewish traditions can no longer be discerned with certainty. Even if such were the case, it would not make the apostates Christ-believers of Jewish origin (so-called "Jewish-Christians"). The author of the letter to Titus evidently knew this, to the extent that he indulges in pejorative allusions ("Jewish fables") or suspicions ("especially those of the circumcision"). The only certain thing, to begin with, is that we are dealing here with Christians and Cretans (1:12). Should precisely a Cretan of *Jewish* origin be made responsible for the "saying" about the Cretans? Anyone who—like the letter to Titus—speaks so pejoratively about Judaism, has written it off long ago. His concern is clearly to charge the Christian deviants with prejudices about Judaism and to discredit them because of their proximity to Jewish traditions. The author is evidently sure that this argument will have its due effect. I do consider it still possible that with his critical invective against the deviants he is alluding to the letter to the Galatians, in order to place the deviant Christian group in the proximity of the "opponents" against whom the Apostle polemicizes there. The phrases οἱ ἐκ τῆς περιτομῆς (cf. Gal. 2:12), ἀποστρεφομένων τήν ἀλήθειαν (cf. Gal. 2:14; 5:7f.) and φρεναπάται (cf. Gal. 6:3; cf. also Gal. 3:1ff.), may support this suggestion.

The Stigmatization of the Deviant Group with Prejudices concerning the Cretans

Negative labels are also found elsewhere in the New Testament, of which only a few examples can be mentioned here. Jesus' low social background is alluded to in Mk 6:3: "Is this not the τέκτων (labourer/carpenter?), the son of Mary and brother . . .?" Or: Jesus drives out the evil spirits by the aid of "Beelzebub" (Mt. 12:24); he is called "possessed" (Jn 8:48, 52) or a "Nazarene" (Mt. 2:23; 26:71; Jn 18:5, 7; 19:19). Some labels allude to ethnic or geographic origins: Jesus is called "Galilean" (Mt. 26:69) or "Samaritan" (Jn 8:48); one may also

⁵⁴ Cf. Exod. 19:5; Deut. 7:6; 14:2; 1 Pet. 2:9f.

compare Jn 1:46: "Can anything good come out of Nazareth?" These few examples show in their various ways that it is thoroughly typical of Mediterranean culture to characterize people by stereotypes or general social categories.[55] Tit. 1:12 further differs from the above examples, however, in that mention of the Cretan ethnic origins is combined with disparaging categories ("liars," "gluttons") even to the extent that a comparison is made with animals. The letter-writer himself also takes the proverbial character out of the word of the poet by identifying it as fulfilled. The letter presupposes that Paul has left his co-worker in Crete (1:5). Titus himself—about whom, it is true, we hear hardly anything further—is (according to Gal. 2:2f.) a Greek, while the members of the Christian communities (Tit. 1:5 implies several Cretan communities) are Cretans. Even the cutting insult about the Cretans in Tit. 1:12 presupposes that the deviants belong ethnically to the Cretans (τις ἐξ αὐτῶν ἴδιος προφήτης). The hexameter evidently goes back to Epimenides (6th cent. BCE),[56] but the context applies it to the deviant Christians mentioned just before (1:10f.): "Cretans are always liars, wicked animals, lazy gluttons."

The semantics of this sentence cannot be analysed at this point. Its proverbial[57] or discriminatory character suggests that a corresponding analysis would only get entangled in the thicket of other prejudices.[58] The *Carthaginians*, originally from Phoenicia, were also referred to in a discriminatory way, being regarded as devious merchants and tradespeople who were not above cheating. Cicero calls them "deceitful and mendacious" (*fraudulent et mendaces*).[59] And he attributes this supposed national trait to the fact that too many "tradespeople and foreigners" were to be found in the harbours of the Carthaginians. In his view the *Campanians* are arrogant because of the fertility and beauty of their country, the *Ligurians* hard and wild, like all people

---

[55] "It is characteristic of the Mediterranean world to think in terms of stereotypes. Persons were not known by their psychological personality and uniqueness, but by general social categories such as place of origin, residence, family, gender, age, and the range of other groups to which they might belong" (B.J. Malina & R.L. Rohrbaugh, *Social Science Commentary on the Synoptic Gospels* [Minneapolis, 1992], pp. 97f.; cf. Malina 1993, pp. 63ff.).

[56] For a full discussion of this problem cf. Dibelius & Conzelmann (3rd edn, 1955), pp. 101–103.

[57] On the dissemination of prejudices about the Cretans, see Dibelius & Conzelmann (3rd edn, 1955), pp. 101–103.

[58] Cf., e.g., Plutarch, Moralia 490B.

[59] The older Pliny says of them: As the Egyptians invented the monarchy and the Greeks democracy, the Punics invented trade (*NatHist* VII 198).

who have to make rocky soil arable.[60] Anyone who comes from *Tiberias* has a warlike passion, *Scythians* enjoy killing and are little better than wild animals, according to Josephus.[61] The characterization of the Cretans as κακὰ θηρία evidently intends to discredit them as "wicked beasts", i.e. because they are dangerous.[62]

The *Egyptians*, too, were despised in a more or less proverbial way.[63] For an example I shall here cite only Juvenal, who in his argumentation strategy engages prejudices about the Egyptians in a comparable way to the writer of Titus, in order to hurt a nouveau-riche man named Crispinus, who had evidently climbed to high office. It is psychologically interesting here that social envy towards a social climber arouses Juvenal's hatred. The hatred is nourished by ethnic prejudice (*Sat* I 27):

> ... if Crispin, who comes from the rabble of the Nile, born as a slave in Canopus, puts his Tyrian robe over his shoulder and "wafts" his gold ring onto his sweaty fingers for the summer (for he cannot bear to wear a greater weight of jewelry)—then it is difficult not to write satire.

This Crispin thus is subject to contempt for various reasons: He is a born slave (*verna*), formerly belonged to the *plebs* of his home town Canopus, which happens to be considered especially immoral (*Sat* VI 84; XV 46), and he is an Egyptian, and thus according to Juvenal's prejudice a member of an uncivilized people (cf., e.g., XV 46), and in addition he makes an ostentatious display of his wealth. Juvenal devotes a whole satire to his hatred for the Egyptians (*Sat* XV). Their strange—to him—manner of worship arouses mockery and horror: in their madness they venerate monsters (like the crocodile, for instance), but also in their stupidity they do not eat onions of any kind: "O god-fearing people (says Juvenal, with irony), whose divinities grow in the garden." On the other hand he accuses them of

---

[60] Cicero, *De lege agraria* 2:95.

[61] *Jos. Vita* 352; *Contra Apionem* 2:269. Other examples are cited by B.J. Malina, "Is There a Circum-Mediterranean Person? Looking for Stereotypes," in *BTB* 22 (1992), pp. 66–87 (71–74).

[62] Malina (1992, 74) collects a number of texts in which the physiognomy of people is characterized by analogy with particular animals. The "characteristics" of particular animals (e.g. fox, wolf, snake) are transferred onto humans. On this cf., e.g., Lk. 10:3; 13:31f.; Mt. 10:16; 23:33.

[63] On this see the comprehensive treatment by K.A.D. Smelik & E.A. Hemelrijk, "'Who Knows What Monsters Demented Egypt Worships?' Opinions on Egyptian Animal Worship in Antiquity as Part of the Ancient Conception of Egypt," in W. Haase (ed.), *Aufstieg und Niedergang der Römischen Welt. Principat. 17.4* (Berlin—New York, 1984), pp. 1852–2000, 2337–2357.

eating human flesh (cf. *Sat* XV 1ff.). In all respects the ways of the Egyptians fill Juvenal with abhorrence. At their orgiastic festivals even men would dance (*Sat* XV 40ff.). Finally the whole people can only be called worthy of death.

Juvenal's hatred of the Egyptians provides an opportunity to study how *xenophobia* or *heterophobia* works. Anything strange, the otherness of the other, is subject to suspicion and interpreted negatively. There are in principle two areas in which strangers stand out: their different religion and their different social behaviour. People who symbolize their religion in the form of animals—like the Egyptians—are "crazy." For normal behaviour is represented by one's own religion: Romans and Greeks worship their divinities in human form. In the social sphere the negative interpretation of the otherness of strangers frequently goes so far as to deny their humanity. The Cretans are dangerous animals. And the Jews, who kept to their ways and customs even in the Diaspora, were considered—because of their close social intercourse among themselves—anti-human (cf., e.g., Tacitus, *Hist* V, 5).

5. *Critical Reception and Evaluation*

How should we deal with such a text? A shocking example is found in an exegetical commentary by G. Holtz:[64]

The commentator assumes that the "inner life of the community . . . is to a horrifying extent corrupt." The guilty party is clearly "gnostics," among whom "former Jews" are noticeable as "especially uncharitable." "They will have maintained part of their Judaism and a part of paganism and have added a bit of Christianity to it." This group is not only "present in frightening numbers," but is also violent. They "storm the houses," appear to be "magicians" and "make empty and fantastic propaganda speeches." Among them, "Jews by birth" are "leaders" and "especially dangerous." For "because they come ἐκ τῆς περιτομῆς, they think they have special rights and make great demands." And what about the Cretans! They are "a rough, work-shy, gluttonous lot." This must be true, because—as Holtz puts it—a

---

[64] G. Holtz, *Die Pastoralbriefe* (Theologischer Handkommentar zum Neuen Testament; Berlin, 1965), pp. 211–16.

"native" is cited as "chief witness." And to reinforce what he has said, the commentator maintains: "the heathen really did speak prophetically." The violent language of the text does not worry Holtz. For the false teachers are "sick in sins" and threaten "the whole community with their infectious germs . . ., if it has not already been infected." "Pastoral care" of course has its "work cut out" here. For "the Jewish gnostics in Crete" have set up "new, but human commandments." The matters concerned—as is to be expected an anti-Jewish prejudice—are "the casuistry of clean and unclean." But "anyone who lives in eucharistic piety is released from the casuistry of the food commandments." The false teachers, on the other hand: even their "thinking is repulsively soiled." All this finally leads to Holtz's "exposing" them as "stewards of hell."

The commentator has become the victim of the communicative strategy of the author. He takes this black-and-white characterization at face value. Even the anti-semitic or racist prejudices fall on fertile soil as far as he is concerned. Indeed, the recipient even increases the negative aspects of the text by supplementing them with prejudices of his own. And finally he prepares a "spiritual" end ("stewards of hell") for the deviants.

A critical exegesis of the Titus text under discussion, in contrast to this reception, will analyse and thus also *evaluate* the New Testament author's prejudice structure and its significance in the historical context of its time. In so doing it will take account of the contingent factors of its situation. What appears to us to be intolerant may certainly have been the understandable reaction to negative experiences in a specific historical situation.[65] In the case of the letter to Titus one should consider the possibility that the author saw the stability of the Christian communities in Crete as threatened by the deviants; at least it is conceivable that he had this subjective view. But his criticism is excessive and his strategy is interested only in enforcing the conventional position. Also to be borne in mind are the standards of ancient culture, to which the text itself belongs. There, ethnocentrism, linked in part with the stereotypical denigration of other peoples, seems to have been common. The scale of discrimination thus ranges from an ambivalent attitude to the members of

---

[65] Cf. B.V. Malchow, "Causes of Tolerance and Intolerance Toward Gentiles in the First Testament," in *BTB* 20 (1990), pp. 3–9.

another people (e.g., Herodotus' attitude to the Egyptians)[66] through to racist prejudices. In the case of the letter to Titus, the dual question arises: Are its statements about the Jews anti-semitic, or those about the Cretans racist? The answer depends on the definition of what may be called anti-semitic or racist.

Anti-semitic Prejudice in Tit. 1:10-16

If anti-semitism is "a fundamental and systematic hostility toward Jews"[67] it may be stated that the letter to Titus does not provide evidence of a systematic hostility towards the Jews. It gives rather the impression of a clear distance from Judaism. The letter does, however, appear to *imply* a fundamental contrast with Judaism. If anti-semitism is taken to mean the "denigration" of and "contempt" for Jews and one sees precisely in this a Christian continuum (as does J. Isaac, see above), then the Titus text under discussion can be called anti-semitic. It must be borne in mind that the author is not directly concerned with "anti-Jewish polemic."[68] Rather, it makes use of anti-Jewish prejudices, with which it aims to attack its intra-Christian "opponents." This form of Christian anti-semitism is unfortunately still current.

Racist Prejudice against the Cretans in Tit. 1:10-16

The nasty words about the Cretans, cited by Tit. 1:12, doubtless show not only an ambivalent attitude to a foreign people. But it can hardly be called ethnocentric, since the concern here is not to put one's own people on a pedestal in contrast to other ethnic groups.[69] In my view, our text reflects an ancient form of racism. For in the dreadful proverb about the Cretans their ethnic origins are linked with negative quasi-biological features. It assumes that all members of the ethnic group of the Cretans have negative characteristics, which disqualify them morally and in the end place them outside the human

---

[66] Herodotus II 35f.

[67] J.G. Gager, "The Origins of Anti-Semitism," in *Attitudes toward Judaism in Pagan and Christian Antiquity* (New York & Oxford, 1983), p. 17.

[68] So, correctly, Hasler (2nd edn, 1992), p. 582.

[69] Ethnocentrism is expressed, for example, in the common opposition between Greeks and Barbarians. It is also evident in statements which take the Romans, for example, to be the most virtuous of all people (cf. Pliny, *NatHist* VII 40).

race. And neither the historical situation of the letter to Titus, nor the general mentality of Mediterranean culture, which presumably took little offence at the text's anti-semitic and racist prejudices, can "justify" its prejudice structure. In any case the ancient situation and mentality can be no criterion for its reception today. It is not, however, simply a question of a critique of the New Testament text and of its Christian exegesis. Rather, historical criticism is always also a criticism of the present, in which, as always, in church and theological discourses anti-semitism and racism are encountered and are not infrequently justified on the basis of biblical texts.

PART II
CULTURE AND INTERPRETATION

BIBLICAL INTERPRETATION FROM THE PERSPECTIVE OF INDIGENOUS CULTURES OF LATIN AMERICA (MAYAS, KUNAS, AND QUECHUAS)

Pablo Richard

Introduction

Over the past ten years I have tried to do an interpretation of the Bible from the perspective of indigenous cultures, especially among the Mayas of Guatemala, the Kunas of Panama, and the Quechuas of Ecuador. This has not been an easy task, for the indigenous have suffered a historical trauma associated with the Bible, through its use in the spiritual conquest of these peoples. The Bible was used to legitimize the conquest and destruction of the culture and religion of the indigenous peoples. Furthermore, almost all interpretation of the Bible in the present day is carried out from within the dominant liberal and modern European culture, which completely ignores the non-occidental cultural world of the Third World. Even to the present time, the churches also continue to interpret the Bible from the perspective of a European culture that is both ethnocentric and occidental.

In the dialogue between Bible and Culture, the Bible must participate with great humility, for the indigenous peoples have lived for thousands of years without the Bible. Since the occidental conquest, those peoples have survived by the strength of their own religion and culture, in confrontation with Christendom. There is in those cultures a deep and significant revelation of God, which profoundly challenges our interpretation of the Bible. Evangelization, if it intends to be liberating and not follow the model of conquest, must begin its work by listening, discerning, and interpreting the presence and revelation of God in indigenous religion and culture.

This article has two parts. The first presents historical and theological foundations for a liberating hermeneutic that permits us to carry out a project of biblical interpretation from the perspective of indigenous cultures. The second part presents our work of biblical interpretation among the indigenous peoples of Latin America, and the theoretical reflection that we have been able to develop up to this point.

A. *Historical and Theological Foundations of a Hermeneutic of Liberation*

1. *The Spirit of Occidental Colonial Domination*

Christianity arrived in Latin America, Africa, and Asia with the colonial expansion of the occident. This is an objective historical and global reality that does not negate specific positive actions, or the generosity and good intentions of many missionaries. The original inhabitants of these three continents endured the arrival of Christianity as the imposition of an occidental colonial system of domination. From the sixteenth century to the present, this process has continued, be it in its Catholic or Protestant versions. This fact, moreover, has meant a profound spiritual and hermeneutical perversion in the very heart of Christianity.

We propose to illustrate this phenomenon by a concrete and significant example. We will take up the work of the sixteenth century author who best represents the spirit of conquest of occidental Christianity, namely Juan Ginés de Sepúlveda. We will use as our reference his principal work, *"Tratado sobre las justas causas de la guerra contra los indios"* ("Treatise on the Just Causes of the War Against the Indians").[1]

a. The Texts

In this essay I will not go into all the complexity of this work and of the discussion of this theme in the sixteenth century.[2] We will look only at a few texts where the author presents the fundamental argument of his work in order to justify the war against the indigenous peoples. Thus, he says,

> ... it is just and natural that prudent, wise, and humane people have dominion over those who do not have those qualities ... (therefore) the Spaniards have a perfect right to rule over these *barbarians of the New World* and adjacent islands, who in prudence, intelligence, virtue, and humanity are as inferior to the Spaniards as *children* are to adults and *women* to men, having between them as great a difference as that between *savage and cruel peoples* and the most merciful peoples ..., and, I would even say, between *monkeys* and human beings. (p. 101)

---

[1] Passages cited in this article are translations of the bilingual (Latin and Spanish) edition of that treatise published in 1979 by the Fondo de Cultura Económica in Mexico City. Page numbers in parentheses following the citations refer to that edition, and the emphasis in each case is that of the author of this article.

[2] For that discussion, see Fernando Mires, *En nombre de la cruz. Discusiones teológicas*

Here we have established the correlation: the inhabitants of the new world are barbarians. They are like children, women, savage and cruel people—practically like monkeys. In contrast, the Spanish Conquistador is adult, male, a most merciful person—in a word, a Human Being (as opposed to a monkey).

The war of the Spaniards against the Indians is just, because

> ... being by nature slaves, barbarian, uncultured, and inhumane, they refuse to accept the domination of those who are more prudent, powerful, and perfect than they—domination that would bring them the greatest benefits, being, moreover, a just thing, through natural law, that *substance* obey *form*, the *body* obey the *soul*, *appetite* obey *reason*, *beasts* obey *human beings*, a *wife* obey her *husband*, *sons and daughters* obey their *father*, the *imperfect* obey the *perfect*, the *worse* obey the *better*, for the universal good of all things. (p. 153)

In another place he adds:

> What more appropriate and salutary thing could happen to these barbarians than to remain subject to the dominion of these whose prudence, virtue, and religion have transformed them from *barbarians*, such as hardly merit the name of human beings, into *civilized people* insofar as they can become that; from people who are *stupid and libidinous*, into people who are *wise and honorable*; from *impious people* and *slaves of demons*, into *Christians* and *worshipers of the true God*? (p. 133)

In this way total domination is justified:

> ... [W]hat is natural and just is that the *soul* rules over the *body*, that *reason* presides over the *appetite*, ... therefore that *wild beasts* be subdued and subjected to the dominion of *humanity*. *Therefore* the *man* rules over the *woman*, the *adult* over the *child*, the *father* over his *sons and daughters*, that is to say, the most *powerful and perfect* over those who are *weakest and most imperfect*. ... (p. 85)

The thought of Juan Ginés de Sepúlveda represents the feeling and thinking of the entire undertaking of conquest and colonization of what is called Latin America, and what today we prefer to call "Abya Yala."[3] This author says what the majority of the Conquistadors and evangelizers feel, think, and do. He is not a marginal author, but

---

y políticas frente al holocausto de los indios (período de conquista) (San José, Costa Rica: Editorial DEI, 1986).

[3] Abya Yala is the name that the Kuna Indians of Panama give to our continent. For us the name "Latin America" is a colonial name and lacks meaning. In the Kuna language Abya Yala means ripe land, big mother land, land of blood. See Aiban Wagua, "Present Consequences of the European Invasion of America," *1492–1992: The Voice of the Victims* (ed. Leonardo Boff and Virgil Elizondo; *Concilium* 1990/6; Philadelphia: Trinity Press International, 1990), p. 56 n. 6.

rather the typical representative of an entire colonial transformation of the society and of Christianity.[4]

b. The Global Reality of Domination

The fundamental and founding relationship in colonial thought is the binomial *Spaniard-Indian*. Of the Spaniards it is said that they are a most gentle people; superior in prudence, intelligence, and virtue; more powerful; and perfect. The Indians, on the contrary, are considered barbaric, uncultured, intemperate, a savage and cruel people. The Spaniards are humane and represent humanity. The Indians are inhumane, hardly merit being called human, and instead are like monkeys. Ginés always calls them, in Latin, *homunculi*—"little men."[5] The salvation of the Indians is given through the subjection that transforms them from barbarians into civilized people, from stupid and libidinous people into wise and honorable ones, from impious people and slaves of demons into Christians and worshipers of the true God.

The binomial "Spaniard-Indian" is equivalent to the other binomials of man-woman, adult-child, father-son or daughter. Finally, it is compared to the relationship of human being to animal. Thus we have the following coordinates:

Spaniard	Man	Adult	Father	Human Being
Indian	Woman	Child	Son, Daughter	Animal

The Spaniard is like the man, the adult, the father, the human being. The Indian is like the woman, the child, the son or daughter, or the animal. The relationship between the members of each pair is that of domination.

The intrinsic relationship among colonial domination (Spaniard-Indian), domination of *gender* (man-woman), domination of one *generation* over another (adult-child), and domination of *nature* (human being-animal) is evident. Colonial domination is thus global and includes every dimension of the human being and of nature.

---

[4] Pablo Richard, "1492: The Violence of God and the Future of Christianity," *1492–1992: The Voice of the Victims*, pp. 59–67.

[5] Ginés writes: "Compare now these qualities of prudence, wisdom, magnanimity, temperance, humanity, and religion (of the Spaniards) to the qualities possessed by those little men in whom you will scarcely encounter vestiges of humanity (*homunculos illos in quibus vix reperies humanitatis vestigia*)" (p. 105).

c. Metaphysical, Necessary, and Natural Character of Domination

The relationship of colonial domination is identified with the relationship of domination of *form over substance, of the soul over the body, and of reason over appetite.*[6] The Spaniard is to the Indian as the soul to the body. The same thing happens with the relationship of domination over the woman, the child, and nature. Moreover, the relationship of domination is presented as the relationship of the powerful over the weak, of the perfect over the imperfect, of what is better over what is worse. Ginés adds, "This is the natural order, which the divine and eternal law commands always to observe."[7] All of this is proven conclusively on the authority of Aristotle, Augustine, and Aquinas, who are cited frequently.[8]

According to this form of argumentation, the Conquistador (and also the man, the adult, and the human being) is the one who creates order, who brings a spiritual dimension, and who imposes rationality. The Indian (and also the woman, the child, and nature) is matter, body, irrational, appetite, and therefore is not human, does not have a soul, and is like a savage wild beast—like a monkey. Thus, as the soul must exercise violence against the body, especially when it rebels against the soul, so also the Conquistador can and should exercise violence against the Indian, the man against the woman, the adult against the child, the human being against nature. It goes against natural and divine law for an Indian to rule over a Spaniard, a woman over a man, or an animal over a human being. That would represent the triumph of appetite over reason, of the material over the spiritual.

2. *500 Years of Spiritual Resistance Against the Colonial Occident*

Colonial thought, which we have exemplified by the work of Juan Ginés de Sepúlveda, was the theoretical expression of the conquest and of all of its human, ecological, economic, political, social, cultural, and religious destruction. In the sixteenth century we experienced a

---

[6] See the citation, above, from p. 153. I include the Latin text here to gauge the precision of the terms: *justum est eo jure naturae, quo materia formae, corpus animae, appetitus rationi, hominibus animalia bruta, viris mulieres, patribus filii, imperfecta, scilecet, perfectis, deteriora potioribus, debent, ut utrisque bene sit, obtemperare.*

[7] *Hic est enim ordo naturalis, quam divina et aeterna lex ubique servari jubet.* (p. 153)

[8] The influence of Aristotle on Juan Ginés de Sepúlveda is determinative and

genocide of sixty million indigenous people, and subsequently of some twenty million Blacks brought from Africa. It is the most massive genocide known in the history of humanity, accomplished integrally within the context of occidental Christendom.[9]

Resistance to the conquest and to colonial domination followed different paradigms. In the first place, we have the prophetic resistance among the Spaniards themselves, whose best known representative is Fray Bartolomé de las Casas.[10] In addition to him, there is a generation of prophetic bishops, religious, and theologians in the sixteenth century who defended the Indian and made possible a liberating Evangelization. Although the dominant position in the Church was that of collaboration and legitimization of the colonial power, despite that domination and in contrast to it, an authentic Evangelization took place ("Evangelization itself constitutes a type of grand jury for the indictment of those responsible for such abuses").[11]

In addition to the prophetic resistance of some missionaries, we have the indigenous resistance. This had two principal expressions: the Indian resistance that maintained its identity in silence, in secrecy, in the mountains and forests; and the Indian resistance that maintained its identity in dialogue with the Christian religion itself. In this way there arose what today is called "Indian-Indian Theology" and "Indian-Christian Theology".[12] Years later a similar process took place among the Blacks brought as slaves from Africa, which also gave rise to an Afro-American theology that today has seen significant development.

In this Indian and Afro-American resistance of five hundred years, we have the most profound and significant historical root of resis-

omnipresent, with citations in particular from the philosopher's treatise on *Politics* (cf. Book 1, Chap. 3). On the other hand, his *Ethics* are cited very little, and then in a purely literal and proof-texting fashion.

[9] For a discussion of the concept of Christendom, see Pablo Richard, *Death of Christendom, Birth of the Church* (Maryknoll: Orbis, 1987).

[10] Gustavo Gutiérrez, *Las Casas: In Search of the Poor of Jesus Christ* (transl. Robert R. Barr; Maryknoll: Orbis, 1993).

[11] See the documents of the Conference of Santo Domingo (October 1992), no. 18.

[12] Today an abundant literature exists on Indian Theology. Most of it is in the form of mimeographed publications or occasional leaflets (what we could still consider oral tradition). Two important publications are *Teología India. Primer Encuentro Taller Latinoamericano* (Mexico [Cenami] and Ecuador [Abya Yala], 1991), 329 pages; and the September 1991, issue of the Mexican journal *Christus* (no. 7), which is entirely dedicated to the theme of Indian Theology.

tance to occidental colonial domination, and of the construction of possible alternatives to that domination. Our continent will be able to reconstruct its life, its identity, and its autonomy only on the basis of this indigenous and Afro-American resistance. The struggle of the Indian and Black peoples for their life, for their culture, and for their religion is the only radical (in the sense of root) perspective that allows us to become aware of occidental colonial domination and to develop a theological, hermeneutical, and spiritual reflection that is a liberating alternative to occidental domination.

The struggle of the indigenous for their life, for their culture, and for their religion, against the occidental colonial domination, was a struggle in which the reality of women and of nature was always integrated. In all of the indigenous cultural currents of Latin America or Abya Yala, from the North to the South of the continent, there has existed from the beginning the unity of woman and man, and the identity of both with nature. God is always woman and man; nature also is always woman and man. The earth is Mother Earth, and in it is the fullness of God. If the colonial domination was founded on the domination of man over woman and of the human being over nature, the indigenous resistance encountered its root and its power in the equality of woman and man and of nature and humankind. The indigenous dimension of gender and nature, and the identification of God with this dimension, was the millenarian root that made possible the confrontation with occidental domination.

Today the resistance to colonial domination—domination in its present form of the "New International Order"—exhibits the same original form that we encountered in the deep roots of our identity. In the present time resistance is developed through a consciousness in which the unity of *culture* (indigenous, Black, and Mestizo), of *gender* (women), and of *nature* (the earth, the body, the cosmos, the environment) is a given. The unity of *culture-gender-nature* founded on the alliance of Indians, Blacks, women, young people, workers, nature, and earth is a consciousness and a movement that are differentiated and multiple, but also deeply united in their resistance to the present colonial domination. This consciousness or historical movement we call symbolically *SOUTH*, given that after the Cold War and the confrontation of East and West, the contradiction of North and South must be recognized as dominant. The centers of power are found principally in the North, while the assaulted and plundered masses are found mostly in the South, where the poorest 80%

of humanity live.[13] This new consciousness that is being born from the South, in which the dimension of culture-gender-nature is united, requires also a *Hermeneutic of the South*, which orients a new biblical interpretation over against the dominant occidental colonial consciousness (constituted by the imposition of the European over the Indian, of man over woman, of the adult over the child, and of humankind over nature, and founded metaphysically on the dominion by "natural law" of the soul over the body, of reason over the appetite, of form over substance).

3. *The Reconstruction of the Spirit Over Against Occidental Christendom*

The fundamental axis of the thought of Juan Ginés de Sepúlveda, and perhaps of all Greco-Latin-occidental thought, is the dualism of *body and soul*. What was new in the colonial conquest was the identification of the relationship of body and soul with the relationship of *Indian and Spaniard*. The Spaniard is identified with Christianity and with the worship of the true God. The Indian is a savage (barbarian-pagan) and worshiper of demons. In the colonial vision the Spaniard is to the Indian as the soul is to the body, as God is to the demons, and as Grace is to Sin. The Spaniard, like the soul, is the expression of what is spiritual and divine. The Indian, like the body, is the expression of the material and the demonic. Salvation takes place in the soul, in the dominion of the soul over the body, in the repression of the body, and, in a definitive form, when the soul is freed from the body. Furthermore, the salvation of the Indians takes place when they cease to be Indian, abandon their identity, their culture, and their religion, and become Christian. If they resist, it is legitimate to exercise violence against their bodies in order to save them, just as the individual exercises violence against the body to save himself or herself. This whole design is reinforced when Ginés, following the Aristotelian tradition, identifies the relation of soul and body with that of form and substance, and of reason and appetite.

The same schema is used for the domination of women, of children, and of nature. The man is identified with the soul, and therefore he is spiritual and rational; the woman is body, carnal appetite, irrational. The man is close to God; the woman is identified with

---

[13] Pablo Richard, "El Sur existe y tiene su teología," *Envío* 137 (May 1993), published in Nicaragua.

sin, and at least with the demonic (the witches). Similarly, the child in contrast to the adult is presented as unformed substance and an irrational being. The same opposition of soul and body, reason and appetite, form and substance is applied to the dominion of humankind over nature. The spiritual Human Being dominates and exercises violence against material nature and against the body. The destruction of nature and of the body, like the destruction of the Indian or the woman, is not important for the occidental spiritual identity.

The colonial expansion of occidental Christendom, by identifying the spiritual and the rational with the domination of the Spaniard over the Indian, of the man over the woman, of the adult over the child, and of the human being over nature, destroyed profoundly the spiritual dimension present in the Indian, in the woman, in the child, in nature, and in the body. The occidental Conquest imposed a rationality and spirituality that are ethnocentric, patriarchal, authoritarian, against nature, and against the body.

In the Indian religion there is an deep identification among *Indian-woman-nature-God*. God and the divine Spirit, in all indigenous traditions, is always present in the community (culture), in the person (woman and man), in nature, and in the earth. The occident denies the Spirit in the very place where the Indians experience it. These five hundred years of indigenous resistance have been five hundred years of *spiritual resistance* against occidental colonialism.

We can say the same thing about that consciousness that arises today in the civil society and in the social movements in Latin America and in what is called the South. For us, today, culture-gender-nature is the privileged space of the spiritual, of the rational, of the presence and revelation of God. The movement of liberation of oppressed people—which is the sum of the indigenous, Afro-American, workers' and *campesinos'* (peasants') movements, movements for women's liberation, ecological movements, movements for children and youth, national liberation movements, and so forth—is a movement for life, but at the same time it is also a *spiritual movement*. The movement for liberation, in contrast to occidental colonial thought, identifies the spiritual and the rational with the liberation of Indians, Blacks, women, youth, the body, and nature. *The liberation of oppressed people is redeeming the meaning of the spiritual today in history.* The movement of liberation radically subverts occidental colonial thought, and redeems the Spirit precisely where domination denies it. The movement of liberation is fundamentally a spiritual movement. The South is poor in money, technology, and armaments, but it is rich in Spirit, in Humanity, and in Culture. The power of God in the South is not manifested in the power of arms and of money, but in the spiritual power of Indians, Blacks, *campesinos*, youth, women, the earth, and nature. The hermeneutic of liberation is also an authentically universal hermeneutic, for the liberation of oppressed people is what makes possible the liberation of everyone—oppressed and oppressors, both equally dehumanized by the structures of domination.

4. *Bible: Conquest and Resistance*

The occidental pattern of domination *profoundly perverted the meaning of the biblical tradition*. The Bible was read and interpreted according to colonial and occidental interests. Even to the present time, the indigenous peoples of Latin America or Abya Yala have experienced a trauma related to the Bible. All of the Bible was interpreted against the spiritual experience of the Indian peoples. The biblical schema of the conquest by Joshua of the Canaanite people was applied to the conquest of the indigenous peoples. Indigenous religions were fought by using the prophetic tradition of opposition to idolatry. The New Testament was read from the perspective of an imperial Christology and a patriarchal and authoritarian ecclesiology. The spiritual was identified with occidental culture, with the dominion of man over woman and of the human being over nature. This spiritual perversion, accomplished by the Greco-Latin-occidental tradition, placed the Bible at the service of colonial domination, and equally at the service of a domination that is patriarchal, against the body, and against nature. The Judeo-Christian tradition was inverted and transformed into its opposite. For that reason, Juan Ginés de Sepúlveda was so easily able to utilize the Bible and occidental Christian thought in order to justify the most horrible genocide in the history of Christendom.

As long as we do not recover the Bible from the perspective of the spirit with which it was written, no exegesis will succeed in discovering the Word of God as a Word different from the dominant occidental culture. It is not a matter of recovering the Bible exegetically, verse by verse, but rather of recovering the Spirit with which the Bible was written in its totality and its profundity (cf. Dei Verbum No. 12). The recovery of this Spirit takes place today in the experience of the Word of God in the movements of liberation; it is here that our faith discerns the Word of God, illuminated by the same Spirit that inspired the Bible.

Biblical anthropology is defined basically by the opposition of *life and death*. The *spirit (pneuma)* is the tendency of the human being (in his or her body and soul) toward *life*. The opposite of the spirit is the *flesh (sarx)*, which is the tendency of the entire human being (in body and soul) toward *death*. Thus it is written in Rom. 8:6, "To set the mind on the flesh is death, but to set the mind on the Spirit is life and peace." The man or woman who is "carnal," or "defined by the flesh," is the man or woman who is oriented, in body and soul alike, toward death. The "spiritual" man or woman is the man or woman oriented, in body and soul alike, toward life. It is the triumph of life over death that defines that which is spiritual. Salvation is the overcoming of death in body and soul. The Holy Spirit brings to its fullness the tendency toward life, even beyond death, in the resurrection of the human being in body and soul. The opposite of this is sin, which reinforces in our body and soul the tendency toward death. Thus St. Paul can say, "For the law of the Spirit of life in Christ Jesus has set you free from the law of sin and of death" (Rom. 8:2).[14]

The Indian peoples, in spite of the Conquest and of occidental Christendom, began to read the Bible in a different way. Today an Indian Hermeneutic or an Indian reading of the Bible already exists.[15] Highly valued in this Indian hermeneutic are the "seeds of the Word" present in Indian religion before the arrival of Christianity. Today there also exists in Latin America a movement that is called "Pastoral Reading of the Bible" or "Communal Reading of the Bible." Others call it "Popular Reading of the Bible."[16] What is important is that the Bible is read and interpreted by the poor in what are called Ecclesial Base Communities, in a climate of prayer and commitment. The Bible is read and interpreted in the heart of the indigenous,

---

[14] Pablo Richard, "Espiritualidad para tiempos de revolución. Teología espiritual a la luz de San Pablo," in Eduardo Bonin (ed.), *Espiritualidad y Liberación en América Latina* (San José, Costa Rica: Editorial DEI, 1982).

[15] Pablo Richard, "Hermenéutica India," *Revista de Interpretación Bíblica Lationamericana (RIBLA)* 11 (1992), pp. 9–24.

[16] Carlos Mesters, *Defenseless Flower: A New Reading of the Bible* (transl. Francis McDonagh; Maryknoll: Orbis, 1989). See also RIBLA 1 (1988). This entire issue, with the title *Lectura Popular de la Biblia en América Latina: Una Hermeneutica de la Liberación,* is dedicated to the theme of "popular" reading of the Bible. See especially the article with that same title written by Pablo Richard (pp. 30–48), and "La Lectura Bíblica en las CEB's," by Neftalí Vélez (pp. 8–29).

Afro-American, and workers' and *campesinos'* movements; of movements
for women's liberation; of ecological movements; and of movements
of youth. The experience of the Spirit does not take place in the
soul as opposed to the body, but in the affirmation of life as opposed
to death. Life is clearly affirmed as the full life of the body, the life
of the poor, the life of indigenous people, the life of Blacks, the life
of women, the life of youth, the life of nature. The space of the
Spirit is the world defined by the relationship body-culture-gender-
work-nature.

B. *Biblical Interpretation From the Perspective of Indigenous Cultures*

In the previous section we have analyzed the radical restoration of
the Spirit, from the perspective of the Third World and over against
colonial domination. No hermeneutic is effective if we do not become conscious of the place of the Spirit in history. Having completed this earlier indispensable task, we will go on to elaborate some
hermeneutical and theoretical principles that I have been developing
on the basis of my practice of doing biblical interpretation from the
perspective of indigenous cultures, especially the Maya, Kuna, and
Quechua cultures of Latin America.

1. *Some Fundamental Hermeneutical Priorities*

The interpretation of the Bible in an indigenous context imposes a
series of priorities:

a. Priority of Life over the Bible

The principle of all liberation evangelization is *to save the life* of those
we want to evangelize. Today the indigenous are threatened with
death by a system of free market economy and by occidental modernity. The Bible comes after; first comes the commitment of the Church
to defend the earth and indigenous culture and communities. It is
that commitment of the Church to the concrete life of the indigenous people that makes possible the rapprochement with indigenous
peoples and the dialogue between Bible and culture. This is the
fundamental commitment of all evangelization.

b. Priority of the Present Over the Past

What comes first is the experience of God in the present spirituality of the indigenous peoples. This spirituality is expressed in *fiestas*, in traditional singing, in the symbols and myths, in dance, in painting, in prayers and rituals. The Bible cannot be presented as something archeological, like a history of the past that one attempts to actualize. The Bible must be interpreted beginning with the present spirituality of the indigenous peoples.

c. Priority of the Revelation of God Over the Biblical Text

The starting point is the Revelation of God in nature and in indigenous culture and religion. We can explain this priority by reference to the affirmation of St. Augustine that the Bible is the "second book of God," and it was written to help us decipher the world, to give us back the gaze of faith and of contemplation, and to transform the whole of reality into a great revelation of God.[17] We express the same thing in our work in the following fashion: God wrote two books, the book of life and the book of the Bible. The book of life is the "book" of the cosmos or of creation, the "book" of indigenous cultural tradition and religion. That is the first and fundamental book of God. The Bible is the *second* book of God, to help us read the first, to transform the book of life into a great revelation of God, to return to us the gaze of faith that allows us to discern God's Word and Revelation present in the book of life—the book of indigenous culture and religion. This priority is fundamental in order for the indigenous peoples to be able to accept approaching the Bible. They do that only insofar as their natural, cultural, and religious world is valued and prioritized as the first book of God. The Bible is accepted, but as an instrument of discernment of their own indigenous tradition. The Bible is not considered as an absolute text, but as a "canon"—a measure or criterion—to discern the Word of God in the present natural, cultural, and religious reality of the indigenous peoples. The text is relative. What is absolute is the Word of God, present both in the book of life and in the Bible.

---

[17] This affirmation of St. Augustine is discussed in Mesters, *Defenseless Flower*, pp. 30–32.

d. Priority of the Indigenous Interpreter as Subject, Over the
Professional Evangelist or Biblical Scholar

The indigenous accept the Bible as the second book of God and as
a canon or criterion of interpretation of their own religious tradition,
on the condition that they themselves are the principal subject of
biblical interpretation. The biblical scholar or evangelist can carry
out the function of delivering the Bible to the indigenous community
or of building an access road to its comprehension, leaving to the
indigenous subject the responsibility of its interpretation. The Bible
is an instrument or criterion of interpretation of the Word of God
present in the indigenous tradition, on the condition that that instrument be utilized by the indigenous person himself or herself. This
presupposes a process of appropriation of the Bible on the part of
the indigenous. Insofar as this process goes forward, the indigenous
person as subject and interpreter of the Bible begins to interpret the
Word of God each time with more authority, legitimacy, security,
autonomy, and power. The process of interpretation of the Bible
from the perspective of these cultures strengthens the indigenous people
as a historical subject capable of a discernment of the Word of God,
both in their own tradition and in the biblical tradition.

2. *The Process of an Indigenous Hermeneutic*

The interpretation of the Bible in an indigenous context generates a
hermeneutical process that is extremely challenging and creative. The
indigenous community that reads the Bible begins to transform the
biblical text, but at the same time the biblical text begins to transform the indigenous community. The community reads the text, and
the text reads the community.

The Bible that arrives in the community is not a neutral book,
but a book already profoundly interpreted over hundreds of years of
tradition of biblical interpretation in the context of the dominant
European and occidental culture. It has become necessary, therefore,
to redeem the Bible starting from the spirit with which the Bible was
written, which requires reconstructing the Bible in the historical context
in which the literal meaning of the text was written and redeemed.
The Bible that comes to the community as the sacred scripture of
European Christendom is transformed into the sacred scripture of
the indigenous community that reads and interprets the Bible. This

requires a process of cultural deconstruction and reconstruction of the text. At that point, a fascinating process of cultural struggle within the biblical text itself begins.

The consequence of all the foregoing is the general affirmation on the part of the indigenous communities, which they themselves express in summary fashion as follows: "The more we know our indigenous tradition, the more we understand the Bible. And vice-versa: The more we know the Bible, the more we understand our indigenous tradition." The recovery and defense of the indigenous culture and tradition does not come into contradiction with the process of appropriation and interpretation of the Bible. The indigenous culture values the Bible insofar as the Bible values indigenous culture. A re-encounter between Culture and Bible in a hermeneutical process that may go on for many years, and that presupposes all of the previously noted priorities, begins to take place.

This hermeneutical process can have important variations according to the concrete historical circumstances of the indigenous peoples. Simplifying this complex picture, we could identify three models that more or less correspond to my experience with different indigenous communities in the last ten years of my work.

a. In the first model, the indigenous people preserves in an integral way its own cultural and religious tradition. This is the case for the Kuna Indians of Panama. It is a people that has lived very isolated geographically, and that has a structure for the preservation of its own tradition. The culture and religion are lived out daily and in a significant way in every village. They possess an oral tradition organized in specific codes (historical, legal, and ecological), and it is preserved and interpreted by persons who have authority in the community. In this case the approach to the Bible acquires a character that is secondary and subordinate to the study and interpretation of the indigenous tradition. The Bible must come in these cases with much humility, assuming its role as a second book. There is interest in the Bible, but always beginning with their own indigenous tradition, and in function of the Word of God present in both traditions. When the indigenous tradition is preserved in an integral manner and has a greater significance and power, it is the Bible, confronted with the indigenous tradition, that has to be reconstructed after having suffered centuries of destruction by a biblical interpretation that is too European, ethnocentric, colonial, and patriarchal. In this situation it is the indigenous tradition that helps to reconstruct the Bible.

b. In the second model, the indigenous culture and tradition have been almost completely destroyed by the occidental conquest and colonization. That is the case with the Quechua Indians of Ecuador. Using an image that I heard from them themselves, we might say that their culture is like a pitcher broken into a thousand pieces. They possess loose fragments of the tradition, but the global content and meaning of the culture and religion themselves have been lost. In these cases the interest in the Bible is greater, because the knowledge of the biblical tradition permits the reconstruction of their own indigenous tradition. The Bible serves as a model by which to reconstruct the pitcher broken into a thousand pieces. This reconstruction of their own indigenous tradition in light of the Bible permits, in turn, the Bible itself to be understood with greater depth.

c. In the third model, the indigenous religion survives integrated with Christianity in a situation of perfect syncretism. This is the case with the Maya religion in Guatemala. In this situation the Mayan culture and religion are interpreted in part in the symbols and categories of the biblical tradition, and vice-versa: the Bible is interpreted in part in the symbols and categories of the Mayan tradition. In this situation, which we consider to have positive value, the dialogue between Bible and Culture has already gone on for centuries, and the subject of the dialogue has been fundamentally the same indigenous community. In this case the hermeneutical process must begin with a long and arduous task of discernment of this Maya-Christian religiosity, seeking simultaneously to recover Mayan culture in itself, and the biblical tradition already interpreted through the aforementioned Mayan culture. The recovery does not seek to separate Bible and culture, but rather a better knowledge of indigenous culture beginning with the Bible, and a better knowledge of the Bible beginning with indigenous culture.

3. *The Hermeneutical Space Necessary for a Biblical Interpretation From the Perspective of Indigenous Cultures*

We call hermeneutical space the institutional *place* where a specific subject realizes a specific reading or interpretation of the Bible. There are two traditional hermeneutical spaces: the academic space and the ecclesial space (liturgical and instructional). The *academic space* is constituted by the faculties of theology, the seminaries, or the specialized theological institutes. In this space the subject is normally the exegete or biblical specialist, who carries out a historical critical or socio-critical reading and interpretation of the Bible. The *ecclesial space* is constituted both by the liturgical space (the celebration of the Word of God with its corresponding interpretation) and by the institutional space (every manifestation of the Tradition and of the Magisterium in the official actions and documents of the Church). In this space the subject is normally the ordained minister or the duly constituted hierarchical subject, who carries out a kerygmatic, magisterial, and normative reading and interpretation of the Bible.

Both the academic space and the ecclesial space are fully necessary, legitimate, and effective hermeneutical spaces. Both scientific interpretation and liturgico-magisterial interpretation of the Word of God will always be necessary and pressing. But a liberating hermeneutic necessary for a biblical interpretation from the perspective of indigenous cultures must create *a new hermeneutical space*, different from the previous ones, although intimately joined to them. This new hermeneutical space must be created beginning from the indigenous communities and without provoking a rupture with those communities. To create a space means first of all to create a small community interested in biblical study, respecting the hermeneutical priorities and the hermeneutical process we have described above. Second, what is indispensable is a minimal biblical introduction that places at the disposal of the community the basic elements to enter both the biblical text itself (literal meaning), and the history behind the text (historical meaning). Armed with these biblical instruments, the community begins to read and appropriate the text. Third, the community seeks to interpret the text and to transform it into Sacred Scripture. In that moment the biblical text is already theirs, it is in their hands, in their mind, in their heart. Finally, the text already appropriated and transformed begins to transform the community itself. In this entire process it is most important that the indigenous community not lose its identity and its tradition. In times of colonizing evangelization, when the gospel was being opposed to culture, the indigenous would experience a tragic spiritual schizophrenia, when Christianity was introduced in opposition to their own indigenous cultural and religious identity. In a liberating evangelization, with a liberating hermeneutic, the Bible is made present in the indigenous community with all of its liberating Spirit and power, without losing its biblical identity proper.

Conclusion

The interpretation of the Bible from the perspective of indigenous cultures has great importance for the indigenous peoples themselves. It seeks to save the life of these peoples who today are tragically threatened, to save their land and the environment in which they live, to save their community and organization, and above all to save their culture and religion, their spirituality, and their liberating presence in the construction of the reign of God in history. But this evangelization from the perspective of these cultures can also have a great importance for the churches, which today are also tragically captive to a European, ethnocentric, and colonial culture. In the indigenous communities is given the harmonious integration of culture, nature, and spirit, which could be the root of a new global alternative to the crisis of modernity and of the present free market economic system. The peoples of the Third World are poor in money and technology, but they are rich in humanity, culture, and spirit. A reconstruction of Christianity from the perspective of the Third World should take the indigenous tradition as the root for a global reconstruction of humanity.

Translated by Sharon H. Ringe

DOES GOD SPEAK MISKITU? THE BIBLE AND ETHNIC IDENTITY AMONG THE MISKITU OF NICARAGUA

Susan Hawley

> *"At first we had the land and you had the Bible.*
> *Now we have the Bible and you have the land."*
> *(Lantenari; 1963: 5)*[1]

This paper will look at the way that the Bible is used by the indigenous Miskitu people on the Atlantic Coast of Nicaragua as a means of defining and redefining their ethnic identity. I will argue that the Bible, though a global script, is well suited to local usage, and that in the case of the Miskitu it was the referent at two key moments of their history by which they redefined their collective social identity in relation to concrete social and political change. At both these moments, the Bible was used by the Miskitu in two distinct yet related ways: as a text, a book, a very material thing with specific and concrete cultural significance, and as a narrative within which the Miskitu chose to situate themselves in order to make sense of and to attempt to control the circumstances in which they found themselves. As I will show, the Bible was for them at one and the same time, a structural limitation, as the dominant colonial discourse of the Europeans, and a vehicle for asserting their agency, as they appropriated the biblical symbols as their own.

The two key junctures at which the Bible came to be used by the Miskitu to assert different identities correspond to two distinct social and political contexts. The first context was that of colonialism, in which the Miskitu converted to Christianity, acquiring a new social identity in the process, which helped them to adapt to the changed circumstances that colonialism had brought. The Bible was one of the key "gifts" which missionaries brought to indigenous peoples around the world in exchange for their obedience to the church (be it Protestant or Catholic) and, in many situations, to the colonial powers from whose centres the missionaries emanated. At this stage the Bible was used as a tool of homogenisation by the missionaries

---

[1] Lantenari quotes this as a summarisation of "the cry of native agitators to the whites" in Africa.

who supposed it to be the text of "civilisation." The Bible was seen by the Miskitu meanwhile, as by many other indigenous peoples around the world (Lantenari, 1965; Saunders, 1988; Worsley, 1968) as the key to the white man's power and wealth.

The second context was that of the rise of the pan-Indian movement as a powerful new social force in the 1960s. This context was one in which increasing value was given to the currency of identity politics or cultural identity as a mode of political "being." In this context, the Miskitu mobilised their ethnic identity politically, using the Bible as a means of differentiation between themselves and other groups. The biblical narrative, and particularly that of the Hebrew Bible, became a cultural-political weapon with which the Miskitu Indians identified in order to struggle against the nation-state. In this struggle, the Miskitu used motifs of the Promised Land and Old Testament Kings as symbols with which to articulate their new political ethnicity.

The Miskitu Indians of the Atlantic Coast of Nicaragua constitute an exogamous and heterogeneous group of roughly 75,000 people, whose origins lie in the intermarriage between Indians, Europeans and Africans. The majority of Miskitu Indians were converted to Christianity about a century ago, mostly by the Protestant Moravian Church, though a significant percentage (roughly about 40%) have since become Catholic, and Catholic missionaries have played an influential role along the Rio Coco home to some 25–30,000 Miskitu Indians, particularly in the transmission of indigenous theology after Vatican II.

Ethnicity and Identity

To analyse the way in which the Bible intersects with ethnic identity, in the Miskitu case, necessitates some prior discussion of what ethnicity is. The definition of ethnicity used here will be that it is: a mode of collective social identity that has as its framework or points of reference a set of inherited or "invented" cultural symbols, which are used selectively and strategically in interaction between groups (Barth, 1969) and in mobilisation of a particular group within the political sphere (A. Cohen, 1974; Worsley, 1984). Such an identity is never fixed, but always in the process of creation, though it often gains its legitimacy and authenticity through its apparent immutability and primordial nature.

The ethnic mode of identity is a form of communication which is structured by the socio-political, and historico-cultural context in which it is made. This communication of identity also structures the context itself. The ethnic mode of identity is thus produced as a result of what Bourdieu calls "the dialectic of the internalisation of externality and the externalisation of internality" (Bourdieu, 1977: 72). Such a communication of identity is always strategic because it involves a set of choices about what cultural symbols are relevant or not to be communicated in a given context. Yet, these choices are only made within the limits inherent to that context. The communication of an ethnic identity can be the source of major ideological conflict. It is linked up in very direct ways to the competition for resources between groups, between a group and the nation-state and also within groups (Olzak, 1983; Urban and Sherzer, 1991; Yinger, 1984).

The formation of ethnic identity involves a process of collective identification. This process of identification is one by which the sameness and unity of the social group, at the same time as its essential difference from every other group, is asserted. Friedman notes that "identification is the rendering to someone of identity" (Friedman, 1992: 332). Identification is thus a means of representation which presupposes an audience, the presence of the Other, without whom the group's "sameness of essential character" (Webster, 1948: 494) could not be conveyed. This combination of the need for Sameness and Difference is characteristic of the act of identification, which turns it into a "structured representation which only achieves its positive through the narrow eye of the negative" (Hall, 1991: 21).

An understanding of identification predicated solely on difference (Hall, 1991; Laclau, 1994; Smith, 1994) is, however, insufficient for an understanding of the Bible and identity. Identification also involves a more extroverted process. It can be the identification *with*, or the assertion of Sameness with, groups external to ones' own. It is the inclusion of others into the definition of the group as a positive and not a negative process. It involves for instance the absorption of extrinsic symbols, which are neither historically nor culturally specific to a certain group, into the narrative of the group's cultural meaning. I will call this "extroverted identity."

Extroverted identity among groups that have converted to or come in contact with Christianity often involves the identification with heroes or events within the Bible, who are moulded into and merged with local traditions or symbols. Such an identification is similar to Ricoeur's

understanding of "appropriation." Ricoeur observes that the insertion of subjects into the text, results in "appropriation [which] is the
process by which the revelation of new modes of being . . . gives the
subject new capacities for knowing himself" (Ricoeur, 1981: 192).
While Ricoeur's concern is with the subject, my concern here is with
group or collective identity. The process is similar in that the insertion of a group into the biblical narrative via a collective hermeneutic
provides an alternative mode of shared identity. This new mode of
identity, however, is only ever made relevant insofar as it is exercised in relation to the social and historical context in which the
hermeneutical interpretation takes place. Thus, not only will the identity "appropriated" be different in each context in which the Bible is
read, it will also both be limited by that context, as well as intrinsically affecting the context.

I will now turn to a brief discussion of two different contexts in
which "appropriation" of a new identity from the Bible occurred,
and make some general observations before going on to look at the
Miskitu case in detail.

Conversion

As Lantenari has shown, the Bible has been typically appropriated
by indigenous peoples in colonial situations in two manners: resistance and assimilation (Lantenari, 1985; 1963). Old Testament passages, for instance, were used by irredentist movements as a "xenophobic" model of resistance to the colonial powers, while the New
Testament was used in integrative (assimilationist) movements as a
"xenophilic" model of acceptance of these powers (Lantenari, 1985:
152–4). In the former movements, Jesus and the New Testament
were rejected as symbols belonging exclusively to the white man. By
identifying with the Jews in the Hebrew Bible, these groups appropriated a new mode of identity that both appeared as a continuation
of the symbolic forms of their previous identity, yet provided a more
potent means of resisting their colonisers. For instance, these groups
found reflections of their own polygamy and shamanism in Old
Testament passages about the Hebrews. At the same time, they found
a narrative of resistance whose symbols were instantly familiar to
those against whom they were directed.

In the cases where groups were open to Christianity and the colonial
power, for example the Miskitu Indians, conversion was seen as a

means to secure a new identity which was part of "a powerful and efficacious system for warding off moral disarray, physical calamities and disease" (Lantenari, 1985: 154). Conversion was also, in many cases of this type a "statement of affiliation with wealthier and more powerful outsiders" (Saunders, 1988: 187). Those who converted in this way saw the Bible as the symbol of their new status and the guarantor of the benefits of their new mode of identity. The Bible was always interpreted, however, both as a material object and a narrative in relation to the previous religious framework and traditions of each group.

The Bible in the colonial setting was thus the cultural code of the dominant powers, which indigenous groups learned to master either in order to resist or merely to survive the new social, political and economic situation into which they were thrust. Some have seen this as evidence that the Europeans were successful in forcing their terms on the peoples they colonised since the latter were "compelled to fight on the linguistic and conceptual terrain of the whites" (Comarroff & Comarroff, 1991: 307). Yet in the process of appropriating a new mode of ethnic identity from the Bible, colonised peoples both made the narrative their own, and spoke to the colonisers in terms that they would understand. Conversion, as the acquisition of a new mode of social identity, was therefore strategic. It took place in the context of domination and vulnerability, and it was an attempt by these colonised peoples to control that situation.

The Rise of Indigenous Consciousness: Political Mobilisation

Indigenous movements, as a continent-wide phenomenon in the Americas, began in the 1960s. They developed into a international movement which incorporates several major organisations (such as the World Council of Indigenous Peoples, WCIP), and advocacy groups (such as the International Work Group on Indigenous Affairs, IWGIA; Cultural Survival) during the 1970s. This political mobilisation of culture came to be known as the Pan-Indian movement which one observer described as "the expression of a new identity . . . the attempt to create a new ethnic group" (Thomas, 1965: 77). This movement provided an indigenous identity grounded in "strategic essentialism" (Warren, 1992: 210); that is, in a claim to and identification with an inner "essence" which all indigenous people are said to have in common. This "essence" is characterised by an intense relationship with the earth, democratic-communal form of self-governance and an innate spirituality. The steps between claims to this "essence" and to political demands for self-determination and political autonomy are fairly short (Hale, 1994: 20).

Many indigenous communities in Latin America were introduced to this strategic ethnic identity by progressive Catholic priests and theologians. Radicalised by the Second Vatican Council, these priests and theologians developed an indigenous theology, in response to the marginalised position of indigenous peoples with whom they worked and influenced by the growth of the Pan-Indian movement (Marzal, 1991; Pollock, 1993; Shapiro, 1981; Smutko, 1975; Taylor, 1981). The Bible which had previously been used by missionaries as a text of "civilisation" became a text for mobilisation. Whereas in the past the Bible had been the ultimate colonial weapon of the suppression of indigenous culture, it now became the tool with which to demand recognition of indigenous cultural and political rights. Indigenous history was read into the biblical narrative, and a political resistance was read out of it.

Rigoberta Menchu, a Guatemalan indigenous woman, now a Nobel Peace Prize holder, describes how when the Guatemalan Indians started to organise politically they:

> began to study the Bible as our main text. Many relationships in the Bible are like those we have with our ancestors, our ancestors whose lives were very much like our own. . . . We began looking for texts which represented each one of us. We tried to relate them to our Indian culture. We took the example of Moses for the men, and we have the example of Judith, who was a very famous woman in her time and appears in the Bible. . . . This gave us a vision, a stronger idea of how we Christians must defend ourselves. It made us think that a people could not be victorious without a just war. (Menchu, 1983: 131)

Indigenous people had been reading the Bible through their own traditions, and appropriating its heroic figures as their own, ever since the Bible first arrived amidst them. But the conscious reading of the Bible that was introduced by indigenous theology was different; it had as its goal, the redefinition of a community's political identity and from there its political behaviour.

This new relationship to the Bible, some suggest, involved as much a process of conversion as the original conversion to Christianity itself (Pollock, 1993: 188). And not all groups were converted. Some groups saw the missionaries' new approach as a duplicitous attempt to conceal true knowledge from them and to force them back into their old culture, which earlier missionaries had proved to them was futile and interior (French Smith, 1988: 38–9). Among the Miskitu Indians, however, consciousness raising courses by a Catholic missionary had a very profound effect on their incorporation of Pan-Indian symbols into a new collective indigenous identity that they began to develop in the 1960s and 70s.

The Miskitu and the Bible: Conversion

The Miskitu Indians converted to Christianity relatively late in the colonial process. They had a long history of contact with Europeans (in particular the English and Dutch) from the sixteenth century onwards, first with buccaneers and later, during the eighteenth and nineteenth century, more formally with the British government. Moravian missionaries, who made the first sustained effort to convert the Miskitu, arrived in 1849. Despite strong support by the Miskitu king and the British government, the missionaries were unsuccessful for the first 30–40 years of their efforts. The Miskitu Indians showed little interest in Christianity, until the 1880s when the missionaries reported a "Great Awakening."[2] After this the Moravian Church spread into almost every village between 1880 and 1940, erecting churches and training local pastors. By 1950, most Miskitu Indians were nominal Christians. Thus, Christianity is a recent arrival among the Miskitu dating back only three or four generations at most.

Missionary Methods

Being Protestant, the Moravian missionaries put a strong emphasis on the Bible and saw one of their key tasks as bringing the gospel to the Indians in their own tongue. In their first year in the region, one of the missionaries, Lundberg reported that:

> these poor people sit in gross darkness. One of them, when lately speaking with me, said: 'The English have a book which speaks of God, and therefore they know more of God than we do. God loves the English alone; he does not take notice of the Indians.' (Periodical Accounts, 1849: 525)

---

[2] The number of converts to the church increased by 100% during the decade of the 1880s, when the "Great Awakening" was taking place (from 1,030 to 3,294, out of a total population of 45,000).

The missionaries' consciously stated aim in translating the Bible into Miskitu, parts of which had been completed by the 1890s (Freeland, 1994: 6–7) was to rectify this perception. Such a re-evaluation of the Miskitu culture and language in positive terms (Freeland, 1994; Rossbach, 1986) and the act of conferring full humanity upon the Indians within the Christian cosmology by giving them the Bible in their own language was crucial to the way that Miskitu Indians came to review their perceptions of themselves as a group. It was also fundamental to their adoption of a Christian identity.

The Bible was however the site of contradictory messages offered by the missionaries. On the one hand they conveyed the worthiness of Miskitu culture by making the Bible a Miskitu text. On the other, the missionaries represented the Bible as the means by which the Miskitu could change their culture, and be raised "to a higher state of civilisation by the power of the Gospel" (P.A., 1949, December 22, p. 316). Indeed, a sign of behaving in this "civilised" and Christian manner was the quoting of the Bible regularly in daily life, in what the missionaries called a "truly Christian conversation" (P.A., 1849: 316). The missionaries themselves used biblical passages as a running commentary on daily events.[3]

Nominal Christianity was not enough for the Moravians. They emphasised the need for a full understanding of the Christian message and an ability to understand the Bible as requisites before they would baptise people. This made the process of "becoming Christian" one necessitating education and the ability to read, or at least memorise, "the book." However, the missionary methods were once again contradictory. While emphasising that conversion was a process and not achieved instantly, the missionaries also tended to stress the urgency of their message and use situations of mortality as key moments in which to divulge the mysteries of Christianity. Soon after their arrival, one missionary, Pfeiffer, noticed that an outbreak of measles which caused many deaths was a "judgement [which] has been the means of revealing to some the deeply rooted disease of their souls" (P.A., 1851: 102).

Not surprisingly these contradictions led to "misunderstandings" by the Miskitu Indians of what the Bible was intended for. In one instance:

---

[3] For instance, in the 1930s, the north american Superintendent of the Church in Nicaragua, observing lots of bush fires in the region, noted that "what springs to one's mind spontaneously is the passage about the burning bush that Moses saw." (Grossman, 1938: 12).

A half Indian . . . living with a Woolvah[4] woman, was lately very ill, and those around him thought he would die. Upon this the woman came to my wife, begging her to ask me to look into the Bible, and see what might be good for the man! This gave me a good opportunity to tell her, that the Bible points out remedies for the soul, not for the body. (P.A., 1859: 112)

This episode reveals how the missionaries were far from being in control of how their message was received. The Bible was a signifier of the passage which the Indians could take to civilisation, which connoted European-ness in the missionaries' view. In attempting to convert the Miskitu they often portrayed Christianity as a means to healing the "sickness" that was Indian culture. The Miskitu, however, understood the Bible within the rubric of their previous experience of foreigners, of their comprehension of institutions (particularly that of the Miskitu King) through which they had previous experience of education, and of their own concepts about health and sickness.

Indigenous Response: (1) The Bible as Foreign Object

Before the arrival of the missionaries, the contact that Miskitu Indians had had with foreigners was based primarily on trade. This began with the buccaneers of the sixteenth century who exchanged guns and rum in return for the help of the Miskitu in fighting the Spanish, and providing them with food and women. The Miskitu King and those few Miskitu who lived in the main town had contact with the British government whose actual physical presence in the eighteenth and nineteenth century was sporadic but at times included a permanent representative, based in the region.[5] The majority of Miskitu Indians, however, who lived in the rural areas, saw foreigners as traders.

More than once the contact that missionaries had with Miskitus was conditioned by this previous experience. In their first year, the missionaries noted:

---

[4] The Woolvah were another indigenous group living in the region, who were dominated and enslaved by the Miskitu Indians. The Miskitus, led by their King, were well known for their slaving raids amongst the other Indians of the region. They all but decimated most of these groups, of whom only 7,000 have survived, and are known under the generic name 'Sumu,' which means 'stupid' in Miskitu.

[5] In 1844 the British government sent its first formal representative, the British Resident, Patrick Walker, and this presence was maintained until 1860, when the region became a Reserve.

the first thing an Indian asks you for is tapla (rum) and tobacco. If we tell them that we do not keep these articles, they are displeased, or express their regret with a smile. (P.A., 1949: 316)

During the 1870s the missionary Smith noted that in several villages where he visited, people were surprised that he had not sent ahead a message of his arrival so that they could have caught venison for him, and were disappointed that he had not brought rum (P.A., 1876: 281:284). He offered them news of the "Saviour of sinners" and the word from the Bible instead. It is not surprising that in these times when conversion rates were low, and where contact with foreigners was characterised by economic exchange, the Miskitu would have understood the Bible as a new form of exchange between them and the latest foreigners: the missionaries. The Bible in this setting would most probably have been seen by the Miskitu as a new type of commodity, and as having, a material property.

During the 1880s several US companies became active in the region, and by 1890 north americans controlled 90% of all commercial activity (Jenkins, 1986: 107). The influx of goods and the availability of labour meant that the Miskitu Indians were drawn into the cash economy more than ever before. It was precisely during this period when the mass conversion of Miskitu Indians to the Moravian Church began. In this situation of the penetration of capitalism, conversion to Christianity, as has often been the case in other parts of the world (Saunders, 1988; Taylor, 1981; Worsley, 1968), was seen as a means to attaining some of the "god-wealth" that white people wielded (Taylor, 1981: 647). As white north american presence increased, the symbols of "white" power, such as the Bible, were seen as a more efficacious than their own, and a Christian identity was seen as more strategic in order to deal with the new situation.

Indigenous Response: (2) Bible as Continuation of Local Form—
The Miskitu King

The institution of the Miskitu kingship was introduced in 1661 by the British. With the crowning of Old Man I, the British extended their indirect rule over the Atlantic Coast of the Central American isthmus, as part of their struggle with the Spanish for regional control (Helms, 1986; Dennis and Olien, 1984). By the time that the missionaries arrived, the Miskitu kingship had developed as an institution to the extent that it had, in each community, a king's house, and a local representative (Roberts, 1827: 125). The Miskitu king also had a Quartermaster who would travel to different communities to give "upla smalkaya" or instructions/teachings. These instructions took the form of announcing certain laws in the name of the king, punishing offenders and ironing out local conflicts (Rossbach, 1986: 65).

The missionaries had a good deal of communication with the Miskitu king when they first arrived. Indeed they took the king's sisters into their house and were responsible for the education of the king. When they travelled into the rural areas, they depended upon the king's contacts, for which reason they came to be seen as new commissioners of the king who had come to give the local people instruction (Rossbach, 1986: 65). Some missionaries did in fact act as local magistrates and officials of the king. Feurig, for instance, acted as Adviser to the king in the 1850s, and was asked to settle disputes in the villages he visited (P.A., 1858: 512). This meant that when the missionaries came to preach, they were assured a hearing from villagers. Grunewald, a missionary during the 1850s, noted that when they preached to the Indians they always got an attentive audience who would reply "It is so" to what the missionaries said (P.A., 1858: 512). This suggests that the Indians had some previous experience of being an audience, and of how they were expected to respond.

The king's instructions were sometimes sent out in the form of a letter. In a predominantly oral society, written text would have commanded an authoritative status. That this was so is shown in an incident in the 1820s, when an English trader was asked to carry a letter from the king to one of the regional chiefs with whom the king had had a dispute. As the trader recorded, another regional chief was to go with him in order to explain that "the paper which spoke, was the king's own self order, and must be obeyed" (Roberts, 1827: 139). The missionaries introduction into rural communities of a whole book of written text, in the form of the Bible, was therefore likewise considered with a great deal of awe and respect by the Miskitu. Just ten years after their arrival, one missionary, Kandler noted how people were arriving from "far off places . . . with the goal of informing themselves about the path of salvation and on the work of the big book (the Bible)" (Missionblatt, 1860: 127, quoted in Rossbach, 1986: 65).

Yet, despite the proximity to the Miskitu king, and despite the delivery of text, the missionaries did not make much headway. It was not until the Miskitu kingship was under threat, that the church began to make inroads into the communities. From 1880 onwards, the kingship was menaced with extinction owing to international politics. In 1860, the British, in deference to the increasing power of the United States in the hemisphere, had pulled out of the region. They made provisions, in their retreat, that the region should be an autonomous Reserve. The United States, however, with an eye to building a canal through Nicaragua, backed the newly formed Nicaraguan State's claim to the region. In 1894, the Nicaraguan State, under Zelaya, invaded the region and took it over by force, referring to the event as the "Reincorporation." The Miskitu king fled to Jamaica where he later died.

The importance of their king to the Miskitu, despite the fact that the monarchy was in practice no more than a puppet of the British for most of the two centuries of its existence as an institution, should not be underestimated. In healing rituals carried out by traditional healers—*sukias*—observed by missionaries during the 1870s, three wooden figures were used: those of the King, the Counsellor and the Gaoler. These were either waved over the patient or put in the patient's bed (P.A., 1873–4: 224). While this was a reflection on the one hand of the local iconography, since it was believed that sick people were the prisoners of the mountain spirit king Asampaca, its striking similarity to the actual institution of kingship suggests there was some overlap between spiritual iconography and political mode of governance, each of which reinforced the other.[6]

It is not surprising then, considering that one of the Miskitus' main cultural institutions was under serious threat during the 1880s and 90s leading to its eventual dissolution, that the Miskitus should start to look for a new identity to cope with the stress inherent within such a situation. The mass conversions of the Great Awakening thus appear as a revitalisation movement, i.e., as "a deliberate, organised, conscious effort by members of a society to construct a more satisfying culture" (Wallace, 1956: 265). In the face of cultural and political crisis, the Miskitu Indians chose a Christian identity as a means of adapting to a new set of circumstances which demanded a quick

---

[6] As Taussig has noted (1980: 182–213), spiritual iconography of indigenous communities changed with the transformation of political circumstances. Icons came to reflect the new property relations of the colonial situation (1980: 183–4) so that spirits that had previously only lived on mountains, became the owners of the mountains, and changed from being benevolent to malevolent. Among the Miskitu, as among the examples Taussig cites, spirits are seen as white and rich.

and strategic response if cultural survival were to be achieved.

The Moravian Church as an institution, which spread into the Miskitu communities after the 1880s, was remarkably similar to the institution of the Miskitu king. The Moravians erected a church in each village, constructed by the members of the community, and this constituted the only communal building in each village, as the king's house had been. The church also introduced its own regulations as to behaviour, similar to the king's laws, and a means of punishment for those who transgressed which consisted of sanctions, and in particular, exclusion from holy communion or even from the congregation itself.

Indigenous Response: (3) The Bible as Local Form—A More Powerful Medicine

While the king was the regional centre of power, the most powerful leaders at the local level were the traditional healers or *sukias*. In some villages, the *sukia* was also the chieftain.[7] Most of Miskitu cosmology both before and after the arrival of the missionaries was intricately related to the maintenance of health. Ill health was attributed to the capriciousness of evil spirits, or the malevolence of one's neighbours, who had poisoned one. The *sukia* was the person (they were often female) who could, for the right price, offer protection against the spirits and who could determine who had planted the poison either in the victim's food or buried along a path the victim was accustomed to use.

The missionaries came into contact with the *sukias* soon after their arrival. They viewed them as proof of "the whole sad hopelessness of heathenism" (P.A., 1910: 496) and directed much of their energy to providing western medicine as an alternative to traditional medicine. Because of this, the missionaries came to be perceived as new and more effective "poison masters," as the missionary Heath exclaimed,

---

[7] The relationship between the King and the *sukias* was not always an easy one. As Ranger has shown in Africa (Hefner, 1993: 73–5) traditional religious leaders led movements against the political chieftains or kings at times, and by no means just maintained the political status quo, as they are usually portrayed as doing. The fact that the Miskitu king similarly felt the *sukias* to be a potential threat to his power was revealed when in the 1870s he banned the making of a living by means of witchcraft (P.A., 1874: 352). This may also have been a sop to the missionaries, but was the result of an incident when a *sukia* refused to heal the king, saying that he was unable to do so.

"thanks to Livingstone College" (P.A., 1915: 377–8). And the source
of their efficacy was seen not just in the medicaments that they handed
out, but also in the book that they brought with them.

By presenting the Bible as the handbook of the different cosmology that went with western medicine, the missionaries offered a whole
different meaning system for understanding illness, and hence the
world. The new regulations as to "Christian" behaviour that they
offered as a counterpart to this cosmology came to be seen by the
Miskitu as similar to the proscriptions that the *sukias* gave out after
healing someone (Rossbach, 1986: 165–6).[8] The emphasis that *sukias*
gave to these proscriptions was that if they were broken, then the
state of health of the patient would be jeopardised. In one incident,
the missionaries living in a village were admonished by the local
leader for not keeping the new rules that the missionaries themselves
had imposed:

> a baby was recently born to a missionary, and of course, its clothes
> were washed and changed even on Sundays . . . The *wita* [literally: judge]
> appeared before the missionary, reproached him, forbade him to do it
> again and threatened him with sanctions if he were to do so.
> (Missionblatt 1891: 370; quoted in Rossbach, 1986: 166)

This failure by the missionaries, to keep the very laws that they had
introduced through the Bible, was seen as imperilling the benefits
that the local population had been promised if they kept the rules.

It was from the *sukias* that the missionaries, not surprisingly, encountered the most resistance. The missionary accounts report that
some local healers saw the Bible as the site of great power and therefore as a threat to their own position. Many *sukias* seem to have
converted to Christianity in an obvious attempt to try to retain their
authority by mastering the new "medicine." This didn't mean, however, that they accepted the Bible, which was after all the carefully
guarded property of the white missionaries. At the turn of the century, one missionary, Grossman, came across a *sukia* who announced
that he rejected the Bible since God made His revelations direct to
him, and that he therefore had a greater claim to the truth
(Missionblatt, 1906: 189; quoted in Rossbach, 1986: 141). A decade
later, Heath reported that a local "sorcerer" called Teodoro Ribera,

---

[8] These involved not eating certain types of food and not having people walk on
one's windward side. If the sick person did not get better it was alleged by the *sukia*
that one of the prescriptions had been broken.

told him that the demons would keep him awake at night and make him say such things as:

> Christians know nothing; the Bible is nothing at all: I am the man who knows something. (P.A., 1915: 378)

While some resistance was directed against the Bible as an object, and as the source of power, antagonism was also expressed at times towards the biblical symbols. In one community on the Coco River, a man called George (we are not told if he was a *sukia* or not) claimed that he had killed Jesus with bullets and that he wanted to be called the Holy Spirit (Missionblatt, 1906: 187; quoted in Rossbach, 1986: 140).

To this day, the Bible is used as a form of talismanic protection, in healing and divination rituals among the surviving *sukias*, who are often members of the church.[9] Meanwhile, indigenous pastors and staunch Miskitu Christians reject all such shamanistic practices and assert that such practices are against the Bible. Yet, at the same time the Bible is seen by them as a means of protection against such practices, as is shown by the proscription laid down by the indigenous pastors, in a very obvious carry over of the *sukia*'s regulations, that menstruating women must not touch the Bible (personal communication, 1994).

Summary: The Bible as New Wine in Old Wineskins or Old Wine in New Wineskins

The establishment of the Moravian Church among the Miskitu Indians was in part the result of the decline of the main cultural institution of the Miskitu, the kingship, which led to the loss of Miskitu political autonomy. At the same time the Miskitus were being incorporated more fully into the capitalist economy. In this situation, the message that the Church brought in the shape of the Bible was filtered by the Miskitu through their own experience and cultural traditions. Yet at the same time, Christianity appeared to the Miskitu

---

[9] One *sukia* in the village of Sisin places a metal pin through the spine of the Bible, and puts a finger at one end while the patient puts their finger at the other. The Bible is then asked questions, and if it spins, the answer is affirmative; otherwise, it is negative. Motifs from the Bible are also incorporated into the healing rituals such as the "angel doctor." One *sukia* in another village, Klar, sings: *"Insal duktar tahabi sakan aiwinara briba"* which means "angel doctor baptise what he [the patient] has in his body."

as a fundamentally more efficacious system, "ideologically and organisationally preadapted to the macrocosm" (Hefner, 1993: 28) into which the Miskitu were thrust.

There is a dialectical tension inherent to the process of conversion. Extrinsic symbols, such as the Bible, are given legitimacy through their re-interpretation as local symbols. Yet at the same time, the foreignness and alien nature of these symbols are seen as the source of their power. This tension between local legitimacy and foreign power is played out differently in different contexts, with varying degrees of conflation, divergence and contradiction. Thus, while the adoption of a new mode of collective identity can be experienced as a radical break from one's previous mode of identity, it can also be experienced as a means of continuing that previous identity in a different and renewed form.

Christianity took hold in Miskitu communities in a dialectical process in which Christianity became miskitu-ised and the Miskitu became christianised. Thus, as the Miskitus used the symbols of the Bible as pointers to their new identity, they also appropriated them as old Miskitu symbols. For instance, many Miskitus consider that Miskitu history really began with the arrival of the church among them, and take "as their historical baseline the beginning of missionary work. Everything prior to this period is considered heathen by definition and therefore best forgotten" (Helms, 1971: 217). Yet, a converse understanding of their history is also common, especially among Miskitu elders, which is that the Moravian Church dates back to the birth of the Miskitus (Lucas, personal communication, 1994). To conclude, the Miskitu Indians relationship to the Bible was one of "appropriation" or insertion of themselves as a group into the biblical text: situating themselves within the biblical text was a means of identifying with the "civilised" modern European world, and also of finding their own history and hence their agency within its narrative.

The Miskitu and the Bible: political mobilisation

The 1960s was a decade of sharp decline in the economic conditions of the Atlantic Coast, where the Miskitu live. In 1960, the Miskitus of Nicaragua lost a large chunk of fertile land on which they had had their crops, when it was handed over to Honduras as a result of a ruling in the International Court at the Hague. This coincided with the exit of most of the transnational logging, banana, and gum companies, which left the Miskitu, who were now dependent on the cash economy, without labour, and without the means to buy the commodities they were accustomed to (Helms, 1971). Somoza, whose family dynasty (backed by the US) ruled Nicaragua for forty years, began to pay some attention to the region at this time, and ordered an education project to be undertaken there, to teach the Miskitus Spanish.[10] Thus, as the north american presence disappeared from the region, there was an increase in the number of "Spaniards" (as Miskitus still call the mestizos of the pacific Coast), and of the institutions of the nation-state.

It was during the 1960s that the Catholic Church began to grow among the Miskitu. Previously the Catholic Church could hardly compete with the Moravians while it was still giving mass in Latin, and while it effectively excluded Miskitus from church leadership because of the strict and lengthy training that ordinands had to undertake.[11] During the 1960s however, the Catholic church, under the aegis of the north american Father Gregory Smutko, began to train delegates of the word and catechists. The influence of Father Gregory's work, however, spread much further than the Catholic Church, owing to his ecumenical, political and pastoral work.

Biblical Symbol as the Basis for Political Mobilisation

Father Gregory had studied anthropology in the US and was deeply committed to the changes that the Second Vatican Council had brought about. His conscious aim when he arrived on the Rio Coco in 1967 was to implement the "option for the poor" and "liberating education" (as recommended by Paulo Freire and by the Council of Medellin) among the indigenous people of the region (personal communication, 1994). Father Gregory, in the process of training delegates of the word, undertook consciousness-raising courses in which he encouraged an indigenous exegesis of the Bible.

---

[10] Previously Somoza had left the region almost entirely in the hands of the foreign companies, but their departure coincided with an increase in political unrest on the Pacific side of the country, and Somoza wanted to ensure that the inhabitants of the Atlantic Coast inhabitants would not also turn on him.
[11] One of the greatest impediments to the Catholic Church handing over leadership of the church to Miskitu Indians, which still stands today, is the celibacy ordinance, since respect and authority within Miskitu communities is usually contingent upon age and the number of children one has.

In these courses, Father Gregory also revitalised Miskitu history, on which he conducted a considerable amount of research, by fusing it with biblical narrative. An example of this was the Miskitu salvation history which was produced in a workshop in 1970 and later written up in Father Gregory's book *Pastoral Indigenista* in 1975.[12] This Miskitu salvation history included a detailed comparison between Miskitu history and that of the Hebrews. For instance, the mythical leader Miskut who:

> came from Honduras with his tribe to Sita-Awala ... and lived there because the land was good to work on and he had peace, deer and abundant food, as well as trees of every species

is compared to "the great leader Moses who brought his people from Egypt to the Promised Land" (Smutko, 1975: 56). And while:

> under the kings, David and Solomon, the Israelites conquered many of the neighbouring tribes ... and defeated their enemies with the help of Almighty God

so it was that "the Miskitu conquered more than twenty neighbouring tribes ... [and] the dominion of the Miskitu kings was much greater than the dominion of the kings of Israel" (ibid.). One of the conclusions of this course was that:

> As God, with his powerful arms, liberated the people of Israel from the slavery of the Egyptians, in the same manner, he gave strength and courage to our fathers in order to defend themselves from the Spanish who were never able to conquer them. (Smutko, 1994: 12)

Father Gregory's courses about Miskitu history and the Bible, were in some ways only a catalyst for a process of ethnic revitalisation which had been gathering momentum during the 1960s before his arrival. In her fieldwork in the mid-60s, the anthropologist, Mary Helms noted that:

> in discussing their discontent and their helplessness to change conditions, a few informants claimed that the king would some day be restored to his position and that the Miskito again be an independent 'nation.' (Helms, 1969: 83)

The symbol of the Miskitu king, had in fact been kept alive as an oral memory, partly by the biblical narrative and with the encouragement of some Moravian missionaries. In the early part of this

---

[12] Father Gregory provided the material, historical and biblical for this history though it was actually written up by Miskitu catechists.

century, for instance, one missionary, Dannenburger introduced what was to become an annual festival in celebration of the Miskitu king (Dennis, 1982: 395). This involved a re-enactment of the king's return to the Atlantic Coast for a day.[13] Furthermore, Old Testament passages about the Israelite kings were read avidly by the Miskitu (Dennis, ibid.). This tendency on the part of the Miskitu to use biblical symbols as a commentary on their history is also evident in the reminiscence of a middle-aged Miskitu professional:

> Since our infancy we have had this hope that the king and queen would return. . . . The daughter of the king was living in Belize and she sent a letter to us saying that she wanted to come back and live with the Miskitus . . . This letter was circulating here in the 1960s . . . and people were quoting passages from the Psalms to justify her return. (Personal communication, 1994)

What Father Gregory introduced, however, was the idea that the revitalisation of Miskitu culture could form the basis for political organising, and most importantly, that being indigenous meant that one should and could fight for certain political rights. As the conclusion to the Miskitu salvation history notes: "the nations that don't fight in order to overcome are the slaves of others" (Smutko, 1975: 59). In 1967, he set up co-operatives on the Rio Coco which in 1970 became the Association of Agricultural Clubs of the Rio Coco (ACARIC). This organisation lobbied Somoza's government for Miskitu political representatives, the removal of brutal National Guardsmen, and demanded fair prices from the merchants for the rice and beans that were grown on the River. As Smutko proudly noted himself, "ACARIC was the first organisation of all the Miskito on the Rio Coco since the death of the last Miskito King in 1914" (Smutko, 1994: 19).

Indigenous Pastors: Guardians of Text, Guardians of Identity

While Father Gregory provided the model of indigenous exegesis with his courses, and the model for political indigenous organising with his co-operatives, it was the Miskitu Moravian pastors which began to take up his message and consciously to articulate an indigenous-Miskitu nationalism. Miskito Moravian pastors asked Father Gregory

---

[13] The king was chosen from among the young men of a village, had foreign money pinned to him, and would speak in a non-Miskitu language, either Spanish or more usually English.

for copies of his courses on the salvation history of the Miskitu, and
these were used in the communities of the Rio Coco for some ten
years afterwards (Smutko, 1994: 12–13). Many of these indigenous
Moravian pastors also worked with Father Gregory in ACARIC, which
was, for the most part, run by Moravian Miskitus.

By the 1960s, the Moravian church had been training indigenous
pastors for some thirty years in their Bible Institute on the Rio Coco[14]
and had pulled out almost all its foreign missionaries.[15] The indigenous pastors were sent out as itinerant preachers, into communities
other than their own,[16] for three year periods. The pastors were totally
dependent upon the community they stayed in for food—and labor
in building both the pastoral house and the church. Yet they maintained a great deal of respect and authority within the communities,
and were often the arbiters of social conflict there. This position of
authority was accorded to them because they were the only members of the community who had any education.

Proof of this privilege was their imparting of the knowledge of the
Bible through their sermons. The pastors had almost exclusive access
to the Bible and were therefore the owners of the "cultural capital"
of Miskitu society, having access, as they did, to "the monopolisation
of the instruments for appropriation of these [symbolic] resources
(writing, reading and other decoding techniques)" (Bourdieu, 1990:
125). The pastors also controlled such cultural capital because of their
command over "text" in general. As I have noted earlier, text had
very material properties for the Miskitu and was seen as the site of
power and in a predominantly oral society, the ability to master text
was the source of personal authority. The significance of text can be
seen in the fact that the binary opposite of the Bible in the communities is a book of sorcery called simply the "blak buk."[17]

---

[14] There were about 66 Miskitu pastors by 1970. The pastors were taught by
north american pastors who demanded rote learning of the Bible rather than any
exegetical practice. There were a couple of Moravian missionaries, however, and in
particular one, Richard Steiner, who is remembered by the Miskitu pastors to this
day for teaching them that indigenous peoples had political rights which they should
demand from the government.

[15] Indeed the church became fully nationalised in 1974, though there were only
one or two missionaries in the region during the 1960s.

[16] This model was justified by the biblical passage now oft quoted by Miskitu
pastors, that "a prophet is not without honour, except in his own country, and
among his own kin, and in his own house" (Mark 6:4).

[17] Any text that is not a Moravian text, or otherwise recognisable (such as a
school book) has on occasions been suspected by zealous community leaders of being

The Bible was viewed as a communal symbolic resource which provided the basis for the Christian identity of the Miskitus. The pastors, as guardians of the Bible were thus also viewed as the guardians of this identity. There was a strong tendency on the part of the laity to delegate responsibility for the maintenance of the collective Christian identity to the "specialists" (in this case the pastors). On the one hand, this was a structural effect of not having access to education. On the other hand, however, it was also a means of escaping the uncomfortable contradiction (or "cognitive dissonance," as Saunders puts it, 1988: 190) arising from the fact that the Miskitu had maintained certain practices pertaining to their traditional religion which were expressly forbidden by the church. By delegating responsibility to the pastors for the upholding of the Miskitu Christian identity, the laity were free to visit *sukias*, poison their neighbours, commit adultery and drink. Pastors who did so, however, were seen as threatening to undermine the smooth functioning of the collective social identity.[18]

The pastors became the main purveyors of the new indigenous identity, filtering it through Miskitu history, and through the biblical narrative. The land (as a conflation of the Promised Land and the territory of the Miskitus) and the king (as a conflation of Old Testament kings and the Miskitu kings) became symbols which were reference points for the new politicised ethnicity of the Miskitu. Thus when Father Gregory left the region in 1971 and ACARIC was dismantled, it was a Miskitu Moravian pastor, Wycliffe Diego, who agitated for the creation of an indigenous political organisation. This organisation, which was called ALPROMISU (the Alliance for the Progress of the Miskitus and Sumus) was founded in 1974 and the majority of its activists were Miskitu Moravian pastors. One of these Moravian pastors, Reverend Mullins Tilleth, who was influential in the movement, began to incorporate indigenous motifs in sermons

---

the black book. In a recent case, a Jehovah's Witness book, in the possession of a young man accused of black magic, was used as evidence against him by community leaders, who were unable to read, in the village of Sandy Bay. A trial took place which was jeopardised, however, by the arrival of the pastor who could read the book and knowing what it was, tactfully suggested that the document in question was most likely not the book they were after (Personal communication, 1994).

[18] This partially explains the seemingly paradoxical relationship between an extremely punitive disciplinary system enforced by the indigenous Moravian church, and the hypocrisy with which these standards are (or are not) kept.

which focused Miskitu political aspirations on the return of the Miskitu king. According to Wycliffe Diego, who worked with him, Tilleth:

> was preaching about the kings and the land. He said that the Miskitus had to rule the land because it says in the dictionary that the word 'indigenous' means 'the owners.' (Personal communication, 1994)

Political Conflict: The Bible and Holy War

In 1979, Somoza's dictatorship was toppled in a revolution spearheaded by the Sandinista National Liberation Front (FSLN). The revolutionary war left the Atlantic Coast virtually untouched, and very few Miskitus took part in it. On the one hand, this revolution created expectations among the Miskitu for an improvement in their political situation, and even for a political space within which their aspirations for the return of the king, and the reestablishment of the Miskitu nation would be fulfilled. On the other, however, the Sandinistas, who had a left-wing orientation and were influenced by Liberation theology, were viewed with suspicion, particularly by the older Miskitus and Moravian pastors, who had been inculcated with a strong anti-communism by the north american Moravian missionaries.[19]

Soon after the revolution, a new indigenous political organisation was formed out of the older one, ALPROMISU. It was renamed, MISURASATA (Miskitus, Sumus, Ramas, Sandinistas United Together). Although this organisation still had Miskitu pastors as its main activists, its leaders were a group of students who had been at university in Managua during the 1970s. These leaders, because of their university education, came to hold an even greater monopoly over the cultural capital of the Miskitu than the pastors had. But it was only through their alliance with the pastors that they were able to mobilise the Miskitu behind the banner of indigenous identity, because the pastors were still the keepers of the Bible and of the Miskitu Christian identity.

Tension arose between MISURASATA and the Sandinista government within just a year of the revolution. The Sandinistas supported MISURASATA, and backed their proposal for a literacy campaign in the indigenous languages, and for communal land rights.

---

[19] Dennis notes that during his fieldwork in 1978–9 among the Miskitu, he heard sermons in the rural villages given by lay pastors "warning that if Somoza left, the Communists would gain control and religion would be outlawed" (Dennis, 1981: 282).

However, in early 1981, when they found out that MISURASATA were planning to lay claim to one contiguous land title that covered nearly 40% of the national territory, they threw the leaders in jail, accusing them of separatism. The charges were not totally unfounded. While the leadership of MISURASATA presented their demands to the Sandinistas as indigenous rights, they were telling the Miskitu people something else. As a Miskitu doctor recounted:

> The leaders ... promised a lot, ... that we were going to have our own independence and have our own everything. We were saying that we wanted independence from the beginning. (Personal communication, 1994)

According to a Miskitu teacher, the leaders were also saying that "the Sandinistas were communists who wanted to finish with God and the Bible, so the pastors got angry" (Pers. comm. 1994). This was corroborated by the wife of Mullins Tilleth who noted that the trouble started because:

> On top of it all, the Sandinists wanted to bring in communism and that's why the Church stood up—we believe in God and we grew up with that and you can't get that out of us ... on the Atlantic Coast, we are not communist, we are Christians, Protestants. (Pers. comm. 1991)

By 1981, the Miskitu leaders, released from jail by the Sandinistas, fled to Honduras where they were supported by the US and became the indigenous front for the Contras. The war was permeated and even structured by biblical symbols and narrative. Some of the first indigenous fighters were divided into bands known as "Los Astros" (The Stars) and "Las Tropas Cruces" (The Troops of the Cross), who all wore white crosses sown to their clothes, and who carried Bibles. In the words of a pastor who fought with the Contra:

> each military group had to have a pastor with them ... they had to have a weapon in one hand and a Bible in the other in order to give prayer services to the troops. (Pers. comm. 1994)

Once again, the Bible for the Miskitu had very material properties, as a form of amulet against bullets. It was also a narrative within which the Miskitu situated themselves. The Bible became a commentary on the war, in which the Sandinistas were identified variously as Antiochus Epiphanes, the Egyptians, Babylon and Rome, oppressing the Miskitus. The Sandinistas were also portrayed as Canaanites and Philistines, whom the Miskitus must drive out of the land. The Miskitus referred to various of their commanders as Moses, Joshua, Gideon and David (Wilde, 1989: 974). Meanwhile, the Rio Coco was seen as the Red Sea. Biblical imagery pervaded the daily events of war in an affirmation of the righteousness of the Miskitu warriors who, like the Israelites under Joshua, were waging their holy war.

Summary

As the Miskitu were incorporated more fully into the nation-state during the 1960s, they came into increasing contact with "the Spanish" from the Pacific Coast of Nicaragua who connoted for the Miskitu everything that was negative and opposed to their positive relations with the Anglo world (Hale, 1994; Helms, 1989). In this situation, the Miskitus deployed biblical symbols as a means of differentiation between themselves and "the Spanish." At the same time, Father Smutko introduced them to a means of utilising the Bible as a cultural-political tool with which to demand rights from the nation-state, which was perceived unerringly by the Miskitu as a "Spanish" institution.[20]

However, as the Bible became part of the communication of Miskitu ethnic identity, it was not just a means of differentiating themselves from the Spanish. It was also an affirmation of allegiance towards the powerful Anglo domain, in which the Miskitu had embedded themselves when they converted to Christianity. It was this allegiance which led the Miskitus to side with the US in their covert war to topple the Sandinista government. In a vignette which reveals the relationship between Miskitu "Anglo-affinity" (Hale, 1994) and war, Helms observed in the 1960s the Miskitus' fascination with Vietnam:

> People talked incessantly about keeping an eye out for aeroplanes and awaiting an attack. Yet beneath the tension was a feeling that it was a mark of importance and recognition to have a war on the river, or, in other words, if warfare were part of the modern world, the Miskito should be involved also. (Helms, 1971: 221)

This fascination for war as a motif of modernity in which the Miskito wanted to participate as long as it was part of the Anglo world, was coupled with an avid reading of Old Testament passages about the

---

[20] Although there was some denominational conversion to the Catholicism at this time, this was because the Catholic church among the Miskitu was run entirely by north americans, and had no contact whatsoever with the Catholic church of the Pacific Coast.

kings and about Joshua's conquering of the Promised land, in which warfare was a common theme.

Thus when the Sandinistas came to power, the Miskitus appropriated the Bible as a means of articulating strong differences with the new government. They saw themselves as caught up in a conflict between good and evil, in which they were the Christians against the communists. They also inserted themselves into the biblical narrative as the Israelites fighting for their king and their land. As a Sandinista leader, Luis Carrion, noted, "the indigenous people found their past in the Bible" (Ohland and Schneider, 1983: 241). They also found their present there.

Conclusion

I have argued throughout this paper that the Bible has been an important means by which the Miskitus of Nicaragua have defined and redefined their ethnic identity. This identity has been strategically articulated within the social and political context in which the Miskitus have found themselves. The first context was that of colonialism when they converted to Protestant Christianity. In the process of conversion, they both interpreted the Bible through their own local traditions, and appropriated it as a symbol of their new "modern" Christian identity.

The second context was that of political mobilisation in the 1960s in which the Miskitus situated themselves within the biblical text in order to articulate their political aspirations for the return of the Miskitu king and for control over their own territory. In this context, the Bible was both a means of differentiation from "the Spanish" of the Pacific Coast of Nicaragua, and a continuing affirmation of Miskitu affiliation with the Anglo world.

The dialectical manner in which the Miskitu have appropriated the Bible as a symbol which is intrinsic to their own culture and at the same time as an extrinsic symbol of their affiliation with the Anglo world from which it came, is perhaps best summed up in the anecdote told by a Miskitu, Rodolfo, to an English traveller who was in the region during the late 1980s:

> an *ingles de color* [an Englishman of color] who lived with my aunt, he used to say . . . that Moses was a Miskito. (Ford, 1992: 184)

List of References

Barth, F., ed.
1969   *Ethnic Groups and Boundaries: The Social Organization of Culture Difference.* Oslo: Universitetsforlaget.
Bourdieu, P.
1977   *Outline of a Theory of Practice.* New York and London: Cambridge University Press.
Bourdieu, P.
1990   *The Logic of Practice.* Cambridge: Polity Press.
Cohen, A.
1974   *Two-Dimensional Man.* London: Tavistock.
Comaroff, J. & Comaroff, J.
1991   *Of Revelation and Revolution: Christianity, Colonialism and Consciousness In South Africa, Vol. 1.* Chicago: University of Chicago Press.
Dennis, P.
1982   "Coronation on the Miskitu Coast." *The Geographical Magazine.* July.
Dennis, P. & Olien, M.
1984   "Kingship Among the Miskito." *American Ethnologist*, 11:4:718–773.
Ford, P.
1992   *Tekkin a Waalk.* London: Harper Collins.
Freeland, J.
1994   "'Why to Go School to Learn Miskitu?': Changing Constructs of Bilingualism and Literacy among the Miskitu of Nicaragua's Atlantic Coast." Paper given at Society at Latin American Studies Conference, Liverpool, 24–26 March.
French Smith, M.
1988   "From Heathen to Atheist on Kairuru Island," in Saunders, G. (ed.), *Culture and Christianity: The Dialectics of Transformation.* Connecticut: Greenwood Press.
Friedman, J.
1992   "Narcissism, roots and postmodernity: the constitution of selfhood in the global crisis," in Lash, S. and Friedman, J. (eds.), *Modernity and Identity.* Oxford, UK and Cambridge, US: Blackwell Publishers.
Grossman, G.
1938   *Nicaragua: Pais y Costumbres y el Tratado de la Hermandad en Nicaragua y Honduras.* translation 1983, Managua, Nicaragua: CIDCA.
Hall, S.
1991   "Old and New Identities, Old and New Ethnicities," in King, A.D. (ed.), *Culture, Globalization and the World-System.* London: Macmillan Press.
Hale, C.
1994   "Between Che Guevara and Pachamama: Mestizos, Indians and Identity politics in the anti-quincentenary campaign." *Critique of Anthropology*, 14(1):9–39.
Hefner, R., (ed.)
1993   *Conversion to Christianity: Historical and Anthropological Perspec-*

tives on a Great Transformation. Berkeley: University of California Press.

Helms, M.
1971   *Asang: Adaptations to Culture Contact in a Miskitu Community.* Gainesville: University of Florida Press.

Helms, M.
1986   "Of Kings and Contexts: ethnohistorical interpretations of Miskito political structure and function." *American Ethnologist*, 13:3:506–52.

Helms, M.
1989   "Symbols of Ethnicity: Geo-Politics and Cosmography among the Miskitu of Eastern Central America." Paper given at XV International Congress of the Latin American Studies Association.

Jenkins Molieri, J.
1986   *El desafio indigena en Nicaragua: el caso do los Miskitos.* Managua: Editorial Vanguardia.

Laclau, E.
1994   *The Making of Political Identities.* London: Verso.

Lantenari, V.
1963   *Religions of the Oppressed: A Study of Modern Messianic Cults.* London: MacGibbon and Kee.

Lantenari, V.
1985   "Revolution and/or Integration in African Socio-Religious Movements," in Lincoln, B. (ed.), *Religion, Rebellion, Revolution.* London: Macmillan Press.

Marzal, M.
1991   *Rostros Indio de Dios: Los Amerindios Cristianos.* Ecuador: Abya-Yala.

Menchu, R. & Burgos-Debray, E.
1983   *I, Rigoberta Menchu: an Indian Woman in Guatemala.* London: Verso.

Moravian Church
1847–1961   *Periodical Accounts.*

Ohland, K. & Schneider, R.
1983   *National Revolution and Indigenous Identity: The conflict between Sandinistas and Miskito Indians on Nicaragua's Atlantic Coast.* Copenhagen: IWGIA document, 47.

Pollock, D.
1993   "Conversion and 'Community' in Amazonia," in Hefner, R. (ed.), *Conversion to Christianity.* Berkeley: University of California Press.

Ricoeur, P.
1981   *Hermeneutics and the Human Sciences.* Cambridge: Cambridge University Press.

Roberts, O.
1827   *Narrative of Voyages and Excursions on the East Coast and in the Interior of Central America.* Edinburgh and London: Constable and Chance.

Rossbach, R.
1986   *Protestantismo en la Costa Atlantica. La Iglesia Morava de 1949 a 1894.* Hannover: Unpublished manuscript.

Saunders, G.
1988   *Culture and Christianiaty: The Dialectics of Transformation.* Connecticut: Greenwood Press.

Shapiro, J.
1981   "Ideologies of Catholic Missionary Practice." *Comparative Studies in Society and History*, Vol. 23 No. 1 Jan. 1981: 130–149.

Smith, A.M.
1994   "Rastafari as Resistance and the Ambiguities of Essentialism in the 'New Social Movements'," in Laclau, E. (ed.), *The Making of Political Identities*, London: Verso.

Smutko, G.
1975   *Pastoral Indigenista.* Bogota: Ediciones Paulinas.

Smutko, G.
1994   *El Apostolado con los Miskitos (1939–1979).* Chap. 10 of unpublished history of the Vicariate in Nicaragua.

Taussig, M.
1980   *The Devil and Commodity Fetishism in South America.* Chapel Hill: University of North Carolina.

Taylor, A.
1981   "God-Wealth: The Achuar and the Missions," in Whitten, N. (ed.), *Cultural Transformations and Ethnicity in Modern Ecuador.* Urbana: University of Illinois Press.

Thomas, R.K.
1965   "Pan Indianism," in Levine, S. and Lurie, N.O. (eds.), *The American Indian Today.* Florida: Everett/Edwards.

Urban, G. & Sherzer, S. (eds.)
1991   *Nation-States and Indians in Latin America*, Austin: University of Texas Press.

Wallace, A.
1956   "Revitalisation Movements," *American Anthropologist*, 58:264–281.

Warren, K.
1992   "Transforming Memories and Histories: The Meanings of Ethnic Resurgence for Mayan Indians," in Stepan, A. (ed.), *Americas: New Interpretive Essays.* Oxford: Oxford University Press.

Wilde, M.
1989   "Faith and Endurance in Eastern Nicaragua," *Christian Century*, Nov. 1: 973–4.

Worsley, P.
1984   *The Three Worlds: Culture and World Development.* London: Weidenfeld & Nicholson.

Worsley, P.
1968   *The Trumpet Shall Sound.* London: Schocken Books.

Yinger, J.M.
1985   "Ethnicity," *Annual Review of Sociology*, 11:151:80.

ETHNICITY, IDENTITY AND HERMENEUTICS: AN INDIAN TRIBAL PERSPECTIVE

Thanzauva and R.L. Hnuni

1. *Introduction*

In all aspects of life today, it is possible to see a dialectical movement towards unity *and* diversity. This is especially clear in the struggle to combine autonomy in politics and co-operation in economics. Similarly, the movements for contextualisation and ecumenism have become integral parts of contemporary Christianity. In this situation, biblical hermeneutics no longer remains the monopoly of Western scholars; it has local dimension as well. The publication of *Voices From the Margin: Interpreting the Bible in the Third World*, edited by R.S. Sugirtharajah, is one of the concrete examples illustrating that there are multiple ways of reading the Bible. It provides clear supporting evidence for J. Moltmann's claim, "reading the Bible with the eyes of the poor is a different thing from reading it with a full belly."[1] This article is concerned with how the tribal people, the most Christianized ethnic group in India, do read and should read the Bible. In the Indian context, the tribal groups can be seen as distinct from the two dominant communities, the Hindus and Muslims, who first drove them out from their land and subsequently tried to assimilate them ignoring their distinct identity and values.

2. *Ethnicity*

Human societies throughout history have lived with some sense of ethnic classification, but the term "ethnic" has been often used to connote a stigmatized and marginalized group. It is usually a dominant group which refers to another as an "ethnic" community. We will begin this article with a brief investigation of the ways this concept has been used in the Bible and in sociology.

---

[1] J. Moltmann, *The Church in the Power of Spirit* (London: SCM, 1978), p. 17.

2.1 Ethnicity in the Bible

The term *ethnos* and its cognate words, *ethnikos* and *ethne*, were used for nation, people in general, and for the Gentiles as distinct from the Jew or Christians.[2] The use of *ethne* in the New Testament, as a technical term for the Gentiles as distinct from the Jews or Christians, corresponds in some measure to *gerim* in the Hebrew Bible. This is particularly evident in the LXX: *ethnos* is almost always used to translate *ger* and *laos* is used for *'am*.[3] An investigation of the use of *ger* in the Hebrew Bible, and a social description of the *gerim* and their condition, will help us to understand biblical ideas of ethnicity. T.M. Mauch suggested that "sojourner" should be the basic translation of *ger*,[4] but D. Kellerman and Christiana von Houten prefer "alien." F.A. Spina argues for "immigrant."[5] The Israelites were once the aliens (*gerim*) before their settlement in Canaan, and that experience became the basis for their responsibility to care for people from other ethnic groups. "You shall not oppress a stranger (*ger*), for you were strangers (*gerim*) in the land of Egypt" (Exod. 23:9). The term *ethnos*, therefore, with its corresponding Hebrew term *ger*, primarily refers to people who are vulnerable, weak, dependent and marginalized as distinct from the dominant group of a society.

2.2 Ethnicity in Sociology

In much of the older social scientific literature, the biblical notion of the ethnic as alien is more or less maintained.[6] In North America, until the Asian immigrants began to form significant communities, the term was often used to describe the Polish, Italian, Lituanian, Bohemian, Slovakian groups who had common problems, interests and concerns. Today it is used more to describe Cambodians, Vietnamese, Indians, and to a certain extent, the Afrikaners and the

---

[2] G. Bertram and K.L. Schmidt, "ἔθνος, ἐθνικός," in *TDNT*, vol. 2, pp. 364–372.

[3] Bertram, p. 365

[4] T.M. Mauch, "Sojourner," in *IDB*, pp. 397–99.

[5] D. Kellerman, "*ger*" in *TDOT*, pp. 440–442; Christina van Houten, *The Alien in Israelite Law* (Sheffield: JSOT Press, 1991), p. 19; F.A. Spina, "Israelites as gerim: Sojourners in Social and Historical Context," in C.L. Meyer and M. O'Connor (eds.), *The Word of the Lord Shall Go Forth: Essays in Honour of David Noel Freedman in Celebration of his Sixtieth Birthday* (Winona Lake: Eisenbrauns, 1983), pp. 321–35.

[6] B. Dattaray, *Tribal Identity and Tension in North East India* (Guwahati: Western Book Depot, 1989), p. 1.

Amerindians; the European immigrants have been integrated into the mainstream.

Fredrik Barth, on the other hand (who is very influential in modern ethnology), discusses another definition of an ethnic group as a population which (a) is largely biologically self perpetuating; (b) shares fundamental cultural values, realised in overt unity in cultural forms; (c) constitutes a category distinguishable from other categories of the same order.[7] This allows any racial or tribal group that has a common cultural tradition to be "ethnic," without particular reference to a minority or weaker status in society.

In India, ethnicity is not a common term. The term "tribe" and "caste" are commonly used for stratification of the society. Many ethnic groups in India (originally tribals) have been absorbed into the Hindu caste structure in which they became either the low or the out-caste, but now they identify themselves as *dalits*, which primarily means the oppressed people. The remaining tribes, unlike *dalits*, belong neither to Hindu social structure nor to Muslim communities. In their tribal relationships, an ethnic co-existence is conditioned by a mutual repulsion and disdain which nevertheless allows each ethnic community to preserve its dignity. By contrast, the caste structure brings about a social subordination and an acknowledgement of "more honour" in favour of the privileged caste and higher status groups.[8] There is, then, a fundamental difference between the *dalits* and *tribals*. Most of the tribes in India are not immigrants; they are indigenous communities alienated from their land and culture.

3. *The Bible and Tribal Identity*

Tribal religion, known today as primal religion, does not depend on a written Scripture but on the experience of the peoples' encounter with their environment in their day to day life. Rather than reading written Scriptures, they read nature and their own life in order to understand God's intention for them. Their conversion to the scriptural religions, particularly to Christianity, brought about radical changes

---

[7] Fredrik Barth (ed.), *Ethnic Groups and Boundaries: The Social Organization of Cultural Difference* (Boston: Little Brown, 1969), pp. 13ff.

[8] H.H. Gerth and C. Wright Mills (eds.), *From Max Weber: Essays in Sociology* (New York: Free Press, 1958), p. 189.

in their lives and became an important factor for the emergence
of a new tribal identity. At the same time, however, the Bible might
be said to be responsible for the present identity crisis in the tribal
societies.

The translation of the Bible into the tribal languages is not merely
making a written book available in the tribal language; it means much
more than that. Since belief in *mana* (impersonal supernatural power)
is the core of primal religion, the Bible also came to be regarded as
mana, having impersonal supernatural power. In fact, the *Mizo*[9] called
it *Pathian Lehkhabu* (the Holy Book of God) and venerated it so highly
that 35% of the funds raised in India for the Bible Society of India
came from the tiny state of Mizoram. Having this notion of the Bible,
it is not surprising that the tribal churches readily accepted a doctrine of verbal inspiration of Scripture. The Bible for the tribal
Christians is a propositional truth about God and human life super-
naturally communicated to human beings by the Holy Spirit.

The translation of the Bible into the tribal languages has had a
significant impact on the tribal societies. A new common history for
the tribals was created as they shared the same faith and the same
story through the Bible. This broke the barrier of narrow village
mentality and "tribalism," and paved the way for the emergence of
a new and larger tribal identity. The translation of the Bible introduced a common dialect for some tribes, and this has to some extent
helped to overcome linguistic differences.[10] Reading one Bible in one
language was an important factor in the development of tribal
ecumenism, and if a common dialect had not been developed in this
way, the tribals in North East India would have been compelled to
speak and use Bengali.[11] Indeed, it was through the efforts of the
missionaries, and tribal Christians themselves, to enable the Christian community to read the Bible that the literacy rate is signifi-

---

[9] Mizo is a tribal community living in the north eastern corner of India who
embraced Christianity in the beginning of this century. They respect and dearly
love the Bible, and they express this in the composition of many scriptural songs.

[10] The *Awe* dialect was used for the Garo tribe in Meghalaya, the *Cherrapunji*
dialect for the Khasi tribe in Meghalaya, the *Ukhrul* dialect for the Tangkhul Nagas
in Manipur, the *Changki* dialect for the Ao Nagas in Nagaland, the *Duhlian* dialect
for the Mizos in Mizoram, the *Serkawr* dialect for the Mara tribe in Mizoram and
so on.

[11] Since the British administrators had learned Bengali (also spellt "Bangali") and
trained the Bangali people, they had a policy to introduce Bangali as a court language. It was the Christian missionaries who developed and reduced the tribal dia-
lects to written form.

cantly higher among the tribal Christians than their neighbouring peoples. It was this concern which led church leaders in the Khasi Hills to take the decision that no convert would be granted full membership in the church until he/she could read.[12] The translation of the Bible, therefore, made a significant contribution towards social transformation.

Having acknowledged the significant contribution of biblical translation, it is also important to acknowledge that the tribal concept of the Bible also creates enormous problems in the area of hermeneutics. The tribal Christians are mostly biblicists who try to use the Bible as a magical book to solve their problems. The Bible was an important instrument in the search for their own identity, but it also alienated them from their own culture. It is our thesis that since the influence of the Bible has already been felt by the tribals, a fresh hermeneutic could once again produce a socially dynamic and liberating influence in our new historical context. Social identity is, especially in the modern world, dynamic.

4. Tribal Hermeneutics

What kind of hermeneutics will best serve in the tribals in the Indian context?[13] The question of a biblical hermeneutic is not merely how do I know the text but how I know myself in the process of knowing God through the text, and how will I be transformed by that knowledge? Paul Ricoeur, with his idea of the autonomy of the text and its surplus of meaning, provides an appropriate philosophical basis for hermeneutics. As opposed to oral discourse, texts achieve a "semantic autonomy;" they can mean more than what the author intended. "[The author's] intention is often unknown to us, sometimes redundant, sometimes useless, and sometimes even harmful as regards to the interpretation of the verbal meaning of his work."[14] There

---

[12] F.S. Downs, *History of Christianity in India, Vol. 5, Part 5: North East India in the Nineteenth and Twentieth Centuries* (Bangalore: Church History Association in India, 1992), p. 200.

[13] According to Clodovis Boff, biblical hermeneutics means (a) a set of canons of exegesis; (b) actual interpretation of the Bible; and (c) theology. *Theology and Praxis: Epistemological Foundations* (Maryknoll, NY: Orbis Books, 1987).

[14] Paul Ricoeur, *Interpretation Theory: Discourse and the Surplus of Meaning* (Fort Worth: Texas Christian University, 1976), p. 76.

is a distancing of the text from the original audience, and this autonomy from the original readers opens up a range of potential readers and potential interpretations.[15] This approach makes possible a new tribal hermeneutic.

The older (and even many of the present) habits of biblical interpretation amongst the tribals do not, in fact, take the tribal, social and cultural conditions into consideration. As a result, the Bible continues to contribute towards alienation of tribals from their culture. This problem, of adequately addressing the present social and economic problems, has been only dimly perceived in the past.

4.1   *Evidence from Missionary Experience*

In retrospection of their first ten years' experience in Mizoram, the two Baptist missionaries, Rev. J.H. Lorrain and F.W. Savidge, expressed in their report,

> Our first message, as soon as we could speak the language, was to proclaim a Saviour from sin. But the people had no sense of sin and felt no need for such a Saviour. Then, we found a point of contact. We proclaimed Jesus as the vanquisher of the Devil as the One who had bound the "strong man" and taken away from him "all his armour wherein he trusted" and so had made it possible for his slaves to be free. This to the Lushais (now known as Mizos) was "Good News" indeed and exactly met their great need.[16]

It is evident from the statement above that what was considered a meaningful message, for missionaries trained in England, was no longer meaningful when it was preached to a different culture. The task for the two missionaries was to re-interpret the gospel in the context of Mizoram.

4.2   *Inadequacy of Historical-Critical Interpretation*

With the exception of fundamentalist circles, historical criticism remains a dominant method for interpreting the Bible in all theological seminaries. In this approach rationalism reigns supreme, demanding

---

[15] Ricoeur, pp. 29–32.
[16] J. Herbert Lorrain and F.W. Savidge, "After Ten Years: Report for 1913 of the BMS Mission in the South Lushai Hills, Assam," in *The Annual Report of BMS on Mizoram 1901–1938* (Serkawrn: Mizoram Gospel Centenary Committee, 1994), pp. 93–94.

the subjugation of the biblical texts to a critical examination apart from the dogma of ecclesiastical authority. The result has generally been a low estimate of the reliability of the biblical texts, since the world view implied by the texts seem so inferior to the contemporary perspective.[17] H.S. Reimarus and H.E.G. Paul, for example, sought to reconstruct a purely historical life of Jesus, free from the "simple-minded supernaturalism" of the first century.[18] While some scholars emphasized historical factuality of the biblical texts, some entertained the notion that the biblical narratives could be factually erroneous and yet religiously meaningful.[19] This resulted in the hermeneutical method of demythologization by the liberals and the historical reconstruction of events by the conservatives. Neither of these approaches helped the tribal Christians in their self understanding, mission and ministry. Rather, they seemed it to make Christianity more and more irrelevant, precisely because they reflected Western cultural dynamics in response to the Enlightenment.

4.3   Inadequacy of Dialogical Interpretation in India

P.D. Devanandan, Raymond Panikkar, Bishop A.J. Appasamy and others have responded to the religious and ideological pluralism in India. In recent years, Paul Gregorios and Stanley Samartha have argued that we should not take authority of the Christian Scripture as self-evidently valid, rejecting other Scriptures; this would simply invite counter claims from other religious groups. In such a situation, so it is argued, the task of hermeneutics is to work out a larger framework of neighbourly relationships within which the insights of different sacred texts can be related to each other for mutual enrichment, yet without denying their particularities.[20] Similarly, R.S. Sugirtharajah advocates that biblical scholars must be sensitive to the scriptural

---

[17] For further study see W.G. Kümmel, *The New Testament: The History of the Investigation of Its Problems* (tr. S. Maclean Gilmour and Howard Clark Kee; Nashville: Abingdon, 1972); Hans W. Frei, *The Eclipse of Biblical Narrative: A Study in Eighteenth and Nineteenth Century Hermeneutics* (New Haven: Yale University Press, 1974).

[18] Larry Chouinard, "Gospel Christology: A Study of Methodology," *Journal for the Study of New Testament* 30 (1987), pp. 21–37. Albert Schweitzer, *The Quest of the Historical Jesus: A Critical Study of its Progress from Reimarus to Wrede* (New York: Macmillan, 9th printing, 1968), pp. 13–67.

[19] *Ibid.*, p. 22.

[20] S.J. Samartha, *The Search for New Hermeneutics in Asian Christian Theology* (Bangalore: Board of Theological Education of Serampore College, 1987); Paul Gregorios, "Hermeneutics in India Today in the Light of the World Debate," in R.S.

texts of others faith and the spiritual sustenance they provide for
many adherents. They should re-read some of the biblical materials
in the light of the multi-faith context.[21] All of these writers are concerned with discovering truth from other Scriptures and synthesizing
it with Christian truth found in the Scripture, a process which might
be called dialogical hermeneutics. This represents a radical shift from
the approach of "decoding" the biblical texts for people of other
cultures.

While dialogical hermeneutics may be appropriate in pluralistic
contexts, it is not directly relevant in the tribal context. The idea of
Scripture, first of all, is itself alien to the tribals. Moreover, reading
the Hindu, Muslim and Buddhist Scriptures, will be further alienating since these derive from the dominant cultures which impinge on
the tribals. The Bible, on the other hand, has already been internalized and is part of their identity. It would be much more rewarding
for the tribals to read the new "Scriptures" being written by God in
their day-to-day struggle for authentic existence, rather than reading
the ancient texts of other Scriptures.

4.4   Dalit *Hermeneutics as Liberation Hermeneutics in India*

Dalit hermeneutics is one form of liberation herementics in India which
attempts to address the *dalits'* aspiration for liberation. It was the
liberation theologians who developed a new way of interpreting biblical data, and rescued the Bible from abstract, individualized and
"neutralized" reading.[22] Expanding on the insights of Latin American liberation hermeneutics, the *dalit* theologians develop their interpretative style and strategies. While liberation theologians in Latin
America interpret biblical texts to criticise the class structure, the
dalit theologians attack the caste system and support struggle of the
dalits for liberation from the oppressive system.[23] The concern of *dalit*
hermeneutics is similar to that of the tribal hermeneutics: in both
cases liberation is the goal and task of hermeneutics. However, in

---

Sugirtharajah and Cecil Hargreaves (eds.), *Readings in Indian Christian Theology*, Vol. 1
(Delhi: SPCK, 1993), pp. 176–185.
    [21] R.S. Sugitharajah, "Inter-faith Hermeneutics: An Example and Some Implica-
tions," in *Voices from the Margins: Interpreting the Bible in the Third World*, pp. 352–363.
    [22] R.S. Sugitharajah, "Introduction," p. 1.
    [23] D. Carr, "Development of Interpretative Perspective and Academic Study,"
The SATHRI Journal 1 (Jan. 1991), pp. 16–51; M. Azariah, "Doing Theology in
India Today," in *Readings in Indian Christian Theology*, pp. 37–45.

the detailed interpretation of the Bible, tribal hermeneutics has to be distinctive for they have a different agenda and different hermeneutical tasks, as indicated above.

4.5   Tribal Hermeneutics and its tasks

Tribal hermeneutics is certainly a sister hermeneutics of the *dalit* hermeneutics and a part of liberation hermeneutics. But the tribal people read the Bible in the context of an identity crisis—alienation from their land and culture, exploitation and economic dependency. All this requires a re-interpretation of the Bible to address these problems. Unless the tribals are allowed to be different in their interpretation of the Bible, the Bible will not only lose its significance, Christianity will remain superficial without really taking root into the tribal culture. In fact, Christianity is quite visible and popular in the tribal society of North East India, and to a great extent it appears indigenized. In depth study reveals, however, that Christianity has not taken root, deep within the tribal culture. The indigenous forms arise from translation of Western Christianity into the tribal language and context. What is needed, we argue, is a form of Christianity arising from the tribal culture, and this in turn requires tribal hermeneutics.

We may, however, find points of contact with some of the discussions of narrative theology and the reader-oriented criticism influenced, in particular, by Ricoeur and Gadamer. The tribal hermeneutics will treat the biblical texts as narrative statements and the "evangelists" as narrators whose intent is to narrate "the story with certain loaded words, in a certain order, and with various rhetorical techniques, in order to encourage a certain response from the readers."[24] An authentic interpretation involves intensive and sincere listening to the story narrated by the authors, combined with sensitivity to the readers' own context, through which the horizon of the text and the readers' context fuse together, generating a new meaning of the text. This approach abandons any historical-critical concerns for historicity or demythologization and engages with the evangelists' forms of

---

[24] Larry Chouinard, "Gospel Christology: A Study of Methodology," *JSNT* 30 (1987), p. 27. This is obviously different from the form critic who assumes that the evangelists merely framed and combined materials which were already in circulation in the communities before the composition of the Gospels.

the text. The narrative approach maintains the unity of the text and tries to understand how the narrators used various materials for their own purpose. Our own narrative approach is combined with a particular orientation towards the tribal reader: we expect the readers to discover their own mission from, and be inspired by, the story. The hermeneutical task here is not merely understanding—though understanding is a part of the process—but transformation of society.

We are therefore proposing a multi-task hermeneutics, encouraging people to understand themselves in the process of understanding the text, that they may be inspired to respond to the issues that confront them. As F.S. Downs points out, the struggle of tribes in India is mainly for the preservation of their unique identity.[25] In the light of this struggle, the tribal theologians resist traditional interpretations of the Bible which tend to take an "integrationist" approach to minority cultures: we are no more interested in being integrated into an homogeneous hermeneutics than we are into that form of nationalism which tries to integrate diverse cultures into one nation. The attempt to create a tribal hermeneutics is an ongoing struggle for autonomy both in politics and in the interpretation of the Bible.

Having sketched some preliminary suggestions regarding the methodology of tribal hermeneutics, we turn now to the substantial matters of content which concern us—existential problems such as alienation from land, exploitation, economic dependency, and so on.

5. *Tribal Hermeneutical Clues*

Some hermeneutical clues are indicated here to show the possibility of tribal hermeneutics. Our purpose in introducing these examples is not to provide a detailed treatment of the interpretation of the selected texts, but simply to indicate the possibility of tribal hermeneutics.

5.1   *Promised Land*

Alienation from tribal land is a common problem throughout India. Transfer of tribal land to non-tribals is now prohibited, yet this legal strategy fails to protect tribals; the laws are easily circumvented. Many

---

[25] F.S. Downs, "Identity: The Integrating Principle," *Journal of Social Sciences and Humanities of North Eastern Hill University* 9/3 (1991), pp. 7ff.

of the tribes have been reduced to landless wanderers. This situation has to be understood in the context of two competing views of land: while the tribals treat land as an essential part of their communal identity (land can only be "owned" by becoming a member of the community who live in the land), the non-tribals regard it as property which can be owned by legal fiction—bought, sold and claimed.

In this context, the tribals may re-read the following biblical passages concerning the promised land: they may put themselves into the role of the Israelites who have been afflicted and humiliated (cf. Deut. 26:5ff); they also might receive the promise of God which came through Joseph: "God will visit you one day, bring you back to the land which he swore to your fathers, Abraham, Isaac, and Jacob" (cf. Gen. 50:24); they might see an analogy with their own experience when God called the tribal leader Moses and asked, "Go and gather the elders of your own tribe, and say to them, "The Lord, the God of your fathers has appeared to me, saying, 'I have observed you and what has been done to you in this land, and I promise that I will bring you out of this affliction'" (cf. Exod. 3:16–17).

Abraham, Jacob, Joseph and Moses are all landless, but they are caught up in a journey towards the promised land. Their story can shape the tribals' struggle for homeland. Most of the tribal movements in India today—such as the *Jarkhan* movement in Bihar; the *Gurkha* movement in Bengal, the *Bodo* and *Karbi* movement in Assam, the *Kuki* movement in Manipur, the tribal movement in Tripura— are fundamentally struggles for a homeland *in their own land*. Unlike the patriarchal story, this Indian experience represents the hope of returning to a land that was, at an earlier time, already theirs. But the idea of promised land can become an impetus, or a motivating analogy, for the tribals' struggle.

5.2   *Pentecost that Revives and Empowers (Acts 2:1–17)*

The coming of the Holy Spirit on the day of Pentecost revived and transformed the disciples of Jesus Christ. In spite of the fact that the Pentecost movement was the origin of the Christian church, today the revival or charismatic movement has gained very little room in the mainline churches. While the mainline churches have had a very low opinion of revivalism, it is one of the distinctive characteristics of the tribal churches. In spite of constant critiques and objections from missionaries and theologically trained leaders, this element remains.

Renthy Keitzer, and a few other scholars in this region, have rightly observed that the revival movement among the tribal churches is in fact an expression of suppressed traditional animistic religion.[26] Keitzer observes that missionaries in Nagaland were able to suppress tribal emotionalism and traditional religious practice. But in Mizoram, this was not the case; the tribal emotionalism has always been a feature of religious practice from the beginning of Christian influence until today. Instead of suppressing this movement, we should guide and transform it. In this context, it is necessary to re-discover and re-read texts concerning the gift of the Holy Spirit on the day of Pentecost and in the subsequent history of the Church.

The re-reading of texts concerning the gift of the Holy Spirit needs to be undertaken without the rationalist prejudices which so often underlie Western biblical interpretation. The same Holy Spirit is received by different people, and manifested differently, depending on the culture, environment and nature of the society. As far as the scriptural texts are concerned, the Holy Spirit inspires and guides kings, prophets, Jesus Christ, the disciples, the church and individual believers. Here we would like to discuss briefly the work of the Holy Spirit in the tribal context of revivalism.

(a) Revival as inculturation: Today inculturation or indigenization is a central concern of churches in Third World countries. Efforts towards inculturation have been made in India since the inception of Christianity by missionaries like De Nobili, William Carey and many others. While De Nobili tried to identify himself with Hindu Brahmins and used Brahmanical language to present the Christian gospel, Carey translated the Bible into the vernacular languages. Some of the Christian intellectuals, such as Chenchiah, Chakkaraiah and others, used Hindu categories to interpret the Christian gospel. Similarly, Robin Boyd used *advaita* philosophy. The success of these efforts has been limited; the churches remain alienated and Christianity remains a foreign religion in India. Comparatively, the tribal churches in the hills appear much more indigenized. Christianity has become their new identity, and this is reflected in some of the tribal churches who mostly sing their own indigenous Christian songs. It is beyond doubt that the revival movement is the primary factor which internalized Christianity in tribal society. In the tribal context, Christian-

---

[26] Renthey Keitzer, "Common Features of Theological Trends in North East India," *ETC Journal* 4 (1991), p. 28.

ity does not remain a foreign religion. However, this does not mean that Christianity is perfectly indigenized in the tribal areas; it is *comparatively* indigenized. We have to move beyond this situation to contextualize Christianity more fully, for which task a tribal hermeneutics is necessary.

(b) Revival as Praxis: Just as the disciples were empowered by the Holy Spirit on the day of Pentecost to witness, so the first Christians of the tribal community—who felt inferior to others and longed for their old ways of life—were empowered by the revival movement. It was the revival movement that enabled the new converts, a marginalized group of the society, to accept themselves and to take up their mission. In much of the debate about mission in India, the priority of praxis has been emphasized, but most of the churches stand still. It is time to realise that real praxis begins with revival or renewal of the churches.

5.3   *Protection of the Aliens in the Deuteronomic Laws*

Since the laws in Deuteronomy are more comprehensive than those in the Book of Covenant, especially in relation to aliens, we can get a more comprehensive picture of the legal treatment of aliens by focussing on Deuteronomic laws. The references to aliens in Deuteronomy are: 1:16; 5:14; 10:18, 19; 14:21, 29: 16:11, 14; 24:14, 17, 19, 20, 21; 26:11, 12, 13; 27:19; 29:11; 31:12. In Deuteronomy, we find that since the Israelites themselves were once aliens, therefore they must care for the aliens in their own land (24:18, 22; cf. Exod. 22:20; 23:9). The aliens must be helped (Deut. 14:28, 29; 24:19, 20, 21, 22), they must not be oppressed (Deut. 5:12–15), they must be allowed to participate in Covenant ceremonies and worship (29:9, 10; 31:12). Justice must be done to the aliens (Deut. 24:14, 17, 19, 21, 22).

The Israelites are instructed to be kind and generous to the aliens, but it is clear that they do not have the same social standing; the law is made by Israelites and addressed to them. It is only the Israelite who is responsible under the law. The alien cannot enforce the law, but is dependent upon the Israelite to uphold it.[27] Since they are vulnerable they must be protected and helped. All the members

---

[27] Christiana van Houten, *The Alien in Israelite Law*, p. 97.

of the Israel community must be taken care of, including the aliens
so that there should be shalom in the society. Social justice for all is
of paramount importance for the Deuteronomic legal collection. This
concern is made necessary because of the existence of a well-to-do
upper class and an impoverished lower class. In particular, it was the
rise of the monarchy which brought with it a hierarchical social structure. It created a royal family, a national cult, a patrician class centred
in the cities, and a semi-free artisan and peasant class.[28]

As indicated before, the tribals in India may be understood as
"aliens" for the following reasons: (a) they do not belong to the
dominant racial groups of the Aryans and Dravidians; (b) they do
not belong to the major religious communities of the Hindus and
the Muslims; (c) they are a vulnerable minority; (d) landless; (e) dependent upon the assistance of the Central Government, and (f) victims of alienation, oppression and exploitation.

The texts identified above may be understood and applied to the
tribal context in India: the Government policy towards tribal communities should combine both legal protection and promotion. The
British administration adopted a policy of protection, isolating the
tribal communities and protecting them from the interference of others
in tribal affairs. This policy has been continued until recently. The
Central Government's intention today to lift *The Inner Line Regulation*—
introduced in Arunachal Pradesh, Nagaland and Mizoram for the
purpose of protecting the tribal people from others—could well lead
to even greater hardships for the tribals. This will be a radical change
in the tribal policy. Any weaker section of any society will need a
certain degree of protection, without which no emancipation will take
place. Protection must be seen as an integral part of the development process.

Protection, however, important as it may be, is not sufficient in
itself. True protection means empowering the people—caring, teaching, training and organising the people to enable the tribal community to protect themselves. Empowering the tribals would also involve letting them participate in the formulation and execution of
the laws. It would also involve economic development, because economic vulnerability is one of the primary factors which has allowed
oppression of the tribal people. Moving beyond protection to em-

---

[28] Van Houten, p. 93, cf. F.S. Frick, *The City in Ancient Israel* (SBLDS, 36; Missoula:
Scholars Press, 1977), p. 205.

powerment might take us beyond the legal vision of Deuteronomy to encompass Ezekiel's radical exhortation to allot resident aliens an inheritance within the boundaries of the land (47:22–23), thereby allowing aliens to participate in the theology of promised land.

These are just some hints to show the possibility of re-reading and re-interpreting the Bible in the tribal context in India. Rather than contributing towards the alienation of tribal people, the Bible's social and spiritual visions could empower them in their struggle for social transformation.

THE RAINBOW SERPENT, THE CROSS, AND THE FAX MACHINE: AUSTRALIAN ABORIGINAL RESPONSES TO THE BIBLE

Lynne Hume

Some years ago anthropologist Laura Bohannan wrote an article entitled "Shakespeare in the Bush" in which she discussed her own recounting of Shakespeare's *Hamlet* to some Tiv people of West Africa during a stint of fieldwork.[1] She recounted the story because she had been reproved by the Tiv; they had told her many things, they said, and so they would like to hear a story from her. During her story-telling Bohannan was constantly interrupted by questions about the central characters and their kin relationships, as well comments about the appropriateness or inappropriateness of their actions and behaviour according to the Tiv people's own social and moral codes.

Story telling among the Tiv is considered to be an art; their standards are high and the audiences are critical. Thinking that the story of Hamlet was one that was universally intelligible, Bohannan was therefore taken aback at their responses. Before getting too far into the main plot of the story, and while explaining who the characters were, she was interrupted by one of the listeners who made the following statement to the rest of Bohannan's audience:

> I told you that if we knew more about Europeans, we would find they really were very like us. In our country also, the younger brother marries the elder brother's widow and becomes the father of his children. Now, if your uncle, who married your widowed mother, is your father's full brother, then he will be a real father to you. Did Hamlet's father and uncle have one mother?

Bohannan's reaction to this question, which, to the Tiv, was an absolutely vital component of relationships between people and therefore crucial to the story, was to respond, rather uncertainly, that she thought they had the same mother but wasn't sure—the story didn't say, at which point an old man reprimanded her and pointed out that these genealogical intricacies made all the difference to the story

---

[1] Laura Bohannan, "Shakespeare in the Bush," *Natural History* 75 (1966), pp. 28–33.

and that when she returned to her home she must ask the elders of her group about these details. Other omissions of cultural significance were pointed out by the Tiv in the process of her relaying the rest of *Hamlet*.

This conversation about Shakespeare's play, written in a time, place and culture far removed from the worldview and epistemology of the West African Tiv, would no doubt have subsequently altered Bohannan's own understanding of *Hamlet*, and the Tiv reaction exemplifies the multiplicities of meaning according to perspective. The Tiv's re-telling of *Hamlet* is indicative of the cognitive processes of interpretation of a Western literary work in light of another culture's epistemology. Their reaction highlights the importance of locating a text within a cultural context. It is useful to keep this notion in mind when making sense of modern Australian Aboriginal biblical exegeses.

Interpreting the Bible through the lenses of white Westerners, has imparted only one point of view, yet one which, as West[2] points out, has exerted considerable influence, especially when subsequently conveyed through the missionization process to indigenous audiences. If we are to employ indigenous perspectives on the Bible, in a manner similar to the Tiv's interpretation of Shakespeare, we may arrive at a somewhat changed point of view with regard to both the biblical meaning *and* the worldview of Aboriginal Australians. We might even reconsider our own theologies in the wake of such hermeneutics and rediscover a richness to the texts that were hitherto not contemplated. But for the moment, an Aboriginal Australian hermeneutic is still in its infancy, and in light of some of the conflicts between the fundamental premises of traditional Aboriginal religion and Western interpretations of Christianity, it would seem that there exists a huge impasse.

However, Christianity has not only flexed its muscles in other cultures, but has been flexible enough to adapt to many different milieus and has managed to survive, albeit somewhat changed in format, in various cultures throughout the world. It is the purpose of this paper to present some of the complexities of translating scripture in indigenous Australia and ways in which Aborigines are dealing with the issues. Suffice, for now, to pose some introductory questions:

---

[2] Gerald West, "Difference and Dialogue: Reading the Joseph Story with poor and marginalized communities in South Africa," *Biblical Interpretation* 2/2 (1994), p. 160.

What is the basis of "traditional" Aboriginal spirituality? How can we, as Westerners, look through an Aboriginal lens: what parts of the Bible convey themes and concerns which most adequately address those of Aboriginal people, and how are Aboriginal Christians overcoming and communicating these difficulties?

Central features of traditional Aboriginal religion reiterated throughout Australia, in spite of the vastness of the continent and regional variations are: The Dreaming, and the integral link between human-land-Dreaming ancestors-totems. The Dreaming is atemporal; it encompasses the past, the present and the future, and has been referred to as "everywhen" to articulate its ahistoricity. Dreaming events and narratives are abiding and enduring. Dreaming ancestors rose up from beneath the earth to shape and mould into form that which already existed, and their journeys imbued the landscape with special significance. As they paused at certain locations, they left traces of the essence of themselves, transforming the country and endowing it with immanent significance.

Traditionally, individuals gained knowledge of their own spiritual identity—as beings who were manifestations of the sacred essence of a specific geographical location or *place*—through cognitive acquisition from initiated elders. Aborigines thus gained an understanding of their own existential being in terms of *place* and *space*,[3] not in terms of time and linear evolution.

The Dreaming is more precisely referred to as The Law which is the sacred knowledge, wisdom and moral truth permeating the entire *beingness* of Aboriginal life, derived collectively from Dreaming events. This focus on *place*, what Swain[4] has termed "geosophy," is knowledge and wisdom derived through the Dreaming, and is an alien concept for the rational Western mind with its emphasis on temporality, history and a linear progression of factual events.

Relationships were (and are) of prime importance in Aboriginal culture: relationships between people, people and land, people and totems. Places were linked by networks of sacred paths made by Dreaming ancestors on their journeys across the land and subsequently travelled by living Aborigines as they moved across that same territory pursuing a nomadic lifestyle. "Country" needed to be cared for;

---

[3] Tony Swain, *A Place for Strangers* (Cambridge: Cambridge University Press, 1993), p. 2.

[4] Swain, *A Place for Strangers*, p. 25.

paths needed to be "sung" and ancestral journeys dramatically re-
enacted in ritual in order to maintain the cosmic balance. The land-
spirit-human interconnectedness was the essence of Aboriginal identity.

Soon after European settlement more than two hundred years ago,
Christian missionaries arrived in Australia intent on spreading their
interpretations of the Word of God to the "barbarous savages." Convinced of the absolute rightness of their own beliefs and values they
set about imparting a foreign and incomprehensible religion to a people
whose own belief system was far removed from their own. Aboriginal ritual and belief was not recognized as religion but as misguided
or evil practices to be opposed and replaced. The recruitment of
Aboriginal people to mission stations (sometimes by kidnapping
children of mixed descent from Aboriginal mothers) effectively suppressed, in many cases, the use of Aboriginal languages, and contributed to the disintegration of traditional knowledge, especially the
secret-sacred knowledge which necessitated interactions over a long
period of time with knowledgeable elders and the deep spiritual link
to "country" which is an absolute and incontrovertable aspect of
Aboriginal spirituality.

Missionaries of various denominations employed different tactics:
some permitted the retention of cultural elements, recognizing, perhaps, the basic tenets of both belief systems to be of value, while
others aggressively attempted to suppress all traditional customs and
beliefs, adamantly refusing to tolerate any vestiges of traditional lore.
The responses to the missionary presence varied from outright rejection (if choice were possible), to acceptance, or a synthesis of the
Christian message with their own beliefs.

It is therefore not surprising that Aborigines today are attempting
a theology that is based principally upon scriptural references to land,
relationships, links between people and the land, and issues of liberation and freedom from oppression. In the light of a deeper understanding of Western responses to the Bible, Aboriginal theologians
are now beginning to question the validity of European biblical interpretations and are attempting to construct a hermeneutical structure of their own, thus creating an emerging indigenous theology,
one that is culturally relevant and contextually appropriate to the
Aboriginal situation.[5] As yet, however, Aborigines search for equiva-

---

[5] See Lynne Hume, "Delivering The Word the Aboriginal Way: the Genesis of
an Australian Aboriginal Theology," *Colloquium* 25 (1993), pp. 86–95.

lences, excluding dissimilarities or avoiding contentious points in order to circumvent disjunctions between the two belief systems.

Through an Aboriginal Lutheran pastor, George Rosendale, and a Uniting Church Aboriginal minister, Djiniyini Gondarra, we see the hermeneutical process evolving. Rosendale uses Aboriginal symbols and metaphors to translate Aboriginal Dreaming stories in Christian terms, using references from both the Old and New Testaments to convey the essential moral messages contained in both. He discusses several Aboriginal myths containing messages pertaining to moral living, and how easily these relate to specific biblical passages, therefore communicating Christian messages through traditional Aboriginal channels.

Rosendale writes:

> I have been able to understand and communicate Western Christianity [to other Aborigines] because I have been trained in European culture. But it was still very painful for me when I noticed that my people were straining desperately as they attempted to understand and grasp the deep meaning of the gospel. Only when I began to learn their stories and customs and used them as pictures to see and understand the gospel did I notice their faces light up. To hear comments such as: "Aah! It's like our story!" made me very happy to share the gospel with my people.[6]

This type of hermeneutical pedagogy, using mythological analogies to assist in the education of Aboriginal ministers, is also advocated by Don Carrington, Coordinator of Theological Studies at Nungalinya College, Darwin, who reports its success in contributing to Aboriginal understanding of the scriptures. Carrington writes that "vital hermeneutical insights are gained when there is a lightning flash of insight by people who are thinking about and living out these stories."[7] This is perhaps best illustrated by the aforementioned quotation of George Rosendale.

Moralising, pointing to exemplary figures, or drawing out certain principles, are not enough in themselves, as Carrington rightly indicates. To convey the original impact and authenticity of the biblical message one needs to work creatively with another story or symbol that "produces a comparable dynamic in a contemporary cultural

---

[6] George Rosendale, "Reflections on the Gospel and Aboriginal Spirituality," *Occasional Bulletin* [Darwin: Nungalinya College] 42 (1989), pp. 1–7.

[7] Don Carrington, "Jesus' Dreaming: Doing Theology through Aboriginal Stories" in J. Houson (ed.), *The Cultured Pearl: Australian Readings in Cross-Cultural Theology and Mission.* (Melbourne: Victorian Council of Churches, 1986), pp. 261–272.

milieu."[8] To this end, the College's distance education scheme, which educates Aboriginal ministers while they remain at their community base enables them to combine Christian ideology with Christian praxis in the appropriate cultural setting thereby transposing the message into a meaningful Aboriginal context.

The Reverend Djiniyini Gondarra, an Elcho Islander and the first Aborigine to be ordained in the Uniting Church in Australia with full theological training, has also lectured at Nungalinya College. Gondarra is probably the best-known writer and champion of Aboriginal Christianity. He is aware that the Western approach to theology has both its plums and its pits, and points out that Western theology is "moulded by Western philosophies" (thus echoing Gerald West), and "preoccupied with intellectual concerns, especially those having to do with faith and reason."[9] Gondarra believes that Westerners reduce the Christian faith to abstract concepts which might have answered the questions of the past, but which fail to deal with today's issues—such as land rights, racism and oppression, and social problems such as alcohol abuse—and have done little to change these situations.

Gondarra sees the need for reconciling the tension between traditional Aboriginal values and Western values. He advocates breaking away from the individualism and rationalism of Western theology in order to allow "the Word of God to work with full power" and to fulfill its task in the Aboriginal Church. He also lays much emphasis on the notions of power and freedom, quoting biblical texts to articulate the powerlessness of the Aboriginal people in the face of colonial imperialism and the need for freedom from oppression. He sums up evangelical theology in quite an orthodox manner: the love and justice of God; the uniqueness and finality of Jesus Christ; the regenerating and empowering of the Holy Spirit; the need for repentance and faith; the life and witness of the church; and a belief in the personal return of Jesus Christ. At the same time, however, he sees in the Western church context "captivities" which have to be overcome.

On the question of an Aboriginal theology his answer is that Christ must be promoted as "the living and acceptable part of their own [Aboriginal] ceremony and culture" and that Aboriginal Christian

---

    [8] Carrington, "Jesus' Dreaming," p. 270.
    [9] Djiniyini Gondarra, "Overcoming the Captivities of the Western Church Context," in *The Cultured Pearl*, pp. 176–182.

leaders need to "plant Christ in Aboriginal soil rather than transplant Western forms of Christianity."[10] He quotes the Hebrew Bible with analogies to the Aboriginal situation in what may be called a discussion of Aboriginal hermeneutics. He cites 2 Samuel 12, the story of the poor man's lamb being taken by the rich man, as one with which Aborigines can readily identify. In this story, the poor are equated with the Aborigines and the rich are seen as white Australians.

Even more pertinent to the Aboriginal situation is the biblical example in 1 Kings 21 of the abuse of power by both civil and religious authorities. The story of Naboth's vineyard relates to the possession of Naboth's land by King Ahab of Samaria. One can see how Aborigines easily identify this biblical passage with their own situation. When Ahab demands that Naboth give him his vineyard and vegetable garden, Naboth replies:

> The Lord forbid that I should give you my ancestral heritage.

After Naboth is stoned to death, Gondarra point out:

> Elijah is told, "Go to King Ahab of Samaria. You will find him in Naboth's vineyard, about to take possession of it. Tell him that I the Lord, say to him, 'After murdering the man, are you taking over his property as well?' Tell him that this is what I say: 'In the very place that the dogs licked up Naboth's blood they will lick up your blood!'"
> When Ahab saw Elijah, he said, "Have you caught up with me, my enemy?" "Yes" Elijah answered. "You have devoted yourself completely to doing what is wrong in the Lord's sight."

The obvious connection made here is to the past mistreatment of Aborigines at the hands of whites, and the dispossession of Aboriginal land. Gondarra believes that there is conflict between human law and the law of God, and it is the duty of Christians to "confront the injustice of the oppressive and unjust laws and to obey God."[11] He then elucidates on the theme of freedom as being the keynote of Christ's mission to the world. Here we can see parallels with liberation theology. He sees that Christ's message is really focussed on the unfree, the poor, the captive, the oppressed and those who are deeply hurt. He equates the poor with the Aborigines and cites Luke 16:19–24, the parable of the poor man Lazarus who desired to be fed the crumbs from the rich man's table, as pertinent to the Aboriginal situation:

---

[10] Gondarra, "Captivities," p. 177
[11] Gondarra, "Captivities," p. 179.

I see the poor man Lazarus is like the black Australians who are struggling to maintain their identity in the midst of the foreign white man's
world.

The appeal is for release from oppression. He quotes Galatians 5:1:

For freedom Christ has set us free; so stand firm and do not submit
again to the yoke of slavery.

The theme of freedom from white domination is quite clear in
Gondarra's article. The terms "power, oppressed, deprived" recur
frequently in this discourse. The notion of powerlessness is one which
has particular relevance to Aboriginal people as they have felt completely powerless in the past. The "good news" is that freedom can
be brought about by the freedom that Jesus Christ advocated.
Gondarra then proceeds to discuss how denominational fragmentation of the Christian message created disunity among Aborigines and
contributed to their powerlessness. He advocates an Aboriginal theology in order to effect an Aboriginal Christian solidarity.

In a recent publication,[12] George Rosendale compares Aborigines,
who were forced off their homeland area into one which suited white
Australians, with the Israelites in Egypt. Rosendale refers to Exod.
3:1-10 as being of relevance:

God saw how the Egyptians were oppressing them. He heard their
cry. With his eyes he saw what was going on in that place. He saw
and heard. He said to Moses, "I am coming to rescue my people. I
am sending you to do that for me."

When he hears this story, he says, he often thinks of the history of
Hopevale.[13] The Israelite story, he says, is very much like Aboriginal
history:

We were taken from our land and brought down to Woorabinda. We
had to live in exile and people threw stones at us. I see not only our
life and Hopevale, but my life as an individual very much like this.

[12] George Rosendale, *Spirituality for Aboriginal Christians* (Darwin: Nungalinya College, 1993), p. 19.
[13] A Lutheran mission station first established near Cape Bedford, North
Queensland, in the 1880s. Later the mission was moved to Hope Valley, then in
1943 the mission people were shipped south, without warning, some to Palm Island
and some to Woorabinda (near Rockhampton, south-central Queensland), a government settlement for Aboriginal people established in 1926. Around 1951 some of
the Woorabinda people who were descendents of Cape Bedford Aborigines, chose
to move back to Hopevale.

The white people came and took these kids from their mothers' arms, sent them away never to be seen again. Just imagine the pain and suffering the parents had to go through. Where it affected them most was in the area of their spirituality.

Nowadays, in the 1990s, many urban-dwellers and those whose parents and grandparents grew up on a mission station, have very tenuous links to a "traditional" Aboriginal spiritual heritage and possess only a vague knowledge of the beliefs and ritual activities of their ancestors, having been denied access to this knowledge through the processes of missionization, modernization and urbanization. For some Aborigines, Christianity is their first religion, having been indoctrinated into the missionary message and enculturated into Western ways for two or more generations. Some negate the plausibility or even desirability of looking to traditional beliefs as an essential ingredient of their own lives.

The Reverend Eddie Law, a Uniting Church minister and an Aborigine, takes an approach which attempts to reconcile the two belief systems. Born and raised on the outskirts of Eidsvold, a small town inland from the coastal town of Bundaberg and Maryborough in south-east Queensland, he learned about traditional Aboriginal spirituality from his grandfather and later trained in Christian ministry at the Uniting Church's Nungalinya College.

His own way of synthesizing tradition and Christianity is to reflect on stories his grandfather told him and to relate these incidents to passages in the Bible. He works with his own people in the Brisbane area, usually by first recounting an Aboriginal story and then looking to the Bible for equivalences, instead of the reverse. Often he meets with people in a Brisbane park frequented by Aboriginal people and tells them Dreaming stories and their scriptural equivalences. The story-telling *modus operandi*, in an outdoor setting, promotes a typically Aboriginal style of discourse.

Eddie Law's own conversion experience is interesting to relate since it included components of both Christianity and Aboriginal culture and influenced his ministerial approach. Before doing so, however, it is necessary to give a brief description of one relevant aspect of Aboriginal culture: the *wandjina*, a figure from antiquity which appears in cave and rock art in certain regions of Australia; this figure is pertinent to Law's conversion.

There is no English equivalent which appropriately conveys the notion of *wandjina*, described variously by anthropologists as: a generalized power, a vital, (yet often destructive) personified force, both regenerative and reproductive, a force which is in both nature and in human beings.[14] A comparable notion is *ungud*, usually portrayed graphically as a rainbow, or a rainbow serpent. The region in which the word *ungud* is used is remarkable for paintings of *wandjina*—images of heads surrounded by an aura of rays emanating from the head, bounded by a horse-shoe shaped curved line; the faces have eyes and a nose but no mouth and sometimes lack bodies. The word *ungud* is put to many uses: sometimes it means a person, sometimes a far-off time, so it corresponds to The Dreaming, and is used as an ultimate explanation of things as they are.[15] *Ungud* makes spirit babies and brings them down in the rain, and *wandjina* pictures are *ungud*.

In order to explain the synthesis between Aboriginal culture, Aboriginal spirituality and Christianity, Eddie Law interprets these *wandjina* as visions that "clever men" or medicine men experienced (and then conveyed through their art) of humankind being made in God's image, thus skilfully bending and shaping an intrinsically traditional Aboriginal concept into a well-formulated Christian belief.

Like many other Aborigines who have turned to Christianity as a means of release from alcohol,[16] Eddie had a sudden conversion one night while extremely intoxicated. His own accounts of this night parallel those of many others. During the conversion experience (the incident which led him to become a born again Christian) a Church of Christ minister, whose name was David Birrell, spoke to him about Christ accepting him just the way he was:

> The night I gave my heart to the Lord, I was blind, blind drunk and this minister guy came up to me and said, "give your heart to the Lord Eddie." I said, "Ah no, wait till I sober up, then I will. He said, "Ah no, God wants you the way that you are, he will take you." All the while I knew there was God and I had nowhere else to turn. I said, "O.K. I will give my life to Christ." Straight away I stood up, no

---

[14] Kenneth Maddock, "The World-Creative Powers," in M. Charlesworth, H. Morphy, D. Bell and K. Maddock (eds.), *Religion in Aboriginal Australia* (St. Lucia: University of Queensland Press, 1992), p. 97.

[15] Maddock, "World-Creative Powers," p. 97.

[16] See for example, Lynne Hume, "Christianity Full Circle: Aboriginal Christianity on Yarrabah Reserve," in T. Swain, and D.B. Rose (eds.), *Aboriginal Australians and Christian Missions* (Adelaide: Australian Association for the Study of Religions, 1988), pp. 250–262; Maggie Brady and Kingsley Palmer, "Dependency and Assertiveness: Three Waves of Christianity among Pitjanjatjara People at Ooldea and Yalata," in *Aboriginal Australians and Christian Missions*, pp. 236–249.

> more drink after that, never touched a drink. I felt a clean feeling all
> through me. That man who came to me [the minister guy] his name
> was Birrell.

What is different about Eddie Law's conversion is his later interpretation of the experience when he was sober. He realised that "Birrell"
had the same sound as the Goreng word *birril* which has the same
meaning as *wandjina*. Law explained, and sketched, *birril's* visual appearance as exactly like that of the *wandjina*: a face with two eyes
and nose but without a mouth, with rays emanating from the outline
of the face. While other Aboriginal Christian conversion narratives
tell of seeing or sensing images of Christ, or a Christ-like figure,
Law's was intriguingly different as it synthesised the two belief systems in a most remarkable way. He interpreted his encounter with
David Birrell (whom he subsequently felt to be symbolic of *birril*) as
a calling from God, after which he turned to Christ and espoused a
Christian lifestyle, and some time later attended Nungalinya College
to train for the ministry.

The sketch he drew to illustrate *Birril/wandjina* he described as:

> around the edges, red ochre, the divisions represent the future blood
> of what was to come, each painted different colours: red, black, yel-
> low—representing different races. We know in our mind, the future to
> come was Jesus Christ.

The *wandjina* of traditional Aboriginal culture is thus depicted as *encoding
prophetic images* of the coming of Christ to Aborigines. Eddie feels that
the *wandjina* was a type of Aboriginal revelation akin to that experienced by John the Baptist. What Eddie Law calls *Birril* is the same,
he says, as this image of the *wandjina*, which is the same thing as
ungud and is a rainbow, which he further interprets as symbolic of
the covenant God established with his people after the flood, mentioned in Genesis 9:12–16:

> God added: "This is the sign that I am giving for all ages to come, of
> the covenant between me and you and every living creature with you.
> I set my bow in the clouds to serve as a sign of the covenant between
> me and the earth. When I bring clouds over the earth, and the bow
> appears in the clouds, I will recall the covenant I have made between
> me and you and all living beings, so that the waters shall never again
> become a flood to destroy all mortal beings. As the bow appears in the
> clouds, I will see it and recall the everlasting covenant that I have
> established between God and all living beings—all mortal creatures
> that are on earth."

Thus, says Law, God's covenant with Aboriginal people was revealed to them through the Dreaming concept of the rainbow:

> God put covenant in the rainbow, so rainbow and Birril, represent: God didn't live here [in Australia] and leave. He made a covenant. If you look in Acts 17:26, you will see that it says: From one man god created all races of mankind and made them live throughout the Earth. He himself fixed the set time and the limit of places they would live. He placed Aborigines in Australia. God made covenant with Aboriginal people in this land, giving us culture and spirituality so we can look for him through our culture. Our culture and your culture all point towards the same god.[17]

The link between the rainbow of Aboriginal lore and the biblical covenant is also espoused by Rosendale:[18]

> What happened afer the flood, when Noah came out? God made covenant. What was the sign of the covenant? THE RAINBOW. In my language [Guugu Yimithirr] we call this rainbow "Yirmbal"[19] and in the Kimberleys they call him "Wandjina." In other places they call him different names.
>
> When we Aborigines talk about rainbow, we have a rainbow-God and all the stories about it. Now what God says in the covenant sign is that he's not going to send flood any more, that he's not going to destroy mankind any more like he did. He repented, he was sorry he destroyed his own creation. So he sent us his Son.

Both Eddie Law and George Rosendale are synthesising The Dreaming and biblical tradition. Further, Eddie Law feels that the absence of a mouth in the *wandjina* figures symbolizes the voice God gave to Aboriginal elders to live in accordance with divine law and teach it to Aboriginal people, enabling them to evangelize in an Aboriginal way, just as Christian evangelists spread the word of God to their people. He suggests that those who accept Jesus as Lord and Saviour also become the mouth. The theme of communication is further taken up by Eddie Law to express his understanding of totems. He sees totems as the connecting link between God, people and land.

Totems, he says, were given to the people by God to remind them of their own cultural values and, like angels, are messengers of God:

---

[17] Interviews with Reverend Eddie Law conducted by several students at University of Queensland in September 1994, and by the author in April 1995.

[18] Rosendale, *Spirituality for Aboriginal Christians*, pp. 5 and 9. On pages 9 and 49 of this monograph are illustrations of the *wandjina*.

[19] "Yirmbal" means both "rainbow" and "rainbow serpent" and refers also to an amethyst python which lives underground in water channels. [Personal communication, Professor Bruce Rigsby, Department of Anthropology and Sociology, University of Queensland].

e.g., two angels were sent by God to save Lot in response to Abraham's plea for help; stars (stars are also Aboriginal totems) guided the Wise Men to Jesus' birthplace. Other instances of symbolic divine communication are also reflected in the cry of a totemic bird which warns of immanent danger or conveys a message to Aboriginal people that a relative is ill or about to die. Thus, totems provide communication between God and people through the medium of nature, and are God's fax machines:

> If we look at the birth of Jesus, no telephone or fax machine to tell people. God spoke to the people in what they were doing, in the same way he spoke to the Aboriginal people, through their cultural values . . . so our totems become like a fax machine.

This is an innovative way of linking modern technology, Aboriginal concepts and Christianity around the central and essential message of communication between the transcendent and the human, via the animal kingdom—though perhaps sliding over the intricacies and complexities of each one in a kind of postmodern pastiche. Both the fax machine and the totem become metaphors for human links to God.

Law, and other Aboriginal ministers, believe that there are ways in which the gospel can and should be preached to Aborigines without destroying their own ancestral culture, ways which most missionaries failed to recognize. When Law became a Christian in the early 1980s and began studying the Bible, he became aware of similarities between Aboriginal culture and materials in both the Old and New Testaments. He made correspondences between The Dreaming stories and the parables of Jesus; just as Jesus used events from people's daily lives to convey meaningful messages, the parables could be likened, he thought, to the everyday life experiences of Aboriginal people.

Law feels that Aborigines *can* continue to follow their own spirituality while being Christians, and in fact, when they retain their culture they are more complete people because they know who and what they are. He recited Acts 17:26 as indicative of the quality of all humans:

> God made from one the whole human race to dwell on the entire surface of the earth, and he fixed the ordered seasons and the boundaries of their regions.

The idea of boundaries is one that is also adopted by George Rosendale, who sees boundaries as marking off those sacred Aboriginal areas whose access is permitted only to knowledgeable, initiated men. He reads into Exod. 19:12, 21, 24 specific understandings of ancient sacred boundaries:

> Mark a boundary around the mountain that the people must not cross. (v. 12)
> Go down and warn the people not to cross the boundary ... if they do, many will die. (v. 21)
> Go down and bring Aaron back with you. But the priests and the people must not cross the boundary ... (v. 24)

The sacredness of land to Aboriginal people is of paramount importance to traditional spirituality and is of increasing political importance in a country like Australia which bases many of its economic assets on mining and other land-exploitative industries. Land has become a sensitive and explosive political issue. To the Western mind, land is to be controlled and used for its economic riches; to Aborigines it is there, not to be owned, but to be "looked after." Aborigines speak of "taking care of country;" there is the notion of guardianship of land rather than ownership. It is therefore not surprising that biblical materials which deal with land are investigated by Aboriginal theologians.

George Rosendale[20] highlights the role of Aborigines as caretakers of the land:

> When we talk about land, we say, this is our land. Actually it is not our land, we are *caretakers* of this land. Each family within that tribe has certain responsibilities in caring for the land.

He makes an admirable attempt[21] at extracting from scripture this notion of guardianship when he writes that God gave mankind *responsibility* for the land, reading Gen. 2:15:

> Then the Lord God placed the man in the Garden of Eden to cultivate it and guard it ...

and commenting:

> See what God said to him, "*cultivate it and guard it.*" They [Aborigines] guarded it when Captain Cook came here but the guns had the best of it.
> Why are the Aborigines angry about land? Right back through the generations God gave it to their ancestors to *look after*. Naboth would not sell that land because he had no right to sell that land, it wasn't his. Powerful King Ahab wanted it for himself. It was the same with

---

[20] Rosendale, *Spirituality for Aboriginal Christians*, p. 2.
[21] Rosendale, *Spirituality for Aboriginal Christians*, pp. 5, 13.

Aborigines. That land has been handed down to him through his ancestors. You see why there is so much pain today with us? Because the same thing has happened here, some powerful fellow comes along and he takes the land.

. . . They killed our grandfathers for this land. So there's going to be pain and suffering for a long long time . . . There's no compensation, nothing for it, and there's no reconciliation with us. We'll be arguing about land for the next hundred years if we don't go back to God the Saviour.

The importance of *place* and its precedence in Aboriginal thought is again brought to the fore by Djiniyini Gondarra:[22]

The people of the Bible understood the significance of a sacred place. Sacred places in Israel were places where worship of Yahweh was deepened and personal renewal was experienced. Their understanding of places where the law was retained and remembered is very close indeed to the understanding the Aboriginal peoples have of sacred sites. In Aboriginal culture, when persons approach a sacred site, a sacred object, or a totem, it is as if they are approaching the tablets of stone Moses brought down from the mountain.

The central importance of place and landforms to Aboriginal spirituality creates, however, a stumbling block when the attempt is made to include this aspect in any search for cultural equivalences. Guboo Ted Thomas tries but somehow fails to convince. In his article,[23] Thomas takes us for a walk in a part of south-eastern Australia to point out the importance of the land, even in the modern context, for Aboriginal people and the special reverence for certain sites and natural land formations. As he says, "one can sense spiritual significance and the presence of spirits." Sacredness, power and energy seem to emanate from nature, and rocks take on meaning the more you dwell on them:

Seeing these faces in the rocks is what I call the spirit. When you are there you get a feeling of our ancestors roaming all through the area thirty or forty thousand years ago.

In fact, some places are so powerful, says Thomas, that if you touch them "your hand will be pushed to the ground." That, he says, is "Koorie [Aboriginal] power." The rocks were not made by human

---

[22] Djiniyini Gondarra and Don Carrington, "Commentary on 'Sacred Sites'," in R.A. Evans and A.F. Evans (eds.), *Human Rights* (Maryknoll: Orbis, 1983), pp. 113–118.

[23] Ted Guboo Thomas, "The Land is Sacred: Renewing the Dreaming in Modern Australia," in G.W. Trompf (ed.), *The Gospel is not Western: Black Theologies from the Southwest Pacific* (Maryknoll: Orbis, 1987), pp. 90–94.

hands but by the Almighty. The sharp distinction between Aboriginal and European reverence towards the land is poignantly articulated in his last paragraph. When he showed the sacred areas of his valley to people from the Department of Forestry they failed to understand what is to Aborigines the sacred meaning of *place*, instead:

> I could see in their eyes they had no clue as to what I was talking about. They wanted to see stained-glass windows or statues of angels— something like that would make a place sacred.

Thomas's description of his feelings towards the land are aptly conveyed to the sensitive reader, but when he compares the close connection between Aboriginal spirituality and the land and the sacredness of the land in biblical accounts, the latter somehow do not quite connect. For example, he sees the mountains as important in the Bible because Moses was given the commandments when he went up on a mountain; water gushed out when Moses struck a rock; Jesus went up in to the mountains to pray; most churches have been built on top of hills. However, in making this link between biblical references and land formations, he is making a rather large hermeneutical leap.

What Aboriginal theologians fail to address, except for Rosendale's attempt, is the question of Aboriginal guardianship or stewardship of land, which is the heart and soul of Aboriginal spirituality; theological arguments which attempt to address this issue become superficial and tenuous. The Dreaming contains concepts and events that are not comparable with Christianity and only marginally more analogous with material in the Hebrew Bible. The land and The Dreaming are one and are linked by a spiritual kinship such that it is impossible to separate one from the other; animals, birds, country, humans, and ancestors are inextricably linked for all time. This, together with the secret-sacred nature of The Dreaming, is the insurmountable obstacle to a thorough synthesis of Christianity and traditional Aboriginal spirituality. Non-initiated men may not have access to, or knowledge of, the secrets, and they are unlikely to be held by a trained Aboriginal Christian minister.

While a fully Aboriginal theology is yet in its infancy, and we have yet to see a more comprehensive Aboriginal exegesis as far as the written word is concerned, there are, doubtlessly, oral interpretations which can be gained through more research in Aboriginal Christian communities, especially research undertaken by Aboriginals.

Oral and visual media of communication fit more comfortably with Aborigines, and these would be profitable avenues for research. We already have some outstanding examples of visual imagery which conveys Christian themes in Aboriginal artwork. Rosemary Crumlin's *Aboriginal Art and Spirituality*[24] contains several paintings by Aboriginal artists: "Crucifixion" (artist Mawalan Marika), "The Crucifixion of Jesus" (Naidjiwarra Amagula), "The Ascension of Jesus" (Naidjiwarra Amagula), "The Dead Christ in the Tree" (Hector Sundaloo Djandulu), "Christ and the Battle" (Paddy Williams), "Moses and God and the Ten Commandments" (Jarinjanu David Downs), "Last Journey of Jesus" (Greg Mosquito and other Balgo men) and "Stations of the Cross" (Miriam-Rose Ungunmerr-Baumann). Each one of these paintings uses traditional techniques and forms and incorporates Aboriginal motifs—Australian country in abstract form, totemic animals and birds, death as a tree burial, and Ungunmerr-Baumann's depictions of Jesus show a Christ in abstract form with a head not unlike the *wandjina*. These works of art demonstrate that the spirituality of Aborigines is often a synthesis of traditional rituals and ceremony with more recent Christian stories.[25]

Some of these paintings could best be described as icons. Anglican Bishop John Lewis's reaction to pictorial representations of visions seen by Yarrabah Christians was that they were similar to church iconography.[26] The icon belongs to the domain of revelation and is a pictorial realisation of the Word. Thus, the work of an iconographer has not only an artistic dimension, but an intellectual and theological one. Like scripture, an icon has an ontological dimension, providing spiritual communion for those who contemplate it; it is a window through which the viewer can contemplate deity and the mysteries which the iconic image suggests. Icons usually portray an admixture of the human and the divine and can evoke strong emotions of a spiritual nature through contemplation. They combine sense impressions with spiritual intuitions in a way which scriptural words may not, especially for peoples whose cultural knowledge is not derived from written sources.

---

[24] Rosemary Crumlin (ed.), *Aboriginal Art and Spirituality* (Melbourne: Collins Dove, 1991).

[25] Crumlin, *Aboriginal Art and Spirituality*, p. 42.

[26] See Lynne Hume, *Yarrabah: Christian Phoenix*. (Unpublished Ph.D. dissertation; Brisbane: University of Queensland, 1990), pp. 203–204.

This is particularly pertinent to peoples such as Aboriginal Australians whose tradition of imparting secret-sacred knowledge is principally through material images such as bark paintings, cave paintings, sacred objects and the natural environment. The Aboriginal world is alive with evidence of the creative ancestors; beings who roamed the land and metamorphosed into the landscape itself, resting at certain places and imbuing the land with the essence of their sacredness. There is an intimate association of painted images and the powers they represent. Dreaming stories of the travels of these ancestors are conveyed through images which mean very little to non-Aborigines but have multiple levels of meaning to Aboriginal people themselves, the knowledge painted into the image being "read" at several levels: one level may be the appreciation of a Dreaming story as a type of geographical map; another level may convey a certain amount of knowledge required to adequately "read" the story (the particular myth surrounding this ancestor and his travels); yet a third level of meaning would be realised by one who is initiated, and certain items within the painting itself would relay the mystery and knowledge permitted only to those few.

Iconography is therefore a particularly relevant way of conveying an Aboriginal theology. Using Aboriginal styles of graphic imagery (albeit with modern technology and materials), the essence of the message is conveyed in a peculiarly Aboriginal way. Paintings such as those by Patricia Marrfurra ("Easter"), and Dominica Katyirr ("Christ is Born") are demonstrative of this style of art. These two women, among several others, form part of Merrepen Arts, an enterprise of the Aboriginal women of Nauiyu, Daly River, Northern Territory who are well known for their artwork and have become self supporting by marketing greeting cards from the designs of their own paintings.

Marrfurra's "Easter" (figure 1) is abstract. At top centre is an ovoid, with rays emanating from it in much the same way as tracks are depicted in a painting of a traditional mythological story. The colours are black, white and ochreous reds and yellows. The impression one gets from looking at this painting is one of an essential central eminence from which all things emerge. Marrfurra's explanation of her painting is that the focus is on Jesus as the Light of the World, through the Resurrection. Black and white represent the sorrows and joys of Christ's journey through life. Palms are strewn in his honour and the blaze of light is the risen Christ.

1. *Easter.* © Patricia Marrfurra (artist), 1993.

2. *Christ is born.* © Dominica Katyirr (artist), 1991

Katyirr's "Christ is Born" (figure 2) is of a dark brown baby lying in a paperbark crib within the centre of a circle from which four straight lines emerge and extend to the sides of the picture. Four diagonal wavy lines, again like tracks, emanate from the baby's bed to reach to each of the corners of the painting. They represent the way in which rain brings new life to the earth as Jesus represents New Life. The wave from top right to left is a new rainbow, again a reminder of Jesus. The central circle is painted in white, brown, black and ochreous reds and yellows to show that Christ was born for all people of the earth.

The typicality of Aboriginal traditional designs are present in both these paintings, as well as in those painted by many other women of Merrepen Arts. The paintings vary from totally abstract to more graphic figures which resemble the mother and child iconography of Byzantine influence. In all these paintings, landscape, flora and fauna are graphically or figuratively Australian. The essence of Aboriginal Australia is blended with the essence of Christianity, as perceived by these artists.

Jerry Jangala's "The Christmas Story" (described as a Warlpiri Iconograph)[27] contains the essence of the story of the birth of Christ, mixed with the Aboriginal importance of landscapes. God (as three persons) sends an angel to Mary and Joseph in Nazareth; donkey and human tracks mark the path they take to Bethlehem; a shining star shows the three wise men travelling on camels to Bethlehem and returning to their country by another route; angels appear to shepherds around their campfire; Mary and Joseph flee with the baby from Bethlehem to Egypt and return eventually to Nazareth. Throughout the total picture all characters are represented as abstract U-shapes (traditional artistic symbols for persons) and the voyage throughout is marked by human and animal tracks. Both story-telling and painting are traditional means of passing on knowledge and they are being synthesized to convey Christian messages in an appropriately Aboriginal way.

The postmodernists have warned us of the power and peril of discourse, of its temporality and uncertainties. But it is perhaps through the medium of images, rather than discourse, that some meaningful coalitions can be formed between two disparate worldviews. As we

---

[27] Reproduced in John Harris, *One Blood: 200 Years of Aboriginal Encounter with Christianity, a Story of Hope* (Sutherland: Albatross Books, 1990), p. 799.

absorb the beauty of ancient works of art and listen to the music of past centuries, the tension between discourse and cognition dissipates and is replaced by an intuitive cognitive concordance. The perils of interpreting the nuances of meaning through the distortions of translations from one language to another, and through time and space, are somewhat displaced by the *image* which conveys polyvalent messages through the medium of unspoken symbols.

Conclusion

Although some Aborigines regard Christianity as a "Whitefella" religion, for many it is the religion of their parents and their chosen religion. Aboriginal Christians are therefore searching for their own understandings of Christian scriptures without the cultural baggage of the Whites. The future directions for Aboriginal Christian leaders, as envisaged by Gondarra, Law, Rosendale and others, is powerful biblical preaching, replacing what they regard as intellectual games of the Whitefellas with a simplicity of speech and deep personal experience; the intellectual approach they regard as particularly White. Aboriginal people want the freedom to make their own decisions and to organize themselves in an Aboriginal way, which means bringing indigenous cultural components into meetings, services and in all areas of organization.

It is a curious irony that while Aboriginal Christians are trying to equate an imposed belief system with their own very ancient past, many non-Aborigines have become disillusioned with Christianity and are looking to indigenous belief systems (such as Amerindian and Aboriginal), and to an ancient Celtic pagan past, to create a new spiritual identity for themselves. Aboriginal Guboo Ted Thomas, who takes white folk into the bush to partake in a Renewing of the Dreaming ceremony at Wallaga Lakes[28] realized this anomaly when he said "I try to show them that we are part of the trees, part of the bush, part of everything, and it is wonderful, *because this is what so many whites are searching for* in Australia."[29]

To return, finally, to the beginning, let us allow the Tiv of West

---

[28] He reports that in spring and summer over a hundred non-Aboriginal people participate in this revival at the lakes and in the mountains.

[29] Thomas, "The Land is Sacred," p. 94 (my emphasis).

Africa to have the last word. At the completion of Laura Bohannan's account of Shakespeare's *Hamlet*, the old man made soothing noises and poured her some more beer, saying:

> You tell the story well, and we are listening. But it is clear that the elders of your country have never told you what the story really means. No, don't interrupt! We believe you when you say your marriage customs are different, or your clothes and weapons. But people are the same everywhere.
>
> Listen and I will tell you how it was and how your story will go, then you may tell me if I am right. Sometime you must tell us some more stories of your country. We, who are elders, will instruct you in their true meaning, so that when you return to your own land your elders will see that you have not been sitting in the bush, but among those who know things and who have taught you wisdom.

READING AS A PHILISTINE: THE ANCIENT AND MODERN HISTORY OF A CULTURAL SLUR

David Jobling and Catherine Rose

Edward Said subtitles a review article on Michael Walzer's *Exodus and Revolution* "A Canaanite Reading" (Said, 1988; Walzer, 1985). Writing as a Palestinian, Said critiques the logic whereby Walzer applies the biblical "exodus" paradigm first to liberation in general, and then to the politics of modern Israel. The problem lies, of course, not in the "exodus" paradigm as such, the release of slaves from their oppressors (Egyptians), but in the sequel to the Exodus story, the conquest of Canaan. From a Canaanite perspective, the conquest story tells how one's own people have to be dispossessed to fulfil a promise of liberation to another people; and this is the position in which modern Palestinians are placed by the application of the exodus/conquest paradigm to the creation of the state of Israel. An analogous example is found in Robert Warrior's "Canaanites, Cowboys, and Indians." Writing as a Native American in response to the white conquest of North America, Warrior likewise identifies with the Canaanites. Both Said and Warrior see the biblical Canaanites as a group whose narrative subjectivity the text has submerged, and by restoring that subjectivity they assert by analogy the submerged subjectivity of their own groups in current discourse.

What we offer here is a Philistine reading of the Philistines in the Bible. Such a reading seems at first sight to be different in principle from the Canaanite readings. There are, so far as we know, no current political groups which seek to assert their interests through analogy with those of the biblical Philistines.[1] But this lack is offset, we think, by the fact that, at least since the end of the seventeenth century, people in the West have called each other "Philistines," most lately to imply artistic illiteracy. As we shall see, such usage also functions to submerge the subjectivity of specific groups.

---

[1] It may, however, be more than a historical irony that Said's Palestinian community, typologically "Canaanites," are etymologically "Philistines." A rumour that we have been unable to confirm has it that some Palestinians in the *intifada* refer to themselves as "Philistines."

In fact, in attempting a Philistine reading, we are, like Said and Warrior, writing on our own behalf, on behalf of groups of which we are a part. But this will emerge only at the end of our discussion, and for now we can justify our enterprise on more general grounds. We see it as *always* methodologically appropriate and necessary to restore submerged subjectivities in texts, since such textual strategies of submersion will inevitably prove to be part of cultural systems of exclusion. The more culturally important the text, and the more prominent the group whose subjectivity the text submerges, the more vital is this work of analysis. The centrality of the Bible in our culture, and the prominence of the Philistines in the Jewish Bible, do not need to be argued. We can be confident *a priori*, therefore, that what the Bible does with the Philistines will be implicated in systems of exclusion in our own biblically shaped culture. This would be so even if it were not strikingly and oddly confirmed by the modern history of the term "Philistine."

Still, it was that history that provided us with our impulse, and it will structure our paper. Our reading is *intertextual*; we put the text of the Bible, as it treats of the Philistines, alongside the "text" of the modern western discourse about Philistines (including cases where this seems to have diverged far from any biblical roots), to see how these texts may interpret each other. We begin not with the Bible but with the cultural logic of the modern usage, and only then ask how this usage informs and is informed by the reading of the biblical text. Our analytic categories begin with Terry Eagleton's "triptych of . . . class, race and gender" (5), but various other critical categories will emerge along the way. Based on this analysis, we will finally exploit in a direct way the special nuance of "Philistine reading" as *anti-aesthetic* reading. We will take on ourselves the subjectivity of modern "Philistines," to press the question of how a certain recent fashion of approaching the Bible as high literary art is complicit, by its failure to engage feminist and other interested discourses, in the system of exclusions which our work will identify.

1. *Philistines in Modern Discourse*

We do not pretend to cover all of the ground implied in this heading. So far as we are aware, there have been no significant turns in the common usage of "Philistine" in the twentieth century, and no major writing on the subject. It has become one of those terms whose meaning everyone "just knows." The vagueness of the term, the feeling that it needs no justification, is very much a part of the way it does its cultural work.

We choose to go back to earlier, formative stages. We begin in Germany, first with the term *Philister* in student language, and then with the extremely important developments among the Romantics. These developments are associated above all with the name of Goethe, but we shall confine ourselves largely to a satire by Clemens Brentano entitled "The Philistine Before, In and After History,"[2] which is of particular value for our study because it includes a section on the Philistines in the Jewish Bible, so that it is possible to observe Brentano's own understanding of the relations between Philistines ancient and modern.

Leaving Germany for England, we shall then consider the work of the person most responsible for making "Philistine" a popular English word, the nineteenth-century writer and educator Matthew Arnold.

A. *Germany: From Jena to Brentano*

A very sporadic use of "Philistine" is attested in English from about the end of the seventeenth century: "Persons regarded as 'the enemy', into whose hands one may fall, e.g. bailiffs, literary critics, etc.; formerly, also . . . the debauched or drunken" (Oxford University Press: 2:2153). This suggests two distinct lines of meaning: on the one hand, a meaning related to the people themselves, that their habits are despicable; on the other, a meaning based on one's relationship to them, that they may have *power* over the person who designates them "Philistine." These double lines of meaning will prove important.

But the first consistent modern meaning of "Philistine" appears at about the same time, among German students, beginning in Jena, to designate the non-student townsfolk. In the constitution of the German states, students enjoyed enormous advantages over townsfolk. The town was dependent economically on the students, and the laws were heavily biased towards their interests. Students became heavily indebted to the townsfolk who sold and rented things to them. In student songs about the Philistines, two themes stand out. One is utter *contempt*, which sees townsfolk, in their settled, conservative, small-

---

[2] See works cited. There is, so far as we know, no English translation.

town way of life, as inferior and existing merely to be exploited in any way possible. The other is *indebtedness*; the students need the Philistines, and their extravagance may eventually give the Philistines power over them (for this summary, see Westerkamp: 4–11).

The story goes that this use of "Philistine" originated when a clergyman chose as the text for his burial sermon for a student who had died in a town-gown skirmish, "The Philistines are upon you, Samson!" (Judg. 16:9, etc.; see Westerkamp: 13; Grimm and Grimm: vol. 12, 1826). While this story may be apocryphal, there is certainly a link between the use of "Philistine" and the Samson story. "A student in his first term was . . . a *Fuchs* (Fox). When the second term came round he became a *Brandfuchs*—and . . . he was, metaphorically speaking, let loose with implicit sanction to lay waste the vineyards and gardens of the Philistines" (Dawson: 98; the reference is to Samson's exploit in Judg. 15:4–5).

We shall return to some specific aspects of the student usage. Before moving on, it is worth underlining that this first consistent modern usage of "Philistine" portrays those using the term in a worse light than their opponents! There is little development of the usage in Germany in the eighteenth century until the rise of the Romantic movement, and especially the appearance of Goethe. Then, "Philistine" rapidly takes on a rather broad meaning, one which still owes much to the student usage, in that it mocks small-town conservatism and self-satisfaction,[3] but which also extends into the artistic and intellectual spheres, as the rebellion of the Romantics against the stagnation which they see to be the result of the Enlightenment. The apparent triumph of reason had led, for the Romantics, to a smug self-satisfaction, an assumption that all human problems were on their way to being solved, a sense of domination over nature through technology. All this is "Philistine" (Westerkamp: 20–52).

In 1811, Clemens Brentano[4] was a member of a dining club in Berlin, made up of intellectual leaders "mostly from the high Prussian aristocracy" (Westerkamp: 97), and his "The Philistine Before, In and After History" was produced *ad hoc* to provide an evening's

---

[3] Westerkamp (5) disagrees, seeing the student and Romantic usages as independent. Brentano's work in particular seems to us to bring the two together.

[4] 1778–1842. Best known for his collaboration with Achim von Arnim on *Des Knaben Wunderhorn* (1805–8), one of the most important early collections of German folk literature.

entertainment for the club. It was not intended for publication. Brentano sets out to parody a pedantic scholarly work, to produce, in fact, a Philistine treatise on the Philistines; it is, it seems, merely to give the work an appearance of scientific completeness that he even includes the biblical section. It is not a part of his agenda to answer *our* question, why the ancient term "Philistine" should have been chosen as a modern category. Nonetheless, within the loose structure and the humorous treatment, striking links do get made between past and present, and our question does get answered at a certain level.

The three sections enumerated in Brentano's title—"Before History," "In History," and "After History"—in fact make up less than half of his parody. They are preceded and followed by various comments on the Philistines of his own time, with emphasis on provincial dullness (190–98, 213–29; unattributed page references in this section are to Brentano). The material on the biblical Philistines is in the section "In History." But before considering this, it is useful to look at "Before History" (198–201). Here, Brentano draws on the mystic Jakob Böhme to present a thoroughly dualistic view of creation. In the beginning, the principles of Yes and No were united in the divine being. Then Lucifer, the No principle, tried to raise itself above the Yes, and was thrown to earth. Lucifer is, for Brentano, "the first Philistine or the idea of the Philistine" (199). This was the first Fall, and it was from the Ideal into the Material, the Material being identified with the Philistine. In a second Fall, the Idea (Adam) was again overcome by the material (Eve), whence sprang the sin— likewise identified with the Philistine—on account of which God brought the flood. But the Philistine idea survived the flood in the person of Noah's son Ham (Brentano uses Gen. 10:14, which includes the Philistines among Ham's descendants). A good example of Brentano's way of linking past and present is his comment that modern Philistines hold the "scientific view" that the rainbow, the sign of the covenant, is an optical illusion (201). In the "Before History" section, then, all in the greatest fun, "Philistine" is raised into a universal dualistic category, connoting above all the materialism of the Enlightenment in its opposition to Romantic idealism.

Before reading in detail the most important section, "In History" (202–208), we make a general comment on Brentano's attitude to Jews. Despite the fact that to call people Philistines would seem to put oneself in the position of a Jew, Brentano shares the anti-semitism of his time. The club for which the parody was written explicitly excluded from its membership both Jews and Philistines (Westerkamp: 97)! Brentano sees the Philistines as the enemies of the Jews only up to the time when the Jews, in crucifying the Son of God, gave up not only their election but also "the conflict with the Philistines," so that Jews and Philistines have now come to "represent the two poles of perversity" (204).

Brentano's reading of the biblical Philistines begins with the Genesis 10 genealogies, playing on the Philistines' Cretan origin, and the classical view that "all Cretans are liars" (202). He next turns to Genesis 26: "Even in their best period they stopped the Israelites' wells," he notes, drawing conclusions about Philistine quarrelsomeness (204). But his attention is drawn mainly to Samson, whom he sees as "a rare hero" (ibid.), whose constant motive was to make war on the Philistines. On the riddle incident (Judges 14) he comments that "No Philistine ever *guessed* anything, but rather *betrayed*" (205, playing on German *erraten/verraten*). In his anti-Semitic vein he calls the Judahites' handing over of Samson to the Philistines (Judg. 15:13) "a truly Jewish reward" for his services (ibid.; it is interesting how easily he can separate Samson from the Jews!). He complains of the modern Philistines' rationalistic disbelief in miracles, reporting how a Philistine told him that "jawbone" was actually the name of a general (ibid.).

Samson, however, became a bit of a Philistine himself, for he got involved in "whoredom," which Brentano sees as a Philistine institution:

> ... I call that kind of thing Philistinism, since to satisfy the most glorious human instinct disgustingly and conveniently, without passion, without sanctification by a priest or sanctification by valour, adventure and danger, is a Philistine thing, ... it is only because of Philistine attitudes that the protection of such sinful women can become established in a state. (206)

Philistine women belong to this culture of whoredom. Delilah, who "tormented ... the hero as much as a Philistine woman can," was "another courtesan" (ibid.).

Concluding his reading of Samson, Brentano asserts that no Philistine can even comprehend such a hero's death, and he toasts all the heroes who have died fighting Philistines (207). He has relatively little to say about 1 Samuel. He has some fun with the plague of haemorrhoids (1 Sam. 5:6, etc.). Goliath he refers to as the "chief

Philistine." On David's sojourn among the Philistines, he ironically comments that the Philistines built their policy on the expectation that David would betray his own people. Such baseness in politicking[5] is a major characteristic of Philistines (207).

Before moving to "After History" (210–13), which deals mostly with the student use of "Philistine," Brentano makes a key comment. The Philistines, in their rationalistic approach to religion, which regards the old biblical stories as superstition, could never make the connections that he has been making. "Philistines can never grasp" that history repeats itself in various "modifications," and that everything, including what they call superstition, must always come back in new forms (209). This suggests that Brentano perceives some ground, outside of opportunistic wit, for drawing connections between ancient and modern Philistines.

Several threads run through the German data. One is the rebellion of youth against age—Brentano seems to have drafted his parody already in 1799, when still a student (Westerkamp: 72–73)—writ large in the rebellion of the Romantics against the Enlightenment. Another is the individual against the mass. Modern Philistines are almost always referred to as a group, displaying predictable characteristics; they are rarely considered as individuals, and one of the many things they cannot grasp is individual talent and "genius." A third thread is the spiritual against the material. The students see their transactions with the Philistines over material matters as a necessary evil, particularly annoying since their taken-for-granted intellectual superiority is not respected in these transactions. Brentano raises the distinction between those who value "ideas" (his own group) and those concerned only for material prosperity and comfort (the Philistines) into a cosmic principle.

Though class is rarely an explicit theme, it is everywhere implicit. The difference between students and townsfolk is class-based. But the class situation is not so simple in Brentano. He keeps aristocratic company, and often projects a privileged intellectual contempt for the middle class. But the Romantics' real fight is against an earlier privileged intellectual generation; through the Enlightenment, Philistinism has taken over the universities and the arts, as well as the political and social spheres, so that the inner-class is as important as the inter-class struggle. Perhaps our best approach to the

---

[5] "Staatsklugheit, mit Niederträchtigkeit verbunden."

issue of class is through the idealist-materialist division. The Enlightenment attitude to the material world was, as the Romantics no doubt
intuited, redrawing the class map of Europe. As will appear in
Matthew Arnold, a new capitalist aristocracy of industrialists and
financiers, and a quite new kind of working class, were being born.

The work of ideology, according to Fredric Jameson (87 and passim),
is the production of class fantasy, and we shall trace this work in all
the data we are looking at. The students' sense of themselves as
Samsons or foxes despoiling the Philistines is such fantasy-work, and
so is Brentano's satire. Into the fantasy the themes of gender and
race are woven. We begin with *gender*. The students were all male,
and their sexual abuse of the town women is one of the things com-
plained of by the townsfolk and celebrated in the students' own songs
(Westerkamp: 6, 9). Brentano's *coterie* is also virtually all-male. A familiar kind of sexism is to be found in his contrast of Adam as the
spiritual with Eve as the material principle, or in his treatment of
Delilah as a nagging woman (Philistine women are apparently worse
nags than others). But gender enters his analysis perhaps most significantly in his upholding the sanctity of marriage over against the
Philistines who, he claims, do not; the culture of prostitution is part
of the Philistine social system. In contrast to the students, who can
identify with the sexual side of Samson's prowess, Brentano wants to
idealize women and sexuality. Even if heroism can "sanctify" sex as
well as a priest can,[6] it does *need* to be sanctified. In fact, Brentano
is able to have it both ways, to despise Philistine women while idealizing those of his own class.

There is, of course, no *racial* difference between the German Philistines and their detractors, but this does not prevent the theme of
race from entering deeply into Brentano's fantasy. The very choice
of "Philistines" as a category implies the Bible's quasi-racial sense of
difference, which Brentano draws out in his reference to the curse
on Canaan, Ham's son, in Gen. 9:25–27. Brentano extends the curse
to all Ham's descendants, including, of course, the Philistines (202).[7]
Even more revealing is his peculiar interplay of Philistines and Jews,
which brings the category of Philistines within the orbit of German
anti-Semitism. A club that excludes both groups expresses, perhaps,

---

[6] See our earlier quote from Brentano (206): "sanctification by a priest or sanctification by valour, adventure and danger."

[7] The use of Genesis 9 with a racist purpose is well known from recent South
Africa.

a wish that the Philistines *were* racially different, so that they might be readily identified.

Such a wish is, in fact, overtly expressed by the Romantic philosopher Johann Gottlieb Fichte just a year after Brentano's satire, and in exactly the same context, a speech to a dining club. Fichte worries about how one may differentiate oneself from a Philistine. Differentiating oneself from a Jew is easy; it is just a matter of not being circumcised. But in combatting the Philistines, one can scarcely avoid becoming one oneself; Philistinism may even consist in thinking that you aren't one![8]

This anxiety over one's own identity vis-à-vis the Philistines is easy to trace also in Brentano, for example in the following telling passage:

> It needs particularly to be noted, that the outward marks... by no means suffice to make someone a Philistine; rather, it always depends on how, given these marks, he faces life. The very person who exhibits all the contrary marks can be a Philistine.... Ah, who can be sure that he is not himself already threaded on a string, and that, if ever the devil tightens the cord, he will not be hung with other Philistines like a row of onions around the neck of Satan's grandmother? (212)

Brentano attempts to distance himself from the Philistines rhetorically by his repeated assertion that they *don't know what's going on*, that an essential part of being a Philistine is an inability to grasp things. The Philistines don't know that they *are* Philistines.[9] In fact, the whole German discourse about Philistines imposes a character on them and suppresses their own subjectivity. The correctness of one's own version of social and other relationships is established rhetorically by the claim that the "others," precisely because of who they are, are incapable of any rational version of their own. There is absolutely no rhetoric of debate between equals. It is as if allowing the Philistines their own voice would make the differences start to disappear.

---

[8] "Ja ihm sitzt die Philisterei/Gerade im Denken, dass er's nicht sei!" Quoted by Westerkamp (99).

[9] One could have some deconstructive fun identifying the contradictions Brentano gets into. He himself humorously notes that his thoroughgoing idealism denies the reality of the very earth on which he is standing (199). His Lucifer (ibid., shades of Milton's *Paradise Lost*) is just such an individual hero as he elsewhere admires. There is some reason to believe that he was unsure of his standing among his aristocratic friends.

B. *Matthew Arnold*

> The whole scope of the essay is to recommend culture as the great
> help out of our present difficulties; culture being a pursuit of our total
> perfection by means of getting to know, on all the matters which most
> concern us, the best which has been thought and said in the world,
> and, through this knowledge, turning a stream of fresh thought upon
> our stock notions and habits, which we now follow staunchly but
> mechanically, vainly imagining that there is a virtue in following them
> staunchly which makes up for the mischief of following them mechani-
> cally. (Arnold: vol. 5, 233–34; unattributed references in this section
> are to Arnold by volume and page).

This is how Matthew Arnold introduces his essay *Culture and Anarchy*.
Writing during a time of social upheaval brought about by industrialization and the introduction of universal male suffrage (this is what
he means by "our present difficulties"), Arnold seeks to quell the
conflict brought about by the growing political power of the middle
and lower classes. "Philistine" is a key term in his campaign for a
central authority that rises above and can mediate the conflict. He
seeks to establish the claims of the disinterested intellectual against
the claims of a self-interested middle class.

"Philistine" is thus in Arnold preeminently a *class* term. He divides
England into three classes, the aristocracy, whom he calls Barbarians,
the middle class and organized labour, who are the Philistines, and
the working class, or Populace. Arnold uses the term "Philistine" to
create a class fantasy in the service of a real class struggle, a struggle
for the "hearts and minds" of the Populace—he wants to maintain
control of the education of the Populace, to keep it out of the hands
of the middle class, who would philistinize the Populace.

But Arnold is not able to see his project in terms of class struggle.
He sees himself as representative not of a threatened intellectual class,
but of those who have risen above class struggle altogether. He distinguishes between the "ordinary self" and the "best self" (5, 134).
Our ordinary self, the self determined by our class, is "separate,
personal, at war." Our best self is "united, impersonal, at harmony."
To cultivate the best self is the task of education; intellectuals, freed
by the power of letters, transcend class conflict to claim their
humanity: "So far as a man has genius he tends to take himself out
of the category of class altogether, and to become simply a man"
(5, 130).

Arnold offers education to the Populace as a means of self-
improvement. Looking to the state as a centre of authority that could

rise above class politics and mediate social conflict, he was a strong advocate of public education.[10] But the unstated price the Populace must pay for this improvement through education is domination by a new intellectual elite. Claiming to eliminate class conflict, he in fact reinscribes *aristo*cracy, in the sense of rule by the best. Arnold stakes the claim of a white male literary elite to be arbiters of cultural change during a time of social upheaval. His use of "Philistine" is part of this strategy.

In an essay on Heinrich Heine, Arnold summarizes the meaning of the term "Philistine" as it has developed in Germany:

> *Philistine* must have originally meant, in the mind of those who invented the nickname, a strong, dogged, unenlightened opponent of the chosen people, of the children of the light.... They regarded their adversaries as humdrum people, slaves to routine, enemies to light; stupid and oppressive, but at the same time very strong. (3, 112)

Arnold fantasizes the Philistines as provincial, narrow, and self-regarding, as worshipping mere externals, what he calls "machinery"—size, power, numbers, wealth—while neglecting the idea, reason, and the good. The biblical image of the Philistine provides Arnold with the portrait of people who have technological superiority while being *culturally* inferior. He describes the England of the industrial middle classes as "the very headquarters of Goliath" (3, 111) where "the sky is of brass and iron" (3, 113).

Though he regards a certain kind of individualism as a Philistine trait, Arnold does not individualize the Philistines. In contradistinction to the disinterested intellectual (the servant of the idea) who has extricated himself from narrow sectarian interests, the Philistine is preeminently a member of a class and acts in that class's interest. Arnold wants to set up a link between individual and state that is not mediated by class and that transcends class interest.

Along with self-interest, the Philistine's key characteristic is a worship of the freedom *to do as one likes*.[11] This is the meaning for Arnold of *anarchy*, which is the opposite of culture. With the passage of the Second Reform Bill, Philistines formed the majority in Parliament, and their desire to do as they liked was combined with the power to do just exactly that. Arnold is particularly concerned that the Populace,

---

[10] For many years he served as Her Majesty's Inspector of Schools.
[11] "Doing as One Likes" is the title of a chapter of *Culture and Anarchy* (5, 115–36).

as their political power rapidly increases, may become philistinized in this sense. In the following passage he draws on the image of Goliath to describe the damage wrought by their clumsy assertion of power:

> while the aristocratic and middle classes have long been doing as they like and with great vigour, he has been too undeveloped and submissive hitherto to join in the game; and now, when he does come, he comes in immense numbers, and is rather raw and rough ... our laws give our playful giant, in doing as he likes, considerable advantage. (5, 122–23)

Despite all of this, Arnold acknowledges that the Philistines are instrumental in the development of the nation. The industrial revolution that has brought the middle and working classes to power has had the good effect of destroying feudalism in England. But Arnold hopes to deal with the social power of the Philistines by seeing them as a necessary but passing phase:

> Now, culture admits the necessity of the movement towards fortune-making and exaggerated industrialism, readily allows that the future may derive benefit from it; but insists, at the same time, that the passing generations of industrialists,—forming, for the most part, the stout main body of Philistinism,—are sacrificed to it. (5, 105)

This is another level of class fantasy. The Philistines are necessary at the moment, but will be "sacrificed" to a better future. They are merely an *instrument* of an historical purpose that transcends them.

Arnold's class fantasy leads him deep into the politics of gender and race. We begin with *gender*. A particular way of thinking about relationships between men and women is implied in Arnold's use of the term Philistine. He characterizes the Philistine attitude towards women as crude and unrefined. The industrial revolution not only brought about changes between the classes but affected the relationship between the sexes as well. Throughout his work Arnold trivializes this change and downplays its depth. In *Culture and Anarchy*, his examination of sexual politics is reduced to a discussion of a proposed bill that would allow a man to marry his deceased wife's sister. The advocates of this bill argue for it on the basis that it does not contradict Levitical laws. Arnold depicts them as exhibiting "that double craving so characteristic of our Philistine ... the craving for forbidden fruit and the craving for legality" (5, 206). He goes on to deploy the rhetoric of ethnology as a persuasive strategy, characterizing advocates of the bill as having a Semitic attitude towards women:

> Who . . . will believe, when he really considers the matter, that where
> the feminine nature, the feminine ideal, and our relationship to them,
> are brought into question, the delicate and apprehensive genius of the
> Indo-European race, the race which invented the Muses, and chivalry,
> and the Madonna, is to find its last word on this question in the in-
> stitutions of a Semitic people, whose wisest king had seven hundred
> wives and three hundred concubines? (5, 208)

Arnold's "enlightened" attitude towards women idealizes them as
possessing spiritual influence, even as it denies them material power.
In *Culture and Anarchy*, Arnold's discussion of marriage to in-laws is
made in terms of male desire rather than female desire. In his discussion of divorce in *God and the Bible* (7, 225–29), Arnold similarly
expresses male rather than female motivation and interest. He characterizes John Stuart Mill, who argued for legalizing divorce as well
as for extending economic and political rights to women, simply as
an advocate of adultery. He never takes up Mill's argument for the
enfranchisement of women, or places the discussion of marriage in
the larger context of Mill's concern for women's equality. Mill's
advocacy of free love becomes a crude and regressive desire for
unlimited sexual expression. Arnold here employs a nature/culture,
animal/human framework in his discussion of sexual relationships.
He sets up a contrast between nature, polygamy and polytheism and
culture, monogamy and monotheism. He links the first set of terms
to the biblical image of the "strange woman." Mill's proposal to change
marriage laws is portrayed as a threat to monotheism and civilization that leads us back into the dark age of unbridled ecstasy symbolized by the Witch of Endor (see 7, 221). These allusions to the
biblical "other" belong to the same set of ideas as the Philistine
"craving for forbidden fruit,"[12] and serve his strategy of keeping women
as the medium of male desire with no independent subjectivity.

There is reason to think that Arnold's "dark age" is as recent as
the Regency period, the end of the eighteenth and the beginning of
the nineteenth century! During that time, the opportunities for women
in the public and economic sphere were much greater, and their
sexual behaviour was much less rigidly controlled than in Arnold's
time. Mill's suggested change in marriage laws would in fact have
brought England back to norms that governed society in the Regency period. During the mid-nineteenth century, there was a rapid

---

[12] Arnold refers, in this discussion, to the Philistine Abimelech in Genesis (7, 218).
For Delilah as the "strange woman," see below, pp. 399–400.

trend to confine women to the private sphere. Anna Clark argues that it was industrialization and the rise of the middle class that brought this change (232–34). She shows how women's sexual reputation was used as a tool to further this confinement; for example, "whore" is used not only in its literal sense, but also of women who engaged in commerce (240–42). It is ironic that Arnold's attitude towards women reflects this middle class morality; if Clark is correct, the stick Arnold uses to beat the Philistines over sexual morality is a stick that he got from them!

As to *race* or ethnology, we have already seen how Arnold deploys it along with gender in his idealizing of women. This leads us into an examination of the ethnic implications of the term Philistine. His equation of Philistine attitudes with Semitic values points up a latent anti-semitism which runs throughout his work. He adopts the ethnological theory that there are two major cultural and linguistic groups, the Indo-European (Aryan) and the Semitic, and argues that Indo-European values are more natural to the English Saxons than Semitic ones.

This set of attitudes also gets displaced, in an ethnographically curious but revealing way, onto his work on Celtic culture. In a series of lectures on this subject, Arnold depicts the Saxons as Philistines and the Celts as children of the light. He emphasizes the impact of Celtic culture on English literature. The sentimental Celts with their fancifulness and quickness of perception, he suggests, have added a much needed leaven to the culture of the steady-going but dull Saxons. However, just as he idealizes women as Muses while refusing to take their demands for political and economic power seriously, so too he ascribes a spiritual force to Celtic culture while refusing to grant material power to it:

> It is not in the outward and visible world of material life that the Celtic genius of Wales or Ireland can at this day hope to count for much; it is in the inward world of thought and science. What it *has* been, what is *has* done, let it ask us to attend to that, as a matter of science and history; not to what it will be or will do, as a matter of modern politics. It cannot count appreciably now as a material power; but, perhaps, if it can get itself thoroughly known as an object of science, it may count for a good deal,—far more than we Saxons, most of us, imagine,—as a spiritual power. (3, 298)

In objectifying Celtic culture as an object of scholarly interest, Arnold dismisses the desire of the Irish and Welsh for political sovereignty and for the re-introduction of the Celtic languages as living media of communication. He ends his addresses with a proposal to undermine Philistinism "through . . . the slow approaches of culture, and the introduction of chairs of Celtic" (3, 386). The study of Celtic culture would provide the Philistine Saxons with the opportunity to acquire culture through the disinterested study of things outside of themselves.

This ethnic farrago of Celts, Saxons, Indo-Europeans and Semites, further mixed up as it is with gender issues, is hard for us now to take seriously. But it forms an integral part of Arnold's pressing of the cultural claims of the literary establishment in its struggle with the Philistines.

Like Brentano, Arnold uses satire and mockery to critique the middle classes while suppressing real class analysis. Unlike Brentano, however, he does not use the Philistine tag merely to objectify and distance his opponents. He is a controversialist, delivering lectures and publishing his work in newspapers and popular magazines. He often quotes his critics' assessments of his arguments and in this way gives a voice to the Philistines. In fact, he often seems to delight in the way his opponents produced satires of his satires, mocking his use of biblical rhetoric. A satire of Arnold by Frederick Harrison, a prominent liberal thinker at Oxford University, so amused Arnold that it led him to develop the fiction, in *Friendship's Garland*, that his Prussian protagonist had broken off correspondence with Arnold and taken it up with Harrison instead (5, 424).

But Arnold is not free of anxiety about his own identity vis-à-vis the Philistines. In *Culture and Anarchy* he describes himself as someone who, while being "properly a Philistine," has been converted to culture:

> I myself am properly a Philistine,—Mr. Swinburne would add, the son of a Philistine. And although, through circumstances which will perhaps one day be known if ever the affecting story of my conversion comes to be written, I have, for the most part, broken with the tea-meetings of my own class, yet I have not, on that account, been brought much the nearer to the ideas and works of the Barbarians or of the Populace. (5, 144)

Arnold's lack of clarity about the degree to which he has separated himself from his Philistine background conveys a sense of unease. Has he been *converted* or has he only broken with his class "for the most part"? To what extent would he admit that his class background influences his ideas and work?

2. *Intertextual Reading of Modern and Biblical Philistines*

In this section, we read the biblical traditions about the Philistines, especially in Judges and 1 Samuel, but also in Genesis, in a way that is organized by our findings from the modern data, drawing connections where appropriate.

A. *The Philistines and class fantasy*

The modern use of "Philistine" we have found to belong essentially to a class discourse, that of an intellectual elite confronting an emergent middle class. The usage is a focus of class anxiety for two reasons; because the Philistines are very powerful, and because it is hard to separate oneself from the Philistines. This class anxiety generates class fantasy, the development of which draws freely on other discourses, notably those of gender and race.

In the biblical presentation, ethnicity rather than class seems to define the relations between Israelites and Philistines (we shall return to the ethnic issues). But there are significant traces of class discourse in the Philistine traditions, and recent developments in biblical studies have made us more sensitive to these.[13] The theme of Israelite *servitude* to the Philistines is prominent (e.g., 1 Sam. 4:9; cf. Samson's involuntary, and David's voluntary, service to Philistines). The Philistine monopoly on iron (13:19–22) makes better sense as a class difference among people sharing the same space than as an ethnic difference. It is interesting that, while the Israelites' special name for the Philistines, the "uncircumcised," may suggest ethnicity, the Philistines' special name for the Israelites, "Hebrews," is likely a class indicator.[14] The iron monopoly, and other indications, suggest that the Philistines were materially more advanced than the Israelites. It has been suggested (beginning with Gunkel), that Samson is opposed to the Philistines as nature to culture, and that the Samson cycle

---

[13] We refer to the recent trend associated above all with Norman Gottwald. See for example Gottwald, 1993.

[14] We refer to the discussion of a link between "Hebrew" and "apiru," the latter very likely being a designation for a disenfranchised and disadvantaged group (e.g., Gottwald, 1979: 419–25). It has been suggested that David's band, which hires itself to a Philistine king, has a resemblance to *apiru* bands. In 1 Samuel, "Hebrew" is used five times by the Philistines (4:6, 9, 13:19, 14:11, 29:3), once by Saul (13:3), and once by the narrator (14:21). It is also the term by which the Egyptians tend to refer to the Israelites in Exodus.

should be read as resistance literature of the oppressed against a culturally superior oppressor (Exum: 90–91, with reference to Niditch).

Such a class picture has points of contact with the modern data (though varying definitions of "culture" complicate the matter). The Romantics set a cult of nature over against a stultifying middle class culture. Arnold, using culture in a different sense, has to admit the Philistines' technological superiority as he mocks their want of culture.

The Philistines are as much a fantasy creation in the Bible as in the modern scene, and thematic connections to the latter are many. The biblical Philistines almost always appear as a *group*, and even when they speak or act as individuals, there is a good deal of stereotyping. In the Samson cycle, the only individualized Philistines are his bride-to-be (14:15–17), her father (15:1–2), and Delilah.[15] The two women speak and act in virtually identical ways, for the same purpose, and only at the instance of a (male) Philistine collectivity. The father-in-law has only one brief speech. The first individualized Philistine voice in 1 Samuel is Goliath's (17:8–10, 43–44), and his words (like the collective Philistine voice elsewhere—Judg. 16:23–25, 1 Sam. 14:11–12) consist entirely of taunts proved unjustified in the event. Much the most interesting individual Philistine voice is that of Achish, King of Gath, in his dealings with David (21:10–15 [11–16], 27:5–28:2, 29), to which we shall return.

Against this collectivity is set the Israelite individual. The theme of the hero who successfully battles a multitude of Philistines recurs frequently. It defines the entire Samson cycle, and is also found in Shamgar (Judg. 3:31), Jonathan and his attendant (1 Sam. 14:6–15),[16] and David (1 Sam. 18:25–27). David's other great exploit, the fight with Goliath (1 Samuel 17), is a simple transformation, replacing multitude with magnitude.[17] There is particular stress on these as *youthful* exploits (Samson, Jonathan, David). This theme of the struggle of the individual (often youthful, often a solitary "genius") against the mass, is one which, as we have seen, is very prominent in the German evidence.

The theme of Philistine materialism, particularly the iron monopoly, has already been raised in connection with class issues; Philistine power

---

[15] If she is a Philistine—it is never so stated. But all popular mythologies make her one.

[16] The number of Philistines here is more modest, twenty, but their death leads to a general panic.

[17] Cf. 2 Sam. 21:15–22, 23:9–17.

over Israel has a material basis. At the fantasy level, the description
of Goliath prepared for battle (1 Sam. 17:5–7) is grotesquely *metallic*,
in contrast to David, who refuses armour (vv. 38–39).[18] This fits well
with Arnold's association of Philistinism with the industrial revolution, and his frequent pejorative use of the term "mechanical." Other
suggestions of Philistine materialism in the Bible are thin. Delilah's
relation to the Philistines (as Brentano stresses) is mercenary (Judg.
16:5). Both in the ancestral stories (Genesis 21, 26) and in the ark
story (1 Samuel 5–6) the Philistines see monetary tribute as the right
way to expiate an offense.

In most of their appearances, the Philistines are at war with Israel.
They are cruel foes, as witness their treatment of Samson and of
Saul's corpse (1 Sam. 31:8–10). They are arrogant and boastful (usually as a foil for the Israelite hero), but can also be reduced to cow-
ardly panic (1 Samuel 4, 7, 14). Several of these themes appear in
the modern data, but perhaps more important than the particular
themes is the sense that conflict with the Philistines is important enough
to be thought of in terms of warfare.

But the Philistines are also portrayed in the Bible as figures of fun,
simple-minded and easily deceived. In the Samson cycle, though, they
are made to look foolish by their inability to deal with Samson in
combat. Sometimes they can get the better of him by shrewdness
and deceit; but even there they are finally out-smarted. In 1 Samuel
4–6, the disasters which fall on the Philistines while they have the
ark are likely meant humorously, especially if the "tumours" were
haemorrhoids. David is able to deceive Achish, king of Gath, first by
feigning madness (chap. 21), then in ingratiating himself with the
Judahites while seeming to Achish to be doing the opposite (chap.
27). Achish's trust in David never wavers.

The biblical picture as we have presented it so far matches the
modern data well, for example our quote earlier from Arnold (but
referring directly to German usage), to the effect that Philistines are
"unenlightened" and "stupid," but also "very strong." The German
students regard the townsfolk as figures of fun, and are confident of
their ability to outwit them, but they are also aware of the Philistines' *power* over them. They are engaged in a battle of wills; as one

[18] Cf. the "Destroyer with three heads" in 13:17, immediately before the reference to the iron monopoly; the word is the same as the destroying angel of the
Passover (Exod. 12:13).

student song puts it, "I cheat only those who cheat me" (Westerkamp: 9). The emphasis in Brentano is heavily on ridicule, but Philistine power also emerges clearly in his discourse (e.g., 218–23, referring to Philistine control of the German theatre). With Arnold, the strength of the Philistines, the threat they pose to national life, has become central, and the element of satire and making fun has relatively receded.

The biblical fantasizing of the Philistines makes its own use of race and gender. The sense of ethnic or even racial difference from the Philistines is centred in two issues: their descent from Ham (Gen. 10:14, emphasized by Brentano), whereby they belong to a quite different section of humanity from Israel, and the common designation "uncircumcised," which suggests that the Philistines are even more different than Israel's other neighbours. The Septuagint translation of "Philistines" in Judges and Samuel, *allophuloi* ("strangers" or "others"), also suggests fundamental difference. In Hebrew, the term "Philistine" does not function to suppress the subjectivity of the other, for the biblical Philistines (unlike modern ones) *call themselves* Philistines (1 Sam. 4:9, 17:8, 29:7, 9, and several other times if Delilah is a Philistine), with the odd effect that in the Septuagint they call themselves *allophuloi*. But "the uncircumcised" *does* function in this way; the Philistines do not use it of themselves, nor do we hear anything about their views on circumcision.

Turning to gender, we start with the Samson cycle. In a treatment of "Samson's Women," J. Cheryl Exum suggests that the saga tends to *conflate* women and the Philistines, both being the "other" in relation to Israel's patriarchal and xenophobic mindset (Exum: 61–93). Part of her argument is based on the familiar "foreign woman" syndrome in the Bible. Another part is based on the structure of the stories—the Philistines succeed in defeating Samson only when a woman helps them. Their means of fighting is womanish, in the conventional sense of using deceit rather than force. Yet another part of Exum's argument, of particular interest because of its specificity to the Philistines, is the term "uncircumcised." The sign of Israelite identity which most serves to exclude Philistines is a *male* sign, which therefore also excludes women. Exum sees Samson as attracted by the Philistine/female "other," and as escaping from it only in death (whereby he is reincorporated into male Israel). Both Brentano and Arnold, as we have seen, glorify monogamous marriage, and link whatever threatens it, including (in Brentano) whoredom, with

Philistinism. In Brentano's case, this limits his otherwise great admiration for Samson; the German students, on the other hand, seem as keen on Philistine women as Samson was.

Further on the gender issue, we may mention the Medium of Endor.[19] Her geographic location in Endor raises the possibility that she may be a Philistine, or perhaps a "liminal" woman from the borderland between Israel and the Philistines.[20] It is no coincidence, in the light of our earlier discussion of women's increasing confinement in the nineteenth century, that Arnold chooses her to symbolize the "dark age" of unbridled ecstasy (i.e., of loose sexual behaviour) before the "cultural conquest" which introduced marriage. For she is one of the few women in 1 Samuel who wields public power.

Gender is brought together with race and class in the episode of the brideprice (1 Sam. 18:17–29). After Saul fails to carry through on his offer of Merab, his older daughter, to David as wife, Michal, his younger daughter, falls in love with David. Saul agrees to this match, but specifies as a brideprice "a hundred foreskins of the Philistines" (thinking to bring about David's death). David, however, secures two hundred, and marries Michal.

The treatment of gender here is interesting. David appears reluctant to take up Saul's offer. The initiative is Saul's, and Michal cooperates by declaring her love for David. But David expresses no reciprocal desire. As later with Abigail, Michal is depicted as choosing him, rather than vice versa. It seems that the David of 1 Samuel, unlike Samson (and unlike the David of 2 Samuel!) does not fall victim to a desire for women/the other. As a result, perhaps, they act on his behalf. In the patriarchal dichotomy of mother/whore, which Exum (32, 65) suggests is the grid underlying biblical representations of women, Michal and Abigail fall on the good mother side.[21] In contrast to Samson, who desires women and who is betrayed by bad women who act like whores, David, who does not desire women, is nurtured by good women who act like mothers. To carry the contrast further, where Samson refuses male bonding, by

---

[19] For the connection of the Philistines with the occult, see Isa. 2:6.

[20] Delilah's home region, "the valley of Sorek" (Judg. 16:4), may be liminal in the same sense.

[21] They tend to act as maternal figures to David. Exum (47) has suggested reading the scene where Michal lowers David out of her window as a symbolic reenactment of birth. Abigail's action of bringing food to David and his men in the wilderness may also be seen as motherly.

separating himself from male-identified Israel and by rejecting his bridal companions, David valorizes male bonding. Exum (52–53) notes that the emotional depth which is lacking from David's interest in Michal (and in Abigail, as we have seen) is reserved for his relationship with Jonathan, which is marked with tears and expressions of lasting loyalty.

The biblical tendency to see women as either whores or mothers is shared by Brentano and Arnold. We have seen how Arnold portrays advocates of "free love" as having fallen victim to the wiles of the "strange woman," and lifts up the Madonna, the Lady (of medieval chivalry) and the Muse, images of women whose spirituality is related to their confinement and sexual unavailability, as figures that represent a proper appreciation of women. Likewise, we have seen how in Brentano the contrast between the mores of the Philistine system and of enlightened society is expressed in terms of female sexuality. The Philistine is a man (!) who does not control, but is subject to a desire for, women. Like Samson, but unlike David, the Philistine gives in to a desire for "forbidden fruit." The valorization of male bonding is also evident in the modern data. The educational institutions of Europe are part of an all-male system, and the relationship of women to the intellectual culture which this system establishes is tenuous at best.

The brideprice episode foregrounds the issue of race in its unsavoury use of circumcision. It would be hard to imagine a more extreme denial of subjectivity than presenting people only as bits of body (cf. Goliath's head), trophies to David's potency and his claim to the throne. Focalizing the Philistines as uncircumcised is not only a racist but also a sexist strategy, if we follow Eilberg-Schwartz's suggestion that circumcision signified to the Israelites fertility and genealogy (144 and the whole chapter [141–76]). According to him, circumcision is a way of establishing kinship ties between men, and descent through the father over against the mother, so that from the Israelite point of view a community that does not practise circumcision is female-defined. By circumcising the Philistines, David removes "the other" as a threat to the male Israelite community.[22]

---

[22] Gender and race fantasy about the Philistines reaches an extreme in the rabbinic story that Goliath was descended from Orpah, Ruth's sister-in-law, as a result of rape. As Orpah returned home after she chose not to accompany Naomi, she was raped by a hundred Philistines and a dog (the dog comes from 1 Sam. 17:43, the hundred Philistines from the foreskins in chap. 18). David and Goliath descend

To complete these comments on the brideprice episode, we note how it functions as a class fantasy. What is stressed is the contrast between the poverty of David and the wealth of Saul. As in his struggle against Goliath, David is fairy tale hero, a poor man from an insignificant family who makes his fortune by service to the king. The foreskins are one more trial for the hero hoping to win the king's daughter. In defeating the Philistines, David symbolically achieves wealth at their expense, exchanging his poverty with them. The text may be read as a piece of class fantasy on behalf of the poor, by means of which they imagine an improvement in their own status. But in fact, they succeed only in raising up a new oppressor for themselves. In the same way, Arnold offers education to the lower class as a means of self-improvement, but the price of the deal is in fact domination by a new intellectual elite. Arnold, like David, may be seen as a figure who escapes class disadvantage to establish himself as the leader in a new system of domination.

B. *An alternative biblical view of the Philistines?*

In the Bible, then, the Philistines are a focus of anxiety which needs to be resolved through fantasy. Some texts direct to the Philistines a fear and hate hardly paralleled in biblical attitudes towards any other group. They are those who have power over us, and they are those who are wholly other than we, and this combination gives them an archetypical awfulness.

On the other hand, there is considerable nuancing of the stereotype features of the Philistines, even in 1 Samuel where these features are prominent. Their war-hungriness is called in question by the fact that the Masoretic text of 1 Sam. 4:1 makes Israel the aggressors (the Septuagint sees it the opposite way). The Philistine mutilation of Saul's corpse, brutal as it is, is not more so than David's mutilation of the corpses of Goliath, and of the two hundred Philistines in 1 Sam. 18:27. Philistine deceptiveness is matched by David's deception of Achish. We could extend the list. Robert Polzin (55–79) suggests that there is a programmatic attempt in 1 Samuel 4–7 to draw parallels between Israelites and Philistines.

---

in parallel lines from Ruth and Orpah—the difference between an Israelite and a Philistine is turned into a difference between two kinds of female behaviour. See *Midrash Rabbah* on Ruth 1:14 (Freedman and Simon: vol. 8, 38–39).

The extent to which the Philistines are figures of fun is also not to be exaggerated. Polzin's suggestion (58) that an Israelite audience would be amused by the Philistines' ignorance of Israel's history—their supposing that Israel is polytheistic and that the plagues of Egypt happened in the wilderness (4:8)—is dubious, for 5:7 and 6:6 show that the Philistines know the truth about these things. When in 6:9 the Philistine theologians propose a test to decide whether Israel's god is behind their disasters or whether they happened "by chance," are they being thick-headed, or subtle? Perhaps they are calling the bluff of the god of Israel. If he exists, and is powerful, then he must prove it by taking the ark back, saving the Philistines further trouble. If not, then the Philistines win the theological debate, and perhaps get to keep their booty.[23] The last section suggestive of Philistine gullibility, the relations between David and Achish, King of Gath, is also ambiguous. David is indeed able to deceive Achish. But the rest of the Philistines have David's measure. In chap. 21, Achish's own servants raise the alarm about David, and in chap. 29, the commanders of the Philistines by no means share Achish's misplaced confidence.

Israel's victories over the Philistines are heavily fantasized. Only in 1 Samuel 7 does Israel win on account of being as a nation in right relation to God. Otherwise, the victories are by individual heroes against absurd odds, and they seem to have no lasting effect. The broader picture is of Israelite and Philistine armies confronting each other on a relatively equal basis, with victory going sometimes to one side, sometimes the other, but with the Philistines having the edge overall.

Such a picture of national rivalry and general equality is greatly strengthened when we move from Judges and 1 Samuel to the other book where Philistines are prominent, Genesis. There, the upshot of the relationship between Israel's ancestors and the Philistines is the establishment of a *treaty* (made in 21:22–34, tested and perhaps even broken, but reestablished in chap. 26). This treaty follows considerable conflict, in which, arguably, the Israelites are more the aggressors (at any rate, they are the newcomers). There is nothing here of the Philistines as uncircumcised, nor of their false gods—indeed Abimelech appears as a God-fearer who readily acknowledges Yahweh. Given the later relations between Israel and the Philistines, it is interesting that the treaty excludes "false dealing" (21:23).

---

[23] Further on 6:9, see below, pp. 412–13.

In the Bible's ideological geography, the Philistines are a different *kind* of enemy from the Canaanites. The latter inhabit space which is to be Israel's; this is a problem to be solved by their extermination or expulsion to some other place. The Philistines, on the other hand, are invaders from the outside; they have their own space, which is not (at least Judges and 1 Samuel) claimed by Israel. They wish to establish themselves in Israel's space, and must be expelled from it and confined in their place. One might suggest a paradigm of Israel and the Philistines as *rival* claimants, by conquest, for the territory of the Canaanites. This even fits the standard historical view that the Exodus Israelites and the Philistines arrived in Canaan at much the same time (ca. 1200 BCE).[24] But this is not the view of the Deuteronomistic History, which sees Israel as conquering the land, and becoming established there under its judges, before the conflict with the Philistines. Genesis stands in an interesting relationship to these views. It allows to the Philistines a greater antiquity in the land than Israel, but it establishes a division of the land by treaty.

In 1 Samuel, the Philistines certainly act like rival claimants to the land, and this paradigm accounts well for the form of relationship which we have found to be most specific to 1 Samuel: *national* conflict which swings back and forth, with successes for both sides, and with no sense, at least in the short run, of a predestined winner. Philistine identity switches (perhaps already in Judges, and certainly by 1 Samuel 7), from being *one in a series* of nations sent by Yahweh to chastise Israel to being the assailant *par excellence*. But they do not (as we shall show) cease to be the instrument of Yahweh; rather, they become the instrument of a different purpose, to establish the kingship of David (who will successfully claim Philistine territory for Israel).

What would happen if one were to look at Judges-Samuel through the eyes of Genesis? There is early evidence that Jewish commentators saw and feared this possibility! Rabbinic sources insist that the Philistines of Judges and Samuel were different people altogether from the Philistines of Genesis.[25] This parallels a shift in the Septuagint's translation of Hebrew *pĕlištîm*. Before Judges, it uses the neutral transliteration *phulistiim*, but beginning with Judges it switches to the pejorative *allophuloi*.[26]

---

[24] Such a paradigm gets encouragement from Amos 9:7: "Did I not bring up Israel from the land of Egypt, and the Philistines from Caphtor . . .?"

[25] *Midrash Tehillim* on Psalm 60 (Braude: vol. 1, 513); the issue here is precisely whether Israel should have been obliged, later, to keep the Genesis treaty.

[26] See above, p. 399. To be precise, Codex Alexandrinus starts using the new

To what extent, then, do the accounts of the Philistines in Judges and Samuel, marked as they are by the uncertainties, anxieties and fantasies of resistance literature, function as a way of excluding an alternative view of the Philistines, one which would allow them more real subject status? Reading through the eyes of Genesis, might we not see a people whose first concern is coexistence (to their own maximum economic advantage, given their greater resources), but who reacted naturally to Israelite unification and aggression? Do the extreme expressions of Philistine otherness cloak an uncomfortable sense of closeness, a sense of a shared past?

Even Brentano (204) comments that Genesis shows the Philistines in their "best period." We can go further and say that if the alternative biblical view that we have identified were dominant, "Philistine" would never have become a cultural slur.

The students in a class at St. Andrew's College, Saskatoon, were asked to put themselves in the position of Israelites and give their views of the Philistines, deliberately using a rhetoric analogous to that of racism or sexism—"Philistines are . . ." (cf. "blacks are . . .," "women are . . ."). The answers ranged widely. There was some emphasis on sheer otherness, defined particularly in religious terms: Philistines are sacrilegious, polytheistic, and hence excluded from the people of Yahweh. Their lack of circumcision was a focus of this otherness; one student equated this with "having no morals." Some extreme adjectives were offered: bestial, subhuman. More common were the attributes of warriors and conquerors. The Philistines were perceived as powerful, arrogant, oppressive, brutal, barbarous towards defeated enemies and (in the incident of the wells in Genesis 26) capriciously destructive. Several students found them "war hungry," assuming them to be the initiators of conflict. In adversity, they were seen mostly as fearful and confused, but sometimes as brave (1 Samuel 4). Perhaps most interesting were the students' suggestions about the Philistines' intellectual capacities. Some found them "stupid, simple-minded," but others found them shrewd, in getting rid of the ark of the covenant (1 Samuel 6) and in keeping Israel disarmed. Despite all of these negatives, some students noted that the Philistines *were* after all culturally superior, and usually victorious.

---

translation at the beginning of Judges and uses it invariably thereafter; Vaticanus likewise switches at the beginning of Judges, but reverts to *phulistiim* on six occasions later in Judges, the last of which is 14:2.

These answers can all be supported from the biblical text, but they stress the negative side heavily, with little sense of the alternative picture of the Philistines which we have just sketched. The interesting question is, to what extent were the students reading the biblical Philistines through eyes conditioned by the negative uses of "Philistine" from much later times, and to this day?

C. *Deep-structural links: instrumentality and anarchy*

To consider a series of critical categories (gender, etc.), and to enumerate characteristics, as we have done in the foregoing, is not yet to get to the heart of what is going on in the biblical treatment of the Philistines. Two of the issues raised particularly by Matthew Arnold will take our intertextual reading to deeper levels.

In Arnold's view of history, the Philistines are a group who are necessary at the moment, but who will disappear in the movement to a better future, will be "sacrificed" to that future (vol. 5, 105; see above, p. 392). This view, which we have called *instrumental*, is underlined by the way Arnold, through his deployment of ethnological theories, makes one race serve the interests of another. Such instrumentality can be traced also in the German material; in a crass form among the students—the townsfolk are an absolutely necessary nuisance—and in a cosmic form in Brentano, where the Philistine "idea" is part of the eternal battle of good and evil.

The instrumental view corresponds to one of the most conspicuous aspects of the Philistines in Judges and 1 Samuel, that they are instruments of Yahweh's purpose. They are Yahweh's instrument to punish sin, as part of the regular judge pattern (Judg. 10:7, 1 Samuel 7), and in the particular case of the sin of the house of Eli (1 Samuel 4). The events of the Samson cycle, the reader is told, unfold as they do because Yahweh "was seeking a pretext to act against the Philistines" (Judg. 14:4). The issue of whether the Philistines are directly instrumental in bringing about the appearance of kingship in Israel is complex, and we shall return to it; but it is evident, once kingship is in place, that the Philistines are instrumental in the transition from Saul to David; there is hardly any reference to them after 1 Samuel 13 which does not directly serve this end. And as soon as this transition is accomplished, at the end of 1 Samuel, the Philistines very suddenly lose importance. They do not need, like the Canaanites, to be literally exterminated; they are exterminated *textually*, as they move from a position of dominance, at the end of 1 Samuel, to being little more than a footnote in the account of David's triumphs in 2 Samuel.

This instrumentality if put in even sharper focus if we pursue further Exum's idea of a conflation of women and Philistines. At first glance, both of David's women in 1 Samuel, Michal and Abigail, attain a subjectivity unusual for women in the Bible. Both take powerful initiatives (Michal in 19:11–19, where she warns David of Saul's intention to kill him and helps him escape). But these women's apparently independent subjectivity is entirely in the service of David in his rise to the throne. Significantly, these women who assist his rise are marginal in the kingdom that he eventually establishes. It is not a son of Michal or Abigail that inherits the throne, but the son of Bathsheba, the first woman that David sees and desires. Just like the Philistines (and, as we have seen, in a complex relation to them) women are merely *instrumental* in the rise of David.

The second issue in Arnold is *anarchy*. Perhaps the most important aspect, for him, of being a Philistine is the desire to do as one likes; as a result, his Philistine class lacks the social discipline that makes for state coherence. The importance of this for Arnold is indicated by his including "anarchy" in the title of his major work on the Philistines.

There is a curious ambiguity as to what is problematic for Israel in the period immediately before the people's request for a king in 1 Samuel 8. On the one hand, the problem is the Philistine occupation. This begins in Judges 10, within the logic of the judge-cycles, but it does not (as that logic demands) end in Judges; rather, it continues into 1 Samuel, up to the time of Israel's demand for a king (Jobling, 1986:49–53). On the other hand, the problem is that every Israelite is "doing what is right in his own eyes," a formula so close to Arnold's "doing as one likes" that it is hard to believe he did not have it in mind. This formula, with which Judges concludes (21:25, cf. 17:6) and which sets the agenda for 1 Samuel, is directly connected to the lack of a king. These two problems, Philistines and anarchy, are not narratively connected—they are simply juxtaposed as two aspects of one problem. In the biblical narrative the Philistines do *not* precipitate the rise of kingship (despite the opposite conclusion reached by most historians of Israel), since they are comprehensively defeated (1 Samuel 7) immediately before the people's demand. (Anarchy is not clearly said to be the cause either, but the logic of the narrative suggests that it is.)

It is tempting to read the Philistine occupation and Israelite anarchy as representing external and internal aspects of the same situation of national demoralization and religious apostasy. But such a move brings us squarely into the logic of Arnold's view of the Philistines of his time. He simply equates what the Bible juxtaposes, Philistines and anarchy, and he sees powerful state control (cf. kingship in Israel) as the only remedy.

In his presentation of his class opponents as an anarchic force within the state, and as an instrument which, though necessary, will be "sacrificed" to the state's historical development, Arnold is not only deploying powerful rhetorical tools. He is working with a logic that is extremely close to that of the biblical treatment of the Philistines in Judges and 1 Samuel. How does this relate to his explicit use of the Bible? We will suggest an answer in our final section.

4. *Philistine Readers of the Bible*

In Arnold's project of educating the Populace in such a way as to reduce the conflict and upheaval brought on by the extension of the franchise, the Bible has an important role to play. He aims to use the Bible to present a view of human history as a connected whole, with a coherence beyond sectarian interests and class conflict. The Bible is particularly fitted to this task of "civilizing" the newly enfranchised masses because it is part of popular culture in a way that Greek and Latin texts are not. He writes:

> If poetry, philosophy, and eloquence, if what we call in one word *letters*, are a power, and a beneficent wonder-working power, in education, through the Bible only have the people much chance of getting at poetry, philosophy and eloquence. (Arnold: vol. 7, 503)

Seeking to present the Bible in a way that reduces the impression of contradictions and fragmentariness, Arnold mines it for "some whole, of admirable literary beauty in style and treatment" (7, 506). He creates a reader based on the last 27 chapters of Isaiah, and his understanding of biblical education as a way to reduce class conflict is clear from the hopes he expresses for this reader:

> Whoever began with laying hold of this series of chapters as a whole would have a starting point and lights of unsurpassed value for getting a conception of the course of man's history and development as a whole.... There are numbers whose crosses are so many and com-

forts so few that to the misery of narrow thoughts they seem almost driven and bound; what a blessing is whatever extricates them and makes them live with the life of the race. (7, 72)

John Henry Newman applauds the intention, though he has problems with the choice of Isaiah (because the messianic passages might lead to disputes over dogma). In 1872, he writes to Arnold suggesting that he develop a popular edition of 1 Samuel for school children: "If I was obliged to throw out some alternative for popular education, I should recommend the 1st book of Samuel; which is a perfect poem . . ." (Newman: vol. 26, 95–96).

It is at least odd, and we would claim significant, that Newman should recommend to Arnold, the great scourge of the Victorian Philistines, the part of the Bible which most treats of the ancient Philistines! In fact, Newman's words, in their context, summarize all the points we shall deal with in this final section: the desire of a threatened intellectual class to take control of a highly centralized public education; the assumption that the Bible is an apt vehicle for education designed to erase class difference; the choice of 1 Samuel as especially apt for this project; and the reference to its artistic perfection.

Arnold's project, in a word, is to save the masses from the Philistines. He wants to take responsibility, over the head of the Philistine middle class, for the religious education of the lower class, the Populace. And he believes that this can happen only in a strong statist political framework. There is an invitation here to pursue further the deep-structural link between Arnold and the Bible which we proposed in the last section. For the adoption of kingship in Israel, the move to a strong statist system, is presented at least by some parts of Judges and 1 Samuel as a way of saving the ordinary Israelite from the "Philistines," whether these are thought of as a literal foreign oppressor or as an externalization of decentralizing tendencies in Israelite society (cf. "everyone doing what is right in his own eyes").[27] It is integral to the ideology of kingship to claim that it exists by popular acclaim, since this justifies its suppression of other structures of power (Jobling, 1992:20–21).

The same logic of appeal to the masses over the heads of other interests can be found in Brentano. The form of his appeal to the

---

[27] It is not our intention here to examine what the decentralizing tendencies might be. On these issues, see Gottwald, 1986.

masses is his life's work of bringing folk-literature to a place of prominence in national life; this is a way of overcoming the modernizing influence of the (Philistine) Enlightenment.

The establishment of this pattern brings us to the topic of this final section—the recent use of "Philistine" to mean artistically illiterate, and the current movement to read the Bible as high literary art. For the same logic as we have traced in Judges, 1 Samuel, Brentano and Arnold, emerges again in the practitioners of this movement. It is this logic which governs, for example, Meir Sternberg's "foolproof composition," which he puts forward as a (even the) foremost characteristic of biblical poetics. His key passage on this issue is worth quoting *in extenso*:

> By foolproof composition I mean that the Bible is difficult to read, easy to underread and overread and even misread, but virtually impossible to, so to speak, counterread. Here as elsewhere, of course, *ignorance, willfulness, preconception, tendentiousness*—all amply manifested throughout history, in the religious and other approaches—may perform wonders of *distortion*. No text can withstand the kind of methodological *license* indulged in by the rabbis in contexts other than legal, or by critics who mix up their quest for the source with the need to *fabricate a new discourse*. Still less can it protect itself against being yoked by *violence*, in the manner of the christological tradition, with a later text whose very premises of discourse (notably "insider" versus "outsider") it would find incomprehensible. Nor can it do much to keep out *invidious assumptions* about Israelite ethics and culture.... In a hermeneutic and *moral* as well as a theological sense, interpretation may always be performed *in bad faith*.
>   Short of such *extremes*, biblical narrative is virtually impossible to counterread. (Sternberg: 50, our emphasis.)

Sternberg here makes a gesture to the common reader. Although the audience of his book will be readers capable of a more "plenary" understanding (56) the common reader need not worry that the simpler message which he or she is able to derive will be different in principle from the more sophisticated one. Sternberg makes this gesture, though, over the heads of a great multitude of readers whose existence he first declares "virtually impossible"—the "counterreaders." Given that counterreading is so very hard, it is astonishing how many readers Sternberg is able to include in this category—aggadic readers in general, a great many Christian readers, and various readers "in bad faith." He does not specify the bad faith readers, but one is tempted to believe that some of them would be the kinds of reader whom Robert Alter and Frank Kermode exclude from the purview of their *Literary Guide to the Bible*: Marxist and psychoanalytic critics,

Deconstructionists [sic] and some feminist critics, and, more vaguely, "critics who use the text as a springboard for cultural or metaphysical ruminations."[28] Certainly such critics (including us) want (in Sternberg's words) to "fabricate a new discourse" that brings biblical discourse into critical new relationships.

Reviewing recent work on 1 Samuel, David Jobling (1993:20–21) argues that this sort of methodological exclusion expresses a sense of anarchy in current biblical studies, a sense that "every one is doing what is right in his/her own eyes," and implies a demand for some sort of consensus, a "king in Israel" (Judg. 21:25). The consensus proposed is based on the Bible as literature, and its advocates often make far-reaching claims for the Bible's literary quality (for example, "Scripture emerges as the most interesting as well as the greatest work in the narrative tradition" [Sternberg: 518]). Jobling further notes that the consensus-seekers distance themselves from political discussion of the Bible, and are not in dialogue with those who read it out of overt political commitment. Arnold's notion that the Bible transcends class difference is near at hand.

But are the readers over whose heads Sternberg addresses the common reader of the Bible *Philistines?* Two considerations suggest so. First, we omitted from the long quote from Sternberg (see the lacuna) his only specific example of bad faith reading. He disapproves of the following words by Bruce Vawter:

> [The Bible develops] the sort of themes that would appeal to rough humor and rouse the chuckles of the fairly low audience for whom they were designed, who doubled with merriment at the thought of the "uncircumcised." (Vawter: 359)

Sternberg does not explicitly call Vawter a Philistine; but that his sole example of reading in bad faith directly evokes the Philistines strikes us as a (non-)coincidence on a par with Newman's recommending 1 Samuel to Arnold. To put words in Sternberg's mouth, his complaint about Vawter is that to accuse the ancient Israelites, the biblical audience, of taking a Philistine attitude to the Philistines is, well, Philistine.[29]

---

[28] Alter and Kermode: 6. The gesture of this General Introduction is the same as Sternberg's, for Alter and Kermode's exclusion of these kinds of literary criticism is part of a broad appeal to educated readers. For such readers, they present Matthew Arnold as a model, though now scarcely attainable (p. 3).

[29] Despite the coincidence in the vertical code, Vawter's *low* reader is a very different character from Sternberg's *under*reader!

Second, Sternberg refers elsewhere in his book (162) to "all qualified observers, pointedly excluding unbelievers like the afflicted Philistines or waverers like Gideon." It is true that he is talking here of
inner-biblical observers, those who are "qualified" to take divine hints
(like Abraham's servant in Genesis 24, drawing conclusions about
the divine will from the indications in his encounter with Rebekah).
But there is hardly a distinction in Sternberg's hermeneutical circle
between the qualification of biblical characters to interpret right, based
on their belief, and the qualification of modern readers to do so,
based on their good or bad faith.

Sternberg's "unbelievers like the afflicted Philistines" return us to
the text of 1 Samuel. He is referring to 1 Sam. 6:9, where the Philistines, afflicted with plagues, consider the possibility that their suffer-
ings may be "by chance" rather than from Yahweh; their unbelief,
then, consists in their keeping open an explanation of their experience which differs from the narrator's (Sternberg: 105). Sternberg's
argument is illuminated by Robert Polzin's treatment of 1 Sam. 6:9.
But before turning to this, some more general comments on Polzin
are necessary.

He prefaces his treatment of the Philistines with part of a quote
from Arnold which we also have used: "Philistine must have originally
meant, in the mind of those who invented the nickname, a strong,
dogged, unenlightened opponent of the chosen people, of the children
of the light" (Polzin: 55, Arnold: vol. 3, 112; it is not clear what
Polzin intends by this epigraph, since he never refers to it afterwards).
He also uses the word "mechanical" in a way directly reminiscent of
Arnold.[30] We have seen how this is one of Arnold's favourite epithets
for the Philistines; but he also refers to the "mechanical" criticism of
some German biblical scholars of his time (7, 203). Polzin's usage is
slightly more complicated; he is referring not to different critics, but
to the different views that critics take of the biblical author/editor.
Polzin contrasts critics like himself who affirm the aesthetic achievement of the ancient storyteller with other critics who see 1 Samuel
as the "mechanical" work of a "crude" editor. But, by transference,[31]

---

[30] In the section, "The Mechanical Author" (9–11), where he is arguing the case
for the Bible as high literary art, and often elsewhere.
[31] We use the psychoanalytic term "transference" (and its cognates) in literary
criticism in much the way that Jane Gallop (1985) does—to trace the ways in which
the dynamics *in* the text get reproduced in the interpretation *of* the text. See also
Jobling, 1994.

there is little difference here; critics see ancient writers as mechanical when their own critical procedures are mechanical, while critics need aesthetic competence to appreciate the storyteller's aesthetic achievement.[32]

Polzin's treatment of the biblical Philistines in 1 Samuel 4–7 is ambiguous in a way reminiscent particularly of Brentano and Fichte—making fun of the Philistines while worrying about whether one is really different from them.[33] On the one hand, he sees the presentation of them as prejudicial; "the fairly comical struggles of the Philistines" (4), the "almost playful picture" of them as "misguidedly ignorant" (58). On the other hand, he finds, as we have seen, a powerful pressure to *parallel* Israel and the Philistines.[34]

To return to 1 Sam. 6:9, the transferential relationships between text and reading come to the fore in Polzin's comment on this verse:

> What the Philistine sorcerers say about God's "heavy hand" is relevant as the reader ponders the nature of the intricate compositional connections between chapters 4–6 and their literary context. The text offers two alternatives; the intricacy happened "by chance" or "it is *his* hand that strikes us" (6:9). Is the narrative hand "crude"—what critics usually mean when they write *redactional*—or "careful"—what I mean when I write *authorial?* (Polzin: 56–57.)

The transference which we made above in discussing Sternberg is precisely accomplished in this quote from Polzin! Commentators who reject Polzin's (or Sternberg's) view of the narrator's view are putting themselves in the place of the Philistines! The question whether every textual phenomenon represents the conscious will of the narrator becomes *the same as* the theological question of whether all phenomena are due to the will of God (note how, in the quote, God's hand expressly becomes the narrator's hand!).

"Others abide our question. Thou art free." These opening words of Arnold's sonnet on Shakespeare (see Stephens, *et al.*: 511), with their assertion that Shakespeare, by some mysterious quality, exempts himself from the critique we bring to bear on other poets, may apply *a fortiori* to the Bible, the biblical narrator, and eventually the biblical

---

[32] When Polzin critiques the "patronizing and disdainful attitude" of the "generic" critics towards the biblical storyteller, he does not, any more than Sternberg, avoid displaying just such an attitude towards the critics (e.g., Polzin: 90).

[33] See above, p. 389.

[34] E.g. Polzin: 55. A particularly clear case of this contradiction is to be seen on p. 65: contrast "as humorously ridiculous a light as the narrator can devise" with "God's heavy hand against Israelite and Philistine alike."

God.[35] The approaches of Sternberg, Polzin, Alter and Kermode, for all their dazzling technical achievements, finally constitute an elaborate way of excusing the Bible from "abiding our question." Sternberg's exclusion of counterreaders, Alter and Kermode's exclusion of a variety of methodological options, rule out *a priori* questions which many people are now urgently putting to the Bible—just such questions of class, race and gender as we have pressed here. 1 Sam. 6:9 evokes a whole history of empirical approaches to reality, with which the history of the term "Philistine" is tightly bound up; both Brentano and Arnold are locked in bitter struggle with a commonsense empirical approach to the world which is increasingly disinclined to accept the claims of "high" culture.

The current methodological ferment in biblical studies has less to do with anarchy than with making the Bible, and the institutional governors of its interpretation, "abide our question." "When is a plague just a plague?" ask the biblical Philistines. "Isn't the rainbow just a meteorological phenomenon?" ask Brentano's Philistines. "When is the biblical narrator's skilful use of repetition just the same word being used twice?" ask critics unimpressed by extreme claims about the narrator's skill and control of "his" material. "And when is 'his' 'art of persuasion' in the service of gender or class privilege?"[36]

What is a Philistine reading? Who is the Philistine who reads? A Philistine reading is one which unpacks how "Philistines" ancient and modern have been used, by people who defined their own identity over against the Philistine "other," to found ideologies from which any subjectivity of the other is absent—ideologies which exist precisely to deny the subjectivity of the other. It probes the limits of such ideologies—their dependence on a residue of the very subjectivity they deny—and will build counterreadings. It presses the question of whether the difference can really be established between the Philistine and the non-Philistine. A Philistine reader is one who is ready, in the pursuit of such goals, to become a Philistine from the point of view of some "chosen people." Opting out of the new biblical-literary orthodoxy imposed by a Sternberg, she will go on considering the

---

[35] Indeed, the language of Arnold's sonnet seems to deify Shakespeare:
   Planting his steadfast footsteps in the sea,
   Making the heaven of heavens his dwelling place, etc.
[36] See Sternberg: 441–81, and on this The Bible and Culture Collective: 182 (this work, *The Postmodern Bible*, deals throughout with the methodological issues we are raising in this section).

other possible explanations. A Philistine reading is one which tries to be "uncircumscribed"[37] by the systems of exclusion which define right and wrong readings according to authorized and unauthorized readers—and is sensitive to the need to avoid creating new exclusions.

List of References

Alter, Robert and Frank Kermode, eds.
1987   *The Literary Guide to the Bible.* Cambridge, MA: Harvard University Press.
Arnold, Matthew
1960–77   *The Complete Prose Works of Matthew Arnold.* Ed. R.H. Super. 11 vols. Ann Arbor: University of Michigan Press.
Bible and Culture Collective, The
1995   *The Postmodern Bible.* New Haven: Yale University Press.
Brentano, Clemens
1935   "Der Philister vor, in und nach der Geschichte: Aufgestellt, begleitet und bespiegelt aus göttlichen und weltlichen Schriften und eigenen Beobachtungen." Pp. 190–229 in Andreas Müller (ed.), *Satiren und Parodien.* Leipzig: Reclam. (Orig. 1811.)
Clark, Anna
1989   "Whores and Gossips: Sexual Reputation in London 1770–1825." Pp. 231–48 in A. Angerman *et al.* (eds.), *Current Issues in Women's History.* London and New York: Routledge.
Dawson, William Harbutt
1904   *Matthew Arnold and His Relation to the Thought of Our Time: An Appreciation and a Criticism.* New York and London: Putnam's.
Eagleton, Terry
1990   *The Ideology of the Aesthetic.* Oxford: Blackwell.
Eilberg-Schwartz, Howard
1990   *The Savage in Judaism: An Anthropology of Israelite Religions and Ancient Judaism.* Bloomington: Indiana University Press.
Exum, J. Cheryl
1993   *Fragmented Women: Feminist (Sub)versions of Biblical Narratives.* Journal for the Study of the Old Testament Supplement Series 163. Sheffield: Sheffield Academic Press.
Gallop, Jane.
1985   *Reading Lacan.* Ithaca, NY: Cornell University Press.
Gottwald, Norman K.
1979   *The Tribes of Yahweh: A Sociology of the Religion of Liberated Israel 1250–1050 B.C.E.* Maryknoll, NY: Orbis.
1986   "The Participation of Free Agrarians in the Introduction

---

[37] We have spared the reader this joke up to now. But it was part of our original concept, and we have tried to offer just such an uncircumscribed reading of the term "Philistine."

of Monarchy to Ancient Israel: An Application of H.A. Landsberger's Framework for the Analysis of Peasant Movements." *Semeia* 37:77–106.

1993   "A Hypothesis about Social Class in Monarchic Israel in the Light of Contemporary Studies of Social Class and Social Stratification." Pp. 139–64 in *The Hebrew Bible in Its Social World and Ours*. Atlanta: Scholars Press.

Grimm, Jacob and Wilhelm
1889   *Deutsches Wörterbuch*. Ed. Matthias von Lexer. 16 vols. Leipzig: Hirzel.

Jameson, Fredric
1981   *The Political Unconscious: Narrative as a Socially Symbolic Act*. Ithaca, NY: Cornell University Press.

Jobling, David
1986   *The Sense of Biblical Narrative*. Vol. 2. Sheffield: JSOT.
1992   "Deconstruction and the Political Analysis of Biblical Texts: A Jamesonian Reading of Psalm 72." *Semeia* 59:95—127.
1993   "What, if Anything, is 1 Samuel?" *Scandinavian Journal of the Old Testament* 7:17–31.
1994   "Transference and Tact in Biblical Studies: A Psychological Approach to Gerd Theissen's *Psychological Aspects of Pauline Theology*." *Studies in Religion* 22:451–62.

Midrash Rabbah
1939   *Midrash Rabbah*. Trans. under the editorship of H. Freedman and Maurice Simon. 10 vols. London: Soncino.

Midrash Tehillim
1959   *The Midrash on Psalms*. Ed. William G. Braude. 2 vols. New Haven: Yale University Press.

Newman, John Henry
1973–84   *The Letters and Diaries of John Henry Newman*. Ed. Ian Ker, Thomas Gornall, S.J., *et al*. 31 vols. Oxford: Oxford University Press.

Niditch, Susan
1990   "Samson as Culture Hero, Trickster, and Bandit: The Empowerment of the Weak." *Catholic Biblical Quarterly* 52:608–24.

Oxford University Press
1971   *The Compact Edition of the Oxford English Dictionary*. 2 volumes. Oxford: Oxford University Press.

Polzin, Robert
1989   *Samuel and the Deuteronomist. A Literary Study of the Deuteronomic History Part Two: 1 Samuel*. San Francisco: Harper & Row.

Said, Edward W.
1988   "Michael Walzer's *Exodus and Revolution*: A Canaanite Reading." Pp. 161–78 in Edward W. Said and Christopher Hitchens (eds.), *Blaming the Victims: Spurious Scholarship and the Palestinian Question*. New York: Verso.

Stephens, James, Edwin L. Beck and Royall H. Snow, eds.
1934   *Victorian and Later English Poets*. New York: American Book Company.

Sternberg, Meir
1985   *The Poetics of Biblical Narrative: Ideological Literature and the Drama of Reading.* Bloomington: Indiana University Press.
Vawter, Bruce
1977   *On Genesis: A New Reading.* Garden City, NY: Doubleday.
Walzer, Michael
1985   *Exodus and Revolution.* New York: Basic Books.
Warrior, Robert
1989   "Canaanites, Cowboys, and Indians: Deliverance, Conquest, and Liberation Theology Today." *Christianity and Crisis* 29:261–65.
Westerkamp, Ulrich
1912   *Beitrag zur Geschichte des literarischen Philistertypus mit besonderer Berücksichtigung von Brentanos Philisterabhandlung.* Doctoral dissertation, University of Munich.

ORIENTALISM, ETHNONATIONALISM AND TRANSNATIONALISM: SHIFTING IDENTITIES AND BIBLICAL INTERPRETATION

R.S. Sugirtharajah

We need no longer offer explanations . . . It matters not whether we are good or bad, civilized or barbarian, so long as we are but ourselves.

Gora–Rabindranath Tagore

"Actually, we're all possessed by cultural otherness in one way or another, aren't we?" he asked.

"Except, at this moment in time it can be sort of hard to say what makes for a cultural self and what's an other" . . . "People like us are this impossible collage, aren't we?".

"Tell me about it!" Firoze shouted back.

. . . "You know," Gita reflected, "When I first came here I used to see everything in terms of dichotomies: America was this big lonely place, and so when I thought of India it was mostly in term of happy things. I also used to think there was a space I could arrive where I'd understand everything and be contented ever after."

"But when you got older, and you saw that everything is mixed up, every horizon opens onto another even more complicated one, and no solution is ever final," said Firoze.

"Exactly," Said Gita.

Love, Stars And All That–Kirin Narayan

It is becoming increasingly clear that nationalities, self-identities and cultures are constructed in response to the Other. Edward Said has been instrumental in initiating a lively academic interest in what have now come to be known as colonial discourse studies. His *Orientalism* (1985 [1978]) focuses on how, in a variety of ways, the West has been able to produce texts and codify knowledge about the Other, especially in the form of those who were under its colonial control. He defines Orientalism as dealing with the Orient "by making statements about it, authorizing views of it, describing it, by teaching it, settling it, ruling over it: in short, Orientalism as a Western style for dominating, restructuring, and having authority over the Orient" (1985: 3). In his view, it is a systematic discipline "by which European culture was able to manage—even produce—the Orient politically, sociologically, militarily, ideologically, scientifically, and imaginatively during the post-Enlightenment period" (1985: 3). In other words,

Orientalism results in not just a textualizing of the Orient, but a textualizing on behalf of it and a representing of it, thus making it amenable to certain kinds of control and manipulation. In effect, what Orientalism achieved was that "European culture gained in strength and identity by setting itself off against the Orient as a sort of surrogate and even underground self" (1985: 3). In characterizing and defining the Other, the West characterized and defined itself— as a superior culture "in comparison with all the non-European peoples and cultures" (1985: 7). Inevitably Said's thesis elicited a great amount of controversy and interest among both Western and post-colonial intellectuals. As a consequence of the debate, Said himself has gone on to address some of the criticism and widen his focus to explore the lasting legacy of colonialism—its cultural and intellectual control (*Culture and Imperialism*, 1993).

Said's thesis has mainly to do with European attitudes to the Middle East and Islam and has no direct relevance to biblical materials, though he points out that during the early nineteenth century, the Orient meant only India and the Bible lands (1985: 4). This present essay engages Said's thesis, highlighting the traces of Orientalist ideas, habits and categories in biblical scholarship, and exploring how both Western and Third World[1] scholars have made use of orientalistic formulae to define their identities. It tries to move the debate a step further by discussing the role of the biblical interpreter at a time when national identities, geographical borders and cultural boundaries are being redrawn, re-mapped and re-designed

Oriental Mannerisms and Biblical Interpreters

One can often identify signs of Orientalism in the writings of biblical scholars. As a way of illustrating this I would like to use the works of Joachim Jeremias, and especially his *The Parables of Jesus* (1963), a near-classic in which countless Third World biblical scholars were schooled. Several of the exegetical conclusions Jeremias arrives at betray his euro-centric perception of the Other. The negative carica-

---

[1] The term, "Third World," is used not in a numerical or geographical sense but as a socio-political designation of a people who have been excluded from power and authority to mould and shape their own lives and destiny. For discussion of the term see my *Voices from the Margin: Interpreting the Bible in the Third World* (Maryknoll, NY: Orbis Books, 1991), p. 3.

turing of the characters, condescending remarks he makes about the narrative style of indigenous story-tellers, the stereotyping of the landscape, are all akin to the travel writing, novels and other literary productions of the colonial era rather than to the marks of a biblical scholarship which professes to be rooted in objective science. For him the East is hot (1963: 140); the Orient is full of beggars (1963: 159); the people in the Orient go to bed early (1963: 157); Oriental women are fertile, inferior and submissive (1969: 375); the rich in the East are brutal (1963: 195); and Oriental story-tellers exaggerate and hype their materials. For instance, in the Parable of the Talents, when Matthew boosted up the amount of money and Luke increased the number of servants, Jeremias attributes this hype to the Oriental story-teller's penchant for large numbers, which "led to embellishment in both versions of the story" (1963: 28). Similarly, the fruitful harvest in the Parable of the Sower is dismissed as "abnormal tripling, after the oriental fashion" (1963: 150). Even Jesus does not escape Jeremias' euro-centric jibe. The inflated contract figures in Luke 16:1–9 are dismissed as "the oriental story-teller's love for large numbers" (1963: 181).

The Parables also perpetuates the notion that the Other is lazy and unreliable. When commenting on the Parable of the Labourers in the Vineyard (Matt. 20:1–19), he states that the excuse the labourers who were standing around came out with, that no one had hired them, was their "cover for their typical oriental indifference" (1963: 37, 137). Such exegetical comments are based not so much on the economic realities of the time, or the employment opportunities available to the labourers, as on the euro-centric view of the Oriental as a lazy native.

Look again at the comments he makes on the Parable of the Wicked Servant (Luke 16:1–9). When the steward adjusts the accounts of the debtors, Jeremias' reaction is very interesting. He attributes the extraordinary behaviour of the steward to the people in the East not knowing anything of book-keeping or audits (1963: 181). At a stroke, he not only elevates European achievements in accounting but also rules out the possibility of the contributions Chinese, Indians and Egyptians have made towards the development of present-day mathematics—a point very cogently argued by George Gheverghese Joseph in his recent book, *The Crest of the Peacock: Non-European Roots of Mathematics* (1991). Such a claim also demonstrates the euro-centric parochialism of Jeremias which denies the possibility of other people having different ways of accounting. The exegetical comment on the same parable by Margaret Gibson, during the height of the colonial period, is worth recalling. Her considered view was that the behaviour of the steward was a custom that prevailed "whenever Orientals are left to their own methods, uncontrolled by any protectorate of Europeans" (1902/3: 334).

Jeremias also reinscribes the 19th century binary typology which posited that there were ontological differences between Eastern and Western mentalities (Said 1985: 259). He writes: "It is not the purpose of either parable (The Mustard Seed and the Leaven) merely to describe a process; that would be the way of the western mind. The oriental mind includes both beginning and end in its purview, seizing the paradoxical element in both cases" (1963: 148). Such comparisons reinforce essentialism and become the template for racial determinism and the inferiorising of the Other, in contrast to Western rationality and superiority. Those who have been part of the colonial experience are well aware that stereotyping is one of the mechanisms by which the colonializer distorts and dominates the Other. Jeremias' comments resemble those of the colonial administrators and missionaries who sought to define the Other by contrasting the superiority of Western civilization with noble savages and inferior races. As Said has pointed out, "the Orient has helped to define Europe (or the West) as its contrasting image, idea, personality, experience" (1985: 1–2).

One of the ideas embedded in Orientalism is the view that Orientals are prone to emotionalism and incapable of rational analysis. Translated into biblical scholarship, this means that Western exegetical efforts are a cerebral and intellectual activity, whereas ours are vague and practical. They investigate and interrogate texts, and engage in critical analysis; we deal with people and their pressing social, theological and spiritual concerns. They get to think, meanwhile we feel for the weak and the vulnerable. I would like to use the recent volume that I edited, *Voices from the Margin: Interpreting the Bible in the Third World* (1991), as an example of this perception. When reviewing the book, even a scholar like Christopher Rowland, who is sympathetic to our cause, comments that "the strength of the Third World exegesis does not lie in its ability to revitalize the historical-critical method by supplying information hitherto unavailable. Rather, the insights it has to offer arise from the articulation of a way of reading in which the perspective of the marginal sheds fresh light on the texts and how they may contribute to our understanding of discipleship" (1992: 45, 6). One comment in the "Books Received" section of the *Journal of Biblical Literature* is equally interesting: "This volume contains 34 essays, including an introduction and postscript by the editor, by 28 Latin American, Asian, Native-American, African and African-American contributors. Only those essays in 'Part II: Re-use of the Bible: Examples of Hermeneutical Explorations' are of biblical interest" (1991: 759). The implication seems to be that all historical, exegetical, intellectual activities are assigned to Western scholars and we are asked to articulate from the realm of emotion and experience.

Such attitudes, however sincere they may be, reinscribe the popular perceptions of Third World interpretation, namely, that we are good at drawing theological implications but weak at undertaking original historical investigation. Western biblical scholars extract deep historical truths from the texts, but we provide homiletical guidelines for Christian living. Such a division of labour not only raises questions about the nature and purpose of historical investigation but also rules out the possibility of culturally-informed historical research. Two examples—from Malawi and India—come to mind. A.C. Musopole places witchcraft terminology, which is often dismissed by Western scholars brought up with Enlightenment values as illogical and antisocial, in its socio-medical context, and from this angle investigates Ps. 18:2 and John 6:50–71. His re-reading of these two texts is an example of how cultural nuances can provide critical resources to illuminate the historical context of the texts (Musopole 1993: 347–354). Similarly Daniel L. Smith-Christopher has shown how Mahatma Gandhi's culturally-conditioned reading of Daniel 6 as Hebrew *bhakti* and social resistance literature anticipated the current textual critical questions (1993: 321–338). The interpretative task, then, requires that we read from our social and cultural locations, and interrogate the texts with our different historical questions, exploring insights about what the texts might have meant historically and what they mean today. The introduction of cultural data, both past and present, will help to expand the historical base of the narratives.

One of the notions Orientalism reinforced was the image of the Eastern Other inhabiting a world seen as eternal and timeless. The Oriental world is represented as static and incapable of any change. Biblical scholars often unconsciously replicate this notion that the non-Western nations sometimes lack vitality and creativity, living with conditions, categories and customs that have barely changed since biblical times. Here is one example:

Those like myself who attempt to teach biblical texts from the social science perspective often find that once the ancient Mediterranean world view has been established, and the text explicated in the light of it, Western students find themselves farther from rather than closer to the text, and are left with the question, "so what?". On the contrary, those who attempt the same approach in a non-Western context, find that the text comes alive to students in a way that it was not before. This is because they are hearing the text unfolded in their own social categories, according to their own world view, instead of through the filter of the Western post-enlightenment paradigm with which they do not identify. (Osiek 1992: 94)

There are two presuppositions behind these sincere words. First, non-Western societies are the same as they always have been. The core cultural values such as honour/shame, pollution/purity which Osiek speaks of are static, regardless of the lapse of time. The possibility of development and change are denied. Such an attitude also neutralizes the differences between and within our cultures and amalgamates our particular histories into one, concocting a unitary subject. The other is the assumption that diverse cultural and religious traditions can be bifurcated into two neat divisions—Western and non-Western.

Natives going Oriental

Orientalism is not something confined to Western critics. Traces of it are evident in the writings of Third World biblical scholars as well. For example, some posit the view that there are reasonable similarities between the conflict-ridden Palestine of Jesus' time and present-day Latin America or Asia. The formal similarities such as poverty, oppression and religious authoritarianism which were prevalent in the Roman-occupied setting of Jesus' ministry are seen as resembling those of the current South American situation. The following two statements, replicate the internal Orientalism of Third World scholars:

The socio-political situation in Jesus' day presents striking parallels to the situation that gave rise to Liberation theology in Latin America. (Boff 1980: 103).
[T]here is a clearly noticeable resemblance between the situation here in Latin America and that in which Jesus lived. (Sobrino 1978: 13).

Likewise, the Japanese theologian Hisako Kinukawa sees striking cultural parallels between first-century Palestine and modern-day Japan:

[W]e notice many parallels and similarities between the modern Japanese and ancient Mediterranean cultures. We who share the social scenarios that shaped the perspectives of the people of the early Christian age have an advantage experientially in understanding them. (1994: 22)

Such statements take note of formal similarities between first-century Palestine and present-day Latin America or Japan but fail to note the critical differences between the exploitation of first century Palestine and the neo-colonial exploitation of Latin America today, or between ancient Mediterranean cultures and modern Japanese cultures.

The Natives Deploying Orientalism for Nationalist Ends

While the West has been using Orientalism to define itself, we also used the constructions of Orientalism to define our identities. The Orientalist projection of a glorious Indian past was seized upon by Indian intellectuals to revive nationalistic fervour, affirming the superiority of Eastern spirituality over decadent Western material values. Even the denigrated traits were turned into positive characteristics. Richard Fox's term for this is "affirmative orientalism" (1992: 152). The backward rural village is now seen as a self-contained, consensus-led and de-bureaucratised community; passivity becomes non-violence; lack of initiative is seen as mark of non-possessiveness, and otherworldliness is turned into spirituality. More importantly, Indian Christian theologians played a critical role in creating a national consciousness. Viewed by the majority Hindus as anti-nationalist, Christian interpreters delved into the ancient Hindu texts to earn their acceptability as true nationals. These Christians followed the path set by the orientalists, and saw the recovery of the Indian sacred texts (the *Vedas*, the *Upanishads*, the *Dharmashastras* and the *Bhagavadgita*), the use of the indigenous literary theories such as *dhvani*, and the employment of various philosophical and logical systems, as a way of entering into the mainstream national life. Comparative studies such as those on the *Gita* and the Fourth gospel (Amaladoss 1975), *Manusmrti* and the Pentateuch (Manickam 1977), and the deployment of the *dhvani* method (Vandana 1981) are all seen not only as celebrating India's glorious past but also as recovering an authentically Indian identity for Christians. Such hermeneutical endeavours have enabled Indian Christians to get rid of their anti-patriotic label, but also have enabled them to invent a self-image. Such constructions

of nationalism were not only a by-product of the internalization of
Orientalism, but were worked out within the framework of the Indian classical Sanskritic tradition at the expense of India's vernacular, oral and folk categories.

Another aspect of internal Orientalism is the privileging of foreign
languages and foreign texts. For instance, those who write in English
are accorded a privileged status over those who use vernacular languages. One of the achievements of colonial education was to produce a false consciousness among the colonialized that knowledge in
any field of learning—whether in science, theology or technology—
could be acquired only through the mediation of modern western
texts. The internalization of this belief has led to the neglect of modern
sources outside European tradition and scholarship. Some Asian
scholars hardly cite works from our own regions. Even when writing
about pain and suffering we rush to Moltmann's *The Crucified God*
(1974), almost forgetting Kitamori (1966). I am not arguing against
foreign influence or borrowing but against our failure to recognize
our own worth.

Acquiring New Identities

Currently, the idea of nationalism itself is going through a severe
reappraisal. Two categories of uprooted people raise special questions for national identity. One is voluntary exiles and the other is
internal exiles. The former are the de-localized transnationals—cf.
Appadurai's term "Postnational" (1993: 417)—who are part of the
diasporic culture which moves across borders and feels at home everywhere and nowhere; the latter are the de-rooted nationals who find
themselves refugees in their own countries, or move to another country
and live in refugee camps and re-settlement reserves. What unites
these two groups is that they both long for a home. The reality of
homelessness is increasingly becoming a new framework for hermeneutics, and it evokes contrary responses. On the one hand, the global theorists propound a borderless transnationalism which scales the
boundaries of nations, territories and states, while on the other hand,
minority communities are engaged in ethnonationalist struggles in-
voking various kinds of age-old tribal and indigenous sentiments.
Makarand Paranjape calls this sub-nationalism (1994: 76).

In the face of the increasing assault on identity, the challenge for some one like myself is to create a contemporary identity which is eclectic, flexible, peaceful, and (in my case) Sri Lankan. However, Sri Lanka itself has become a highly contested site. In overlapping and multiple axes of identification, two negotiating options are generally held to be open to us: either to say that there is no such thing as Sri Lankanness because it is non-existent or unclarifiable, or go to the other extreme and fashion a very narrow and one-dimensional notion of ourselves in territorial and linguistic terms, as various ethnic groups are trying to do. I think there is a third alternative. That is, to position ourselves between and betwixt cultures and countries and engage in a processual hermeneutic. JanMohamed calls this limbo state the "interstitial cultural space" (1992: 97). It is a vantage point from which those who are caught amidst several cultures and groups, and are unable or unwilling to feel "at home" in any, can come up with unlimited alternative forms of group identity and social arrangement. This is not only a mediating position between communities, cultures and nations, but it also enables us to subject them to "analytic scrutiny."

It is in this uncolonialized space, if there ever is one, that contemporary hermeneutical praxis must reserve for itself the freedom to mix and harmonize, change and retain various ingredients. Locking oneself into any one position will be to deny oneself available options. This is precisely what Iqbal Ahmed Chaudhary, the narrator in Adib Khan's novel, *Seasonal Adjustments* (1994) did not want to happen to his daughter, Nadine. *Seasonal Adjustments* is a novel about moving between Bangladesh and Australia and also about coming to terms with mixed marriage—Catholic and Muslim. Keith, the Australian father-in-law, a Catholic, is keen that his grand-daughter, Nadine should be baptized so that she can preserve the family tradition. But the child's father, Chaudhary, is not particularly happy with Keith's brand of Christianity. He feels that the narrowness of a single tradition may be a handicap to his daughter who is growing up in multi-cultural Australia. He is more concerned that Nadine should be exposed to different views and ideas before she works out her own religious stance. In a heated conversation at a family party, Keith, who represents the old single-culture Australia, says in a desperately arrogant voice: "Every child is born into a tradition." Chaudhary replies in an equally irritant tone: "Nadine will be among a slowly growing minority which will learn how to combine traditions. It will not be easy" (1994: 85). It is in this "interstitial cultural space" that the post-nationals in their metropolis and the subnationals in their refugee settlement, will work out a relevant hermeneutics. This, as Chaudhary says, will not be easy.

List of References

Amaladoss, M.A.
1975   "An Indian Reads St. John's Gospel." Pp. 7–24 in C. Durai-
            singh and Cecil Hargreaves (eds.), *India's Search for Reality and
            the Relevance of the Gospel of John*. Delhi: ISPCK.
Appadurai, Arjun
1993   "Patriotism and its Futures." *Public Culture* 5/3:411–29.
Boff, Leonardo
1980   "Christ's Liberation via Oppression: An Attempt at Theo-
            logical Construction from the Standpoint of Latin America."
            Pp. 100–34 in Rosino Gibellini (ed.), *Frontiers of Theology in
            Latin America*. London: SCM Press.
Fox, Richard G.
1992   "East of Said." Pp. 144–56 in Michael Sprinker (ed.), *Edward
            Said: A Critical Reader*. Oxford: Blackwell.
Gibson, Margaret D.
1902/3   "On the Parable of the Unjust Steward." *The Expository Times*
            14:334.
JanMohamed, Abdul R.
1992   "Worldliness-without-World, Homelessness-as-Home: Toward
            a Definition of a Specular Border Intellectual." Pp. 96–120
            in Michael Sprinker (ed.), *Edward Said: A Critical Reader*. Ox-
            ford: Blackwell.
Jeremias, Joachim
1963   *The Parables of Jesus* (revised edition). London: SCM Press.
—— 1969   *Jerusalem in the Time of Jesus*. London: SCM Press.
Joseph, George Gheverghese
1991   *The Crest of the Peacock: Non-European Roots of Mathematics*. Lon-
            don: Penguin Books.
Khan, Adib
1994   *Seasonal Adjustments*. St. Leonards NSW: Allen and Unwin.
Kinukawa, Hisako
1994   *Women and Jesus in Mark: A Japanese Feminist Perspective*. Mary-
            knoll, NY: Orbis Books. English edition: SPCK: London.
Kitamori, Kazoh
1966   *Theology of the Pain of God*. London: SCM Press. Japanese edition
            1946.
Manickam, T.M.
1977   *Dharma According to Manu and Moses*. Bangalore: Dharmaram
            Publications.
Moltmann, Jürgen
1974   *The Crucified God*. London: SCM Press.
Musopole, A.C.
1993   "Witchcraft Terminology, The Bible, and African Christian

Theology: An Exercise in Hermeneutics." *Journal of Religion in Africa* 23/4:347–54.

Osiek, Carolyn
1992   "The Social Sciences and the Second Testament: Problems and Challenges." *Biblical Theology Bulletin* 22/2:88–95.

Paranjape, Makarand
1994   "Indian (English) Criticism." *Indian Literature* 160:70–78.

Rowland, Christopher
1992   Review of *Voices from the Margin*. *Theology* 95:45–6.

Said, Edward
1985 (1978)   *Orientalism*. Harmondsworth, Penguin Books.
—— 1993   *Culture and Imperialism*. London: Chatto and Windus.

Smith-Christopher, Daniel L.
1993   "Gandhi on Daniel: Some Thoughts on a 'Cultural Exegesis of the Bible.'" *Biblical Interpretation: A Journal of Contemporary Approaches* 1/3:321–28.

Sobrino, Jon
1978   *Christology at the Crossroads: A Latin American Approach*. London: SCM Press.

Sugirtharajah, R.S.
1991   *Voices from the Margin: Interpreting the Bible in the Third World*. Maryknoll, NY: Orbis Books. English edition, London: SPCK.

Vandana, Sister
1981   *Waters of Fire*. Bangalore: Asia Trading Corporation.

CULTURAL BIAS IN EUROPEAN AND NORTH AMERICAN BIBLICAL SCHOLARSHIP

John Riches

The present reflections are prompted by engagement in an international research project whose principal focus is on interpreting the Bible in African contexts.[1] If African scholars wish to use the methods of contemporary biblical criticism to interpret the biblical texts, to what extent are they taking over methods and modes of reading which are transcultural (like algebra), to what extent are they taking over a set of questions and procedures which are rooted in a very different economic, political and cultural context and which may reflect concerns which are not theirs and indeed attitudes which are positively inimical to them?

The kind of inculturation hermeneutics which many African scholars are now developing[2] has a number of identifiable aims. It seeks in the first place to use the resources of one's own culture to *understand* the biblical texts. Thus it is argued that African beliefs and experience may provide important analogies with ancient texts, which are not available or readily available to scholars from other cultures (e.g., belief in spirits, patterns of social organisation). And it also seeks to read the texts in such a way that they may illumine the profound questions which engage a particular cultural group at a particular time and therefore to show how those texts can be appropriated and given social embodiment in that culture (renewal of African identity, questions concerning personal survival beyond death and the place of the ancestors in a religious world-view).

Put like this, it can be fairly easily seen that very similar aims

---

[1] This project was coordinated by Dr. Justin Ukpong of the Catholic Institute of West Africa and is supported by the Department of Biblical Studies, Glasgow University, the Department of Religion and Classics, University of Zimbabwe, the Institute for the Study of the Bible, University of Natal, Pietermaritzburg. A full report of its Glasgow consultation is available on request to me.

[2] See e.g., J.S. Ukpong, *Proclaiming the Kingdom: Essays in Contextual New Testament Studies* (CIWA Publications, P.O. Box 499, Port Harcourt, 1993); J.S. Ukpong, T. Okure, et al. (ed.), *Evangelization in Africa in the Third Millenium: Challenges and Prospects* (CIWA Press, Port Harcourt, 1992); P. Schineller, *A Handbook on Inculturation* (New York: Paulist Press, 1990).

have in fact been pursued by many European and North American biblical scholars. It has been an accepted principle of historiography that the historian should seek to understand the meaning of the texts and documents which he/she studies by the use of analogy.[3] And scholars as diverse in their cultural and social context as Martin Luther and F.C. Baur have approached the biblical texts with leading questions which reflect their own different settings and concerns. Luther's question "How do I get a just God?" and Baur's attempt to show how the biblical texts contribute to the expression of a new stage in the development of the human consciousness[4] are both defining questions in the sense that they set the direction for many years for the subsequent efforts of scholars and so define a whole epoch of scholarship.

This is not to deny that the tradition of European and North American scholarship which still holds the ascendancy in the professional associations of biblical scholars was also responsible for the development of "purely historical" methods (Baur) which seek to answer these questions in ways which are publicly accountable. It is rather to draw attention to the importance of particular cultural questions, experiences and beliefs in the ways in which different generations of scholars understand and appropriate their texts and therefore to raise the question of cultural bias in such work. How far may this—quite proper—cultural dimension of biblical interpretation lead to distortion, to bias? And how can this be defined and identified?

Cultural bias may enter in at different points of this exercise. We may in the first instance too easily overlook certain aspects of ancient culture and overemphasise others by pressing analogies with our own. Tyrrell's famous taunt that Harnack looked down the well of history and saw his own, Liberal Protestant, face reflected at the bottom,[5] if true, is a devastating indictment of one of the major historians of his generation who believed that he could indeed discriminate between those elements which were central to Jesus' religious faith (his sense of the presence of God in his heart) and those which were merely the husk of such beliefs (his belief, shared with

---

[3] Ernst Troeltsch, *Gesammelte Schriften*, *II* (Tübingen: J.C.B. Mohr, 1913), pp. 729–753; "Historiography," in J. Hastings (ed.), *Encyclopaedia of Religion and Ethics* (New York: Charles Scribners, 1914), VI, pp. 716–723. See too, V.A. Harvey, *The Historian and the Believer* (London: SCM, 1967).

[4] For a somewhat fuller discussion see my "A Future for New Testament theology?," *Literature and Theology* 8/4 (1994), pp. 343–353.

[5] G. Tyrrell, *Christianity at the Cross-roads* (London, 1909) p. 44.

many of his time, in the imminent end of the world).[6] And yet, others (Albert Schweitzer, E.P. Sanders)[7] have argued persuasively that Jesus can be understood properly only when we see the central role which such apocalyptic beliefs in an imminent end play in Jesus' religious beliefs. Our attempts to read the historical evidence in the light of analogies between ourselves and Jesus may, that is to say, equally lead us to a sense of the strangeness between Jesus and ourselves, as Schweitzer saw.[8] It is not so much the role of the analogical imagination in historiography which is at fault but the desire to conform the subject of our study to those aspects of our experience which provide the closest analogies, which leads to bias and distortion.

Again, the questions which we pose to the texts may serve both to illumine and to distort them. If Luther wrestles with the meaning of Rom 1:17 in order to discover the meaning of the "righteousness of God" and to deliver himself from his own pangs of conscience and fears of judgment, then he may (does, I would want to argue) discern elements in the text which are genuinely liberative. But as we shall see there is a danger in this. In pressing answers to our questions we may too easily overlook questions and concerns in the texts which are not our own and thus constrict our view of the text. More disturbingly perhaps, the very fact that we succeed in appropriating the texts may easily lead to their annexation: to a sense that the texts are ours and that we are specially privileged in respect of these texts. This is of course one easy way of fuelling one's sense of one's own importance, of producing a sense (similar to that engendered by Harnack's identification of his religious sensibilities with those of Jesus) of cultural superiority. If the texts speak to our cultural concerns so directly, then is it not true that we are uniquely their heirs?

In what follows I want to pick out a few examples from the history of biblical scholarship which may serve to illustrate the workings of such cultural bias and distortion, as well as showing how enormously fruitful such culturally specific readings have been. At the same time it will be important to consider the role of historical methods in these examples. In this way one may be able to argue both for a proper, if self-critical, role for inculturation hermeneutics

---

[6] A.V. Harnack, *What is Christianity?* (Philadelphia: Fortress, 1957), p. 55.

[7] A. Schweitzer, *The Quest for the Historical Jesus* (London: A&C. Black, 1936); E.P. Sanders, *Jesus and Judaism* (London: SCM 1985).

[8] See my "Apocalyptic-Strangely Relevant," in W. Horbury (ed.), *Templum Amicitiae* (Sheffield: JSOT Press, 1991), pp. 237–263.

and to suggest that there are aspects of historical work which are to be seen as transcultural.

Lutheran interpretations of Paul and, by extension, Judaism have recently been the subject of fierce criticism[9] which has on occasion come close to accusations of racism and religious prejudice. Do such criticisms do justice to Luther's own search for liberty and self-identity? Luther was tormented by the question: how do I get a just God? In a situation where he was encouraged to believe that only by following the rigours of late Mediaeval penitential discipline could he satisfy a relentless and almighty God, he turned to Paul and Rom. 1:17: in it (the gospel) the righteousness of God is revealed. This he had been taught to read as referring to the formal or active righteousness of God: that by which God is himself righteous, that which he exercises in punishing sinners and rewarding the righteous. As if it were not enough that the Law should reveal to him the wrath of God to sinners, the gospel was to reinforce it too. But by battling away at the text, by reading it in the context of the Psalms and of the Fathers, but more importantly in the context of the chapter in Romans: "he who is righteous through faith shall live," he eventually came to see that the genitive "of God" referred not to the righteousness which belongs to God but to the righteousness which comes to men and women as a gift from God and which is received in faith. All at once, Luther tells us the meaning of Scripture was opened up to him and a whole new world came to birth as he ran through Scripture in his mind.[10]

The significance of this reading of Romans was of course enormous for Europe—and therefore for all who subsequently had the fortune or misfortune to be involved in the history of Europe. Let me make some brief points.

This was essentially a grammatical reading of the text. Luther was using, passionately, but nonetheless responsibly and indeed in an exemplary way, the methods of humanist scholarship to break open the meaning of the Pauline text. An awareness of grammar, syntax, of the relation of Paul's text to its context and to other biblical texts, of the possibility of readings other than the standard orthodox, church

---

[9] Notably by E.P. Sanders, in his *Paul and Palestinian Judaism*, (London: SCM 1977), pp. 33–59. But see too S. Westerholm, *Israel's Law and the Church's Faith* (Grand Rapids: Eerdmans, 1988).
[10] Preface to the Latin Writings, *Luther's Works*, Vol. 34 (St. Louis: Concordia, 1960), pp. 336f.

readings: all this informs Luther's search for "what Paul intended" and has inspired countless works of sharp-eyed and scholarly exegesis. Against such there is no law.

Nevertheless his reading is directed by questions about his identity which were able to move large sections of his society. In his *de libertate christiana*[11] Luther makes it clear that his search is for a realm of freedom which would lie outside the control of the ecclesiastical authorities, where the believer would be lord of all, prophet, priest and king, and where he/she also would know herself to be a servant of all. It is in this sphere of inwardness, of faith, that the believer's relationship to her God is rooted, not in the outward sphere of "works-righteousness" which can be controlled by church discipline and canon law. The believer's works *ad extra* may still be ambiguous and subject to the discipline of the state, but in faith he knows himself to be *simul justus et peccator* and can discover a new sense of liberty, calling and service. It is here—and only here—that believers meet their God in Christ and find life and self-worth.

The consequences of this are far-reaching: on the one hand there grows out of this a strong sense of group identity which is closely linked, though not identical with various German regional identities.[12] On the other hand, it leads Luther to make a radical distinction between those who live by faith and *all* those who do not. Thus he divides the world into two: all those who imagine that by their own efforts they can gain life and salvation: monks, philosophers, Turks, Jews[13] and those who know that salvation rests in accepting God's gift of righteousness in faith.

It is not difficult to see why Luther's reading of Paul was so powerful and liberative for him and for subsequent generations of scholars and believers. It forged a new family of communities with a strong sense of group identity and released the emergent German nation

---

[11] de libertate christiana, *WA*, 7.50, 5–30; for a somewhat fuller discussion, see my "Nachfolge," *TRE* XXIII (Berlin: W. de Gruyter, 1994), p. 692.

[12] Cf. the introduction to G. Ritter, *Luther: His Life and Work* (London: Collins, 1963), where he asserts that "[t]o a German, Luther's character has always borne an unmistakably national stamp and he has appeared as one of the most important architects and personalities of the national, intellectual tradition and way of life." (15) He goes on to say, however, in the light of the catastrophe of the Second World War that this is now superseded and that Luther's life "now bears upon the whole question of our spiritual existence, with those basic questions on whose solution the formation of human culture is completely dependent." (16)

[13] Commentary on Galatians *ad* 2.16, *Luther's Works*, Vol. 26 (St. Louis: Concordia, 1963), p. 140.

from its Babylonian captivity to the Church of Rome. But questions remain as to its cultural bias: both in relation to its understanding of the texts and in relation to the attitudes which it may engender towards other cultures and people.

In the first place, emphasis on justification by faith as the fundamental experience of God through which the Christian discovers life and freedom leads to a neglect of other elements in Paul: his concern with the history of God's dealings with the peoples of the world, not least with Israel; his striving to give a positive account of the Law and of the place of ethical imperatives in the Christian life. The danger of pressing too hard on the analogy between "Lutheran" experience of liberation from a troubled conscience (and the Babylonian captivity of the Church) and Paul's sense of freedom and life in Christ is great and easily leads to a one-sided interpretation of Paul.[14] Secondly, Luther's question, seen as a question about group and national identity leads him to see all cultures in terms of a simple dualism of faith and "works-righteousness"; the world is recast in these terms and therefore all who do not find the way to faith are to be categorised as those who seek their "own righteousness."

Theoretically this could lead to a quite different attitude to other cultures: recognising that there may indeed be others who do not seek their "own righteousness" and therefore leaving judgments on others open. In practice, it all too easily leads into a Lutheran doctrine of the necessity for salvation of the acceptance of the Gospel as taught by D. Martin Luther and to a traducing of all other cultures, foremost among them Judaism, as they are forced into the mould of "works-righteousness."

Nevertheless while it is true that much Lutheran scholarship has indeed pressed the analogy between Lutheran experience of faith and Paul's theology too hard, it needs to be seen that Lutherans like Krister Stendahl[15] and Ernst Käsemann,[16] as well as other scholars like E.P. Sanders, have, diversely and indeed antagonistically, attempted to correct the balance by historical argument and scrutiny of both Pauline and Jewish texts. Again, careful attention to what is

---

[14] Cf. K. Stendahl, "The Apostle Paul and the Introspective Conscience of the West," in *Paul Among Jews and Gentiles* (Philadelphia: Fortress, 1976), pp. 78–96, with particular reference to Phil. 3 and Rom. 9–11.

[15] *Paul Among Jews and Gentiles*.

[16] *Perspectives on Paul* (London: SCM, 1971).

said and to the context in which it is said, may serve to highlight the differences between Protestant/Lutheran senses of liberation and Paul's.

My second example is that of F.C. Baur, the German Protestant theologian who dominated New Testament studies in the nineteenth century. Baur's social and cultural context was very different from that of Luther's. Coming from an orthodox Lutheran family, he sought as a university professor in the burgeoning culture of nineteenth century Germany to give an account of Christianity which would show its entitlement to a central place in the new bourgeois culture. If Luther was a revolutionary, counter-cultural figure overthrowing the great mediaeval synthesis of church, state and society, Baur's concern was to justify theology's place within the academy to its "cultured despisers," something he did with astonishing success. Accordingly in his *Church History*[17] he sets out to place Christianity in its context in world history. The Christian religion came into being at the time when the Roman Empire had established a measure of unity in the Mediterranean world. The period saw the emergence of a more universal consciousness in world history, which found its religious expression in Christianity with its rejection of the particularities of local cults and codes. For it was a religion in which there would in Christ be neither Jew nor Gentile, slave nor free, male nor female (in theory at least).

Baur's purpose may have been apologetic but his methods and arguments needed to be those which would carry weight in the academy. Thus he sought to offer an account of Christianity which was "purely historical." And again one must say that much of the work which he did was exemplary. He it was who scrutinised the Pauline epistles in an attempt to determine which were from Paul and which were not and who was responsible for setting biblical studies on a firm historical footing. He it was who first seriously attempted to give an account of the development of early Christianity, showing how it moved from the teaching of Jesus with his universalist ethic but his still particularist understanding of himself as the Jewish Messiah via Paul with his Law-free doctrine of the Spirit, through the struggles between Pauline and Petrine Christianity with its emphasis on the Law, to a final synthesis in early Catholicism. Thus Baur portrays the growth of early Christianity as a new form of culture

---

[17] *The Church History of the First Three Centuries* (London: Williams and Norgate, 1878–9).

which gave expression to a new universal religious self-consciousness. Those who were in Christ were new creatures who transcended the old particularist cultures, Judaism and the pagan cultures of the ancient world. Judaism with its monotheistic developments was in many ways superior to other Hellenistic religions, but it was still, with its particular codes, inferior to Christianity.

There can be no denying Baur's contribution to the development of historical studies of the New Testament. At the same time we must notice his limitations and the place at which distortion may creep in. Baur was heavily dependent on Hegel's philosophy of *Geist* for the account which he offered of the development and history of the Christian religion out of Jewish and Hellenistic religion. It was through the Spirit that there gradually and dialectically emerged a new, more universal self-consciousness which was, as Christ-consciousness, at the same time a consciousness of the universal spirit which manifests itself by entering into the limitations of human culture and gradually transcending the particularities of local cultures and religions. Baur's key-witnesses in all this were texts like 1 Cor. 2:10–16: "no one comprehends the thoughts of God except the Spirit of God . . . we have the mind of Christ." Yet as Schweitzer, Wrede and later E.P. Sanders pointed out, to lay stress on the possession of the Spirit in this sense is to miss the profoundly eschatological/apocalyptic character of Paul's thought. It was too, as W. Heitmüller would argue, to overlook the strong parallels between Paul's use of "spirit" and that of popular Greek religion with its enthusiasm and sacramental rites. Spirit for Paul was more closely related to the notion of spirit possession than to the heightening of moral and religious consciousness which Hegel described in his philosophy of *Geist*.[18]

Furthermore there is no mistaking the sense in which Baur's portrayal of Christianity as the expression of the new universal moral, religious self-consciousness is the means of a massive annexation of Christianity by Protestant bourgeois culture (in this respect it was truly European and could be enthusiastically embraced in England, Scotland and elsewhere in Europe). It shows *Kulturprotestantismus* as the highest form of religion with all others subordinate to it. It does not, like Luther, relegate all others to the status of false religions; rather it encourages attempts to grade different religions into higher

---

[18] See my *A Century of New Testament Study* (Cambridge: Lutterworth, 1993), pp. 31–49.

and lower. But it does make it quite clear who is at the top. And most importantly it shows—a particular cultural form of—Christianity as replacing other forms of religious culture as outmoded and superfluous. But while it thus showed nineteenth century European Christianity to be superior to other religions it left open the question of the debt of Christianity to other forms of religion. To what extent did Christianity arise out of other forms of religion; to what extent in its subsequent development was it indebted to the different cultures in which it took root?

Baur had many sons. Perhaps the most interesting of his followers were the so-called History of Religions School, scholars like H. Gunkel and W. Bousset. Their goal was to plot the development of religious beliefs in the ancient world and in particular to examine the degree to which Christianity had borrowed from, emerged out of other contemporary religions: Judaism, the Mystery religions and the other pagan religions of the Mediterranean. This in turn raised the question of the relation of Christianity to the other forms of religion from which it emerged. How indeed does one identify the "essence of religion" among all its varied forms? Scholars like Bousset reacted sharply to attempts simply to identify the essence of Christianity with the essence of religion, or to distinguish between natural and supernatural or revealed religion. They insisted that the history of the Old and New Testaments shows them as so closely interwoven with the general history of religion that "a distinction between revealed and natural religion becomes an impossibility." What it does show is "a movement from below, a slow growth from the imperfect to the perfect." Nevertheless while Bousset is concerned to stress the continuities between Christianity and other forms of religion, there is no doubt where in this process of gradual development Christianity stands. "The religion of the Old and New Testament however represents . . . the line of the purest expression of religion, the Gospel is, to say the very least, until now highest and most perfect instantiation."[19]

It is illuminating to consider the rather different history of this kind of liberal cultural imperialism in Germany and England. Liberal theology in Germany was largely discredited after the carnage and defeat of the First World War. Liberal Protestant culture was fatally weakened and unable to withstand the attacks of nationalism, socialism

---

[19] W. Bousset, *Das Wesen der Religion dargestellt an ihrer Geschichte* (Halle: Gebauer-Schetschke, 1904), p. 8.

and national socialism. In their different ways both Barth[20] and Bultmann[21] sought to make a sharp break between religion and the gospel/kerygma and to seek meaning and self-understanding, not in the heritage of religious culture but in the transcendent *viva vox evangelii*.

In England, by contrast, Liberal theology emerged alive and well. One of the more remarkable examples of this unrepentant cultural (and military) triumphalism is to be found in A.C. Headlam's *The Life and Teaching of Jesus the Christ*.[22] Like most Liberal theologians, Headlam wished to interpret the Kingdom of God as the power of God at work in history and to make a more or less close connection between it and Christianity. "It is," he wrote, "a process which is now working, not a new revelation to come from heaven, so it might be described as Christianity or the Christian dispensation, the new state of things inaugurated by the preaching of Jesus."[23] In this there is nothing new. What is striking is the way in which he can identify this process with the course of the War. He draws parallels between the British Army's advances from Egypt to Palestine and ancient battles of the biblical times and the crusades: "English and Australian cavalry fought where Coeur de Lion had fought"; and he rejoices in the hope that Jesus' land "may never again be brought under the blighting influence of Turkish and Mohammedan rule."[24] He even goes so far as to express approval of the Allies' treatment of the Germans at the Treaty of Versailles!: "we can (and have attempted to) treat our enemies justly."[25] Such self-delusion exposes with all desirable clarity the dangers of this kind of identification between the fortunes of one's own group and the divine purposes in history.

And Liberalism lived on, in a rather different vein, in the works of C.H. Dodd, interestingly in *The Meaning of Paul for Today*,[26] to my mind quite disturbingly in *The Founder of Christianity*.[27] In the latter work Dodd spelled out his belief that Jesus came to found Christianity and that there is a relatively straight line running from Jesus

[20] See particularly his attack on the notion of religion in his *The Epistle to the Romans* (Oxford: Oxford University Press, 1968).
[21] "Die liberale Theologie und die jüngste theologische Bewegung," in *Glauben und Verstehen, I* (Tübingen: J.C.B. Mohr, 1961), pp. 1–25.
[22] London: John Murray, 1923.
[23] *ibid.*, p. 255.
[24] *ibid.*, vii.
[25] *ibid.*, p. 225.
[26] London: Swarthmore Press, 1920.
[27] London: Collins, 1971.

through the history of the Mediaeval Church and the Reformation on, "with some unfortunate accompaniments"[28] into the Europe of the modern era. The accompaniments referred to are the religious wars of the seventeenth century which ravaged the population of central Europe, leaving a third of it dead and reducing it to a state of virtual anarchy. This is another clear case of cultural bias, where someone, because of his conviction that his, in this case European Christian culture, is God-given is unable to look the facts of history squarely in the face. In some not always clearly specified sense there is an identification here between the gospel, the church and European culture, "Christendom."

I have so far not said anything about developments in NT studies in North America. Here the situation is complex with a great range of different approaches from the conservative New Right, which is at least as culturally imperialistic as any former Liberalism, to the pluralism of those who teach in non-denominational schools and colleges, often alongside colleagues of other faiths. There is too a major division between those who continue to espouse historical critical modes of reading the Bible and those who seek to replace them with some form of literary reading. I shall here be concerned only with one example from those who continue to pursue historical critical studies, and from among them with E.P. Sanders and D. Boyarin.

Sanders' major work has been concerned to re-evaluate the Judaism of the first century and to attack the portraits which had previously been offered particularly by German Lutheran scholars. Within that framework he also seeks to give an account of the religion of Jesus and Paul. Sanders' enquiry owes much to the *religionsgeschichtliche* method but can be sharply distinguished from the work of scholars like Bousset in a number of ways. In the first place he is fiercely critical of the way they have portrayed and evaluated Judaism. In a devastating critique in *Paul and Palestinian Judaism*[29] he shows how biased their reading is. But more fundamentally he effectively side-steps one of the central aims of the school, which was to portray the historical *development* of religions, to show how one religion emerged out of, had its roots in another or others. Sanders does not deny the interest of such questions: they arise naturally from his portrayal of Pauline Christianity as essentially different from Palestinian Judaism. What

---

[28] *ibid.*, p. 13.
[29] Pp. 33–59.

he wants to offer however is an account of the patterns of religion which are to be found in these two types of religion, to show how they function, how people move through them and shape their lives in their terms. When it comes to evaluating the two, he refuses. "In short, *this is what Paul finds wrong in Judaism: it is not Christianity* . . . In saying that participationist eschatology is different from covenantal nomism, I mean only to say that it is different, not that the difference is instructive for seeing the error of Judaism's way."[30] When it comes to the question of the derivation of Pauline Christianity from other forms of contemporary religion, Jewish or Hellenistic, Sanders is prepared to speculate briefly but his conclusions are largely negative and his inclination is to see Paul's pattern of religion as largely his own creation, with some debts to Jewish apocalyptic and Hellenistic portrayals of the human plight.[31]

In what sense, then, does such a study aid our understanding? Again Sanders' method differs significantly from the models of scholarship which we have so far considered. He does not readily appeal to analogies with present experience and indeed denies outright that there we have such analogies available for understanding Paul's participationist eschatology. "We seem to lack a category of 'reality'—real participation in Christ, real possession of the Spirit—which lies between naive cosmological speculation and belief in magical transference on the one hand and a revised self-understanding on the other." But, although he does not have a new category to propose, and while interpretations in terms of magical transference and new self-understandings do not capture what Paul was saying, he can at least assert that Paul had such a category of reality. And this is to say that "[t]o an appreciable degree, what Paul concretely thought cannot be directly appropriated by Christians today."[32] Of course there are elements in Paul's thought which are more easily transferable to our present day: the language of "trust, obedience, renunciation of one's own striving" but that does not mean that these represent the "real and exhaustive interpretation of what Paul meant."[33]

It is interesting to consider what is happening here. Attempts to inculturate Paul into contemporary American culture are being re-

---

[30] *ibid.*, p. 552.
[31] *ibid.*, pp. 553–6.
[32] *ibid.*, pp. 522f.
[33] *ibid.*, p. 523.

sisted or, perhaps better, relativised: those who make them may draw strength and comfort from them but they risk imposing their own interpretation on that which fundamentally eludes interpretation and they therefore inevitably distort and misread. Such readings can at best catch only part of what Paul was saying and we need therefore to be extremely cautious about evaluative religious judgments. In the light of the history of Christian anti-Semitism, it is not difficult to understand such reticence.

This is not of course to deny any explanatory role to Sanders' own work. What he presents is intended to be "helpful for under-standing" and it achieves this by careful comparison of different patterns of religion, comparing that is, whole with whole. What dis-tinguishes one religion from another is not that they disagree on important central tenets (that may occur between members of the same family of religions) but that "there is a *significance* to a basic agreement or disagreement with regard to a whole pattern, and that basic agreement can exist despite agreement on even important ele-ments."[34] And this in turn sheds light on Sanders' leading question which is a functionalist one: how do these religions work? How does someone get in and stay in? Such questions sit neatly alongside those of social anthropologists who do not seek analogies between their own sense of self-understanding or indeed other forms of religious experience and those of the religions they study, but who rather attempt to describe as closely as they may how the beliefs and rituals of a particular religious group lead to the functioning of the group as a whole. There is, that is to say, no attempt to appropriate the religion, simply to understand its operation. And in a secular aca-demic institution with colleagues of different faiths and none, such an approach *may* help to preserve a certain neutrality. Just as, in a multi-cultural society, the relativisation of all attempts to appropriate religious traditions and the refusal to evaluate one religious tradition against another *may* assist the growth of tolerance and co-operation.

Sanders has undoubtedly rendered great service to Christian and Jewish studies of the first century by purging (largely at least) the discipline of its anti-Jewish bias, the portrayal of first century Juda-ism as "works-righteousness." But there is also a reluctance to try to learn from these ancient texts, to seek answers from them, however

[34] *ibid.*, p. 552.

critically, to our present cultural concerns, even though such concerns clearly underlie Sanders' own work.

It is then perhaps not surprising that these should be taken up by other scholars. Notable among these is the Jewish Rabbinic scholar, Daniel Boyarin in his *A Radical Jew: Paul and the Politics of Identity*.[35] Boyarin gratefully accepts Sanders' contribution to the understanding of first century Judaism and his corrections of, largely, Lutheran misreadings. But he is interested in a cultural reading which precisely may find links between the experience of groups different from the dominant "European" cultural groups and Paul's texts and which also may have its own political agenda.[36] Specifically he wants to read Paul in the light of his own knowledge of Jewish religious and hermeneutical traditions which he judges to be very close to those from which Paul sprang. And he wants to read Paul in the light of Jews' experience of cultural difference, more bluntly of the violence done to Jews "in the name of Paul's text."[37] Thus whereas Sanders is reluctant to address the question to what extent Paul was critical of Judaism, Boyarin supposes Paul to be concerned with questions of the difficulties of combining belief in a universal God with the particularities of Jewish practice. "Why would a universal God desire and command that one people should circumcise the male members of the tribe and command food taboos that make it impossible for one people to join in table fellowship with all the rest of his children?"[38] He thus portrays Paul as a cultural critic who seeks to universalise Judaism by allegorising it and contrasts Paul's reading with rabbinic/midrashic readings which emphasise the particularity of the prescriptions of Torah and their literal application in the flesh. That is to say, Boyarin's political experience and agenda will precisely not allow him simply to portray the differences between Pauline Christianity and Judaism; it is essential for him to understand their interrelation and to tease out Paul's own evaluative judgments.

---

[35] Berkeley: University of California Press, 1994.

[36] "'Cultural reading' has two senses. On the one hand, it refers to exegetical advances that 'European' interpreters of the Bible gain by paying attention to the insights of Bible-readings from 'other' cultures that may have practices and knowledges important for the understanding of biblical texts. It refers as well to the politicized readings of the Bible generated by people who have been the object of colonialist or racist practices carried out in the name of the Bible." *A Radical Jew*, p. 40.

[37] *ibid.*, p. 40.

[38] *ibid.*, p. 39.

Whereas Sanders portrays Paul as someone who has found a new religious life which is essentially different from his former Judaism, Boyarin sees Paul as a Jew who is striving to give Judaism a new direction.

Thus Boyarin sees Paul as reacting to first century readings of Torah which stress the concrete, physical bond between Yahweh and his people, the marking of that relationship in the flesh. The divine name ShaDaY is inscribed in the body, the *shin* in the nose, the *dalet* in the hand and the *yod* in the circumcision (see *Tanhuma Tsav* 14). In midrashic interpretation "this mark of natural or naturalized membership in a particular people is made the center of salvation. These texts, in their almost crude physicality, register a strong protest . . . against any flight from the body to the spirit with the attendant deracination of historicity, physicality, and carnal filiation which characterizes Christianity."[39] Equally Paul's reaction is seen to be analogous to present Jewish concerns about their own cultural particularity and the dangers that it has brought. Paul's reaction to culturally particular readings of the tradition was to embrace a wide-spread counter-tendency of his own times: neo-Platonism. This was not foreign to Judaism. Philo of Alexandria was deeply attracted to it. But Paul in the allegory of Hagar and Sarah seeks to universalise Jewish culture, to relegate Jewish observance of Torah to the sphere of the transitory, the "flesh," and to relocate—and recast—Jewish traditions in the sphere of the spirit (Gal 5:17, where flesh is taken to mean the circumcised flesh of the penis). The old cultural distinctions are thus relegated to the past (3:28); in Christ a fundamental underlying unity is discovered which supersedes the old dispensation. The tragedy is that this new dispensation with its "universal" self-consciousness may then turn on those who still hold to a particularising reading of their traditions and subject them to sustained and terrible violence. Again what is happening here is that Boyarin refuses a reading which is content to trace the pattern of a religion without consideration for its long-term political implications. The meaning of Pauline texts like Gal. 5:17 needs to be spelled out in terms of its history of effects, and these include not only its spawning of a rich history of Christian piety and interiority, but the traducing of Judaism as it is portrayed as standing in fundamental opposition to Christian life in the Spirit.

---

[39] *ibid.*, p. 37.

It would of course be intriguing to enter into a fuller debate with Boyarin. In the end there would be similar debates to those which have been conducted with the other figures discussed above. Does an allegorising interpretation of Paul do justice to the other aspects (notably the more sharply apocalyptic ones) of his thought? How accurately does Boyarin represent the pervasiveness of a certain kind of platonising universalism? Does concentration on themes of political and cultural identity bring us so close to the heart of Paul's concerns that we may see in them the principle explanation of his "conversion"? Are all the "effects" which flow from particular Pauline texts to be accepted as a proper indication of their *Sinnpotential?* All questions, again, in which a careful historical scrutiny of the evidence will play an important role in resolving the debate.

As Boyarin himself recognises, his questions and approach to Paul bear interesting resemblance to those of F.C. Baur. What is distinctive about his own work is that he filters these questions about the emergence of a more universalising consciousness in the West through the consciousness of those who have rejected such universalising tendencies and have therefore found themselves marginalised and victimised. And, just as importantly, he wants to claim Paul for his own tradition. There are, he argues, important cultural critical messages for Judaism in Paul's writing which can contribute to their own search for identity, and so, indirectly at least, to the self-understanding of Christians.

I have been trying to show in this article the extent to which major European and, more recently, North American readings of the Bible are cultural readings. Those who now, in Africa and elsewhere, consciously seek to develop their own readings from a different cultural standpoint should not be portrayed as engaging in a fundamentally different type of activity. Nor should they suppose that the tools of historical criticism cannot serve their purpose. The ways in which these have been employed on either side of cultural debates provides evidence of that. But while African and Jewish cultural readings are written from the point of view of the oppressed and marginalised, the readings of European and North American modernity have been written by middle class academics who were members of powerful nations. The principal danger that we have noticed with such readings is the tendency to annexation: towards a too easy identification of one's own cultural appropriation of particular texts with their meaning *tout court*, a tendency to universalise one's own reading and therefore to impose it on others, together with its high estimation and privileging of one's own culture. At the root of this lies the too easy conversion into *identities* of perceived *analogies* between present (culturally determined) experience and belief and that of the communities which first produced the texts being studied.

If, then, we want to uphold the validity of cultural readings, we need to stress the importance of cultural interaction in such readings. Different voices may serve to disturb the too ready identification of elements in a particular group's experience with those of, e.g., Paul and his community. And historical argument and scrutiny may then help to undermine the distortions to which the overpressing of cultural analogies can lead. But precisely insofar as historical work is informed by analogies and its questions are framed within a particular community, it too is subject to a limitation of perspective which can be corrected only by complementary views from members of different cultural groups. And since most of the major studies of Christianity have in fact been written from a position of power and privilege there is an urgent need to listen to the readings of the marginalised and oppressed which may press on those in the West different questions and perspectives.

In a recent article,[40] David Tracy has called for a greater recognition of the diversity of centres in theology. In one sense this is a call for the overcoming of the "grand narratives" of modernism of which Baur's construction of Christian history is a rich example. It is a call to attend to the "voices of subjugated knowledge: the voices of all those marginalised by the official story of modern triumph."[41] But in seeking to overcome the colonising tendencies in modernism, we should not abandon the appeal to reason (including historical reason) as a means of addressing the key questions of our own society and of enabling communication between people of different cultures and with different interests. Nor should we simply exult in the rediscovery of local traditions. Rather, and here Tracy appeals to Levinas,[42] "the face of the genuine other should release us from all desire for totality and open us to a true sense of infinity. The face of the other should also open us to the Jewish rather than the Greek

---

[40] "On Naming the Present," in David Tracy, *On Naming the Present: God, Hermeneutics, and Church* (London: SCM, 1994), pp. 3–24.

[41] *ibid.*, p. 20.

[42] *Totality and Infinity: An Essay on Exteriority* (Pittsburgh: Duquesne University Press, 1980).

realities constituting our culture. For the face of the other can open us to ethical responsibility and even to the call of the prophets to political and historical agency and action."[43] The challenge to those who engage in cultural readings of the Bible lies precisely here: so to read the texts that they may discern the reality of the infinite God of life in the concrete situations of their own culture; at the same time as being always ready to hear the voices of others who from their culture, their situation of difference, of suffering and oppression may critique and enlarge that understanding of God.

---

[43] Tracy, "Naming the Present" p. 17.

ON NEW TESTAMENT INTERPRETATION
AND ETHNOCENTRISM

Pieter F. Craffert

1. *Introduction*

New Testament interpretation is inevitably cross-cultural. This should
be reason enough for taking note of the important debate on ethnocentrism in cultural anthropological studies. In the wake of "the interpretive turn" (the recognition of the centrality of interpretation in
all human affairs) it is claimed that the idea of neutrality towards
one's own context is nothing but a display of ethnocentric blindness.
Thus, some have questioned whether ethnocentrism can in fact be
avoided. We urgently need an investigation of the reasons for the
different views and how they may influence biblical studies.

The issue of ethnocentrism poses serious moral and ethical questions for anyone involved in cross-cultural interpretation. Is it possible to present other cultural practices and beliefs in such a way as
to do justice to them, and if so, how should it be done? Is it possible
for modern people to respect the cultural strangeness from which the
New Testament texts emerged? Are those scholars who claim to avoid
ethnocentrism deceiving themselves and their readers?

2. *On Ethnocentrism and the Interpretive Turn*

2.1 *Varieties of Ethnocentrism*

Briefly, ethnocentrism maintains that beliefs and practices in another
culture should, or cannot but, be interpreted according to the standards of one's own culture. The obverse, cultural relativism, maintains that such beliefs and practices should be evaluated relative to
the culture of which they are part (see Lett 1987:71; Winthrop
1991:235–237). The one attaches special privilege to one's own community while the other asserts a tolerance for every other group. But
at least three different aspects of ethnocentrism should be considered: factual, moral and epistemological.

First, if ethnocentrism implies "judgments based on irrational preferences incapable of rational validation" (Bidney 1968:546), then a
degree of "factual" ethnocentrism is found in all societies and cultures;
both conscious and unconscious preferences for inherited practices
and beliefs are facts of socialisation. Second, the moral side of ethnocentrism is constituted not by the fact of a preference for one's
own cultural values, but by the "uncritical prejudice in favour of
one's own culture and the distorted, biased criticism of alien cultures"
(Bidney 1968:546). The epistemological side of ethnocentrism is related to the factual aspect: here we find the notion that one cannot
do otherwise than interpret alien cultures from one's own perspective, and in this sense "everybody is ethnocentric" (Rorty 1985:13).

As with Rorty, Hoy finds no evil in ethnocentrism as the notion
that "we see the world through our own self-understanding," only in
expecting "every other self-understanding to converge with ours"
(1991:175). The benign ethnocentrism suggested by him would do
all it could to keep from imposing its own views on others, but would
not do so with the intention of overcoming ethnocentrism which he
regards as an inevitable part of the interpretive turn (see Hoy
1991:171). According to this view, ethnocentrism is inevitable and
the moral obligation lies in avoiding undue imposition. Rorty maintains that we "would rather die than be ethnocentric, but ethnocentrism is precisely the conviction that one would rather die than share
certain beliefs" (1986:525). Geertz also reminds us that all ethnography is in the last analysis the product of the describer's description.
Any pretension that ethnography is "more than the representation of
one sort of life in the categories of another is impossible to defend,"
due to the "un-get-roundable fact that all ethnographical descriptions are homemade" (Geertz 1988:144–145). So also Bohman: "since
we can interpret things only from 'our' point of view, interpretation
is inevitably ethnocentric. It is impossible to understand others as
they understand themselves: we understand them only according to
'our own lights'" (1991b:113).

In the name of the interpretive turn, Hoy insists that ethnocentrism is not easy to avoid and that the very idea of neutrality towards
one's own context is really a blindness towards context-dependence
(see 1991:156, 170). Part of the trouble with enthnocentrism is that
it impedes us from discovering at what sort of angle we stand to the
world and "what sort of bat we really are" (Geertz 1986:112).

2.2 Ethnocentrism and New Testament studies

Ethnocentrism, and its avoidance, is closely linked to the ways in which the interpretive turn is understood. Primarily three responses to the issues of ethnocentrism and the interpretive turn can be identified in New Testament studies. They can best be described as responses of denial, of avoidance and of celebration. Traditional New Testament studies have often operated in the mode of denial, or even ignorance, of ethnocentrism. On the other hand, social-scientific approaches have made conscious attempts to avoid ethnocentrism by explicitly making use of social scientific models and by acknowledging the theory dependence (or model dependence) of all interpretation. All exegetes use models, and traditional New Testament scholarship's apparent ignorance of this fact exposes them to justifiable accusations of ethnocentrism (see Craffert 1992:217, 224–225 for a discussion and references).

This attempt to avoid ethnocentrism takes at least two directions (see Craffert 1994b:9–10): some believe that the use of etic (outsiders') models ensures that ethnocentric imposition is avoided, while others believe that the use of emic (insiders') concepts will achieve the same end. But whether emic or etic categories are used, the very same dilemma has to be faced: how does one do justice to the subjects' cultural system? In fact, even switching between native and observers' concepts does not necessarily lead to the avoidance of ethnocentrism.

The third response, therefore, is not at all surprising: since readers' socio-political contexts always influence their interpretations (we are all trapped in our frameworks), ethnocentrism should not be avoided; instead, readers should *celebrate* this condition in that their readings should be explicitly reflecting their socio-political choices (see Schüssler Fiorenza 1988; West 1991 and Craffert 1994a for many more examples). In order to evaluate these responses, we need a closer examination of this "interpretive turn."

2.3 What is the so-called interpretive turn?

The interpretive turn, in a variety of disciplinary circles, represents agreement on the essential role of interpretation in all human inquiry (see Bohman, Hiley & Shusterman 1991:10). There are no such things as isolated, individual facts or atomistic propositions; there is always a contextual "background" which is implicated and which requires interpretation. The concept of "holism" is used to indicate this state of affairs (Dreyfus 1980:3–4; Bohman 1991b:113). But there are two elements of the interpretive turn, each of which raises a distinct set of problems for epistemology.

The first may be called *hermeneutic universalism*—"the claim that interpretation is a universal and ubiquitous feature of all human activity" (Bohman, Hiley & Shusterman 1991:7). Contrary to the idea of an observer-independent perspective, this maintains that there is "no privileged position, no absolute perspective, no final recounting" (Rabinow & Sullivan 1979:6). In Dreyfus's words (see Bohman, Hiley & Shusterman 1991:7), there are only *interpretations all the way down* with no appeal to experience, meaning, or evidence that is independent of interpretation or more basic than it. The only ground for an interpretation can only be other interpretations (see Taylor 1977:103, 111, 126).

The second element may be called *hermeneutic contextualism* which means that interpretation always takes place within some context or background (see Bohman, Hiley & Shusterman 1991:7). Both observer and observed are always enmeshed in a culture which implies that "we see the lives of others through lenses of our own grinding" (Geertz 1984:275). While hermeneutic universalism holds that everything is interpretation, contextualism implies that truth is relative to some context or interpretive circle.

Depending on the exact formulation of the above elements, both a strong and a weak holist position are possible. Put differently, one's formulation of the interpretive turn can move in at least two directions on a continuum: towards a weak or towards a strong formulation of it. Strong and weak holism differ with regard to at least two aspects: first, their theoretical and philosophical foundations, and second, with regard to their descriptions of the interpretive process. Consequently they produce different aims, and claims, regarding the issue of ethnocentrism.

3. *The Theoretical Foundations of Strong and Weak Holism*

It is one thing to agree that all interpretation is homemade, but quite another to agree on what conclusions should be drawn from such a position; it is one thing to agree on the essential role of interpretation in human affairs, but quite another to agree on the form and direction that role should take. In my view, "strong holism" leads in the direction of interpretive skepticism. A summary of this position is cogently provided by Bohman (1991b:116):

> (1) Interpretation is circular, indeterminate, and perspectival (the thesis of the "hermeneutical circle").
> (2) Interpretation occurs only against a "background," a network of unspecifiable beliefs and practices (thesis of the "background").
> (3) The background is a condition for the possibility of interpretation which limits its epistemic possibilities of correctness (thesis of transcendental limits).
> (4) All cognitive activities are interpretive (thesis of the universality of interpretation).
> (5) *Therefore*, the conditions of interpretation are such that no "true" or "correct" interpretations are possible (interpretive skepticism).

Thus ethnocentrism cannot be avoided.

Weak holists, however, argue that the challenge is how to present another life form in a way which does justice to both the interpreter's culture and the one to be examined (see Geertz 1988:144; Bohman 1991a:151; 1991b:130, 132). A nonskeptical holism accepts the theses of the hermeneutical circle and the necessity of a background, but it tries to show that there is no reason for skepticism in a properly understood circularity. In accepting the thesis of the hermeneutical circle, weak holism argues that circularity is non-vicious. A summary, is again provided by Bohman (1991b:125):

> (1) Interpretation is circular, indeterminate, and perspectival (thesis of the "hermeneutical circle").
> (2) Its circularity may be defined by the necessity of a "background," a set of shared and accessible conditions of possibility (the background as a reflective-transcendental concept).
> (3) As a formal condition of possibility, the background acts as an enabling condition and not a limiting condition (given a distinction between "enabling" and "limiting" conditions).
> (4) The conditions of interpretation are neutral with regard to the *warrants* of knowledge claims, including claims about interpretations (the denial of hermeneutic universality).
> (5) *Therefore*, interpretation can produce revisable, public knowledge based on evidence.

The weak holistic argument maintains not only that "circularity is nonvicious but also that it is based on enabling conditions analysed as shared background constraints" (Bohman 1991a:146). Such constraints are not strong enough to act as fixed limits or to make it impossible to decide normatively between interpretations on the basis of evidence. Ultimately, it is the limit thesis which sustains the strong holist position. The limit thesis holds that "the involvement in the shared practices and beliefs that make up any particular 'background' or culture are so strong that we cannot take any distance from them" (Bohman 1991b:119). This is the case, for example, in Gadamer's account of prejudice which holds that "understanding consists exclusively of judgments, most of which remain tacit *Vorurteile*, prejudgments or prejudices" (Hoy 1991:166–167). At least two arguments in the weak holistic account oppose the limit thesis.

The first is the argument against the *myth of the framework* which exaggerates a difficulty into an impossibility. Although we are always prisoners caught in the framework of our theories, expectations, experiences and language, Popper maintains that "we are prisoners in a Pickwickian sense: if we try, we can break out of our framework at any time. Admittedly, we shall find ourselves again in a framework, but it will be a better and roomier one; and we can at any moment break out of it again" (Popper 1970:56).

Along the same lines, Bohman suggests that the limit thesis rests on the assumption that by being socialised into a world there are interpretive orientations which serve as background and which *cannot* be brought under reflective control. However, not only can such orientations be brought under reflective control and be submitted to public scrutiny (see Bernstein 1991:336; Bohman 1991b:119–120), but they may also be changed. In the end there is a world of a difference between the idea that we are sometimes imprisoned in our cultural categories, and the radical view that we are always trapped beyond the point of escaping from them (see Hirsch 1985a:194). Ultimately, it is an empirical question whether and to what extent a certain set of background practices or beliefs indeed distorts an interpretation (see Bohman 1991b:120). All this does not mean that overcoming one's framework is an easy or obvious task. Skinner reminds us that coming to a historical text, "we may have to engage in extremely wide-ranging as well as extremely detailed historical research" (1988:275). The same applies to cross-cultural and textual interpretation.

The second argument against the strong holist thesis of universal contextualism (background) has to do with its transcendental argument: it confuses enabling conditions with limiting conditions. There are several differences between these two types of conditions (see Bohman 1991b:121–123 for detail). Speaking a particular language, for example, is an enabling condition of communication and not a fixed limit on the capacity to communicate with others, since it may be expanded to include new contexts and possibilities of understanding (see Bohman 1991b:123). A certain background should therefore be seen as a set of flexible constraints rather than as being tied to fixed limits. In short, Bohman argues (1991a:144):

> skeptical strong holists infer determinate and empirical limits on knowledge from the holistic but enabling conditions of interpretation. The confusion begins in the universality thesis, since the holist loses sight of the fact that holism is itself a formal theory resulting from transcendental reflection on the general conditions of interpretation and not an interpretation itself. If holistic concepts like the background are formal, reflective, and interpretive, the premises of the holistic argument violate its own anti-theoretical account of interpretation as always contingent and context dependent.

In my view, the "celebration" response stands in the tradition of strong holism while the "avoidance" responses have elements of the weak holistic view. It remains a question, however, whether the avoidance responses as they stand are adequate in dealing with the issue of ethnocentrism.

4. *The Interpretive Process*

Strong and weak holism employ different descriptions of the interpretive process. Although they agree that interpretation presupposes at least two perspectives (or horizons), due to their different theoretical positions, they have mutually exclusive views on the interpretive process which deals with these two horizons. On the one hand, strong holists tend to blend the two perspectives into that of the interpreter, and on the other hand, weak holists attempt to keep the horizons apart. Consequently, strong holists recognise a single task in the interpretive process while weak holists allow for a multiple-task process in interpretation.

4.1 *The fusion of horizons in a single task process: strong holism*

In emphasising hermeneutic contextualism, strong holism not only promotes the inevitable privilege of the interpreter's viewpoint, but also blends two distinct horizons within a single phase of interpretation. While some think that it is impossible not to blend these horizons, others agree that even if it were possible, it is not worthwhile to pay much attention to past or alien horizons. Gadamer, for example, argues that understanding the past (and therefore also foreign cultures) undoubtedly requires a historical horizon (1979:271), but projecting such a horizon is only a phase in the process of understanding: the horizon while being projected, is simultaneously removed (see 1979:273). This is also confirmed by Hoy's understanding of Gadamer's "fusion of horizons." The past or alien horizon is not totally constructible because that would mean that there exists "a historical *Gegenstand an sich* that the historical sciences could aim to uncover" (Hoy 1991:165). Hoy maintains that while context conditions understanding, understanding also conditions the context. There is a circular or feedback relation between background and interpretation (1991:166).

Similarly, Rorty believes that the alien or past horizon has a limited value, although he admits that interpretation should pay attention to placing texts within their own benighted times and context, as well as engage them as contemporary conversational partners: "There is nothing wrong with self-consciously letting our own philosophical views dictate terms in which to describe the dead. But there are reasons for *also* describing them in other terms, their own terms" (Rorty 1984:50). The first he calls *rational reconstructions* and the latter *historical reconstructions*. He objects, however, to the idea that historical reconstruction can first be done and rational reconstruction later (1984:53 n. 1):

> The two genres can never be *that* independent, because you will not know much about what the dead meant prior to figuring out how much truth they knew. These two topics should be seen as moments in a continuing movement around the hermeneutical circle, a circle one has to have gone round a good many times before one can begin to do *either* sort of reconstruction.

Thus, one of the criteria for establishing the historical or subject's point of view remains the interpreter's estimate of how much truth they know.

The main reason for a curiosity with historical reconstructions, Rorty maintains, is to help us recognise that there have been different forms of intellectual life than ours (see 1984:51). The minimal sort of understanding of what the others were up to, is like being able to exchange courtesies in a foreign language without being able to translate that into one's own language since translating an utterance means fitting it into our practices (see 1984:52 n. 1).

It is not surprising that from a strong holist conception of the interpretive process, ethnocentrism is inevitable and to be celebrated. However, from a weak holistic perspective a rather different interpretive process can be envisaged.

4.2 Separate horizons in a multiple-task process

I endorse the descriptions of Taylor (see 1985b:118) and Geertz (see 1973:27) on the interpretive process as a dual task which consists of, first, uncovering or mastering the subject's conceptual structures and self-description and, secondly, of a comparison between those structures and the interpreter's cultural system. From this viewpoint, responsible interpretation requires existence in two worlds at once, the world of the past and the world of the present, the culture of the subject and the culture of the interpreter (see Hirsch 1985b:16; Jeanrond 1988:45). In such a weak holistic perspective a different view of the interpretive process emerges, and consequently the issue of ethnocentrism is dealt with differently.

4.2.1 Supplementing the model of the hermeneutical circle

Anthropologists and historians have long recognised that the interpretive process escapes perfect description due to the inevitable tension inherent within it (see Peacock 1986:76). It operates under the paradoxes of antithetic affirmations: "Identification and distancing, which are antithetic, are affirmed at the same time" (Todorov 1988:4). Thus, the the notion of a multiple-task interpretive process places considerable strain on the metaphor of the hermeneutic circle; this metaphor should be supplemented by that of "bracketing" (see Hirsch 1976:5).

Bracketing is like "learning a second first language" (Bernstein 1991:336; and see Skinner 1988:252; Hirsch 1985a:196); it entails restraint of one's own background and a presumption of otherness. The idea of brackets, which has been taken from Husserl, does "in fact represent something that most of us believe we experience in [any] verbal discourse, namely, an alien meaning, something meant by an implied author or speaker who is not ourselves" (Hirsch 1976:6; and see Hirsch 1960:467–469; 1984b:204). But for an alien meaning to be intelligible, it has to be compared, in some sense, with our own background. Bracketing and comparing suggests a multiple-task process. Similarly, Bohman has identified the limitations of the hermeneutical circle and allows for different types of interpretation, namely, contextual[1] and rational interpretations. Contextual interpretations take us only so far as to constitute *their* world in *our* terms. Such interpretations should, however, be supplemented by rational comparative interpretations which bring tests for adequacy within a hermeneutic circle (see 1991b:132, 143).

Each interpretive task, within the multiple-task process, resembles a hermeneutical circle. Although the unity in this process should be emphasised, taking note of the individual tasks will be an important feature in any attempt to deal adequately with the issue of ethnocentrism. Therefore, I will briefly introduce each of the three tasks.

4.2.2 Paying attention to the subject's cultural system

Bernstein reminds us that the basic condition for all understanding requires one to test and risk one's convictions and prejudgments in and through an encounter with what is radically other and alien. "To do this requires imagination and hermeneutical sensitivity in order to understand the 'other' in its strongest possible light" (Bernstein 1991:4). The very nature of human action, Taylor maintains, requires that "we understand it, at least initially, in its own terms; that means that we understand the descriptions that it bears for the agents. It is only because we have failed to do that that we can fall into the fatal error of assimilating foreign practices to our own familiar ones" (1985a:149). Therefore, unless we begin with a characterisation of a society in its own terms, we shall be unable to identify the matter that requires explanation (see MacIntyre 1971:223; Skinner 1988:271).

Insisting on the insider's perspective, as the source for all reflection, also expresses something about our own rootedness in culture, history and language. This finitude is, however, not seen as a constraint, but as an enabling condition which serves as a window onto ourselves and our world (see Guignon 1991:96–97). Adequate interpretation struggles first and foremost with what the subjects are up to.

Pressing as far as possible towards making sense of the subjects' point of view is, however, not the same as saying that the interpreter

---

[1] It should be noted that the *contextual* type of interpretation in Bohman's sense differs from the contextual or engaged kind of interpretations encountered in the celebration response. Contextual in this sense refers to historical (or true to the subject's point of view) as opposed to contextual as interpretation reflecting the interpreter's point of view.

should adopt their point of view. Turning native rules out the possibility of showing cultural beliefs or practices as wrong, confused or deluded (Taylor 1985b:123). Turning native, if really successful, simply adds one more subject to be understood by outsiders. Making sense of the subjects' viewpoint is not the same as saying that their viewpoints make sense in our terms.

4.2.3   Paying attention to the interpreter's cultural system

An adequate interpretation theory can, however, not stop at the point of examining (bracketing) the subjects' world since, as Taylor reminds us, "it will frequently be the case that we cannot understand another society until we have understood ourselves better as well" (1985b:129). And if this is the case, then an adequate interpretation also includes a grasp of ourselves as agents in the world—which means, at least in our case, an industrialised, scientific world. Unfortunately, as Jarvie remarks, "despite what they *say* a good deal of the time, anthropologists do not begin from an understanding of our own culture" (1986b:163). Is it any different with New Testament scholars?

Modern scientific culture, "marks this society of ours and makes it different in many ways from all the other societies there have ever been" (Jarvie 1986b:163). Besides being the culture within which this interpreter chooses to live, it happens to form the background from which the otherness of the pre-industrial nature of the first-century world can be recognised. What then are some of the basic features of this late-twentieth century modern scientific culture which force themselves onto the interpretive task?

One of the practices that has helped to create the modern culture is the disengagement of thought from social embedding and embodied agency. In short, it calls on each of us "to become a responsible, thinking mind, self-reliant for his or her judgments" (Taylor 1991:307). It pushes towards greater clarity and deeper criticism of our nature as knowing agents and linguistic beings which is crucial to our moral and spiritual beliefs (see Taylor 1987:479). In fact, Lett points out that the term humanism (of which science is a necessary, but not sufficient component) includes the conviction that human beings are solely responsible for discerning and defining the meaning of human life and the conviction that they should do so through the exercise of skeptical reason while respecting the freedom and moral equality of all individuals (see 1991:323).

A second feature of scientific culture is related: it fosters the *separation* of understanding reality from the practice of putting ourselves in tune with reality (cf. Taylor 1985b:128). Scientists claim provisional knowledge based on the cumulative results of a never-ending process of skeptical inquiry. In case something better comes along, understanding cannot be anything but tentative (see Jarvie 1986c:224). Nevertheless, it stands opposed to mysticism (faith, revelation and intuition) as an alternative worldview (see Sono 1994:xv). In non-scientific cultures, understanding what reality is, and putting oneself in tune with it, are not separable activities (Taylor 1985b:128).

In view of the modern "separationist" project, it is not only the general features of the pre-industrial world of the New Testament which strike modern people as strange, but especially the beliefs in magic, revelations, demons and the like, as the primary motors for social and personal actions. These issues constitute the real challenge for modern interpreters claiming to avoid ethnocentrism; the cultural gap between us and the people of the first-century is huge. It is easy enough to insist that the interpreter's context shapes interpretation, but it is only when it is realised that what is at stake are incommensurable *realities*, rationalities, beliefs and practices that the significance becomes apparent. When it is remembered that *we* also construct dreams, illusions, fantasies, myths and fictions (see Jarvie 1986c:220), it is misleading to insist that the real world is simply a construct. Incommensurability between cultural beliefs and practices can be identified exactly because it is assumed that we can give historically contingent and indeed fallible (not definitive foundational) reasons for our beliefs, both about ourselves and about other cultures (see Bernstein 1991:277). So is it possible in an encounter with the first-century world to be faithful to a scientific culture without being ethnocentric?

4.2.4 The task of cross-cultural comparison

Once weak holism's route has been taken (that an interpreter should push as hard as possible to grasp the viewpoints of the subjects in their strongest possible light while also pushing towards an understanding of his/her own position), cross-cultural comparison follows as subsequent task. The more successfully the first task can be conducted, the more progress can be made in comparing the two systems. We should note, however, that the idea of comparison between incommensurable beliefs and practices in weak holism not only excludes the fusion of horizons idea in strong holism; it also excludes the view (a false ally) that the subjects' self-descriptions are incorrigible. "The incorrigibility thesis" rules out an account which may show cultural beliefs or practices to be wrong, confused or deluded (see Taylor 1985b:123–125). The indifference inherent in such a version of comparison results, paradoxically, in another kind of ethnocentrism. Taylor rightly emphasizes that an interpretive, comparative social science should allow for the possibility of critique.

Following Habermas, Bohman also argues that because humans are inevitably participants in a background of practices, they must always *evaluate* in order to understand and relate others' beliefs and norms to their own. In fact, adequate interpretation "requires evaluation to the extent that what is at stake in the interpretation is a 'validity claim,' a claim that the action is justifiable relative to some form of shared knowledge" (Bohman 1991b:137–138). Especially when cultural beliefs and practices (which are incommensurable with those of the interpreter) occupy the same space, assessment cannot be avoided. As Taylor points out, someone seriously practising magic in a modern scientific society will be considered to have lost his/her grip on reality (see 1985a:146). Incommensurable ways of life insistently raise the question of who is right. Yet if interpreters begin by asserting, on scientific ground, that magical practices are not true, then their scientific language—which allegedly neutral—ends up being ethnocentric (see Taylor 1986b:126). Similarly, Rorty affirms the necessity of ethnocentrism by saying that successful reconstructions "can only be performed by people who have some idea of what they themselves think about the issues under discussion, even if only that they are pseudo-issues" (Rorty 1984:53 n. 1).

5. Can Weak Holism overcome Ethnocentrism?

Once it is accepted that it is not totally impossible to transcend one's background (see, for example, Hoy 1991:159), the principle has been granted that it can occasionally be done by means of critical and public scrutiny. The celebration of being ethnocentric can then no longer be seen as epistemologically inevitable but becomes a matter of choice. If, on the other hand, an escape into the subject's point of view neither avoids ethnocentrism nor counts as adequate interpretation (going native just adds one more subject to be interpreted) the question remains whether ethnocentrism can actually be overcome in the process of comparison.

5.1   Cross-cultural comparison: a matter of perspicuous contrast

In order to avoid either privileging one's own understanding (ethnocentrism) or accepting the incorrigibility of the others' self-understanding, adequate interpretation aims at critical comparison of incommensurable cultural beliefs and practices. Really overcoming ethnocentricity, Taylor says, "is being able to understand two incommensurable classifications" (1985a:145). He rejects the idea that "the language of a cross-cultural theory has to be either theirs or ours" (1985b:125). Interpretive social science, he maintains, "requires that we master the agent's self-description in order to identify our *explananda*; but it by no means requires that we couch our *explanantia* in the same language. On the contrary it generally demands that we go beyond it" (Taylor 1985b:118). It will almost always be the case that the adequate language in which we understand another society is not our language of understanding, or theirs, but rather what one could call a language of perspicuous contrast. This would be a language in which we could formulate both their way of life and ours as alternative possibilities in relation to some human constants at work in both (see 1985b:125).

Understanding magic in alien societies perfectly illustrates what this involves (see Taylor 1985b:127–128). In a scientific world, there might be nothing corresponding to magical practices and therefore such practices should not be seen as "either proto-technology or expressive activity, but rather as partaking of a mode of activity in which this kind of clear separation and segregation is not yet made" (Taylor 1985b:118). This implies that in a language of perspicuous contrast an account is given of procedures in both societies.

For some scholars, Taylor's notion of human constants (such as birth, death, marriage, drought, plenty, etc.) too heavily relies on the metaphysical assumption that there are indeed uninterpreted human constants (see Bohman 1991b:133). Therefore, following Habermas, it is argued that "the presence of certain 'learning processes' establish commonalities across cultural boundaries" (Bohman 1991b:138). These commonalities allow the interpreter to act as a virtual participant in a culture in the sense that the reasons for certain practices are understood (see MacIntyre 1971:228–229). Seeking out commonalities and pointing out differences and conflict is a task marked by the model of dialogical encounter (see Bernstein 1991:336–337). Understanding does not only entail agreement but includes conflicts and differences.

5.2 Avoiding ethnocentric imposition?

The idea of a multiple-task process of interpretation works against accusations of ethnocentrism in at least two ways. First, understanding other peoples' self-understanding as clearly as possible protects one from ethnocentric imposition or projection. Second, it explicates the angle from which an interpreter looks at the world. Knowing what kind of people we are, works against the grain of ethnocentric imposition. The process of clarifying and getting a better understanding of the kind of knowing, speaking and acting agents we are, also creates the space for discovering that which is different.

The skepticism about avoiding ethnocentrism on an epistemological level need not be accepted. "Once the illusions of contextualism are seen through, interpretation again becomes part of our attempt to know the world and others in it" (Bohman 1991a:153). Keeping in mind that there is no claim here of reaching an objective, disengaged and value-free position, the notion that interpretation is (epistemologically speaking) inevitably ethnocentric, can be laid to rest. Performing a multi-task process allows for the avoidance of the blending, and consequently the overtaking of the other horizon by that of the interpreter. In short, it escapes *ethnocentric imposition* when understanding alien beliefs or practices. Hoy (see 1991:172) is, however, correct in maintaining that, at least from his perspective, ethnocentrism has not really been avoided in this approach; the issue of critical assessment has to be dealt with.

5.3 Critical assessment

It has been argued that adequate interpretation demands comparison, and comparison cannot take place without assessment. It should be noted that assessment in interpretation takes at least two routes. One kind of assessment is needed for understanding alien cultural beliefs and practices, while the second kind has to do with the acceptance or rejection of such beliefs and practices once they have been understood. The first, it has been argued, is dealt with by means of perspicuous contrast. There is, however, a second kind of assessment involved in cross-cultural comparison. That is what Jeanrond refers to as the assessment of the subject matter and of the situation of interpretation (see 1988:65).

Contrary to the idea that interpretation consists of a fusion of horizons, the multiple-task view on interpretation recognises that "not all otherness and difference are to be celebrated" (Bernstein 1991:313). Some cultural practices and beliefs are just not real options for us— at least not without self-deception or paranoia (see Rorty 1985:18 n. 13). On the other hand, as Taylor reminds us, criticism is inseparable from self-criticism (see 1985b:131). Cross-cultural interpretation is challenging in that it constantly confronts an interpreter with choices of truth. It can challenge our own self-definitions and practices and point out the falseness of beliefs on which they are based (see Jarvie 1977:202). Going through the process in a critical *and* self-critical way may turn out either way—showing beliefs and practices of either culture to be wrong, confused or deluded. Ethnocentrism, when it represents the choices made in the face of alternative ways of life, is not the same as ethnocentric imposition.

Strong holism ends up in ethnocentric imposition, but weak holism forces a decision. Although background constraints on evaluation eliminate the possibility of "uniquely true interpretations" (Bohman 1991b:125), in a weak holistic argument there is a non-skeptical notion of interpretive circularity: the evaluation of conflicting interpretations will be "comparative, fallibilistic and revisable" (Bohman 1991b:125) but "also governed by epistemic norms like coherence and correctness" (Bohman 1991b:126).[2] We can be passionately committed to the beliefs that regulate our actions when they are based on the stongest possible historically-contingent justifications (see Bernstein 1991:280). This is different from declaring our vocabulary final, immune to criticism, or the norm for evaluating others. Paying lipservice to a plurality of voices or viewpoints is easy enough. It is however, much more difficult to *live* the challenges of plurality.

6. *Some Concluding Remarks*

The issue of ethnocentrism is important first and foremost not because there is a general consensus that it can and should be avoided,

---

[2] A viable alternative to foundationalism, Bernstein argues, is fallibilism "where

but because it confronts all involved in cross-cultural interpretation with some fundamental issues, both epistemological and ethical. While there is no longer any defence for denying the role of ethnocentrism in New Testament studies, there should also be a moral question directed to those who "celebrate" its presence. If ethnocentric imposition can be avoided in interpretation, then the explicit choice for political-contextual interpretations (in the strong holistic tradition) can no longer be defended as inevitable.

Adequate interpretation cannot be satisfied with either turning native (using only emic concepts) or imposing etic concepts. The interpretive process is structured by dialogue between incommensurable cultural beliefs and practices and not by choosing between them. The multiple-task process is not only much more challenging to perform than the rival suggestions; it is also much more rewarding. If knowledge of others is not only a possible route towards knowledge of oneself but the only one, as Todorov maintains (see 1988:4), then cross-cultural interpretation is not without its dividends; it can lead to a better and more critical self-understanding. It challenges an interpreter on the level of fundamental cultural beliefs and practices. In short, it confronts one with alternative ways of being human and consequently with the challenge of taking a stance with regard to the question of truth. The central question New Testament scholars have to face is what to do with the strangeness and alienness encountered in cross-cultural interpretations of the Bible.

List of References

Bernstein, R.J.
1991   *The new constellation: The ethical-political horizons of modernity/ postmodernity*. Cambridge: MIT Press.
Bidney, D.
1968   "Cultural relativism." s.v. *International Encyclopedia of the Social Sciences*.
Bohman, J.F.
1991a   "Holism without skepticism: Contextualism and the limits of interpretation." Pp. 129–54 in J.F. Bohman, D.R. Hiley, and R. Shusterman (eds.), *The interpretive turn: Philosophy, science, culture*. Ithaca: Cornell University Press.

we realise that although we must begin any inquiry with prejudgments and can never call everything into question at once, nevertheless there is no belief or thesis—no matter how fundamental—that is not open to further interpretation and criticism" (1991:327).

466   PIETER F. CRAFFERT

—— 1991b   *New philosophy of social science: Problems of indeterminacy.* Cambridge: Polity Press.

Bohman, J.F., Hiley, D.R. and Shusterman, R.
1991   "Introduction: The interpretive turn." Pp. 1–14 in J.F. Bohman, D.R. Hiley, and R. Shusterman (eds.), *The interpretive turn: Philosophy, science, culture.* Ithaca: Cornell University Press.

Capra, F.
1982   *The turning point: Science, society, and the rising culture.* London: Flamingo.

Craffert, P.F.
1992   "More on models and muddles in the social-scientific interpretation of the New Testament: The *sociological fallacy* reconsidered." *Neotestamentica* 26(1):217–39.

—— 1994a   "Reading and divine sanction: The ethics of interpreting the New Testament in the New South Africa." Paper read at the International Conference on Religion and Rhetoric, Unisa, Pretoria, South Africa.

—— 1994b   "Taking stock of the emic-etic distinction in social-scientific interpretations of the New Testament." *Neotestamentica* 28(1):1–21.

Dreyfus, H.L.
1980   "Holism and hermeneutics." *Review of Metaphysics* 34:1–23.

Gadamer, H.-G.
1979   *Truth and method.* London: Sheed & Ward.

Geertz, C.
1973   "Thick description: Toward and interpretive theory of culture." Pp. 3–30 in *The interpretation of cultures: Selected essays.* London: Hutchinson.

—— 1984   "Anti anti-relativism." *American Anthropologist* 86:263–78.
—— 1986   "The uses of diversity." *Michigan Quarterly Review* 25:105–23.
—— 1988   *Works and lives: The anthropologist as author.* Cambridge: Polity Press.

Guignon, C.B.
1991   "Pragmatism or hermeneutics? Epistemology after foundationalism." Pp. 81–101 in J.F. Bohman, D.R. Hiley, and R. Shusterman (eds.), *The interpretive turn: Philosophy, science, culture.* Ithaca: Cornell University Press.

Hirsch, E.D. (Jr)
1960   "Objective interpretation." *Publication of the Modern Language Association* 75:463–79.

—— 1976   *The aims of interpretation.* Chicago: University of Chicago Press.

—— 1984a   "Criticism and countertheses: On justifying interpretive norms." *Journal of Aesthetics and Art Criticism* 43:89–91.

—— 1984b   "Meaning and significance reinterpreted." *Critical Inquiry* 11:202–25.

—— 1985a   "Back to history." Pp. 189–97 in G. Graff and R. Gibbons (eds.), *Criticism in the university.* Evanston: Northwestern University Press.

—— 1985b   "Counterfactuals in interpretation." Pp. 15–28 in *L'herméneutique texte, lecture réception.* Texte: Revue de critique et du

Theorie Litteraire, 3. Toronto: Texte Trinity College.

Hoy, D.C.
1991 "Is hermeneutics ethnocentric?" Pp. 155–75 in J.F. Bohman, D.R. Hiley, and R. Shusterman (eds.), *The interpretive turn: Philosophy, science, culture*. Ithaca: Cornell University Press.

Jarvie, I.C.
1977 "Understanding and explanation in sociology and social anthropology." Pp. 189–206 in F.R. Dallmayr and T.A. McCarthy (eds.), *Understanding and social inquiry*. Notre Dame: University of Notre Dame Press.
—— 1986a "Anthropologists and the irrational." Pp. 233–56 in *Thinking about society: Theory and practice*. Dordrecht: D. Reidel.
—— 1986b "Anthropology as science and the anthropology of science and of anthropology." Pp. 162–82 in *Thinking about society: Theory and practice*. Dordrecht: D Reidel.
—— 1986c "The problem of the ethnographic real." Pp. 212–32 in *Thinking about society: Theory and practice*. Dordrecht: D Reidel.

Jeanrond, W.G.
1988 *Text and interpretation as categories of theological thinking*. New York: Crossroad.

Lett, J.
1987 *The human enterprise: A critical introduction to anthropological theory*. Boulder: Westview Press.
—— 1990 "A field guide to critical thinking." *The Skeptical Inquirer* 14(2):153–60.
—— 1991 "Interpretive anthropology, metaphysics, and the paranormal." *Journal of Anthropological Research* 47:305–29.

MacIntyre, A.
1971 "The idea of a social science." Pp. 211–229 in *Against the self-images of the age: Essays on ideology and philosophy*. London: Duckworth.

Mouton, J. and Pauw, J.C.
1988 "Foundationalism and fundamentalism: A critique." Pp. 176–86 in J. Mouton, A.G. Van Aarde, and W.S. Vorster (eds.), *Paradigms and progress in theology*. Pretoria: Human Sciences Research Council.

Peacock, J.L.
1986 *The anthropological lens: Harsh light, soft focus*. Cambridge: Cambridge University Press.

Popper, K.
1970 "Normal science and its dangers." Pp. 51–58 in I. Lakatos and A. Musgrave (eds.), *Criticism and the growth of knowledge: Proceedings of the international colloquium in the philosophy of science*. Cambridge: Cambridge University Press.

Rabinow, P. and Sullivan, W.M.
1979 "The interpretive turn: Emergence of an approach." Pp. 1–21 in P. Rabinow and W.M. Sullivan (eds.), *Interpretive social science: A reader*. Berkeley: University of California Press.

Rorty, R.
1981 "Method, social science, and social hope." *Canadian Journal of Philosophy* 9(4):569–88.
—— 1984 "The historiography of philosophy: Four genres." Pp. 49–75

in R. Rorty, J.B. Schneewind, and Q. Skinner (eds.), *Philosophy in history: Essays on the historiography of philosophy*. Cambridge: Cambridge University Press.

—— 1985   "Solidarity or objectivity." Pp. 3–19 in J. Rajchman and C. West (eds.), *Post-analytic philosophy*. New York: Columbia University Press.

—— 1986   "On ethnocentrism: A reply to Clifford Geertz." *Michigan Quarterly Review* 25:525–34.

Schüssler Fiorenza, E.
1988   "The ethics of biblical interpretation: Decentering biblical scholarship." *JBL* 107(1):3–17.

Shusterman, R.
1991   "Beneath interpretation." Pp. 102–28 in J.F. Bohman, D.R. Hiley, and R. Shusterman (eds.), *The interpretive turn: Philosophy, science, culture*. Ithaca: Cornell University Press.

Skinner, Q.
1988   "A reply to my critics." Pp. 231–88; 326–41 in J. Tully (ed.), *Meaning and context: Quentin Skinner and his critics*. Oxford: Polity Press.

Sono, T.
1994   *Dilemmas of African intellectuals in South Africa: Political and cultural constraints*. Pretoria: University of South Africa.

Taylor, C.
1977   "Interpretation and the sciences of man." Pp. 101–31 in F.R. Dallmayr and T.A. McCarthy (eds.), *Understanding and social inquiry*. Notre Dame: University of Notre Dame Press.

—— 1985a   "Rationality." Pp. 134–51 in *Philosophy and the human sciences: Philosophical papers 2*. Cambridge: Cambridge University Press.

—— 1985b   "Understanding and ethnocentricity." Pp. 116–33 in *Philosophy and the human sciences: Philosophical papers 2*. Cambridge: Cambridge University Press.

—— 1987   "Overcoming epistemology." Pp. 464–88 in K. Baynes, J. Bohman, and T. McCarthy (eds.), *After philosophy: End or transformation?*. Cambridge: MIT Press.

—— 1991   "The dialogical self." Pp. 304–14 in J.F. Bohman, D.R. Hiley, and R. Shusterman (eds.), *The interpretive turn: Philosophy, science, culture*. Ithaca: Cornell University Press.

Todorov, T.
1988   "Knowledge in social anthropology: Distancing and universality." *Anthropology Today* 4(2):2–5.

West, G.O.
1991   *Biblical hermeneutics of liberation: Modes of reading the Bible in the South African context*. Pietermaritzburg: Cluster Publications.

Winthrop, R.H.
1991   "Relativism." s.v. *Dictionary of concepts in cultural anthropology*.

RACIAL AND ETHNIC MINORITIES IN BIBLICAL STUDIES

Fernando F. Segovia

According to the rationale that accompanied the invitation to contribute to this project, the present volume was conceived with two
primary factors in mind: the eruption of the issue of ethnicity on the
global scene in recent years and the perceived and corresponding
responsibility on the part of biblical scholars to address the subject
on an explicit and sustained basis. Both concerns are clearly reflected
in the title of the volume—*Ethnicity and the Bible*. The rationale further identified two specific goals for the project: in pursuing the issue
of ethnicity, the volume would also serve to highlight the diversity in
method and theory presently to be found in the discipline as well as
offer a new model for doing biblical theology in the contemporary
scene, a model based on a broadly conceived theological reflection
on the Bible in the light of the new methodological and theoretical
pluralism in the discipline. Both aims are clearly reflected in the structure of the volume. While a first part brings together a variety of
different approaches to ethnicity in the Bible, with corresponding
sections on the Hebrew Bible and the Christian Scriptures, a second
part focuses on ethnicity in the contemporary world, with sections
on the relationship between the Bible and present-day ethnic issues
as well as the politics of biblical interpretation. Thus, the rationale
argued for an approach to the new and pressing question of ethnicity
from the point of view of both the text (ethnicity in the Bible) and
the readers of the text (ethnicity in the interpretation of the Bible).[1]

---

[1] On both counts the rationale for the volume closely parallels the earlier rationale for the journal itself, as outlined in the Editorial Statement of the first issue
(*Biblical Interpretation* 1 [1993] i–ii). With regard to motivating factors, the editorial
statement cited the recent burgeoning of new approaches to textual interpretation as
well as the need for biblical studies to become more public and pluralistic. With
regard to goals in mind, the statement presented the journal as both a forum for
the fresh interpretation of texts through the use of the new critical approaches and
a forum for theoretical debate regarding the theological and political implications of
such new developments. Thus, the boldness behind the new journal—with its open
criticism of the leading journals in the field for their failure to reflect the new pluralism within the discipline—was reflected in the boldness behind the proposed volume:

My own contribution to the project belongs decidedly within the second part of the volume. Indeed, I see my task in this study as that of providing an overall critical view of the life and role of ethnic and racial minorities[2] in biblical studies, by which I mean both the discipline and the profession, especially in the light of the profound and radical changes at work at the end of the twentieth century, hence the rather broad title for the essay.[3] As such, I am not interested here in the construction of ethnicity or race in the Bible or even in the relationship between ethnicity or race and biblical interpretation; rather, my particular concern is with ethnicity and race within the field and the guild of biblical studies and thus with the politics of interpretation from both a disciplinary and professional perspective.

---

in effect, given the rise of ethnicity as a global and public critical issue, it was imperative for biblical scholars to take an open and systematic stand on the topic, with particular attention to be given to the diversity of reading strategies in the discipline as well as broad theological reflection in the light of such pluralism.

[2] The expression "ethnic and racial minorities" represents a combination of the terms "ethnic group" and "racial group" as well as the term "minority group," all of which are basic concepts in the study of intergroup relations; see, e.g., J.R. Fegin, *Racial and Ethnic Relations* (Englewood Cliffs, NJ: Prentice Hall, 3rd edn, 1989) esp. pp. 4–19. A word of explanation is in order. With regard to the first two terms, "ethnic group" and "racial group," these are concepts whose definitions vary widely not only in terms of historical usage but also with regard to perspective and ideology. In other words, neither "ethnicity" nor "race" are self-evident and fixed concepts grounded in nature or genetics, but social constructs with an underlying historical and ideological base. My own use of these terms is social in nature and follows that of Fegin: ethnic and racial groups as social groups, singled out as such for social interest, whether good or bad, either from inside or outside the differentiated groups, on the basis of certain cultural or physical characteristics, respectively. With regard to the third term, "minority group," this is a concept that is often used of both ethnic and racial groups and that implies the existence of a "majority group" and the presence of ethnic or racial stratification. In other words, the term "minority group" is not just a descriptive classification but also an evaluative category. At times, the terms "dominant group" and "subordinate group" are preferred in the literature, in order to reflect the fact that a "minority group" in terms of stratification may actually be a "majority group" with regard to numbers. My own use of the term in this study implies both numbers and stratification.

In sum, I employ the expression "ethnic and racial minorities" to mean individuals from social groups, whether culturally (ethnic) or physically (racial) identified as such, who have traditionally been considered inferior within a scale of stratification set up by the West and operative in all the theological disciplines, including biblical criticism. In effect, such individuals may be described as critics of non-Western origins or descent who either live in their respective countries or reside within the West itself. Moreover, while they invariably represent, as a whole, a numerical majority in the world in terms of their own socioreligious affiliation, they represent a minority both in terms of stratification and numbers within the theological disciplines in general and biblical criticism in particular.

[3] This study is a revised version of a presentation given at the 1994 Annual

I should like to begin, therefore, with an analysis of a number of factors that I see as constitutive for our situation at the turn of the century and then conclude with a description of the life and role of ethnic and racial minorities in the light of such a context.[4] It is my firm belief that ethnic and racial minorities have a fundamental role to play in the future direction of the discipline and the profession in what I would describe as the post-Western, postcolonial world of religious studies and theological studies in general and biblical criticism in particular. It is also my firm belief, however, that such a role is not at all an easy one to play; in fact, it involves and calls for struggle as a way of life. In the end, however, I would argue that such struggle is for life, and a very promising life indeed.

Racial and Ethnic Minorities in Biblical Studies at the Turn of the Century

There are three factors at work in the contemporary scene that I regard as fundamental for the life and role of ethnic and racial minorities in biblical studies at the turn of the century—that pregnant period of time, which has come to be known in intellectual history as the *fin de siècle* and which we have already properly entered as such, marking the close of one century and the beginning of

Meeting of the Society of Biblical Literature in Chicago, Illinois, in a session sponsored by the Committee on Underrepresented Racial and Ethnic Minority Persons in the Profession. I should like to express my gratitude hereby to all of my colleagues on the committee for their very kind invitation to serve as the keynote speaker for the session as well as to all the members of the panel who responded to my presentation out of their own particular histories and experiences (Professors Victor Paul Furnish, Southern Methodist University, Dallas, TX; Gale A. Yee, University of St. Thomas, St. Paul, MN; Cyris Moon, San Francisco Theological Seminary, San Anselmo, CA; and Renita J. Weems, Vanderbilt University, Nashville, TN).

[4] As my use of the first person plural adjective indicates, my approach to the question is from an emic rather than etic perspective—the perspective of the insider, a representative of ethnic and racial minorities in the field and the guild. It is a perspective with a number of interrelated and interdependent layers of meaning, which I would describe as that of (a) a critic of non-Western origins; (b) with birth and primary socialization outside the West (in Latin American culture and, more specifically, within its Caribbean variant); (c) with secondary socialization and permanent residence, indeed citizenship, in the West (the United States); (d) and hence, a member of an ethnic minority group within the United States, the Hispanic Americans, constituting at present approximately nine percent of the population (close to twenty-two million people) and widely recognized and differentiated as such both by the group itself and the majority culture. I would define the group as follows: people of Hispanic descent, associated in one way or another with the Americas, who now live permanently, for whatever reason, in the United States.

another and so laden with meaning of all sorts, both before and after the fact. One such dimension of meaning that I would associate with the present *fin de siècle* has to do with the drastically changed nature of doing theology or criticism in a postcolonial, post-Western world. The first factor concerns the world of global affairs—the geopolitical context; the second, the world of biblical criticism—the disciplinary context; the third, the world of the biblical guild—the professional context.

Geopolitical Context: The World of Global Affairs

To begin with, a few remarks are necessary with regard to the geopolitical scene at large. In a recent and much-debated article on world politics, Samuel Huntington, Eaton Professor of the Science of Government and Director of the John M. Olin Institute for Strategic Studies at Harvard University, has argued that global politics is presently entering a new and different phase of development altogether.[5] It is an argument that I find, on the whole, insightful as well as

---

Such a perspective I have characterized in terms of the diaspora. For a sharper delineation, see: (a) regarding its hermeneutics: "Toward a Hermeneutics of the Diaspora: A Hermeneutics of Otherness and Engagement," in Fernando F. Segovia and Mary Ann Tolbert (eds.), *Reading from This Place. Volume One: Social Location and Biblical Interpretation in the United States* (Minneapolis: Fortress Press, 1994), pp. 57–73; and "Toward Intercultural Criticism: A Reading Strategy from the Diaspora," in Fernando F. Segovia and Mary Ann Tolbert (eds.), *Reading from This Place. Volume Two: Social Location and Biblical Interpretation in the Global Scene* (Minneapolis: Fortress Press, 1995) pp. 303–30. (b) Regarding its theological locus and mode: "Two Places and No Place on Which to Stand: Mixture and Otherness in Hispanic American Theology," *Listening. A Journal of Religion and Culture* 27 (1992), pp. 26–40; and "In the World but Not of It: Exile as Locus for a Theology of the Diaspora," in Ada María Isasi-Díaz and Fernando F. Segovia (eds.), *Aliens in the Promised Land: Voices of Hispanic American Theology* (Minneapolis: Fortress Press, 1996), forthcoming.

[5] Samuel P. Huntington, "The Clash of Civilizations?" *Foreign Affairs* 72 (Summer 1993), pp. 22–49. The ensuing discussion may be traced as follows. First, a number of responses appeared in the very next issue of *Foreign Affairs* 73 (September–October 1993): Fouad Adjami, "The Summoning," pp. 2–9; Kishore Mahbubani, "The Dangers of Decadence: What the Rest Can Teach the West," pp. 10–14; Robert L. Bartley, "The Case for Optimism," pp. 15–18; Liu Bynian, "Civilization Grafting," pp. 19–21; and Jeane J. Kirkpatrick et al., "The Modernizing Imperative," pp. 22–26. Then, Huntington himself responded in a second article: "If Not Civilizations, What?" *Foreign Affairs* 72 (November/December 1993), pp. 186–94. Since then, a number of studies have contributed further to the discussion, e.g., Robert D. Kaplan, "The Coming Anarchy," *The Atlantic Monthly* 273:4 (February 1994), pp. 44–76; and Matthew Connelly and Paul Kennedy, "Must It Be the Rest Against the West?" *Atlantic Monthly* 274:6 (December 1994), pp. 61–84.

persuasive and reproduce here in its essentials as an appropriate preamble to, and overall framework for, my own reflections regarding the state of affairs in the discipline and the profession.

For Huntington, this new phase in question is marked not so much by the end of history, the return of traditional rivalries among nation-states, or the decline of the nation-state in the face of tribalism and globalism—as many would have it—but rather by a new source of conflict in the world, neither economic nor ideological but *cultural*. As such, nation-states will neither disappear nor go into a period of decline; to the contrary, they shall continue to function as the most powerful actors in world affairs. At the same time, however, global conflict will be increasingly defined not by conflicts among nation-states—a development which would signify a return in principle to a previous phase of evolution, as outlined below—but rather by conflicts between nations and groups of different *civilizations*, with the "fault lines" between such civilizations as the "battle lines" of the future.[6]

This new phase, moreover, represents the fourth and latest stage in the evolution of conflict in the modern political world. Thus, while in the past conflict has been by and large the result of conflicts *within* Western civilization, with all non-Western peoples and governments as objects of history, from this point on conflict will be driven by conflicts *between* civilizations. The earlier development of conflict, encompassing the last three hundred and fifty years of Western history (1640s–1990s), Huntington traces in terms of the following three stages:

---

[6] Huntington ("Clash of Civilizations," pp. 23–25) defines a "civilization" as: (a) a cultural entity—not unlike villages, regions, ethnic groups, nationalities, and religious groups, all of which are said to have distinct cultures at different levels of cultural heterogeneity; (b) of the most comprehensive sort—involving the highest cultural grouping of people and the broadest level of cultural identity on the part of people. The concept carries a number of other connotations as well. First, civilizations include objective (language; history; religion; customs; institutions) as well as subjective elements (the self-identification of people). Second, civilizations are fluid rather than fixed concepts, insofar as people can and do redefine their identities with a resulting change in the composition and boundaries of civilizations. Third, civilizations may involve large numbers of people (e.g., China) or a very small number of people (e.g., the Anglophone Caribbean). Fourth, civilizations may include several nation-states (e.g., Islam, Latin America, and the West) or one (e.g., Japan). Fifth, civilizations blend and overlap and thus may include subcivilizations. Here, the example of the West is very much to the point, with its two major variants (Europe and the United States), although there are other examples as well (as in the case of Islam, with its Arab, Malay, and Turkic variants). Finally, civilizations are dynamic, not only dividing and merging but also rising and falling.

1. To begin with, for about a century and a half after the Peace of Westphalia (1648–1789)—that is to say, from the end of the Thirty Years War and the emergence of the modern international system in 1648 to the outbreak of the French Revolution in 1789—conflict in the West consisted largely of conflicts among princes: emperors, absolute monarchs, and constitutional monarchs, all attempting to expand their bureaucracies, armies, mercantilist economies, and territories.

2. Subsequently, for the next one hundred and twenty-five years (1789–1914/18)—namely, from the aftermath of the French Revolution (1789) to the conclusion of the First World War in 1918—conflict in the Western world took the form of conflicts between or among nation-states: as princes expanded the territories over which they ruled, nation-states came into being and clashed with one another over the long course of the nineteenth century and right into the first decades of the twentieth century itself.

3. Then, for the last seventy years and hence the greater part of the twentieth century (1918–1989)—in effect, from the aftermath of World War I (1918), especially in terms of the Russian Revolution and the reaction against it, until the implosion of the Soviet Empire and the end of the Cold War in 1989—conflict in the West consisted of conflicts involving ideologies. Such conflict involved two distinct stages: first, prior to the Second World War (1918–1939/45), among communism, fascism-nazism, and liberal democracy; subsequently, during the Cold War (1945–1989), between communism and liberal democracy, as embodied in the struggle between the two superpowers, the Soviet Union and the United States, neither of which was a nation-state in the classical sense and each of which defined its identity in terms of its ideology.

Again, all such conflicts amounted to conflicts within Western civilization, Western civil wars as it were. However, with the collapse of the Union of Soviet Socialist Republics and the end of the Cold War, Huntington sees international politics as moving beyond its long Western phase, with enormous and radical consequences for the world at large, including the West. On the one hand, non-Western peoples and governments begin to move thereby from a position as objects of history—or, perhaps more accurately, its targets—to a position as movers and shapers of history alongside the West, as "subjects of history," as Liberation Theology has so often and so aptly put it.[7]

---

[7] This, however, is an aspect of the discussion that, in my opinion, Huntington

On the other hand, conflict takes on as a result the form of conflicts involving civilizations.[8] On one level, such conflict involves the different civilizations, with eight identified as major in this regard—African, Confucian, Hindu, Islamic, Japanese, Latin American, Slavic-Orthodox, and Western.[9] On another level, such conflict also involves "the West and the Rest," given not only the undisputed primacy of Western civilization but also its long history of imperialism and colonialism.[10]

---

does not engage or pursue in adequate fashion. While quick to draw numerous implications for the West, both short-term and long-term, of this tectonic change in international politics and fully cognizant of how the global discussion has been controlled for centuries by the West with its own fundamental interests in mind, he fails to give sufficient attention to the grave responsibility borne by the West for the present state of affairs. After all, the legacy of the West in this regard—an often-bypassed but intrinsic part of Western civilization and culture—is a most heavy burden indeed: from the centuries of colonialism, involving the widescale domination, exploitation, and extermination of other peoples; to the technological perfection of displacement, forced labor, and genocide by Germany, in the name of a *Herrenvolk*, in the course of the present century; to the ongoing and unchecked ethnic cleansing at work in the Balkans and the growing resentment of and hostility toward immigrants and refugees in the West, especially those from the non-Western world. In other words, the magnificent legacy of the West—its great "creed," for which see n. 11 below—extended only so far and was accompanied throughout by political domination and economic exploitation, social and cultural disdain, ethnic and racial prejudice and discrimination, ultimately leading to the slavery and extermination of millions upon millions of peoples. Indeed, it was the failure of the West to extend its "creed" to the rest, to see the other in the light of its own "creed," that is largely responsible for the situation faced by the world as it begins to move into the twenty-first century.

[8] Huntington ("Clash," pp. 25–29) sees such a coming state of affairs as inevitable for a variety of reasons: (a) Differences among civilizations are real and basic, the product of centuries. (b) As the world becomes a smaller place, the increasing interactions between peoples of different civilizations intensify civilization-consciousness, both in terms of similarities within civilizations and differences between civilizations. (c) The processes of economic modernization and social change separate people from their local identities, not only weakening thereby the nation-state as a source of identity but also giving rise to fundamentalist religious movements across the globe, which rush in to fill the void. (d) The dual role of the West: a West at the peak of its power, but also a West that no longer calls forth imitation but rather a return-to-the-roots movement in the non-West. (e) Cultural characteristics and differences as less mutable and less easily compromised than political or economic ones. (f) An increase in economic regionalism, both grounded in and reinforcing civilization-consciousness. The end result is an overall growth in an "us versus them" relationship between civilizations.

[9] From the point of view of the "us versus them" mentality, such conflicts take place at both a micro and a macro level. At the micro level, adjacent groups along the "fault-lines" struggle for control of territory and each other. At the macro level, states from different civilizations compete for relative military and economic power, struggle over the control of international institutions, and promote their own political and religious values.

[10] The phrase is borrowed from an earlier piece by Kishore Mahbubani ("The

From a geopolitical point of view, therefore, ethnic and racial minorities in biblical studies, whether based in their respective countries and cultures or in the West itself, represent by and large the children of cultures (1) formerly controlled by the West during its long period of global hegemony and as a result of its extensive process of colonial expansionism and domination in the world at large; (2) trapped until very recently as pawns within the dualistic struggle between the "free world" or first world and the "communist world" or second world; and (3) only now beginning to attain a measure of self-identity, self-consciousness, and self-determination, cultural and otherwise. Those living in the West—mostly by way of its North American variant (the United States) and including individuals of African, Asian, Caribbean, and Latin American descent—further represent a significant and increasingly unwelcomed presence of non-Western cultures at the very heart of the West, no matter how inscribed in the West they may be or how devoted to its foundational creed and principles.[11] In the end, the broad geopolitical shift outlined by Huntington will

---

West and the Rest," *The National Interest* [Summer, 1992], pp. 3–13). From the point of view of the "us versus them" mentality, the efforts of the West to promote democracy and liberalism as universal values, maintain its military predominance, and advance its economic interests are met with countering responses from other civilizations, with an increasing appeal to common religion and civilization-identity in this regard.

[11] In the past few years, the backlash against immigrants and immigration from outside the West into the West has increased sharply, in Europe as well as in the United States. It is a presence that is seen as harmful to the West, its culture and way of life, and even as ultimately leading to its demise. For the European scene, with an informative breakdown of the numbers and countries of origin involved, see Félix Monteira, "Ser extranjero en Europa, algo poco recomendable," *El País*, (30 July 1990), int. ed.: 4. In the United States in particular, the projections of the Census Bureau have thrown fear into the heart of the majority and dominant culture, with its estimates to the effect that by the year 2050, given the continuation of present levels of immigration, the American population will be 23 percent Hispanic-American, 16 percent African-American, and 10 percent Asian-American—in effect, just under 50 percent of the population will be of non-European origin. See, e.g., William A. Henry III, "Beyond the Melting Pot," *Time* (9 April 1990), p. 28. The question raised by commentators from the dominant culture is posed in explicit ethnic and racial terms: whether such immigrants will espouse the "twin bedrocks" of the country—European culture and the "American Creed" of liberty, equality, individualism, and democracy. See, e.g., Bruce D. Porter, "Can American Democracy Survive?" *Commentary* (November, 1993), pp. 37–40; and Huntington, "If Not Civilizations," esp. pp. 189–190, from whom I have borrowed the terms in quotation marks above.

See also the recent book by Peter Brimelow, which takes the argument to a new and alarming level of discourse (*Alien Nation: Common Sense about America's Immigration Disaster* [New York: Random House, 1995]). Brimelow, himself an immigrant from England, argues for a drastic curtailment of present immigration policy on the part

have a further and inevitable effect on ethnic and racial minorities in all the theological disciplines, including biblical criticism, as these individuals and groups proceed to reflect more and more on what it means to do theology from their own social locations and to read and interpret the Bible from their own places.

Disciplinary Context: The World of Biblical Criticism

Some remarks are in order as well with regard to the present state of affairs in the discipline we practice, what I call "biblical criticism" for lack of a better name, given the inevitable but unintended canonical connotations of such a designation.[12] It is a discipline that finds itself at present in a situation of seemingly stable anomie or liminality, due in part to a number of theoretical and methodological developments within the discipline itself in the course of the last twenty-five years or so but also in part to certain important sociocultural developments as well.[13] It is this latter aspect that I should like to highlight in the present context.

---

of the United States, in effect since the Immigration and Naturalization Act of 1965, which opened the doors widely to immigrants from outside the European continent. This clarion call for a respite in immigration again reveals strong and stereotypical ethnic and racial connotations: a focus on the reunification of families has turned immigration into a kind of civil right for inhabitants of third-world countries; the new immigrants are disproportionately prone to poverty, crime, and welfare dependency; and new racial minorities, such as Asians and Hispanics, will alter the very nature of the American nation-state, traditionally white in character.

In the end, such arguments reflect the traditional position of the Protestant Anglo-Saxon dominant culture of the country and were being voiced not too long ago, during the last great wave of immigration into the country from the 1890s to the 1920s, against such "races" as the Jews and other ethnic groups of southern and eastern European extraction, Catholic and Orthodox to boot. Nowadays, the face of the enemy has changed: it is no longer the Jew, the Greek, the Slav, or the Italian but the non-European or non-Westerner that has become the target of suspicion, fear, and even hatred. That too, I am afraid, is part of the legacy of Western civilization—a profound and persistent contradiction at the heart of its "creed" of liberty, equality, individualism, and democracy.

[12] By "biblical criticism" I mean, therefore, from my Christian perspective, the study not only of the canonical texts of the Bible as such—however defined, whether one follows the Catholic tradition or the Protestant tradition—but also of all the other extant texts of ancient Judaism and earliest Christianity. I mean as well not only the study of literary texts and other cultural artifacts but also the study of the interpretation of such "texts." I readily acknowledge the need for a more comprehensive term for the discipline, a term that would include but not privilege the "canon" as such, that would place the canon within the wider framework of the socioreligious world in question; I also confess that so far I have found none to my satisfaction.

[13] For a personal plotting of the course of the discipline in the present century in

In effect, following a pattern at work not only across a broad disciplinary spectrum but also within religious and theological studies in general, biblical criticism, which had remained since its inception as a discipline, in the aftermath of the French Revolution, exclusively the preserve of Western males—Western male clerics, to be more precise—has witnessed during the last twenty years or so an influx of outsiders into the discipline, individuals who had never formed part of the field before and who were now making their voices heard for the first time: Western women; non-Western theologians and critics; ethnic and racial minorities from non-Western civilizations in the West.[14]

Such individuals, to be sure, received their training almost exclusively in the academic institutions of the West, where historical criticism—the first paradigm—still reigned supreme by and large and where they were duly introduced to the fundamentals of the method at the hands of Western male scholars in their role as *Doktorvätern* or "doctoral fathers," master researchers and teachers as well as founders or links in all-important, patriarchal pedigree lines. As such, these outsiders were very much subject to the powerful centripetal and

---

terms of four paradigms or umbrella models of interpretation (historical criticism; literary criticism; cultural criticism; and cultural studies), see my "'And They Began to Speak in Other Tongues': Competing Modes of Discourse in Contemporary Biblical Interpretation," *Reading from This Place. Volume One*, pp. 1–32. For a delineation of the fourth and most recent paradigm, what I call "cultural studies," see my "Cultural Studies and Contemporary Biblical Criticism: Ideological Criticism as Mode of Discourse," *Reading from This Place. Volume Two*, pp. 1–17.

[14] On the globalization of the discipline, see the section on "Reading the Field" in the first issue of *Biblical Interpretation* 1 (1993), pp. 34–114, esp.: David A.J. Clines, "Possibilities and Priorities of Biblical Interpretation in an International Perspective," pp. 67–87; and David Jobling, "Globalization in Biblical Studies/Biblical Studies in Globalization," pp. 96–110. See also John R. Levison and Priscilla Pope-Levison, "Global Perspectives on New Testament Interpretation," in Joel B. Green (ed.), *Hearing the New Testament: Strategies for Interpretation* (Grand Rapids: Eerdmans, 1995), pp. 329–48. For similar though earlier developments in other fields and their consequences, see: (a) from the point of view of historical studies: Joyce Appleby, Lynn Hunt, and Margaret Jacob, *Telling the Truth about History* (New York and London: W.W. Norton, 1994), pp. 126–59 (Chap. 4: "Competing Histories of America"); and Peter Novick, *That Noble Dream: The "Objectivity Question" and the American Historical Profession* (Cambridge: Cambridge University Press, 1988), pp. 469–521 (Chap. 14: "Every Group Its Own Historian"). (b) From the point of view of literary studies: Vincent B. Leitch, *Cultural Criticism, Literary Theory, Poststructuralism* (New York and Oxford: Columbia University Press, 1992), pp. 83–103 (Chap. 5: "Pluralizing Poetics"). (c) From the point of view of social studies: Steven Seidman, *Contested Knowledge: Social Theory in the Postmodern Era* (Oxford and Cambridge, MA: Blackwell, 1994), pp. 234–80 (Chap. 7: "The New Social Movements and the Making of New Social Knowledges").

homogenizing forces of this training, with its emphasis on the classic
ideals of the Enlightenment: all knowledge as science; the scientific
method as applicable to all areas of inquiry; nature or facts as neutral and knowable; research as a search for truth involving value-free
observation and recovery of the facts; the researcher as a giant of
reason who surveys the facts with disinterested eyes.[15]

A further though much more implicit dimension of this process of
academic socialization, quite in keeping as well with the cult of
modernity emerging from the Enlightenment, should be noted as well:
the profound conviction that such training not only represented
progress over against traditional interpretations of the Bible (the triumph of light over darkness and reason over tradition) but also the
superiority of the West over against all other cultures (the hermeneutics
of over/against and the white man's burden). In other words, historical criticism was not only perceived and promoted as the sole
and proper way to read and interpret the texts of antiquity but also
as the ultimate sign of progress in the discipline, the offer of the
West to the rest of the world and the means by which the backward
and uncivilized could become modern and civilized.

Despite such overwhelming academic enculturation, it did not take
long before a good many of these individuals began to question the
character and agenda of such criticism, especially with respect to the
unquestioned and unquestionable construct of the scientific researcher,
objective and impartial—the universal and informed reader—operative in one form or another not only in historical criticism but also
in the other two emerging paradigms of literary and cultural criticism and to raise instead the radical question of contextualization
and perspective. This growing insistence on the situated and interested nature of all reading and interpretation brought additional,
pointed, and unrelenting pressure on biblical criticism—already in
serious turmoil as a result of internal methodological and theoretical
challenges—to come to terms with the question of real readers, the
flesh-and-blood readers.

In so doing, of course, the long-standing project of the Enlightenment, as embodied in historical criticism and continued by and large
by its emerging rivals—at least at first—was ultimately being called

---

[15] For an excellent analysis of the operative model of history at the heart of
traditional historical criticism, see Appleby, Hunt, and Jacob, *Telling the Truth*, pp.
15–90 (Chapter 1: "The Heroic Model of Science").

into question as well: the character of biblical studies as "science" and the use of the "scientific" method; the nature of "history;" the possibility of "value-free" observation; the role of the "rational, disinterested" researcher; the notion of "progress." In the process, historical criticism, along with the new competing paradigms, began to be analyzed—like the Enlightenment itself—in terms of contextualization and perspective, social location and agenda, inextricably tied as these were to the gender and origins of its practitioners—Western male clerics. In other words, the thoroughly gendered and thoroughly Western character of the discipline, lying just behind the scientific façade of the universal and informed reader, began to be systematically exposed and critiqued.

From a disciplinary point of view, ethnic and racial minorities in biblical studies, whether outside the West or within the West, have resisted and continue to resist, given their cultural origins outside the West, any view of criticism as timeless and value-free, seeing it instead as thoroughly enmeshed in the public arena and thus as irretrievably political in character and ramifications, both from the point of view of the narrower meaning of this term (the realm of politics within the sphere of the sociopolitical) and its broader meaning (the realm of power within the sphere of the ideological). In other words, ethnic and racial minorities insist on reading with their own eyes and making their own voices heard, while challenging their colleagues in the West to do the same, in an explicit and public fashion. In this regard, the profound geopolitical transformation at work outlined above will only magnify this twofold resistance on the part of ethnic and racial minorities against the construct of the universal and learned reader, with its corresponding vision of a non-ideological reading, and insistence on the construct of the flesh-and-blood reader, with its corresponding vision of all reading as ideological to the core.

Professional Context: The World of the Biblical Guild

Finally, some remarks are in order as well with regard to the profession and its guilds, that is to say, its network of learned organizations. There is a wide range of such groups in existence: while some have a distinctly local, national, or regional focus, others are more international in scope. Among the latter, some focus on the study of either the Christian Scriptures (e.g., the Society for the Study of the New Testament) or the Hebrew Bible (e.g., the International Organization for the Study of the Old Testament), while others encompass both areas of specialization (e.g., the Catholic Biblical Association and the Society of Biblical Literature). All of these international organizations have, quite understandably from both a historical and an economic point of view, their origins in the West. Moreover, although their membership is open in principle to non-Western critics, their overall character and orientation as well as actual attendance at the annual meetings remain overwhelmingly Western in character. Consequently, at a time when the number of biblical critics from outside the West is clearly on the rise, there is still no international organization in the field with a primary base outside the West; no occasion when non-Western critics from across the globe can meet on their own, as the West so often does; no meeting in the West where non-Western critics ever represent more than a handful of participants; and no gathering anywhere where the West and the non-West, the colonizers and the colonized, can come together on a regular basis for dialogue in sufficient numbers from both sides.

Yet, an exception may be in the making, by way of the Society of Biblical Literature. First, the Society is beginning to hold its annual international meetings outside Europe on a regular basis, with a first such meeting held in Australia in 1993 and a second scheduled for South Africa in 1998. Second, as part of its Challenge Campaign, a multiyear drive for funds and endowment, the Society has established as one of its primary goals for the future the expansion of the circle of voices participating in biblical studies, with increased contacts and interaction between the West and the non-West as a concrete desideratum.[16] Third, the makeup of the Society within the United States, its home base, is also beginning to change. Such changes should come as no surprise, given the broader demographic currents at work in U.S. society at large. Two recent sets of statistics should be especially noted in this regard.

First, not long after the national census of 1990, the U.S. Census Bureau reported a profound shift at work in the society: while in 1980 U.S. citizens of non-European descent represented one fifth or 20 percent of the nation's population, by 1990 they accounted for

---

[16] For the scope and goals of this Challenge Campaign, see the news release and report of the Executive Director in *Religious Studies News* 10 (February, 1995), pp. 15–18. The report indicates that SBL members come from eighty countries and that 10 percent of the membership resides outside North America.

one fourth or 25 percent of the population—a development of unbelievable proportions.[17] Second, in 1987, a few years before the census, the Hudson Institute published a report, entitled "Workforce
2000," which has turned out to be quite influential in the national
discussion.[18] The report predicted, among other things, that the labor force of the not too distant future would be increasingly diverse,
more and more composed of women, members of minority groups,
and other alternatives to the traditional white, male breadwinner.
Thus, what the Hudson Institute report of 1987 had anticipated for
the year 2000, the census findings of 1990 had begun to confirm in
no uncertain way.

Such demographic changes and projections, involving a rapidly
growing presence of individuals of non-Western origins or descent,
were bound to have, sooner or later, an impact on the academic
profession, its graduate programs, and its guilds. Neither biblical
criticism nor the Society of Biblical Literature have been exceptions
in this regard. Indeed, a look at program offerings and institutional
structures shows that the Society is gradually beginning to reflect
such larger societal changes as well. For example, for some time now
two such groups have been hard at work: the African-American
Theology and Biblical Hermeneutics Group and the Bible in Africa,
Asia, and Latin America Group; in addition, two more have been
recently formed and approved: the Asian and Asian-American Biblical Studies Consultation and the Bible in Caribbean Culture and
Tradition Consultation. Similarly, for the last three years the Committee on Underrepresented Racial and Ethnic Minority Persons in
the Profession has endeavored to provide leadership, community, and
advocacy within the Society for minority concerns and issues.

Given such developments within the SBL in the United States,
the Society could very well become, if it were to reach out and incorporate—in keeping with its stated goals—the ever-growing number of scholars from outside the West in biblical criticism, the first
truly international organization in the profession, with enormous and

---

[17] See, e.g., Felicity Barringer, "Census Shows Profound Change in Racial Makeup
of the Nation," *The New York Times*, (11 March 1991), nat. ed.: A1. It is this trend
that is reflected in the Census Bureau's long-range progressions for the year 2050,
when the percentage of the non-European population of the nation is expected to
reach just under 50 percent. It is also this trend that is causing increasing concern
among U.S. citizens of European descent. See n. 12 above.

[18] William B. Johnston, *Workforce 2000: Work and Workers for the 21st Century* (Indian-
apolis: The Hudson Institute; Washington: U.S. Department of Labor, 1987).

healthy ramifications for both Western and non-Western critics alike. Indeed, there is no other group on the horizon that could even come close to such a reality—or would want to, for that matter. To be sure, even within such a transformed vision of the Society, the West would continue to predominate, not only by way of governance and numbers but also in terms of discourse and practice; at the same time, however, a vital space would be open thereby for dialogue between the West and the rest, with sufficient numbers in attendance from both camps to ensure a balanced discussion and engagement.

From a professional point of view, ethnic and racial minorities in biblical studies have begun to see their numbers increase and their concerns and interests expand both inside and outside the West. Such a presence will continue to grow as our numbers in theological education and graduate programs continue to expand, and expand they will: outside the West, not only because of the fundamental geopolitical changes taking place in the world but also because of the continuing power and impact of Liberation Theology in all of its various forms, with its clear call for conscientization—for a sense of self-identity, self-consciousness, and self-determination; inside the West, on account of the continuing factors of high immigration, a relatively young population, and a high birthrate among ethnic and racial minorities, alongside a similar impact on the part of Liberation Theology.

Concluding Comments

Such, then, is my assessment of our overall situation as ethnic and racial minorities in biblical studies at the turn of the century. To summarize: (1) From the perspective of world affairs, we represent, whether at home or in the diaspora, the children of non-Western cultures at a defining time in international politics, a time when the long era of Western global domination begins to draw to a close and "the rest" begin to regard and exert themselves as subjects of history. The impact of such geopolitical developments on all academic disciplines, including religious studies and the classical theological disciplines, is only bound to increase as this process continues to unfold, gradually but inexorably. (2) From the perspective of the discipline, we call into question the dominant Western and modernist myth of the impartial and objective observer, the ideal and universal reader, and call instead for an explicit focus on real readers, on place and ideology. In so doing, we argue for a different approach to the discipline, involving critical analysis of contextualization and perspective at all levels of inquiry, as well as a different approach to pedagogy. (3) From the perspective of the profession, we witness our presence in the guild—our numbers and influence; our concerns and interests— very much on the rise. Highly conscious of the fact that we are no longer solely inscribed in the West, we begin to look toward our own cultures and histories for grounding and inspiration. With this general context in mind, therefore, I should like to turn at this point to an analysis of our life and role in the discipline and the profession.

Life and Role of Ethnic and Racial Minorities in Biblical Studies

Such a state of affairs, while seemingly quite promising and attractive on the surface, is, to say the least, not without untoward consequences. In an earlier analysis of the life and role of ethnic and racial minorities in theological education and scholarship, I described our situation in terms of struggle, as a *lucha*, constant and unrelenting but also worth fighting.[19] I am afraid I cannot but describe our situation in biblical studies, whether with reference to the discipline or the profession, in similar terms of struggle, unremitting and everpresent but worth engaging as well. In what follows, then, I begin with a few observations regarding the nature of this struggle, with recourse to the same three factors invoked above, as a point of departure for a final reflection on the need to take up the struggle.

Life as Struggle

First, from a geopolitical perspective, biblical criticism is perceived as both alien and alienating by ethnic and racial minorities. On the one hand, the roots and moorings of our discipline and profession have been, as pointed out above, profoundly and understandably Western. As such, the canon of works and authors to be read, the issues and concerns in question, the historical contexts and perspec-

---

[19] Fernando F. Segovia, "Theological Education and Scholarship as Struggle: The Life of Racial/Ethnic Minorities in the Profession," *Journal of Hispanic/Latino Theology* 2 (1994), pp. 5–25. In so doing, I borrowed from the popular religion of my cultural group, as filtered through the prism of my own family, the focal vocabulary of life as both struggle and counterstruggle.

tives to be studied, and the interpretive frameworks and traditions to be used in the analysis of such works, issues, and perspectives have been those of the West. As ethnic and racial minorities enter the discipline and the profession from outside the West, they find that neither the content nor the mode of discourse is their own. The situation proves to be in many ways, therefore, an alien one. Such individuals find themselves—their works and authors; their issues and concerns; their contexts and perspectives; their interpretive frameworks and traditions—not only out of place but also out of sight.[20] For such individuals, therefore, to pursue biblical studies is to enter yet another dimension of the Western world and to see the biblical world as re-constructed and re-presented by the West.

On the other hand, the problem is not only one of different contents and modes of discourse but also one of sociocultural perception and attitude. At this point, one must keep in mind the dynamics of hegemony and colonialism—the relationship between the center and the margins, the dominant group and the subordinate groups, the majority group and the minority groups. Colonial discourse and practice function largely in terms of binary oppositions: a primary opposition of center/margins engendering and supporting a number of other oppositions, such as superior/inferior, civilized/savage, advanced/primitive—all coalescing in the end in the traditional geopolitical opposition of the West/the rest. Consequently, ethnic and racial minorities, coming as they do from non-Western cultures, enter not only an alien context in biblical studies but also an alienating context, a context where the content and mode of their discourse are not acknowledged, much less accepted or respected, as an equal, as a different or alternative vision of reality. For such individuals, therefore, to pursue

---

[20] For a constantly expanding discussion, see, e.g., Itumeleng J. Mosala, *Biblical Hermeneutics and Black Theology in South Africa* (Grand Rapids: William B. Eerdman's, 1989), esp. pp. 1–42; Cain Hope Felder, *Troubling Biblical Waters. Race, Class, and Family* (Maryknoll: Orbis Books, 1990), esp. pp. 3–21; idem, (ed.), *Stony the Road We Trod: African American Biblical Interpretation* (Minneapolis: Fortress Press, 1991); R.S. Sugirtharajah (ed.), *Voices from the Margins: Interpreting the Bible in the Third World* (Maryknoll: Orbis Books, 1991), esp. pp. 1–6 and 434–44; Patrick J. Hartin, *Third World Challenges in the Teaching of Biblical Studies* (Occasional Papers 25; Claremont: The Institute for Antiquity and Christianity, 1993); Kathleen O'Brien Wicker, "Teaching Feminist Biblical Studies in a Postcolonial Context," in Elisabeth Schüsler Fiorenza (ed.), *Searching the Scriptures. Volume One: A Feminist Introduction* (New York: Crossroad, 1993), pp. 367–80; R.S. Sugirtharajah, "The Bible and Its Asian Readers," *Biblical Interpretation* 1 (1993), pp. 54–66; and idem, ed., *Commitment, Context and Text: Examples of Asian Hermeneutics*, spec. issue of *Biblical Interpretation* 2 [1993], pp. 251–376.

biblical studies is to enter further into the world of social stratification set up by the West vis-à-vis "the other."[21]

To be sure, what is true of biblical studies is true of all other theological disciplines as well. I should like to recount in this regard a personal vignette that Gustavo Gutiérrez, the Peruvian theologian, shared with me sometime ago in the course of a conversation on theological studies from an international perspective. I do so not only because it is truly a classic, a perfect example of the sense of struggle I am striving to convey, but also because of the individual in question. Gutiérrez recalled how, during his days as a doctoral student in theology at the University of Lyon, a fellow student of his from Europe, told him how hard he found it to accept that he (Gutiérrez) *could have anything to teach him at all.* This is a story with which all ethnic and racial minorities can readily identify; a situation that we have all faced at one time or another in the course of our socioeducational journey in the West, whether in England, France, Germany, or the United States; and a story that I hear in endless variations not only from graduate students but also from seasoned scholars on a fairly regular basis. In fact, as one such scholar once put it, one is often made to feel like the man born blind of John 9, as he is told by the powers that be, "You were born in utter sin and you dare to teach us!"

From the point of view of biblical studies in particular, I should like to share one such close encounter of my own, which took place some years ago at an international meeting of the discipline. It involved a young German scholar who, having heard a presentation of mine partially grounded in a hermeneutics of liberation, asked, in a tone of arrogance and disdain such as I have seldom seen in the whole of my professional life, what this all had to do with him. This reaction was what I would call a variation of the center-of-the-world syndrome: a thoroughly uncritical acceptance of European concerns and hermeneutics as pivotal for the world at large, with a corresponding dismissal of all other hermeneutics and concerns as inferior and irrelevant. To such individuals, it would come as a complete and unfathomable surprise for any of us to answer the question, as well we could, with the counterquestion, what does anything you do have to do with us? Except that our sense of dialogue, of being in-

---

[21] On prejudice and discrimination from the point of view of inter-group relations, see Fegin, *Racial and Ethnic Relations*, pp. 15–17.

scribed in various discourses and practices at one and the same time, theoretically prevents us from doing so, since in fact we see all hermeneutics and concerns as ultimately interrelated.

I could go on, of course, recounting stories that either I myself have experienced or that others have shared with me over the years. The point is clear, however: it is very difficult for the West to enter into serious dialogue with the non-West, given the enduring psychological and cultural dynamics of hegemony and colonialism; in fact, it is well-nigh impossible for the West to listen to the critique from the non-West, radical and severe as it often is and must be, in the light of the intervening historical and political relationship. It is quite understandable: how can a position that has been dominant for so long accept the worth, let alone the critique, of the subordinate? How can in-subordination be tolerated, much less engaged?

Second, from a disciplinary perspective, ethnic and racial minorities tend to be quite conscious and upfront about their agenda and social location, while Westerners still hold on, by and large, in practice if not in theory, to the construct of the impartial and objective observer. Their own perspective and contextualization are not acknowledged, much less analyzed, because the construct of a universal and disinterested gaze prevents them in effect from doing so. From such a normative gaze, therefore, what ethnic and racial minorities do, especially since it is foregrounded as such, is seen as contextual and limited; what they themselves do, however, is seen as world-encompassing and significant. As a result, a historical experience and cultural reality as particularized and contextualized as any other is bracketed and universalized thereby as normative human experience and reality—the reality and experience of the center, with the rest unable to transcend their own social locations—the realities and experiences of the margins.

Again, let me offer a personal story by way of illustration. This one has to do with a young English scholar and a conversation, in the course of another international meeting, on the character and aims of traditional historical criticism. Visibly angry and turning surprisingly emotional, this individual protested that the method had no agenda as such, that its goals of impartiality and objectivity were solid, and that the basic problem was that people such as I were trying to politicize the discipline and derail it from its established scientific path. This reaction reflects what I would call a variation of the innocence syndrome: a belief to the effect that interpretation of the Bible is beyond any and all agendas and thus entirely removed from the political realm. For such individuals, it is impossible to see that the myth of innocence is in itself a highly political agenda.

Third, from a professional point of view, it should also be kept in mind that Western institutions having to do with religion, and thus including academic guilds and graduate programs, function by and large out of a liberal-humanist paradigm and thus presuppose a structuralist-functionalist model of society and religious groupings. As such, they replicate the profound contradictions at work in the paradigm: on the one hand, one finds within such institutions an open and heartfelt commitment to openness and tolerance; on the other hand, one also finds a much more subtle but equally forceful emphasis on consensus and conformity. Thus, while harmony and cohesion are much loved and emphasized, conflict is greatly feared and studiously avoided, with solutions to conflict generally sought behind the scenes rather than face to face.

When conflict originates with those who are not only outsiders, expected to be grateful, happy, and compliant for their very admission into such circles of privilege, but also outsiders who are by nature, as children of the colonized, perceived as marginal and inferior, the situation becomes especially problematic, almost intolerable, above all if such conflict has to do, as it usually does, with issues of justice and representation. The paradigm finds it very hard, if not altogether impossible, to deal with such a situation and paternalism usually kicks in as a result: How could those for whom we have done so much react in such a way? The charges that follow are well-known: malcontents; ungrateful; difficult; and my favorite, politicized.

Again, a personal story will serve to illustrate this aspect of the struggle. It concerns a young Belgian scholar and involved a conversation, during yet another international meeting, on the relationship between colonialism and hermeneutics. While quite aware of the historical consequences of Western religious expansionism in the world, involving an onslaught on all native religious beliefs and traditions as primitive or idolatrous, this individual held on for dear life to the belief that in the end the West had done far more good than evil for its colonies throughout the world. This reaction represents what I would call a variation of the all-we-have-done-for-you syndrome: a failure to realize that the rest of the world never had much of a choice regarding this Western program of doing good onto others and its offer of salvation. For such individuals, it proves impossible to deal, theologically and otherwise, with that other and highly destructive side of Western civilization.

In sum, it is not difficult to see why the discipline and the profession of biblical studies should prove a struggle for so many ethnic and racial minorities. It is very difficult to deal with a discourse and practice that are not one's own, that do not regard one's discourse and practice as on a par with those of the reigning paradigm, that refuse to see themselves as particularized and contextualized as any other, and that have a visceral or structural aversion to conflict and confrontation. Within such a paradigm, ethnic and racial minorities are constantly reminded, whether actively or passively, of their marginal status and role in both discipline and profession. Such conditions give rise to and enthrone that sense of struggle which so distinguishes our life in biblical criticism. I would argue that there should be no illusions in this regard: it is a way of life that must be accepted as inevitable, not only for the time being but also, as the stories above indicate, for the foreseeable future, given the age of the interlocutors in question. At the same time, I believe it is a way of life that is very much worth fighting and engaging, insofar as it is a struggle for life.

Struggle for Life

It seems to me that ethnic and racial minorities in biblical studies, as in religious studies or the other classical theological disciplines, embody a profound contradiction at the turn of the century. There is a very real sense in which, from any number of perspectives, the course of events favors us greatly: our recent and irreversible emergence as subjects of history on the world stage; the utter demise of the modernist construct of the ideal observer and narrator and its replacement with the postmodernist construct of the always situated and engaged narrator and observer; our growing presence in the profession, both outside and inside the West, with a corresponding focus on our own concerns and interests, our own readings and interpretations. At the same time, and precisely because of such reasons, our life and role in the discipline and the profession will continue to be one of struggle. Times of change are never easy, especially for those used to power: it is very hard for the center, even traumatic, to come to terms with the loss of center; to have to admit that the center has not only shifted but actually disintegrated, giving rise to a multiplicity of voices; and to engage all such other voices in dialogue as one among many.

In the end, however, I would also argue that our future is a most promising one. Several factors compel me to argue in this direction. First, postmodernism is unstoppable, as more and more new faces join the discussion and re-claim their voices, especially when attempts are made to squash or derail such developments. Second, our numbers and our coalitions, which are crucial, will continue to push the movement forward and make it ever stronger and more sophisticated. Finally, we do have many well-meaning friends as well among our Western colleagues. Here I have in mind not those whom I would call cultural transvestites, who not only love to be one of us but also wish to show us, as our leaders, the way to the promised land, but rather those who are willing to listen and perhaps even follow, for a change.[22] The future of biblical studies—like the future of religious and theological studies in general—I am convinced is a post-colonial, post-Western future, and in that future racial and ethnic minorities will have a fundamental and decisive role to play, whether outside the West or in the trenches in the West. It is a future in which the reading and interpretation of the Bible will be pursued and analyzed from any number of different contexts and perspectives, social locations and agendas, places and ideologies. It is a future with such tasks as the following before us:

(a) First and foremost, a re-reading and re-interpretation of the biblical texts from outside the Western context, with a focus on such issues as the following: the self-construction of the early Christian groups; their construction of the "other"—of all those outside the boundaries of the group—and of their relationship vis-à-vis such

---

[22] For the same problematic from the perspective of gender, see Elaine Showalter, "Critical Cross-Dressing: Male Feminists and The Women of the Year," *Raritan* 3 (1983), pp. 130–49. I will never forget in this regard a planning conference for a biblical project with global pretensions to which a number of ethnic and racial minorities, including myself, had been invited to attend. It gradually emerged in the course of the discussions that no minority had taken part in the planning stages of the project; that an extensive charter document had already been drafted for the project, to which we were expected to react; and that we would not benefit at all from the large funding in question despite the fact that our ideas and our names would serve as the backbone for the revised draft of the document. Needless to say, all of us left the conference with a rather bitter taste in our mouths, the taste of having been used yet again. This is something against which we must be constantly on the watch, putting our hermeneutics of suspicion to good use over and over again.

"others;" their construction of the political realm and of their relationship to this realm, whether at the imperial level or at the local level; their visions of a different world, a world in which peace and justice prevail.

(b) A critical reading of the re-construction and re-presentation of early Christianity on the part of the West, with a focus on such questions as: how it was presented, or the poetics of construction; why it was presented in the way it was presented, or the rhetoric of the construction; and for whose benefit or detriment it was presented as presented, or the ideology of the construction.

(c) A thorough analysis of the relationship between biblical interpretation and Western hegemony and colonialism, especially in the course of the nineteenth and early twentieth centuries, when both the formation of the discipline and the process of expansionism find themselves at their respective peaks.

(d) Beyond a re-reading of the texts, a critical dialogue and engagement with the texts, their constructions and ideologies, in the light of one's own contextualization and perspective. In this regard, I believe there is an urgent need to engage the Bible not so much in the light of events in Europe in the present century—what is often referred to as the post-holocaust context—but rather in the light of events outside the West, in its colonies and territories, in the course of the last five hundred years—what I referred to earlier as the other face of Western culture and civilization. In other words, there is a need to address the wider question of how to read and interpret the Bible in the aftermath of centuries of domination, discrimination, exploitation, and the wholesale displacement and extermination of countless "others" who stood in the path of Western progress. While the question of doing theology in the light of the holocaust could hardly be ignored by the West, given its occurrence at the very heart of Europe, the question of doing theology in the light of colonialism has not received as much attention or sympathy on the part of the West, no doubt given the removed nature of such policies and events.

(e) The pursuit of a new kind of dialogue among the colonized themselves, that is, a dialogue between and among the different non-Western groups and cultures in the absence of the West. This is not to say that the dialogue between the West and the rest must come to an end but rather that the dialogue must be expanded to cover a variety of axes without necessary inclusion of the West at every step of the way.

It is in the light of tasks such as these that I describe the future of biblical studies as a future that is very much worth the struggle, a future full of life and, as I said at the beginning, a very promising life indeed. As a product of the diaspora and thus as someone deeply inscribed in the West, I would further describe it as a future in which the admirable "creed" of the West—and admirable it is indeed—is carried forward one step further and extended to all human beings regardless of ethnicity or race.

INDEX OF AUTHORS

INDEX OF BIBLICAL REFERENCES

APOCRYPHA

NEW TESTAMENT